T5-BPZ-652

 Wissenschaftliche Untersuchungen
zum Neuen Testament · 2. Reihe

Herausgeber / Editor
Jörg Frey (München)

Mitherausgeber / Associate Editors
Friedrich Avemarie (Marburg)
Judith Gundry-Volf (New Haven, CT)
Hans-Josef Klauck (Chicago, IL)

 230

Clint Tibbs

Religious Experience of the Pneuma

Communication with the Spirit World
in 1 Corinthians 12 and 14

Mohr Siebeck

CLINT TIBBS, born 1971; 2006 PhD (The Catholic University of America, Washington, D. C.); teaching Religion, Bible and Philosophy at Delta State University.

BS
2675.6
.G47
T63
2007

ISBN 978-3-16-149357-7

ISSN 0340-9570 (Wissenschaftliche Untersuchungen zum Neuen Testament, 2. Reihe)

The Deutsche Nationalbibliothek lists this publication in the Deutsche Nationalbibliographie; detailed bibliographic data is available in the Internet at *http://dnb.d-nb.de*.

© 2007 by Mohr Siebeck, Tübingen, Germany.

This book may not be reproduced, in whole or in part, in any form (beyond that permitted by copyright law) without the publisher's written permission. This applies particularly to reproductions, translations, microfilms and storage and processing in electronic systems.

The book was printed by Laupp & Göbel in Nehren on non-aging paper and bound by Buchbinderei Nädele in Nehren.

Printed in Germany.

In Memoriam

Dr. Michael Patrick O'Connor
1950 – 2007

שלום

Preface

This book is a revision of a dissertation completed for a Ph.D. in Biblical Studies at The Catholic University of America, Washington, D.C., November, 2005. In it, I argue that First Corinthians 12 and 14 provide a context for the study of religious experience in earliest Christianity. While religious experience has been done some justice in Biblical Studies, as Chapter Two indicates, First Corinthians 12 and 14 have yet to be discussed in any detail as religious experience. First Corinthians 12 and 14 are often read as concerning "spiritual gifts." This heading, however, highlights only one component of Paul's polemic, "gifts," to the neglect of other and equally important terms. The experiences Paul mentions in these texts, "speaking in a spirit," "prophecy," "glossolalia," "saying a blessing in a spirit," as well as the mention of "spirits" in three different places, suggest that Paul was actually writing about communication with the spirit world. This was one of the main religious experiences of the earliest Christians, evidenced elsewhere in *Didache* 11, the Shepherd of Hermas, *Mandate* 11, and Montanism. This book is also a reevaluation of the early Christian understanding of "the Holy Spirit." Biblical scholars routinely read "the holy spirit" in the New Testament as it came to be understood during the fourth century as a Deity, "the Holy Spirit." I conclude that early Jewish pneumatology is a more appropriate prism through which to view "holy spirit" in early Christianity than is Athanasian-Cappadocian pneumatology of the fourth century. The phrase "the holy spirit," as a collective noun, referenced "the holy spirit world."

I would like to thank, first and foremost, my dissertation director, Dr. Raymond F. Collins, whose seminar on First Corinthians in the Fall of 1997 at The Catholic University of American provided me the basis from which this book took form. Dr. Collins's knowledge of Paul's First Letter to the Corinthians served as a tremendous guide in the rhetoric of Paul's exposition on "spiritual things," as his commentary masterfully shows. Dr. Collins was always patient and guided my writing carefully and thoroughly. He was ever keeping me abreast of the most recent research on my topic, supplying me with articles and monographs I had overlooked. This book would not be what it is without Dr. Collins's gracious acceptance to guide me through the labyrinths of writing such a work.

My two readers, Dr. Francis J. Moloney and Dr. Francis T. Gignac, provided insights into format and content that improved the work and clarified my thinking on pivotal points. Any mistakes, however, are my own, not theirs. Dr. Gignac's training in Greek (however rigorous!) proved rewarding by bringing the Greek text (and all of its problems) to life. Dr. Moloney's seminars on the gospels of Mark and John proved very insightful and exposed me to the field of the historical Jesus and gospel studies. These scholars have played a leading role in my development as a biblical scholar. Thanks to them both.

Other scholars have also made long-lasting impressions during my graduate studies. Dr. Michael Patrick O'Connor offered sound training in Hebrew and Akkadian and also served as a significant guide in student-related matters. As a professor, O'Connor provided for the academic needs and advisement of graduate students as well as showing a genuine concern for their work and development as scholars. He will be missed. Dr. Douglas Gropp's training in Hebrew poetry and Aramaic was an indispensable resource and learning experience. Dr. Frank Matera's seminar on New Testament Theology introduced me to the "theology-religious experience" problem that is dealt with in this book. Sound tutelage in Old Testament studies, Syriac, and Second Temple literature was provided by Dr. Alexander Di Lella, Dr. Joseph Jensen, Dr. Christopher Begg, Dr. Joseph A. Fitzmyer, and Dr. David Johnson.

Commentaries are a dime-a-dozen. But the following scholars are those whose commentaries on First Corinthians that I have profited from greatly: Raymond F. Collins, Simon J. Kistemaker, Gordon D. Fee, David E. Garland, Richard B. Hays, Anthony C. Thiselton, and Hans Conzelmann.

A word of thanks goes to other individuals who have played a role during graduate studies. Thanks to Dr. Curt Lamar for his advisement during undergraduate days to pursue graduate studies at The Catholic University of America; Dr. James A. Scarborough for his conversations on "spiritual things"; Dr. Daniel (Donny) Kirsch for insightful talks over a Paulaner Salvatore; Evan Smith with help in Latin; Dr. Mary Katherine Birge, Pauline scholar in her own right, with gracious help during my initial ventures into Greek and Hebrew way back when; and Amy E. Pinky-Phillips for her library assistance during research pursued at the Harvard Divinity School library, Spring, 2004.

I also wish to express my appreciation to Dr. Henning Ziebritzki and the editorial staff of Mohr Siebeck Publishing House and Professor Jörg Frey and his team for accepting this work for publication in the *Wissenschaftliche Untersuchungen zum Neuen Testament*; and a special thanks to Bettina Gade.

Last but not least, I wish to give a thanks of appreciation to Mom and Dad and to the Dr. and Mrs. Robert C. Tibbs Fund for the Humanities in Religious Studies that allowed me to pursue graduate studies for so many years. Dad did not live long enough to see this book through. I dedicate this book to him and to Mom. Thanks to both of you for all of your support. I also wish to dedicate this book to my grandmother (Me-Maw) who passed away several weeks before Dad's passing. Above all, I thank Him who makes all things possible.

Cleveland, Mississippi, March 2007   Clint Tibbs

Table of Contents

Preface VII

Abbreviations XV

Introduction 1

Chapter 1. "Now Concerning Spiritual Gifts": The State of
Research on the Interpretation of Prophecy,
Glossolalia, and πνεῦμα Terms in First Corinthians
12 and 14 21

1. Introduction 21
2. Prophecy and Glossolalia in First Corinthians 12 and 14 23
3. Old Testament Prophecy and Paul 25
4. Greco-Roman Prophecy and Paul 27
5. Prophecy and Glossolalia: Trance 29
6. Glossolalia as a "Sign" 31
7. Glossolalia: Human Language? 33
8. Glossolalia: Social Science and Contemporary Pentecostalism 38
9. Retrospect on Prophecy and Glossolalia 41
10. πνεῦμα Terms in First Corinthians 12 and 14 42
11. Backgrounds to Paul's use of πνεῦμα in First Corinthians 43
12. πνευματικά in 1 Cor 12:1 44
    12.1. "Spiritual Persons" 45
    12.2. "Spiritual Gifts" 45
    12.3. "Spiritual Things" 46
13. πνευματικά in 1 Cor 14:1 47
14. πνευματικά versus χαρίσματα 47
15. πνεῦμα and πνεύματα 49
    15.1. πνεῦμα θεοῦ and πνεῦμα ἅγιον 49
    15.2. 1 Cor 12:10 διακρίσεις πνευμάτων 50
    15.3. 1 Cor 14:12 ζηλωταί πνευμάτων 51
16. Retrospect on πνεῦμα Terms in First Corinthians 12 and 14 53
17. Prospect: First Corinthians 12 and 14 as Religious Experience 54
18. The Spirit World in Paul 60
    18.1. Third- and Fourth-Century Patristics: The Emergence
          and the Defense of the Deity of the Holy Spirit 62

18.2. The Theology of the Holy Spirit and Biblical Studies 69
18.3. The Spirit World of the Earliest Christians 71

Chapter 2. Religious Experience and Biblical Studies:
            A Survey of the Discussion 77

1. Introduction 77
2. The Emergence and Graphic Portrayal of Religious Experience 77
    2.1. Hermann Gunkel 77
    2.1. Heinrich Weinel 80
    2.3. Paul Volz 83
    2.4. Henry Barclay Swete 86
    2.5. Elmer H. Zaugg 87
    2.6. Henry Wheeler Robinson 90
    2.7. Percy G. S. Hopwood 91
    2.8. Retrospect 93
3. The Reemergence of the Portrayal of Religious Experience 94
    3.1. James D. G. Dunn 94
    3.2. Gordon D. Fee 96
    3.3. John R. Levison 98
    3.4. Luke Timothy Johnson 101
    3.5. John Ashton 103
    3.6. John Eifion Morgan-Wynne 106
    3.7. Retrospect 108
4. Conclusion 108

Chapter 3. Communication with the Spirit World in
            First-Century Greco-Roman and Jewish
            Literature: Plutarch (δαίμων), Josephus, Philo
            (πνεῦμα θεῖον), and Pseudo-Philo
            (*spiritus sanctus*) 113

1. Introduction 113
2. Plutarch: *De Def. Orac.* 414E, 418C–D, 431B 115
3. Josephus: *A. J.* 4.6.5 §118, §119, and §121 119

4. Philo: *Her.* 259, 265–66; *Mos.* 1.274, 277, 283; and *Spec.* 4.49 123
5. Pseudo-Philo: *L.A.B.* 28.6, 10a, and 62.2 131
    5.1. *L.A.B.* 28.6, 10a: Kenaz 132
    5.2. *L.A.B.* 62.2: Saul 135
6. Pre-Platonic Evidence for Prophetic Amnesia 138
7. Prospects for the Old Testament and Early Christian Literature 141
8. Conclusion 144

Chapter 4. "Now Concerning Spiritism": Communication with the Spirit World as Religious Experience in 1 Cor 12:1–3 147

1. Introduction 147
2. 1 Cor 12:1a περὶ δὲ τῶν πνευματικῶν, "Now Concerning Spiritism" . . 148
3. 1 Cor 12:2–3: Grammar and Confession 155
4. 1 Cor 12:2–3: Contrast and Analogy 157
5. 1 Cor 12:2: NonChristian Spiritism 159
6. 1 Cor 12:3: Christian Spiritism 165
7. 1 Cor 12:3: The Holy Spirit or a holy spirit 170
8. 1 Cor 12:1–3: A Translation and Explanation 174
9. 1 Cor 12:1–3: Theme and Variations 178

Chapter 5. The Manifestation of the Spirit World: 1 Cor 12:4–11 181

1. Introduction: πνεῦμα as "Spirit World" in Translation 181
2. The Meaning of "the Spirit" in 1 Cor 12:4, 7 184
3. The Meaning and Use of "One" in 1 Cor 12:9, 11 188
4. 1 Cor 12:4–7, 11: The Manifestation of the Spirit World 195
5. 1 Cor 12:8–10: The Activities of the Spirit World 201
    5.1. Verse 8: λόγος σοφίας, λόγος γνώσεως, "Message of
        Wisdom" and "Message of Knowledge" 202
    5.2. Verse 9a: πίστις, "Faith" 203
    5.3. Verse 9b: χαρίσματα ἰαμάτων, "Gifts of Healings" 204

5.4. Verse 10a: ἐνεργήματα δυνάμεων, "Effective Acts
       over Evil Spirits" 205
5.5. Verse 10a: προφητεία, "Prophecy" 207
5.6. Verse 10a: διακρίσεις πνευμάτων, "Discernment of
       Spirits" 207
5.7. Verse 10b: γένη γλωσσῶν, "Different kinds of Tongues,"
       and ἑρμηνεία γλωσσῶν, "Interpretation (Translation)
       of Tongues" 213
6. Conclusion 213

Chapter 6. Prophecy and Glossolalia: The Direct
            Communication of Spirits through Human
            Mediums in First Corinthians 14 215

1. Introduction 215
2. Prophecy and Glossolalia: Ecstasy 217
3. Prophecy and Glossolalia: Verbal Communication from the
    Spirit World 219
4. Glossolalia: A Spirit that Speaks a Foreign Language
    through a Prophet 220
5. Prophecy: A Spirit that Speaks the Language of the Christian
    Congregation through a Prophet 221
6. 1 Cor 14:1b–3: A Translation and Explanation 227
7. 1 Cor 14:4–5: Spirits Should Speak in the Language of the
    Spectators Unless a Translator is Present 230
8. 1 Cor 14: 6–11: The Unintelligibility of Glossolalia – Paul's
    Musical Instrument Analogies and an Example Taken from
    Human Languages 233
9. 1 Cor 14:12: A Variety of Spirit Beings Required for the
    Church 236
10. 1 Cor 14:13–19: The Need for Intelligible Communication
     from the Spirit World 242
11. 1 Cor 14:20–25: Intelligible Communication from the Spirit
     World Convicts Nonbelievers of the Reality of Spirit
     Communication 252
12. 1 Cor 14:26–33: Regulations for Communication with the
     Spirit World 258

13. 1 Cor 14:37–40: Paul's Final Comments on Communication
    with the Spirit World of God 266

Conclusion 269

Appendix 1. Greek Text and English Translation of
             1 Cor 12:1–11 and 1 Cor 14:1–33, 37–40 279

1.1. 1 Cor 12:1–11 279
1.2. 1 Cor 14:1–33 280
1.3. 1 Cor 14:37–40 283

Appendix 2. The Meaning and Usage of the Term
             "Spiritism" 285

1. Spiritism and Popular Culture 285
2. Spiritism and English Versions of the Bible 288
3. Spiritism and Biblical Necromancy 291
4. Spiritism: Continuity with Prophetic Activity in the Torah,
   the Prophets, and the Writings 294
5. Consulting the Spirit World: דרש, שאל, בקש 298
6. The Term רוח the Basis for Spiritism 302
7. Conclusion 304

Appendix 3. A Statistical Analysis of πνεῦμα as "holy spirit"
             in the New Testament 307

1. Articular forms of πνεῦμα as "the holy spirit" 307
2. Anarthrous forms of πνεῦμα as "a holy spirit" 310
3. Plural forms of πνεῦμα denoting evil spirits 311
4. Plural forms of πνεῦμα denoting good spirits 312
5. Plural forms of πνεῦμα denoting both good and evil spirits ... 312
6. Singular forms of πνεῦμα, anarthrous and unqualified 312
7. The dative ἐν πνεύματι in reference to "holy spirit" 313
8. Analysis of Data 314
9. Conclusion 318

Bibliography 321

1. Commentaries on First Corinthians 321
2. Primary Literature 322
3. Secondary Literature 323

Index of Ancient Sources 339

Index of Modern Authors 359

Index of Subjects and Key Terms 365

Abbreviations

The abbreviations of journals follow the Catholic Biblical Quarterly style sheet. Otherwise, names of journals are spelled out in their entirety. Abbreviations for biblical books also follow this style sheet.

1. Ancient Editions of Biblical Texts

LXX	Septuagint (Greek translation of the Old Testament, ca. third–second century B.C.E.)
NT	New Testament
OT	Old Testament

The numbering of chapters and verses of the OT follows the Hebrew MT (masoretic text).

2. Names of Biblical Books (with Apocrypha)

Gen	Genesis	Matt	Matthew
Exod	Exodus	Mark	Mark
Lev	Leviticus	Luke	Luke
Num	Numbers	John	John
Deut	Deuteronomy	Acts	Acts
Judg	Judges	Rom	Romans
1 Sam	1 Samuel	1, 2 Cor	1, 2 Corinthians
1 Kgs	1 Kings	Gal	Galatians
Isa	Isaiah	Eph	Ephesians
Jer	Jeremiah	Phil	Philippians
Ezek	Ezekiel	Col	Colossians
Zech	Zechariah	1, 2 Thess	1,2 Thessalonians
Ps (*pl.* Pss)	Psalm	1 Tim	1 Timothy
Job	Job	Phlm	Philemon
Dan	Daniel	Heb	Hebrews
1, 2 Chr	1, 2 Chronicles	Jas	James
Jdt	Judith	1, 2 Pet	1, 2 Peter
Sir	Sirach	1 John	1 John
Tob	Tobit	Jude	Jude
Wis	Wisdom	Rev	Revelation

3. The Dead Sea Scrolls

1QH[a]	*Thanksgiving Hymns*
1QHf	*Hymns*
1Q3	*1QLeviticus*
1QM	*War Scroll*
1QS	*Rule of the Community*, formerly *Manual of Discipline*
1QSb	*Rule of the Blessings*
4QShirShabb[a]	*Songs of the Sabbath Sacrifice*
4QS1	*Sapiential Work*
4Q502	*Ritual of Marriage*
4Q504	*Words of the Luminaries[a]*
4Q511	*Songs of the Sage[b]*
8Q5	*Hymn*
CD	*Damascus Document*

4. Other Jewish Literature

1 Enoch	*Ethiopic Enoch*
T. 12 Patr.	*The Testaments of the Twelve Patriarchs*
T. Asher	*Testament of Asher*
T. Dan	*Testament of Dan*
T. Gad	*Testament of Gad*
T. Levi	*Testament of Levi*
T. Jud.	*Testament of Judah*
T. Reub.	*Testament of Reuben*
T. Sim.	*Testament of Simeon*
T. Ben.	*Testament of Benjamin*
T. Iss.	*Testament of Issachar*
Jub.	*Jubilees*

5. Targums

Tg. Onq.	Targum Onqelos
Tg. Ps.-J.	Targum Pseudo-Jonathan

6. Early Christian Texts

Herm. *Mand.*	The Shepherd of Hermas, *Mandates*
Did.	*Didache*
Eccl. Hist.	Eusebius *Ecclesiastical History*
Haer.	Epiphanius *Panarion* (Against Heresies)
De princip.	Origen *De Principiis*
ad Serap.	Athanasius *Epistles to Serapion*
Hom. 24	Basil *Against the Sabellians, Arius, and the Anomoeans*

7. Plato, Plutarch, Josephus, Philo, Pseudo-Philo and Related Works

Ion	Plato *Ion*
Symp.	Plato *Symposium*
Phaed.	Plato *Phaedrus*
Mor.	Plutarch *Moralia*
De Def. Orac.	Plutarch *Obsolescence of Oracles*
A.J.	Josephus *Jewish Antiquities*
Fug.	Philo *On Flight and Finding*
Her.	Philo *Who is the Heir of Divine Things*
Mos.	Philo *Life of Moses*
Prov.	Philo *Foresight*
Spec.	Philo *The Special Laws*
Q.G.	Philo *Questions and Answers in Genesis*
L.A.B.	Pseudo-Philo *Biblical Antiquities*
Phars.	Lucan *Pharsalia* (*Bellum civile*, Civil War)
De bell. civ.	Lucan *On the Civil War*
De Div.	Cicero, *On Divination*
Geo.	Strabo *Geography*
De myst.	Iamblichus *On the Mysteries*
Pyth.	Heraclitus *The Pythia*

8. Reference Works

ABD	David Noel Freedman et al. (eds.), *The Anchor Bible Dictionary* (6 vols.; New York: Doubleday, 1992)
ANF	*Ante-Nicene Fathers* (10 vols.; Peabody, MA: Hendrickson, 1994)
ANRW	H. Temporini and W. Haase (eds.), *Aufstieg und Niedergang der römischen Welt* (93 vols.; Berlin/New York: de Gruyter, 1972–)
BAGD	W. Bauer, *A Greek-English Lexicon of the New Testament and Other Early Christian Literature* (trans. F. W. Gingrich and F. W. Danker; 2d ed., rev. F. W. Danker; Chicago: University of Chicago Press, 1979)
BDAG	W. Bauer, *A Greek-English Lexicon of the New Testament and Other Christian Literature* (3d ed., rev. and ed. F. W. Danker; Chicago: University of Chicago Press, 2000)
BDB	F. Brown, S. R. Driver and C. A. Briggs, *Hebrew and English Lexicon of the Old Testament* (Oxford: Clarendon, 1974)
BDF	F. Blass and A. Debrunner, *A Greek Grammar of the New Testament and Other Early Christian Literature* (trans. R. W. Funk; Chicago: University of Chicago Press, 1961)
CAD	Ignace J. Gelb et al. (eds.), *The Assyrian Dictionary of the Oriental Institute of the University of Chicago* (21 vols.; Chicago: The Oriental Institute, 1956–)
CWDNT	Spiros Zodhiates (ed.), *The Complete Word Study Dictionary New Testament* (Chattanooga, TN: AMG, 1992)
DDD	Karel van der Toorn et al. (eds.), *The Dictionary of Deities and Demons* (Leiden: Brill, 1995)
EDB	Adrianus van den Born, *Encyclopedic Dictionary of the Bible* (trans. Louis F. Hartman; New York: McGraw-Hill, 1963)
EDNT	Horst Balz and Gerhard Schneider (eds.), *The Exegetical Dictionary of the New Testament* (5 vols.; Grand Rapids, MI: Eerdmans, 1990)

ISBE	Geoffrey W. Bromiley et al. (eds.), *International Standard Bible Encyclopedia* (5 vols.; Grand Rapids, MI: Eerdmans, 1979)
LCL	Loeb Classical Library
LSJ	H. G. Liddell and R. Scott, *Greek-English Lexicon* (Oxford: Clarendon Press, 1996)
Nestle-Aland[27]	E. Nestle and K. Aland, *Novum Testamentum graece* (27th ed.; Stuttgart: Deutsche Bibelgesellschaft, 1993)
NCE	M. R. P. McGuire et al. (eds.), *New Catholic Encyclopedia* (19 vols.; New York: McGraw-Hill, 1967)
NPNF	*Nicene and Post-Nicene Fathers* (Ser. 2; 14 vols.; Peabody, MA: Hendrickson, 1994)
OTP	James H. Charlesworth (ed.), *The Old Testament Pseudepigrapha* (2 vols.; New York: Doubleday, 1983–1985)
TDNT	Gerhard Kittel (and G. Friedrich), *Theological Dictionary of the New Testament* (trans. Geoffrey W. Bromiley; 10 vols.; Grand Rapids, MI: Eerdmans, 1964–76)
TDOT	Helmer Ringgren (and Johannes Botterweck), *Theological Dictionary of the Old Testament* (trans. John T. Willis; 14 vols.; Grand Rapids, MI: Eerdmans, 1974–)
PG	J. P. Migne (ed.), *Patrologia graeca* (Paris: J. P. Migne, 1857–1887)
PGL	G. W. H. Lampe, *A Patristic Greek Lexicon* (Oxford: Clarendon Press, 1961; 19th impression, 2005)
UBS	United Bible Societies Handbook Series

9. Journals, Serials

AcOr	*Acta orientalia*
AfO	*Archiv für Orientforschung*
AO	*Aula Orientalis*
BASOR	*Bulletin of the American Schools of Oriental Research*
Bib	*Biblica*
BSac	*Bibliotheca Sacra*
BT	*Bible Translator*
BZ	*Biblische Zeitschrift*

BTB	*Biblical Theology Bulletin*
CBQ	*Catholic Biblical Quarterly*
CTR	*Covenant Theological Review*
EvQ	*Evangelical Quarterly*
ExpTim	*Expository Times*
GOTR	*Greek Orthodox Theological Review*
HTR	*Harvard Theological Review*
Int	*Interpretation*
ITQ	*Irish Theological Quarterly*
JAAR	*Journal of the American Academy of Religion*
JAOS	*Journal of the American Oriental Society*
JBL	*Journal of Biblical Literature*
JEH	*Journal of Ecclesiastical History*
JETS	*Journal of the Evangelical Theological Society*
JJS	*Journal of Jewish Studies*
JQR	*Jewish Quarterly Review*
JR	*Journal of Religion*
JSJ	*Journal for the Study of Judaism in the Persian, Hellenistic, and Roman Periods*
JSNT	*Journal for the Study of the New Testament*
JSOT	*Journal for the Study of the Old Testament*
JSSR	*Journal for the Scientific Study of Religion*
JTS	*Journal of Theological Studies*
Noet	*Noetestamentica*
NovT	*Novum Testamentum*
NTS	*New Testament Studies*
OrAnt	*Oriens antiquus*
PSB	*Princeton Seminary Bulletin*
RHPR	*Revue d'histoire et de philosophie religieuses*
SBLSP	*Society of Biblical Literature Seminar Papers*
SJOT	*Scandinavian Journal of the Old Testament*
SJT	*Scottish Journal of Theology*
TBT	*The Bible Today*
TLZ	*Theologische Literaturzeitung*
TS	*Theological Studies*
TynBul	*Tyndale Bulletin*
VC	*Vigiliae christianae*
VT	*Vetus Testamentum*
VTSup	Supplements to VT

WTJ	*Westminster Theological Journal*
ZAW	*Zeitschrift für die alttestamentliche Wissenschaft*

10. Bible Versions

ASV	*American Standard Version*
BBE	*Bible in Basic English*
CEV	*Contemporary English Version*
DBY	*Darby Bible*
DRA	*Douay-Rheims Bible*
KJV	*King James Version*
NKJ	*New King James Version*
NRS	*New Revised Standard Version*
NAB	*New American Bible* (St. Joseph Edition, 1986)
NAS	*New American Standard Bible*
NIV	*New International Version*
NJB	*New Jerusalem Bible*
NLT	*New Living Translation*
REB	*Revised English Bible*
RHM	*The Emphasized New Testament: A New Translation* (J. B. Rotherham)
RSV	*Revised Standard Version*
TAY	*Living Letters: The Paraphrased Epistles* (Kenneth N. Taylor)
TEV	*Today's English Version*
TOB	*Traduction œcuménique de la Bible*
WNT	*The New Testament: An Expanded Translation* (Kenneth S. Wuest)

11. Other Abbreviations

B.C.E.	before the common era (= B.C.)
ca.	circa
C.E.	common era (= A.D.)
cf.	confer, compare
chap.(s.)	chapter(s)
Contra	against, in disagreement with

diss.	dissertation
ed.	edited by
e.g.	*exempli gratia*, for example
esp.	especially
et al.	*et alii*, and others
fl.	*floruit*, flourished (used with a date to indicate the productive years of a historical figure whose birth and death dates are unknown)
ibid.	*ibidem*, "in the same place" (in the same previously mentioned work)
idem	*id*, the same (author)
i.e.	*id est*, "that is"
masc.	masculine
n.(nn.)	footnote(s)
n.p.	no publisher
p.(pp.)	page(s)
Pace	with due respect, but differing from
repr.	reprinted
rev.	revised by (rev. ed. = revised edition)
ser.	series
sg.	singular
s.v.	*sub verbo* ("under the word," dictionary entry)
trans.	translated by
v.(vv.)	verse(s)
vis-à-vis	in relation to, compare to
vol.(s.)	volume(s)

Introduction

This research is an attempt to explain the meaning of πνεῦμα, prophecy, and glossolalia in First Corinthians 12 and 14. While many studies evaluate these terms from the perspective of contemporary pentecostalism or through historical-critical research worked out within a Christian theology of the Holy Spirit, I will argue from the perspective of religious experience. This perspective will be driven by historical-critical methodology but with an eye to the realm of spirits.[1]

A religious experience may be described as an experience that brings together human beings and spiritual realities from a world "beyond" the physical. The origin of the term "religion" is in the Latin *religio*. In the Classical and Roman understanding *religio* had to do with that which "binds" people to the gods whom they serve. This suggested the threshold at which both the world of humanity and the world of the gods converged or met during community rituals and festivals devoted to the celebrations of certain gods.

By the seventh century the term "religious" seems to have lost its "pagan" associations among Christian communities in which the term *religio* was used as a designation for those people who dedicated their lives to the service of God. These were the *religiosi*, a term that gave rise to the English expression "religious," describing those who belonged to an order committed in faith to serving God.[2]

In contemporary society the expression "religious experience" covers a broad range of feelings, emotions, and activities from both religious and secular realms. The expression sometimes suggests an "awesome" event in a person's life. It may also be used to describe experiences of mystics who believe that they have visions and/or auditions of a divine world. A person who is deeply committed to his or her faith through a rich prayer life may also be considered "religious." The expression is reserved for some extraordinary experience (religious or secular) that transcends the usual daily experiences of most human beings who go about their lives of work, rest, and play.

---

[1] Historical criticism traditionally restricts itself to that which can only be known through empirical sources. The "spiritual" or "transcendental" is something that history is unable to explain. See Edgar Krantz, *The Historical-Critical Method* (GBS; Philadelphia: Fortress, 1975) 36–37.

[2] So Ernst Feil, "From the Classical Religio to the Modern Religion: Elements of a Transformation between 1550 and 1650," in *Religion in History: the Word, the Idea, the Reality* (ed. Michel Despland and Gerard Vallee [Waterloo, Ontario: Wilfred Laurier University Press, 1992] 31–43) 32.

The social sciences attempt to define religious experience through the study of religious movements and their impact on the lives of individuals. These works cut across three related disciplines, sociology, anthropology, and psychology. Sociology and anthropology describe religious experience in the context of social and cultural conditions.[3] Psychology studies the personal psychological conditions associated with religious experience in order to define the nature of that experience.[4]

Much of this work tends to define religious experience as an opium or "hallucination," a reaction to a dysfunctional or stressful lifestyle within a given culture. In the social sciences, "deprivation theory" defines religious experiences as those formed out of the need of individuals who are "deprived" of social status and stability. These individuals look for an outlet in a form of cultic experience that gives them a sense of power over their lives.[5] Thus, the perspective of social and anthropological theorists reduce the experience to "psychological" or "cultural." A sympathy for the category of "spirit" in religious experience in these studies is undermined.

The anthropologist Erika Bourguignon, however, has provided biblical scholars with material from anthropological field research in the areas of possession, trance, and altered states of consciousness.[6] Her student, Felicitas Goodman, explores possession and exorcism in the modern world, revealing the beliefs in and the experiences with spirit beings.[7] The work of these two

---

[3] See the classic work William James, *Varieties of Religious Experience* (New York: Longmans, Green, 1902; repr. New York: Vintage Books, 1990); and more recently Ioan M. Lewis, *Ecstatic Religion: A Study of Shamanism and Spirit Possession* (Hammondsworth, England: Penguin, 1971; repr. New York: Routledge, 2003); and C. Daniel Batson and W. Larry Venti, *The Religious Experience: A Social-Psychological Perspective* (Oxford: Oxford University Press, 1982).

[4] See André Godin, *The Psychological Dynamics of Religious Experience* (Birmingham, AL: Religious Education Press, 1985; trans. Mary Turton of *Psychologie des expériences religieuses: La désir et la réalité* [Paris: Le Centurion, 1981]).

[5] Sometimes, this theory, or a variation of it, is applied to women in Greek antiquity who were empowered by daemons. See Ruth Padel, "Women: Model for Possession by Greek Daemons," in *Images of Women in Antiquity* (ed. Averil Cameron and Amélie Kuhrt; Detroit: Wayne State University Press, 1983; repr. 1993) 3–18. See also Ioan M. Lewis, "Spirit-Possession and Deprivation Cults," *Man* 1 (1966) 307–29.

[6] See Erika Bourguignon, *Religion, Altered States of Consciousness, and Social Change* (Columbus: Ohio State University Press, 1973); and idem, *Possession* (San Francisco: Chandler & Sharp, 1976; repr. Prospect Heights, IL: Waveland Press, 1991).

[7] See Felicitas Goodman, *How about Demons? Possession and Exorcism in the Modern World* (Bloomington: Indiana University Press, 1988).

scholars is utilized by some biblical scholars to explain phenomena related to trance states, possession, and visions in the NT.

John J. Pilch is one of the foremost biblical scholars to profit from the work of Bourguignon and Goodman. A biblical scholar who works with social scientific models for interpreting the bible, Pilch uses the anthropological field research of Goodman to explain trances and visions in the NT within a cultural context.[8] Pilch's work is quite effective in explaining religious phenomena in the NT from contemporary religious experiences in the modern world. Despite theological prejudices against religious phenomena outside of Christianity,[9] Pilch's work shows that experiences in third-world countries are useful models for interpreting similar experiences in the world of the NT.[10]

Sometimes experiences of spirit possession in the biblical, historical, and contemporary record are studied within the fields of psychology and psychiatry, but only in the "negative" sense of demonic possession. Both the Protestant and Catholic churches believe and teach that demonic possession is the actual invasion by an evil spirit of the body of the person who becomes the spirit's victim, not unlike the reports of demoniacs in the NT.[11] In psychology, however, the belief in spirits is usually cast aside as an archaic, pre-modern, and pre-scientific explanation for what is otherwise diagnosed as a psychological disorder, e.g., schizophrenia or multiple personality disorder, whose provenance is located in an organic aberration.

One of the foremost proponents of the psychological argument is Juan B. Cortés, S.J., who believes that what the·biblical authors lacked in knowledge

---

[8] See John J. Pilch, "Appearances of the Risen Jesus in Cultural Context: Experiences of Alternate Reality," *BTB* 28 (1998) 52–60; idem, "Paul's Ecstatic Trance Experience near Damascus in Acts of the Apostles," *Hervormde Teologiese Studies* 58 (2002) 690–707; and idem, *Visions and Healing in Acts of the Apostles: How the Early Believers Experienced God* (Collegeville, MN: Liturgical Press, 2004).

[9] See Karl Rahner below, pp. 5–6.

[10] See also Stevan L. Davies, *Jesus the Healer: Possession, Trance, and the Origins of Christianity* (New York: Continuum, 1995), who uses the research of Bourguignon and Goodman to explain prophets, prophecy, and spirit possession in the NT. I disagree, however, with Davies's conclusion that Jesus was a "spirit-possessed prophet" (ibid., 51). Jesus possessed the spirit in that he had access to the realm of divinity or spirit that enabled him to perform miracles and healings. It seems unlikely that spirits possessed Jesus and spoke out of him.

[11] See Adolf Rodewyk, *Possessed by Satan: The Church's Teaching on the Devil, Possession, and Exorcism* (Garden City, NY: Doubleday, 1975; trans. Martin Ebon of *Die Dämonische Besessenheit* [Aschaffenburg: Paul Pattloch Verlag, 1963]).

about the human psyche, modern-day psychology more than makes up for.[12] This perspective reduces the biblical belief in possession to something that is not inherent to it: psychology and psychiatric medicine. The synoptic gospels, at times, seemed to have distinguished illnesses from demonic possession as if to suggest possession was not always considered a physiological illness (cf. Matt 8:16).

The application of psychology may not always adequately explain the effects of πνεῦμα in the NT. Admittedly, the symptoms of possession and of psychological disorders may be similar, as attested in antiquity.[13] But if "spirits" are to be explained as a psychological disorder in the negative spiritual experiences in the NT, then positive experiences with spirits, e.g., prophetic possession, are to be likewise reduced to the disorders of the psyche. This reduction, historically, does not explain the beliefs of the early Christians. Apart from demonic possession, spirits may also serve a community positively by communicating divine knowledge via prophetic possession. The knowledge and information conveyed during the possession state that is beyond the possessed person's normal intellectual capacity gives rise to two different perspectives: biblically, the divine knowledge is that of a communicating spirit; in the psychology of modernity, the provenance of the knowledge is the subconscious.

Philosophy has also contributed to the study of religious experience. The work of Edmund Husserl concerning the phenomenology of philosophy is a major contribution.[14] Husserl's study serves as a method for understanding the nature of metaphysics and epistemology. Essentially, phenomenology is based on the realities designated by two terms that Husserl introduced, *noema* and *noesis*. *Noesis* refers to a subject's experience and *noema* refers to the subject known. The interplay between these two realities is taken into careful consideration while "bracketing" (*epoché*, holding in suspension) judgments about the metaphysical existence or non-existence of that which is perceived by the subject. Luke Timothy Johnson has recently applied Husserl's

---

[12] Juan B. Cortés and Florence M. Gatti, *The Case Against Possessions and Exorcisms: A Historical, Biblical, and Psychological Analysis of Demons, Devils, and Demoniacs* (New York: Vantage Press, 1975). See also Adam Crabtree, *Multiple Man: Explorations in Possession and Multiple Personality* (New York: Praeger, 1985).

[13] See Chapter Three, 141 n. 119 below.

[14] See Edmund Husserl, *Cartesian Meditations: An Introduction to Phenomenology* (trans. Dorion Cairns; Boston: Kluwer Academic Publishers, 1950); and idem, *Ideas Pertaining to a Pure Phenomenology and to a Phenomenological Philosophy* (trans. W. Boyce Gibson; Boston: Nijhoff, 1983).

phenomenology to a study of religious experience in earliest Christianity with effectiveness.[15]

Theology has also contributed to delineating religious experience. Both Protestant and Catholic theologians have written at length on the experience of "spirit" in the early church. One of the main contributors from the Protestant tradition is Jürgen Moltmann, who approaches the subject from a holistic, ecumenical perspective.[16] Moltmann describes the historical experiences of the spirit denoted by the Hebrew noun רוח, "wind," "spirit," in the OT as experiences of divine energy and divine power in the lives of the patriarchs and the Israelites.[17] Moltmann sees the OT experience of spirit continued in the NT. The experience is a "Trinitarian experience of the spirit," a spirit christology initiated in the synoptic gospels and continued by Paul and John, who have a "christological doctrine of the Spirit."[18]

In the Catholic theological tradition, Karl Rahner contributes a volume to the experience of the spirit.[19] The phenomena of the spirit in the NT and the early church is treated in a chapter entitled "Religious Enthusiasm and the Experience of Grace."[20] From the beginning of his exposition, Rahner claims that the comments of a dogmatic theologian are unable to express the "concrete and specific characteristics" of experiences of the spirit. He attempts to locate the description of experiences of the spirit within dogmatic theology, particularly within the theology of divine grace.

Rahner notes that phenomena of the spirit and charismatic enthusiasm (glossolalia) in and of themselves are not inherently Christian for they may occur in different sects, both inside and outside of Christianity. Thus, Rahner proposes that only the doctrine of divine grace as outlined in the Jesuit tradition can define an experience of the spirit as truly "Christian." Otherwise, phenomena related to charismatic enthusiasm, which may or may not be

---

[15] Johnson's work is surveyed in Chapter Two. In the field of philosophy, see further John E. Smith, *Experience and God* (New York: Oxford University Press, 1968); William P. Alston, *Perceiving God: The Epistemology of Religious Experience* (Ithaca: Cornell University Press, 1991); and Louis Roy, *Transcendent Experiences: Phenomenology and Critique* (Toronto: University of Toronto Press, 2001).

[16] Jürgen Moltmann, *The Spirit of Life: A Universal Affirmation* (Minneapolis: Fortress, 1992).

[17] Ibid., 39–57.

[18] Ibid., 58.

[19] Karl Rahner, *Experience of the Spirit: Source of Theology* (Theological Investigations 16; trans. David Morland; New York: Crossroad, 1983).

[20] Ibid., 35–51.

Christian, would reduce Christianity to the level of other religions.[21] In the final analysis, Rahner limits his perspective to a contemporary theory of divine grace without allowing the insights of exegesis to inform his exposition of the phenomena of the spirit any further.[22]

Within theology, the unwillingness to deal with "spirit" in terms of experience has been somewhat of a conundrum.[23] This stems partly from the way in which the study of theology and the study of religion are treated in the academy. Traditionally, theology and religion are two different disciplines within academia: theology deals strictly with Christianity (whether biblical, historical, or systematic theology) and religion deals with practically everything else, both western (Judaism, Islam) and nonwestern (Buddhism, Taoism, and Hinduism) religious traditions.[24] Sometimes, however, the demarcation between "theology" and "religion" is not always clear.[25]

At a deeper level, theology tends to focus on ideas that originated from individuals whose writings reflect "thinking about God." Sometimes these writings contributed to the formulation of Christian doctrine that later served as a documentation of the beliefs of the church.[26] As such, theology deals with

---

[21] Ibid., 39.

[22] Ibid., 35, 40. Rahner revealingly states, "One might in certain circumstances regard such phenomena as very useful or as an inevitable concomitant of religion, but the exact elucidation of their origin would be a question in which dogmatic theology could happily declare itself to have no interest" (p. 40).

[23] This is especially the case within academic theology such as Moltmann and Rahner. Rahner admits of no interest (happily so!) in his exposition of phenomena related to experiences of the spirit except within the limits of divine grace. In contemporary society, however, theology has sometimes engaged that branch of fringe science known as psychical research or occultism. This has brought theology into a conversation with explicit experiences of "spirit" in present-day society, e.g., dreams, mediums, trance states, visions, Marian apparitions, Eucharistic miracles, etc. See Alois Wiesinger, *Occult Phenomena in the Light of Theology* (trans. Brian Battershaw; Westminster, MD: Newman Press, 1957; repr. Fort Collins, CO: Roman Catholic Books, 1999); and Donald I. Bretherton, "Theology and Psychical Studies," in *Life, Death & Psychical Research: Studies on Behalf of the Churches' Fellowship for Psychical and Spiritual Studies* (ed. J. D. Pearce-Higgins and G. Stanley Whitby; London: Rider, 1973) 240–57.

[24] See Gillian R. Evans, *Old Arts and New Theology: The Beginnings of Theology as an Academic Discipline* (Oxford: Clarendon Press, 1980); and Edward Farley, "The Place of Theology in the Study of Religion," *Religious Studies and Theology* 5 (1985) 9–29.

[25] See Paula M. Cooey, "Fiddling While Rome Burns: The Place of Academic Theology in the Study of Religion," *HTR* 93 (2000) 35–49. Judaism possesses a body of work that is, arguably, theological, i.e., the Talmud and the Mishnah. Moslems also possess the Quran.

[26] I say "sometimes" because many of the writings in church history that bear on "theology" were not always accepted as orthodox by the church. Classic examples are the Arian controversy and Origen, whose views on salvation and reincarnation did not follow those of the

topics that might not always reflect the NT itself, but rather reflect what a certain writer thinks the NT might be saying or its possible implications. The writer may even elaborate and embellish in ways that go beyond what a NT text actually says, yet remain within the realm of theology. This commitment to "thinking about God" gives the added legitimacy to extraneous theological musings as authoritative affirmations for certain NT texts. The origin of doctrine and dogma arises from such theological musings.[27]

The German history-of-religions school argued that later doctrinal developments in church history, having become theological perspectives of scholars, obscure the views expressed in the NT. The experiences in the NT have been recast with theological verbiage that do not accurately depict those original experiences. Hence a line was drawn between "theology" and "experience" by the history-of-religions school.

Peter Balla offers a brief yet insightful summary of the challenges that religious experience poses to theology.[28] He debates the contributions of the history-of-religions school to the dividing line between "theology" and "experience." Any theological interpretation of the NT ran the risk of introducing doctrinal beliefs that were not clear in the NT. The affirmation that theology was somehow inadequate for the study of the NT was common to the history-of-religions approach. Balla notes that this approach assessed theological ideas (e.g., of Paul) as secondary theories meant to interpret the experiences mentioned in the NT text.[29]

In an attempt to extend the range of theology beyond that of doctrine, Balla modifies the traditional view of theology to include a wide range of religious phenomena.[30] He argues that the history-of-religions approach is problematic.

---

church at the time. Even ideas from "orthodox" theologians such as Augustine and Aquinas did not always meet with the sanction of the church.

[27] For instance, ὑπόστασις is a term that occurs in Heb 1:3 for the Son of God, but in later Greek theology it described God, Christ, and the Spirit as three "persons," contributing to the theology of the Trinity. The "triadic" position of "father," "son," and "holy spirit" in Matt 28:19 can certainly be seen as the basis from which the idea of ὑπόστασις was elaborated. So, there exists NT precedence for a given theological idea that developed later. But such precedence does not necessarily mean that later theological ideas adequately describe that precedence.

[28] Peter Balla, *Challenges to New Testament Theology: An Attempt to Justify the Enterprise* (Peabody, MA: Hendrickson, 1998) 20–32.

[29] Balla, *Challenges*, 31.

[30] Ibid., 23. Balla's proposition for theology to encompass religious experience is also maintained by Eric O. Springsted ("Theology and Spirituality: Or, Why Religion is Not Critical Reflection on Religious Experience," *PSB* 19 [1998] 143–59) who claims, ". . . theology precisely is 'critical reflection on religious experience,' whether one's own or somebody else's" (p. 151–52).

Balla takes to task the idea of "distinguishing between experience and interpretation." He argues that what might be called a theological affirmation in the NT is, in fact, the only available data to assess the experience described in the affirmation.

Admittedly, the experience that is reduced to writing, i.e., the experience "behind" the text, may not at all be accessible to the historian. Thus, the primary study should be the theological affirmation of the text itself. Any theological reflection of biblical figures or authors who were thinking through an experience that had happened to them and reduced it to writing as their "interpretation" of that experience must serve the historian as primary source material for the experience that may or may not be recoverable from "behind" the text. Balla believes that theology should deal with both experience and its subsequent interpretation in the NT. His thought represents a major advance in the field of theology.

A definition for "religious experience" is not always desired by some scholars. Caroline Franks Davis, for instance, notes that definitions involving the term "God" are difficult since the term "God" connotes a variety of possible interpretations. Because there exist many religious traditions and many types of experiences within each of those traditions Davis evades a definition for religious experience.[31] The term "experience" itself is also difficult to define. One may posit, however, that, despite its ambiguity, an experience is the "acquirement of genuine knowledge furnished by the world considered as external to the mind: the concept thus expresses the empirical sum of one's total knowledge."[32]

An experience of a religious nature needs further qualification. Larry Hurtado notes that Christian religious experience in the NT is expressed in the phrases "Spirit of God" or "Holy Spirit."[33] The key term then for religious experience in the NT is "spirit." The illustrious biblical scholar Hermann Gunkel once stated, "In the history of primitive Christianity the activities of the Spirit [*die Wirkungen des Geistes*] are a factor of greatest significance."[34] The

---

[31] Caroline Franks Davis, *The Evidential Force of Religious Experience* (Oxford: Clarendon Press, 1989) 29. Davis (ibid., 33–65) offers six categories of religious experience: (1) interpretive experiences; (2) quasi-sensory experiences; (3) revelatory experiences; (4) regenerative experiences; (5) numinous experiences; and (6) mystical experiences.

[32] Antoine Vergote, "Religious Experience," in *From Religious Experience to a Religious Attitude* (ed. A. Godin; Chicago: Loyola University Press, 1965) 17–18.

[33] Larry Hurtado, "Religious Experience and Religious Innovation in the New Testament," *JR* 80 (2000) 183–205.

[34] See Chapter Two, nn. 1 and 3 for bibliographic data.

"activities of the Spirit" in the history of early Christianity relate experiences that "bind" the human world with the spirit world – a *religio* experience. Thus, a definition for religious experience that reflects this may be "immediate contact with the realm of the Divine"[35] or "the realms of spirit."[36]

The term "spirit" (Hebrew רוח, Greek πνεῦμα, and Latin *spiritus*) has a varied and complex history extending from the Bible and Stoicism to nineteenth-century scholastic philosophy. The meanings originally denoted by the term "spirit" relate the idea of an invisible and active force: wind, vapor, divine breath, moving air. By analogy these meanings were applied to an equally invisible yet real sentient reality: "a spirit." The same term was used for both "wind" and "a spirit" because both were thought of as penetrating or pervading material objects. It is from the analogous meaning of πνεῦμα, that of "a spirit," that this study delineates religious experience or "immediate contact with the realms of spirit."

The concept of "a spirit" is rarely discussed. Before we proceed any further it is necessary to discuss what is meant by "a spirit." Until twenty-five years ago, little investigation was made into the concept of a spirit by philosophers of religion. According to P. J. Sherry, there were two reasons for this reluctance: 1) Rudolph Bultmann's demythologizing that led to a rejection of a belief in spirits and angels as archaic, outdated nomenclature for the modern world; and 2) the rejection of a dualistic concept of a person as both body and spirit for a person as a single psycho-physical organism. This second point hinges on the belief in a resurrection of the body and not of the spirit.[37]

Sherry observes that recent trends in the philosophy of religion define a spirit as "a person without a body," an "incorporeal agent," or an "incorporeal personal substance." From an empirical perspective, a major flaw in such definitions is that the qualification "incorporeal" negates the identifying content of the term "substance."[38] Sherry ultimately adopts an alternative definition for a spirit as "a non-physical power permeating creation, particularly men's

---

[35] Vergote, "Religious Experience," 19.

[36] Some studies that use "religious experience" in relation to the OT, NT, and Judaism have nothing to do with explicating religious experience in terms of contact with the realms of spirit. See William J. Hutchins, *The Religious Experience of Israel* (New York: Association Press, 1919), a theology of the OT; Percy Gardner, *The Religious Experience of Saint Paul* (London: Williams & Norgate, 1911), a theology of Pauline thought; and Eugene Mihaly, *Religious Experience in Judaism* (Cincinnati: Hebrew Union College–Jewish Institute of Religion, 1957), whose focus on "keeping God's law" serves his definition for religious experience.

[37] Patrick J. Sherry, "Are Spirits Bodiless Persons?" *Neue Zeitschrift für systematische Theologie und Religionsphilosophie* 24 (1982) 37–52, esp. 37–38.

[38] Ibid., 38–39.

hearts."[39] This definition reflects the way in which Stoicism conceived of πνεῦμα as a non-personal substance that permeated the universe and through which everything in creation was in sympathy.

Part of the problem raised by the phrase "incorporeal substance," i.e., "non-physical substance" (an oxymoron) among contemporary philosophers was not so much of a problem among early Jews and Christians. The term πνεῦμα denoted both the substance of a spirit (a non-physical substance) and the spirit being itself, i.e., πνεῦμα was "a kind of immaterial substance proper to spiritual beings" and "of angels' substance."[40] From this vantage point, spirits were non-corporeal, in the sense of non-physical, beings, but this did not deny them a body, a spiritual body.[41]

Sherry notes that biblical texts make use of both personal and impersonal language for the spirit. Some of the impersonal language, e.g., the spirit is "poured out," is "given to men to drink," "fills" men, or is "quenched" by men, is metaphorical language not appropriate to a person but rather more appropriate for a power. On the one hand, the terms "person" and "power" as they relate to the concept of a spirit are distinguished. On the other hand, Sherry states that "the different terms 'power' and 'person' both indicate that a spirit exists independently of men and has causal efficacy."[42]

Thus, as Sherry observes, the idea of a spirit as "a power" of some kind can only be identified with reference to a substance or a person. The issue of "power" and "person" for the meaning of "spirit" in the NT is sometimes related to Greek grammar. Since Greek does not possess the English indefinite article "a," the anarthrous forms of πνεῦμα in the NT can be rendered as "holy spirit." Translating anarthrous forms as simply "holy spirit" might suggest that spirit here denotes a material or a substance, e.g., "he has holy spirit," not unlike the use of "silver" in the phrase "the coin is silver." The anarthrous form of "spirit," however, is indefinite in meaning and so the translation into English as "a spirit" is also appropriate. This translation holds the possibility that "spirit"

---

[39] Ibid., 48.

[40] *PGL*, s.v. πνεῦμα; and Philo, *Q.G.* 1.92 wherein the "substance" (οὐσία) of angels is "spiritual" (πνευματική), and *Mos.* 1.274,277 wherein angels are "spirit beings" (πνεύματα).

[41] The phrase σῶμα πνευματικόν, "spiritual body," is oxymoronic in Greek, for the term σῶμα refers to the living physical (flesh, bone, blood) body of a human being (see LSJ, s.v. σῶμα). Paul seems to have been aware of this, for in 1 Cor 15:44 he takes care to distinguish the σῶμα ψυχικόν, "natural body," of mortals from the σῶμα πνευματικόν, "spiritual body," of spirits, i.e., the "resurrection body." This distinction is also made in Luke 24:39, . . . πνεῦμα σάρκα καὶ ὀστέα οὐκ ἔχει . . ., ". . . a spirit does not have flesh and bones . . ."

[42] Sherry, "Spirits," 47.

refers to a sentient being, "*a* spirit," one from among an indefinite number of sentient spirit beings. In some cases it is possible to speak of spirits in the same way as people speak of ghosts and the dead.

Such beings are regarded as incorporeal (at least in the sense of being without ordinary physical bodies), and as having personal attributes, e.g. speaking through mediums, being happy or unhappy, and, in the case of poltergeists, manipulating material objects.[43]

Recently, Phillip H. Wiebe contributed to a theory of spirits wherein he defends the argument of the early Christian claim that spirits are real.[44] Part of Wiebe's argument deals with the broader relationship between arguments for the reality of spirits and arguments for the existence of God. The existence of God and the existence of spirits are often treated separately. Wiebe fills this gap in the philosophy of religion.

Weibe observes that among the more than thirty definitions of "spirit" cited in the *Oxford English Dictionary*, one of the definitions relates the notion of a spirit as a person: "A supernatural, incorporeal, rational being or personality, usually regarded as imperceptible at ordinary times to the human senses, . . ."[45] Weibe notes that this definition captures one of the senses with which the term is used in contemporary society. This is also one of the primary definitions of "spirit" in the NT and early Christian literature.[46]

Despite the fact that, for the modern reader, there exist invisible forces besides spirits that affect the observable world, such as the wind, radiation, viruses, and germs, the effects of an invisible sentient being are sometimes accompanied by an observable phenomenon that distinguishes it as an intelligent being: the capacity for cognitive communication in a given language. Wiebe argues that by observable effects spirits might be accounted for by different phenomena that are attributed to them. Wiebe takes as an example the demoniacs in the gospels and argues that from these reports, "Postulating a sentient spirit for intelligible but peculiar speech does not seem to be an irresponsible use of the spirit hypothesis."[47] Weibe also notes Paul's caution to the Corinthians that idol worship makes one become "partners with demons" and that these demons exhibit a measure of rationality.[48] The idea that spirits

---

[43] Ibid., 41.

[44] Phillip H. Wiebe, *God and Other Spirits: Intimations of Transcendence in Christian Experience* (Oxford: Oxford University Press, 2004).

[45] Ibid., 141.

[46] See BDAG, s.v. πνεῦμα; and *PGL*, s.v. πνεῦμα.

[47] Weibe, *God and Other Spirits*, 35.

[48] Ibid.

communicate with intelligible language in biblical texts, such as the voice emanating from the burning bush in the presence of Moses and the spirits that are responsible for the behavior and speech of the Gadarene demoniacs, leads Wiebe to conclude that the reality of a spirit "is secured primarily by the phenomena it is said to have caused."[49]

The analogy with "breath" or "wind" highlights the observable phenomena or the effects of a spirit's action. Gunkel's statement comes to the fore in describing the active or effective (*Wirkungen*) presence of spirit beings in the lives of the earliest Christians. Philosophy and theology sometimes distinguish between the effects of "a spirit," denoted in the analogy with "breath" and "wind," and "a spirit" as a personal agent. According to Sherry the analogy with "breath" is useful "in giving us the idea of an invisible and independent agent, but it misses the characteristic of *personal* agency."[50]

The analogy, alone, may not give evidence of personality. But in the NT "spirits" communicate intelligible language as seen in the reports of demoniacs in the gospels and in the life of Paul in Acts 16:16,18 and 23:9. "Spirits" can also "teach" (cf. John 14:26; 1 Cor 2:13; and 1 Tim 4:1). Such evidence shows that a spirit is not only felt or known by its effects, but is also known through its "immediate contact" in the form of verbal communication with human beings. Spirits might also manifest themselves in the form of human beings and walk among humans as one of them as seen in the lives of Lot, Abraham, and Tobit. These appearances are sometimes known as "angelic visitations." Thus, in biblical material, spirits are personal sentient beings that make themselves known in the physical world through their effects, materializations, and by means of their articulate communications either in person (during angelic visitations) or invisibly through the possession of a human being or through some other medium such as an idol.

This book will show that one of the primary source texts for religious experience in the NT is First Corinthians 12 and 14. Paul uses πνεῦμα here in several ways: (1) anarthrous – πνεῦμα, "spirit"; πνεῦμα ἅγιον, "holy spirit"; πνεῦμα θεοῦ, "spirit of God"; (2) articular – τὸ πνεῦμα, "the spirit"; and (3) in the plural – πνεύματα, "spirits." Exegesis usually explains πνεῦμα, in both articular and anarthrous forms, as "the Holy Spirit" or "the Spirit of God" and the plural πνεύματα as "gifts" or "manifestations" of the Holy Spirit.

As Balla challenges theology to begin looking at the idea of "experience"

---

[49] Ibid., 129. Thus, "spirits are postulated entities that can be understood primarily by the causal relationships they have with objects whose existence is not in doubt" (ibid., 130). Spirits, despite their invisible nature, become, indirectly, an epistemic possibility.

[50] Sherry, "Spirits," 42 (emphasis his).

more closely in NT theology, so will my argument challenge theological exegesis of πνεῦμα in First Corinthians 12 and 14.[51] A sympathy for what Martin Hengel calls "strange and difficult" in the NT seems to be lacking in much scholarship on πνεῦμα in First Corinthians 12 and 14.[52] Hengel notes that when dealing with NT texts on angels, demons, and apparitions, the historian must be sympathetic to that thought-world and be open to the possibility of transcendent experience.[53] In addition, Rick Strelan has observed that traditional biblical scholarship steers away from the "other" world of spirit in the NT:

> In general, New Testament scholars have shown scant interest in things like angels, dreams, visions and supranormal experiences. Having been driven for over a hundred years by a scientific method that ruled out the supernatural, *a priori*, few academics would put their credibility and academic acceptability on the line by publishing on this material. If they did publish on it, it was to debunk it as historically unreliable or as illustrative of precritical thought.[54]

I will argue that the term πνεῦμα in First Corinthians 12 and 14 reflects the first-century Jewish and Christian experiences of a spirit world from which were derived intelligent, sentient yet invisible beings; not unlike the conception of "a spirit" in the ancient world as an "invisible person."[55] The phrase "spirit world" denotes a plurality of spirits that inhabit multiple dimensions (also known as "spheres" or "planes" in esoteric literature) that transcend both time and space as we know it. When we say "spirit world" we refer to "worlds of spirit" that encompass both the "higher" dimensions, known as the heavens, and the "lower" dimensions, know as the hells. The dimensions "higher" and "lower" are so-called in relation to that dimension in which the Earth inhabits. Thus, the phrase "spirit world" is used in the singular to denote a plurality of dimensions

---

[51] An earlier study on experiences of the spirit in Paul can be found in R. Birch Hoyle, *The Holy Spirit in St. Paul* (Garden City, NY: Doubleday, 1928). Hoyle admits of the "spirit-problem for theology" (ibid., 5) and proceeds to explain the Pauline experiences in their modes of thought and expression.

[52] Martin Hengel, "Problems of a History of Earliest Christianity," *Bib* 78 (1997) 131–44, esp. 133.

[53] Ibid., 134–35. See Peter Stuhlmacher, *Historical Criticism and Theological Interpretation of Scripture: Toward a Hermeneutics of Consent* (trans. Roy A. Harrisville; Philadelphia: Fortress, 1977; repr. Eugene, OR: Wipf & Stock, 2003) 84–85.

[54] Rick Strelan, *Strange Acts: Studies in the Cultural World of the Acts of the Apostles* (BZNW 126; Berlin: Walter de Gruyter, 2004) 9.

[55] See E. J. Dingwall, *Ghosts and Spirits of the Ancient World* (London: Kegan Paul, Trench, Truebner, 1930).

that are inhabited by myriad spirit beings whose attitude and disposition toward themselves, toward their neighbor, and toward God run the spectrum of vices and virtues and determine the dimension to which each spirit inhabits. These dimensions are sometimes referenced in early Jewish and Christian texts. In the *Martyrdom and Ascension of Isaiah* "seven heavens" are mentioned; in 2 Cor 12:2 Paul writes of a "third heaven"; and in John 14:2 the gospel author records ἐν τῇ οἰκίᾳ τοῦ πατρός μου μοναὶ πολλαί εἰσιν, "in my Father's house there are many rooms."[56] From the early Christian perspective, then, holy spirits would inhabit the higher spiritual dimensions that come under the direct rule of God and Christ, and evil spirits would inhabit the lower spiritual dimensions ruled by Satan. Early Christian literature is rife with comments and descriptions of the activities of spirits both good and evil.[57]

In the NT, the world of good spirits was frequently denoted as a corporate plurality in the phrases "the spirit," "the holy spirit," or "the spirit of God." The world of evil spirits was likewise denoted collectively as "the spirit of antichrist" or "the spirit of error." The spirits who placed their allegiance in Christ and God were known as "holy spirits" or what Clement of Alexandria referred to as the "spirits of Christ."[58]

Over time the phrases "the spirit," "the holy spirit," and "the spirit of God" came to signify a reality other than a world of good spirits. The theology of

---

[56] In contemporary after-life research on "higher" and "lower" dimensions, see George W. Meek, *After We Die, What Then?* (Atlanta, GA: Ariel Press, 1989) 92–96, 102, 109, 129.

[57] The Shepherd of Hermas, *Mandate* 11; *Epistle of Ignatius to the Ephesians*, 9; *Epistle of Ignatius to Hero* 2; 113; Justin Martyr, *1 Apology* 5, 9, 14, 18, 26, 39, 54, 56, 62; *Dialogue with Trypho* 7, 82; *Hortatory to the Greeks* 8, 35; Irenaeus, *Against Heresies* 1.13.3; 1.16.3; 3.11.9; 3.24.1; 4.20.6; 4.33.6; 5.6.1; Tatian, *Address to the Greeks* 14, 16; Theophilus, *To Autolycus* 2.9, 33; Athenagoras, *A Plea for Christians* 7, 9, 26, 27; Clement of Alexandria, *Exhortation to the Heathen* 3, 4; *The Instructor* 2.4; *The Stromata* 1.17, 6.8; Tertullian, *Apology* 22, 23, 26; *The Shows* 10, 12; *A Treatise on the Soul* 9, 11, 28, 46, 58; *Against Marcion* 5.8; Minucius Felix, *The Octavius* 27, 35; Commodianus, *Instructions* 18; Origen, *De princip.* 2.7.3; 3.3.3; *Against Celsus* 3.2,29,37; 4.92,95; 6.45; 7.3–7,35,67–70; 8.11,48,61–63; Hippolytus, *Refutation of All Heresies* 9.8; *Treatise on Christ and Antichrist* 2; *Against the Heresy of Noetus* 1; Cyprian, *Epistle* 9.4, 74.7,10; *Treatise* 6.6,7; Novatian, *Concerning the Trinity* 29; Methodius, *Oration Concerning Simeon and Anna* 12; Arnobius, *Against the Heathen* 1.56,62; 4.12; Lactantius, *The Divine Institutes* 2.16,17; 7.24; *Epitome of the Divine Institutes* 28; *Of the Manner in which the Persecutors Died* 11; Asterius Urbanus, *Extant Writings* 1,2,4,7,8,9,10; *Constitutions of the Holy Apostles* 7.2.21; 8.1.2; 8.2.3; Clement, *Recognitions* 5.20,31,33; *Homilies* 9.10,11,13,14,15,16, 17; 17.14,17; and *First Clement to the Corinthians* 42. An English translation of these texts can be found in *Ante-Nicene Fathers: The Writings of the Fathers Down to A.D. 325* (ed. Alexander Roberts, James Donaldson, et al.; 10 vols.; Peabody, MA: Hendrickson, 1994).

[58] Clement, *Fr. 1, Comments of the First Epistle to Peter*. ANF 2. 570.

Athanasius of Alexandria and Basil of Caesarea redefined "the holy spirit [world]" as "the Holy Spirit," a single Person of the Godhead that exists in an ontological relationship with God and Christ.[59] The position of "the Holy Spirit" in the Godhead was formulated during the fourth century. According to William H. C. Frend,

> It was not sufficient just to confess "three persons." One had to try to express in human language the reality of Father, Son, and Holy Spirit sharing the common essence (*ousia*) of the Godhead yet retaining each their identifying quality or *hypostasis*. God was Father, the Son "was begotten," the Holy Spirit "proceeded" but together they equally composed the Godhead.[60]

This theology of the Holy Spirit won out at the Council of Constantinople in 381. This theology contributed, however, to a departure from the understanding of "spirit" of the earliest Christian communities by artificially distinguishing "the Holy Spirit" as a divine Person from the rest of spirit creation. The ideas and terminology for the theology of the Holy Spirit represent developments that served the interests of the church to formulate its doctrine of the Godhead (e.g., ὑπόστασις, πρόσωπον, *persona*, *filioque*), a doctrine that the church struggled with for centuries.[61] This theological, sometimes philosophical, venture became an authoritative affirmation of Scripture. The preponderance of contemporary scholarship on πνεῦμα as "holy spirit" or "spirit of God" in the NT assumes this theology as inherent in the NT. The writings of later Fathers and Doctors of the church are credited with bringing this theology to light.

A challenge for exegesis arises out of the need to look beyond the theology of the Holy Spirit and interpret πνεῦμα within the landscape of early Jewish pneumatology.[62] This landscape (e.g., the Dead Sea Scrolls, *The Testaments of*

---

[59] For an overview of this development, see the authoritative study, Michael A. G. Haykin, *The Spirit of God: The Exegesis of 1 and 2 Corinthians in the Pneumatomachian Controversy of the Fourth Century* (Leiden: Brill, 1994).

[60] William H. C. Frend, *The Rise of Christianity* (Philadelphia: Fortress, 1984) 632.

[61] See Adolf Harnack, *History of Dogma* (7 vols.; Boston: Little, Brown, 1903; repr. 4 vols.; New, NY: Dover, 1961) 4. 108–37; and Edmund J. Fortman, *The Triune God: A Historical Study of the Doctrine of the Trinity* (Philadelphia, PA: Westminster, 1972; repr. Eugene, OR: Wipf & Stock, 2006).

[62] The impact of Jewish studies on the interpretation of the NT has proven significant. No scholar today would deny that Jesus was a Jew. Likewise, the world of the earliest Christians was thoroughly Jewish. The earliest Christians can rightly be deemed a Jewish sect alongside the Pharisees, Sadducees, and the Essenes. On his mission to the Gentiles, Paul brought with him components of his Judaism (however modified!) and even boasted in it. Whereas Paul deviates at times from traditional Judaism (especially with regard to the Law), his pneumatology remains Jewish, with the added dimension of soteriology that he shares with the pneumatology

the Twelve Patriarchs, Philo, and Josephus) provided the basis from which early Christian pneumatology emerged and thrived.[63] Also, discriminations in the translation of the Greek text will ultimately affect interpretation. The occurrences of πνεῦμα without the definite article τό in 1 Cor 12:3 and 14:2,16 are almost always rendered with the definite article in English as "*the* Holy Spirit," implying the third Person of the Trinity. Greek lacks an indefinite article "a." But, as Sherry rightly notes, "This is not to say that we cannot continue to use the term 'a spirit', for there are plenty of Biblical references specifying a particular spirit . . . as well as ones using the plural πνεύματα."[64] An equally grammatically plausible translation for πνεῦμα in the anarthrous is "a spirit," indicating one of many. This not only follows the meaning of the indefinite in Greek, but also reflects the historical milieu of πνεῦμα in first-century Jewish-Christian pneumatology.

The anarthrous form of πνεῦμα in 1 Cor 12:3 and 14:2,16 arguably denotes "a spirit of God," "a holy spirit," and "a spirit." This argument is reinforced further if we understand πνεύματα in 14:12,32 to indicate "spirits" and not "gifts" or "manifestations" of the Holy Spirit. The definite τὸ πνεῦμα, "the spirit," indicates the "spirits" in a collective sense, i.e., "the spirit world." The experience of communicating with the spirit world is found in Paul's list of 1 Cor 12:8–10. The verbal utterances of spirits are denoted by the terms προφητεία, "prophecy," and γλωσσῶν, "tongues" or glossolalia. Paul describes these inspired forms of speech as someone who speaks ἐν πνεύματι, "in a spirit." First Corinthians 12 and 14 will be explained as an explicit example of religious experience in the form of communication with the spirit world.

The invisible, transparent nature of spirits, denoted in the same term for "wind" (πνεῦμα), did not easily promote communication between the physical world and the world of spirits. If communication was desired by human beings with invisible sentient beings called "spirits," then certain physical media were required as well as a keen knowledge of how the media functioned. One of the features of religious experience is that any activity that solicits the spirit world

---

of 1QHᵃ and Jewish Wisdom tradtion. See Robert P. Menzies, *The Development of Early Christian Pneumatology: with special reference to Luke-Acts* (JSNTSup 54; Sheffield: JSOT, 1991), who shows that the historical background for "spirit" in the NT is found within the pneumatological perspectives of the late Second Temple period and Wisdom.

[63] See John R. Levison, "The Pluriform Foundation of Christian Pneumatology," in *Advents of the Spirit: An Introduction to the Current Study of Pneumatology* (ed. Bradford E. Hinze and D.Lyle Dabney; Marquette Studies in Theology 30; Milwaukee: Marquette University Press, 2001) 66–85.

[64] Sherry, "Spirits," 43 n. 14.

"will be conditioned by the physical material in which and with which alone it can work."[65] In First Corinthians 12 and 14, Paul's reference to media for the spirit world is found in the terms προφήτης, "prophet," and εἴδωλα, "idols." In antiquity, prophets and idols were common media used for direct intercourse with the spirit world. The voices of the idols and symptoms exhibited by possessed human mediums were the effects created by spirits that made communication with the spirit world possible.

In contemporary society communication with the spirit world is known as "spiritism" or "spiritualism." Usually, these two terms denote communication with "the dead" during "séances." This definition is a misnomer borne out of American popular culture during the late nineteenth century. Linguistically, the term "spiritism" is based upon the Latin term *spiritus*, the equivalent of the Hebrew term רוח and the Greek term πνεῦμα, terms that denoted any number of spirits both good and evil, human or nonhuman. Paul's exposition in First Corinthians 12 and 14 uses πνεῦμα for "a spirit of God" and "a holy spirit." The term "spiritism" as applied to Paul's exposition then would reflect these spirits in particular.

The religious experience of direct inspiration and communication with the spirit world should not be related to what a mystic might do, even though both the mystic and the prophet experience the spirit world. Eugene Boring observes the two major distinctions between these two types of experiences: The prophet

is different from the mystic in that (a.) he doesn't necessarily seek the deity, but is sought by him and (b.) his 'communion' with the deity (=the experience of inspiration) is not an edifying end in itself for the prophet, but is the means of receiving the message for the community.[66]

Whereas the mystic seeks union with the deity in private, cloistered quarters as an edifying experience unto itself, the prophet serves the community as a channel through which the spirit world communicates. Unlike mysticism, spiritism functions within a congregational setting of believers and worshipers of God who solicit the spirit world via a prophet for edification, guidance, and instruction from spirits themselves. Mysticism is an experience that serves an individual (unless, of course, the mystic is given orders by the divine realm to

---

[65] Joachim Wach, "Universals in Religion," in idem, *Types of Religious Experience, Christian and Non-Christian* (Chicago: University of Chicago Press, 1951) 44.

[66] M. Eugene Boring, "'What are We Looking For?' Toward a Definition of the Term 'Christian Prophet,'" *SBLSP* (1973) 142–54, esp. 148. On mysticism, see Bernard McGinn, *The Foundations of Mysticism: Origins to the Fifth Century* (A History of Western Christian Mysticism 1; New York: Crossroad, 1994).

communicate the experience to others for their benefit, e.g., the Revelation of John).

Chapter One of this book is an overview of recent research on prophecy, glossolalia, and πνεῦμα terms in First Corinthians 12 and 14. This overview will show the many different ways in which scholars have explained these three items in Pauline studies. It will be argued that much of this recent research tends to neglect the experiential nature of "spirit."[67] A way forward will be proposed by arguing for an interpretation of First Corinthians 12 and 14 as religious experience, an interpretation that few scholars, if any, have yet to make. This experience involved direct contact with the good spirit world. The spirit world in Paul is given a brief overview. This overview attempts to show how τὸ πνεῦμα went from designating "the spirit world" in Paul's early Jewish-Christian environment (i.e., the historical context of πνεῦμα) to denoting "the Holy Spirit" as a divine Person in the fourth-century church (i.e., the subsequent theological interpretation of πνεῦμα). It is to the former that NT exegesis must show sympathy.

Next will follow in Chapter Two a survey of scholarly monographs on religious experience of the spirit in both the OT and the NT. These monographs serve as the kind of examples of scholarship that are sensitive to the complex range and experiences of רוח and πνεῦμα in biblical literature. This survey will establish the basis from which to approach First Corinthians 12 and 14 as religious experience.

In Chapter Three, Greco-Roman and Jewish texts contemporary with Paul will be studied for their descriptions of spirits communicating through the agency of prophets. Despite the enlightening work of anthropological field research bearing on the religious experience of spirits,[68] used effectively by

---

[67] See Bernard Cooke, *Power and the Spirit of God: Toward an Experience-Based Pneumatology* (Oxford: Oxford University Press, 2004) who believes that "much remains to be done in clarifying the Spirit as divine 'outreach' to creation" (p. v). Cooke's work, however, relegates "spirit" to a "power" without mention of the possibility for personal spirit beings. His work is meant to serve the needs of the church in contemporary society. Cooke's attention though to an "experience-based pneumatology" reveals a much-needed sensitivity for biblical scholarship to explain πνεῦμα as an agent of empirical experience among humans despite its immediate metaphysical nature.

[68] See most recently David J. Hufford, "Beings without Bodies: An Experience-Centered Theory of the Belief in Spirits," in *Out of the Ordinary: Folklore and the Supernatural* (ed. Barbara G. Walker; Logan, UT: Utah State University Press, 1995) 11–45; Jeannette M. Mageo and Alan Howard, ed., *Spirits in Culture, History, and Mind* (New York: Routledge, 1996); and James L. Cox, "Spirit Mediums in Zimbabwe: Religious Experience in and on Behalf of the Community," *Studies in World Christianity* 6 (2000) 190–207.

some scholars to explain religious phenomena in the NT (Pilch, Davies),[69] I will, instead, draw from first-century Greco-Roman and Jewish texts that give explicit detail for spirits who enter into the bodies of prophets and communicate with the spectators present. This evidence is situated closer in time and in place to the NT, providing a more immediate environment from which to enhance Paul's pithy language in First Corinthians 12 and 14.

Chapters Four, Five, and Six are an exegesis of 1 Cor 12:1–3, 4–11, and 1 Cor 14:1–33, 37–40. The exegesis will attempt to show that Paul's exposition is not so much about "spiritual gifts" as it is about "communication with the spirit world" or "spiritism." The glossolalists that Paul admonishes were mediums through whom spirits spoke foreign languages. The term "medium" is used in English Bibles only in contexts of occult or divinatory activity that is outlawed by Yhwh (see Lev 20:6,27; Deut 18:11–12). A prophet in First Corinthians 14 was likewise a medium who acted as an instrument for spirits. Mediums were not condemned for being "mediums" per se. In the OT, mediums were condemned only for the type of spirit that communicated through them (see Appendix 2).

A conclusion summarizes the research and states the significant contributions. The conclusion is followed by three appendices: (1) the Greek text and a translation of 1 Cor 12:1–11 and 14:1–33, 37–40; (2) the meaning and usage of the term "spiritism"; and (3) a statistical analysis of πνεῦμα as "holy spirit" in the NT. The appendices are meant to provide substantive elaborations on pivotal points in the book.

---

[69] See also Colleen Annette Shantz, "Paul in Ecstasy: An Examination of the Evidence for and Implications of Paul's Ecstatic Religious Experience," (Ph.D. diss., The University of St. Michael's College, 2003), who explains prophecy and glossolalia in Paul via the anthropological research of Goodman on spirit possession.

Chapter 1

"Now Concerning Spiritual Gifts": The State of Research on the Interpretation of Prophecy, Glossolalia, and πνεῦμα Terms in First Corinthians 12 and 14

1. Introduction

The translation of 1 Cor 12:1a as "now concerning spiritual gifts" has long been a beacon for both lay and scholarly audiences who navigate the pithy text of Paul's discourse in First Corinthians 12–14. As early as the *KJV* of 1611, translators inserted "spiritual gifts" in its text, italicizing, however, the word "gifts" to indicate that it does not occur in the Greek text at 12:1a. Yet most modern English versions and many commentaries continue to use the phrase "spiritual gifts" in their translation and explanation of Paul's message.

Scholars are motivated to concentrate on First Corinthians 12–14 as texts that enumerate a variety of "gifts" (12:8–10) and elaborate two of these gifts, namely, prophecy and glossolalia, or speaking in tongues as it is frequently called (14:1–39). The consensus of scholars is that this passage was written by Paul in response to the misuse of spiritual gifts, particularly glossolalia. Some Corinthians had been practicing glossolalia to the exclusion of its usefulness in the community; apparently, interpretation of glossolalia had been ceded to its mere linguistic fascination and a self-serving demonstration of a superior spiritual ability among those who practiced it. Paul attempts to correct this notion by both placing glossolalia in a wider context of related spiritual endowments and establishing criteria to which all spiritual endowments are subject: the Lordship of Christ, Christian love, and the edification of the congregation.

First Corinthians 12–14 functions as a complete rhetorical unit.[1] 1 Cor 12:1a begins with a transitional formula περὶ δέ, "now concerning," introducing a new topic in Paul's discourse: the πνευματικά. This is carried through to First Corinthians 13, a digression on "love," that serves to place the spiritual gifts in proper perspective: without love the greatest spiritual gift is worthless (13:2).

---

[1] Margaret M. Mitchell, *Paul and the Rhetoric of Reconciliation: An Exegetical Investigation of the Language and Composition of 1 Corinthians* (Louisville: Westminster/John Knox, 1992) 266. Sometimes First Corinthians 12–14 is elaborated within a larger block of material dealing with community worship, 11:2–14:40. See Mitchell, ibid., 258–59; and Anthony C. Thiselton, *The First Epistle to the Corinthians* (NIGTC; Grand Rapids: Eerdmans, 2000) 900.

The discourse on πνευματικά resumes in 1 Cor 14:1, wherein Paul focuses on two spiritual endowments: prophecy and glossolalia. The problems that glossolalia had been causing, i.e., glossolalia without interpretation and as a means for self-promotion in the community, force Paul to discuss *intelligible* inspired speech, i.e., prophecy, in antithetical arguments against glossolalia. This exposition is carried through until 14:40. A new topic begins in 1 Cor 15:1 where Paul's use of a disclosure formula, "I want you to know" (8:1 and 12:3), establishes a transition from the previous discussion on spiritual endowments in 12–14.[2] The occurrence of πνευματικά in 12:1 is linked to its occurrence in 14:1. The transitional and disclosure formulas, "now concerning . . . I want you to know," in 12:1,3 and 1 Cor 15:1 establish First Corinthians 12–14 as a distinct rhetorical unit.

Joop F. M. Smit has noted that γλῶσσα occurs twenty-one times and the word groups προφητεία, προφητεύω, προφήτης twenty times in First Corinthians 12–14.[3] Despite this abundance, prophecy and glossolalia are never defined by Paul but simply used in antithetical arguments whereby Paul attempts to give priority to prophecy over that of glossolalia. Hence, scholars have attempted in various ways to identify what prophecy and glossolalia meant for Paul and why he urged the Corinthians to practice prophecy over that of glossolalia.

I will present recent interpretations of inspiration and of πνεῦμα terms in First Corinthians 12 and 14 to show how this research has affected the course of the discussion.[4] Retrospects summarize this research with comments on some major points of it. A prospect suggests an interpretive scheme that moves the discussion forward to take into account the explicit nature of the experiences underlying the terms "spirit," "prophecy," and "glossolalia."

This prospect will challenge traditional scholarship on First Corinthians 12 and 14 by posing the argument that Paul's advice to the Corinthians concerns matters related to spiritism, i.e., communication with the spirit world. Paul's antithetical arguments that give priority to prophecy (intelligible speech) over that of glossolalia (unintelligible speech) are to be understood in the context of spirit communication: Paul advises the Corinthians to seek those spirits who communicate in the mother tongue of the spectators (prophecy) so that all may

---

[2] So Raymond F. Collins, *First Corinthians* (SacPag 7; Collegeville, MN: Liturgical Press, 1999) 533.

[3] Joop F. M. Smit, "Argument and Genre of 1 Cor 12–14," in *Rhetoric and the New Testament* (ed. Stanley E. Porter and T. H. Olbricht; JSNTSS 90; Sheffield: Sheffield Academic Press, 1993) 211–30.

[4] For our purposes, chap. 13 is a digression on "love" and, for the most part, does not serve to inform the discussion on inspiration and πνεῦμα terms in chaps. 12 and 14.

linguistically understand what the spirits are saying. The fact that glossolalia (spirits who communicate in a language unknown by the spectators) should have ever occurred in the first place has generated much scholarly debate with little consensus. In the context of spirit communication, Paul did not intend for glossolalia to remain a novelty or to be practiced for purposes of mere self-promotion in the community.

Given the nature of this somewhat maverick interpretation, proceeding chapters of this book are devoted to a survey of the scholarly discussion on the matter of early Christian experience of the activities of spirit beings and first-century documentation of spirit communication via speaking-trance mediums in Plutarch, Josephus, Philo, and Pseudo-Philo. These chapters will establish a basis from which to spring forward to the argument that Paul's exposition in First Corinthians 12 and 14 relates to the matter of spirits communicating through prophets in the language of the congregation. This argument covers the texts 1 Cor 12:1–3 (Chapter 4), 1 Cor 12:4–11 (Chapter 5), and 1 Cor 14:1–33, 37–40 (Chapter 6). For now, an assessment of recent research on these texts provides a perspective that gives both hindsight on the scholarly debates and a platform from which to move forward.

2. Prophecy and Glossolalia in First Corinthians 12 and 14

Prophecy in NT studies has received considerable attention only during the past thirty years. Several studies have been devoted to the subject, notably those of Nils I. J. Engelsen,[5] Theodore M. Crone,[6] E. Earle Ellis,[7] David Hill,[8] Wayne A. Grudem,[9] David E. Aune,[10] M. Eugene Boring,[11] Thomas W. Gillespie,[12] and

---

[5] "Glossolalia and Other Forms of Inspired Speech according to 1 Corinthians 12–14," (Ph.D. diss., Yale University, 1970).

[6] *Early Christian Prophecy: A Study of Its Origin and Function* (Baltimore, MD: St. Mary's University, 1973).

[7] *Prophecy and Hermeneutic in Early Christianity* (Grand Rapids: Eerdmans, 1978).

[8] *New Testament Prophecy* (London: Marshall Morgan & Scott, 1979).

[9] *The Gift of Prophecy in 1 Corinthians* (Lanham, MD: University Press of America, 1982; repr. Eugene, OR: Wipf & Stock, 1999).

[10] *Prophecy in Early Christianity and the Ancient Mediterranean World* (Grand Rapids: Eerdmans, 1983).

[11] *The Continuing Voice of Jesus: Christian Prophecy and the Gospel Tradition* (Louisville, KY: Westminster/John Knox, 1991).

[12] *The First Theologians: A Study in Early Christian Prophecy* (Grand Rapids: Eerdmans, 1994).

Christopher Forbes.[13]   All of these studies define prophecy as a form of intelligible speech of divine origin, but beyond this point they differ in their methodological approach, concentration, and criticism.

Glossolalia in the NT has also received a great deal of attention from scholars, some of which was motivated by the Pentecostal and charismatic movements of the 1960s and 1970s. Glossolalia occurs together with prophecy as a form of inspired speech in First Corinthians 14, and many of the monographs on prophecy also treat glossolalia in this context. But some studies focus solely on glossolalia, most notably those of Francis W. Beare,[14] Stuart D. Currie,[15] John P. M. Sweet,[16] Stephen S. Smalley,[17] Ernest Best,[18] Roy A. Harrisville,[19] Vern S. Poythress,[20] Anthony C. Thiselton,[21] Wayne A. Grudem,[22] H. Wayne House,[23] Watson E. Mills,[24] Philip F. Esler,[25] and Gerald Hovenden.[26]

Prophecy is commonly understood in present-day society as a "foretelling" of future events. In biblical and extra-biblical material, "prophecy" is a term taken from Greek, the preverb προ- "before" (in a spatial sense) + the verb φημί, "to speak," with a further suffix -της, carrying the sense of forthtelling.[27] Prophetic speech may refer to the past, present, or future; yet it is always a

---

[13] *Prophecy and Inspired Speech in Early Christianity and its Hellenistic Environment* (Tübingen: Mohr, 1995; repr. Peabody, MA: Hendrickson, 1997).

[14] "Speaking with Tongues: A Critical Survey of the New Testament Evidence," *JBL* 83 (1964) 229–46.

[15] "'Speaking in Tongues': Early Evidence outside the New Testament Bearing on 'Glossais Lalein,'" *Int* 19 (1965) 274–94.

[16] "A Sign for Unbelievers: Paul's Attitude to Glossolalia," *NTS* 13 (1967) 240–57.

[17] "Spiritual Gifts and First Corinthians 12–14," *JBL* 87 (1968) 427–33.

[18] "The Interpretation of Tongues," *SJT* 28 (1975) 45–62.

[19] "Speaking in Tongues: A Lexicographical Study," *CBQ* 38 (1976) 35–48.

[20] "The Nature of Corinthian Glossolalia: Possible Options," *WTJ* 40 (1977–1978) 130–35.

[21] "The 'Interpretation' of Tongues: A New Suggestion in the Light of Greek Usage in Philo and Josephus," *JTS* 30 (1979) 15–36.

[22] "1 Corinthians 14:20–25: Prophecy and Tongues as Signs of God's Attitude," *WTS* 41 (1979) 381–96.

[23] "Tongues and the Mystery Religions of Corinth," *BibSac* 140 (1983) 134–50.

[24] *A Theological/Exegetical Approach to Glossolalia* (Lanham, MD: University Press of America, 1985).

[25] "Glossolalia and the Admission of Gentiles into the Early Christian Community," *BTB* 22 (1992) 136–42.

[26] *Speaking in Tongues: The New Testament Evidence in Context* (Sheffield: Sheffield Academic Press, 2002).

[27] See the classic text: Erich Fascher, *Prophetes: Eine sprach- und religionsgeschichtliche Untersuchung* (Gießen: A. Töplemann, 1927). This is an extensive analysis of the uses of προφήτης, προφητεύειν, and προφητεία in both secular and religious Greek texts.

"speaking forth" of such matters. This was usually done by one designated as "a prophet."[28] Glossolalia is usually understood as "speaking in tongues." The Greek is from γλῶσσα, "tongue" or "language," and λαλεῖν, "to utter."

Any discussion of prophecy and glossolalia in First Corinthians 12 and 14 is bound up with the context in which Paul discusses the matter. Paul's discussion is polemical, not theological or philosophical. We have no descriptions of what prophecy and glossolalia were and how they occurred. Paul is not descriptive but rather prescriptive; his discourse is not meant to inform the Corinthians of the nature of these phenomena (for they were all too familiar with them), but rather to advise the Corinthians on how such phenomena should function within the church.

3. OT Prophecy and Paul

Scholars sometimes view prophecy in the OT, Paul's scriptural heritage, as the only true antecedent to Christian prophecy. The Hebrew term נביא, "prophet," is translated into Greek (LXX) as προφήτης, the term used for Christian prophets. Thus, Hill notes that "the prophets of the Christian community share the same title of dignity as the prophets of the old Covenant, *prophētēs*."[29] Hill further notes the connection of early Christian prophecy with an OT prophetic tradition found in Acts 2:16–21 that recalls the end time of prophecy promised in Joel 2:28–29.[30]

Earlier OT scholarship argued for an "evolution" from ecstatic prophecy in Israel's early history (1 and 2 Samuel, 1 and 2 Kings, influenced by the ecstasy of Israel's Canaanite religious environment) to the "literary" prophecy of the major prophets (Isaiah, Jeremiah, Ezekiel), intelligible and without ecstasy, thus reflecting a normative, i.e., canonical, view of prophecy.[31] Gordon D. Fee follows this line of reasoning when he compares NT prophecy with OT

---

[28] See Georg Luck, *Arcana Mundi: Magic and the Occult in the Greek and Roman Worlds* (Baltimore, MD: Johns Hopkins University Press, 1985) who states that a prophet "is a person who speaks for a god, or through whom a god speaks and reveals his plans" (p. 230).

[29] Hill, *New Testament Prophecy*, 11–12.

[30] Ibid., 12. See also Grudem, *Gift of Prophecy*, 47.

[31] See Sigmund Mowinckel, "'The Spirit' and the 'Word' in the Pre-Exilic Reforming Prophets," *JBL* 53 (1934) 199–227; idem, "Ecstatic Experience and Rational Elaboration in Old Testament Prophecy," *AcOr* 13 (1935) 264–91; Charles F. Whitley, *The Prophetic Achievement* (Leiden: Brill, 1963) 1–23; Charles D. Isbell, "The Origins of Prophetic Frenzy and Ecstatic Utterance in the Old Testament World," *WTJ* 11 (1976) 62–80; and Menahem Haran, "From Early to Classical Prophecy: Continuity and Change," *VT* 27 (1977) 385–97.

prophecy. He argues that OT prophetic activity "as it came to be canonized" had little to nothing to do with ecstasy, frenzy, or mania.[32] NT prophets exhibited the rational prophetic activity of the literary prophets rather than the irrational prophetic activity exhibited by Saul's and Samuel's prophets.[33] Thus, NT prophecy finds continuity with "canonical" OT prophecy.[34]

A variation on Fee's position contrasts Paul's Hellenistic environment, wherein prophecy was an ecstatic utterance, with OT canonical prophecy that was without ecstasy, i.e., intelligible utterance. Hill argues that Paul derived his view of prophecy from OT/Jewish models whereas the Corinthians derived their view from "the Greek ecstatic model" akin to the mystery cults and to experiences reflected in the terms "*mainomai, manits* and *enthousiasmos.*"[35] On the basis of Paul's derision of glossolalia among the Corinthians, Hill views Paul's argument in First Corinthians 14 as one that questions the notion of religious ecstasy (glossolalia) among the Corinthians as the legitimate sign for true spirit inspiration.[36]

Raymond F. Collins argues that in 1 Cor 14:22 Paul's contrast between believers and nonbelievers might allude to a distinction between biblical prophecy and prophecy in the Greco-Roman world. Like Hill, Collins distinguishes Hellenistic ecstatic utterance, "sounds expressed by someone in a trance," from biblical prophecy where the prophet "spoke an intelligible utterance."[37] Whereas unintelligible sounds might impress nonbelievers, prophecy serves the greater cause as "an instrument of conversion of the nonbeliever."[38]

---

[32] Gordon D. Fee, *The First Epistle to the Corinthians* (NICNT; Grand Rapids: Eerdmans, 1987) 595.

[33] So Fee (ibid., n. 72) who states, "However one is to understand 'ecstasy' of Saul and the others in 1 Sam. 19:19–24, e.g., it scarcely belongs to the canonical understanding, and the latter is what influenced Christ and the early Christians."

[34] So, too, Leon Morris, *The First Epistle of Paul to the Corinthians: An Introduction and Commentary* (Tyndale New Testament Commentaries; Grand Rapids: Eerdmans, 1985) 168; and Simon J. Kistemaker, *1 Corinthians* (New Testament Commentary; Grand Rapids: Baker, 1993) 479.

[35] Hill, *New Testament Prophecy*, 121.

[36] Ibid., 121–22.

[37] Collins, *First Corinthians*, 508.

[38] Ibid.

4. Greco-Roman Prophecy and Paul

Scholars have traditionally looked to extra-biblical literature, especially Hellenistic, to shed light on the nature of the phenomenon of prophecy and glossolalia in Paul. The nature of prophecy is sometimes defined on the basis of Paul's intent to distinguish prophecy from glossolalia. The view that the Corinthian practice of prophecy occurred in the manner of existing Hellenistic ecstatic speech brings glossolalia into the broader arena of ecstatic speech. Thus, Engelsen and Crone argued that for Paul prophecy was ecstatic, and on this basis prophecy and glossolalia were not distinct among the Corinthians.[39] According to Engelsen, Paul is the first to differentiate between two forms of ecstatic speech, the one intelligible, prophecy, and the other unintelligible, glossolalia, while the Corinthians themselves made no real distinction as such.[40]

Scholars often compare the ecstatic speech of oracular shrines, especially the Delphic oracle, with the unintelligible nature of glossolalia in First Corinthians 14. The idea is that the ecstatic nature of Delphic inspiration produced unintelligible speech like that of glossolalia among the Corinthians.[41] Joseph Fontenrose, however, has argued for a different picture of Delphic inspiration wherein the Pythia instead spoke an intelligible utterance.[42] The ecstatic nature of Delphic inspiration does not imply that oracular speech was unintelligible. Rather, ecstasy describes the psychic condition in which intelligible speech was spoken.

The inspired or ecstatic nature of the Pythia refers to the god putting her "out

---

[39] Engelsen, "Glossolalia," 204; and Crone, *Early Christian Prophecy*, 219, 226.

[40] Engelsen, "Glossolalia," 100, 189.

[41] So Johannes Behm, "γλῶσσα," *TDNT* 1. 719–26; Frederick F. Bruce, *1 and 2 Corinthians* (New Century Bible; London: Oliphants, 1971) 117; Luke T. Johnson, "Norms for True and False Prophecy in First Corinthians," *American Benedictine Review* 22 (1971) 29–45; Hans Conzelmann, *1 Corinthians: A Commentary on the First Epistle to the Corinthians* (Hermeneia; Philadelphia: Fortress, 1975) 234; House, "Tongues and the Mystery Religions," 134–50; Terrance Callan, "Prophecy and Ecstasy in Greco-Roman Religion and in 1 Corinthians," *NovT* 27 (1985) 125–40; and Joop F. M. Smit, "Tongues and Prophecy: Deciphering 1 Cor 14,22," *Bib* 75 (1994) 175–90.

[42] Joseph Fontenrose, *The Delphic Oracle* (Berkeley: University of California, 1978) who states that a "close study of all reliable evidence for Delphic mantic procedures reveals . . . no frenzy of the Pythia, no incoherent cries interpreted by priests. The Pythia spoke clearly, coherently, and directly to the consultant in response to his questions" (p. 10).

of herself" in order to control her vocal chords and speak intelligibly through her.[43] Ecstasy is no indicator of the manner of speech, whether intelligible or unintelligible, but simply the inspired state in which speech is delivered.[44] Forbes has argued on the basis of this evidence that Christian glossolalia is not a linguistic parallel phenomenon with Hellenistic oracular speech, for oracles normally spoke in plain Greek.[45]

Whereas glossolalia is sometimes distinguished linguistically from Hellenistic oracular speech, Christian prophecy as inspired *intelligible* speech is seen as a comparable phenomenon to prophecy in the Greco-Roman world. Aune argues that both Hellenistic prophecy and Christian prophecy were intelligible verbal messages communicated by a god/spirit through an inspired human medium.[46] Forbes is clear that Hellenistic prophecy and Christian glossolalia, although both inspired, were different speech forms, the former intelligible, the latter unintelligible. But Christian prophecy was similar to Hellenistic "inspiration manticism" that "shares with early Christian prophecy the belief that revelation from the gods characteristically takes the form of statements made by persons believed to be under the influence of the god(/s), who declare his/their will in a particular matter."[47] Max Turner follows Aune and Forbes with a detailed critique of NT concepts of prophecy, most notably the psychology of prophecy, the content of prophetic speech, and charismatic exegesis.[48]

---

[43] The interpretation of Delphic oracular speech as "frenzied," hence unintelligible, is derived from the contributions of late Latin writers such as Lucan who translated the Greek term μανία, "inspiration," "rapture," by the Latin terms *insania* and *vercordia*, with the result that depicts a mad and raving Pythia. Plutarch does not deny the inspired state of the Pythia (ἐνθουσιασμός, "possessed by a god") but claims that her speech was intelligible. See Plutarch, *Mor.* 407 BC.

[44] So Plutarch, *Mor.* 623 A, "to those possessed by a god (ἐνθεαζομένοις) it is given to chant oracles in metre and few madmen can one find whose ravings are not in verse and song."

[45] Forbes, "Early Christian Inspired Speech and Hellenistic Popular Religion," *NovT* 28 (1986) 257–70. So, too, André Mehat, "L'Enseignement sur 'les choses de l'esprit' (1 Corinthiens 12, 1–3)," *RHPR* 63 (1983) 395–415, esp. 397–98; and Charles H. Talbert, *Reading Corinthians: A Literary-Theological Commentary on 1 and 2 Corinthians* (New York: Crossroad, 1992) 89.

[46] Aune, *Prophecy in Early Christianity*, 201, 339.

[47] Forbes, *Prophecy and Inspired Speech*, 280.

[48] Max Turner, *The Holy Spirit and Spiritual Gifts in the New Testament Church and Today* (Peabody, MA: Hendrickson, 1998) 200–12.

5. Prophecy and Glossolalia: Trance

In a related aspect, some scholars look at whether prophecy and glossolalia were conscious speech acts, i.e., whether or not trance was involved. Turner has recently asked, "Were New Testament 'Tongues' Ecstatic?"[49] Turner complains about the misuse of the term "ecstasy" in NT studies and states that little can be known from the Greek text about the psychological state of glossolalia.[50] He concludes with Engelsen that glossolalia was neither more nor less ecstatic than prophecy.[51]

Allen R. Hunt argues that Paul distinguishes between intelligible, edifying non-ecstatic prophecy from ecstatic, unintelligible glossolalia in 1 Cor 14:13–19.[52] Hunt argues that the nonuse of the νοῦς, "mind," during the occurrence of glossolalia is evidence for a trance state, for the mind remains ἄκαρπος, "unfruitful" (14:14).[53] Prophecy is a nontrance speech act, for inspired prayer and song occur with the use of the "mind" (τῷ νοΐ) and "with the spirit" (τῷ πνεύματι) in tandem (14:15). "This use of the νοῦς proves crucial when seeking to illumine Paul's understanding of the nature of inspired speech."[54]

Forbes argues that 1 Cor 14:14 gives no clear evidence for a trance state: "that the mind is unfruitful does not necessarily mean that it is unconscious."[55] Instead, the issue involves for whom the mind is unfruitful, the glossolalist or the congregation who do not understand the glossolalist. Forbes believes that Paul is not concerned with the existence of trance during glossolalia but rather that Paul's argument concerns intelligibility.[56]

---

[49] Ibid., 237.

[50] Ibid., 238. Following Forbes (*Prophecy and Inspired Speech*) who states, "'Ecstasy' is one of the most misused terms in the vocabulary of New Testament scholarship in our area" (p. 53).

[51] Turner, *The Holy Spirit and Spiritual Gifts*, 238 n. 66.

[52] Allen R. Hunt (*The Inspired Body: Paul, the Corinthians, and Divine Inspiration* [Macon, GA: Mercer University Press, 1996]) states, "Paul does not understand prophecy to involve an ecstatic or trance-like state . . . tongues require such a state of ecstasy" (p. 125).

[53] According to Hunt, an "unfruitful mind" is akin to an ecstatic state wherein the mind is temporarily suspended and "wanders" beyond the body.

[54] Hunt, *Inspired Body*, 126. So, too, Callan, "Prophecy and Ecstasy," who distinguishes between nonecstatic prophecy from tongues accompanied by trance (p. 137).

[55] Forbes, *Prophecy and Inspired Speech*, 64.

[56] Ibid. So, too, David E. Garland, *1 Corinthians* (Baker Exegetical Commentary on the New Testament; Grand Rapids: Baker Academic, 2003) who states, "Nowhere does Paul refer to the mental state of the speaker, and he does not use a Greek word that implies some ecstatic state or trance" (p. 585).

Fee, however, argues that neither prophecy nor glossolalia were ecstatic utterance. He bases this view on Paul's description for "order" in the Corinthian congregation (14:27,28).[57] Fee believes that, on the basis of 1 Cor 14:23–25, 32, Paul rejects any form of Spirit-inspiration that borders on ecstatsy. Prophets were to be linguistically understood and the glossolalist must practice restraint and self-control in the congregation if no one is present to interpret.[58] Fee identifies the psychic condition of ecstasy with unintelligible speech and frenzied physical behavior.

Callan devotes an article to the question of whether NT prophecy was a trance phenomenon. He begins his thesis, though, in an unusual way. NT prophecy is a matter of spirit possession whereby "a spirit enters the human body and takes control of it."[59] Callan then intends to discern whether NT prophecy involved trance, i.e., "whether or not the ordinary consciousness of the prophet is replaced by another."[60] Callan ultimately concludes that prophecy in First Corinthians 12–14 did not involve trance. But if NT prophecy is a matter of spirit possession, as Callan claims, then spirit possession would include a trance state as Callan defines it, "the consciousness of the prophet replaced by another," i.e., by a spirit. Callan creates an untenable paradox: NT prophecy is spirit possession but is not a trance phenomenon.

Callan claims that whereas Greek mantic prophecy was accompanied by trance, prophecy in Hellenistic Judaism, as seen in Philo, did not involve trance. This showed Philo's fidelity to the scriptural presentation of prophecy.[61] Paul is similar to Philo in seeing prophecy as something that does not involve trance in fidelity to the OT נביא. By identifying prophecy with glossolalia, however, the Corinthians understood prophecy to be accompanied by trance. Paul's antithetical arguments for distinguishing prophecy from glossolalia in First Corinthians 14 were meant to correct this view: prophecy is rational and

---

[57] Fee, *First Epistle*, 595, 598.

[58] Ibid., 598, 696. So, too, Robert Gundry, "'Ecstatic Utterance' (NEB)?" *JTS* 17 (1966) 299–307, who states, "These rules imply that in normative Christina glossolalia the speaker was not seized with uncontrollable excitement, but maintained self-control with the ability to wait or to keep completely quiet" (p. 306).

[59] Callan, "Prophecy and Ecstasy," 126.

[60] Ibid.

[61] Ibid., 129, 134–35. Callan states, "In ordinary Greek usage *prophētēs* is most commonly used to designate the entranced mantis of an oracle . . . , and less commonly to designate spokesmen who are not entranced. But when *prophētēs* is used to translate *nabi*, the proportions are reversed. In the OT *prophētēs* is used most commonly to designate those who are at least not clearly entranced and less commonly to designate those who are clearly in a trance" (ibid., 133).

intelligible (νοῦς, 14:15,19) and glossolalia involved trance because it was unintelligible (ἄκαρπος, 14:14).[62]

6. Glossolalia as a "Sign"

The ecstatic nature of tongues is elaborated by some scholars to be a "sign" (σημεῖον) of divine activity. Gillespie believes that glossolaliac outbursts occurred immediately after prophecy as a legitimizing sign for the divine nature of intelligible prophetic speech.[63] But this interpretation of glossolalia tends to reduce it to terms that are not clearly perceptible in Paul's discourse as something that works simply as a sign for prophetic confirmation. Sweet argued that the contrast is not ecstasy (glossolalia) versus rationality (prophecy) but rather unintelligible speech versus intelligible speech, so that, in practice, prophecy was no less a "sign" for divine activity than was glossolalia.[64] The distinction that Paul draws between prophecy and glossolalia was meant not to suppress glossolalia but to regulate it.[65]

Glossolalia has also been seen in Paul as a "sign" of divine judgment. This is based on Paul's reference to Isa 28:11 in 1 Cor 14:21, wherein Paul begins a new stage in his argument for prophecy over tongues by stating that tongues are a "sign." Grudem notes that in the NT "sign" can mean "an indication of God's approval and blessing . . ." or "an indication of God's disapproval and warning of judgment."[66] Grudem argues that tongues are a sign of God's disapproval of unbelievers. Hence, Paul's loose quotation of Isa 28:11 ("with foreign languages and with lips of foreigners I will speak to this people") is adapted by him as an oracle of divine judgment on those who speak uninterpreted tongues. Paul would rather have unbelievers come to the Christian faith. Prophecy, as a sign of God's presence and blessing on believers, makes a positive impression

---

[62] Ibid., 136–37.

[63] See Gillespie, *First Theologians*, 129–64. So, too, Antoinette C. Wire, *The Corinthian Women Prophets: A Reconstruction through Paul's Rhetoric* (Minneapolis: Fortress, 1990) 140.

[64] Sweet, "A Sign for Unbelievers," 247. So, too, Ben Witherington, *Conflict and Community in Corinth: A Socio-Rhetorical Commentary on 1 and 2 Corinthians* (Grand Rapids: Eerdmans, 1995) 275, 279; and Hovenden (*Speaking in Tongues*) who states, "The contrast between tongues and prophecy is not 'ecstasy' versus 'rationality', but 'unintelligibility' versus 'intelligibility'" (p. 150).

[65] Sweet, "A Sign for Unbelievers," 254.

[66] Grudem, "God's Attitude," 390.

on unbelievers that brings them into the fold (cf. vv. 22b, 24-25).[67] Sweet argues that uninterpreted tongues create the divisions that Paul attempts to rectify between those Corinthians who speak in tongues and those who do not. Sweet suggests that the abuse of glossolalia was seeing it as a sign of spiritual superiority. In an attempt to curtail this sense of superiority, Paul was responding to a Corinthian slogan: "tongues are a sign for believers."[68] Thus, the glossolalists believed their gift to be a "sign" of God's approval of them as πνευματικοί, "spiritual ones," for the benefit of believers. The practice of glossolalia without interpretation is for Paul a "self-indulgent use of unintelligible noises"[69] that only separates believers from one another. Glossolalia that gave glossolalists a sense of superiority over others led to arrogance.[70]

Bruce C. Johanson argues that "sign" has a positive context in 1 Cor 14:22. He believes the contradiction between v. 22 and vv. 23–25 is reconciled once we read v. 22 as a rhetorical question that expresses not Paul's views but that of the glossolalist's: tongues are for unbelievers, prophecy is for believers.[71] Paul's rebuttal comes in vv. 23–25 where he rejects the (positive) view of those who believe that glossolalia is a sign for unbelievers. Glossolalia, instead, is madness (μαίνεσθε) to unbelievers, while prophecy convinces unbelievers that God is in their presence.[72]

Karl O. Sandnes argues on the basis of the topos of common advantage that the context of "signs" in 1 Cor 14:20–25 is not meant to combat factionalism between spiritually superior-feeling glossolalists and other Corinthians, but rather to advise the practice of prophecy at the expense of tongues.[73] Although Sandnes is in agreement with Grudem that a "sign" can denote judgment or salvation, he argues that glossolalia is not meant as a sign of judgment against the glossolalists. Whereas the OT context of Isa 28:11–12 is one of judgment against Israel, Paul uses it as a proof-text that glossolalia cannot convey

---

[67] Ibid., 395–96. Cf. David E. Lanier, "With Stammering Lips and Another Tongue: 1 Cor 14:20–22 and Isa 28:11–12," *CTR* 5 (1991) 259–86.

[68] Sweet, "A Sign for Unbelievers," 241.

[69] Thiselton, *First Epistle*, 1075.

[70] See Richard A. Horsley, "'How can some of you say there is no resurrection of the dead?' Spiritual Elitism in Corinth," *NovT* 20 (1978) 202–31; and Dale B. Martin, "Tongues of Angels and Other Status Indicators," *JAAR* 59 (1991) 347–89.

[71] Bruce C. Johanson, "Tongues, a Sign for Unbelievers?: A Structural and Exegetical Study on 1 Corinthians XIV. 20–25," *NTS* 25 (1979) 180–203, esp. 193.

[72] Ibid., 194.

[73] Karl O. Sandnes, "Prophecy–A Sign for Believers (1 Cor 14,20–25)," *Bib* 77 (1996) 1–15. Contra Sweet, Horsley, and Martin.

understanding of God's message.[74] Sandnes wonders that if the effect of prophecy and tongues on the unbeliever is related in vv. 23–25 from v. 22a, and the effect of prophecy on the believer is not picked up again from v. 22b, then "What is the sign character of prophecy for the believers in light of vv. 24–25?"[75]

Sandnes suggests that the negative impact of glossolalia on the outsider is used by Paul to persuade *believers* which gift of inspired speech to practice: prophecy. Verse 22 is a rhetorical teaching device for Christians (believers) that illustrates the effects of prophecy and glossolalia from the perspective of outsiders. Glossolalia is a "sign" to unbelievers or outsiders that they remain outside of the Christian community, for they do not understand the tongue. Hence, Paul's aim is to convince believers to practice prophecy rather than glossolalia for the sake of unbelievers.[76]

7. Glossolalia: Human Language?

A matter related to the argument "intelligible speech" versus "unintelligible speech" is whether glossolalia conveyed cognitive content like prophecy, or whether it was a noncognitive language. This is sometimes elaborated by scholars in relation to the Pentecost event in Acts 2:1–13 where Luke speaks of ἑτέραις γλώσσαις, "other tongues," a phenomenon that might reflect xenolalia, i.e., speaking an unlearned cognitive language.[77]

Sometimes xenolalia is distinguished from what Paul means by glossolalia on the basis that, unlike Luke, Paul never qualifies tongues as an "other" (ἕτερος) language. On the one hand, Paul's use of the term ἑτερογλώσσοις in his quote of Isa 28:11 (1 Cor 14:21; Isa 28:11 [LXX]: γλώσσης ἑτέρας, referring to the language of the Assyrians) provides evidence that glossolalia might have

---

[74] Ibid., 7–11.

[75] Ibid., 13–14.

[76] Ibid., 14–15.

[77] Cyril G. Williams (*Tongues of the Spirit: A Study of Pentecostal Glossolalia and Related Phenomena* [Cardiff: University of Wales Press, 1981]) states whether "the Lukan account of tongues at Pentecost (*lalein heterais glōssais*–'to speak in other tongues', Acts 2:4) refers to a phenomenon identical with the Corinthian experience described by Paul (*lalein glōssais* 'to speak in tongues,' 1 cor 14:5 . . .)" (p. 25).

involved real human language for Paul.[78] On the other hand, others argue that by the use of "foreign languages" in the passage in the book of Isaiah Paul makes not an identity but an analogy for glossolalia.[79] This argument is reinforced by Collins who observes that Paul also compares "speaking in tongues with the inarticulate sounds of musical instruments (14:8)."[80]

The phrases "human tongues" and "angelic tongues" in 1 Cor 13:1 are sometimes thought to show that glossolalia was a real human language. Forbes cites the "human tongues" as Paul's way of implying that foreign languages are what a glossolalist spoke. He concludes that glossolalia involved foreign languages: "the *miraculous ability* to speak foreign languages otherwise unknown to the speaker."[81]

Similarly, Hovenden argues that the angelic, heavenly language of Job's inspired daughters in the *Testament of Job*, an Egyptian Jewish text of the first century B.C.E. or first century C.E., was meaningful and whose content was praise.[82] Depending on the dating of the *Testament*, Hovenden argues that the angelic languages might depict the same phenomenon that Paul means by the phrase "tongues of angels."[83] Thiselton criticizes this view and believes that

---

[78] So Hovenden, *Speaking in Tongues*, 129. Hovenden (ibid.) further suggests that γλῶσσα can mean "language" in Greek usage and glossolalia had content as genuine communication on the basis of 1 Cor 14:2 (ὁ γὰρ λαλῶν γλώσσῃ . . . λαλεῖ . . . θεῷ). So, too, Gundry, "'Ecstatic Utterance' (NEB)?": "The use of the term [γλῶσσα] for understandable language far exceeds its use for obscure speech, especially in biblical Greek" (p. 299). Harrisville ("Speaking in Tongues") notes, however, that the term γλῶσσα appears together with the verb λαλεῖν seven times in the LXX, and while γλῶσσα by itself might indicate a language in biblical Greek, "the Septuagint translator appears to have known nothing of a technical term for speaking in tongues" (pp. 38–39).

[79] So Esler, "Glossolalia and the Admission of the Gentiles," 139; and Steve Summers, "Out of My Mind for God: A Social-Scientific Approach to Pauline Pneumatology," *JPT* 13 (1998) 77–106, esp. 103. Esler believes that xenolalia never existed in Christian circles and that Luke, who depicts xenolalia in Acts 2, does so in error by relying on "earlier traditions which have become distorted over as glossolalia died out among the Christian communities and the nature of the phenomenon became misunderstood in the absence of first-hand experience" (p. 141).

[80] Collins, *First Corinthians*, 455–56.

[81] Forbes, *Prophecy and Inspired Speech*, 63.

[82] Hovenden, *Speaking in Tongues*, 126–27.

[83] Ibid., 127. Thus, "if, as is possible, the *Testament* is reflecting an awareness of the phenomenon of tongues, it might be that it also reflects a belief that tongues are linguistically meaningful." So, too, Bruce, *1 and 2 Corinthians*; Conzelmann, *1 Corinthians*, 221 n. 27; Fee, *First Epistle*, 630–31; Richard B. Hays, *First Corinthians* (IBC; Louisville, KY: John Knox, 1997) 223; Turner, *The Holy Spirit and Spiritual Gifts*, 228; Collins, *First Corinthians*, 475; and Garland, *1 Corinthians*, 585.

the nature of tongues is better explained on the analogy of "sighs too deep for words" (Rom 8:26).[84]

Garland argues that glossolalia was not a miraculous ability to speak in unlearned languages, as Forbes maintains. Garland believes that the term γλῶσσα can, indeed, mean "language."[85] He observes, however, that glossolalia is addressed to God (1 Cor 14:2,14,28) and not to humans (14:2,6,9), that it consists of "mysteries" unintelligible to humans (14:2) that benefit only the speaker (14:4), and that it communicates with God in ways that normal human language does not (14:15).[86] Thus, glossolalia is not a known human language, for, initially, it serves to communicate with God. Garland follows the argument of Esler: Paul's reference to foreign languages in Isa 28:11 is used as an analogy to explain glossolalia in 1 Cor 14:10–11. Glossolalia was not identical to a foreign language but only akin to it.[87]

For those who argue that glossolalia was bona fide human language, the "interpretation of tongues" (ἑρμηνεία γλωσσῶν) raises a related matter as to whether "interpretation" means "translation," and therefore the translation of a known language. The "interpretation of tongues" is complementary to speaking in tongues, and Paul urges that glossolalia should not be practiced in public unless accompanied by interpretation.

Thiselton has argued that "interpretation" does not mean "translation" but rather "putting into articulate speech." He bases his argument on the usage of διερμηνεύω, ἑρμηνεία, and διερμηνευτής in Philo and Josephus as meaning "put into words."[88] Thiselton suggests that glossolalia is merely a gift for the inarticulate and illiterate that the Corinthians are urged to give up as "childish ways" (1 Cor 13:11).[89] He reads 1 Cor 14:6–11 as examples of a communicative barrier that points to the probability that glossolalia did not take the form of a foreign language that an "interpreter" might translate.[90] He defines glossolalia as "a kind of non-conceptual, pre-rational outlet for a powerful

---

[84] Thiselton, *First Epistle*, 973.

[85] The Greek word γλῶσσα also means the physical tongue (Luke 16:24) and regular speech (1 John 3:18).

[86] Garland, *1 Corinthians*, 584.

[87] Ibid. So, too, Fee, *First Epistle*, 598.

[88] Thiselton, "'Interpretation,'" 15.

[89] Ibid., 31. Thiselton argues that Paul intended that tongues should never occur in public on the basis of 1 Cor 14:13, which Thiselton renders, "he who speaks in a tongue should pray for the power to produce articulate speech" (p. 36).

[90] Thiselton, *First Epistle*, 1109.

welling up of emotions and experiences."[91] Similarly, Garland argues that "interpretation of tongues" is not a word-for-word translation but rather an interpretation of what was said or an explanation of the experience.[92]

Hovenden, however, believes that Thiselton's argument misses Paul's personal testimony in 1 Cor 14:18 that gives some merit for the existence of glossolalia.[93] Hovenden argues that Paul does not prohibit glossolalia but wants any occurrence of glossolalia to be accompanied by interpretation.[94] He claims that Thiselton reads 1 Cor 13:11, "childish ways," with a significance that it was not meant to convey.[95] Hovenden concludes that Paul likely believed that glossolalia was human language. The intended meaning for "interpretation of tongues" must be "to translate" or "to interpret."[96]

Forbes offers a detailed critique of Thiselton's position. Forbes states that, whereas ἑρμηνεύω and διερμηνεύω can mean "to articulate" or "to put into words" an inarticulate utterance, as Thiselton argues, many occurrences of these terms require the rendering "to translate" or "to interpret or expound."[97] Forbes concludes that such a comparison does not do justice to the Pauline evidence that always refers to the interpretation "of tongues." Unlike Philo and Josephus where the phrase "interpretation of tongues" does not occur, the meaning of

---

[91] Thiselton, "'Interpretation,'" 30. Thiselton (*First Epistle*) states that the phenomenology of glossolalia in 14:4 is best expressed in the terms of Gerd Theissen and Krister Stendahl who explain that "these utterances well up, in experiences of wonder and praise as the Holy Spirit releases inhibitions and censors, in ways which reflect pre-conscious yearnings, sighings, or 'building up' which evade cognitive objectification and formulation" (p. 1108).

[92] Garland, *1 Corinthians*, 586. Fee (*First Epistle)* is a little unclear: "Although this term could mean something like 'translation,' it can also mean 'to put into words'; in this context it probably means to articulate for the benefit of the community what the tongues-speaker has said" (p. 598).

[93] Hovenden, *Speaking in Tongues*, 116–17.

[94] See Fee (*First Epistle*) who similarly states, "The problem is not speaking in tongues per se but speaking in tongues without interpretation—which from the context seems very likely what the Corinthians were doing" (p. 659).

[95] Hovenden, *Speaking in Tongues*, 115–16.

[96] Ibid., 119. Turner (*The Holy Spirit and Spiritual Gifts*, 227–28) also believes that Thiselton's proposal is unconvincing in the light of the loosely quoted Isa 28:11, "other tongues," that Turner believes serves as a parallel to glossolalia. Thus, "interpretation of tongues" would more likely mean "translation." Contra Fee, Summers, Esler, and Garland, who see Isa 28:11 functioning as an analogy to glossolalia.

[97] Forbes, *Prophecy and Inspired Speech*, 65.

"interpretation" in Paul cannot be separated from the meaning of the "tongue" to be interpreted.[98]

According to Robert Zerhusen, the problem posed by glossolalia was not a matter of a miraculous (inspired) ability to speak unlearned foreign languages. Instead, glossolalia was simply the use of non-Greek native languages spoken by multilingual individuals that went untranslated during the worship service.[99] Zerhusen appeals to research that describes Corinth as a highly multilingual seaport city, a culture that was best described as dyadic or "group-oriented" instead of individualistic.[100]

While many Corinthian Christians spoke Greek as a second language (the language of prophecy at Corinth), some might have been compelled to praise God in their native language without the thought of translating for others. Zerhusen argues that 1 Cor 14:5,13,27 urges those who speak in their native non-Greek language to translate for the others present: "Paul wants people whose native languages are not Greek to be able to freely worship God in the language most familiar to them (as long as they translate)."[101] Zerhusen claims that scholarly preoccupation with the psychology of glossolalia is misdirected. Instead, scholars should focus on the cosmopolitan makeup of the Corinthian congregation as the source for the problems posed by glossolalia.

---

[98] Forbes (ibid., 70) states, "General lexicographical considerations ought not to be allowed to dominate immediate, contextual exegesis–especially when lexicography itself provides an alternative, and more exegetically suitable, meaning for ἑρμηνεύω anyway." See Thiselton's response to Forbes's criticism, *First Epistle*, 975–77.

[99] See Robert Zerhusen, "The Problem Tongues of 1 Cor 14: A Reexamination," *BTB* 27 (1997) 139–52. Zerhusen observes that "Paul never explicitly states whether or not the language-speaker knew or understood the language that he was using," and that "Paul's emphasis throughout the chapter is . . . on the hearer of the problem languages, not the speakers" (p. 145).

[100] Ibid., 150: "At Corinth, while everyone knew the *lingua franca* (i.e., Greek), people came from all over the Roman Empire bringing their non-Greek native languages with them. These languages ranged from widely spoken languages such as Aramaic to more remote 'local' languages like Lycaonian or Demotic Egyptian."

[101] Ibid., 146.

8. Glossolalia: Social Science and Contemporary Pentecostalism

Studies on glossolalia in Paul are sometimes informed by the researches of the social sciences[102] and the experiences of contemporary Pentecostal and charismatic groups.[103] Contemporary experiences of glossolalia are thought to represent the same gift of tongues mentioned in 1 Cor 12:10. J. Massyingberde Ford argued that studies on glossolalia that do not take into account contemporary phenomena "appear to speak from the standpoint of persons who have no empirical experience of the phenomenon which they wish to evaluate."[104]

Many linguists who have recorded and analyzed contemporary glossolalia conclude that modern examples of tongues are not a known human language and are lexically uncommunicative.[105] James R. Jaquith concludes that the contents of contemporary glossolalia are not cognitive language but "verbalizations which superficially resemble language in certain of its structural aspects."[106] Poythress has suggested that contemporary glossolalia is a coded

---

[102] See L. Carlyle May, "A Survey of Glossolalia and Related Phenomena in Non-Christian Religions," *American Anthropologist* 58 (1956) 75–96; James R. Jaquith, "Towards a Typology of Formal Communicative Behaviors: Glossolalia," *Anthropological Linguistics* 9 (1967) 1–8; Felicitas D. Goodman, *Speaking in Tongues: A Cross-Cultural Study of Glossolalia* (Chicago: University of Chicago Press, 1972); John P. Kildahl, *The Psychology of Speaking in Tongues* (San Francisco: Harper and Row, 1972); Vern S. Poythress, "Linguistic and Sociological Analyses of Modern Tongues-Speaking: Their Contributions and Limitations," *WTJ* 42 (1979) 367–98; H. Newton Malony and A. Adams Lovekin, *Glossolalia: Behavioral Science Perspectives on Speaking in Tongues* (Oxford: Oxford University Press, 1985); Esler, "Glossolalia and the Admission of the Gentiles," 136–42; and Summers, "Out of My Mind for God," 77–106.

[103] Anthony A. Hoekema, *What About Tongue-Speaking?* (Grand Rapids: Eerdmans, 1966); Frederick D. Bruner, *A Theology of the Holy Spirit: The Pentecost Experience and the New Testament Witness* (Grand Rapids: Eerdmans, 1970); William J. Samarin, *Tongues of Men and Angels: The Religious Language of Pentecostalism* (New York, NY: Macmillan, 1972); René Laurentin, *Catholic Pentecostalism* (Garden City, NY: Doubleday, 1977); Williams, *Tongues of the Spirit*; Morton T. Kelsey, *Tongues Speaking: The History and Meaning of Charismatic Experience* (New York, NY: Crossroad, 1981); Frank D. Macchia, "Sighs too Deep for Words," *JPT* 1 (1992) 47–73; and Mark J. Cartledge, *Charismatic Glossolalia: An Empirical-Theological Study* (Burlington, VT: Ashgate, 2002).

[104] J. Massyingberde Ford, "Towards a Theology of Speaking in Tongues," *TS* 32 (1971) 3–29, esp. 15.

[105] Samarin, *Tongues of Men and Angels*, 121–49.

[106] Jaquith, "Toward a Typology," 6. Likewise, Goodman (*Speaking in Tongues*) describes her personal experience with glossolalists: "The meaningful speech slowly dissolves, as if wiped away, and the patterns of glossolalia take over" (p. 94). See her linguistic analysis, ibid., 99–

language that the interpreter of tongues deciphers by means of a supernatural "key."[107] Patterns emerge in the vocalizations of modern glossolalia and the discerned structures are what amounts to language patterning.[108]

First-person accounts of glossolalia have been recorded by social scientists. The initial experience of glossolalia is described as an emotional conversion or a feeling of release and freedom.[109] Other personality effects of glossolalia include feelings that are described with biblical antecedents such as being "born again" or "baptized in the Spirit." Phrases such as "falling down" or "slain of the Spirit" are based on the physiological/psychical experience of the initial onrush of glossolalia. Once the experience has transpired, the person feels "wonderful."[110]

Noncognitive, nonlexical glossolalia of contemporary society is sometimes considered a poor example for the evidence in First Corinthians 14. Gundry observes that the verb λέγω, "to say," is used for both glossolalia (14:16) and for normal human speech. The verb λαλέω, "to speak," is used in connection with speaking with the mind which implies intelligible speech (14:19) and for prophetic speech (14:29).[111] Hence, γλῶσσα + λαλεῖν can arguably refer to cognitive language in Paul.

Donald A. Carson suggests that while contemporary glossolalia might be more akin to a computer program as a coded "language," a nonhuman language yet conveying real information, the evidence in Paul is in favor of glossolalia as a human language. Carson observes that 1 Cor 12:10,28 refer to different kinds (γένη) of tongues, some of which may have been human languages.[112] Carson concludes that the relationship between the content of glossolalia and its subsequent interpretation into intelligible language shows that in Paul

---

123, and her conclusion, 124, that contemporary glossolalia is "a vocalization pattern, a speech automatism, that is produced on the substratum of hyperarousal dissociation, reflecting directly, in its segmental and suprasegmental structure, neurophysiological processes present in this mental state."

[107] Poythress, "Linguistic and Sociological Analyses," 375–76.

[108] See Virginia J. Hine, "Pentecostal Glossolalia: Toward a Functional Interpretation," *JSSR* 8 (1969) 211–26. An example of transcribed glossolalia appears in this way: "aish nay gum nay tayo" (Kildahl, *Psychology of Speaking in Tongues*, 36).

[109] Goodman, *Speaking in Tongues*, 24–57; Maloney and Lovekin, *Glossolalia*, 161–85.

[110] Goodman, *Speaking in Tongues*, 6.

[111] Gundry, "'Ecstatic Utterance' (NEB)?" 304.

[112] Donald A. Carson, *Showing the Spirit: A Theological Exposition of 1 Corinthians 12–14* (Grand Rapids: Baker, 1987) 86–87. So, too, Zerhusen ("Problem Tongues") who states, "Differentiation into individual, particular tongues seems to imply language of some kind" (p. 141).

glossolalia bore cognitive content. Despite this interpretation of the Pauline evidence, researches and experiences in modern glossolalia show that there is no univocal cognitive content in contemporary tongues.[113]

Contemporary xenolalia (xenoglossy, xenoglossai), i.e., the inspired ability to speak real but unlearned human languages, is sometimes suggested as a modern example of the Pentecost event in Acts 2 and the gift of glossolalia in Paul.[114] During the early part of the twentieth century, the xenolalia of Carlos Mirabelli, a Brazilian medium born in Botucatu, Sao Paolo (1889–1951), of Italian parentage, was documented in a 73-page account of his mediumistic abilities.[115] Mirabelli was observed to speak in a trance not only his own language and local dialects but also the following languages: German, French, English, Dutch, Czech, Arabic, Japanese, Russian, Spanish, Hebrew, African dialects, Albanian, Latin, Chinese, ancient and modern Greek, Polish, and Egyptian, none of which he knew in his waking state.

More recent research in xenolalia appears in the studies of Ian Stevenson who documents occurrences of those who speak human languages unknown to them.[116] Such contemporary evidence might enlighten arguments for glossolalia in Paul as a cognitive human language much like that portrayed in Acts 2:4–13. Both Luke and Paul use the same term to indicate unknown language spoken by the prompting of the spirit, γλῶσσα.

Luke T. Johnson, however, not only questions the legitimacy of comparing the glossolalia in Paul with the xenolalia in Acts 2:4–13 but also defines xenolalia as a phenomenon that occurs in the hearing rather than in the speaking (Acts 2:8). The gift is to *hear* one's own language, and not everyone is given this gift (2:13). In contrast with Acts, Johnson states that Paul "could hardly make clearer his conviction that tongues are an intrinsically noncommunicative form or utterance (1 Cor. 13:1; 14:2, 4, 7–9, 16–17, 23)."[117]

---

[113] Carson, *Showing the Spirit*, 87–88.

[114] See Thiselton (*First Epistle*) who notes that as early as the commentator Charles Hodge, both Acts 2:4–11 and First Corinthians 14 were understood to relate the same phenomenon. Quoting Hodge, Thiselton states that glossolalia in Paul was "the ability to speak in languages primarily unknown to the speakers. The nature of this gift is determined by the account given in Acts 2:4–11 . . ." (p. 975). See n. 77 above.

[115] Rodolpho H. Mikulasch, ed., *O medium Mirabelli: o que ha de verdadeiro nos seus milagres, e a sua discutida mediumnidade posta em prova* (Santos, Brazil: Graphic Radium, 1926). See also Hans Gerloff, *Das Medium Carlos Mirabelli* (Tittmoning: Walter Pustet, 1960).

[116] Ian Stevenson, *Xenoglossy: A Review and Report of a Case* (Charlottesville, VA: University Press of Virginia, 1974); and idem, *Unlearned Language: New Studies in Xenoglossy* (ibid., 1984).

[117] Luke T. Johnson, "Tongues, Gift of," *ABD* 6. 597.

9. Retrospect on Prophecy and Glossolalia

Prophecy and glossolalia are usually, although not always, thought to be some kind of inspired speech whose impetus is the Holy Spirit. The presence of trance in prophecy and glossolalia is made on the basis of whether the speech is intelligible or unintelligible. The state of mind of the prophet and the manner of speech are seen as accompanying components.

On the one hand, some argue that Paul does not distinguish between rational and irrational states of mind because he provides no language for trance states. Rather, Paul distinguishes between intelligible and unintelligible forms of speech. On the other hand, whereas some argue that a rational state of mind was necessary for rational speech, rational speech might also occur in an irrational ("ecstatic") state of mind. Paul is concerned for the primacy of prophecy if glossolalia cannot be interpreted, but the prophet's state of mind may not have had any effect on whether his speech was intelligible or unintelligible.

Glossolalia is considered to be either a human language with cognitive content or a nonhuman language with no cognitive content. Each point of view is argued on the basis of the NT Greek text, Hellenistic sources, and on the reports of modern charismatic and Pentecostal experiences and the social sciences. Social-science models have provided questionable comparative data for glossolalia in the NT. The evidence in the NT suggests the possibility that glossolalia was either a noncognitive or a cognitive human language. Social-science research, however, concludes that present-day glossolalia communicates only noncognitive content. Given this scenario, the occurrence of xenolalia in present-day society as bona fide cognitive language possibly serves as a model for both Acts 2 and First Corinthians 14.

Prophecy is usually interpreted from the OT, early Judaic and Hellenistic sources contemporary with Paul, but it is hardly ever interpreted from present-day occurrences of prophecy. This is mainly because glossolalia occurs most frequently in Pentecostal and charismatic groups as the true sign for the presence of the Holy Spirit. Intelligible speech does not have the legitimizing effect for the Spirit's presence in Pentecostal churches. The preponderance of glossolalia in Pentecostal churches serves as the only model for "Holy Spirit speech" for social scientists to investigate within an institutional context.

Thus, prophecy in modern society is usually studied by anthropologists within nonwestern primitive societies in present-day African countries.[118] As such, prophecy in modern primitive society stands outside of the institution of the Christian churches. Even though glossolalia in present-day Pentecostalism is the prevalent social-science model for inspired speech in the NT, some scholars have ventured into the social sciences for modern models to enlighten our knowledge of NT prophecy.[119]

Despite the many different scholarly views of what, why, and how prophecy and glossolalia were among the Corinthians, one matter is relatively clear from Paul's discourse as it has come down to us: Paul attempts to advise the practice of inspired speech in the Corinthian congregation by emphasizing intelligible speech over that of unintelligible speech.

10. Πνεῦμα Terms in First Corinthians 12 and 14

We now turn to the component of prophecy and glossolalia that gave them their inspired nature: πνεῦμα, "spirit." The number of πνεῦμα terms in First Corinthians 12–14 comes to twenty, 13 in chap. 12 and 7 in chap. 14. By ratio, this represents the highest concentration of πνεῦμα terms in any one chapter of the Pauline or disputed Pauline letters. The term χαρίσματα, "gifts," occurs three times in chap. 12 and, in conjunction with πνεῦμα terms, is read by many scholars as Paul's discourse on the proper use of "spiritual gifts" within the Corinthian gatherings.

---

[118] For example, Edward E. Evans-Pritchard, *Nuer Religion* (Oxford: Clarendon Press, 1956); Bengt Gustaf M. Sundkler, *Bantu Prophets in South Africa* (2nd ed.; London: Oxford University Press, 1961); and John Beattie and John Middleton, *Spirit Mediumship and Society in Africa* (New York: Africana Publishing, 1969).

[119] NT scholarship has been influenced by the work of the social sciences in general, for example, see the works of Bruce J. Malina, John J. Pilch, and Jerome H. Neyrey. Davies has contributed a study that explores the idea of spirit possession from the field studies of anthropologists as an application to prophets and prophecy in the NT (*Jesus the Healer*, 22–24, 43–51). Aune (*Prophecy in Early Christianity*) utilized terms coined by the anthropologist Erika Bourguignon, "possession trance" and "vision trance," to describe early Christian prophecy and revelation (pp. 19–22). See also Pilch (*Visions and Healing*) who uses the anthropological work on altered states of consciousness by Felicitas Goodman to inform the phenomenon of trance states in Acts.

11. Proposed Backgrounds to Paul's Use of πνεῦμα in First Corinthians 12 and 14

The term πνεῦμα was originally used in Greek to denote "air" or "moving wind." In anthropological and cosmological contexts it was used to denote a fine material substance that made up the universe and was a component of physical vitality.[120] Paul's understanding and use of πνεῦμα is sometimes seen to come from his Hebrew/Jewish roots. The LXX provides the phrase πνεῦμα θεοῦ as a translation for the Hebrew רוח אלוהים. Thus, the spirit of God in Paul (1 Cor 12:3) is a derivative of OT usage.[121]

Paul's usage of πνεῦμα in relation to prophecy in First Corinthians is not far afield from the understanding of the spirit in Judaism as the spirit of prophecy. In Judaism, the spirit of God was known as "the spirit of prophecy." Targums Onkelos and Pseudo-Jonathan use the phrase "the spirit of prophecy" as a translation for "the spirit of God" in the Torah.[122] The phrase "the spirit of prophecy" is found in *Jub.* 31:12 and in Philo, *Fug.* 186 and *Mos.* 1.277. It has been argued that, like Jewish authors, Paul views the spirit as the spirit of prophecy (cf. 1 Thess 5:19–20 and 1 Cor 12–14).[123]

Other backgrounds and influences have been proposed for Paul's use of πνεῦμα. James A. Davis provided a study that attempted to relate the Jewish wisdom tradition, e.g., the Wisdom of Solomon, to the use of πνεῦμα in Paul.[124] Walter Schmithals authored a study of a possible Gnostic background to πνεῦμα in Paul.[125] Birger Pearson argued that Hellenistic Judaism is the appropriate

---

[120] See Alexander of Aphrodisia, *De mixtione* 216.14–17: ὑποτίθεται τὴν σύμπασαν οὐσίαν, πνεύματός τινος διὰ πάσης αὐτῆς διήκοντος, ὑφ' οὗ συνέχεταί τε καὶ συμμένει καὶ σύμπαθές ἐστιν αὐτῷ τὸ πᾶν, "the whole of substance is unified by *pneuma* which wholly pervades it through which the universe is made kept together, is stable, and is made intercommunicating (sympathetic)."

[121] So Walter C. Wright, "The Source of Paul's Concept of Pneuma," *CovQ* 41 (1983) 17–26.

[122] See the texts *Tg. Onq.* Gen 41:38; Num 11:25–29; 24:2; 27:18; *Tg. Ps.-J.* Gen 41:38; 45:27; Num 11:25–29.

[123] See Archie Hui, "The Spirit of Prophecy and Pauline Pneumatology," *TynBul* 50 (1999) 93–115.

[124] James A. Davis, *Wisdom and Spirit: An Investigation of 1 Corinthians 1:18–3:20 against the Background of Jewish Sapiential Traditions in the Greco-Roman Period* (New York: University Press of America, 1984).

[125] Walter Schmithals, *Gnosticism in Corinth: An Investigation of the Letters to the Corinthians* (trans. J. E. Steely; Nashville: Abingdon, 1971). For criticism, see Robert M. Wilson, "How Gnostic Were the Corinthians?" *NTS* 19 (1972) 65–74; and Judith L. Kovaks,

backdrop to view πνεῦμα in Paul, especially the way in which Philo uses the term in prophecy.[126] Non-Jewish Hellenistic Greek sources such as Plutarch are rarely cited for Pauline pneumatology. A recent study by Terence Paige, however, attempts to use First Corinthians as indirect evidence for a Corinthian, i.e., a Hellenistic Greek, view of πνεῦμα, a view with which Paul was familiar and which he attempts to correct.[127]

These are some of the major backgrounds presented for Pauline pneumatology by scholars. Paul's pneumatology reflects LXX usage wherein the phrases πνεῦμα θεοῦ and πνεῦμα ἅγιον both occur (see 1 Sam 19:23 [LXX] and Isa 63:10,11 [LXX]). As a Jew, Paul would have been familiar with the LXX usage; πνεῦμα θεοῦ and πνεῦμα ἅγιον both occur in 1 Cor 12:3. Prophecy then for Paul was a matter of inspiration by the "spirit of God."

12. πνευματικά in 1 Cor 12:1

The meaning of 1 Cor 12:1a, περὶ δὲ τῶν πνευματικῶν, is unclear. Its precise meaning has caused much debate among scholars. The plural τῶν πνευματικῶν is an adjective used substantively in the genitive case. The genitive case is ambiguous and therefore may be read as either neuter ("spiritual things") or masculine (and feminine) ("spiritual persons").[128]

"The Archons, the Spirit, and the Death of Christ: Do We Need the Hypothesis of Gnostic Opponents to Explain 1 Cor 2:6–16?" in *Apocalyptic and the New Testament: Essays in Honor of J. Louis Martyn* (ed. J. Marcus and M. L. Soards; JSNTSS 24; Sheffield: JSOT, 1989) 217–36.

[126] Birger Pearson, *The Pneumatikos-Psychikos Terminology in 1 Corinthians: A Study in the Theology of the Corinthian Opponents of Paul and its Relation to Gnosticism* (SBLDS 12; Missoula, MT: Scholars Press, 1973) 44–47.

[127] Terence Paige, "Spirit at Corinth: The Corinthian Concept of Spirit and Paul's Response as Seen in 1 Corinthians" (Ph.D. diss., University of Sheffield, 1991). See also Paul Meyer, "The Holy Spirit in the Pauline Letters," *Int* 33 (1979) 3–18, who gives the Corinthian view of the spirit.

[128] As Collins (*First Corinthians*, 446) rightly observes. The ambiguity of this adjective is apparent in translations of its occurrence in 1 Cor 2:13, πνευματικοῖς πνευματικά συγκρίνοντες: "expressing spiritual truths in spiritual words" (*NIV*); "describing spiritual realities in spiritual terms" (*NAB*); and "teach spiritual things to spiritual people" (*CEV*).

12.1 *"Spiritual Persons"*

Some scholars argue that since πνευματικῶν refers to "spiritual persons" elsewhere in First Corinthians (2:15; 3:1; 14:37), then πνευματικῶν in 12:1a is to be understood as a masculine plural. The idea is that, given the ambiguity of gender, priority should be given to the masculine. For some who interpret the term as "spiritual persons," the distinction between neuter and masculine makes little difference in 12:1a; in the words of Barrett, "spiritual persons are those who have spiritual gifts."[129] Others view "spiritual persons" as Corinthian gnostics whose self-imposed "wisdom" (γνῶσις, 1 Cor 2:13–15) sets them apart from other Corinthians.[130] Similarly, John D. Ekem argues that τῶν πνευματικῶν is a rhetorical tool used by Paul to address "spiritual persons" whose ecstatic excesses went beyond Paul's prescriptions for the practice of spiritual gifts in the church.[131]

12.2 *"Spiritual Gifts"*

For many scholars, however, περὶ δὲ τῶν πνευματικῶν is often seen within the context of v. 4 that begins with the χαρίσματα, "gifts, graces." The enumeration of gifts in 12:4–10 and the proper use of two of them, prophecy and glossolalia, in 14:1–40, is the primary concern in the unit 12–14. Considering the nature of Paul's discourse on the χαρίσματα, many scholars understand the "things" (τῶν) to be referring to the "gifts," rendering 12:1a as a heading to the unit, "Now

---

[129] Charles K. Barrett, *The First Epistle to the Corinthians* (HNTC; New York: Harper & Row, 1968) 278. So, too, Morris, *1 Corinthians*, 163; Bruce, *1 and 2 Corinthians*, 117; Roy A. Harrisville, *1 Corinthians* (ACNT; Minneapolis, MN: Augsburg, 1987) 205; Craig L. Blomberg, *1 Corinthians* (NIV Application Commentary; Grand Rapids: Zondervan, 1994) 243; Christian Wolff, *Der erste Brief des Paulus an die Korinther* (THKNT 7; Berlin: Evangelische Verlagsanstalt, 1996) 282; and Robert Omara, *Spiritual Gifts in the Church: A Study of 1 Cor 12:1–11* (Rome: Pontificia Universitas Urbaniana, 1997) 5–6. Wolfgang Schrage (*Der erste Brief an die Korinther* [EKKNT 7/1–4; Zurich: Benziger/Neukirchen-Vluyn: Neukirchener, 1991–2001] 3. 118–19) suggests that since gifts are given to persons, "gifts" and "persons" go together. He believes that the masculine is the Corinthian position, "spiritual persons," and the neuter is Paul's position, "spiritual things." Garland (*1 Corinthians*) states, "The translation 'spiritual ones' matches its usage at the conclusion of the discourse in 14:37" (p. 564).

[130] So Schmithals, *Gnosticism in Corinth*, 171–72; and Pearson, *Pneumatikos-Psychikos*, 47.

[131] John D. Ekem, "'Spiritual Gifts' or 'Spiritual Persons'? 1 Corinthians 12:1A Revisited," *Noet* 38 (2004) 54–74. Ekem (ibid., 61) agrees with Barrett (*First Epistle*, 278) that "spiritual persons" is an inclusive reference to persons in whom spiritual gifts are at work.

concerning spiritual gifts."[132] Thus, πνευματικά and χαρίσματα are considered identical terms in Paul's context. A few scholars understand the neuter in a broader sense than, but not excluding, "spiritual gifts."[133]

12.3 "Spiritual Things"

Some scholars who opt for the neuter maintain a distinction between "things" that relate specifically to "gifts" and "things" that relate to "things [whatever they may be] that come from the spirit." Fee argues that the emphasis in distinction reflects the root words πνεῦμα and χάρισμα: "When the emphasis is on the manifestation, the 'gift' as such, Paul speaks of *charismata*; when the emphasis is on the Spirit, he speaks of *pneumatika*."[134] Fee translates 12:1a as "things of the Spirit," referring to spiritual manifestations form the perspective of the Spirit.

Richard B. Hays states that the translation "now concerning spiritual gifts" is an interpretive paraphrase of the Greek text that, instead, reads "now concerning spiritual things."[135] The spiritual things refer to spiritual manifestations in general without discrimination. Hays observes that the "gifts" come into the discussion only later in v. 4 and are meant to enumerate the spiritual manifestations about which the Corinthians should be concerned,

---

[132] So Archibald Robertson and Alfred Plummer, *A Critical and Exegetical Commentary on the First Epistle of St Paul to the Corinthians* (Edinburgh: T & T Clark, 1991) 259; Jean Héring, *The First Epistle of St Paul to the Corinthians* (London: Epworth, 1962) 122–23; Arnold Bittlinger, *Gifts and Graces: A Commentary on 1 Corinthians 12–14* (Grand Rapids: Eerdmans, 1967) 13; Conzelmann, *1 Corinthians*, 204; Talbert, *Reading Corinthians*, 81; Grudem, *Gift of Prophecy*, 157–60; and Carson, *Showing the Spirit*, 22. Kistemaker (*1 Corinthians*) states, "The Greek adjective *pneumatikōn* (spiritual) appears alone in the original text, so that we are compelled to add a word. We complete the thought . . . with the noun gifts (compare 14:1)" (p. 412). Siegfried S. Schatzmann ("Purpose and Function of Gifts in 1 Corinthians," *Southwestern Journal of Theology* 45 [2002] 53–68) states, "The terms 'spiritual gifts' (*pneumatika*) and 'gifts of grace' (*charismata*) will be considered as complementary, if not synonymous" (p. 53); and Craig S. Keener, *1–2 Corinthians* (New Cambridge Bible Commentary; Cambridge: Cambridge University Press, 2005) 100. This follows most English versions.

[133] So Collins, *First Corinthians*, 446–47; and Turner, *The Holy Spirit and Spiritual Gifts*, 261 n. 2.

[134] Fee, *First Epistle*, 576.

[135] Hays, *First Corinthians*, 207.

specifically, those manifestations that are recognizably God's gifts of grace (χάρις).[136]

Similarly, Thiselton argues that translations that render "things" as "gifts of the spirit" is to overtranslate the Greek text. He believes that the Corinthians used the term πνευματικόν to refer to a wide range of spiritual feeling states and phenomena, whereas Paul, with his use of χαρίσματα, was more focused on "gifts of the spirit." Thiselton argues that the Greek should translate, "Now concerning things that 'come from the Spirit.'"[137]

13. πνευματικά in 1 Cor 14:1b

The phrase ζηλοῦτε δὲ τὰ πνευματικά in 14:1b, as an introduction to Paul's exhortation on prophecy and glossolalia in chap. 14, is sometimes understood to refer to inspired speech gifts. Scholars who viewed πνευματικά in 12:1a as "things" or "persons" now see it as "gifts of inspired utterance" in 14:1b.[138] Collins observes that whereas Paul had been using "gift" language (χάρις-) in chap. 12, he resumes "spirit" language (πνεῦμα-) in chap. 14 from 12:1a. This allows Paul to return from his digression on love in chap. 13 to the topic of "spirit" gifts, namely prophecy.[139] Usually, πνευματικά in 14:1b is rendered as "spiritual gifts," a meaning that is thought to resume 12:1a.

14. πνευματικά versus χαρίσματα

The occurrence of πνευματικά in 1 Cor 12:1a and χαρίσματα in 12:4 is sometimes thought to show a transition in Paul's line of exhortation to the Corinthians. In a paper delivered in 1949, Ernst Käsemann first argued that Paul substituted πνευματικά with χαρίσματα as a theological critique in an

---

[136] Ibid., 208. Marion L. Soards (*1 Corinthians* [NIBC; Peabody, MA: Hendrickson, 1999]) argues similarly that the subject of 1 Cor 12:a is "spiritual matters" (p. 252), and that "the use of *charismata* emphasizes that whatever spiritual gifts occur in the Corinthian congregation, those gifts are by God's grace (*charis*)" (p. 255).

[137] Thiselton, *First Epistle*, 910, 930.

[138] Fee, *First Epistle*, 654; Hays, *First Corinthians*, 235; Thiselton, *First Epistle*, 1083; and Garland, *1 Corinthians*, 632.

[139] Collins, *First Corinthians*, 490–92.

attempt to refocus the Corinthian perspective.[140]   The term πνευματικά expressed the Corinthians' concern for spiritual manifestations whereas χαρίσματα expressed Paul's recommendation for where the Corinthians should place their concern, namely, "gifts" freely given of God.

Many scholars since have followed Käsemann on this point. A distinction is maintained between the terms πνευματικά and χαρίσματα based on an argument for Paul's terminological shift. Kenneth S. Hemphill argues that Paul introduced the idea of "gifts" given to every believer in 1 Cor 12:4 as a corrective to the term "spiritual persons" in v. 1 that denoted only certain persons who prided themselves as "spiritual" above others.[141] Wolff suggests that Paul uses "die Begriffe 'Gnadengaben' und 'Geistesgaben'" to avoid the Corinthian obsession with spiritual manifestations ('Pneumatiker'-Terminologie) by steering their attention instead to the "grace-given" character of spiritual manifestations.[142] Collins observes that the shift from πνευματικά to χαρίσματα, though jarring, is not without intent. He believes that with the use of the term "gifts" Paul "provides a theological corrective to the popular Corinthian notion of spiritual phenomena."[143] This reinforces Paul's point that authentic spiritual manifestations are "gifts" whose source is God. Similarly, Thiselton follows Käsemann and argues that by the use of "*persuasive definition* or *code switching* Paul redefines what counts as spiritual by talking about what God freely gives."[144]

In a related aspect, πνευματικά is sometimes understood to relate two specific spiritual abilities, that of prophecy and speaking in tongues prided by those

---

[140] Ernst Käsemann ("Ministry and Community in the New Testament," in idem, *Essays on New Testament Themes* [SBT 41; London: SCM, 1964] 63–134; trans. W. J. Montague of an essay that appeared in *Exegetische Versuche und Besinnungen 1* [2nd ed.; Göttingen: Vandenhoeck & Ruprecht, 1960] 109–34), originally given as a paper in 1949 in Herborn, in which he states, "We must not, however, fail to observe that Paul usually displaces, or rather forcibly removes, the term πνευματικά and substitutes for it the idea of charisma; because he takes such pains to do this, it is clearly meant to be the starting-point of a theological critique. This critique becomes explicit in 1 Cor 12:2" (p. 66).

[141] Kenneth S. Hemphill, *Spiritual Gifts: Empowering the New Testament Church* (Nashville: Broadman, 1988) 58.

[142] Wolff, *Der erste Brief,* 282. Ekem ("'Spiritual Gifts' or 'Spiritual Persons'," 62) agrees with Wolff that Paul attempts to shift the Corinthians' concern from a preoccupation with a self-promoting spiritual ability to the fact that God, not a Corinthian ecstatic elite, is the source of spiritual endowments.

[143] Collins, *First Corinthians,* 452.

[144] Thiselton, *First Epistle,* 930 (emphasis his). But Grudem (*Gift of Prophecy*) sees no real corrective measure on Paul's part: "There is no explicit indication by Paul that he is attempting to correct their understanding of the term πνευματικός" (p. 159).

Corinthians who practiced them. In contrast, Paul speaks of χαρίσματα that referred to a variety of spiritual gifts that were equally as important. The close proximity of πνευματικά in v. 1 to "speaking in the spirit" in v. 3 gives the impression of a relationship between the two. Paul's introduction of "gifts" in v. 4 is meant to show the Corinthians that inspired speech (πνευματικά) should conform to God's purpose for its use, not for the Corinthian use of an exhibition of spiritual power.[145]

15. πνεῦμα and πνεύματα

The use of the anarthrous πνεῦμα in the singular (1 Cor 12:3; 14:16) and in the plural (1 Cor 12:10; 14:12,32) has led to many interpretations. In many cases, the singular and plural forms are interpreted in the light of Paul's phraseology in 1 Cor 12:4, 8, and 9: τὸ αὐτὸ πνεῦμα, "the same spirit," τὸ πνεῦμα, "the spirit," and τῷ ἑνὶ πνεύματι, "the one spirit."

15.1 πνεῦμα θεοῦ *and* πνεῦμα ἅγιον

Most commentators usually render πνεῦμα θεοῦ and πνεῦμα ἅγιον in 1 Cor 12:3 as "the Spirit of God" and "the Holy Spirit." But few scholars note that the Greek text in 12:3 lacks the definite article τό, "the," and therefore, following Greek grammar, can read "a spirit of God" and "a holy spirit."[146] Reginald St John Parry observed that πνεύματι θεοῦ might translate as "a spirit from God" and πνεύματι ἁγίῳ as "a holy spirit."[147] Kirsopp Lake also noted that in 1 Cor 12:3 those who confessed Jesus as Lord were inspired by "a holy spirit." Lake makes the point that the article is explicitly absent in Paul's text: "St. Paul says

---

[145] See Donald W. B. Robinson, "Charismata versus Pneumatika: Paul's Method of Discussion," *Reformed Theological Review* 31 (1972) 49–55; E. Earle Ellis, "Spiritual Gifts in the Pauline Community," *NTS* 20 (1973–1974) 128–44, esp. 128–29; David L. Baker, "The Interpretation of 1 Corinthians 12–14," *EvQ* 46 (1974) 224–34, esp. 229; House, "Tongues and the Mystery Religions," 144; Enrique Nardoni, "The Concept of Charism in Paul," *CBQ* 55 (1993) 68–80, esp. 72; Gillespie, *First Theologians*, 77–78; Hays, *First Corinthians*, 207–08, and Garland, *1 Corinthians*, 563.

[146] See BDF § 257: "τὸ ἅγιον πνεῦμα . . . without article as a divine spirit."

[147] Reginald St John Parry, *The First Epistle of Paul the Apostle to the Corinthians* (Cambridge Greek Testament Commentaries; Cambridge: Cambridge University Press, 1926) 176–77. Parry states, quoting Hort, "Each operation or manifestation of 'the Holy Spirit' may be represented, and in the N. T. is most commonly represented, as immediately due to 'a holy spirit'" (p. 176).

πνεύματι ἁγίῳ, not τῷ πνεύματι ἁγίῳ."[148] Ellis believes as well that 12:3 might refer to "a spirit" or "a holy spirit."[149]

Fee, however, argues that a plurality of good spirits in Paul is untenable. He notes that Paul's explicit use of "the one spirit" and "the same spirit" does not allow for an indefinite number of holy spirits.[150] The majority of commentators do not believe that Paul spoke of a multitude of holy spirits. The "one spirit" and the "same spirit" become the definitive phrases for Paul's understanding of "holy spirit": only *one* exists.

Many scholars never discriminate between the articular/anarthrous use of πνεῦμα. Their silence on the matter in tandem with their use of the phrases "the Spirit" or "the Holy Spirit" (even in the anarthrous) implies that such discrimination is unnecessary and has little to offer for understanding Pauline pneumatology.

15.2 1 Cor 12:10 διακρίσεις πνευμάτων

The plural forms of πνεῦμα in First Corinthians 12 and 14 are often read in the light of "the one spirit" and "the same spirit" as well. The "discernment of spirits" in 12:10 might refer to a discernment of "spiritual manifestations" that emanated from the Holy Spirit,[151] "the Holy Spirit" from "evil spirits,"[152] or "the Holy Spirit" and "human spirits" wherein the prophetic utterance is that of the human spirit moved by the Holy Spirit.[153] Thiselton argues that Paul never uses the term πνεῦμα to refer to "an evil spirit," and so the gift lies in the capacity to discern the genuine activity of the spirit from human attempts to replicate such activity.[154]

---

[148] Kirsopp Lake, *The Earlier Epistles of St Paul* (London: Rivingstons, 1911) 207 n. 1.

[149] Ellis, "'Spiritual Gifts'," 132.

[150] See Fee (*First Epistle*) who notes in this regard: "Parry, following Hort, makes a point of the anarthrous use of πνεῦμα as though it implied an 'intermediate sense' in which each manifestation is the work of 'a holy spirit.' But that is to miss Paul's usage altogether. V. 9 alone indicates that such is not true ('by the same Spirit'; 'by the one Spirit')" (p. 578 n. 43).

[151] So Robertson and Plummer, *First Epistle*, 267; and Garland, *1 Corinthians*, 583.

[152] So Barrett, *First Epistle*, 286; Grudem, *Gift of Prophecy*, 59; Kistemaker, *1 Corinthians*, 425; and Robert L. Thomas, *Understanding Spiritual Gifts: A Verse-by-Verse Study of 1 Corinthians 12–14* (Grand Rapids: Kregel, 1978; repr. 1999) 35.

[153] So Fee, *First Epistle*, 597; and Rien Van Vliet, "Discerning of Spirits. What Does it Really Mean?" *Eastern Journal of Practical Theology* (1998) 19–28. William F. Orr and James A. Walther (*1 Corinthians: A New Translation* [AB 32; Garden City, NY: Doubleday, 1976] 282) believe that "spirits" in 12:10 refers to the Spirit, humans spirits, and evil spirits.

[154] Thiselton, *First Epistle*, 967.

Gerhard Dautzenberg argued that the gift refers to interpreting revelations of the spirit spoken through prophecy.[155] Others argue similarly that the gift of "discerning spirits" is a discernment between true prophetic utterances and false prophetic utterances.[156] Grudem critiques Dautzenberg saying that if Paul meant interpreting "prophecies" he would have used the term for that, προφητεία. Instead, Paul uses the term πνεύματα, "spirits," and so the meaning remains "distinguishing between spirits."[157] Engelsen stated that "spirits" refers to both false spirits and true spirits.[158] Likewise, Aune, even though he ultimately prefers to understand "spirits" as "prophetic utterances," notes that the *NEB* translation, "the ability to distinguish true spirits from false," remains defensible.[159]

15.3 1 Cor 14:12 ζηλωταί πνευμάτων

Just as Paul speaks of "discernment of spirits," in 14:12 he also observes the Corinthians' "zeal for spirits." The plural noun "spirits" is interpreted here as components that belong to "the Spirit," functioning in the capacity of "manifestations" or "powers of the Spirit."[160] Grudem believes that "spirits" here refers to the plural manifestations of the one Spirit of God.[161] Fee argues that the Corinthians are zealous for their own "human spirits" as a mouthpiece

---

[155] Gerhard Dautzenberg, "Zum religionsgeschichtlichen Hintergrund der διάκρισις πνευμάτων (1 Kor 12, 10)," *BZ* 15 (1971) 93–104.

[156] So Bruce, *1 and 2 Corinthians*, 119; Conzelmann, *1 Corinthians*, 209, who thinks that "discerning spirits" is explained by 1 Cor 14:24–25; Fee, *First Epistle*, 596–97; Soards, *1 Corinthians*, 260, who follows Fee; Collins, *First Corinthians*, 455; Paul Kairiuki Njiru, *Charisms and the Holy Spirit's Activity in the Body of Christ: An Exegetical-Theological Study of 1 Corinthians 12,4–11 and Romans 12,6–8* (Gregorian Theological Series 86; Rome: Gregorian University, 2002) who states, "the language of 'spirits' . . . refer[s] to the prophetic utterances that need to be discerned" (p. 162); Garland, *1 Corinthians*, 583; and Keener, *1–2 Corinthians*, 101.

[157] Grudem, "A Response to Gerhard Dautzenberg on 1 Cor. 12.10," *BZ* 22 (1978) 253–70, esp. 266–67.

[158] Engelsen, "Glossolalia," 222.

[159] Aune, *Prophecy in Early Christianity*, 220.

[160] So Robertson and Plummer, *First Epistle*, 311; Bruce, *1 and 2 Corinthians*, 131; Thiselton, *First Epistle*, 1107; and Garland, *1 Corinthians*, 638.

[161] Grudem, *Gift of Prophecy*, 123.

for the Spirit in speaking in tongues.[162] Other scholars argue that "spirits" here, as manifestations of the Spirit, is identical to "gifts."[163]

The plural noun "spirits" is sometimes taken literally to refer to "spirit beings," either in a negative or in a positive context. On the one hand, some understand Paul's use of "spirits" to be a Corinthian term that denotes their interest in a multitude of spirit beings, a so-called "animistic perspective."[164] Paul accommodates this language, but does so with irony and rebuke.[165] Paul's own language preference for spiritual manifestations is the plural "gifts" and the "one Spirit."[166]

In contrast, a few scholars argue that Paul uses the plural noun "spirits" to refer to a multiplicity of "good spirits" responsible for the manifestations. Héring argues that "spirits" refers to individual good spirits given to prophets, "spirits of the prophets," in both 14:12 and 14:32.[167] Barrett translates πνευμάτων as "spiritual gifts" but comments that the term is literally "spirits" and that in 14:12 it refers to "various spiritual agencies producing various spiritual gifts."[168] Ellis argues that "spirits" are not charismatic manifestations ("gifts") but rather "the powers that lie behind and attend those manifestations." He believes that in both 14:12 and 14:32 a plurality of good spirits is to be inferred.[169]

Donatus Udoette believes that "spirits" in 14:12 refers to "manifestations of Spirits" that Paul exhorts the Corinthians to seek for the purpose of building up

---

[162] Fee, *First Epistle*, 666.

[163] So Morris, *1 Corinthians*, 189–90; Conzelmann, *1 Corinthians*, 237; Kistemaker, *1 Corinthians*, who states, "The plural noun *spirits* refers to the Holy Spirit distributing many of his spiritual gifts to his people" (p. 488); Wolff, *Der erste Brief*, 331; Hays, *First Corinthians*, 236; Soards, *1 Corinthians*, 285–86; and Keener, *1–2 Corinthians*, 105. Collins (*First Corinthians*, 499) translates πνευμάτων as "spiritual realities" that are held to the same standard by which all spiritual gifts are measured.

[164] Richard E. Oster, *1 Corinthians* (College Press NIV Commentary; Joplin, MO: College Press, 1995) 335.

[165] So Robertson and Plummer, *First Epistle*, 311; Engelsen, "Glossolalia," 154–55; Harrisville, *1 Corinthians*, 232–33; and Oster, *1 Corinthians*, 335.

[166] So David Hill, *Greek Words and Hebrew Meanings: Studies in the Semantics of Soteriological Terms* (SNTSMS 5; Cambridge: Cambridge University Press, 1967; repr. Eugene, OR: Wipf & Stock, 2000) who states, "The Corinthians probably believed in many spirits, giving many varied gifts: for Paul, there are many gifts, but only *one Spirit* (12:4)" (p. 266, emphasis his).

[167] Héring, *First Epistle*, 149.

[168] Barrett, *First Epistle*, 319.

[169] Ellis, "'Spiritual Gifts'," 134.

the church.[170]　While Udoette includes the term "manifestations" in his translation, a term used by others to denote "powers" that emanate from "the one Spirit," he nonetheless provides the translation "Spirits." This translation seems to accommodate language for "the Holy Spirit" by using a capital "S" while maintaining the plurality of the Greek text, thus, creating a theological tension between "the Holy Spirit" and many "[Holy?] Spirits."

16. Retrospect on πνεῦμα Terms

In First Corinthians 12 and 14, πνεῦμα terms tend to be read as "the Holy Spirit," "the Spirit of God," "gifts," and "manifestations." While the term πνευματικά in 12:1a is sometimes rendered as "spiritual persons," scholars usually believe it anticipates Paul's exhortation on χαρίσματα and so is rendered as "spiritual gifts" or "spiritual things" in a broader sense that includes "gifts." But the terms "spirit" and "gift" are different in meaning, as some scholars admit. They cannot be identical because each term belongs to a different semantic domain.

Paul's insistent use of "the same spirit" and "the one spirit" clashes with his use of the plural noun "spirits." The numeral "one" (ἕν) is understood to indicate a numerically singular "spirit." Translations of the plural noun πνεύματα in 1 Cor 14:12,32 as "gifts," "prophetic utterances," "inspirations," "manifestations," or "powers" attempt to accommodate for "the one/same spirit" phrases that many scholars believe denotes "the Holy Spirit himself" in 1 Cor 12:4 (τὸ αὐτὸ πνεῦμα), 12:9 (τῷ ἑνὶ πνεύματι), and 12:11 (τὸ ἕν καὶ τὸ αὐτὸ πνεῦμα).

Accordingly, Paul's mention of "the one spirit" rules out the possibility for "spirits" to mean a plurality of "holy spirits"; hence, "spirits" must indicate "manifestations" or "powers" of the Holy Spirit. But the term "spirits" bears neither the meaning "manifestation" nor "power" in Greek; a Greek term already exists for each, namely φανέρωσις and δύναμις, as in 1 Cor 12:7, φανέρωσις τοῦ πνεύματος, "manifestation of the spirit," and in Luke 4:14, τῇ δυνάμει τοῦ πνεύματος, "the power of the spirit." Likewise, Grudem has shown that "spirits" cannot mean "prophetic utterances," for if Paul meant "prophecies" he would have used the term for it.

Some scholars argue that "spirits" in 1 Cor 12:10, 14:12,32 refer to a plurality

---

[170] Donatus Udoette, *Prophecy and Tongues: A Pauline Theology of Charismata for Service in the Church [1 Cor 14]* (Rome: Pontifica Universitas Urbaniana, 1993) 124.

of "spirit beings," the meaning the term "spirits" had in the first century. The tension that this interpretation creates with "the one spirit" is not explained by these scholars. Consequently, their interpretation of "spirits" as many good spirits is not reconciled with Paul's use of the term "one" as a qualifier for "spirit."

Fee argued that "spirits" are "human spirits" moved by the one Spirit. But it is improbable that Paul would have called the Corinthians "spirits" or have said that they are "zealous" for their own "human spirits." Textual variants give some indication that scribes believed that the plural noun "spirits" in 14:12, 32 referred to the spirit that was without and not the human spirit within.[171]

17. Prospect: First Corinthians 12 and 14 as Religious Experience

What seems to be lacking in much of this study is a deeper understanding of the experiences that underlie these terms. Texts that speak of individuals who "speak in a spirit" (1 Cor 12:3; 14:2,16), who are in the presence of the "manifestation of the spirit" (1 Cor 12:7), who are "zealous for spirits" (1 Cor 14:12), or who are in the presence of "God" (1 Cor 14:25) relate experiences that transcend our normal Western boundaries of reality, i.e., conscious, physical, biological life. In the NT, these experiences are said to occur by the action of πνεῦμα. "Spirit," by definition, is invisible; yet, like the wind, it becomes a real presence through its effects.

In the NT, the interaction between humans and spirit often occurs within a context of visionary experiences (cf. Acts 10:3–7, 10–16; 2 Cor 12:2–4; Rev 1:10; 4:2) or of a divine service accompanied by inspired utterances (cf. 1 Thess 5:19–21). The experience is a "religious experience," an experience that is based on spirit in general and whose *modus operandi* is accessing spirit for the purpose of revelation in particular. Prospectively, the use of πνεῦμα and πνεύματα in First Corinthians 12 and 14 provide the kind of evidence for this experience. Despite this, Thiselton has raised doubts:

---

[171] See the variants in Nestle-Aland²⁷. 1 Cor 14:12, πνευματικῶν (for πνευμάτων), P 1175 *pc* a r vg^mss sy^p co; and at 1 Cor 14:32, πνεῦμα (for πνεύματα) D F G Ψ* 1241ˢ pc a b vg^mss sy^p. These variants attest to a possible uneasiness with the plural "spirits." The first variant, πνευματικῶν, "spiritual things," recalls the same term in 1 Cor 12:1a, hence not human spirits. The second variant, πνεῦμα, "spirit," might have been understood as "the Spirit of the prophets," i.e., the Holy Spirit operating through the prophets and not the prophets' own human spirits.

It goes against the grain of Paul's emphasis in the thanksgiving . . . to focus attention on the 'religious experience' of 1 Corinthians 12–14 rather than on the generosity of God's sovereign gift of himself in a variety of ways.[172]

In a recent study of Pauline pneumatology, Friedrich W. Horn expresses caution with regard to studying spirit phenomenon as a means to identify true Christian religious experience apart from nonChristian religious experience. He argues that Hellenistic and early Christian sources show that the relationship between the perception and the interpretation of spirit experiences is dictated by the person's socially and culturally conditioned point of view.[173] A particular spirit phenomenon may be interpreted differently by a Greek, a Jew, or a Christian. Thus, Horn argues that specifically Christian spirit phenomena did not exist because such phenomena were too ambiguous. Different religious and cultural groups might interpret the selfsame phenomena as coming from either good or evil spirits. That which a Christian might view as the presence of the spirit of God, a Jew might view as the presence of the devil.[174]

By citing the ambiguity of spirit phenomena, Horn provides a caveat for the study of religious experiences of spirit in early Christianity. This ambiguity was a genuine problem that was never completely overcome by early Christians. The institution of "discerning" or "testing" spirits was an attempt to deal with it. But there remained a potential loophole that deceptive spirits could exploit by masquerading as good or truth-bearing spirits.[175] The NT canon yields no clear consensus about procedures for "testing the spirits." In 1 John 4:2 the spirits came from God only if their statements were in accord with a Christological tradition: ". . . that Jesus Christ has come in the flesh . . . ." But this criterion might not have prevented a lying spirit from disguising itself by stating an equivalent Christological expression, appearing as, in the words of Paul, an "angel of light" (2 Cor 11:14). Indeed, Paul mentions the gift for "discernment of spirits" (1 Cor 12:10) but gives no illustration about how to unmask a deceptive spirit.

The activities of good spirits and evil spirits were nearly identical to all outward appearances (for "a spirit of falsehood" might claim to be "a spirit of truth"). This near identity gives evidence for one of the fundamental variables

---

[172] Thiselton, *First Epistle*, 98.

[173] Friedrich W. Horn, *Das Angeld des Geistes: Studien zur paulinischen Pneumatologie* (Göttingen: Vandenhoeck & Ruprecht, 1992) 20.

[174] Ibid., 20. Horn states further, "Phänomene sind, weil auf Interpretation angewiesen, vieldeutig und nie an sich ein eindeutiger Beweis für eine Gottes- oder Geisteserfahrung" (p. 21). See Matt 12:24,27–28.

[175] Cf. 2 Cor 11:4; 1 Tim 4:1–2; and 1 John 4:1–3.

that governed the perception and interpretation of spirit phenomena in the first century C.E. The ambiguity that might arise from the empirical presence of spirits among humans stemmed not so much from human perceptions but from the nature of spirits themselves: like the wind, spirits were (1) invisible to humans, which provided deceptive spirits with an obvious advantage for stealth; and (2) spirits were known through their effects. These effects might be produced by either a good or an evil spirit. Thus, the potential for construing the selfsame spirit phenomenon as the work of either a good or an evil spirit was always present.

This ambiguity, however, does not dismiss a study of spirit phenomena as something that can be reliably gauged as specifically Christian. The invisible nature of spirits introduced an unavoidable consequence for those who communicated with the spirit world: invisible beings remained elusive to verification despite their empirical presence as seen through their effects; hence, deception was always possible. The purported phenomena that spirits produced through an individual, whether a demoniac or a prophet, were usually the only evidence available for scrutiny among those who did not otherwise possess the ability for clairvoyance, seeing the spirits, or clairaudience, hearing the spirits. Certain individuals, however, may have been able to sense or feel the spirits through clairsentience that aided in the discernment process. These abilities, that in present-day society might be called "psychic," probably played a role in unmasking deceptive spirits.[176] Some persons may have had the ability for both seeing and hearing the spirits. Those who were not clairvoyant and/or clairaudient relied on the physical effects produced by spirits through mediums.

The activity of a spirit was usually determined by the actions and/or statements of the human instrument through whom a spirit was believed to operate. This is illustrated in the NT when "prophets" give voice to spirits that are either from God or not from God (Matt 7:15–20; Gal 5:22–26; 1 John 4:2–3). The identical activities of good and evil spirits was an unchangeable factor with which Christians had to cope. Thus, Christians instituted the "discerning" or "testing" of not only spirits but also of the persons through whom spirits acted.[177]

---

[176] See John J. Heaney, *The Sacred and the Psychic: Parapsychology and Christian Theology* (New York: Paulist Press, 1984).

[177] For the "life of the prophet" as a testament to the spirits that speak through him, see *Did.* 11:8, οὐ πᾶς δὲ ὁ λαλῶν ἐν πνεύματι προφήτης ἐστίν, ἀλλ᾽ ἐὰν ἔχῃ τοὺς τρόπους κυρίου. ἀπὸ οὖν τῶν τρόπων γνωσθήσεται ὁ ψευδοπροφήτης καὶ ὁ προφήτης, "However, not everyone who speaks in a spirit is a [true] prophet, but only if he exhibits the Lord's ways. By his conduct, therefore, will the false prophet and the [true] prophet be recognized"; and Herm. *Mand.* 11.16,

The spirits who operated through prophets were not always immediately identifiable as either holy or demonic. In Christian circles, the utterances of invisible spirit beings through the intermediary of a possessed prophet demanded adjudication by observers. Such engagement acted as a means to avoid deception by unmasking an impostor spirit. This should be embraced as a starting point from which to study early Christian religious experience.[178]

Despite Thiselton's dismissal of religious experience and Horn's reservations about it, Hurtado has devoted a study on the contributions of religious experience to earliest Christianity:

It is clear that earliest Christianity was characterized by a rich and varied assortment of religious experiences, ranging all along a continuum from the quiet and inward to the dramatic and outward categories. The rhetoric of the New Testament attributes all these Christian religious experiences to the Spirit of God, the "Holy Spirit." The success of earliest Christianity and its appeal and credibility in the eyes of converts seem to have been very heavily connected with its ability to provide religious experiences that corresponded to its rhetoric of being "gifted," "filled," "anointed," and "empowered" by the Spirit of God.[179]

Hurtado observes that the primary rhetoric for religious experience in the NT is "spirit." Charles H. Talbert notes that "spirit" was the category by which Christian religious experience was distinguished from nonChristian religious experience in a *particular* sense, for "not all religious experience is Christian." This particular sense is found in the discernment of spirits for which the only true Christian criterion was the acknowledgment of Jesus as Lord by the spirits.[180] Hurtado states that prophecy uttered in Christ's name in terms normally reserved for the God of Israel, "Lord" (יהוה, κύριος), was an

---

ἔχεις ἀμφοτέρων τῶν προφητῶν τὴν ζωήν. δοκίμαζε οὖν ἀπὸ τῶν ἔργων καὶ τῆς ζωῆς τὸν ἄνθρωπον τὸν λέγοντα ἑαυτὸν πνευματοφόρον εἶναι, "You now have descriptions of the life of both kinds of prophets. Therefore test by his life and his actions the person who claims that he is moved [to speak] by a spirit."

[178] Horn (*Angeld*) does not completely discredit such a study: "Die Interdependenz von Wahrnehmung und Interpretation verbietet einen positivistischen Einsatz bei Tatsachen, sie hat vielmehr den theologie- und religionsgeschichtlichen Horizont abzustecken, unter dem die urchristliche Rede vom Geist sich überhaupt entfaltet" (p. 21).

[179] Hurtado, "Religious Experience," 183. Particularly for Paul, see Alan F. Segal, *Paul the Convert: The Apostolate and Apostasy of Saul the Pharisee* (New Haven, CT: Yale University Press, 1992) who states, "In order to fully appreciate Paul's letters, they need to be read in light of religious experience . . ." (p. xiii).

[180] Charles H. Talbert, "Paul's Understanding of the Holy Spirit: The Evidence of 1 Corinthians 12–14," in *Perspectives on the New Testament: Essays in Honor of Frank Stagg* (ed. Charles H. Talbert; Macon, GA: Mercer University Press, 1985) 96.

innovation that identified religious experiences of the spirit in the first century as uniquely Christian.[181]

Frequently, scholars simply use the phrase "the spirit" as a gloss without clarifying what they actually mean by it. Consequently, the imagination is left to roam indiscriminately in a thought world that covers anything related to the "spiritual." In English versions of the NT, "spirit" is capitalized and this in itself is an interpretive flourish on the Greek that made no such distinction. In many cases it is tacitly assumed by scholars that "the spirit" is "the Holy Spirit" of Christian theology, making further clarification unnecessary.

Spirit is understood in different ways in the NT. Sometimes it is thought to be an impersonal power from texts that pair πνεῦμα and δύναμις.[182] Fee argues that in Paul the terms "spirit" and "power" are sometimes interchangeable.[183] The idea of spirit is also thought to stand behind terms that might suggest either semipersonal beings or impersonal powers such as ἀρχή and ἐξουσία.[184] Marie E. Isaacs argues that the meaning of "spirit" can be metaphorical, indicating mood or inclination.[185]

Among first-century Jews and Christians the semantic range of the term "spirit" covered more than mere metaphor for divine power or driving force. The term "spirit" extended into the range of personality, not from the perspective of "third Person" denoted in later Christian tradition (Latin *persona*, Greek ὑπόστασις, πρόσωπον), but instead from the perspective of the LXX and

---

[181] Hurtado, "Religious Experience," 199. Hence, despite Horn's claim that ambiguous spirit phenomena made phenomena unique to Christianity nonexistent, there seems to have been statements and actions that were meant to verify specifically Christian religious experiences apart from nonChristian ones.

[182] See Luke 1:17; Acts 10:38; 1 Cor 2:4; 1 Thess 1:5.

[183] Fee (*First Epistle*) states, "To speak of the Spirit is automatically to speak of power" (p. 95). Indeed, "power" is one idea behind the term "spirit," for the primary meaning of πνεῦμα, "moving air," denotes energy and force.

[184] Rom 8:38 (ἀρχαί), 1 Cor 15:24 (ἀρχήν, ἐξουσίαν, δύναμιν).

[185] Marie E. Isaacs, *The Concept of Spirit: A Study of Pneuma in Hellenistic Judaism and Its Bearing on the New Testament* (HM 1; London: Heythrop College, 1976) 71. Cf., however, an earlier commentary by Marvin R. Vincent, *Word Studies in the New Testament* (4 vols.; New York: Scribner's, 1887; repr. Grand Rapids: Eerdmans, 1989) who states, "πνεῦμα, spirit, is never used in the New Testament of temper or disposition." (3. 387).

Second Temple literature that imbued the Greek noun πνεῦμα, as a translation for רוח, "spirit," with attributes of a sentient being.[186]

---

[186] See Menzies, *Early Christian Pneumatology*, 53–111. Other studies on spirit have similarly concluded that πνεῦμα was modified by the LXX. See William R. Shoemaker ("The Use of רוח in the Old Testament, and of πνεῦμα in the New Testament," *JBL* 23 [1904] 13–67) who states, "Since the Greeks had nothing that corresponded to this Hebrew concept (the Spirit of God), it is not strange that they lacked a terminology to express it.... It was only natural that the translators should extend the term used for wind and breath (πνεῦμα) to cover this meaning also" (p. 37); Ernest de Witt Burton (*Spirit, Soul, and Flesh: The Usage of* πνεῦμα, ψυχή, *and* σάρξ *in Greek Writings and Translated Works from the Earliest Period to 180 A. D.; and of their Equivalents* רוח, נפש, *and* בשר *in the Hebrew Old Testament* [Chicago: Chicago University Press, 1918]) states, "The LXX use of πνεῦμα to denote an unembodied being neither human nor divine finds no parallel in earlier Greek writers.... Only in the Greek translated from the Hebrew do we find the expression spirit of God, πνεῦμα θεοῦ, or holy spirit, πνεῦμα ἅγιον.... It is in this literature only that we find spirit of man, or spirit meaning a shade, an angel, or a demon" (p. 153, 170–71); Edwyn Bevan (*Symbolism and Belief* [Port Washington, NY: Kennikat Press, 1968; repr. of 1938 edition]) states, "When the terms of Jewish religion had to be translated ... into Greek ..., *pneuma* was taken as the regular word to represent the Hebrew *ruakh*.... By being used to translate *ruakh* it acquired for Jews and Christians a new connotation, that of *ruakh*, which in some of its meanings indeed overlapped with the connotation of *pneuma*, but in others was used in a way which would have been hardly intelligible to a Greek of the time of Plato.... Personal beings without bodies, whether non-human beings, angels and devils, or disincarnate humans spirits, could now be spoken of as *pneumata*" (pp. 181–83); Hill (*Greek Words and Hebrew Meanings*) who states, "The Septuagint translators reveal a strong tendency to render the Hebrew word רוח by πνεῦμα, and this in spite of the fact that the Hebrew had a wider range of meanings than the Greek. The survey of Greek usage showed that πνεῦμα covered the meanings 'wind', 'breath of life' and 'air', but did not denote 'spirit', either human or divine: in biblical Greek πνεῦμα is employed to render רוח when it bears this meaning" (pp. 217–18); Isaacs (*Concept of Spirit*) who states, "... Hebrew ideas have been introduced into the Greek concept of πνεῦμα.... The LXX introduced a new dimension into the usual Greek usage.... In faithfully translating the Hebrew term *ruach* as πνεῦμα when it applied not only to wind, breath and life, but also to God, the LXX played a significant part in the development of its meaning in subsequent Greek literature" (pp. 15, 17); Georg Kretschmar ("Der Heilige Geist in der Geschichte: Grundzüge frühchristlicher Pneumatologie," in *Gegenwart des Geistes: Aspekte der Pneumatologie* [ed. K. Rahner and H. Schlier; QD 85; Freiburg: Herder, 1979] 92–130) states, "Die rûah (רוח) des Alten Testamentes und des palästinensischen Judentums, schon in der Septuaginta durch 'Pneuma' (πνεῦμα) wiedergegeben, kann den Wind meinen, eine anthropologische Größe, Engel und Dämonen, die schöpferische Kraft Gottes, in der er auch Menschen ergreift und als Propheten oder Amtsträger in seinen Dienst stellt" (p. 101); Joseph A. Fitzmyer ("The Role of the Spirit in Luke-Acts," in *The Unity of Luke-Acts* [ed. J. Verheyden; Leuven: Leuven University Press, 1999] 165–83) who states, "... the Jewish belief in intermediate beings such as angels and spirits, especially in the postexilic period, has clearly modified the Hellenistic understanding of *pneumata*. Hence, if the Lucan references to 'unclean' or 'evil spirits' are related to Hellenism, they are related to it via the LXX" (pp. 168–69); and Terence Paige ("Who Believes in 'Spirit'? *Pneuma* in Pagan Usage and

In the NT, spirits were intelligent beings who, although invisible, made their presence empirically known in a variety of ways. One of the explicit ways spirits presented themselves was through the agency of a human being. The gospels and Acts tell of accounts of spirits (πνεύματα, δαίμονες) who speak in the first person from individuals they temporarily possessed.[187] Spirits also presented themselves by "materializing" in human form. Raphael appeared to Tobit as one of the seven angels of heaven (Tob 12:12–22), and Jesus' resurrection appearance was thought to have been as πνεῦμα (Luke 24:36–37). A sentient spirit being might be a spirit power in the same way that a human being is called "a power" (δύναμις, Acts 8:10) who performs wonders. In either case, the idea of "power" does not suggest anything less than something personal.[188]

Since the NT world was populated with intelligent spirit beings, malevolent (Matt 8:16) or benevolent (Heb 1:14; Rev 1:4), we can begin to clarify our meaning for "spirit" in early Christian religious experience. Talbert's observance of the "discernment of spirits" as one of the ways in which true Christian religious experience was assessed among the earliest Christians points in the direction of understanding the meaning of "spirit" in early Christian religious experience. The plural "spirits" suggests a "spirit world" in which exist myriad spirit beings.

18. The Spirit World in Paul

The phrase "spirit world" is not one that many scholars normally use for Pauline pneumatology. The phrase "the Holy Spirit" is the usual expression from which Pauline pneumatology is delineated. Nonetheless, the spirit world has been the

---

Implications for the Gentile Christian Mission," *HTR* 95 [2002] 417–36) states, "Though we know Jews and Christians brought a new, specialized meaning to *pneuma*, what we cannot say with certainty is exactly when or why this use passed into pagan language and writing. As it occurs in the Septuagint, this usage must have been employed by Jews in Egypt and elsewhere from the middle of the third century B.C.E. onwards" (p. 434).

[187] Matt 8:29–31; 12:43–45; Mark 1:23–26; 5:2,7–10; Luke 4:33–35; (John 11:51?); Acts 16:16; 19:15.

[188] See Geoffrey H. W. Lampe, *God as Spirit* (Bampton Lectures; Oxford: Clarendon, 1977), who states, "'Spirit' has the further advantage over some other 'bridge' concepts that it is an analogy drawn from personal life. Unlike 'power' (*dynamis*), it need not denote an abstract power or impersonal force" (p. 43). See also Herm. *Sim.* 9.13 where personal "holy spirits" are called "powers": Αὗται, φησίν, ἅγια πνεύματά εἰσι . . . . δυνάμεις εἰσὶ τοῦ υἱοῦ τοῦ θεοῦ, "They, he said, are holy spirits . . . [they] are powers of the Son of God."

subject of several studies on Paul's use of the term πνεῦμα, as well as ἄγγελοι, ἀρχή, ἐξουσία, δύναμις, στοιχεῖον, and δαιμόνιον. Otto Everling presented one of the earliest studies of the spirit world in Paul.[189] Martin Dibelius followed later with a monograph that focused the use of "angel," "Satan," and "demons" in Paul.[190]

More recently, scholars have contributed substantially to the discussion of the spirit world in Paul. In many cases, the discussion of the spirit world in Paul focuses on the terms ἐξουσίαι, "authorities," ἀρχαί, "principalities," στοιχεῖα, "elements," and δυνάμεις, "powers."[191] Many of these terms occur in the disputed Pauline letters, Colossians and Ephesians. But the undisputed Pauline letters include them as well (see Rom 8:38; 1 Cor 15:24).

While studies of the spirit world focus on the terms "angels," "elements," "principalities," "authorities," and "powers," the Greek phrases πνεῦμα ἅγιον, "holy spirit," and πνεῦμα θεοῦ, "spirit of God," are usually believed to indicate a spiritual reality that is set apart (theologically) from a spirit world that otherwise includes only "minor" entities such as angels, demons, and powers. The Holy Spirit and the Spirit of God (e.g., see English versions of 1 Cor 12:3) are treated as something other than "spirits" of a spirit world.[192] Theological

---

[189] Otto Everling, *Die paulinische Angelologie und Dämonologie: Ein biblisch-theologischer Versuch* (Göttingen: Vandenhoeck & Ruprecht, 1888).

[190] Martin Dibelius, *Die Geisterwelt im Glauben des Paulus* (Göttingen: Vandenhoeck & Ruprecht, 1909).

[191] See George B. Caird, *Principalities and Powers: A Study in Pauline Theology* (Oxford: Clarendon, 1956); Heinrich Schlier, *Principalities and Powers in the New Testament* (Freiburg: Herder, 1961); Hendrikus Berkhof, *Christ and the Powers* (Scottdale, PA: Herald, 1977); Wesley Carr, *Angels and Principalities: The Background, Meaning and Development of the Pauline Phrase hai archai kai hai exousiai* (Cambridge: Cambridge University Press, 1981); Pierre Benoit, "Pauline Angelology and Demonology: Reflexions on the Designations of the Heavenly Powers and on the Origin of Angelic Evil According to Paul," *Religious Studies Bulletin* 3 (1983) 1–18; Walter Wink, *Naming the Powers* (Philadelphia: Fortress, 1986); Clinton E. Arnold, "The 'Exorcism' of Ephesians 6.12 in Recent Research: A Critique of Wesley Carr's View of the Role of Evil Powers in First-Century AD Belief," *JSNT* 30 (1987) 71–87; Eduard Schweizer, "Slaves of the Elements and Worshipers of Angels: Gal 4:3, 9 and Col 2:8, 18, 20," *JBL* 107 (1988) 455–68; and Clinton E. Arnold, "Returning to the Domain of the Powers: Stoicheia as Evil Spirits in Gal 4:3,9," *NovT* 38 (1996) 55–76.

[192] See Clinton E. Arnold, *Powers of Darkness: Principalities and Powers in Paul's Letters* (Downers Grove, IL: Inter-Varsity, 1992), who states that the Holy Spirit "is of a qualitatively different nature than the spirits known by people in the Hellenistic religions" (p. 117), who, like the Jews, "believed in the existence of good and evil spirits" (p. 91); Stephen F. Noll, *Angels of Light, Powers of Darkness: Thinking Biblically about Angels, Satan and Principalities* (Downers Grove, IL: Inter-Varsity, 1998), who states that "the Holy Spirit was [n]ever an angel" (p. 89); and Victor C. Pfitzner, "The Spirit of the Lord: The christological focus of Pauline

treatments of the spirit world tend to discuss "spirit" within two separate categories: (1) "spirit" as angels and demons; and (2) "spirit" as "the Holy Spirit" that Christian theology would later recognize as a Person of the Trinity.[193]

18.1 Third- and Fourth-Century Patristics: The Emergence and the Defense of the Deity of the Holy Spirit

The use of the term πνεῦμα in the NT does not reflect the theological utility and focus that the term came to have in the later centuries of the Christian West, namely, as a term indicating "one unique Spirit."[194] The term πνεῦμα appears in the NT denoting "angels" (Heb 1:14), "a demon" (Matt 8:16), "a spirit" (Luke 24:37), "a holy spirit" (Acts 2:4), "an unclean spirit" (Mark 5:2), "the spirit" (Mark 1:12), "the holy spirit" (John 14:26), "the evil spirit" (Acts 19:15), "the spirit of truth" (John 15:26), and "spiritual forces" (Eph 6:12). Particularly in First Corinthians 12 and 14 the term πνεῦμα appears in the anarthrous, "[a] spirit of God," "[a] holy spirit," and "[a] spirit" (1 Cor 12:3, 14:2c, 16), in the articular, "the spirit" (12:7,8,9,11;14:15), in the plural, "spirits" (12:10; 14:12,32), and as an adjective used substantively for "spiritual things" (12:1; 14:1) and "spiritual persons" (14:37). From this data, one may legitimately ask, Did the earliest Christians understand there to be one Holy Spirit as espoused by Trinitarian theology?

The sources for Trinitarian theology can be traced to several church fathers of the fourth century: Cyril of Jerusalem; Athanasius of Alexandria; and the Cappadocian fathers, Basil of Caesarea, Gregory of Nyssa, and Gregory of Nazianzus. These fathers contributed to the theology of a divine Holy Spirit who was set apart from the rest of spirit creation. Whereas this theology came to the fore during the fourth century, the Holy Spirit as distinct and unique began to emerge in the third century in the writings of Origen.

Origen (185–ca. 254) is noted as the first Greek father to have contributed

---

Pneumatology," *St. Mark's Review* 178 (1999) 3–11, who states, "The Holy Spirit is not to be identified with any generic spirit" (p. 4).

[193] See Laurence Cantwell, *The Theology of the Trinity* (Theology Today 4; Notre Dame, IN: Fides, 1969); and Rob van der Hart, *The Theology of Angels and Devils* (Theology Today 36; ibid., 1972). Whereas van der Hart discusses the "theology of spirits" (*Angels and Devils*, 9), Cantwell discusses "spirit" as a term that denotes the Holy Spirit who "is at work in every member of the Christian community, and yet *there are not many spirits, but one*, and he 'apportions to each one individually as he wills' (1 Cor 12.11)" (*Trinity*, 25, emphasis mine).

[194] For the fourth-century patristic dialogue and debate about the status, nature, and relationship of the Holy Spirit to the Godhead, see Haykin, *Spirit of God*.

to a systematic treatment of the Holy Spirit. In *De princip*. 1.3 and 2.7, Origen describes the Holy Spirit in terms of a single reality but he remains vague on nature and status. One of the pneumatological debates that would contribute to the divinity of the Holy Spirit in the fourth century was Origen's assertion that nowhere in Scripture is the Holy Spirit said to be a created being.[195] The Spirit was not a creature, and this implied a difference in status and nature apart from the rest of spirit creation.[196] Origen further asserted the personhood of the Spirit (ὑπόστασις) as a member of "the most excellent Trinity (τριάδος)"[197]

Origen also speaks of the existence of both good and evil spirits in *De princip*. 3.3.4:

It is then clearly established, by many proofs, that while the soul of man exists in this body, it may admit different energies, i.e., operations, from a diveristy of good and evil spirits.[198]

A relationship or distinction between the Holy Spirit and other good spirits is not clearly given by Origen. Origen's pneumatology remained less satisfactory for the church than the pneumatology of the subsequent century. Nonetheless, through Origen "the way was opened to the fuller discussion of the theology of the Spirit upon which the fourth century entered."[199]

The distinction between the Holy Spirit as a divine Person and other subordinate spirits emerges more clearly in the fourth century, particularly in the writings of Cyril of Jerusalem, Athanasius of Alexandria, and the Cappadocian fathers. The nature and status of the Holy Spirit in the Godhead was initially defended with resources that had been developed decades earlier for the nature and status of the Son.[200]

---

[195] So ibid., 14–15.

[196] *De princip*. 1.3.3.

[197] *De princip*. 1.3.2.

[198] ANF 4. 336.

[199] Henry Barclay Swete, *The Holy Spirit in the Ancient Church: A Study of Christian Teaching in the Age of the Fathers* (London: Macmillan, 1912) 143. Even though Origen is credited with being the first Greek father to lend any significance to the Holy Spirit, Irenaeus gives a hint of concerted thought on the Holy Spirit. See ibid., 84–94.

[200] So Lewis Ayers, *Nicaea and its Legacy: An Approach to Fourth-Century Trinitarian Theology* (Oxford: Oxford University Press, 2004) 211–21. The motives for the development of orthodox doctrine during the third and fourth centuries are discussed in Maurice Wiles, *The Making of Christian Doctrine: A Study in the Principles of Early Doctrinal Development* (Cambridge: Cambridge University Press, 1967) 18–40. See further Ralph E. Person, *The Mode of Theological Decision Making at the Early Ecumenical Councils: An Inquiry into the Function of Scripture and Tradition at the Councils of Nicaea and Ephesus* (Band XIV der Theologischen Dissertationen; Basel: Friedrich Rienhardt, 1978). More recent, see John Behr,

The Nicene Creed, a product of the first great ecumenical church council that met in Nicaea in 325, present-day Turkey, gives little attention to the nature of the Holy Spirit with the exception to the statement: "And [we believe] in the Holy Spirit." Shortly after the Nicene Council, a sharp line was drawn between the Godhead and the created realm. The Spirit, as a part of the Godhead, was not a creature.[201]   The exegetical efforts of Cyril, Athanasius, and the Cappadocian fathers, subsequent to the Nicene Council, determined the ultimate meaning and shape of their theology of the Holy Spirit.

By a reference to 1 Cor 2:10–12, Cyril argues, ca. 348, for a differentiation between the Spirit and the rest of the created spiritual world:

No created being is equal to him [the Spirit]. Not all classes of angels, not all their hosts together have equality with the Holy Spirit. The all-perfect power of the Paraclete overshadows them all. While they are sent to minister, he searches even the depths of God, according to the Apostle (then follows 1 Cor 2:10–12).[202]

Cyril also distinguished the Holy Spirit from other spirits: "For many things are called spirits. An angel is called a spirit; our soul is called spirit; the wind that blows is called spirit . . . . such is not the Holy Spirit."[203]

Approximately ten years later, bishop Serapion of Thmuis, situated on one of the branches of the river in the Nile delta, wrote to his friend Athanasius (ca. 298–373) asking for advice about how to engage a group of Christians in Egypt who considered the Holy Spirit to be a creature, hence something less than divine. In his reply to Serapion, *Epistles to Serapion* (*ad Serap.*), Athanasius called these Egyptian Christians Tropici, so-called for their manner of interpreting Scripture metaphorically, using allegories and tropes.[204]   The

---

The Nicene Faith (Crestwood, NY: St Vladimir's Press, 2004); and Ramsay Macmullen, *Voting about God in Early Church Councils* (New Haven, CT: Yale University Press, 2006).

[201]   For the period before the Nicene Council, see Georg Kretschmar, "Le Développement de la doctrine du Saint-Esprit du Nouveau Testament à Nicée," *Verbum Caro* LXXXVIII (1968) 5–55.

[202]   Cyril, *Catechetical Letters* 16.23. NPNF ser. 2, 7. 121.

[203]   Cyril, *Catechetical Letters* 16.12–16. NPNF ser. 2, 7. 118–19.

[204]   See Alasdair Heron, "Zur Theologie der 'Tropici' in den Serapionbriefen des Athanasius," *Kyrios* 14 (1974) 3–24. Athanasius notes their position on the Holy Spirit to Serapion, *ad Serap.* 1.1: "You write . . . that certain persons . . . oppose the Holy Spirit, saying that he is not only a creature, but actually one of the ministering angels, but differs from the angels only in degree" (C. R. B. Shapland, trans., *The Letters of Saint Athanasius Concerning the Holy Spirit* [London: Epworth, 1951] 59–60).

Epistles contain the first substantial, direct approach on the nature of the Holy Spirit in relation to the Father and to the Son.[205]

Athanasius claimed that within the realm of spiritual creatures, spirits, and angels, the Spirit stood separate and apart from all of these:

And it is manifest that the Spirit is not one being of the many nor an angel, but one unique being, or rather, he belongs to the Logos who is one, and to God who is one, and is also of the same substance.[206]

As a part of the "unoriginated Trinity" the Spirit has a unique relationship with the Father and the Son. Athanasius reasoned from 1 Cor 2:11,12 that since the Spirit is ἐκ τοῦ θεοῦ, "from God," who is an Uncreated Being, the Spirit's nature is likewise uncreated. In contrast, the creatures come from nothing and originate in a point in time as Athanasius argued from Gen 1:1.[207]

While πνεῦμα may indicate a number of spirit beings, good or evil, in the NT, the specific NT phrases τὸ πνεῦμα τὸ ἅγιον, τὸ ἅγιον πνεῦμα, "the holy spirit," and τὸ πνεῦμα, "the spirit," were later distinguished by Athanasius from other πνεῦμα terms in the NT by virtue of the definite article τό, "the." Athanasius crystalized this view in his *Epistles to Serapion*:

Is there any passage in the divine Scripture where the Holy Spirit is found . . . with the article (μετὰ τοῦ ἄρθρου) so that he is called not simply 'spirit' (πνεῦμα) but 'the Spirit,' (τὸ Πνεῦμα) . . . Unless the article is present, it cannot refer to the Holy Spirit. . . . There is no doubt that it is the Holy Spirit who is intended; especially when it has the article.[208]

The significance of the definite article "the" was for Athanasius the primary textual indicator that "the spirit" was a single reality, separate from the rest of

---

[205] The development of the doctrine of the Holy Spirit is grounded in Athanasius's epistles to Serapion: "It is no exaggeration to say that the subsequent development of the dogma of the Holy Spirit was decisively influenced by them" (Haykin, *Spirit of God*, 59).

[206] Athanasius, *ad Serap.* 1.27, καὶ οὐκ ἄδηλον, ὅτι οὐκ ἔστι τῶν πολλῶν τὸ Πνεῦμά, ἀλλ᾽ οὐδὲ ἄγγελος, ἀλλ᾽ ἓν ὄν, μᾶλλον δὲ τοῦ λόγου ἑνὸς ὄντος ἴδιον, καὶ τοῦ θεοῦ ἑνὸς ὄντος ἴδιον καὶ ὁμοούσιόν ἐστιν (*PG* 26. 593B–C). If Athanasius reflects the Tropici position accurately, we see even in their pneumatology a distinction between "the Holy Spirit" and the angels in that the Holy Spirit "differs from the angels only in degree" (*ad Serap.* 1.1).

[207] Athanasius, *ad Serap.* 1.22; 3.2. Athanasius's exegesis on the Spirit as an uncreated being is analyzed and discussed in Haykin, *Spirit of God*, 77–92. See also Panachiotis Christou, "Uncreated and created, unbegotten and begotten in the theology of Athanasius of Alexandria," *Augustinianum* XIII (1973) 399–409.

[208] Athanasius, *ad Serap.* 1.4. *PG* 26. 536C–537A. Trans. Shapland, *Letters*, 68, 69–70.

spirit creation. Hence, "the spirit" as "the Spirit"[209] was not a spirit τῶν πολλῶν, "of the many [spirits]," but rather ἓν ὄν, "one unique being," indicated especially by the article, τὸ Πνεῦμα, *"the* Spirit" (*ad Serap.* 1.27).[210]

The Cappadocian fathers made a significant impact on the theology of the Holy Spirit. Their debate was waged against the Pneumatomachi, "spirit fighters," who, like the Tropici before them, considered the Holy Spirit to be a creature.[211]

Basil of Caesarea (329–379) distinguished the Holy Spirit from the rest of the spirits and angels that make up the spiritual world. Basil argued, "One does not speak of the Spirit and of the angels as if they were equals."[212] The ministering spirits in Heb 1:14 are creatures but such is not the Holy Spirit: "We are bound to anathematize all who speak of the Holy Spirit as ministerial [a ministering spirit] inasmuch as by this term we degrade him to the rank of a creature."[213] Whereas Basil can implicitly speak of "holy spirits," he does so in such a way that subordinates their nature to the Holy Spirit: "The pure, spiritual, and transcendent powers are called holy, because they have received holiness from the grace of the Holy Spirit."[214]

Basil also reasoned that the Spirit is not a creature because of its procession from the Father: "the Spirit of truth we have been taught to proceed from the

---

[209] Note Athanasius's text, μὴ ἁπλῶς λέγηται πνεῦμα, ἀλλὰ τὸ Πνεῦμα, "he is called not simply 'spirit' but 'the Spirit'" (*PG* 26. 537A), wherein Athanasius takes the liberty of distinguishing "spirit" from "Spirit" by capitalizing the Greek letter π: μὴ πνεῦμα, ἀλλὰ τὸ Πνεῦμα, "not a spirit, but the Spirit." This forged the very theology that the Roman church deemed orthodox during the fourth century. Hence, in present-day English, the capitalization of "spirit" in conjunction with the definite article denotes "the Spirit" as a divine Person.

[210] Athanasius's understanding of the function of the article here might reflect the "particular" use wherein the article particularizes a substantive to denote a particular person, thing, event, or idea. See Stanley E. Porter, *Idioms of the Greek New Testament* (2nd ed.; Biblical Languages: Greek 2; Sheffield: JSOT, 1994) 104. See also Didymus the Blind, *On the Holy Spirit* 15, who states that the article in the context of "holy spirit" is *"singularitatis significator"*; and further about the significance of the article in Didymus, *On the Holy Spirit* 3 and *On the Trinity* 2. 457c.

[211] The Tropici might have been a group of Pneumatomachi. See Haykin, *Spirit of God*, 20 nn. 50 and 52. On the Pneumatomachi, see Peter Meinhold, "Pneumatomachoi," *Paulys Realencyclopadei der classischen Altertumswissenschaft* 11/1 (1951) 1066–1101.

[212] Basil, *On the Holy Spirit* 13.29. David Anderson, trans., *St. Basil the Great: On the Holy Spirit* (Crestwood, NY: St. Vladimir's Press, 1980) 50. See Basil's reaction against those who deny the divinity of the Holy Spirit, 10.24–11.27.

[213] Basil, *Epistles* 125.3. NPNF ser. 2, 8. 195.

[214] Basil, *On the Holy Spirit* 16.38. Trans. Anderson, *Basil*, 62. See further: "If we agree that the Spirit is subordinate, then the choirs of angels are destroyed, the ranks of archangels are abolished, and everything is thrown into confusion" (ibid., 63).

Father, and we confess Him to be of God without creation."[215] Basil seems to have been influenced by Athanasius's use of 1 Cor 2:11,12 as a proof-text for the divine and uncreated nature of the Spirit: "But the greatest proof that the Spirit is one with the Father and the Son is that He is said to have the same relationship to God as the spirit within us has to us (then follows 1 Cor 2:11)."[216]

Gregory of Nyssa (335–394), Basil's younger brother, likewise maintained the position that the Holy Spirit was of a unique nature, separate from the rest of the spiritual world. In his *Against the Macedonians* 2, 5, Gregory writes that the Holy Spirit is out God and is of Christ. He compares the Father, Son, and Holy Spirit to three torches, the first of which imparts its light to the second and through the second to the third. Like Athanasius before him Gregory of Nyssa claims that the nature of the Holy Spirit is the same as that of the Father and of the Son.[217]

While Athanasius, Basil, and Gregory of Nyssa maintained the divinity of the Holy Spirit, they all came short of calling the Holy Spirit God. Gregory of Nazianzus (329–389) is noted as having been the first church father to explicitly declare that the Holy Spirit is God.[218] Gregory engaged in a lengthy but fruitless debate with the Pneumatomachi and ultimately proclaimed them as blasphemers because they did not regard the Spirit as God.[219] Whereas the Pneumatomachi claimed that Scripture does not proclaim the Spirit as God, Gregory argued that the Scriptures contain a gradual revelation of the Godhead. The NT "only hinted at the deity of the Holy Spirit, but now the Holy Spirit lives among us and gives us a clearer manifestation of himself."[220]

In *Letter 58: To Basil*, Gregory recounts a question posed by a "so-called philosopher": "And why on earth do you, my friend, speak so openly of the

---

[215] Basil, *Epistles* 125.3. NPNF ser. 2, 8. 195.

[216] Basil, *On the Holy Spirit* 16.40. Trans. Anderson, *Basil*, 67. So Haykin, *Spirit of God*, 137–47, esp. 140.

[217] See Anthony Meredith, trans., *Gregory of Nyssa* (The Early Church Fathers; New York: Routledge, 1999) 41–42: "But the Holy Spirit . . . is the same as the Father and Only Begotten, ... It [the Spirit] is with all them that are worthy, yet not separated from the Holy Triad." The term "Macedonians" is a misnomer for the Pneumatomachi who were called such by the church historians Socrates and Sozomen. The term comes from bishop Macedonius, defender of the semi-Arian position, who was removed from power as patriarch of Constantinople in 360. See R. P. C. Hanson, *The Search for the Christian Doctrine of God: The Arian Controversy, 318–381* (London: T & T Clark, 1988; repr. Grand Rapids: Baker, 2005) 760–72.

[218] Fortman, *Triune God*, 78.

[219] Gregory of Nazianzus, *Orations* 34.11. NPNF ser. 2, 7. 337.

[220] Gregory of Nazianzus, *Orations* 31.26. NPNF ser. 2, 7. 326.

Spirit as God?" Gregory then appeals directly to Basil: "How far should we come forward in speaking of the Spirit as God? What expressions should we use? . . . We need to have a firm front against those who criticize us!"[221] Elsewhere Gregory writes, "Is the Spirit God? Most certainly. Is he then consubstantial? Yes, since he is God."[222]

Without question the divinity of the Holy Spirit developed during the pivotal fourth century of the church. In an edict given by Theodosius on February 28, 380, the view of the Holy Spirit as a Deity was legalized in Rome as orthodox:

We should believe in the sole deity of the Father and the Son and the Holy Spirit in equal majesty and holy Trinity. We order those following this law to assume the name Catholic Christians, but the rest, since we judge them demented and insane, to sustain the infamy of heretical dogma and their conventicles not to take the name of churches, to be smitten first by divine vengeance, then also by the punishment of our authority, . . ."[223]

The following year the Deity of the Holy Spirit was dogmatically declared at the Council of Constantinople in 381.[224] The phrase "the spirit which is from God" in 1 Cor 2:12 served as a proof-text for the Spirit's uncreated nature akin to God himself. Scripture is used by Cyril, Athanasius, and the Cappadocian fathers as the basis for the divinity of the Holy Spirit. To be sure, however, their exegesis of Scripture determined the Deity of the Holy Spirit.[225]

---

[221] Brian E. Daley, trans., *Gregory of Nazianzus* (The Early Church Fathers; New York: Routledge, 2006) 180.

[222] Gregory of Nazianzus, *Orations* 31.10. NPNF ser. 2, 7. 321. Cyril of Jerusalem did not go as far as Athanasius and the Cappadocian fathers in his doctrine of the Holy Spirit: "There is one God the Father, one Lord, . . . one Holy Spirit . . . This is all we need to know without inquiring curiously about nature or hypostasis. For if it had been in Scripture, we would have spoken of it; let us not presume to speak what is not in Scripture" (*Catechetical Letters* 16.24; Edward Yarnold, trans., *Cyril of Jerusalem* [The Early Church Fathers; New York: Routledge, 2000] 60–61).

[223] *The Theodosian Code* 16.1.2. P. R. Coleman-Norton, trans., *Roman State and Christian Church. A Collection of Legal Documents to A.D. 535* (3 vols.; London: Society for the Propagation of Christian Knowledge, 1966) 1. 354. Gregory of Nazianzus is clear: "I hope it may be always my position . . . to worship God the Father, God the Son, and God the Holy Spirit, three persons, one Godhead, undivided in honor and glory and substance and kingdom . . ." (*Orations* 31.28. NPNF ser. 2, 7. 326–27).

[224] See Anthony Meredith, "The Pneumatology of the Cappadocian Fathers and the Creed of Constantinople," *ITQ* 48 (1981) 196–212.

[225] Haykin (*Spirit of God*) states, "Both Athanasius and Basil firmly believed that the Scriptures had to be the basis of a sound pneumatology. This conviction . . . meant that Scriptural exegesis was central to the pneumatological discussions of the latter half of the fourth century" (p. 229). See ibid., 63–67, 93–100, 114–20, and 123–29. Basil's exegesis is reflected

18.2 The Theology of the Holy Spirit and Biblical Studies

Many commentators assume that τὸ πνεῦμα and τὸ πνεῦμα τὸ ἅγιον in the NT are a kind of "proto-Athanasian" Holy Spirit: what Athanasius said about the Spirit was already inherent in the NT. For instance, Thiselton argues that Athanasius's ontology of the Holy Spirit, although of a later date, is nonetheless "a logical explication of Paul's thought" in First Corinthians.[226]

Joseph Haroutunian gives a reflection on the impact of Athanasius's statement wherein the articular τὸ πνεῦμα was distinguished from a plurality τῶν πολλῶν, "of the many [spirits]": "The Holy Spirit is the one who replaces, neither too clearly, nor too completely, the spirits, the good spirits. . . . The Holy Spirit is the Good Spirit."[227] This statement summarizes the impact of the later fourth-century theology of the Holy Spirit on an earlier historical first-century belief in many holy spirits. The Athanasian-Cappadocian doctrine for the Holy Spirit would come to obscure the NT spirit world's plurality of holy spirits.

Those studies that distinguish the Holy Spirit as qualitatively different from all other spirits in the NT incorporate a theological premise reflective of later Christian thought which postdates the writings of the NT by several centuries.[228]

---

in his discussions on the theological significance of the prepositions ἐν, διά, ἐκ, and μετά which are used in Scripture with regard to the Father, Son, and Holy Spirit (*On the Holy Spirit* 2.4–8.21; 25.58–29.73).

[226] Anthony Thiselton, "The Holy Spirit in 1 Corinthians: Exegesis and Reception History in the Patristic Era," in *The Holy Spirit and Christians: Essays in Honor of James D. G. Dunn* (ed. Graham N. Stanton, et al.; Grand Rapids: Eerdmans, 2004) 207–228, esp. 224.

[227] Joseph Haroutunian, "Spirit, Holy Spirit, Spiritism," *Ex Auditu* 12 (1996) 59–75, esp. 63.

[228] See Steve Swartz, "The Holy Spirit: Person and Power: The Greek Article and *Pneuma*," *BT* 44 (1993) 124–38, who quotes from Nigel Turner, *Grammatical Insights into the New Testament*: "Whenever the Holy Spirit has the article the reference is to the third person of the Trinity (expressed either as *to Pneuma to Hagion* or as *to Hagion Pneuma*), but when the article is absent the reference is to 'a' holy spirit, a divine influence possessing men" (p. 129). While the latter part of this statement conveys one of the meanings for the absence of the Greek article τό, "a holy spirit," the first part of the statement, "the third person of the Trinity," is a theological judgment about the significance of the Greek article whose provenance can be traced back to Athanasius and Didymus. The level to which some authors will take the presence of the article as an indicator that "spirit" is a single divine Person of the Godhead distinct from other spirits can be illustrated from Bretherton, "Theology and Psychical Studies," who states, "The existence of spirit-entities is a Biblical concept . . . But where does the Holy Spirit come into all this? . . . There is *the* Spirit: . . . there are spirits of the departed, some good, some bad . . . We must not confuse the spirits of the departed with THE Spirit–the Holy Spirit, the Spirit of God" (pp. 255–56, emphasis his).

Fourth-century formulation redefined language for the spirit world in the NT with theological verbiage.[229]

The grammatical and semantic range of πνεῦμα in the NT that includes good sentient spirit beings, such as "a holy spirit," is eclipsed by translations that, under the influence of centuries of Christian theological tradition, always translate the Greek anarthrous as either "the Holy Spirit" or simply "Holy Spirit." Steve Swartz notes to this effect, "By long-standing tradition, such references are capitalized, and even with the anarthrous references, the translations almost invariably translate with the English definite '*the* Holy Spirit.'"[230] Theological traditions of the Holy Spirit have been used by many NT scholars as critical benchmarks for studies on "holy spirit" in the NT. But a unique, uncreated Holy Spirit, above and beyond other spirits in status and in nature, is neither a tenable prospect for πνεῦμα in the NT nor indigenous to the NT period.

The theology of the Holy Spirit as a unique being is a product of fourth-century individuals whose readings of the NT text established a new trend for the understanding of "the holy spirit" in the NT: an artificial distinction between "the spirit" and "spirits." As we have seen, much of the work for synthesizing the doctrine of the Deity of the Holy Spirit was accomplished by Athanasius and the Cappadocian fathers. In the pneumatological debates of the fourth century, the phrase "the spirit" took on a life of its own in ways that fundamentally departed from the NT. The Athanasian-Cappadocian interpretations established

---

[229] See Hegumen Hilarion Alfeyev, "The Trinitarian Teaching of St. Gregory Nazianzen," in *The Trinity: East/West Dialogue* (ed. Melville Y. Stewart; Studies in Philosophy and Religion 24; Boston: Kluwer Academic Publishers, 2003) 107–30, who states, "Nowhere in the New Testament is the divinity of the Holy Spirit proclaimed. The term 'Trinity' appears for the first time in the writings of Theophilus of Alexandria, and it is only in the third century that its use can be noted more widely (particularly, by Origen)" (p. 108). Apparently, Gregory of Nazianzus was aware of his own extra-biblical theology. Dong-Chan Chang ("The Doctrine of the Holy Spirit in the Thought of the Cappadocian Fathers," [Ph.D. diss., Drew University, 1983] 114) comments on Gregory's *Orations* 31.26: "To explain the lateness of the recognition of the Spirit as God he produces a highly original theory of doctrinal development," that of the "gradual revelation through Scripture." Gregory further supports the gradual disclosure of the Deity of the Holy Spirit with an allusion to John 14:26 and 16:12,13, "all things should be taught us by the Spirit when He should come to dwell amongst us"; Gregory then adds, "Of these things, one was the Deity of the Spirit Himself" (*Orations* 31.27. NPNF ser. 2, 7. 326). The scribal practice of abbreviating πνεῦμα in some NT Greek manuscripts to denote one of the *nomina sacra*, i.e., πνεῦμα as a "divine name" (ΠΝΑ), has no real bearing on the question of Deity. See David C. Parker, *Codex Bezae: An Early Christian Manuscript and Its Text* (Cambridge: Cambridge University Press, 1992) 106.

[230] Swartz, "Holy Spirit," 125.

the canonized understanding of "the Spirit," "the Holy Spirit," and "the Spirit of God" in the NT.[231]

To be sure, a spirit world populated with many good spirits, often called "angels" by the fathers, is found in the writings of Origen,[232] Cyril,[233] Athanasius,[234] Basil,[235] Gregory of Nyssa,[236] and Gregory of Nazianzus.[237] This is in keeping with the NT evidence. Yet, these church fathers also contributed to the theology of a divine Holy Spirit, a Deity set apart from the rest of spirit creation. This theological invention seems to have occurred when the phrase "the spirit" was argued (through exegesis) to indicate a unique Spirit, the only one of its kind.

18.3 The Spirit World of the Earliest Christians

The notion that there was only one unique Holy Spirit is hardly sustainable for the first century.[238] The earliest Christians reflected upon and recorded their experiences of spirit within the framework of their Jewish world. The spirit world of the earliest Christians is a product of early Jewish pneumatology. Hence, Menzies observes that "the first Christians who thought through the significance of their experience of the Spirit did so in light of their Jewish background."[239] The occurrences of πνεῦμα in the NT, with all of their variety (anarthrous, articular, singular, plural, qualified, and unqualified), tend to reveal

---

[231] A good example of imaginative theological musing about the Holy Spirit is found in Basil, *On the Holy Spirit* 9.22–23 and 16.37–38. Trans. Anderson, *Basil*, 42–44 and 60–65. See also Theodore C. Campbell, "The Doctrine of the Holy Spirit in the Theology of Athanasius," *SJT* 27 (1974) 408–40. Campbell states that Athanasius "makes the question of the divinity of the Spirit a *sine qua non* of the Christian theology of God. One must take a stand on the full divinity of the Holy Spirit" (p. 438).

[232] Origen, *De princip.* 3.3.4.

[233] Cyril, *Catechetical Letters* 16.23.

[234] Athanasius, *ad Serap.* 1.27.

[235] Basil, *On the Holy Spirit* 16.38.

[236] Gregory of Nyssa, *Commentary on the Song of Songs* 15.6,4 (Meredith, *Gregory*, 116); and *On the Soul and the Resurrection*, NPNF ser. 2, 5. 444.

[237] Gregory of Nazianzus, *Orations* 31.29. NPNF ser. 2, 7. 327.

[238] See Raymond E. Brown, *Introduction to the New Testament* (ABRL; New York: Doubleday, 1997), who states, "On the basic point of the Spirit, Christians are now shaped by a trinitarian theology worked out in the 4th century; there is no evidence that Paul had such clarity about the personhood of the Spirit" (p. 532).

[239] Menzies, *Early Christian Pneumatology*, 52. See also Thomas Marsh ("Holy Spirit in Early Christian Thinking," *ITQ* 45 [1978] 101–16) who states that Paul's pneumatology "remains firmly rooted in the Bible and Jewish thinking" (p. 108).

a spiritual reality that reflects, more realistically, the first-century Jewish conception of the spirit world rather than the fourth-century Athanasian-Cappadocian theological world of the Holy Spirit.[240]

The term πνεῦμα in Paul with reference to "holy spirit" and "spirit of God" falls within the range of the first-century Jewish-Christian beliefs in a spirit world; a world that Isaacs observes was already differentiated into good and evil spirits during the Second Temple period: "The inter-testamental period was one in which there was a remarkable development in Jewish thinking about the whole spirit world – good as well as bad."[241]

Texts that contribute heavily to our knowledge of this development in Jewish thinking about the spirit world are the Dead Sea Scrolls, *1 Enoch*, *Jubilees*, and *The Testaments of the Twelve Patriarchs*.[242] The idea of "one unique Holy Spirit" did not exist in early Judaism.[243] Instead, spirit creation (in both its Hebrew guise and Greek guise) was populated with "holy spirits,"[244] "spirits of truth,"[245] and "spirits of God."[246]

---

[240] W. Eugene March ("God With Us: A Survey of Jewish Pneumatology," *Austin Seminary Bulletin* 83 [1967] 3–16), notes that "early Christian 'theologizing' concerning the work of the Spirit and the Spirit's presence was closely kin to the Jewish tradition out of which the first Christians had come" (p. 12). See also Werner Foerster, "Der Heilige Geist im Spätjudentum," *NTS* 8 (1962) 117–34.

[241] Isaacs, *Concept of Spirit*, 110.

[242] The seedbed for this development is found in the OT. See William O. E. Oesterley, *Immortality and the Unseen World: A Study in Old Testament Religion* (New York: Macmillan, 1921) 35–62. One may also include the book of Tobit, the works of Josephus, Philo, and the magical papyri (on texts, see Hans D. Betz, *The Greek Magical Papyri in Translation* [ed. idem; Chicago: University of Chicago Press, 1986]).

[243] As was recognized by Kirsopp Lake (*The Beginnings of Christianity: The Acts of the Apostles* [5 vols.; ed. F. J. Foakes Jackson and Kirsopp Lake; London: Macmillan, 1920–1923; repr. Grand Rapids: Baker, 1979] 5. 102) who stated, "Do the Synoptics, and did the circle of Jewish thought which they represent, think that there were many bad but *only one good spirit*, or did they think that there were many of both, and that both obsessed mankind? If this question is confined to the actual fact of the existence or non-existence of many good spirits, there can be but one answer. *There were many*" (emphasis mine).

[244] רוחות קודש, "holy spirits" (1 QHᵃ 8.12; 4QShirShabbᵃ 40.24.5); πνεῦμα ἁγιωσύνης, "a spirit of holiness" (*T. Levi* 18:11).

[245] כול רוחי אמת, "all the spirits of truth" (1 QM 13.10); τὸ πνεῦμα τῆς ἀληθείας, "the spirit of truth" (*T. Jud.* 20:1).

[246] רוחות אלוהים היים, "spirits of the living God" (4QShirShabbᵃ 40. 24.6); πνεῦμα θεοῦ, "a spirit of God" (*T. Sim.* 4:4).

Qualifications for spirits in the *Testaments* (ca. 200 B.C.E.–ca. 100 C.E.)[247] provide direct correspondence to qualifications for spirits in the NT: πνευμάτων τῆς πλάνης, "spirits of deceit" (*T. Sim.* 3:1) and πνεύμασιν πλάνοις, "deceitful spirits" (1 Tim 4:1); πνεῦμα ἁγιωσύνης, "a spirit of holiness" (*T. Levi* 18:11, Rom 1:4); πνεῦμα θεοῦ, "a spirit of God" (*T. Sim.* 4:4, Rom 8:9, 1 Cor 12:3); ἀκάθαρτα πνεύματα, "unclean spirits" (*T. Ben.* 5:2) and πνευμάτων ἀκαθάρτων, "unclean spirits" (Luke 6:18); πᾶν πνεῦμα τοῦ Βελιάρ, "every spirit of Beliar" (*T. Iss.* 7:7) and πᾶν πνεῦμα . . . ἐκ τοῦ θεοῦ ἐστιν, "every spirit . . . that is from God" (1 John 4:2); τὸ πνεῦμα τῆς ἀληθείας, "the spirit of truth" (*T. Jud.* 20:1, John 14:17, 1 John 4:6); and τὸ πνεῦμα τῆς πλάνης, "the spirit of error" (*T. Jud.* 20:1, 1 John 4:6). All of these qualifications for πνεῦμα are of Jewish thinking.[248]

Christopher Forbes's study of the spirit world in Paul examines Paul's terminology for the spirit world against its first-century Jewish background. He observes the relative paucity of references in Paul to the more traditional terms for spirits, i.e., "angels" and "demons," noting fourteen occurrences of angels in Paul, ten in the undisputed letters and four in the disputed. The term "demon" occurs in only two passages, 1 Cor 10:20–21 and 1 Tim 4:1.[249] Forbes observes that although "Paul clearly believes in angels, demons, spirits and Satan, the vocabulary he seems to prefer to use to describe the 'spiritual world' is different."[250] This "different" vocabulary includes the terms "authorities,"

---

[247] The provenance and date of the *T. 12 Patr.* are notoriously debated. The arguments range from a purely Jewish work closer in time to the Dead Sea Scrolls with later Christian interpolations to a purely Christian work composed during the second or third century C.E. as a sort of midrash on the book of Jubilees. Aramaic fragments of the *Testaments of Levi* and of *Naphtali* (in Hebrew) were found among the Dead Sea Scrolls. The original language of the *T. 12 Patr.*, whether Aramaic or Greek, is also debated. See Martin McNamara, *Intertestamental Literature* (Wilmington, DE: Michael Glazier, 1983) 105; and James C. VanderKam, *An Introduction to Early Judaism* (Grand Rapids: Eerdmans, 2001) 100–01.

[248] For correspondence in the Dead Sea Scrolls see רוח אמת, "spirit of truth," רוח העול, "spirit of deceit" (1 QS 3.18,19; 4.9,20,21b,23); רוחות בליעל, "spirits of Belial" (CD 12.2); רוחות עולה, "spirits of deceit" (1QM 15.14); and רוח קודש, "a holy spirit" (1 QS 4.21a; 9.3). Compare also the use of the 3rd m.s. personal pronoun in Paul and in the Scrolls: τὸ πνεῦμα αὐτοῦ τὸ ἅγιον, "his holy spirit" (1 Thess 4:8) and רוח קדשו, "his holy spirit" (1QS 8.16; CD 2.12).

[249] Christopher Forbes, "Paul's Principalities and Powers: Demythologizing Apocalyptic?" *JSNT* 82 (2001) 61–88, esp. 64–65.

[250] Ibid., 67. As a Pharisee, Paul would have been expected to acknowledge the existence of angels and spirits. See Acts 23:6–8.

"principalities," "powers," and "elements," each of which might be construed as personal, semipersonal, or impersonal according to context.[251]

Paul's vocabulary for the spirit world is full of terminological variety. The Greek noun πνεῦμα is only one of the many terms Paul uses for sentient beings of a spirit world.[252] First Corinthians 12 and 14 use this Greek noun exclusively for indicating experiences with a spirit world. Dibelius stated that with the use of πνεῦμα and πνεύματα in First Corinthians 12 and 14, "It is clear that Paul sees here, as he frequently does, conditions and events that lie . . . within the realm of spirits."[253]   Paul's Jewish pneumatology reflects the "realm," or more appropriately, "realms of spirits" in which exist good and evil spirits. Hence, Craig S. Keener can state, "Early Jewish pneumatology provides a context in which early Christian pneumatic experience may be understood."[254] It is within this interpretive view that I will explore religious experience in First Corinthians 12 and 14.

The plural "spirits" that are committed to God, and thus "holy," poses a historical reality that is obscured by the theology of the Holy Spirit. In order to accommodate Trinitarian beliefs, theology tends to impose fourth-century formulations for the spirit on its description of the spirit world.[255] The fourth-

---

[251] Ibid., 67–74. On the disputed Pauline letters, see Raymond F. Collins, *Letters that Paul Did Not Write: The Epistle to the Hebrews and the Pauline Pseudepigrapha* (GNS 28; Wilmington, DE: Michael Glazier, 1988).

[252] Note that πνεῦμα for "holy spirit" and its equivalences ("spirit of God," "his spirit," and "spirit of the Lord") occurs close to one hundred times both in the disputed and undisputed letters of Paul. Articular references: Rom 8:2,5,16,23,26; 12:11; 15:30; 1 Cor 2:10,11,12,14; 3:16; 6:11; 12:7,8(twice), 9(twice); 14:15(twice); 2 Cor 1:22; 3:8,17(twice); 4:13; 5:5; 12:4,11; 13:13; Gal 3:2,5,14; 4:6; 5:17,22; Eph 1:13; 4:3,30; 6:17; 1 Thess 4:8; 5:19; 1 Tim 4:1; Phil 1:19; Heb 9:8; 3:7; 10:15,29. Anarthrous references: Rom 1:4; 2:29; 5:5; 7:6; 8:4, 9, 11, 13, 14,15; 9:1; 14:17; 15:13,16,19; 1 Cor 2:4,13; 6:19; 7:40; 12:3(twice),10,13; 14:2,12,16,32; 2 Cor 3:3,6; 6:6; Gal 4:29; 5:5,16,18,25; Eph 2:18,22; 3:5; 4:4; 5:18; 6:18; Phil 2:1; 3:3; 1 Thess 1:5,6; 2 Thess 2:13; 2 Tim 1:14; Tit 3:5; Heb 1:7,14; 2:4; 6:4; 12:9,23.

[253] Dibelius, *Geisterwelt*, 74 (translation mine).

[254] Craig S. Keener, *The Spirit in the Gospels and Acts: Divine Purity and Power* (Peabody, MA: Hendrickson, 1997) 27. See Finny Philip, *The Origins of Pauline Pneumatology: The Eschatological Bestowal of the Spirit upon Gentiles in Judaism and in the Early Development of Paul's Theology* (WUNT 1/194; Tübingen: Mohr Siebeck, 2005), who shows that Paul's beliefs about spirit come from Second Temple Judaism; and Menzies (*Early Christian Pneumatology*) shows that "Judaism provided the conceptual framework for the pneumatological reflection of Luke and Paul, as well as the primitive church before them" (p. 52).

[255] For instance, see Thomas A. Noble, "The Spirit World: A Theological Approach," in *The Unseen World: Christian Reflections on Angels, Demons, and the Heavenly Realm* (ed. Anthony N. S. Lane; Grand Rapids: Baker, 1996) 185–223, who states, "The attempt must be made to

century Christian theology for "the Holy Spirit," however, does not adequately explain the "spirit world" as it is known, historically, in the texts of the NT.[256]

The NT does not suggest formulations of the spirit, theological or rhetorical, but rather contains the records of empirical experiences of a spirit world. Hurtado observes that "the religious experiences attested in the sources for early Christianity have not always been done justice in scholarly studies."[257] While this generally remains the case, the survey of the scholarly discussion in the following chapter will show that both past- and present-day scholarship offer a challenge to Thiselton's notion that any discussion of First Corinthians 12 and 14 as religious experience "goes against the grain of Paul."

---

articulate our understanding of the spirit world within the Trinitarian, Christocentric shape of Christian dogmatics" (p. 186); and, "To outline briefly clear Christian doctrine on the spirit world, we shall take the Trinitarian structure of the Nicene Creed as a guide" (p. 192).

[256] This point hinges on what some see to be a dilemma between "what Scripture meant," i.e., its historical context, and "what Scripture means," i.e., as a source for present-day theological reflection in light of centuries of tradition. David M. Williams (*Receiving the Bible in Faith: Historical and Theological Exegesis* [Washington, D.C.: Catholic University of American Press, 2004] 72–75) notes this distinction in an exposition of Raymond Brown's assessment of the historical-critical method. Williams states, "Over the course of those centuries a systematic structure has developed whose relationship to the literal [historical] sense 'is not simple'; the biblical basis for a given doctrine may range anywhere from strong to nonexistent" (p. 72). Admittedly, the church fathers did not engage in historical-critical investigations. They did not differentiate between what a text "meant" and what it "means." Their writings were theological works rather than critical ones. So Haykin, *Spirit of God*, 116. Nonetheless, their exegetical decisions stem from biblical texts.

[257] Hurtado, "Religious Experience," 184.

Chapter 2

Religious Experience: A Survey of the Discussion

1. Introduction

Religious experience of the spirit has received only sporadic attention from scholars over the years. At times it has been as a reaction to theology and dogma in biblical studies. At other times it has served the need to illuminate various spirit phenomena throughout religious history. But usually the study of religious experience understands the language and rhetoric of spirit to be an expression for an ultramundane spirit world. The texts of antiquity are filled with references to phenomena that were believed to be the actions of inexplicable forces that although invisible were nonetheless felt as a reality by their effects.

During the past century and a quarter, a number of major studies of religious experiences of the spirit in the OT, Jewish, Greco-Roman, and Christian texts have appeared. The present survey, from Hermann Gunkel in 1888 to John Eifion Morgan-Wynne in 2006, will show emergence and continuity in the study of religious experience as a means to understand and explicate the wide range and complexity of the language of spirit in the Bible and early Christian literature. The survey is divided into two parts: (1) the emergence and graphic portrayal of religious experience; and (2) the reemergence of the portrayal of religious experience. The studies conveniently fall within these groups chronologically and show the trends of religious experience in scholarship. A conclusion will complete the survey.

2. The Emergence and Graphic Portrayal of Religious Experience

2.1 Hermann Gunkel: Die Wirkungen des heiligen Geistes nach der populären Anschauung der apostolischen Zeit und nach der Lehre des Apostels Paulus (Göttingen: Vandenhoeck & Ruprecht, 1888).

In biblical studies, Hermann Gunkel is best known for his contributions to the OT and is recognized as the father of form criticism. He was one of the leading German scholars of his day in the field of OT and taught many of the luminaries that came after him. His initial effort, however, was devoted not to the OT but to the spirit in the NT. Printed in 1888, his book was published in an English translation ninety-one years later, a testimony to the relevance and significance of the work.[1]

Gunkel's slender volume (110 pages in the German) presents a penetrating analysis of the spirit in two major sections. The first is devoted to "The Popular Views" of the spirit, taken from the synoptics and Acts. The second deals with "The Teaching of Paul" on the spirit as related in his letters.

In the preface to the second edition (1899),[2] Gunkel explains that the essential task of his study was to "ascertain the symptoms by which an effect (*Wirkung*) of the Spirit was recognized."[3] Given the nature of his study, Gunkel distinguishes what he does from studies that view the spirit through the lens of doctrine and dogma. Gunkel was interested in getting at the first-hand experiences of those persons affected by the spirit. According to his analysis, the effects of the spirit were observable by the symptoms exhibited by the person upon or in whom the spirit acted. Gunkel refers to these persons as pneumatics, whose primary function was to serve the spirit as a vehicle for its activities.

Throughout the book Gunkel stresses that spirit in NT times was never the subject of a formulated doctrine. Instead, the effects of the spirit were issues of concrete facts "which were the object of daily experience and without further reflection were directly experienced as effected by the Spirit."[4] Although Gunkel does admit that dogma and doctrine have their proper place as representative of later theological developments, "none of it would exist if real events were not underlying."[5]

Gunkel highlights the Jewish and experiential nature of the primitive church's concept of the spirit. In the primitive church a symptom of the activities of the spirit was recognized within the scheme of cause and effect:

---

[1] *The Influence of the Holy Spirit* (trans. R. A. Harrisville and P. A. Quanbeck; Philadelphia: Fortress, 1979). All quotations are from the English translation. Gunkel's study was originally submitted to the Theology Faculty of Göttingen in 1888 as a dissertation (Gerd Lüdemann and Martin Schröder, *Die religionsgeschichtliche Schule in Göttingen: Eine Dokumentation* [Göttingen: Vandenhoeck & Ruprecht, 1987] 66).

[2] A third edition was published in 1909.

[3] Ibid., 2. The "emergence and graphic portrayal of religious experience," as a heading for the first section of the survey, is Gunkel's language for the explicitness and reality of human experiences with invisible sentient beings, "spirits," as expressed in NT texts: "Diese *lebendige Anschauung* vom Geist herrscht in unseren Quellen durchaus vor" (*Die Wirkungen des heiligen Geistes* [Göttingen: Vandenhoeck & Ruprecht, 1888] 29), "This *graphic view* of the Spirit dominates our sources throughout" (*Influence*, 40).

[4] Ibid., 14.

[5] Ibid., 3.

"Belief in the Spirit is . . . for the purpose of explaining the presence of certain, above all inexplicable, phenomena by means of the transcendent."[6] The presence of the spirit was inferred by those who witnessed a force whose explanation defied conditions prevailing in the world.[7]

According to Gunkel the primitive church conceived the spirit in ways derived from the OT. In Hebrew terminology the word for "wind" and "spirit" (רוח) is the same. The spirit of God was "invisible of course to the naked eye though actually present and thus after the analogy of the wind."[8] The spirit is vividly experienced and thus visualized as substance. This conception of the spirit by Israelites and Jews was based on their own experience, apart from Hellenic influences.[9] According to Gunkel, the substance of the spirit in Judaism was that of light (*1 Enoch* 43:4; 71:1;104:2; Dan 12:3; *Apoc. Ezra* 7:55; *Apoc. Bar.* 51). Jews who became Christians retained these ideas (2 Cor 11:14; Matt 13:43).

Gunkel argues that this exposition of the spirit in the primitive church is the background to Paul's thought and development of the concept of the spirit. Like the primitive church, Paul ascertained the pneumatic origin of the presence of the spirit by its symptoms and believed the spirit to be the source of supernatural power as displayed in glossolalia and prophecy.[10] Paul's concept of the spirit was no less experiential than that of the primitive church: "Paul believes in the divine Spirit because he has experienced it."[11]

Of particular importance was Gunkel's innovative contribution in the area of demonology and pneumatology. He argued that the activity of demons as described in the NT is especially instructive for an understanding of the activities of the spirit.[12] Demons and the spirit shared many similarities: both have their locus of activity in the person through whom they appear from

---

[6] Ibid., 32–33.

[7] According to Gunkel (ibid., 39) the impressions made by the presence of the spirit were ones of "fear" (Matt 9:8; Mark 5:15; Luke 5:26), "amazement" (Matt 12:23; Mark 2:12; Luke 5:26), "astonishment" (Mark 1:27), "marvel" (Matt 8:27), and "shock" (Matt 13:54; Luke 4:32). Gunkel could well have added Acts 2:7, where glossolalia produced similar reactions.

[8] Ibid., 59.

[9] In light of the trend of his day to relegate the origins and ideas of "spirit" in early Christian sources to Greek influences (for example, see Carl von Weizsäcker, *Das apostolische Zeitalter* [Freiburg: J. C. B. Mohr, 1886]; and Carl Friedrich G. Heinrici, *Der erste Brief an die Korinther* [Göttingen: Vandenhoeck & Ruprecht, 1896]), this must be judged to be a progressive observation by Gunkel.

[10] *Influence*, 79–85.

[11] Ibid., 100.

[12] Ibid., 49–59.

without; a demoniac was ἐν πνεύματι ἀκαθάρτῳ, "with an unclean spirit," and a pneumatic was ἐν πνεύματι θεοῦ, "with a spirit of God"; the spirit speaks through the pneumatic and demons through the demoniac; both demons and the spirit grant superhuman knowledge.[13] The reason for the similarity was obvious to Gunkel. Both the spirit and demons were of the same essence, that of "spirit," and could be recognized by the same symptoms.[14]

Gunkel was careful to observe that despite these similarities the manifestations of demons and the spirit must have had distinguishing characteristics in order to avoid any confusion of the spirit world. Demons were pernicious and could be identified as the spirits of evil people. The spirit has more power than demons. Spiritual manifestations that occurred in the name of God or Jesus Christ were perceived with greater certainty as coming from the spirit. But this was not always the case since lying spirits could deceive and mislead the church.[15]

Die Wirkungen des heiligen Geistes is a modest study, the earliest work of a young scholar who matured well beyond his initial effort. But it is a seminal study whose poignant observations laid the groundwork for the modern discussion of the experience of the spirit in early Christianity.

2.2 Heinrich Weinel: Die Wirkungen des Geistes und der Geister im nachapostolischen Zeitalter bis zum Iranäus (Freiburg, Leipzig, and Tübingen: Mohr, 1899).

Weinel's similarly titled work is intended to continue Gunkel's study that appeared a decade earlier. What Gunkel accomplished for the apostolic period through Paul, Weinel does through the third century. He covers early Christian literature that includes the NT, the *Didache*, the Shepherd of Hermas, and Barnabas, as well as works of church fathers such as Justin, Athenagoras, Theophilus, Origen, Tatian, Hippolytus, and Tertullian, and the work of Eusebius. Although there are clear signs of indebtedness to Gunkel, Weinel's study of the effects of spirits (*Geister*), both good and bad, in early Christian communities and thought supersede those of Gunkel, as Gunkel admits: "In this excellent book I recognize the legitimate continuation of my studies and observe with particular delight that in going beyond the results I then obtained, Weinel

---

[13] Gunkel may well have added that just as the spirit can "teach" (John 14:26; 1 Cor 2:13), so do the demons teach "doctrines" (1 Tim 4:1).

[14] *Influence*, 52.

[15] Ibid., 49 and 53–58.

has advanced to views and methods that were also disclosed to me throughout the years."[16]

According to Weinel, the NT and other early sources give evidence for the spirits that operated among the first Christians. The demons, who masqueraded as gods and heroes, felt threatened by the emergence of Christianity as a movement directed by a spirit world of God. The Roman state became the protagonist of these demons against the fledgling movement.[17]

Early Christians experienced demons in a variety of ways: through demons' erring teachings (1 Tim 4:1), through potential communal participation with demons (1 Cor 10:20), through demonic attacks on Christian faith (John 6:70; 13:2,27), and the demons bearing false witness against Christians (Eusebius, *Eccl. Hist.* 5.1.14,23,25,52).[18]

Weinel proceeds with his study in a way that recalls Gunkel's:

Whenever the early church talked about the spirit and spirits, the views were always based on real and frequent experiences. A discrete investigation on the experiences of the holy spirit cannot be made from the later doctrines concerning the spirit, but rather must take, as its starting point, the experiences from which the doctrines arose.[19]

Weinel was interested in experiences in antiquity that reflected "communication with an invisible world of spirits" and the consequences and effects of this communication.[20]

One of the main observations that Weinel draws from his overview is similar to one of Gunkel's ideas, that the effects of demons and of the spirit are identical:

The activities of the holy spirit and those of the demons are, however, phenomena which not only bear a general resemblance to each other, but one and the same phenomena may be construed as the work of either a good or a bad spirit, according to the religious viewpoint of him who records it. What might be considered as the work of good or holy spirits by a Christian Gnostic, might appear to a Catholic as a hallucination produced by demons, and vice versa. . . Therefore, it is inevitably necessary to treat the activities of all spirits together.[21]

---

[16] Gunkel, *Influence*, 1.

[17] Weinel, *Wirkungen*, 11–12.

[18] Ibid., 13–20.

[19] Ibid., 63 (translation mine).

[20] Ibid., 55 (translation mine).

[21] Ibid., 64 (translation mine).

Weinel is able to exploit this further by asserting that a proper organization and study of the effects of the spirit world must include those of all spirits found in the early Christian sources.[22]

According to Weinel, inspired speech is the most explicit effect of the spirits found in early Christian sources. He rehearses the evidence for glossolalia and for spirits that were thought to have entered into human subjects. The Shepherd of Hermas and the apologetic slandering of Montanism give evidence that the same spirit effect may have been interpreted as due to either good spirits or demons. Discernment could not be based solely on the form of speech spoken by the prophet. Spirit speech could be ambiguous, for it was believed that demons could at times speak true things.[23] As to intensity, inspired speech provided one of the most powerful examples of the effects of spirits on the physical organism.

Weinel claims that human impulses were so closely connected with and influenced by spirit agents that the spirits thought to be responsible for certain virtues and vices came to be identified with particular moods, drives, and passions that then could be used as descriptive epithets for spirits. Thus, "a spirit of" whatever virtue or vice was not merely a way of expressing a psychological mood whose origins were endogenous, but rather referred to a spirit that was especially potent in that virtue or vice and which played and tugged at the comparable human virtues and vices for good or for evil.[24] Weinel finds evidence for this in Hermas, Clement, Justin, Barnabas, and Irenaeus as well as in the NT (Eph 4:29–32; James 4:5–7; Heb 6:4; 1 Pet 3:4) and the *Testaments of the Twelve Patriarchs*. Sins were of the devil who tried to thwart the faithful and corrupt the graces and effects of the holy spirit. By the nature of such invisible spirit influences on the psyche, the otherwise extraneous spirit influences could be effectively camouflaged as originating from within the person.[25]

Despite the invisible nature of spirits, Weinel explores texts that give evidence for the belief of persons who could see, hear, or feel the presence of spirits about them. Both good and bad spirits made themselves known in this way. Paul is instructed by Christ through visible intercessions. Polycarp heard a voice of encouragement from heaven as he entered his martyrdom in the stadium, and Ignatius was told of Polycarp's death by an inexplicable voice. A Christian Montanist experienced a visible encounter with a soul that had a body

---

[22] Ibid., 68.
[23] Ibid., 88.
[24] Ibid., 156.
[25] Ibid., 151–61.

of light and that spoke. Weinel observed that these effects of the spirit not only revealed a spirit world beyond the normal human senses but also served as a realization for Christians of the heavenly world that was to be their future possession.[26]

Weinel consults sources that cover a span of two to three centuries. Whereas many scholars treat Christian texts of different times and genres exclusively from one another (even within the NT) for fear of theological cross-contamination, Weinel is able to demonstrate that ideas and beliefs in the effects of the spirit permeated Christian thought with equal vigor and conceptualization from as early as Paul in the mid-first century to as late as Tertullian or Eusebius in the second, third, and fourth centuries.[27]

Weinel's explorations and interpretations of the data fared well under criticism and are considered worthy contributions.[28] He provides material that is pertinent to an understanding of religious experience in early Christianity. He takes seriously the experiences of the spirit world as depicted to varying degrees in early Christian sources.[29]

2.3 Paul Volz: Der Geist Gottes und die verwandten Erscheinungen im Alten Testament und im anschließenden Judentum (Tübingen: Mohr, 1910).

What Gunkel and Weinel accomplished for Christian sources, Volz does for the OT and early Jewish literature, including the LXX, Second Temple literature, and rabbinic literature. He acknowledges the merit of the work of Gunkel and Weinel and attempts to examine the effects of the spirit in the OT and Judaism.

---

[26] Ibid., 191–92.

[27] Weinel also gives examples of like phenomena from religious history: ". . . wo die pneumatischen Vorgänge auf demselben seelisch-leiblichen Gebiet auftreten, ist es höchst auffallend, wie gleichartig sie in allen Jahrhunderten gewesen sind. Der mittelalterliche mönchische Mystiker, der Quäker im protestantischen England, der hugenottische Inspirierte, der Wunderarzt des 19. Jahrhunderts erlebt und thut dann ganz dasselbe wie der Pneumatiker der werdenden Kirche" (p. 65).

[28] See the following reviews: G. Kruger, "H. Weinel, *Die Wirkungen des Geistes und der Geister im nachapostolischen Zeitalter bis auf Irenaeus*," *Archiv für Religionswissenschaft* 2 (1899) 371–80; Adolf Harnack, "Review of *Die Wirkungen des Geistes*, by H. Weinel," *TLZ* 24 (1899) 513–15; and Wilhelm Bousset, "Review of *Die Wirkungen des Geistes*, by H. Weinel," *Göttinger Gelehrte Anzeigen* 163 (1901) 753–76. Unfortunately, Weinel's work has not been afforded the same treatment as Gunkel's with an English translation. This is surprising because Weinel's insights are as important today as they were in 1899.

[29] In a similar vein, see also P. Athanas Recheis, *Engel, Tod und Seelenreise: Das Wirken der Geister beim Heimgang des Menschen in der Lehre der Alexandrinischen und Kappadokischen Väter* (Temi e Testi 4; Roma: Edizioni di Storia e Letteratura, 1958).

His study is divided according to the two major periods in the history of Israel, (1) the preexilic period (*die ältere Zeit*, pp. 1–77) and (2) the postexilic period (*die spätere Zeit*, pp. 78–194).

In the first section of his study, Volz discerns three concepts of Hebrew רוח, "spirit," in the historical and prophetic works: (1) רוח as a demonic agent whose effects were bad and harmful (e.g., the "evil spirit of the Lord" in 1 Samuel was a personal spirit that abused the person it affected physically and psychologically)[30]; (2) רוח as a spirit nature in Judges, where Gideon and Samson are used as a tool by the spirit that seizes and penetrates them (Judg 6:34; 13:25)[31]; and (3) רוח as a kind of fluid-like spiritual matter that remains in the person and can be transferred from one person to another (Num 11:25, Ezek 8:3; 9:24; 11:1).[32] The notion of רוח as spirit matter is derived from that to which it is related, "air."

The term רוח covered a vast array of things spiritual. It could be a spiritual fluid-like agent, an energy, or a personality. The reality designated by רוח was the cosmic makeup of the heavens and its inhabitants.[33] Those that it affected were pneumaticians or spirit people who served as a witness to the רוח and to the reality of divinity. The רוח was a link between the spirit world and the community. The pneumaticians were mediating agents of the רוח for the benefit of the community. The רוח not only served as a testimony to the existence of an invisible world; it was also from this world that the community was informed and strengthened in its faith.[34]

Unlike his predecessors, Gunkel and Weinel, Volz devotes a large portion of his study to the nature of the spirit as person: "Die Geisthypostase" (pp. 145–94).[35] This section constitutes one of the strengths of the study. It begins with a diachronic analysis from texts such as Trito-Isaiah through rabbinic literature (pp. 147–73). It then includes an analysis of possible influences coming from Babylonian and Persian sources and discusses such related topics as *shekhinah*, *logos*, and angels (pp. 174–93).

---

[30] *Der Geist Gottes*, 2–4.

[31] Ibid., 6–7.

[32] Ibid., 23–25.

[33] Ibid., 52.

[34] Ibid., 43, 57.

[35] The term "hypostasis" is derivative from ante-Nicene Greek theology that described the person of the spirit as ὑπόστασις (the Greek preposition ὑπό + the Greek verb ἵστημι, literally "to stand under"). Hypostasis as used by Volz is merely meant to convey the idea of person and not the theological ramifications the term came to have in the Christian West, especially in Origen and later.

Although Volz argues that Judaism regarded the spirit of God as a hypostasis, he also says that it is difficult to determine when this idea begins. Volz discerns various hues of the conception of the personhood of the spirit throughout the postexilic period. At times monotheistic and pantheistic conceptions appear simultaneously in Judaism (Ps 139). At other times the spirit of God is a power independent of Yhwh. It is "sent out" to work through the prophets, guide the community, and act as a mediating power for communication with Yhwh. The spirit can appear to function as an angelic being that leads persons (Isa 63:14; Ps 1:43). Not until Zech 1:9 does the idea of an angelic being clearly emerge. In rabbinic literature the spirit is fully hypostasized as "the holy spirit," an agent from the heavenly sphere with total autonomy from God.

Like Weinel, Volz sees the need to address the relationship between the spirit of God and the rest of the world of spirits, good and bad.[36] However, whereas Weinel merely mentions the relationship as "a problem for pneumatology,"[37] Volz attempts to elaborate the issue. Volz claims that within canonical literature the conception of a varied spirit world was for all purposes suppressed. Only in the literature of later Judaism did the transcendence of God and foreign influences contribute to ideas of a world of spirits.[38] The effects of the spirit of God and of other spirits were analogous. As to nature, the spirit of God was not one of many such spirits, nor was it the highest. It was a power that stood completely unto itself.[39]

Volz, however, implicitly admits the difficulty of maintaining this view that makes the spirit of God "similar yet different and apart" from other spirits. The functions of angels were equal to those of the spirit of God, especially as mediators of divine knowledge. The spirit of God may perform an office that is usually relegated to that of an angelic being. Furthermore, in texts such as *Jubilees* and *The Testaments of the Twelve Patriarchs* there appears a spirit of truth as well as other good spirits that make up the heavenly populace. Their relationship to God is not always clear.[40]

In sum, Volz provides a study that is not only instructive for OT and Judaic scholarship but also for the NT and early Christianity. His study is not of the *Religionsgeschichtliche Schule* but benefits from its contributions. There is a noticeable debt to both Gunkel and Weinel, whose ideas are reflected

---

[36] *Der Geist Gottes*, 181.

[37] Weinel, *Wirkungen*, 68.

[38] *Der Geist Gottes*, 181–82 n. 2.

[39] Ibid., 183.

[40] Ibid., 184–85.

throughout the study. Volz makes important and seminal contributions that go beyond those of his predecessors with a keen analysis of the nature of the spirit (hypostasis) in postexilic and later Judaism that is pertinent not only for Judaism but also for the emergence of Christianity. He was able to demonstrate the complexity and flexibility of the term רוח and how this one term came to be used for myriad spiritual agents, energies, substances, natures, beings, and the spirit world.

2.4 Henry Barclay Swete: The Holy Spirit in the New Testament (New York, London: Macmillan, 1909).

In his exposition of texts dealing with the spirit in the NT, Swete was primarily interested in the early Christians' experience of the spirit. Known for his critical skills, Swete did not devote much effort to literary or historical criticism in this work. He wanted the reader to listen to the voice of the NT as a whole, unencumbered by such critical details. Swete believed that the early Christian testimonies to the experience of the spirit are ultimately unaffected by the concerns of literary or historical criticism.

Swete's study is divided into three sections. Sections one and two are a running commentary on the spirit in the (1) historical narratives of the Synoptics and Acts, and (2) in the teachings of Jesus and Paul and in other NT writings (1, 2 Peter, James, the Johannine Epistles). The third section is a systematic overview in seven categories: (1) the Spirit of God; (2) the Spirit of Jesus Christ; (3) the Spirit in the Church; (4) the Spirit and the Ministry; (5) the Spirit and the Written Word; (6) the Spirit and the Personal Life; and (7) the Spirit and the Life to Come.

The first and second sections of Swete's commentary are very general. The views of other scholars are kept to a minimum. In his portrayal of the spirit, Swete is not as graphic as Gunkel or Weinel, especially with regard to cause and effect. For Swete, the spirit is not simply the source of supernatural power. Rather, the spirit is a guiding force that shaped the lives of Jesus, the apostles, and Paul. The spirit was experienced in the realm of redemption, in love, and in the intimacy of the human consciousness.[41]

Swete used language that appeals to his ministerial side, more liturgical than it is critical. His discourse was theologically driven and less substantive than one might expect for an exposition of religious experience of the spirit. For

---

[41] See, for instance, Swete's commentary on Rom 4:25 and 5:1,3–5 (p. 213), and the commentary on Rom 8:26–27 (p. 221).

instance, Swete described the effect of the outpouring of the spirit at Pentecost as "the new life which sprang up in the hearts of believers, its freshness, its brightness and joy, its unfailing supply, the law of self-extension which it invariably follows."[42] Moreover, Swete's commentary on texts is rather brief.

An "Appendix of Additional Notes" attempts to make up for the brevity of Swete's exposition. In the appendix, Swete treats such topics as demons in the gospels, the Paraclete, the gifts of prophecy and tongues, the laying on of hands, rapture and ecstasy, the inspiration of sacred books, and flesh and spirit.[43] This portion of Swete's study reflects his most concentrated effort in his study of religious experience of the spirit.

Swete is not sympathetic to the spirit as an objective and operative transcendental force recognized as such among early Christians. Rather, the experience that Swete elucidates is one of the religious freedom of those who "walk in the Spirit," a new life in the spirit that is expressed in Christian conduct and righteous living. Swete's assessment of the experience of the spirit is expressed in language that appeals to morality and theology.

2.5 *Elmer Harry Zaugg: A Genetic Study of the Spirit-Phenomena in the New Testament (Menasha, WI: George Banta, 1917).*

Zaugg's study was originally a dissertation completed at the University of Chicago in 1917. It is representative of early American scholarship in NT studies influenced by the research and methods of the *Religionsgeschichtliche Schule* and by the fruits of anthropological and sociological studies of the time.[44] Zaugg's "genetic" study concerns the ideas inherited by the NT from earlier times as well as those of its immediate Hellenistic environment, a deviation from Gunkel, Weinel, and Volz who consulted Jewish and Christian sources. The plan of Zaugg's study is based on the then quite recent theory of the evolution of religion. He subscribes to the idea of the universal course of religious development from a primitive stage (sometimes known as the savage stage) to a higher civilized stage distinguished by an ethical and moral conscience resulting from the influence of certain philosophical schools of thought and a developed transcendental monotheism. This kind of approach,

---

[42] Ibid., 350.

[43] Ibid., 365–405.

[44] Zaugg (*Spirit-Phenomena in the NT*, 1) expresses this in the opening to the Introduction: "The task which we have set before us is an attempt to interpret the New Testament conceptions of spirits and the Spirit in the light of the ideas currently held by the people outside Christian circles who lived at the time when the New Testament books were written."

known as the comparative method, was typical of the American and British version of the German *Religionsgeschichtliche Schule*. Unlike its German counterpart, the American and British comparative method studied religious concepts such as totemism, fetishism, and animism. It explained religion as a progression via Darwin evolutionary theory from "lower" to "higher" forms of expression.[45]

Zaugg addresses how beliefs in spirits and demons arose in a primitive age (the time of Homer and earlier) and how these beliefs and demons were later modified and developed in the Greco-Roman world. According to Zaugg, these primitive ideas persisted throughout the Greco-Roman era.[46] During this era there was an ethical modification of the spirit world; an "evolution" from the primitive view that appropriated no moral standard to spirits. According to Zaugg, the roots of this ethical movement went back only as far as Isaiah and Plato.[47] The emphasis on morality and the dualistic conception of spirit and matter that were developed in the teachings of the Orphics and Pythagoreans led to a division of the spirit world into two opposing camps: the spirits of light and the spirits of darkness. Whereas Jews spoke of these two groups as either angels or demons, the Greeks and Romans used the word daemons for both classes of spirits.[48]

The "evolution" of the concepts of spirits impacted the figure of the prophet. A prophet communicated divine knowledge either by being elevated to heavenly regions or becoming possessed by a spirit that spoke through him.[49] The Christian prophet operated in a time when there was no neutrality in the concepts of the spirit world; because of the ethical movement, spirits were either

---

[45] The "evolution" of religion from a "lower" to a "higher" form was a Darwinian model of religion made popular by the anthropologist Edward B. Tylor in his book *Primitive Culture* (New York: Holt, 1874). It has been criticized as an inappropriate way to understand the complexity of religion. For a useful discussion of the comparative method see Eric J. Sharpe, *Comparative Religion: A History* (Richmond: John Knox, 1975).

[46] This reflects the thinking of Tylor, who claimed that within advanced civilizations there remained survivals of primitive customs and thus provided for evidence of cultural evolution.

[47] Zaugg (*Spirit-Phenomena in the NT*, 17) states that "among the ancient Hebrews there was no application of a moral standard to the acts of a spirit or of Jehova." Some of his examples are 1 Sam 16:14 and 1 Kgs 22:19–23.

[48] Ibid., 18. See also n. 46.

[49] Ibid., 48–51.

good or bad. A prophet could give voice to either a good spirit or an evil one. Thus, it became necessary for people to differentiate among the spirits.[50]

Some of the signs for those who were led or spoke by good spirits involved the power to cast out demons and the ability to state an allegiance to Jesus as Lord and as having come in the flesh (e.g., 1 Cor 12:3; 2 Thess 2:8; 1 John 4:1,2). Zaugg observes that these signs were not foolproof, for even false teachers and prophets arose and claimed allegiance to Christ (e.g., Matt 7:15,22; 2 Cor 11:13,14). The real test was the Christian life and the moral ideal: "By their fruits you shall know them."[51] This ideal was effected by the spirit that transformed the person on the inside. The result was expressed in a virtuous lifestyle. Although the ethical movement had impressed itself on the spirit world, Paul personalized it: the spirit affects change from within.[52]

Zaugg's contribution to the religious experience of early Christians is the American complement to Gunkel, Weinel, and Volz. Zaugg deals with the graphic portrayals of spirits and demons in his sources. Departing from the methods of Gunkel, Weinel, and Volz, Zaugg offered a perspective from the anthropological and sociological views of his day that explained the progress of religious ideas and customs within a Darwinian model of evolution. He interprets this evolution as due to the rise of a more transcendental monotheism and an ethicism within Judaism and Greco-Roman culture that distinguished itself from their predecessors. Christian experiences were distinguished from those of the surrounding culture based on its own ethic, an ethic that was identifiably "Christian."

The use of anthropological data and research has continued within biblical studies to this day, most notably in the social function of divination and prophecy, but it has done so in a way that departs from Zaugg and the earlier methods of the "history-of-religions" approach.[53] Zaugg's study is nonetheless

---

[50] Zaugg (Ibid., 63), like Gunkel and Weinel, observed that "the matter of deciding whether a man was possessed by an evil or good spirit was not an easy task, for the outward manifestations of their operations were quite alike."

[51] Ibid., 64.

[52] Ibid., 69–72.

[53] See e.g., Frederick H. Cryer, *Divination in Ancient Israel and Its Near Eastern Environment: A Socio-Historical Investigation* (JSOTSup 142; Sheffield: Sheffield Academic Press, 1994); and Lester L. Grabbe, *Priests, Prophets, Diviners, Sages: A Socio-Historical Study of Religious Specialists in Ancient Israel* (Valley Forge, Penn: Trinity, 1995). These studies, however, represent a sort of mutation of the "history-of-religions" approach. Instead of taking comparative material from the immediate environment and times of ancient Israel, Judaism, and Christianity, they utilize comparative data taken from the anthropological field studies of modern-day primitive societies such as the Pacific Islands, Indian, and West African societies.

an important one in the discussion of the religious experience of early
Christianity.

2.6 Henry Wheeler Robinson: The Christian Experience of the Holy Spirit (New York, London: Harper, 1928).

The religious experience that Robinson describes is motivated by a kind of
spirit-psychology in which the human spirit and the spirit work together.
Robinson calls the relationship between the (higher) spirit and the (lower)
human organism "kenosis," "a humiliation and an acceptance of the lower as the
medium of the higher."[54] Kenosis creates an upward and a downward dynamic.
Through the upward dynamic the human spirit is changed by the power of
Christ. Through the downward movement the spirit comes through the risen
Christ to those who have faith. The two dynamics in tandem create a new birth.
Robinson illustrates this with a reference to 1 Cor 2:11, in which Paul compares
the spirit in man with the spirit of God. Robinson cites this as a Pauline
example of kenosis, the intimate relationship between God's spirit and the
human spirit.[55]

Revelation occurs within the human psyche through the spirit. The
revelatory experience may involve not only revelation of divinity but may also
encompass moral, intellectual, and aesthetic experiences.[56] Christian experience
is the Christian consciousness of the indwelling of the spirit through Christ
which, according to Robinson, is summed up in Gal 2:20, "I live, and yet no
longer I, but Christ lives in me."[57]

In the area of Christian experience of the spirit as "kenosis," Robinson's

---

The former is representative of the original plan of the history-of-religions school espoused by
Gunkel and Weinel. The latter tries to take the idea a step further in hopes of finding "living"
examples of what is found in the ancient texts of "dead" civilizations. The expectation is to shed
light on otherwise meager textual information in the biblical material. This was the program of
the comparative method.

[54] Robinson, *Christian Experience*, 87. The term "kenosis" is derived from the discussion
of the meaning of Phil 2:7a, ἀλλὰ ἑαυτὸν ἐκένωσεν μορφὴν δούλου λαβών, ἐν ὁμοιώματι
ἀνθρώπων γενόμενος, "but he emptied himself as one taking on the form of a slave, coming in
human likeness." The verb ἐκένωσεν is the aorist of κενόω, "to deprive of power," from which
Greek κενός is derived. Robinson (p. 151) uses this verse as an example of the principle of
kenosis that is found in the "indwelling of the Church by His Spirit"; just as the incarnation was
the limitation and humiliation of Christ, so is the spirit that comes down from heaven and dwells
in the church.

[55] Ibid., 63, 83–85.

[56] Ibid., 99.

[57] Ibid., 135–39.

study is highly speculative. It is an imaginative rendering, an exercise in constructive theology that results in a quasi-psychological theology of the Christian experience of the spirit. Robinson does not express religious experience in the way that is most commonly found in early Christian sources: a spirit world that objectively interacts with a community *from without*. Instead, he overinternalizes the experience of the spirit. He describes the experience as something occurring solely within the person at the level of the subconscious, which may, nevertheless, be a legitimate way the spirit operates among humans.

Robinson admits the reality of a spirit world in the Christian faith and mentions the effects that modernity has had on the belief in a spirit world.[58] However, this does not translate into Robinson's work in such a way as to facilitate his arguments and observations. His explanations of the Christian experience of the spirit are mediated through the arena of consciousness and psychology wrapped in theological dress. The result is an explanation of Christian religious experience via the language of constructive and liturgical theology. Such language is more suited to orthodoxy than it is to a contribution to a critical study of the religious experience of the spirit in early Christianity.

2.7 Percy G. S. Hopwood: The Religious Experience of the Primitive Church: The Period Prior to the Influence of Paul (New York: Scribner's, 1937).

Hopwood suggests that deficiencies in scholarship of his day (e.g., dogmatic theology, historical-criticism, and church history) are due to the nature of the data which is both historical and experiential. He offers what he calls an empirical method that is sensitive to the experiential facets of the life of those surrounding Jesus and of those in the early church. Rather than totally denying the historical, Hopwood believes that an empirical approach is to be integrated within a historical framework. The components in the life of those who experienced the facts come within the purview of the historical.

Hopwood argues that one of the distinctive features of the empirical method is its concern with eyewitness accounts to the "numinous," a term coined by Rudolph Otto.[59] Hopwood elaborates on the empirical significance of the resurrection for the religious experience of the early church. He concludes that the resurrected body was of a spiritual essence not unlike that of angels

---

[58] Ibid., 2, 30, 218–20.

[59] Rudolph Otto, *The Idea of the Holy* (London: Oxford University Press, 1923). See the critique of Otto's use of the term "numinous" in Wayne Proudfoot, *Religious Experience* (Berkeley: University of California, 1985).

appearing in visions, as at the empty tomb (Luke 24:23).[60] The early church emerged on the basis of the religious experience of the resurrection appearances, introducing the reality of spirit in a new way. These appearances confirmed through eyewitness account a heavenly life beyond the tomb.[61]

With the emergence of the early church, religious experiences blossomed with experiences of the spirit. Hopwood devotes a large portion of his study to this; much of it is a graphic portrayal of spirits, not unlike those of Gunkel and Weinel.[62] Hopwood draws on analogies from religious history to help elaborate and explain the NT phenomena further. Like Gunkel, Hopwood refers to the accompaniments of the presence of the spirit as symptoms or effects that were recognized as such by their extraordinary nature. Yet, with his analysis of the experiences of the pre-Pauline church of Acts, Hopwood makes observations that go beyond those of Gunkel.

Experiences of the spirit in the early church involve speaking in tongues at Pentecost, healings, visions and dreams, ecstasy and trance, and the activities of angels. All of these were of an empirical nature, verified and experienced through eyewitness accounts. Physical marvels provided additional empirical evidence for the presence of the spirit in the early church. Philip was bodily taken away from the Ethiopian. Prison doors open of themselves. Hopwood notes that experiences of the spirit may be directed against those who merited God's wrath, as in the sudden deaths of Ananias and Sapphira (Acts 5:3–5,9).[63]

Hopwood observed, like Gunkel nearly fifty years earlier, that the effects of the spirit are identical to those of demons. Empirical evidence shows that the indwelling of the spirit in Jesus was used by his opponents, the scribes and Pharisees, to accuse him of demonic influence in order to discredit his efforts publicly (Mark 3: 22,30). Hopwood deduces that this could be possible only if there had been similarities between the activities of good spirits and demons. Such similarities, according to Hopwood, had the potential for producing a misreading of spirit influences among the undiscerning who were led to ascribe to the spirit what was actually of demonic origin, a situation that would benefit demonic sources that could capitalize on such a scenario through artifice and guile:

---

[60] According to Hopwood (*Religious Experience*, 133–35), this confirms Pharisaic and Pauline belief in a spiritual body and resurrection.

[61] Ibid., 137–41.

[62] Ibid., 145–206.

[63] Ibid., 182–83.

These resemblances between the two orders of 'spirit' experience are accounted for by the psychology of a religious experience which viewed both Spirit and demon possession as an invasion of a supernatural, overpowering energy into human personality.[64]

Hopwood makes an important contribution to the study of early Christian religious experience. He does not define, however, what he means by his "empirical method."

2.8 Retrospect

The foregoing studies have shown a graphic approach to the spirit that achieves perceptive results. Gunkel focused on the experiences of the early church in Acts and Paul. In his study Weinel included early Christian sources and church fathers. Volz focused on the spirit experiences in the OT, early Judaism, and rabbinic Judaism. Zaugg used the comparative method to discern an evolution in the ethical concept of spirits. Hopwood used an "empirical method" to elucidate what he thought was a concrete reality of a numinous spirit world in the lives of early Christians. All of these studies demonstrated that the identical effects of good and evil spirits was instructive for a study of the spirit world's activity.

Swete and Robinson offer insights that are not sensitive to a graphic portrayal of religious experience. Both claim to have done a study of the spirit as experience, but it is a theology of the experience of the spirit. Their studies tend to lack a sympathy for the language of spirit as an experiential sentient force or forces as understood by early Christians. Sometimes, theological reflections on the spirit do not achieve results that show one of the main features of religious experience: effects of the spirit. In Christian theology "the Holy Spirit" is unique and cannot be compared to any other spirit.

---

[64] Ibid., 200.

3. The Reemergence of the Portrayal of Religious Experience

3.1 James D. G. Dunn: Jesus and the Spirit: A Study of the Religious and Charismatic Experience of Jesus and the First Christians as Reflected in the New Testament (London: SCM; Philadelphia: Westminster, 1975).

With the exception of Hopwood's study in 1936, interest in religious experience in biblical studies waned during most of the post-World War I era.[65] Motivated by the dialectical theology movement, biblical studies were devoted to doctrines of the NT. Religious experience was not a topic of exposition during the post-World War II era.[66] Historical-critical work was more concerned with form-criticism, the tradition history of NT writings, and other literary-critical issues.

Dunn attempts to ascertain the religious experiences of the first-generation Christians by delineating what made these experiences authentically Christian. Dunn's interest in analogous contemporary phenomena within the Pentecostal movement is reminiscent of earlier studies cited in this survey that used phenomena from religious history to inform the NT phenomena (see Weinel and Hopwood).

Dunn discusses the experience of the spirit within the earliest Christian community. He claims Christianity began as an eschatological enthusiastic (spirit-inspired) sect within first-century Judaism. Two of the main enthusiastic activities were glossolalia and prophecy. In a discussion of Luke's retrospect of the enthusiastic beginnings of Christianity, Dunn notes Luke's lack of discrimination in the area of spirit. According to Dunn, Luke is not attentive to distinguishing the spirit of God from counterfeits.[67]

Dunn raises a question about visible proofs of the spirit. He concludes that Luke again comes up short.[68] Even though Luke has provided a vivid account of Christianity's enthusiastic beginnings, Dunn believes that because of Luke's lack of discernment in the area of religious experience, Luke offers nothing that

---

[65] One study, however, stands out for this period: W. Warde Fowler, *The Religious Experience of the Roman People: From the Earliest Times to the Age of Augustus* (London: Macmillan, 1922).

[66] Although see Eric R. Dodds, *Pagan and Christian in an Age of Anxiety: Some Aspects of Religious Experience from Marcus Aurelius to Constantine* (Cambridge: Cambridge University Press, 1965).

[67] Dunn, *Jesus and the Spirit*, 167–68, 175, 195.

[68] Ibid., 189–93.

highlights the distinctiveness of early Christianity's experience of the spirit.[69] Paul, who is attentive to "discerning the spirits," stands in stark contrast.

Dunn's study of Paul and the Pauline churches is treated in three parts: (1) spirit and grace; (2) community as the body of Christ; and (3) Paul's distinctively Christian religious experience. According to Dunn, Paul uses the words spirit (*pneuma*) and grace (*charis*) more than any other NT author to speak of the Christian's experience of God. Following Gunkel, Dunn states that for Paul spirit is experiential. Experience of the spirit is not "something hidden in the secret depths, a religion of mere inwardness and 'closet piety.'"[70]

Dunn also discusses the distinctly Christian dimension of early Christian religious experience. Phenomena such as dreams, healing, visions, ecstasy, and inspired utterance occurred in Hellenistic society outside of Christianity. The existence of these Hellenistic phenomena underscored the ambiguity of such phenomena within Christianity. Dunn concludes that charismatic experience as such cannot distinguish the distinctively Christian experience of the Pauline churches from similar phenomena in the Hellenistic world.[71]

Dunn then turns to eschatology. He asks whether the eschatological dimension of Paul's religious experience is unique among the religious experiences of the ancient world. Dunn concludes in the affirmative. According to Paul, the Christ event set up a radically new relationship between God and humanity that determined life's course in light of the imminent end. Salvation is an eschatological good whose wholeness belongs to the future, the "not yet." The experience of the spirit was the "already" of eschatology. The spirit was the metaphorical "first fruits" or "first installment" that Christians experience as the body of Christ. The spirit is the key to the eschatological tension, the already-not yet of Christian experience.[72] The *charismata* occurred within the context of the eschatological tension of Christian experience. Dunn uses the existence of this relationship to argue for the uniqueness of early Christian religious experience in light of the more conventional experiences of visions, ecstasy, healing, and inspired speech in the Greco-Roman world.

It should be clarified that eschatology was not an experience per se; the eschaton was a reference to a particular time frame. The *charismata* are not in and of themselves eschatological; similar phenomena were shown to occur within the noneschatological arena of the Greco-Roman world. For Christians, however, the *charismata* were thought to occur within an eschatological

---

[69] Ibid., 196.

[70] Ibid., 202.

[71] Ibid., 307.

[72] Ibid., 310.

context; they were from the Christian perspective signs of the outpouring of the spirit, heralding the imminent end and the reign of the Kingdom of God.

3.2 Gordon D. Fee: God's Empowering Presence: The Holy Spirit in the Letters of Paul (Peabody, MA: Hendrickson, 1994).

Fee's ambitious, 967-page study offers an expansive analysis on every occurrence of the word πνεῦμα in the Pauline texts. He studies not only those letters generally considered to have been written by Paul (Romans, First and Second Corinthians, Galatians, Phillipians, First and Second Thessalonians, and Philemon) but also those that many believe to be pseudepigrapha (Ephesians, Colossians, First and Second Timothy, and Titus). Fee's study addresses both the academic community and the lay community. He wants his exegetical work not only to explain Paul but also to assist in a revitalization of the spirit in the church today.

In his study Fee argues for an experiential understanding of Paul's notion of the spirit: "For Paul the Spirit was an *experienced* reality."[73] Fee does so with a much more theological orientation than Dunn. This is expressed in Fee's argument that Paul understood the spirit in Trinitarian terms.[74] Fee's blend of theology and experience is reminiscent of the kind of approach found earlier in Swete's study. Fee maintains the importance of the experiential aspect of the spirit in Paul: "Paul's main interest in the Spirit is experiential, so that his Spirit talk is limited basically to the Spirit's activity. . . ."[75]

Fee claims that "God is *experienced* as a triune reality."[76] Fee's discussion, however, is rooted within a Christian orthodoxy that was not fully worked out until several centuries after Paul. The issue is whether the term "Trinity" adequately describes what Paul was saying. The idea that the spirit is something more than an impersonal force or power does not mean that an argument for a personal spirit should be cast in Trinitarian terms.[77]

---

[73] Fee, *God's Empowering Presence*, xxi (italics his).

[74] Ibid., 827–45. Fee describes his book as: "a book on Pauline *theology*. Not the whole of that theology, nor even its chief element, but an aspect of the *experienced faith* of Paul and his churches that stood much closer to the center of things for him–and for them–than seems to be true for us" (p. 1; italics his).

[75] Ibid., 829.

[76] Ibid., 84 (italics his).

[77] Other scholars are committed to a Trinitarian component in the NT. See Joseph Maleparampil, *The "Trinitarian" Formula in St. Paul: An Exegetical Investigation into the Meaning and Function of Those Pauline Sayings which Compositely Make Mention of God,*

Fee's study addresses the relationship between the Pauline churches and modern-day church life. Weinel and Hopwood referred to analogous spirit phenomena throughout religious history. Dunn discussed how the Pauline *charismata* informed the Pentecostal movement of the twentieth century. Fee, however, goes a step farther than Weinel, Hopwood, or Dunn in this respect. He concludes his massive study with what he sees is a disturbing contrast between the Pauline perspective of the spirit and the present situation of the Christian church.

Although Fee sees in the creeds, liturgies, theologies, and institutional life of the present-day church the continued presence of the spirit, he believes that the spirit, dynamically experienced and eschatologically oriented, should be more fully integrated into the life of the church. He argues that the "restorationist" type of early spirit movements is destructive and wonders what a restoring of "the primitive church" would ever mean or would look like in the modern world. Instead of, as he puts it, "tearing down barns and building new ones," Fee opts for the spirit bringing life into the present state of the church. Fee does not want to "return" to the "primitive church," yet at the same time he wants the spirit of that church to be active in the church today:

> The plea of this study, therefore, is not that of a restorationist, as if we could restore 'the primitive church.' . . . Rather, it is a plea for the recapturing of the Pauline perspective of Christian life as essentially the life of the Spirit . . . fully integrated into the life of the church.[78]

In his previously mentioned study, Dunn provides a critique of this sort of argument that undermines graphic religious experiences of the early church (ecstasy, enthusiasm) by reducing them to terms of theology:

> Christian theology has often attempted to reduce Christian experience in effect to a rather bare 'feeling of dependence,' or to the moral earnest of the categorical imperative, and has withdrawn in ill-concealed horror from more extravagant manifestations of religious feeling.[79]

Fee's dismissal of a restoration of the experience of the "primitive church" for an incorporation of the Pauline perspective of the life of the spirit into the contemporary church seems to reflect Dunn's critique. Because of their resemblance to "paganism," Fee does not want "extravagant manifestations," i.e., the enthusiasm and ecstasy of the early church, to flourish in the church of

---

Christ, and the Holy Spirit (European University Studies Series 23; Theology 546; Frankfurt: Peter Lang, 1995).

[78] Fee, *God's Empowering Presence*, 901.

[79] Dunn, *Jesus and the Spirit*, 3.

today. These manifestations are replaced with a contemporary theology of "life" of the spirit, an ambiguous appeal whose theological nuances are more assumed than explained.[80]

Fee applauds the efforts of the spirit movements of the past but does not mention any by name.[81] One of the earliest ones that appeared during the late second century C.E. was that of the Montanists who practiced *ecstatic* prophecy as a continuation of what they believed to be the kind of prophecy that occurred among the earliest Christian communities. Many spirit movements during the past several hundred years exhibited some element of trance, e.g., the Shakers and Camisards.[82] Traditionally, spirit movements began in reaction to the church of their day as an institution and to its theologies. Fee, however, argues against the existence of ecstasy and trance in early Christian prophecy and glossolalia. In light of this, Fee's praise for past spirit movements with their graphic religious experiences, or "extravagant manifestations," seems to counter his argument for a present-day spirit movement in the churches grounded in a theological abstraction, "Life," rather than graphic experiences of the spirit.

Fee claims to deal with the spirit as experience. But this claim would have been better served if the exegesis was sensitive at least to Jewish and Christian concepts of a world of spirits and its effects. Instead, Fee stresses a theological dynamic that is not sensitive to historical experiences with spirits. His vision of the spirit is inhibited by a Trinitarian perspective that yields theological commitments that do not reflect ideas of the first century C.E. Fee's study tries to capture the essence of the spirit but is hampered by theologically constructed views that do not allow the experiential essence, despite Fee's efforts, to shine through clearly.

3.3 *John R. Levison: The Spirit in First Century Judaism (Leiden: Brill, 1997).*

Levison brings an important angle to the discussion by addressing the notions of the spirit in first-century Judaism. His study reveals the broad range of views of the operation, nature, and effects of the spirit in three first-century Jewish

---

[80] To be sure, the nuances of "the spirit of life," a Pauline phrase, are given their explanation within Paul. For example, see Fee, *God's Empowering Presence*, 522–27. But how this is to fulfill the role of "experience" in the church today is something the reader is left guessing.

[81] Ibid., 901.

[82] For a survey of these movements see Ronald Knox, *Enthusiasm: A Chapter in the History of Religion with Special Reference to the Seventeenth and Eighteenth Centuries* (Oxford: Clarendon, 1950; repr. Notre Dame, IN: University of Notre Dame Press, 1995); and the more recent Clarke Garrett, *Spirit Possession and Popular Religion: From the Camisards to the Shakers* (Baltimore, MD: Johns Hopkins University Press, 1987).

authors: Josephus, Philo, and the author (Pseudo-Philo) of the *Liber antiquitatum biblicarum* (*L.A.B.*). Levison demonstrates how the writings of nearly contemporary Greco-Roman authors illuminate the "exegetical movements" of these three Jewish authors.

Levison studies two Greco-Roman authors who wrote more or less within the same period as his three Jewish authors, Cicero (106–43 B.C.E.) and Plutarch (46–ca. 120 C.E.). When exegetical movements concerning the spirit cannot be found within the OT itself or Jewish biblical exegesis, Levison turns to Cicero's treatise *De divinatione* and Plutarch's *De defectu oraculorum* or *De genio Socratis* for evidence.

Levison discusses the modifications of the Balaam story in Numbers 22–24 by both Philo and Josephus. He pinpoints the nature of Balaam's inspiration within the exegetical movements of Philo and Josephus to include the following: prophetic amnesia (loss of mental control) brought on by the invading presence of an angelic spirit; possession by the angelic spirit that gains entry into Balaam; and the utilization from within Balaam's mouth by this divine spirit to produce oracular words of its choosing.

Levison states that, in contrast with the biblical text, Philo and Josephus refer specifically to loss of *mental* control in the presence of the spirit.[83] Philo's and Josephus's descriptions of the invasive action of the angelic spirit resulting in the spirit's use of Balaam's vocal chords have no parallel in the OT. Levison locates the relevant milieu of inspiration in Philo and Josephus in Greco-Roman mantic conceptions.

Levison shows that in *L.A.B.* Kenaz and Saul experience amnesia after a spirit prophesies through them. The cause of the inspiration is expressed in biblical terms but the effect, prophetic amnesia, is not. In *L.A.B.* the biblical basis for Kenaz's inspiration is enhanced with effects that are derived from nonbiblical material.[84] In other passages of *L.A.B.* the spirit "leaps on," "dwells in" Kenaz, and "elevates" his mind in a trance state that later he is unable to recall.[85] This description is common to early Jewish portrayals of visionary ascent. Levison notes that these extrabiblical elements in *L.A.B.* correspond to conceptions of the ascent of the soul in Cicero's *De divinatione* and prophetic experience in Plutarch's *De defectu oraculorum*. Prophetic amnesia is not found in biblical texts; the idea can be traced to Platonic literature.[86]

Levison's work reinforces Martin Hengel's argument that neat lines of

---

[83] See Levison, *Spirit*, 40.
[84] See *L.A.B.* 28.10, 62.2.
[85] See *L.A.B.* 28.6.
[86] Levison, *Spirit*, 109–30.

demarcation cannot be drawn between Jewish and Greek modes of thought.[87]
Levison demonstrates that there are no clear borders separating Diaspora
(Hellenistic) and Palestinian conceptions of the spirit. This blurring of the lines
is explicitly seen in what Levison says are the "astounding *variety of effects* of
the spirit's presence."[88] These are rehearsed and given further implications for
NT studies in Levison's final chapter, "Prospect."

According to Levison, prophecy is one of the most pervasive effects of the
spirit. His research shows that a rigid identification of prophecy as either
Hellenistic or Jewish is a false dilemma that cannot easily be substantiated. The
dilemma, says Levison, is expressed by David Hill, who wrote:

In Philo's writings we find either an acute hellenisation of the Jewish concept of prophecy, or
a hellenistic view of prophecy justified on a biblical basis: whichever view of the matter we take
. . . , it certainly represents a significant departure from what is reflected in other extant Jewish
literature of the general period.[89]

Levison responds by showing how geographically widespread Greco-Roman
conceptions of inspiration were: Philo in Alexandria, Josephus in Rome, and
Pseudo-Philo in Palestine. He questions the usefulness of a "typically Jewish"
concept of inspiration and wonders if the Greco-Roman forms should be
described as a "significant departure" from typical forms of Judaism.

The implications of Levison's insight for Christian prophecy are far-
reaching.[90] As in Judaism, prophecy in early Christianity (originally a sect of
Judaism) cannot easily be identified as either Greek or Jewish. Hill has argued
for the "either-or" scenario for prophecy within Christianity: "Presumably Paul
derived his view of the phenomenon from Old Testament/Jewish models . . . ,
whereas the Corinthians' understanding seems to reflect the Greek ecstatic
model."[91] This neat division must give way to the more nuanced Jewish notions
of the effects of the spirit discussed by Levison.

Levison's study has studied the various ways in which the spirit was

---

[87] Ibid.

[88] Ibid., 238 (emphasis his).

[89] Ibid., 253, taken from Hill's *New Testament Prophecy*, 33.

[90] Levison argues, "Hill's contention concerning Christian prophecy, that '. . . there will be
few scholars, if any, who will wish to claim that prophetic phenomena in Greek and Roman
religion provide *primary* evidence for the understanding of Christian prophecy,' ought perhaps
to be revisited in light of the Greco-Roman elements which permeate, not only Diaspora Jewish
literature, but also a first century Palestinian example of re-written Bible composed in Hebrew"
(*Spirit*, 254).

[91] Hill, *New Testament Prophecy*, 121.

perceived in first-century Judaism. The nature of the spirit could be likened to that of an angel or to a daemon; the effects of the spirit and daemon are identical both in ecstatic prophecy and in contemplative philosophical alertness. Because of the diversity of ideas of the spirit in Josephus, Philo, and Pseudo-Philo, Levison offers a caveat: "In light of the diversity of conceptions that co-exist within the writings of individual first century authors or within a single ancient document, it is ill-advised to attempt to ascertain for each first century author one dominant conception of the spirit."[92]

Levison's study situates Philo, Josephus, and Pseudo-Philo comfortably within a Greco-Roman milieu without effacing their Jewish identity. Doing so, Levison demonstrates that the assimilation of Greco-Roman elements does not compromise their Jewish heritage. His study is an example of the kind of academic insight that was found in the works of Gunkel, Weinel, and Volz.[93] Observing that a good or an evil spirit may produce the same symptoms, Levison continues the legacy of Gunkel's insights. Levison advanced this perspective with his analysis of the descriptions of the analogous effects of daemons in Greek authors and divine spirits in Jewish authors.[94] Levison's study is a testimony to the continued relevance of these insights for the contemporary academic study of the spirit in Judaism and Christianity.

3.4 Luke Timothy Johnson: *Religious Experience in Earliest Christianity*: *A Missing Dimension in New Testament Studies (Minneapolis*: *Fortress, 1998).*

Johnson offers a bold critique of NT studies' treatment – or lack thereof – of religious experience. His own work stresses that the NT is full of experiential language that scholarship had previously left by the wayside. Johnson presents his case in two persuasively argued chapters at the beginning of his work: "What's Missing from Christian Origins" and "Getting at Christian Experience." He then applies his argumentation in three chapters, each devoted

---

[92] Levison, *Spirit*, 242.

[93] In reviewing the work of Volz, Levison comments on how alike these scholars were in their approach: "Following the lead of his predecessors, H. Gunkel and H. Weinel, Volz analyzed the *effects* of the spirit in Early Judaism and Christianity by devoting a considerable section of the book to the effects (*Wirkungen*) of the spirit, such as inspired speech, inspired poetry, prophetic and predictive speech, inspired writing and translation (LXX), and inspired wisdom" (p. 18; emphasis his).

[94] For example, see ibid., 36–38, 48–53, 114–25, 185–86.

to an area of early Christian life that was central to its religious experience: ritual initiation (baptism), glossolalia, and sacred meals.

Johnson argues that the privileging of theology over religion is a matter of the prevalence of an academic orthodoxy that sees "authentic Christianity" in terms rooted in a clerical norm of Catholic and Protestant scholarship. This clerical norm "fixed attention on formal scripture, doctrine, morality, and institution as the appropriate defining elements in Christianity."[95] Such a theological perspective views ecstasy and "negotiating spiritual powers" as things beyond the norm for Christianity; they do not represent "true religion" but a "popular religion."[96] By illuminating the language of religious experience in the NT, Johnson attempts to show how this perspective is misguided. His second chapter describes an epistemology that attempts to apprehend better the realities of which such language speaks.

Johnson asserts that the historical-critical method (he calls it a "model") has paid little attention to the relevance of religious experience. The method has generated a history of theological ideas and social institutions that has given the language of religious experience the appearance of something too subjective or elusive to be of use in historical reconstruction.[97]

Johnson defines a problem in NT studies as a "theoretical refusal to acknowledge any reality beyond that capable of being described 'historically.'"[98] Despite his portrayal of an academia inept in the area of religious experience, Johnson argues that it is possible to construct an approach that does not replace historical analysis but supplements it with a "phenomenological approach."

Along with his arguments for the importance of religious experience in NT studies, Johnson gives helpful caveats for the difficulties encountered in a scholarly, objective analysis of religious experience.[99] One problem is that religious experience may appear suspicious because the purported cause of the experience is incapable of verification. Spirits by nature are invisible. Hence, phenomena attributed to them are susceptible of being interpreted as fraud, human deception, hallucination, or credulity, rather than as the result of the extraneous agency of spirits.

Johnson's analysis of the nature of glossolalia incorporates field research of present-day charismatic and Pentecostal groups. His use of contemporary phenomena is reminiscent of Weinel, Hopwood, and Dunn, who made use of

---

[95] Johnson, *Religious Experience*, 3.
[96] Ibid.
[97] Ibid., 12–13.
[98] Ibid., 41.
[99] Ibid., 53–60.

religious history. Johnson argues that, despite what many modern glossolalists think, the NT evidence does not support the understanding that tongues were real human languages. His claim that glossolalia in early Christianity was "structured babbling" rests on the interpretation of ὅτι μαίνεσθε in 1 Cor 14:23 as "raving" in the manner of mantic prophecy and on the "best" evidence provided by the linguistic analysis of the modern occurrence of glossolalia.[100] Yet recent research has shown that mantic prophecy was not meaningless babble. Instead, oracles spoke intelligibly.[101] The consequence of recent research invalidates his interpretation of 1 Cor 14:23 as an example of so-called "frenzied," i.e., unintelligible, mantic prophecy.

Johnson has demonstrated that scholarly attention to religious experience in early Christianity has diminished of late. The strength of his study lies in the persuasive argument that religious experience is one essential feature of early Christianity that has not been accurately appraised by the scholarly guild. Early Christian religion has been analyzed by scholars in terms of "a manipulation and mapping of human ideological and political interests." Johnson shows that religious experience was a matter of an "other" reality, a spirit reality.[102] A pertinent feature of early Christianity was the belief in a spirit world. The spirit world was not evoked as "imaginary or possible or under construction but as one in which the writers and readers of this literature actually exist."[103]

Johnson's study persuasively establishes the legitimacy of the study of religious experience in early Christianity within the academy. His work shows the need for scholars to begin seriously considering the role and nature of spirit as an invisible and transcendent yet present reality that interacted with early Christian communities on a regular basis.

3.5 John Ashton: The Religion of Paul the Apostle (New Haven: Yale University Press, 2000).

Ashton attempts to delineate the religious experiences of Paul by comparing the accounts with modern-day field reports on shamanism. He states that the

---

[100] Ibid., 113–15.

[101] See Fontenrose, *The Delphic Oracle*; and Forbes, *Prophecy and Inspired Speech*. Johnson admits that evidence suggests that oracles were linguistically intelligible, i.e., were real human languages, and that the presence of glossolalic utterance at Greek oracles is uncertain. Thus his understanding of early Christian glossolalia as babble and, as such, parallel to mantic prophecy is confusing.

[102] Johnson, *Religious Experience*, 39.

[103] Ibid., 9.

impetus for his study derives from two works, Gunkel's *Die Wirkungen des heiligen Geistes* and Ioan M. Lewis's well-known anthropological work, *Ecstatic Religion: A Study of Shamanism and Spirit Possession.* Ashton defines "religion" as a term that covers a variety of practices and beliefs "all relating somehow or other to unseen powers."[104] In contrast, theology is an extended and systematic reflection on religious matters. Paul was a "religious genius" whose life experience "belongs not to theology but to religion" (Deissmann).[105] It is Paul's "original sphere of vital religion" that the phenomenon of shamanism can inform and enlighten.

Ashton asks, "Was St Paul a shaman?" and responds, "Not really," but qualifies this with the assertion that structural resemblances between Paul and shamans are "quite striking."[106] The stages in the life of a shaman are shared in the life of Paul: (1) an early phase – Paul's experience on the road to Damascus was not unlike that of a shaman who is chosen to follow a new life via an encounter with a divine being; (2) a call, and experiences of trance and ecstasy that accompany it – Paul's apostolic career was marked by mastery of spiritual phenomena and authority over his communities; and (3) a subsequent career as a figure of authority over spirits – Paul's relationship with Christ was similar to a shaman's relationship with his spirit guide.[107]

According to Ashton, shamanism may be used at least as a metaphor to stress the similarities between it and the religious features of Paul's life. Comparisons of this sort serve as "a disciplined exaggeration in the service of knowledge."[108] Ashton uses metaphors in the same way the physical sciences might resort to models to explicate physical phenomena that may not lend themselves to an accurate or literal explanation. Like metaphors, models "have the advantage of drawing attention to some particular feature of whatever it is that they are focused on without involving any claim, either explicit or implicit, that this is the *only* way of looking at them."[109]

The last two chapters in Ashton's work, "Paul the Charismatic" and "Paul

---

[104] Ashton, *Religion*, 22–23.

[105] Ashton elaborates on this further with insights from Deissmann: "In a later study, objecting to certain doctrinaire tendencies in nineteenth-century investigations of Paul's teaching on the grounds that they transfer Paul from what he calls 'his original sphere of vital religion' into the secondary sphere of theology, he urges that 'we must try to understand him first in his primitive religious originality'" (ibid., 26).

[106] Ibid., 29–30.

[107] Ibid., 32–33.

[108] Ibid., 57. This is a phrase from Jonathan Z. Smith for which Ashton gives no reference citation.

[109] Ibid., 57–58 (italics his).

the Possessed," deal directly with the topic of the spirit. Ashton states that the term "spirit" in Paul is given to a variety of associations that make it difficult to define. Paul established himself as one with mastery of spiritual gifts, the power to perform miracles, to prophesy and to speak in tongues. These shaman-like qualities were necessary for Paul to have authority over spirit communities.

In a final chapter, "Paul the Possessed," Ashton describes two episodes in Paul's life that relate the phenomenon of spirit-possession: (1) the episode preceding his experience of conversion on the way to Damascus (the episode Ashton claimed earlier was reflected in Rom 7:14–23); and (2) the subsequent experience of being "in Christ." Using deconstruction, a relatively new form of criticism in biblical studies, Ashton spends a great deal of effort to establish Rom 7:13–25 as autobiographical.[110]

Ashton's study is not unlike other studies that have used anthropology to explain biblical material.[111] Notwithstanding the phenomena of religious experience throughout history, within civilizations both ancient and modern, western and nonwestern, "shaman" may not be an appropriate category for Paul. Paul believed in and dealt with a spirit world. Early Christianity was not unique in its dealing with spirits. But one does not have to resort to shamanism to show this.

With his study, Ashton has provided a good example of an academic exercise in comparative religions. To this end he was successful. The life of a shaman has one major component similar to the life of Paul: a relationship with the spirit world. Beyond that, any comparison of early Christian experiences with contemporary nonwestern experiences potentially creates the false impression that references to communicating with a supra-mundane world of spirits in Paul can be explained only from nonwestern sources. Discussions of interactions with the spirit world can be derived from the Pauline texts without resorting to shamanism.

---

[110] For example, see Stephen D. Moore, "Deconstruction Criticism: the Gospel of Mark," in *Mark and Method: New Approaches in Biblical Studies* (ed. J. C. Anderson and S. D. Moore; Minnesota: Fortress, 1992) 84–102.

[111] For prophecy and divination in the Ancient Near East and the OT, see Robert R. Wilson, *Prophecy and Society in Ancient Israel* (Philadelphia: Fortress, 1980). More in line with Ashton's study are Kurt Goldammer, "Elemente des Schamanismus im alten Testament," in *Studies in the History of Religion* (ed. Ugo Bianchi; SupNum 19; Leiden: Brill, 1972) 266–85; and John P. Brown, "The Mediterranean Seer and Shamanism," *ZAW* 93 (1981) 374–400.

3.6 John Eifion Morgan-Wynne: Holy Spirit and Religious Experience in
     Christian Literature ca. AD 90–200 (Paternoster Studies in Christian
     History and Thought; Eugene, OR: Wipf & Stock, 2006).

John Eifion Morgan-Wynne's contribution to religious experience in early
Christianity began as a dissertation completed at the University of Durham
under James D. G. Dunn in 1987. Morgan-Wynne argues that since the
publication of Heinrich Weinel's work, *Die Wirkungen des Geistes und der
Geister*, in 1899 (see above in this chapter), there has not appeared a study on
the experience of the spirit for the period ca. A.D. 90–200. Morgan-Wynne's
work is meant to update Weinel's work. Unlike Weinel's work, Morgan-
Wynne organizes his survey of Christian literature during this period according
to geography. According to Morgan-Wynne this arrangement has the advantage
of showing the wide diversity and variety of church life and Christian
experience of the spirit ca. A.D. 90–200.[112]

    Morgan-Wynne briefly surveys the experience of the spirit in the first two
Christian generations found in the writings of Paul, Pre-Lucan material in Acts,
and Lucan redacted material. He concludes that experiences of the spirit found
in these texts included prophecy, inspired speech, glossolalia, the ability to heal,
visions, pronouncements of judgment, and guidance and direction. Morgan-
Wynne ponders whether these experiences continued unabated among
Christians of the late first century to the end of the second century. His work
affirms that they did.

    Morgan-Wynne's survey of the experience of the spirit covers the gospel of
John, the Johannine epistles, the *Didache*, the *Odes of Solomon*, the gospel of
Matthew, the Pastoral epistles, Jude, 2 Peter, the *Letter of Barnabas*, *Polycarp
to the Philippians*, the *Martyrdom of Polycarp*, 1 Clement, 1 Peter, the
Shepherd of Hermas, the *Passion of Perpetua and Felicitas*, and the writings of
Ignatius of Antioch, Tatian, on Montanism, Justin Martyr, on Valentinian
Gnosticism, Irenaeus, Tertullian, Clement, and Theodotus. Morgan-Wynne
studies these texts with historical-critical methodology and a sensitivity for early
patristic studies.

    The work studies the experience of the spirit in a particular geographical
region as exhibited by Christian texts whose provenance is more or less known:
Syria, Asia Minor, Greece, Rome, Southern Gaul, Northern Africa, and Egypt.
The experiences are elaborated according to three areas: (1) divine presence; (2)
divine illumination; and (3) divine power. Divine presence includes "a sense

---

[112] Morgan-Wynne, *Holy Spirit and Religious Experience*, 16.

of God's wholly-other presence, a sense of the numinous, some sort of ecstatic experience, a sense of being surrounded or pervaded or overwhelmed by or caught up into the divine."[113] This involved inspired prophetic speech and visions, experiences that Christians shared with their Hebraic-Judaic heritage found in the OT. Divine illumination involves guidance by the spirit which leads to a more profound understanding of God's purposes for an individual or for a congregation. This might include two kinds of guidance, that which Morgan-Wynne calls "mediated" guidance whereby the spirit guides and directs those into what is God's will for them, and "immediate" inspiration and guidance whereby the spirit is experienced by an individual through a sudden realization of being confronted and possessed by the truth. Divine power occurs within the arena of ethical empowering. Here, the experience of the spirit is felt within the development of human character and behavior, in the prompting of a course of action, and when dealing with temptations and base desires. Divine presence, illumination, and power may each occur throughout a Christian's life.

Morgan-Wynne also concentrates on how a claim to be guided by or inspired by the spirit was established among early Christians. He shows that earliest Christianity was faced with the problem of evaluating spiritual experiences as those either coming from the spirit or not. Paul dealt with the problem of deciding between conflicting interpretations of the spirit's directive and whether the spirit cancelled an earlier command as seen in Acts 20:2 and 21:4. Morgan-Wynne attempts to ascertain those experiences of the spirit that might have been either subjective or objective.

Morgan-Wynne continues the legacy of Weinel's contribution to the study of the effects of the spirit in early Christianity. His work is not only an update of Weinel's work but also shows the importance of the continued presence of the spirit among the Christians during the era A.D. 90–200. The presence of the spirit was known by its effects that were produced through the human organism. Whether such experiences can be ascertained as either objective or subjective is a matter of debate. Morgan-Wynne shows that experiences of the spirit could be of a highly subjective nature. But he also shows that these experiences could be objective among those who were able to successfully determine whether the spirit was involved in a particular experience.

---

[113] Ibid., 17.

3.7 Retrospect

The reemergence of the interest in religious experience evidences some continuity with earlier scholarship as well as trajectories into unchartered territory. Dunn contributes the idea that eschatology is the defining element for Christian religious experience, but his study is dependent on Gunkel for its summary of various other ideas. Fee's study recalls that of Swete whose theological discussion of the experience of the spirit is carried out much more extensively by Fee. Levison's study uses the insights of the effects of the spirit in Gunkel and Volz. He applies them to Jewish texts of the first century C.E. with results that are reminiscent of these scholars. Levison observes a broad complexity in the use of the term "spirit" in first-century Judaism. Johnson's is the first study to argue persuasively for biblical studies to examine religious experience. His work vindicates the relevance of Gunkel, Weinel, and Volz for scholarship today. Ashton's study recalls the comparative method of Zaugg but goes in a new direction by appealing to the phenomena of shamanism. Finally, Morgan-Wynne updates the work of Weinel and contributes a much-needed study on the earliest experiences of the spirit among Christians and how these experiences continued into the early patristic period.

4. Conclusion

These thirteen studies are of varying worth in the analysis of religious experience in early Christianity. Works that appealed to particular theological explanations of experiences of the spirit are of little value. Swete, Robinson, and Fee reflected theological dynamics that eclipsed experiences of the spirit in early Christian texts with language suited to liturgy (sacraments), conscience (kenosis), pastoral commentary (joy; freedom; sanctification; life), and anachronistic technical terminology (Trinitarian). Dunn, however, stands out as an exception. He has shown that a recognition of religious experience is not dependent on a non-theological approach.

The more convincing works were those sympathetic to the complexity, range, and context of the term "spirit" (רוח or πνεῦμα) within the world of early Jewish and Christian communities. Gunkel, Weinel, Volz, Levison, and Morgan-Wynne grasped and explicated the fundamental principle of experiences of the spirit: the variety of *effects* of the spirit. Through its effects, the invisible spirit realms manifested an objective source from which came divine guidance, instruction, admonishment, and chastisement; the reality of the otherwise invisible spirit world was made more apparent as an active agent within a faith community.

An important observation that emerged from the study of the effects of spirits was the analogous activities of demons and good spirits. Other studies have also noted similarities between holy spirits and evil spirits. Frederick C. Conybeare observed, "Πνεῦμα, so used in the New Testament is, apart from moral qualities, the same sort of agency as δαιμόνιον."[114] Conybeare noted that the identity was most persuasive in the area of possession:

> The New Testament writers believed that the physical constitution of a spirit, whether holy or impure, was akin to moving vapor. . . . The Holy Spirit gave rise in those whom it inspired just the same physical manifestations as did the unclean spirits. . . . The vocal organs of one possessed were controlled by a demon . . . , the Holy Spirit within a man equally took possession of his voice. . . .[115]

S. Vernon McCasland similarly stated, "Possession by the Holy Spirit was differentiated from demon possession by the type personality which the person exhibited under possession. . . . The person's conduct indicated whether he was possessed by a good or an evil spirit."[116] Pamela M. Binyon offered a study whose title suggested an analogy between the terms "spirit" and "demon."[117] Unfortunately, Binyon's study was not detailed and lacked the insights of studies surveyed here.

Dunn, whose work is surveyed above, remarks elsewhere that by "abandoning the dimension of the demonic we may find that we have abandoned also the dimension of the Spirit."[118] The observance of the continuity of demonic activity with spirit activity covers a time period in scholarship that is over a century. Such a range shows its endurance and pertinency for our study.

The modern academic assumptions of "the spirit" in the NT as simply referring to a single sanctifying power or a divine Person that stands apart from

---

[114] Frederick C. Conybeare, "The Demonology of the New Testament," *JQR* 8 (1896) 576–608, esp. 579 n. 3.

[115] Ibid., 579–81.

[116] S. Vernon McCasland, *By the Finger of God: Demon Possession and Exorcism in Early Christianity in the Light of Modern Views of Mental Illness* (New York: Macmillan, 1951) 7.

[117] *The Concepts of 'Spirit' and 'Demon:' A Study in the Use of Different Languages Describing the same Phenomena* (Studies in the Intercultural History of Christianity 8; Frankfurt: Peter Lang, 1977).

[118] Dunn, *The Christ and the Spirit: Pneumatology* (2 vols.; Grand Rapids: Eerdmans, 1998) 2. 68.

the rest of what was "spirit," a sort of "proto-Athanasian Holy Spirit," does not reveal the true range of the term for early Jews and Christians. If there were many good spirits, i.e., holy spirits, in the NT world, the question arises, What does "the Holy Spirit" mean?

The relationship between good spirits and the presumed one good spirit, the Holy Spirit, is never fully addressed or worked out. Dibelius recognized that "a problem exists in the relationship between πνεῦμα (spirit) and πνεύματα (spirits)."[119] Some of the authors surveyed above showed an awareness for both "the spirit" and "good spirits." Gunkel's observation of NT texts that illustrate both grammatical forms τὸ πνεῦμα, "the spirit," and πνεύματα, "spirits," led him to speak of the "tendency in the New Testament age to separate the Spirit of God into various spirits."[120] Weinel recognized the relationship between "the spirit" and many good spirits as an unresolved problem for pneumatology: "One can hardly understand and solve one of the problems of pneumatology: treating separately the good spirits from the spirit and from Christ and God."[121] Volz discussed texts for "the spirit" and "good spirits" but made no suggestions as to how to proceed. Johnson, however, maintained a normative pneumatology reflective of a later age of Christian creeds wherein grammar was raised to the level of theology: *the* Holy Spirit, unique, set apart, above and beyond all other spirits: "There live not only *the spirit* called 'holy' but also *those spirits* called variously demons, unclean spirits, Satan, or the devil, whose own power is sufficient to be taken with deadly seriousness."[122] The earlier studies of Gunkel, Weinel, and Volz demonstrated that such a discrete distinction between "*the* spirit" and "*those* spirits," the former good and the latter evil, is hardly sustainable in light of early Jewish and Christian beliefs in spirits; the plural "spirits" may also refer to good spirits.

Nonwestern metaphors used in the studies of Zaugg and Ashton have the potential for bringing early Christian religious experience into the broader arena of animism or nature religions, the consequence of which does not provide an ample defense for "spirits" in early Christianity. Rather, it inevitably derides the matter of communicating with "spirits" as something nonChristian, more suited to so-called "primitive" forms of religious expression *à la* Tylor and James G.

---

[119] Dibelius, *Die Geisterwelt*, 74 (translation mine).

[120] Gunkel, *Influence*, 44. So, too, Dibelius (*Die Geisterwelt*, 76): ". . ., die zwischen bösen und guten Geistern unterscheidet. . . . Der göttliche Geist äußerte sich auf so mannigfache Art, daß jede von diesen Wirkungen wieder ein besonderes πνεῦμα zum Urheber zu haben schien."

[121] Weinel, *Wirkungen*, 68 (translation mine).

[122] Johnson, *Religious Experience*, 9.

Frazer.[123] Christian theology exploits the "primitive" to explicate an otherwise artificial distinction between language for "the Holy Spirit" (representative of "higher" theology and morality) and language for "spirits" (representative of "lower" forms of religious expression such as animism, ghosts or "spooks" shared by ancient pagan people and present-day nonwestern people).[124] For the purposes of our study, the works of Gunkel, Weinel, Volz, Hopwood, and Levison have yielded the most enlightened arguments.

History also supports their approach. A classic example in the history of early Christianity is second-century Montanism. The speech of spirits through the entranced mediums Montanus, Prisca, and Maximilla was on the one hand claimed as that of holy spirits, while on the other hand opponents construed the same activity as demonic.[125]

The survey provides an impetus for the discussion of an area that has yet to be explored in biblical studies: religious experience of the πνεῦμα in First Corinthians 12 and 14. These texts promise to illustrate early Christian religious experience in its most explicit form, that of receiving communication from the spirit world by the direct speech of spirits through mediums. The act of communicating with spirits through mediums is given the name "spiritism" (or "spiritualism") in present-day society. This activity is expressed in English versions of the Bible, but, unfortunately, only in contexts of occultism and divination that are condemned in the biblical antidivinatory laws. The idea, however, that both good and evil spirits might communicate through the possession of a passive human subject shows that spiritism, by definition, is not simply an infernal, occult art restricted to spirits of the dead or demons, as some English versions claim. Instead, communication with spirits through mediums can be of a divine nature or of a demonic nature (Montanism).

Thus, the idea that First Corinthians 12 and 14 relate the religious experience of spirit communication opens up the possibility for arguing that these texts refer to what might be called "spiritism," i.e., "the art of communicating with the spirit world." The following chapter will show that first-century Greco-Roman and Jewish texts provide evidence for good spirits who communicated through the agency of a human intermediary.

---

[123] James G. Frazer, *The Golden Bough: A Study in Comparative Religion* (New York: Macmillan, 1894).

[124] For instance, see David Burnette, *Unearthly Powers: A Christian's Handbook on Primitive and Folk Religions* (Nashville: Thomas Nelson, 1992).

[125] Eusebius, *Eccl. Hist.* 5.16.7, 16–17; 5.17.1–3. See further Nancy Caciola, *Discerning Spirits: Divine and Demonic Possession in the Middle Ages* (Conjunctions of Religion and Power in the Medieval Past; Ithaca, NY: Cornell University Press, 2003).

Chapter 3

Communication with the Spirit World in First-century Greco-Roman and Jewish Literature: Plutarch (δαίμων), Josephus, Philo (πνεῦμα θεῖον), and Pseudo-Philo (*spiritus sanctus*)

1. Introduction

In antiquity a variety of ways existed for communicating with the spirit world. Cicero gives us the two classic distinctions for such communication: (1) "artificial," which employs methods that require training in the omen literature, and other "technical" methods such as astrology, augury, and the examination of animal entrails; and (2) "natural," which is related to direct inspiration (prophecy), visions, and dreams, employing the use of the human being in some form for communication from the spirit world.[1]

The descriptions that will be analyzed in first-century Greco-Roman (Plutarch) and Hellenistic Jewish texts (Josephus, Philo, and Pseudo-Philo) will bear on "natural" forms of inspiration, specifically that of the direct speech of spirits through the intermediary of human beings. This analysis will serve as examples for the kind of inspiration that Paul depicts with the terms "prophecy," "glossolalia," and the phrase "speaking in a spirit" in an exegesis of 1 Cor 12:1–11 and 14:1–33, 37–40.

The term δαίμων denoted "a spirit" in pre-Christian Greek literature. The term πνεῦμα indicated "a spirit" in Hellenistic Jewish literature, the earliest is in the LXX. In non-Jewish Greek literature πνεῦμα carried this meaning only as early as the magical papyri of the second and third centuries C.E.[2] This is essentially what we find in the authors studied and explored in this section:

---

[1] Cicero, *De divinatione*, 1. 9, 12. For descriptions of artificial and natural divination in the Greek world, see William R. Halliday, *Greek Divination: A Study of its Methods and Principles* (Chicago: Argonaut, 1967; repr. of 1913 ed.). In the OT, see Ann Jeffers, *Magic and Divination in Ancient Palestine and Syria* (SHCANE 8; Leiden: Brill, 1996). Another useful study, although dated, is T. Witton Davies, *Magic, Divination, and Demonology Among the Hebrews and their Neighbors* (London: J. Clarke, 1898; repr. New York: KTAV, 1969).

[2] So Paige, "Who Believes in 'Spirit?'," 434.

Plutarch, Philo, Josephus, and the author known as Pseudo-Philo. Whereas Plutarch does not use πνεῦμα for a spirit being, Philo, Josephus, and Pseudo-Philo not only use πνεῦμα (*spiritus*) but also δαίμων (*daemon*) for a spirit. This can be attributed to their Jewish heritage wherein both πνεῦμα and δαίμων were used in Second Temple literature for denoting "spirits."

Philo uses four terms for a spirit: ἄγγελος, δαιμόνιον, ψυχή, and πνεῦμα. In *Questions and Solutions on Genesis 1*, Philo devotes a treatise "On the Giants" that is a discussion of Gen 6:1–4. In it he states, "It is Moses' custom to give the name of angels (ἄγγελοι) to those whom other philosophers call daemons (δαίμονες), souls (ψυχαί) that which fly and hover in the air."[3] For Philo, souls (ψυχαί), daemons (δαίμονες), and angels (ἄγγελοι) are terms that refer to the same being. He explains, "So if you realize that souls and daemons and angels are but different names for the same one underlying object, you will cast from you that most grievous burden, the fear of daemons or superstition."[4] Philo describes the nature (οὐσία) of angels as spiritual (πνευματική).[5] In his rewriting of Numbers 22–24, Philo identifies angels with πνεύματα, "spirits."[6] This is in keeping with the tradition of the OT such as that found in Ps 104:4 and Job 4:15,18. The quotation of Ps 104:4 in Heb 1:7, ὁ ποιῶν τοὺς ἀγγέλους αὐτοῦ πνεύματα, "he makes his angels spirits," demonstrates the existence of this identification in the first century C.E.

Josephus also uses different terms for entities of the spirit world. According to Morton Smith, τὸ δαιμόνιον covered the whole range of the spirit world in Josephus, designating divine and Satanic powers.[7] Throughout Josephus's writings there is not only a commitment to a god (θεός), i.e., the only "true" God of the Jews, but also a recognition of a multitude of angels (ἄγγελοι), spirits

---

[3] *Gig.* 1.6: οὓς ἄλλοι φιλόσοφοι δαίμονας, ἀγγέλους Μωυσῆς εἴωθεν ὀνομάζειν, ψυχαὶ δ' εἰσὶ κατὰ τὸν ἀέρα πετόμεναι.

[4] *Gig.* 1.16: ψυχὰς οὖν καὶ δαίμονας καὶ ἀγγέλους ὀνόματα μὲν διαφέροντα, ἓν δὲ καὶ ταὐτόν ὑποκείμενον διανοηθεὶς ἄχθος βαρύτατον ἀποθήσῃ δεισιδαιμονίαν.

[5] *Q.G.* 1.92.

[6] *Mos.* 1.274, 277.

[7] See Morton Smith, "The Occult in Josephus" in *Josephus, Judaism, and Christianity* (ed. Louis H. Feldman and Gohei Hata; Detroit: Wayne State University Press, 1987) 241–42. See even earlier, Plato, *Apology* 31D: θεῖον τι καὶ δαιμόνιον, "something divine and daemonic."

(πνεύματα), daemons (δαίμονες), and unspecified powers such as φαντάσματα, "visionary beings," and τύχη, "fate," personified.[8]

2. Plutarch: *De Def. Orac.* 414E, 418C–D, 431B

Plutarch, ca. 46 C.E.–ca. 120s C.E., held a priesthood at the oracular shrine at Delphi from 95 C.E. until his death. He devotes several of his dialogues to the Delphic oracle, *De E apud Delphos*, *De Pythiae oraculis*, and *De defectu oraculorum.* In each dialogue Plutarch treats a specific topic, such as the word *EI* at the shrine's entrance, why oracles were no longer given in verse, and the problem of the decline in oracular activity at Delphi. The discussion of δαίμονες as spirits who speak through human intermediaries is particularly present in *De defectu oraculorum.*[9]

In his dialogue *De defectu oraculorum*, Plutarch does not give a definitive answer why oracles had declined since times past. He simply relates different points of view on the matter to various dialogue partners such as Lamprias, Cleombrotus, Ammonius, Demetrius, Heracleon, and Philip. Part of the dialogue concerns the spirit beings that are responsible for the oracles at Delphi, whether they are θεοί, "gods," or δαίμονες, "daemons." The main views are offered by Lamprias and Cleombrotus.

In his discussion of the function of the oracles, Lamprias maintains the Platonic view that θεὸς δὲ ἀνθρώπῳ οὐ μίγνυται, "A god does not mingle with man" (*Symp.* 203A). Thus Lamprias argues that "no prophetic shrine or oracle is ever abolished by the instrumentality of a god" (*Def. orac.* 414D). The god does not give anything that is perishable; hence, the god does not abolish the oracle. This was the context within which Lamprias maligned the view that the god himself entered into the bodies of prophets. By entering into the bodies of prophets the god reduces himself to a level not in keeping with its majesty; in essence, the god "mingles with man." Lamprias states,

---

[8] For daemonology in the Greek and Roman worlds see Georg Luck, *Arcana Mundi*, 163–225.

[9] See Giulia Sfameni Gasparro, "*Daimôn* and *Tuché* in the Hellenistic Religious Experience," in *Conventional Values of the Hellenistic Greeks* (ed. P. Bilde et al.; Studies in Hellenistic Civilization 8; Aarhus: Aarhus University Press, 1997) 67–109.

Certainly it is foolish and childish in the extreme to imagine that the god himself, after the manner of *engastrimuthous* (who used to be called Eurycleis, but now Pythones), enters into the bodies of his prophets and prompts their utterances, employing their mouths and voices as instruments.[10]

Lamprias's statement does not vitiate possession per se. Rather, the idea that τὸν θεὸν αὐτόν, "the god himself," enters into a prophet is rejected as an untenable prospect.[11] Immediately after Lamprias maligns the view that the god possesses a prophet, he rationalizes his position on a Platonic trajectory that views the transcendency of the gods in the hierarchical system, god-daemon-human:[12] "For if he (the god) allows himself to become entangled in men's

---

[10] *Def. orac.* 414E: εὖηθες γάρ ἐστι καὶ παιδικὸν κομιδῇ τὸ οἴεσθαι τὸν θεὸν αὐτὸν ὥσπερ τοὺς ἐγγαστριμύθους, Εὐρυκλέας πάλαι νυνὶ δὲ Πύθωνας προσαγορευομένους, ἐνδυόμενον εἰς τὰ σώματα τῶν προφητῶν ὑποφθέγγεσθαι, τοῖς ἐκείνων στόμασι καὶ φωναῖς χρώμενον ὀργάνοις. See Acts 16:16 for the girl who prophesies by a πνεῦμα πύθωνα, "a spirit of python." The term ἐγγαστρίμυθος is made up of the preposition ἐν, "in," the noun γαστρί, "stomach" or "inner body," and μῦθος, "myth," literally, "a story in the belly." It carries the sense "one who has a story-telling spirit of divination inside." The term occurs as early as the late fifth and fourth centuries B.C.E. The term is sometimes interpreted as a "ventriloquist" in which the voice of the indwelling spirit was actually the second voice that ventriloquists were known for producing. So Friedrich W. Foerster, "πύθων," *TDNT* 6. 918–19. But the phenomenon of projecting the voice does not adequately describe what is meant in the Greek term ἐγγαστρίμυθος, a spirit that speaks from within the person. Daniel Ogden (*Magic, Witchcraft, and Ghosts in the Greek and Roman World: A Source Book* [Oxford: Oxford University Press, 2002]), uses the term "ventriloquist" with the following qualification, "The term 'ventriloquist' is not used here in its usual modern significance of a shabby entertainer who throws his voice into a sinister dummy but in its original one, that of a person whose stomach is inhabited by a ghost or a demon that speaks through his mouth" (p. 30).

The eponym for this phenomenon was Eurycles who is used by Aristophanes as a metaphor to describe the way he published plays through other playwrights (see *Wasps*, 1019–20: "In imitation of the prophetic method of the Eurycles, he [the poet] entered their stomachs and poured out lots of comedy"). Cf. *Wasps*, scholiast R, scholiast Lh; and Plato, *Sophist* 252C, and the scholia ad and loc. Alfred C. Pearson (*Fragments of Sophocles* [3 vols.; Cambridge: Cambridge University Press, 1917]) states that Aristides, *Dind.* I.30, "indicates . . . that Eurycles was a generic name given to spirits temporarily occupying the body of a man" (1. 37). In the LXX, ἐγγαστρίμυθος translates אוב, "a spirit of divination" or "ghost," indicating both the spirit (אוב) and the practitioner (אשת בעלת־אוב, "female master of a spirit of divination") through whom the spirit spoke (see Lev 20:6,27; Deut 18:11; 1 Sam 28:7,8 and the corresponding LXX version).

[11] Contra Wesley D. Smith, "The So-called Possession in Pre-Christian Greece," *Transactions and Proceedings of the American Philological Association* 96 (1965) 403–36, esp. 416.

[12] For this transcendency see Plato, *Symp.* 202E–203A.

needs, he is prodigal with his majesty and he does not observe the dignity and greatness of his preeminence."[13]

Lamprias may reject the idea that a god is the entity responsible for the oracles, but he presents one of the basic ideas of inspiration among Jews, Christians, and Greeks: a spirit enters into a person and speaks by using the mouth to speak, as would the human spirit under normal conditions.[14] Lamprias uses a musical instrument as a simile for prophecy. He describes the persons as ὄργανα, "instruments." The simile expresses the passivity of a prophet in the hands of a spirit.

Lamprias favors a different theory for the oracles, one that postulates that a vapor rises from the ground and inspires the Pythia. Changes in the sun and the earth led to the cessation of the vapor, resulting in the cessation of oracles.[15] Cleombrotus agrees with Lamprias that the god is not responsible for the oracles.[16] He suggests, instead, that the obsolescence of oracles at Delphi might be attributed to mediating daemons. Cleombrotus claims that many before him held to this view and that it was not unique to his own thinking:

Let this statement be ventured by us, following the lead of many others before us, that coincidentally with the total defection of the guardian spirits [δαιμόνια] assigned to the oracles

---

[13] *Def. orac.* 414E: ἑαυτὸν γὰρ ἐγκαταμειγνὺς ἀνθρωπίναις χρείαις οὐ φείδεται τῆς σεμνότητος οὐδὲ τηρεῖ τὸ ἀξίωμα καὶ τὸ μέγεθος αὐτῷ τῆς ἀρετῆς.

[14] Gordon Clark ("Possession," in *Dictionary of the Apostolic Church* [ed. James Hastings; New York: Scribner's, 1916–1918] 2. 248) states, "As a person's ordinary speech and action sprang from the action of his own spirit, . . . , so extraordinary conduct of any kind was due to the impact of a spirit other than his own."

[15] *Def. orac.* 431E–434C. See further on this theory Herbert W. Parke and Donald Ernest W. Wormell, *The Delphic Oracle I: The History* (Oxford: Basil Blackwell, 1956) 19–26; and Joseph Fontenrose, *The Delphic Oracle.* According to Cicero and Plutarch, the vapors provide the initial impetus for inspiration but do not give utterance to the Delphic priestesses. Lamprias refers to the vapor as τὸ δὲ μαντικὸν ῥεῦμα καὶ πνεῦμα θειότατον, "but the prophetic current and breath is most divine" (*Def. orac.* 432D). Strabo (*Geo.* 9.3.5) calls it πνεῦμα ἐνθουσιαστικόν, "breath that inspires a divine frenzy;" and Chysostom (72.12) says that it fills the priestess, ἐμπιμπλαμένη τοῦ πνεύματος. But the vapor is a natural phenomenon and cannot explain the phenomenon of a spirit speaking through the priestess, as Cleombrotus explains.

[16] *Def. orac.* 414F.

and prophetic shrines, occurs the defection of the oracles themselves; and when the spirits flee or go to another place, the oracles themselves lose their power.[17]

This view seems to go back as far as the fifth century B.C.E. Lamprias's statement that likened the phenomenon of Delphic inspiration to the ἐγγαστρίμυθος (414E) suggests that Cleombrotus's notion of mediating daemons can be traced to the phenomenon of the ἐγγαστρίμυθος. Whereas Lamprias gives the philosophically correct view from a Platonic perspective that a god was not the possessing entity, Cleombrotus gives the historically correct view that the possessing entity was believed to be a daemon, not a god.[18] Cleombrotus does not mention Eurycles or the ἐγγαστρίμυθος by name, but his suggestion for a mediating daemon seems to point in their direction. He also describes the way in which daemons functioned at the oracles: "But when the spirits return many years later, the oracles, like musical instruments, become articulate, since those who can put them to use are present and in charge of them."[19] Like Lamprias, Cleombrotus uses a musical-instrument simile to present how oracles stood in relation to the daemons: as a musician gives voice to his instrument by playing it, so do daemons give voice to the oracles by controlling the vocal organs (= ὄργανα) of the human intermediary. Cleombrotus is clear that the spirits, i.e., the daemons, are behind the oracles, for the spirits, "put them to use," and are "present and in charge" of the oracles.

Later in the dialogue, Lamprias criticizes Cleombrotus's explanation of the function of the oracles with a summary of it before presenting his own explanation (the vapors theory):

For what was said then [i.e., earlier by Cleombrotus], that when the demigods [δαιμόνων] withdraw and forsake the oracles, these lie idle and inarticulate like the instruments of musicians, raises another question of greater import regarding the causative means and power

---

[17] *Def. orac.* 418C–D: καὶ τετολμήσθω μετὰ πολλοὺς εἰρῆσθαι καὶ ἡμῖν, ὅτι τοῖς περὶ τὰ μαντεῖα καὶ χρηστήρια τεταγμένοις δαιμονίοις ἐκλείπουσί τε κομιδῇ συνεκλείπει ταῦτ' αὐτὰ καὶ φυγόντων ἢ μεταστάντων ἀποβάλλει τὴν δύναμιν.

[18] Plato, however, does not always describe episodes of inspiration that correspond to his hierarchical system god-daemon-humanity where daemons act as mediators between the transcendent gods and the lowly humans. For instance, in *Ion* 534D a *god* speaks through a person. Terms for inspiration are based on the term θεός such as ἔνθεος and ἐνθουσιασμός which, if not stated otherwise, implies a god as the mediating source. Whether Plato thought this was inconsistent with his hierarchical system is not apparent.

[19] *Def. orac.* 418D: εἶτα παρόντων αὐτῶν διὰ χρόνου πολλοῦ καθάπερ ὄργανα φθέγγεται τῶν χρωμένων ἐπιστάντων καὶ παρόντων.

which they [daemons] employ to make the prophetic priests and priestesses possessed by inspiration.[20]

Here Lamprias reiterates the simile that oracles are like the instruments of musicians. Lamprias uses language that exemplifies possession by spirits, ποιοῦσι κατόχους τοῖς ἐνθουσιασμοῖς, "making possessed those inspired," that further highlights Delphic inspiration. The agents of inspiration cannot be the gods, for this would offend their majesty, so Cleombrotus suggests that daemons are the agents, maintaining the boundary between the gods and humanity.[21]

3. Josephus: *A.J.* 4.6.5 §118, §119, and §121

Three first-century Jewish authors also depict the communication of spirits through human intermediaries similar to Plutarch. Josephus, Philo, and Pseudo-Philo describe the presence and effects of spirits in vivid terms that are usually considered unique to Greco-Roman thought, i.e., "ecstasy" and "prophetic amnesia." These three authors' Jewishness in an otherwise Hellenistic society shows that the expressions for inspiration available to them would have been typically Greek only from a lexical standpoint. The experiences conveyed by the Greek expressions, however, were akin to the conceptions of inspiration for Jews, Greeks, and, as we shall see later, for Christians.

Josephus, 37–ca. 100 C.E., born of a priestly family, was a descendent of the Hasmoneans. At the age of nineteen he became a Pharisee (*Vita* 10). Later in life, during the Great Jewish War, he sided with the Romans and became a client with an imperial pension. During this period he produced his *Antiquitates Judaicae* and *Bellum Judaicum*. Next to Philo, Josephus is one of the most

---

[20] *Def. orac.* 431B: τὸ γὰρ ἀφισταμένων καὶ ἀπολειπόντων τὰ χρηστήρια τῶν δαιμόνων ὥσπερ ὄργανα τεχνιτῶν ἀργὰ καὶ ἄναυδα κεῖσθαι λεχθὲν ἕτερον λόγον ἐγείρει τὸν περὶ τῆς αἰτίας μείζονα καὶ δυνάμεως, ᾗ χρώμενοι ποιοῦσι κατόχους τοῖς ἐνθουσιασμοῖς.

[21] Cleombrotus's statement brings out caveats from his dialogue partners. Heracleon observes that if daemons are behind the oracles, their sinful nature and their fall from heaven as related by Empedocles creates a religious problem (418E). Ammonius wonders if the daemons are nothing more than the ψυχαί, "souls," referenced in Hesiod (*Works and Days*, 125) who "make their rounds, 'in mist appareled'" (431B). Lamprias wonders if Cleombrotus has adequately explained the mechanics of Delphic inspiration.

important Jewish authors for ideas of the effects of spirit communication during the first century C.E.[22]

Much scholarly work has been done on prophecy and prophetic figures in Josephus.[23] But Levison has rightly complained that modern scholarship on Josephus's interpretation and use of the term πνεῦμα suffers from neglect. Levison lists earlier works that made some contribution to the spirit in Josephus. He claims that these works are inadequate sources that treat πνεῦμα as a sort of curiosity or ignore it all together.[24] Levison shows that Josephus's version of Numbers 22–24 in *A.J.* 4.6.2 §102–4.6.12 §158, the story of Balaam, is a focal point for his understanding of inspiration.[25]

The story of Balaam was important for Josephus.[26] First, the amount of space Josephus devotes to the Balaam pericope suggests its level of pertinency for him.[27] Louis Feldman surmises that Josephus is interested in prophecy in general and the Balaam pericope provides material about a prophetic figure.[28]

---

[22] For an introduction to the writings of Josephus, see Harold W. Attridge, "Josephus and His Works," in *Jewish Writings of the Second Temple Period* (ed. Michael E. Stone; Literature of the Jewish People in the Period of the Second Temple and the Talmud 2; Philadelphia: Fortress, 1984) 185–232.

[23] See Joseph Blenkinsopp, "Prophecy and Priesthood in Josephus," *JJS* 25 (1974) 239–62; David Hill, "Jesus and Josephus' 'Messianic Prophets,'" in *Text and Interpretation: Studies in the New Testament Presented to Matthew Black* (ed. E. Best and R. M. Wilson; Cambridge: Cambridge University Press, 1979) 143–53; Louis H. Feldman, "Prophets and Prophecy in Josephus," *JTS* 41 (1990) 386–422; Rebecca Gray, *Prophetic Figures in Late Second Temple Jewish Palestine: The Evidence from Josephus* (Oxford: Oxford University Press, 1993); and Christopher T. Begg, "The 'Classical Prophets' in Josephus' Antiquities," in *"The Place Is Too Small for Us": The Israelite Prophets in Recent Scholarship* (ed. R. P. Gordon; Winona Lake, IN: Eisenbrauns, 1995) 547–62.

[24] John R. Levison, "Josephus' Interpretation of the Divine Spirit," *JJS* 47 (1996) 234–55.

[25] John R. Levison, "The Debut of the Divine Spirit in Josephus' Antiquities," *HTR* 87 (1994) 123–38.

[26] See Louis H. Feldman, *Studies in Josephus' Rewritten Bible* (Leiden: Brill, 1998) 110–36.

[27] Feldman (ibid., 110) compares the Hebrew of Num 22:2–25:9 with 164 lines and the LXX with 261 lines to Josephus's version of the story with 363 lines.

[28] Feldman (ibid., 114–15) notes that Josephus never calls Balaam a προφήτης, but rather a μάντις. Feldman notes that Josephus uses the terms μάντις, μαντεία, μαντεῖον, and μαντεύομαι with reference to pagan prophets and prophecies. This might deride the character of Balaam. However, Feldman observes Josephus's inconsistency with terminology where he uses the term "prophet" for an otherwise pagan, i.e., non-Jewish, Egyptian prophet (*Ap.* 1.35 §312) and the prophets of Baal opposed by Elijah (*A.J.* 8.13.5 §339). Likewise, the term μαντεία refers to predictions made by Jews who were not prophets, such as Jotham (*A.J.* 5.7.5 §253), and to

Second, Josephus realized that history and prophecy were inevitably bound up with one another, for the prophets were responsible for the recorded history of the Jewish people. Third, biblical prophetic figures were known to Hellenistic Greeks, and the Balaam pericope provided an opportunity for Josephus to relate to his Hellenistic audience effectively.[29]

The character of Balaam presented a problem for Josephus. In the biblical account (Num 22:2–20), Balaam is called upon to curse Israel. Feldman notes that if Josephus "gave too positive a portrayal he would not only be going against the simple meaning of the biblical text but would also be in a position of praising one who sought to curse the Jews."[30] Josephus shifts his focus from Balaam's personality to the historical, military, and political issues between Israel and its enemies, thereby avoiding the character problem.

The manner of inspiration in Num 24:2–3 is given in pithy terms, ותהי עליו רוח אלהים וישא משלו ויאמר, "and a spirit of God came upon him and he lifted his voice and said." Josephus elaborates on the experience of Balaam in three pertinent texts in *A.J.* 4.6.1 §102–4.6.6 §130.

Josephus describes the way in which Balaam delivered the oracle, "Such was the inspired utterance of one who was no longer master of himself but was overruled by the divine spirit to deliver it."[31] Josephus uses the term ἐπεθείαζεν, "inspired," to characterize the manner of speech given by Balaam. This inspired state is described further in two subsequent phrases. The first phrase describes the psychic condition at the moment of inspiration, οὐκ ὢν ἐν ἑαυτῷ, "one who was not in himself." This phrase suggests that some aspect of Balaam, possibly a component of his personality or mind (or spirit), was absent during inspiration. The second phrase makes clear that something other than Balaam himself was responsible for his inspired utterance, τῷ δὲ θείῳ πνεύματι πρὸς αὐτὸ νενικημένος, "but was overruled by the divine spirit to deliver it." These two elements suggest that "not Balaam, but a divine spirit" spoke.

Josephus has Balaam describe the experience to Balak with words that

---

Josephus himself (*B.J.* 4.10.7 §625), (p. 115 n. 12). For Balaam's associations with divination, see Michael S. Moore, "Another Look at Balaam," *RB* 97 (1990) 359–78.

[29] Feldman (*Studies*, 111) notes that according to Origen (*Against Celsus* 4.51) Numenius of Apamea, the Pythagorean, quoted Moses and other biblical prophets in his writings.

[30] Ibid., 134.

[31] *A.J.* 4.6.5 §118: Καὶ ὁ μὲν τοιαῦτ' ἐπεθείαζεν οὐκ ὢν ἐν ἑαυτῷ, τῷ δὲ θείῳ πνεύματι πρὸς αὐτὰ νενικημένος.

continue to elaborate on the manner of his inspired state and utterance: "Do you (Balak) think that it rests with us at all to be silent or to speak on such themes as these, when we are possessed by the spirit of God?"[32] Balaam explains that the spirit "possesses" or "takes hold of" (λάβῃ) him. Balaam then asks if he is in charge of whether he speaks or is silent under the inspiration of the spirit. He answers his own question, "For that spirit gives utterance to such language and words as it will, whereof we are all unconscious."[33] A spirit of God speaks on its own volition and cannot be forced to act through a human intermediary. This reflects the thinking of Sir 39:6, wherein "a spirit of understanding" (πνεύματι συνέσεως) speaks only "if the great Lord wills" (ἐὰν κύριος ὁ μέγας θελήσῃ).

Balaam describes his inspired state as one in which he is not conscious of what he says or does (οὐδὲν ἡμῶν εἰδότων). This recalls the earlier phrase, οὐκ ὢν ἐν ἑαυτῷ, "one who is not in himself," suggesting an ecstatic condition wherein Balaam's spirit or mind is ousted by a spirit of God that uses his vocal organs to communicate. Despite this "ecstatic" condition, Balaam's utterance is completely intelligible.

Balaam mentions his inspired state for a second time to Balak, "For nothing within us, once he has gained prior entry, is any more our own."[34] With this statement put into the mouth of Balaam, Josephus continues to reiterate the nature of the effects of a spirit that speaks through Balaam. The ἐκείνου refers back to τὸ θεῖον, "the divine," or "the deity," in the previous line. The "entry" (εἰσελθεῖν) of divinity into Balaam causes the condition that Josephus has already mentioned twice, "one who is not in himself," and "whereof we are all unconscious." Here, Josephus gives a third characterization, "nothing within us . . . is any more our own." The ultimate antecedent to the demonstrative pronoun ἐκείνου in the phrase "once he (or 'it') has gained prior entry" is πνεῦμα θεοῦ/θεῖον in 4.6.5 §118, §119 which is the cause of the effect of unconsciousness in these lines.

Josephus's description of the effects of the presence of a spirit in Balaam is not far from the kind of characterization that we see in Plutarch for the effects

---

[32] *A.J.* 4.6.5 §119: δοκεῖς ἐφ᾽ ἡμῖν εἶναί τι περὶ τῶν τοιούτων σιγᾶν ἢ λέγειν, ὅταν ἡμᾶς τὸ τοῦ θεοῦ λάβῃ πνεῦμα;

[33] Ibid.: φωνὰς γὰρ ἃς βούλεται τοῦτο καὶ λόγους οὐδὲν ἡμῶν εἰδότων ἀφίησιν. Compare Acts 2:4, καθὼς τὸ πνεῦμα ἐδίδου ἀποφθέγγεσθαι αὐτοῖς, "just as the spirit enabled them to proclaim."

[34] *A.J.* 4.6.5 §121: οὐδὲν γὰρ ἐν ἡμῖν ἔτι, φθάσαντος εἰσελθεῖν ἐκείνου ἡμέτερον.

of the presence of a daemon. These effects are not to be found in the biblical text whose phraseology is terse and laconic: "the Lord put a word in [Balaam's] mouth" (Num 23:5,16) and "the spirit of God came upon him" (Num 24:2). Whereas the idea for the entry of a spirit into a person can be clearly seen in biblical texts such as Lev 20:27, 1 Sam 10–19, 1 Kgs 22:23, 1 Chr 12:19, and 2 Chr 24:20, the detail that Josephus gives for inspiration has a closer parallel in a passage such as Plutarch's *Def. orac.* 418D. Levison attributes the details found in Josephus's account of Balaam's inspiration to the influence of Greco-Roman views of inspiration such as those found in Plutarch.[35]

4. Philo: *Her.* 259, 265–66; *Mos.* 1.274, 277, 283; and *Spec.* 4.49

The kind of detail found for inspiration in Josephus occurs also in Philo. In Philo, however, the description of the effects of the presence of a spirit are much more elaborate than what we have in Josephus. Philo's characterization of inspiration portrays an explicit knowledge of how spirits were believed to communicate through human intermediaries or mediums. He gives more precise details than Josephus does; some of these details are consistent with those of Josephus.

Philo has been the focus of scholarly inquiry for many decades, and deservedly so.[36] Philo wrote within the tradition of Middle Platonism and the

---

[35] Levison, "Debut," 133. Levison shows that Josephus understood the inspiring agent in Balaam to be a spirit being and not an impersonal prophetic vapor, as was one of the theories of Delphic inspiration. The vapors theory was given to ridicule, as seen in both Origen (*Cels.* 3.25) and John Chrysostom (*Hom. in 1 Cor.* 29.1), who claimed the vapor entered the priestess through her vagina as she sat on the tripod above the vapor with legs parted. Levison (ibid., 135) notes that if Josephus had identified the divine spirit with the vapor, he might have faced the potential for misconstrual of inspiration as sexual penetration.

[36] The classic work on Philo is Harry A. Wolfson, *Philo: Foundations of Religious Philosophy in Judaism, Christianity, and Islam* (2 vols.; Cambridge, MA: Harvard University, 1947). For an introduction to the writings of Philo, see Peder Borgen, "Philo of Alexandria," in *Jewish Writings of the Second Temple Period*, 233–82. For bibliographies, *Philo of Alexandria: An Annotated Bibliography 1937–1986* (ed. Roberto Radice and David T. Runia; Supplements to Vigiliae Christianae 8; Leiden: Brill, 1988); and the subsequent bibliographies on Philo in *The Studia Philonica Annual.*

Hellenistic philosophy of his time.[37] His writings preserve concepts pertinent to the world of Judaism, Christianity, and Hellenism of the first century C.E. He adopted the allegorical interpretive traditions, common to his Hellenistic culture, developed and used in Alexandria for studying Homer and other Greek traditions. Philo's Platonism, however, has sometimes been misconstrued as a sort of Gnosticism.[38]

Philo's place within Judaism is significant because his writings are one of the main literary testimonies to Hellenistic Judaism during the Second Temple period.[39] Philo is also an important figure for the NT and subsequent Christian literature.[40] In particular, Philo's writings are believed to share a conceptual background similar to that of the Letter to the Hebrews.[41] Harold W. Attridge notes, "There are undeniable parallels that suggest that Philo and our author [of Hebrews] are indebted to similar traditions of Greek-speaking and -thinking Judaism."[42] Philo lived within an eclectic period and his writings reflect it.

Although little is known of Philo's life, he lived in Alexandria, the single largest Jewish community outside of Palestine. The years of his life (ca. 20 B.C.E.–ca. 50 C.E.), make him a contemporary of Jesus and Paul. According to his own testimony, Philo visited the temple in Jerusalem only once.[43] Philo apparently held a high status among his fellow Jews, for he was selected to lead a Jewish delegation to Rome to meet with Gaius Caligula over a crisis related to the pogrom implemented in his community by the prefect Flaccus in 38 C.E.[44]

Philo is one of the main sources for descriptions of inspiration in the first

---

[37] See David T. Runia, *Philo of Alexandria and the* Timaeus *of Plato* (Philosophia Antiqua 44; Leiden: Brill, 1986).

[38] See Birger A. Pearson, "Philo and Gnosticism," in W. Haase, ed., *ANRW* 2, 21. 1, 295–342.

[39] See Samuel Sandmel, *Philo's Place in Judaism: A Study of Conceptions of Abraham in Jewish Literature* (Cincinnati: Hebrew Union College, 1956); and Ronald Williamson, *Jews in the Hellenistic World: Philo* (Cambridge Commentaries on Writings of the Jewish and Christian World 1.2; Cambridge: Cambridge University Press, 1989).

[40] See David T. Runia, *Philo in Early Christian Literature: A Survey* (Assen: Van Gorcum; Minneapolis: Fortress, 1993); and idem, *Philo and the Church Fathers* (Leiden: Brill, 1995).

[41] See Ronald Williamson, *Philo and the Epistle to the Hebrews* (ALGHJ 4; Leiden: Brill, 1970).

[42] Harold W. Attridge, *The Epistle to the Hebrews: A Commentary* (Hermeneia; Philadelphia: Fortress, 1989) 29.

[43] *Prov.* 2.64.

[44] *In Flaccum* and *De legatione ad Gaium*.

century.[45] In the Greco-Roman world, one of the terms used to convey the psychic condition during which inspiration occurred was ἔκστασις, "ecstasy," a term subject to myriad uses and abuses in contemporary English. Philo himself gives four understandings of the term. He begins with a brief "definition" of ecstasy, ἔκστασις ἡ μέν ἐστι λύττα, "ecstasy, or 'raging madness'"[46] and proceeds to describe four different forms.

The first is madness that produces mental delusion (μανιώδης παράνοιαν ἐμποιοῦσα) brought on by old age or melancholy. The second is surprise or amazement (σφοδρὰ κατάπληξις) due to an unexpected or sudden event. The third is a peaceful state that Philo likens to passivity of mind (ἠρεμία διανοίας). The fourth Philo calls πασῶν ἀρίστη, "the best of all," that of divine possession (ἔνθεος κατοκωχή) and inspiration (μανία) to which prophetic types (προφητικόν) are subject.[47] Philo uses this form of ecstasy to describe prophecy, the way in which spirits communicate through human intermediaries.[48]

Philo elaborates that "a prophet has no utterance of his own, but all his utterance came from elsewhere, the echoes of another's voice."[49] The prophet is the "vocal instrument of God" (ὄργανον θεοῦ ἐστιν ἠχεῖον); he is "smitten and played to sound in an invisible manner by him" (κρουόμενον καὶ πληττόμενον ἀοράτως ὑπ' αὐτοῦ). Thus, a prophet is a passive instrument in the hands of a divinity.

Like Josephus, Philo describes the inspired state of Balaam in his rewriting of Numbers 22–24. Balaam's inspired state is brought on by an angel who tells Balaam,

---

[45] See Mary Jo Weaver, "Πνεῦμα in Philo of Alexandria" (Ph.D. diss.; University of Notre Dame, 1973) 115–41.

[46] *Her.* 249.

[47] Ibid.

[48] See John R. Levison , "Inspiration and the Divine Spirit in the Writings of Philo Judaeus," *JSJ* 26 (1995) 271–323.

[49] *Her.* 259: προφήτης γὰρ ἴδιον μὲν οὐδὲν ἀποφθέγγεται, ἀλλότρια δὲ πάντα ὑπηχοῦντος ἑτέρου· Notice that the verb ἀποφθέγγεται, used here for inspired speech, appears in the same context in *Test. of Job* 48:2 and Acts 2:4.

I shall prompt the needful words without your mind's consent, and direct your organs of speech as justice and convenience require. I shall guide the rein of speech, and though you understand it not, employ your tongue for each prophetic utterance.[50]

This prediction made by the angel to Balaam is fulfilled in the words, "He [Balaam] advanced outside, and straightway became possessed, and there fell upon him the truly prophetic spirit which banished utterly from his soul his art of wizardry."[51] Here, Philo identifies the angel with a divine spirit. These two Philonic passages confirm the idea that angels were spirit agents. Levison observes that, "The prediction of the angel in *Vit. Mos.* 1.274 and the prophetic spirit's accomplishing of this prediction in *Vit. Mos.* 1.277 describe the same event, the former prospectively and the latter retrospectively."[52]

Philo gives a clear description of ecstatic speech, i.e., speech that is spoken by a spirit through a temporarily unconscious person. The angel says that it will direct the organs of speech "without your mind's consent" and shall guide the rein of speech "though you understand it not." This is confirmed later when the inspiration event occurs, ἔνθους αὐτίκα γίνεται, "he immediately became possessed" (1.277). The speech by the indwelling spirit (φλέγοντας ὥσπερ ἑρμηνεὺς ὑποβάλλοντος ἑτέρου θεσπίζει τάδε) is an oracle that is in clear Greek (1.278–79). Hence, an ecstatic state does not indicate "frenzied," unintelligible speech, as is often suggested by scholars who identify the psychic condition of ecstasy with the nature of speech uttered in this condition.

Philo gives another example of an "irrational" state in which "rational" speech is delivered. He states that Balaam "was suddenly possessed, and,

---

[50] *Mos.* 1.274: ὀνήσεις γὰρ οὐδέν, ἐμοῦ τὰ λεκτέα ὑπηχοῦντος ἄνευ τῆς σῆς διανοίας καὶ τὰ φωνῆς ὄργανα τρέποντος, ᾗ δίκαιον καὶ συμφέρον· ἡνιοχήσω γὰρ ἐγὼ τὸν λόγον θεσπίζων ἕκαστα διὰ τῆς σῆς γλώττης οὐ συνιέντος.

[51] Ibid., 1.277: ἔξω δὲ προελθὼν ἔνθους αὐτίκα γίνεται, προφητικοῦ πνεύματος ἐπιφοιτήσαντος, ὃ πᾶσαν αὐτοῦ τὴν ἔντεχνον μαντικὴν ὑπερόριον τῆς ψυχῆς ἤλασε·

[52] Levison, "The Prophetic Spirit as an Angel According to Philo," *HTR* 88 (1995) 189–207, esp. 191. Philip S. Alexander ("The Demonology of the Dead Sea Scrolls," in *The Dead Sea Scrolls After Fifty Years: A Comprehensive Assessment* [2 vols.; ed. J. C. VanderKam and P. W. Flint; Leiden: Brill, 1999] 2. 331–53) notes that nowhere in the Dead Sea Scrolls "do we read of an angel *possessing* a human" (p. 339; emphasis his). On the whole the term "angel" is not used in the context of possession. But Philo reminds us that a spirit speaking through a person does not mean that it was not an angel. Contemporary English has contributed to a sort of categorization that is distinct and rigid: "angels," "spirits," "demons." In antiquity, the categories that these three terms denoted were seamless. All three terms describe the same reality: an invisible sentient being.

understanding nothing, his reason as it were roaming, uttered these prophetic words which were put into his mouth."[53] The following "prophetic words" are intelligible Greek that relates that King Balak will not be successful against the Israelites (1.283–84). Elsewhere, Philo describes Moses as one who is "taken out of himself by divine possession" (οὐκέτ᾽ ὢν ἐν ἑαυτῷ θεοφορεῖται) and delivers clear words (*Mos.* 2.250–52). Whether or not this shows fidelity to the biblical text should not obscure the fact that utterances in an ecstatic state, according to Philo, could be readily understood.[54]

Philo gives a graphic depiction of the onset of a prophet's trance by the invasion of a spirit and the recovery of the prophet's senses once that spirit has left: "This is what regularly befalls the fellowship of the prophets. The mind is evicted at the arrival of the divine spirit, but when that departs the mind returns to its tenancy."[55] This is a clear statement of what is meant by the phrase "ecstatic prophecy," i.e., "speaking forth in an out-of-the-self state." As the spirit enters into the prophet, it "evicts" (ἐξοικίζεται) the mind (νοῦς) of the prophet, which produces a state of unconsciousness. When the divine spirit leaves, the mind "returns" to the prophet (εἰσοικίζεται) who then regains consciousness.

Philo provides more detail of the effect of the presence of an invading spirit being when he states:

For indeed the prophet, even when he seems to be speaking, really holds his peace, and his organs of speech, mouth and tongue, are wholly in the employ of Another, to shew forth what He wills. Unseen by us that Other beats on the chords with the skill of a master-hand and makes them instruments of sweet music, laden with every harmony.[56]

---

[53] *Mos.* 1.283: . . . ἐξαίφνης θεοφορεῖται καὶ μηδὲν συνιείς, ὥσπερ μετανισταμένου τοῦ λογισμοῦ, τὰ ὑποβαλλόμενα ἐξελάλει προφητεύων τάδε.

[54] Aune (*Prophecy in Early Christianity*) observes, "Ecstasy and rationality, however, should not be regarded as two mutually exclusive states of consciousness" (p. 33).

[55] *Her.* 265: τῷ δὲ προφητικῷ γένει φιλεῖ τοῦτο συμβαίνειν· ἐξοικίζεται μὲν γὰρ ἐν ἡμῖν ὁ νοῦς κατὰ τὴν τοῦ θείου πνεύματος ἄφιξιν, κατὰ δὲ τὴν μετανάστασιν αὐτοῦ πάλιν εἰσοικίζεται.

[56] Ibid., 266: ὄντως γὰρ ὁ προφήτης, καὶ ὁπότε λέγειν δοκεῖ, πρὸς ἀλήθειαν ἡσυχάζει, καταχρῆται δὲ ἕτερος αὐτοῦ τοῖς φωνητηρίοις ὀργάνοις, στόματι καὶ γλώττῃ, πρὸς μήνυσιν ὧν ἂν θέλῃ· τέχνῃ δὲ ἀοράτῳ καὶ παμμούσῳ ταῦτα κρούων εὔηχα καὶ παναρμόνια καὶ γέμοντα συμφωνίας τῆς πάσης ἀποτεκεῖ.

The prophet is clearly speaking for, as Philo states, the prophet's "organs of speech" are "employed." But Philo indicates that the prophet only "seems to speak" (λέγειν δοκεῖ) and is really "silent" (ἡσυχάζει). This suggests that the prophet's spirit does not speak (in Philonic terms, "his mind has been evicted"). Instead, "another" (ἕτερος), i.e., "the divine spirit," speaks with the use of the prophet's vocal organs.

Mention of the vocal organs, particularly the mouth, is a common feature in descriptions of inspiration. Philo's depiction of the spirit that operates the organs for speech, καταχρῆται δὲ ἕτερος . . . στόματι καὶ γλώττῃ, "in the employ of another . . . the *mouth* and tongue," is comparable to what Plutarch says of gods and daemons in *Def. orac.* 414E, τοῖς ἐκείνων στόμασι . . . χρώμενον, "employing their [prophets'] *mouths*." Similar experiences are described in 1 Kgs 22:22–23, "a lying spirit in the *mouths* of (בפי [ἐν στόματι, LXX]) his prophets," *Jub.* 24:14, "a spirit descended upon her *mouth*," and 31:12, "a spirit of prophecy came down into his *mouth*." In all five instances, the mouth is described as the organ that a spirit operates from within a person in order to speak its message audibly and intelligibly.

Philo describes an invisible spirit world that operates through a human medium. An audience sees a prophet delivering a message; his physical body informs them by its performance of utterance. Despite the movement of the prophet's mouth for the production of audible speech, it is not his spirit activating his physical body, but rather a divine spirit that has entered him and speaks through him. This is related by the notion that a speaking prophet only "seems to speak" (λέγειν δοκεῖ). A *foreign* invisible agent is the source of the speech from the prophet. Philo states that the activity of the spirit is "unseen by us" or "invisible" (ἀοράτῳ). Hence, Philo is describing divine spirit possession from the perspective of spectators. He continues to elaborate on this inexplicable activity by means of a simile of a musical instrument wherein the spirit "beats on the chords (vocal organs) with the skill of a master-hand and makes them instruments of sweet music."

This simile for prophecy recalls the way in which Plutarch described the activity of daemons speaking through the Delphic priestess, "when the spirits (daemons) return many years later, the oracles, like musical instruments, become articulate" (*Def. orac.* 418D). Philo extends the simile to describe the nature of the speech as "sweet music, laden with every harmony," i.e., intelligible language.[57]

In *De specialibus legibus* Philo gives another depiction of a spirit making use of a deep-trance medium for the purpose of communication:

For no pronouncement of a prophet is ever his own; he is an interpreter prompted by Another in all his utterances, when knowing not what he does he is filled with inspiration, as the reason withdraws and surrenders the citadel of the soul to a new visitor and tenant, the divine spirit which plays upon the vocal organism and dictates words which clearly express its prophetic message.[58]

During inspiration, a prophet's speech is not the product of his own faculties (οὐδὲν ἴδιον ἀποφαίνεται). Instead, his statements are made by "another" (ἑτέρου) while the prophet is unconscious during the event (γεγονὼς ἐν ἀγνοίᾳ). The inspired state of the prophet is characterized by the verb ἐνθουσιάζω, a generic term for spirit possession that is related to ἔνθεος, "within is a god." The possessing agent of the prophet is θείου πνεύματος, "a divine spirit." The unconscious or trance state of the prophet is depicted as a withdrawal of the "reason," perhaps that aspect of the human psyche that defines one as "conscious" (μετανισταμένου μὲν τοῦ λογισμοῦ). The "reason" leaves behind the "citadel of the soul" (ἡ τῆς ψυχῆς ἀκρόπολις), a phrase that refers to the physical body of the prophet.

Once the reason withdraws and the prophet is temporarily unconscious, "a new visitor and tenant" (ἐπιπεφοιτηκότος δὲ καὶ ἐνῳκηκότος), identified as the

---

[57] A simile of a musical instrument is also used by Christian authors of the second and third centuries to describe the way in which spirits communicate through OT and Christian prophets. The most famous of these texts is found in Epiphanius, where the Christian prophet Montanus is described as a passive medium through whom a holy spirit states, "The man is like a lyre and I strike him like a plectrum, the man is asleep [i.e., in a trance] but I am awake" (*Haer.* 48.4). See also Justin Martyr, *Hortatory to the Greeks* 8; Athenagoras, *A Plea for Christians* 7 and 9; Clement of Alexandria, *Instructor* 2.5; Hippolytus, *Treatise on Christ and Antichrist* 2; Theophilus, *To Autolycus* 2.9; and the *Odes of Solomon* 6. 1,2. The significance of these Christian texts shows that Christian experiences of communicating with the spirit world via deep-trance mediums were identical to those of nonChristian Greeks and Jews.

[58] *Spec.* 4.49: προφήτης μὲν γὰρ οὐδὲν ἴδιον ἀποφαίνεται τὸ παράπαν, ἀλλ᾽ ἔστιν ἑρμηνεὺς ὑποβάλλοντος ἑτέρου πάνθ᾽ ὅσα προφέρεται, καθ᾽ ὃν χρόνον ἐνθουσιᾷ γεγονὼς ἐν ἀγνοίᾳ, μετανισταμένου μὲν τοῦ λογισμοῦ καὶ παρακεχωρηκότος τὴν τῆς ψυχῆς ἀκρόπολιν, ἐπιπεφοιτηκότος δὲ καὶ ἐνῳκηκότος τοῦ θείου πνεύματος καὶ πᾶσαν τῆς φωνῆς ὀργανοποιίαν κρούοντός τε καὶ ἐνηχοῦντος εἰς ἐναργῆ δήλωσιν ὧν προθεσπίζει.

divine spirit, enters the citadel of the soul, i.e., the physical body. The performance of a spirit speaking from within a human physical body is characterized as a spirit that "plays upon the vocal organism and dictates words" (φωνῆς ὀργανοποιίαν κρούοντός τε καὶ ἐνηχοῦντος). Philo describes the speech of the indwelling spirit within an unconscious prophet as words that "clearly express its prophetic message" (εἰς ἐναργῆ δήλωσιν ὧν προθεσπίζει), thereby suggesting intelligible utterance.

With these Philonic texts, it is clear that communication with the spirit world was facilitated by means of the direct speech of a spirit through its human medium. The prophet experienced a trance in which he became a passive instrument in the hands of a divine spirit. This experience rendered the prophet temporarily "mindless" (ἐν ἀγνοίᾳ). The ecstatic activity of the wild and frenzied priests, priestesses, and other individuals such as we find in the accounts of Aeschylus,[59] Sophocles,[60] Virgil,[61] Strabo,[62] Lucan,[63] and Lucian[64] is not a sufficient comparison with the behavior that Philo depicts. Philo sometimes uses similar terms, for example, μανία and ἐνθουσιασμός, but his characterization of possession trance includes the means whereby spirits communicated intelligibly and with intent, not the means for erratic behavior or wild, senseless exhibitionism.

The fact that Philo describes the form of ἔκστασις that is marked by ἔνθεος κατοκωχή, "divine possession," and μανία, "inspiration," as the πασῶν ἀρίστη, "best of all,"[65] and a form whose impetus was θεῖον πνεῦμα, "a divine spirit," strongly suggests that this form of inspiration was not in disdain among Jews of the first century C.E.[66]

---

[59] *Prometheus Bound* 875–87, wherein Io refers to the spasm, twitching, madness, whirl of the eyes, and the babbling tongue.

[60] *Ajax* 284–330, wherein Tecmessa describes a fit by Ajax.

[61] *Aeneid* 6.77–82, in which the prophetess thrashes about in the cave in order to rid herself of Apollo while her mouth raves and her heart is wild.

[62] *Geo.* 10.466–68, where he describes the music and frenzy of the Curetes.

[63] *Phars.* 5.173–75, wherein the Delphic priestess, possessed by Apollo, knocks over the tripod; *Bel. Civ.* 5. 169–74, for similar activity.

[64] *Alexander* 12, in which Alexander the Great has a fit of madness and foams at the mouth.

[65] *Her.* 249.

[66] This is also in keeping with the fact that Philo considers the phenomenon associated with the ἐγγαστρίμυθος in a positive light. In his version of Deuteronomy 18, Philo omits the term ἐγγαστρίμυθος from the list of false divinatory practices in 18:11. This seems to indicate that for Philo this form of prophetic experience was a legitimate form of inspiration. Levison (*Spirit*)

5. Pseudo-Philo: *L.A.B.* 28.6, 10a, and 62.2

Like Philo, the author known as Pseudo-Philo gives evidence for spirits that communicate through a human subject who is temporarily rendered unconscious during the event. The writing known as *Biblical Antiquities*, often referred to by the Latin title *Liber antiquitatum biblicarum (L.A.B.)*, is a Latin text that was transmitted along with the Latin translations of Philo's works. Pseudo-Philo, the pseudonymous author of *L.A.B.*, is not the same figure as Philo. According to Daniel J. Harrington, Philo's allegorizing is absent from *L.A.B.* Furthermore, whereas Philo wrote in Greek, Harrington can posit a Hebrew *Vorlage* for the extant Latin texts of *L.A.B.* Harrington argues for a provenance in Palestine, composed no later than 100 C.E. but possibly before 70 C.E.[67]

The pertinency of *L.A.B.* for early Judaism and Christianity is evident in the scholarship devoted to this document. Leopold Cohn is credited with formally reintroducing *L.A.B.* to scholars,[68] as he argues that the Latin text is a translation from the Greek under which lay a Hebrew *Vorlage*.[69] The first English translation was made by Montague R. James.[70] It has since been updated by Louis H. Feldman with a 160-page prolegomenon.[71] Guido Kisch contributed a valuable monograph on *L.A.B.*[72] Subsequently, commentaries on *L.A.B.* have appeared by Christian Dietzfelbinger,[73] Charles Perrot and Pierre-Maurice

---

states, "Because this form of inspiration which Deut 18:11 proscribes belongs, according to Philo, to the positive side of the contrast between artificial and natural divination, and because this sort of inspiration ousted Balaam's abilities of artificial divination, such as augury, and *because it characterizes prophetic inspiration in general*, Philo does not include it in the list of false forms of divination in his version of Deuteronomy 18" (p. 53 n. 62; emphasis mine). Cf. n. 10 above.

[67] Daniel J. Harrington, "Pseudo-Philo," *OTP* 2. 299–300.

[68] Ibid., 298.

[69] Leopold Cohn, "An Apocryphal Work Ascribed to Philo of Alexandria," *JQR* 10 (1898) 277–332.

[70] *The Biblical Antiquities of Philo* (London: Society for Promoting Christian Knowledge, New York: Macmillan, 1917).

[71] *The Biblical Antiquities of Philo* (New York: KTAV, 1971) ix–clxix.

[72] *Pseudo-Philo's Liber Antiquitatum Biblicarum* (Notre Dame: University of Notre Dame, 1949).

[73] *Pseudo-Philo: Antiquitates Biblicae* (JSHRZ 2.2; Gütersloh: Gerd Mohn, 1975).

Bogaert,[74] Frederick J. Murphy,[75] and Howard Jacobson.[76] Jacobson reiterates Harrington's position that *L.A.B.* was originally composed in Hebrew during the second half of the first century or early second century C.E. somewhere in Palestine.[77]

L.A.B. is a rewritten Bible, specifically a history of Israel from Adam to David with imaginative expansions. All extant manuscripts end abruptly during Saul's final speech.[78] *L.A.B.* not only stands as a witness to the understanding of the Bible in Palestinian synagogues prior to 70 C.E., but also, as a Jewish writing composed around the time during which the NT writings were emerging, it is important for the earliest period of Christianity.[79]

Descriptions of inspiration in *L.A.B.* are not as abundant as they are in Philo. The topic of inspiration in *L.A.B.*, however, has been the focus of two recent articles.[80] Two texts in *L.A.B.* demonstrate the notion of spirit communication via a deep-trance medium whereby a spirit enters into a person, rendering him temporarily unconscious, speaks to an audience, leaves, and then the person awakens not knowing what has transpired: *L.A.B.* 28.6,10a and 62.2, the former dealing with Kenaz, the latter with Saul.

5.1 L.A.B. 28.6,10a: Kenaz

The Kenaz cycle of Pseudo-Philo's work is found in *L.A.B.* 25–28. In the OT, Kenaz is the father of the first judge, Othniel (Judg 3:9,11), the younger brother

---

[74] *Pseudo-Philon, Les Antiquités Bibliques* (SC 229–30; Paris: du Cerf, 1976).

[75] *Pseudo-Philo: Rewriting the Bible* (Oxford: Oxford University Press, 1993).

[76] *A Commentary on Pseudo-Philo's* Liber Antiquitatum Biblicarum (2 vols.; AGAJU 31; Leiden: Brill, 1996).

[77] Ibid., 215–24. Hebrew fragments of *L.A.B.* exist. But they are medieval retroversions of parts of *L.A.B.* found in the Hebrew *Chronicles of Jerahmeel*, Bodleian MS Heb. d. 11; 14th century. See Daniel J. Harrington, *The Hebrew Fragments of Pseudo-Philo's* Liber Antiquitatum Biblicarum *Preserved in the* Chronicles of Jerahmeel (SBL; Missoula, MT: University of Montana, 1974). Unfortunately, the Hebrew fragments are of limited use as a textual witness for *L.A.B.* See Harrington, ibid., 5–7.

[78] Harrington, *OTP* 2. 298.

[79] Ibid., 302.

[80] Antonio Piñero, "A Mediterranean View of Prophetic Inspiration: On the Concept of Inspiration in the *Liber Antiquitatum Biblicarum* by Pseudo-Philo," *Mediterranean Historical Review* 6 (1991) 5–34; and John R. Levison, "Prophetic Inspiration in Pseudo-Philo's *Liber Antiquitatum Biblicarum*," *JQR* 85 (1995) 297–329.

of Caleb. In *L.A.B.*, Othniel is not mentioned and Kenaz is depicted as Caleb's son and the first judge; he attains a prominence like that of Moses (*L.A.B.* 9–19), Joshua (20–24), and Deborah (30–33).[81] In *L.A.B.* 28 Kenaz delivers a testamentary speech not unlike Moses and Joshua in other parts of *L.A.B.* Kenaz contemplates Israel's unfaithfulness and destruction by God.

Liber antiquitatum biblicarum 28.6,10a describes an inspiration event similar to those described by Philo. It begins: "And when they had sat down, a holy spirit came down upon Kenaz and dwelled in him and put him in ecstasy, and he began to prophesy, saying."[82] What follows is presumably a "vision," for the prophesy begins, "Behold, now I see."[83] In 28.10a the inspiration experience concludes, "And when Kenaz had spoken these words, he was awakened, and his senses came back to him. But he did not know what he had said or what he had seen."[84]

The phrase *et extulit sensum eius*, literally, "and elevated his senses," admits of a variety of interpretations. The Latin *sensus* can mean mental faculties of perception, self-consciousness, the five senses, or sense perception. The verb *effero* is used here transitively and probably refers to a carrying away of the *sensus*, thus possibly referring to loss of mental or physical sense.[85] Arguably, this can be related to the idea of the ascent of the soul in Cicero's *De Div.* 1.114, wherein the soul, by rising out of the body, is able to see beyond the shackles of the physical body and foretell events that will occur well into the future. Thus, the phrase *et extulit sensum eius* might relate the source of Kenaz's prophetic utterance in 28.6–9: Kenaz's soul rises from his body to see the future.[86]

Other elements in 28.6, however, seem to suggest another source for Kenaz's prophetic utterance. The elevation of Kenaz's senses is due to the action of

---

[81] Murphy, *Pseudo-Philo*, 116.

[82] *L.A.B.* 28.6: *Et dum sederent, insiluit spiritus sanctus habitans in Cenez, et extulit sensum eius, et cepit prophetare dicens.* . . . Latin texts are cited from Harrington and Cazeaux, *Pseudo-Philon: Les Antiquités Bibliques*, 1: *Introduction et Texte critique.* The English translations are from Harrington, "Pseudo-Philo," *OTP* 2. 341–42.

[83] Murphy (*Pseudo-Philo*, 132) describes 28.6–9 as a prophetic vision conveyed in ecstatic speech as Kenaz receives it.

[84] *Et factum est cum locutus fuisset Cenez verba hec, expergefactus est et reversus est sensus eius in eum. Ipse autem nesciebat quae locutus fuerat, neque quae viderat.*

[85] Levison, "Prophetic Inspiration," 308.

[86] So ibid., 309.

spiritus sanctus, "a holy spirit" that *insiluit*, "comes" or "leaps upon," and *habitans in*, "dwells in" Kenaz, with the result that *extulit sensum eius*, "it elevated his senses," or, with Harrington, "put him in ecstasy." Kenaz experiences a possession trance wherein the spirit operates within him for the purpose of communicating to its audience. The holy spirit speaking through Kenaz is saying, "Behold, now I see," which does not necessarily imply a vision, but simply that which the spirit said through Kenaz. The inspiration experience in *L.A.B.* 28.6–9 is not a "vision" of Kenaz, but rather prophetic speech of a holy spirit through a passive Kenaz.

If the experience described here was a vision had by Kenaz's ascended soul, the indwelling holy spirit would be superfluous.[87] Possession is not a necessary accompaniment for an ascent of the soul. Philo's *Her.* 265, "the mind is evicted at the arrival of the divine spirit," comes closer to *L.A.B.* 28.6.[88]

The conclusion of Kenaz's experience in 28.10a describes a state of amnesia: "When Kenaz had spoken these words, he was awakened, and his senses came

---

[87] Compare the experience in the *Martyrdom of Isaiah* 6.10–14: "And as he was speaking in the holy spirit in the hearing of them all, he became silent, and his mind was taken up from him, and he did not see the men who were standing before him. His eyes were indeed open, but his mouth was silent, and the mind in his body was taken up from him. But his breath was (still) in him, for he was seeing a vision. . . . And the people who were standing by, apart from the circle of prophets, did [not] think that the holy Isaiah had been taken up." Robert H. Charles's translation (*The Ascension of Isaiah* [London: Adam and Charles Black, 1900]) is clearer, "And the people who stood near did (not) think, but the circle of the prophets (did), that the holy Isaiah had been taken up" (p. 45). For Ethiopic and Latin texts, see Charles, 100–01. Here, Isaiah's mind is "taken away" (omitted by the Latin versions S L², but, according to Charles [45 n. 10] is genuine in Greek form, ἤρθη ὁ διαλογισμὸς αὐτοῦ) after the holy spirit (in him?) ceases to speak. This is a reversal of what we see in *L.A.B.* 28.6, wherein a holy spirit ousts ("elevates") Kenaz's mind by dwelling within him.

[88] Cicero's description in *De Div.* 114 never suggests possession. The soul leaves the body "inflamed and aroused by a sort of passion" and is "kindled by many different influences." Plutarch, *Def. orac.* 432D, states that the soul grasps the future when its withdrawal (ἐξίσταται δέ) is brought about by inspiration (ἐνθουσιασμόν). Admittedly, these are elements that are used to describe spirit possession. Both the inspired ascent of the soul and spirit possession, however, have a structural similarity that should not identify the two phenomena: the soul/mind is jettisoned from the body. The difference is that in the inspired ascent of the soul the individual experiences a flight from the body that he is able to recall, if in fact it is left to him to deliver the revelation. If the individual is a deep-trance medium for spirits, then his soul/mind is likewise jettisoned (ascends) from the body to make way for the entering foreign spirit that communicates the revelation. Both the inspired ascent of the soul and spirit possession share a common structural bond that the term ἐνθουσιασμός potentially describes. One needs to interpret which phenomenon is being alluded to as much as the text will allow.

back to him. But he did not know what he had said or what he had seen." The inability to recall the inspiration event is evidence for a state of unconsciousness or trance. The phrase *reversus est sensus eius in eum*, "his senses came back to him," also reflects the description in Philo's *Her.* 265, "but when that [the spirit] departs, *the mind returns to its tenancy.*"

Levison traces this idea to Platonic texts such as *Ion* 533D–534E, where poets compose only when they are "possessed" (ἔνθεος), "out of their minds" (ἔκφρων), and when their "mind is no longer in them" (ὁ νοῦς μηκέτι ἐν αὐτῷ ἐνῇ).[89] According to 534C–D a god "takes away the mind of these men . . . in order that we who hear them may know that it is not they who utter these words of great price when they are out their wits, but that it is the god itself who speaks and addresses us through them."[90]

5.2 L.A.B. 62.2: Saul

Liber antiquitatum biblicarum 62.2 is a retelling of Saul's prophetic experience among Samuel's guild of prophets (1 Sam 19:20–24):

And a spirit abided in Saul, and he prophesied saying, "Why are you led astray, Saul, and whom are you pursuing in vain? The time allotted to your kingdom has been completed. Go to your place. For you will die, and David will reign. Will not you and your son die together? And then the kingdom of David will appear." And Saul went away and did not know what he had prophesied.[91]

The introduction and conclusion of this text afford us a view of the presence and effects of a spirit as seen earlier in *L.A.B.* 28.6,10a: the indwelling of a spirit and amnesia once the spirit departs. The first part is reminiscent of biblical forms of communication with spirits: *Et mansit spiritus in Saul et prophetavit dicens*, "and a spirit abided in Saul, and he prophesied saying."[92] The conclusion,

---

[89] Levison, "Prophetic Inspiration," 310. Compare this to Josephus, *A.J.* 4.6.5 §118, οὐκ ὢν ἐν ἑαυτῷ, "one who is no longer in himself."

[90] Philo's *Her.* 266, "the prophet . . . when he seems to speak is really silent . . . his organs are in the employ of Another," reflects this Platonic view as well.

[91] *OTP* 2. 374.

[92] Levison ("Prophetic Inspiration") states, ". . . there is no reason to look further afield than Pseudo-Philo's biblical source to understand the introductory words, 'And [a] spirit abided in Saul, and he prophesied. . . .' The spirit is already central in 1 Sam 19:20–24, and references

however, has no biblical precedent: *Et abiit Saul et non scivit que prophetavit,* "And Saul went away and did not know what he had prophesied."

As with Kenaz's prophetic amnesia, Levison locates the precedent for Saul's prophetic amnesia in Greco-Roman and Christian texts.[93] In *Apology* 22C and *Meno* 99C, Plato says that inspired poets do not know what they are saying (ἴσασιν δὲ οὐδὲν ὧν λέγουσι). In the second century C.E., Aelius Aristides describes the priestesses of Zeus as having no knowledge of Zeus' oracles prior to his communication through them, "nor afterwards do they know anything which they have said, but all inquirers understand it better than they."[94]

Justin Martyr preserves two instances wherein he describes an experience of prophetic amnesia of the Sibyl who cannot recall her statements made under inspiration: "As soon as the inspiration ceased, there ceased also the remembrance of all she had said,"[95] and ". . . the prophetess having no remembrance of what she had said, after the possession and inspiration ceased."[96] John Cassian (ca. fourth century–ca. early fifth century) records two types of demonic possession, those who "are affected by them [demons] in such a way as to have not the slightest conception of what they do and say, while others know and afterwards recollect."[97] Here, Cassian describes a deep trance with amnesia, and a part trance whereby the ecstatic condition is not as intense and the person recalls what the spirit did and/or said through them. Amnesia was the product of either divine or demonic spirit possession.[98]

Levison has demonstrated that the notion of prophetic amnesia was prominent in the Greco-Roman world. The "breadth and longevity of its

---

to prophecy and prophesying, as noun and verb, occur no less than twelve times in 1 Samuel 10 and 19" (p. 302).

[93] Ibid., 304.

[94] *In Defense of Oratory* 43: οὔθ' ὕστερον οὐδὲν ὧν εἶπον ἴσασιν ἀλλὰ πάντες μᾶλλον ἢ ἐκεῖναι.

[95] *Hortatory* 37.2: παυσαμένης δὲ τῆς ἐπιπνοίας ἐπέπαυτο καὶ ἡ τῶν εἰρημένων μνήνη.

[96] *Hortatory* 37.3: καὶ τῆς ἐπιπνοίας μὴ μεμνημένης τῶν εἰρημένων.

[97] *Conferences* 1.12. NPNF, 11. 366.

[98] Antiquity distinguished between a lucid trance (part trance) where the person retains consciousness during possession, and a somnambulistic trance (deep trance) where the person loses consciousness during possession. See Traugott K. Oesterreich, *Obsession and Possession by Spirits Both Good and Evil* (trans. D. Ibberson; Chicago: The de Laurence Company, 1935; repr. *Possession: Demoniacal and Other Among Primitive Races, in Antiquity, the Middle Ages, and Modern Times* [New Hyde Park, NY: University Books, 1966]) 26–90; and Eric R. Dodds, *The Greeks and the Irrational* (Berkeley: University of California Press, 1951) 297.

popularity suggests that Pseudo-Philo could easily have known this tradition without a literary dependence upon these or other Greco-Roman authors."[99] Evidence for prophetic amnesia does not seem to occur in the OT.[100]

---

[99] "Prophetic Inspiration," 305.

[100] See Peter Michaelsen ("Ecstasy and Possession in Ancient Israel: A Review of Some Recent Contributions," *SJOT* 2 [1989] 28–54), who suggests, "If possession trance is always attended by amnesia, it is in principle impossible to prove it in the prophetic books of the Old Testament, inasmuch as these books originate from or pretend to originate from the prophets themselves" (p. 49). This is true for Isaiah, Jeremiah, and Ezekiel. But one cannot use visionary experiences (the revelatory experience of Isaiah and Ezekiel) as evidence that prophetic amnesia did not exist in biblical times, or that remembrance of the prophetic experience was the norm. Visionary experiences, by nature, do not necessarily always require the full removal of the soul/mind/spirit from within the person. For instance, the necromanceress in 1 Sam 28 "sees" the spirit of Samuel while Saul does not. She, however, retains her mental faculties. This "vision" apparently involves no form of trance state, but rather is a clairvoyant episode wherein the person sees the spirit world from within the physical body without having to leave it. Other instances in the OT show that experiences of seeing angelic beings required no trance whatsoever. In Zech 4:1, 4, Zechariah is awakened from a sleep and shown a vision by an angelic being in an awakened state. Sometimes experiences of angelic beings and their revelatory images may have been instances of full materializations that required no clairvoyant or trance ability whatsoever on the part of the person viewing the image or the angelic being. These were instances of angelic visitations such as that found in Gen 18, 19:1, and Tob 12:11–22. A comparison of vision trance with possession trance is a comparison of two different experiences, despite the fact that they might share the notion of the soul's/mind's "removal from the body." Aune (*Prophecy in Early Christianity*, 19–21) distinguishes between a possession trance (possession by spirits) and a vision trance (visions and adventures during the soul's absence from the body). In both instances, an eviction of the soul/mind is required. In the NT, Peter and Paul have ecstatic visionary experiences. In Acts 10:10 Peter has a vision that was initiated when ἐγένετο ἐπ᾽ αὐτὸν ἔκστασις, "a trance came upon him." Yet he was able to recall the vision in 10:28. Likewise, in 2 Cor 12:2–4, Paul cannot tell whether a certain man was "in" or "out of the body" during his vision experience in the third heaven. Being "out of the body" is an ecstatic state, yet the man Paul refers to seems, even fourteen years later, to recall what he saw and heard. Whereas amnesia follows an experience of ecstatic possession, the same condition of ecstasy in visions, wherein the physical body is not inhabited by a foreign spirit but remains "empty" while the soul/mind views spiritual natures and realities while absent from the body, does not usually produce amnesia. The term ἔκστασις does not discriminate the intensity of the trance or "out of the self" state. It may refer to a part trance or a full trance. The fact that a biblical precedent exists for the idea of spirits speaking from within a person may imply that amnesia occurred as well. It is simply never recorded that it occurred.

6. Pre-Platonic Evidence for Prophetic Amnesia

Whereas no clear precedent for prophetic amnesia exists in the OT, evidence for it can be found in the biblical world, particularly in the figure of the *mahhû* and Babylonian diagnostic texts. The prophetic figure of the *mahhû* (feminine *muhhûtu*) is rarely found in ancient Near Eastern texts, but it is known from the earliest periods, Ur III, Old Akkadian (*muhhû*), Old Babylonian (*mahhû*), as well as Middle Assyrian and Neo-Assyrian.[101] It is a figure found in the Mari texts that stem from the Zimri-Lim period (ca. 1750–1700 B.C.E.). For some time these texts provided scholars with a point of comparison with biblical prophecy.[102]

The term *mahhû* is a D-stem verbal adjective derived from the Akkadian verb *mahû*, "to go into a trance," hence, "one brought into a trance."[103] The Sumero-Akkadian lexical lists provide, by means of synonymous comparison, Sumerian equivalents to the Akkadian verb *mahû*: è, "to go out (of one's mind)"; e₁₁, "to ascend, descend."[104] The term *mahhû* has several Sumerian equivalents, two of which present clear evidence for the presence of spirits: *lú-an-dib-ba-ra*, "one who has been seized by a god"; and *lú-an-ne-ba-tu*, "one

---

[101] See Simo Parpola, *Assyrian Prophecies* (State Archives of Assyria 9; Helsinki: Helsinki University Press, 1997) XLV–XLVI.

[102] See John C. Hurd, "Prophetism at Mari and Old Testament Parallels," *ATR* 49 (1967) 397–40; Jimmy J. M. Roberts, "Antecedents to Biblical Prophecy from the Mari Archives," *RQ* 10 (1967) 121–33; Friedrich Ellermeier, *Prophetie in Mari und Israel* (Herzberg: Erwin Jungfer, 1968); William L. Moran, "New Evidence from Mari on the History of Prophecy," *Bib* 50 (1969) 15–56; James F. Ross, "Prophecy in Hamath, Israel, and Mari," *HTR* 63 (1970) 1–28; Jean-Georges Heintz, "Prophetie in Mari und Israel," *Bib* 52 (1971) 543–55; John F. Craghan, "Mari and its Prophets: The Contributions of Mari to the Understanding of Biblical Prophecy," *BTB* 5 (1975) 32–55; Abraham Malamat, "A Forerunner of Biblical Prophecy: The Mari Documents," in *Ancient Israelite Religion: Essays in Honor of F. M. Cross* (ed. P. D. Miller, P. D. Hanson, and S. Dean McBride; Philadelphia: Fortress, 1987) 33–52; idem, *Mari and the Early Israelite Experience* (The Schweich Lectures, 1984; Oxford: Oxford University Press, 1989); and Simon B. Parker, "Official Attitudes toward Prophecy at Mari and in Israel," *VT* 43 (1993) 50–68.

[103] *CAD* s.v. *mahû.*

[104] Parpola, *Assyrian Prophecies*, CIII n. 219. Stephen Langdon ("Note: Mahhu, not Magus," *JRAS* [1932] 391–92) gives Sumerian evidence for a possible case for an ecstatic condition, *ĝur-mu al-è-dé*, "the mind departs" (p. 92).

who has been entered into by a god."[105] By equivalence, the term *mahhû* represents a practitioner who is possessed by spirits for the purposes of communicating with the spirit world.

In the corpus of Mari texts designated ARM X (*Archives Royales de Mari*) two texts give evidence for the god Annunītum that possesses Šēlebum and Ahātum:

In the temple of Annunītum on the third day Šēlebum went into a trance and thus (spoke) Annunītum.[106]

In the temple of Annunītum in the city, Ahātum, the servant of Dagan-mālik, went into a trance and spoke as follows, thus . . .[107]

The verb used in these texts for "to go into a trance" is *mahû*. The first text shows that Šēlebum was a passive instrument through whom Annunītum spoke, not unlike the texts we have seen in Plutarch, Josephus, Philo, and Pseudo-Philo.[108] The second text is probably to be understood similarly.[109]

Alfred Haldar gives evidence for the prophetic amnesia of the *mahhû*: "I am struck down like a *mahhu*, I bring forth what I do not know."[110] This line is from a votary's prayer to the god Nabu.[111] The passage is unique, for it gives us a glimpse into the trance state of a *mahhû*. The first part, "I am struck down (or 'seized') like a *mahhu*," recalls one of the Sumerian lexical equivalents for

---

[105] *CAD* s.v. *mahhû*. For an excellent analysis of *mahhû* and *lú-an-ne-ba-tu* as they occur in the Sumero-Akkadian lexical lists, see Richard A. Henshaw, *Female and Male. The Cultic Personnel: The Bible and the Rest of the Ancient Near East* (Princeton Theological Monograph Series 31; Allison Park, PA: Pickwick, 1994) 156,157,163.

[106] ARM X 7. 5–7, no. 1.

[107] ARM X 8. 5–8, no. 2. For other texts of this nature, see Parpola, *Assyrian Prophecies*, CIII n. 220.

[108] Craghan ("Mari and Its Prophets") states that in this text, ". . . the god and prophet converge to the point of identification" (p. 40).

[109] Moran ("New Evidence from Mari") observes the possibility for the existence of the lucid trance among the *mahhus*. But he suggests that ". . . we may not conclude that this type of trance was the rule. The prophets may often or even regularly have lost consciousness of themselves and become subjectively identified with the god within them" (p. 28).

[110] Alfred Haldar, *Associations of Cult Prophets among the Ancient Semites* (Uppsala: Almqwist & Wiksells, 1945) 25.

[111] For the Akkadian text, transliteration, and a translation, see S. A. Strong, "On Some Babylonian and Assyrian Alliterative Texts I," *Proceedings of the Society of Biblical Archaeology* 17 (1895) 138–39.

mahhû, lú-an-dib-ba-ra, "one who has been seized by a god." The second part, "I bring forth what I do not know," expounds on the results of the "seizure" mentioned in the first part. The verb *ūbal,* "I bring forth," derived from the Akkadian verb *wabalum,* can have the idiomatic sense of "speak forth."[112] Thus, the sense of the text, "I speak forth what I do not know," does not refer to an inability to understand the meaning of a cryptic message spoken by the *mahhû.* Their utterances were clear and succinct.[113] Rather, it seems to point to an unconscious state in which the *mahhû* "brings" or "speaks" forth a message.[114]

Martin Stol has published a study of epilepsy in Babylonian diagnostic texts preserved on clay tablets.[115] In these texts, the patient's sickness is attributed to the "hand" of some god or goddess. Tablet XXVI, 19–22 (20–23) gives a description of amnesia at the withdrawal of a spirit:

If, at the time it overwhelms him, his limbs are paralyzed, it [unconsciousness] is pouring over him and he forgets himself, after it has poured over him his eyes are . . . , his face is red . . . if the conjurer makes that patient 'talk', and he says what he has been made to 'talk'; after it has released him he does not know what he had 'talked': Hand of incubus of fever (?).[116]

According to Stol, the "it" in this text refers to unconsciousness.[117] The incubus in the phrase "hand of incubus" is a name for a type of spirit whose Babylonian name was *lilû,* the central element of which is Sumerian LÍL, "wind," "phantasma."[118] The patient "talks" while in an unconscious state, a state that, apparently, is due to the "hand of incubus," i.e., the intense presence of a spirit. Once the patient regains consciousness, i.e., "after it has released him," the patient is unaware of anything he has said. This phenomenon is comparable to

---

[112] *CAD* s.v. *abālu.*

[113] So Parpola, *Assyrian Prophecies,* XLV–XLVII.

[114] So Haldar, *Associations of Cult Prophets,* 25; and Donald J. Jones, "Ecstaticism and the Hebrew Prophets," *Methodist Theological School* 7 (1969) 33–45, who reiterates Haldar's view for the state of the *mahhû* described in this text as "the absence of normal consciousness" (p. 35).

[115] Martin Stol, *Epilepsy in Babylonia* (Cuneiform Monographs 2; Groningen: Styx, 1993).

[116] Ibid., 61.

[117] Stol (ibid.) states, "The verb 'to pour out' (*rehû*) is used for commencing sleep or lapsing into a state of unconsciousness. . . . It can be used without subject, 'impersonal', meaning that the person loses his consciousness."

[118] Ibid., 46.

prophetic contexts that we have seen in the *mahhû* and in Philo, Josephus, and Pseudo-Philo.[119]

Whereas Plato provides the Greek basis for descriptions of inspiration in the Greco-Roman texts of Plutarch and Philo,[120] the Semitic texts for the *mahhû* show that possession trance and amnesia were widespread in time and geography. The Sumerian equivalents *lú-an-ne-ba-tu* and *lú-an-dib-ba-ra*, the verbal idea of *mahû*, the Mari texts, and the text of a prayer to Nabu, taken together, show the kind of presence and effects of spirits that are found in Greco-Roman texts: an indwelling spirit communicates through an unconscious prophet. Ecstatic prophecy with amnesia was not unique to the Platonic Greek and Greco-Roman world, for the same phenomenon occurs in Mesopotamia centuries earlier.[121]

7. Prospects for the OT and Early Christian Literature

If the Mesopotamian and Greco-Roman evidence for prophetic amnesia suggests that this phenomenon was typical of communicating with spirits via human mediums, this might, at least, imply that such was the case in OT texts

---

[119] The symptoms of illness and those of prophetic behavior are sometimes analogous in antiquity. Jimmy J. M. Roberts ("The Hand of Yahweh," *VT* 21 [1971] 244–51) shows that the expression "hand of x," where x represents a divine name or some term for a god or entity, designates the "disastrous manifestation of the supernatural power" (p. 240). This was especially so in contexts of illnesses that were attributed to the presence of a god or a spirit. Roberts suggests that the Egyptian expression "man in the hand of a god" designated an insane person and resembled the activity found in the Akkadian verb *namhû* (from *mahû*) for Mari prophets and the Hebrew hithpael התנבא used for the behavior of a madman and the ecstatic behavior of a prophet (p. 250). This can be seen in the Greek term ἐπίληψις, "seizure" by a god, from which English "epilepsy" is derived. Hence, Hippocrates called it ἱερὰ νόσος, "the divine illness." Hippocrates (*Epid.* 5. 63) also compared the symptoms of an illness with the prophetic phenomenon associated with the ἐγγαστρίμυθος (see Ê. Littré, ed., *Hippocrates: Ouevres complétes* [10 vols.; Paris: J.-B. Bailliére, 1839–1861] 5. 242). Roberts ("Hand") states that "the expression, 'hand of Yahweh,' was applied to the prophetic phenomenon precisely because that phenomenon bore a remarkable similarity to the symptoms of human illness normally designated by the expression" (p. 250).

[120] So Levison, "Inspiration and the Divine Spirit," 287.

[121] Compare the Akkadian text, "like a *mahhu*, I bring (speak) forth what I do not know," with Philo, *Spec.* 1.65, where the prophet "has no power of apprehension when he speaks but serves as the channel for the insistent words of another's (a divine spirit's) prompting."

that refer to indwelling spirits communicating with an audience, despite the fact
that the OT texts do not detail the phenomenon of amnesia in contexts of inspiration. Hence, the experiences recorded in texts such as Lev 20:27[122], 1 Kgs
22:23[123], 1 Chr 12:19[124], 2 Chr 24:20[125], and the instances in 1 Samuel 10–19
that refer to "a spirit leaping upon" a person (רוח + צלח) might have been
accompanied by amnesia.

Furthermore, one wonders if the Christian material for prophetic phenomena
can be favored as uniquely "Christian."[126] Thiselton has stated that "it becomes
essential to differentiate between components drawn from an Israelite-Jewish
background and those associated with Graeco-Roman paganism."[127] The
opinion that Greek expressions and descriptions of inspiration are somehow a
departure from biblical, Jewish, and Christian notions of inspiration does not
fare well under close analysis of texts ranging from as early as the second
millennium up to the third or fourth century C.E. (John Cassian) that show
evidence for what is considered by some to be unique to Greek ideas.[128]

---

[122] ואיש או־אשה כי־יהיה בהם אוב או ידעני, "a man or a woman who has in them a ghost or
a knowing spirit." See Appendix Two, 295 n. 44.

[123] רוח שקר בפי כל־נביאיך, "a lying spirit in the mouths of all of your prophets."

[124] ורוח לבשה את־עמשי, "and a spirit put on Amasai."

[125] ורוח אלהים לבשה את־זכריה, "and a spirit of God put on [entered into] Zechariah."
See Appendix Two, 296 nn. 45, 46.

[126] Aune (*Prophecy in Early Christianity*) voiced a similar view: ". . . scholars . . . regard
the contribution of Greco-Roman prophetic and oracular traditions as being of little value in
understanding the phenomenon of early Christian prophecy. . . . , neglect of the Greco-Roman
material is based on the implicit notion that whatever is distinctively Greco-Roman is somehow
a corruption of the Christian faith, while continuities with Israelite-Jewish tradition indicate a
faithfulness to biblical (and hence normative) tradition" (p. 17). This is the classic wedge
between the OT and Greco-Roman phenomena and Greco-Roman and Christian forms of
inspiration.

[127] Thiselton, *First Epistle to the Corinthians*, 959.

[128] Such an opinion polarizes biblical and Greek prophecy. Hill (*New Testament Prophecy*)
gives expression to this opinion: "Presumably Paul derived his view of the phenomenon from
Old Testament/Jewish models and possibly from contact with prophets influenced by such
models (like those in Acts), whereas the Corinthians' understanding seems to reflect the Greek
ecstatic model: those who practiced according to it were employed in the mystery cults and their
activities and experience were described . . . by terms like *mainomai, mantis, enthousiasmos*,
etc., terms which are not used of New Testament prophets" (p. 121). Max M. B. Turner
discusses the origins of the spirit of prophecy ("The Spirit of Prophecy and the Power of
Authoritative Preaching in Luke-Acts: A Question of Origins," *NTS* 38 [1992] 66–88) and posits
that spirit possession is more a Greek phenomenon than Jewish: "We also have quite prominent
cases of 'invasive' charismatic speech, though it is notable that the clearest cases (in Philo and

Certainly, the "tests" instituted in Christian circles for spirit phenomena were Christian (e.g., 1 Cor 12:10; 1 John 4:1; *Didache* 11; Hermas *Mandate* 11) but the prophetic experiences that were tested seem to have been close to the kind of experiences analyzed thus far in this chapter. Levison presents this view as follows:

> If Philo in Alexandrian Egypt and Josephus in Rome are accompanied by Pseudo-Philo in Palestine in the process of assimilating Greco-Roman conceptions of prophecy, then one must question the usefulness of a description such as 'typically Jewish' and ask further whether these conceptions of prophecy, which exhibit close affinities with Greco-Roman conceptions of inspiration, ought to be shunted aside as a 'significant departure' from putatively typical forms of Judaism. Moreover, Hill's contention concerning Christian prophecy, that '. . . there will be few scholars, if any, who will wish to claim that prophetic phenomena in Greek and Roman religion provide *primary* evidence for the understanding of Christian prophecy' (Hill, *New Testament Prophecy*, 9), ought perhaps to be revisited in light of the Greco-Roman elements which permeate, not only Diaspora Jewish literature, but also a first century Palestinian example of re-written Bible composed in Hebrew.[129]

In summary, the texts in Josephus, Philo, and Pseudo-Philo relate *Jewish* forms of inspiration. Rhetoric against Greek ecstatic models of prophecy does not occur in Philo, Josephus, or Pseudo-Philo.[130] Instead, possession trance, ecstasy, unconsciousness, and amnesia are effects of the presence of "holy" (*sanctus*) or "divine" (θεῖον) spirits in the writings of these first-century Jewish authors.

The argument that Greek expressions for inspiration (ἔνθεος, ἔκστασις, κατοκωχή, ἄγνοια) are terms meant to convey meaning for non-Jewish (Greek) readers, with the implication that Jewish readers would have known better, is unrealistic.[131] Too often, scholars view the "mindless" (ἄγνοια) prophetic

---

Josephus) are heavily marked by the language of divine possession, or of mantic prophetism (see Plato *Phaedrus* 244A–245C; *Ion* 533D–534E), and to that extent cannot safely be regarded as conveying a *typically Jewish* notion of the Spirit of prophecy" (p. 85; emphasis his).

[129] Levison, *Spirit*, 254 (parentheses mine).

[130] Josephus and Philo are not hesitant at pointing out uniquely Jewish institutions distinct from Greek ones in other areas of Jewish life, such as the temple, Jewish ritual, and Jewish feast days.

[131] Feldman (*Josephus' Rewritten Bible*) implies this argument by stating, "Where the Bible states that a musician played, and 'the hand of the L-rd' came upon Elisha (2 Kings 3:15), Josephus says that Elisha became divinely inspired (ἔνθεος) (*Ant.* 9.35). In this way . . . he has portrayed Elijah in a way that his non-Jewish readers might more readily understand, inasmuch

experience with derision on the basis of a "rational" framework.[132] If the Greek terms did not reflect Jewish ideas in any way, one wonders how Hellenistic Jews would have described experiences of inspiration in the first century C.E.

8. Conclusion

The descriptions of the effects of spirits presented in this chapter recall what is meant by the term "medium," a passive human agent through whom spirits speak to a third party. English Bibles and much scholarly material restrict the idea of a medium to one who traffics with the dead or spirits of divination. Consulting mediums was a sin (see Lev 20:6, 27; Deut 18:11–12). The texts analyzed here show that mediums might also be controlled by good spirits (δαιμόνιον, "a divinity," θεῖον πνεῦμα, "a divine spirit," and *spiritus sanctus*, "a holy spirit") whose duty it was to communicate the will of God (at least in Josephus, Philo, and Pseudo-Philo). Mediums were merely instruments through whom the spirit world (good or bad) communicated.[133] Prophets were mediums

---

as the term ἔνθεος is applied to those who are divinely possessed, as we see, for example, in poets who are inspired (Plato, *Ion* 534B)" (p. 349).

[132] Gerhard Friedrich, "προφήτης," *TDNT* 6. 851; Heinrich Bacht, "Wahres und falsches Prophetentum," *Bib* 32 (1951) 237–67; Grudem, *The Gift of Prophecy*, 150–76; and Turner, *The Holy Spirit and Spiritual Gifts*, who distinguishes "strong forms" of ecstasy as uncontrolled, i.e., "unconscious," trance from controlled, i.e., "conscious," trance wherein the prophet retains his senses. He argues that the controlled form occurred in the Pauline churches and implicitly shunts aside the "strong form" as atypical of Christian and Jewish forms of inspiration (pp. 200–204). Turner, however, misuses the terms "controlled" and "uncontrolled," terms he takes from Aune's *Prophecy in Early Christianity* (p. 34). Aune uses the terms to denote voluntary (controlled) and involuntary (uncontrolled) possession. Turner uses the terms to denote a conscious state (controlled) and an unconscious state (uncontrolled), applying the terms to the psychic condition of the one possessed. Aune's use is derived from the original intent of the terms taken from the anthropological studies of Lewis, *Ecstatic Religion*, and Erika Bourguignon, *Possession*. Turner's application of the terms seems to be an implicit ecstatic–non-ecstatic antithetical contrast wherein Greek prophecy is ecstatic and Christian prophecy in the Pauline churches is not ecstatic.

[133] The term "medium" is usually understood by many NT scholars as a derogatory term for those who traffic with spirits of the deceased and for practices that are related to "paganism" and nonChristian forms of religious experience. But like the term "spiritism," the term "medium" is used for one who is an intermediary for *any* type of spirit, holy or evil, human or otherwise. Aune (*Prophecy in Early Christianity*) describes Christian prophets as "inspired *mediums* of divine revelation" (p. 201) and false prophets as "*mediums* through which evil spirits spoke" (p.

adept in the field of spirit communication, and prophecy was the speech of spirits through mediums.[134]

In the following three chapters of this book we will see that texts in First Corinthians 12 and 14 that refer to the "manifestation of the spirit," "spirits" and "speaking in a holy spirit," i.e., prophecy and glossolalia, promise to illustrate the kind of spirit activity chronicled thus far: the direct speech of spirits through human mediums. This will show continuity with Mesopotamian, biblical, Greco-Roman, and Jewish traditions.

---

229). See also Dibelius (*Geisterwelt*, 74), who states, "Denn der Geist ist eine Macht, die den Menschen überkommt, in ihn hineinfährt und sich nun durch das Medium der Person beim einen so, beim andern so äußert." The term "medium" is applicable to both types of prophets, describing, merely, a prophet's function as one with the ability to become a passive instrument through which the spirit world, good or evil, might communicate intelligently.

[134] To be sure, not all who are called prophets are passive entranced mediums possessed by spirits. Isaiah and Jeremiah are referred to by the term נביאים, but they delivered their prophecies in their own person on the basis of visions and auditory phenomena, or in ways that are unrecoverable from the Hebrew text, e.g., היה דבר יהוה אליו, "the word of the Lord came to him" (see Jer 1:2, 2:1, 7:1; and 11:1).

Chapter 4

"Now Concerning Spiritism":
Communication with the Spirit World as Religious
Experience in 1 Cor 12:1–3

1. Introduction

Over a century ago Heinrich Weinel observed that the early church emerged as a body that was devoted to communicating with a spirit world for guidance and instruction:

Within the ancient world view of the continuous activity of communicating with an invisible world of spirit beings lay the fundamental drive of the new religious and moral life of the early church.[1]

Many of the studies surveyed in Chapter Two showed that evidence for "communicating with an invisible world of spirit beings" in the NT and early Christian sources is found in the descriptions or occasional statements of the effects of intelligent spirit beings. These effects were believed to provide empirical experiences of an invisible spirit world that lay above and beyond the human world. Weinel elaborated:

The meaning of the effects of the spirit for all of the early Christian faith is represented by and based upon the descriptions of these experiences within the complex of religious and moral conceptions, feelings, and expressions which form the new life of the Christian.[2]

Despite Weinel's statements, biblical scholars have offered critical readings of First Corinthians 12 and 14 that suffer from a lack of nuance for and a sensitivity to a "spirit world"; "spirit" in First Corinthians is almost always viewed from the perspective of "the Holy Spirit" within traditional Christian theology. This perspective provides little in the way of truly understanding the meaning and significance of the religious experience of the earliest Christians–experiences of communicating with the holy spirit *world*; a multi-dimensional world of innumerable realms inhabited by spirit beings who act and serve among humanity by the aegis of God and Christ. The arguments in the exegesis in this and the following two chapters will attempt to show that Paul

---

[1] Weinel, *Wirkungen*, 55 (translation mine).
[2] Ibid., 62 (translation mine).

advised the Corinthians to communicate with the spirit world in such a way that would elicit only those spirit messages that could be readily known in the language of the congregation. Thus, my reading of the texts will be facilitated by what was stated in the Prospect of Chapter One, the conclusion of the survey of Chapter Two, and the texts analyzed in Chapter Three that serve as a historical attestation for communicating with spirits through deep-trance speaking mediums in the first century C.E.

Much of the exegetical literature on First Corinthians 12 and 14 was rehearsed in Chapter One, "Now Concerning Spiritual Gifts." The present chapter serves as a counterpoint to Chapter One and will selectively draw from the exegetical comments presented in that chapter.

2. 1 Cor 12:1a: Περὶ δὲ τῶν πνευματικῶν, "Now Concerning Spiritism"

First Corinthians 12–14 form a complete self-contained rhetorical unit. Chapter 12 opens the discourse in general terms, chap. 13 is a digression on "love" to give some perspective for what was said in chap. 12 and as an exhortation to those mentioned in 8:1, and chap. 14 discusses specific phenomena, e.g., prophecy and glossolalia, mentioned in the introductory material of chap. 12.

Paul begins his discourse to the Corinthians in 12:1a with what is widely believed to be a standard literary, introductory formula, περὶ δέ, "now concerning."[3] In 1 Cor 7:1 this formula introduces an issue raised in a previous Corinthian letter to Paul, περὶ δὲ ὧν ἐγράψατε, "now concerning the things that you wrote." Thus, some believe that the formula elsewhere in First Corinthians introduces issues raised in this same Corinthian letter to Paul.[4] The formula, however, might serve simply as an enumerative device that begins a new topic known both to the author and recipient without necessarily implying matter raised in a previous letter.[5] If this is the case in 12:1a, then περὶ δὲ τῶν πνευματικῶν is not likely Corinthian terminology that Paul accommodates as

---

[3] See Margaret M. Mitchell, "Concerning ΠΕΡΙ ΔΕ in 1 Corinthians," *NovT* 31 (1989) 229–56.

[4] See 1 Cor 7:25; 8:1; 12:1; 16:1,12. So John C. Hurd, *The Origins of 1 Corinthians* (New York, NY: Seabury, 1965; repr. Macon, GA: Mercer University Press, 1983) 63–74; and Conzelmann, *1 Corinthians*, 115.

[5] So Mitchell, "Concerning," 234.

a response to the Corinthians. Rather, πνευματικά is Paul's own term for an introduction to his personal thoughts on the matter.[6]

Paul raises an issue that the Corinthians were intimately familiar with, τῶν πνευματικῶν, "spiritual things." Admittedly, the meaning behind this phrase is not readily clear in the Greek text until one has read the complete section of the letter, chaps. 12 through 14. But even then, questions linger. The ambiguity of the gender of τῶν πνευματικῶν introduces an initial problem for interpretation. It can be resolved by context. Whereas many scholars believe that "spiritual things" in 12:1a are the "gifts" enumerated in vv. 4–11, even arguing that "spirit" and "gifts" are identical (as most English versions translate, "spiritual gifts"), the "things" cover a variety of terminology.

Throughout First Corinthians 12 and 14 Paul uses terms and phrases related to the presence, effects, and communication of spirits: εἰπεῖν ἐν πνεύματι, "to speak in a spirit" (12:3), χαρίσματα, "gifts" or "graces" (v. 4), ἐνέργεια/ἐνεργήματα, "works," "activities," or "energies" (v. 6), φανέρωσις τοῦ πνεύματος, "manifestation of the spirit" (v. 7), προφητεύων, "one who prophesies," λαλῶν γλώσσῃ, "one who speaks a tongue," ζηλωταί ἐστε πνευμάτων, "you are zealous for spirits" (14:12), προσευχεῖν τῷ πνεύματι, "to pray [with] the spirit" (v. 15), ψαλεῖν τῷ πνεύματι, "to sing [with] the spirit" (v. 15), εὐλογῆς [ἐν] πνεύματι, "you say a blessing [with] a spirit" (v. 16), πνεύματα προφητῶν, "spirits of the prophets" (v. 32), and πνευματικός, "spiritual persons" (v. 37). The "spiritual things" cover all of these terms, hence, χαρίσματα, "gifts," is only one of the many terms Paul uses in his exposition. A neuter gender for the genitive τῶν πνευματικῶν seems to fit this context.

Several scholars are sensitive to the inclusiveness of the phrase περὶ δὲ τῶν πνευματικῶν. Fee argues that "the things of the Spirit" is a better translation than "spiritual gifts." The terms χάρις and πνεῦμα reflect two different meanings and are not identical.[7] Collins translates "concerning spiritual realities," which has the advantage of introducing all of the phenomena related in the Greek words Paul uses here.[8] Hays and Thiselton also believe that the Greek reads "now concerning spiritual things," or "things that come from the

---

[6] So Njiru, *Charisms*, who states, "From Paul's discussion one does not get the impression that the term πνευματικά was a term used by the Corinthians while χαρίσματα was his own" (p. 90).

[7] Fee, *First Epistle*, 576.

[8] Collins, *First Corinthians*, 445.

Spirit."[9] Alan F. Johnson suggests that the Greek text refers to "matters of the Spirit."[10] Ekem, who although argues for the interpretation "spiritual persons," suggests that a possible alternative rendering might be "spiritual matters" whereby the advantage of such a rendering "lies in its ability to capture the entire scope of the phenomena being addressed in 1 Corinthians."[11] The translations "things" or "matters of the spirit" maintain the true meaning of the Greek without positing an interpretive paraphrase, i.e., "spiritual gifts," that might suggest something other than what Paul actually meant.[12]

Other translations for 1 Cor 12:1a, περὶ δὲ τῶν πνευματικῶν, come closer to the thrust of the phrase in the context of the various operations of spirit phenomena that Paul discusses. Werner de Boor subtitles his exegesis of chaps. 12–14 as "von den Wirkungen des heiligen Geistes" and translates 12:1a as "Über die Geisteswirkungen."[13] De Boor argues that πνευματικά does not merely suggest "gifts" but all spirit activities mentioned by Paul: "Paul is not only concerned with *charismata*, the 'gifts of the spirit,' but he also discusses, more comprehensively, all of the activities of the spirit."[14]

Andreas Lindemann similarly translates 12:1a as "Was aber die Wirkungen des Geistes."[15] Like de Boor, Lindemann places a more traditional alternative translation in parentheses: (oder: die Geistbegabten). The primary translation

---

[9] Hays, *First Corinthians*, 207, and Thiselton, *First Epistle*, 910.

[10] Alan F. Johnson, *1 Corinthians* (Inter-Varsity Press New Testament Commentary Series; Downers Grove, IL: Inter-Varsity Press, 2004) 218.

[11] Ekem, "'Spiritual Gifts' or 'Spiritual Persons'," 66.

[12] See also George T. Montague, *The Holy Spirit: Growth of a Biblical Tradition* (Peabody, MA: Hendrickson, 1976) who states, "The topic was the *pneumatika*, which the translations usually render 'spiritual gifts,' even though the word 'gift' in not in the Greek. It is simply the neuter plural of the adjective 'spiritual,' and it has the most general sense of any kind of manifestation of the spirit" (p. 146). See also Ellis ("'Spiritual' Gifts," 129) who notes that χάρισμα is not synonymous with πνευματικόν, especially since Paul qualifies χάρισμα with πνευματικά in Rom 1:11.

[13] Werner de Boor, *Der erste Brief an die Korinther* (Wuppertaler Studienbibel; Leipzig: R. Brockhaus, 1968) 198.

[14] Ibid., translation mine. See Traugott Holtz ("Das Kennzeichen des Geistes [1 Kor. XII. 1–3]," *NTS* 18 [1972] 365–76): "Sie ist aber nicht eigentlich ein Charisma, sofern darunter die Gaben des Geistes verstanden werden, die sich in besonderen Erscheinungen individuell manifestieren. Vielmehr ist sie für Paulus die Grundlage allen geistgewirkten Tuns, auf der sich die einzelnen Charismen zum Nutzen der Gemeinde, des Leibes Christi, entfalten sollen" (p. 369).

[15] Andreas Lindemann, *Der Erste Korintherbrief* (HNT 9/1; Tübingen: J. C. B. Mohr, 2000) 262. So Holtz ("Kennzeichen") who states, "Paulus sachlich die Gemeinde über die πνευματικά belehrt, über die Wirkungen des Geistes in der Gemeinde" (p. 368).

of both scholars, "die Wirkungen des Geistes" and "die Geisteswirkungen," however, provides the fundamental interpretation that is supported by Paul's terminological variety for activities of the spirit. De Boor and Lindemann provide an interpretation that penetrates the bald Greek text and forges in the direction of what Paul seems to mean.

The translation "die Wirkungen des Geistes" is a direct nod toward the works of Gunkel and Weinel surveyed in Chapter Two, *Die Wirkungen des heiligen Geistes* and *Die Wirkungen des Geistes und der Geister*. The translations of de Boor and Lindemann recall Gunkel's earlier statement: "In the history of primitive Christianity the activities of the Spirit are a factor of greatest significance."[16] Indeed, the activities or effects of the spirit (*Wirkungen des Geistes*) were the driving force behind the early church. They evidenced a spirit world that communicated with Christians during the formative years of the church – which brings us to our interpretation of περὶ δὲ τῶν πνευματικῶν.

Spiritism is an act to solicit communication with the spirit world. The utility of the term "spiritism" covers communication with any type of spirit, good or evil, just as the term πνεῦμα in the NT was ambiguous. Scholars have nonetheless defined "pagan" phenomena in the NT as spiritism, reflecting English Bible versions, scholarly articles, and commentaries that use the term "spiritism" in the exclusive context of necromancy, "divination by the dead," and "pagan" divination in the OT.[17]

In a chapter devoted to "Good and Evil Spirits," George B. Stevens described demon possession and related activities as "the phenomena of spiritism which our sources describe."[18] In an exegesis of 1 Cor 12:3, Arnold Bittlinger argued that "there are no legitimate grounds for making analogies between pagan (i.e., spiritist) and Christian phenomena."[19] J. Stafford Wright discussed mediumship and spiritism (he uses the term "spiritualism") in the popular and restricted context of consulting the deceased. On this basis he concluded that Paul "does not suggest that Christian mediums can put the bereaved in touch with those who have passed on."[20] An entry for "spiritism" appears in *A Dictionary of Early Christian Beliefs*. The texts that are used to illustrate the semantic range

---

[16] Gunkel, *Influence*, 9.

[17] See Appendix Two, "The Meaning and Usage of the Term 'Spiritism.'"

[18] George B. Stevens, *The Theology of the New Testament* (Edinburgh: T & T Clark, 1899; 2nd ed. 1918) 90.

[19] Bittlinger, *Gifts and Graces*, 16.

[20] *The New International Dictionary of New Testament Theology* (ed. Colin Brown; Grand Rapids, MI: Zondervan, 1977) 559.

of the term include matters on sorcery, divination, idolatry, conjuring spirits of the dead, enchantment, and demon possession.[21]

George W. Butterworth argued that the "spiritual gifts" of 1 Cor 12:1 have "no connection with 'spirits', that is, with departed souls."[22] He concluded that early Christians were not in the practice of discerning spirits of the departed but instead discerning the Holy Spirit from evil spirits. If we recall that "the Holy Spirit" may not have been an appropriate prospect for πνεῦμα ἅγιον during the first century, then we might ought, instead, to speak of "holy spirits from evil spirits." No descriptions exist in the NT as to what type of spirits these were (human or otherwise), but simply that they were either "of God" or not.[23] The question of whether the spirits who were active in the spiritual things were either departed humans spirits or not becomes moot, at least from the perspective of the NT. The phrase "a holy spirit" does not identify whether that spirit is a deceased human being. It simply indicates that the spirit in question is a spirit who is from the spirit world of God; a spirit who is under God's authority and who acts on his commands as opposed to an evil spirit.

Butterworth is probably correct that early Christians did not seek to communicate purposefully with departed souls in particular. He states that early Christian religious experience had "little relation or similarity to a séance at which intercourse is sought with the spirits of the dead."[24] This does not mean, however, that communication with the spirit world was not actively sought by early Christians who met in small circles for this purpose (1 Cor 14:26, ὅταν συνέρχησθε, "when you come together"). The spirit world was not restricted to spirits of the dead; it encompassed all spirits, good or evil, human or otherwise–hence, a "séance" ("a sitting") for communications with the spirit world potentially elicited *any* spirit. Early Christians were interested in communicating with only those spirits who could be empirically verified as having been sent from God (see 2 Thess 2:2; 1 John 4:1–3).

Other scholars understand spiritism as applied to first-century phenomena in

---

[21] *A Dictionary of Early Christian Beliefs* (ed. David W. Bercot; Peabody, MA: Hendrickson, 1998) 632–33. Some of the texts cited for spiritism are Deut 18:10–12; Gal 5:19–21; Rev 21:8; *Did.* 7:3, and texts from Tertullian, Hippolytus, Origen, Cyprian, and Lactantius. See further Gábor Klaniczay and Éva Pócs, ed., *Communicating with the Spirits* (Demons, Spirits, Witches 1; Budapest: Central European University Press, 2005).

[22] George W. Butterworth, *Spiritualism and Religion* (London: Society for Promoting Christian Knowledge, 1944) 94.

[23] Josephus (*B.J.* 7.6.3 §185) records that "the spirits of evil men" after death become δαιμόνια, "demons," and possess persons in order to kill them. The term πνεῦμα can also be used of the human spirit in the NT. See Acts 7:59.

[24] Butterworth, *Spiritualism and Religion*, 95.

a less negative sense. Andrew Lang discussed the "discerning of spirits," ancient attempts to prove spirit identity, and Delphic inspiration as evidence for spiritism in antiquity.[25] *The Westminster Dictionary of Church History* defines spiritism ("spiritualism" is used) as "those who appeal directly to the Holy Spirit."[26] Montanism, a second-century Christian movement devoted to spirit communication via human trance mediums, was the "prototype of spiritism."[27]

The classicist Eric R. Dodds argued that Greek oracles were analogues to spiritism.[28] He noted that the Pythia became possessed by the god who entered into her and used her vocal organs as if they were his own "as the so-called 'control' does in modern spirit-mediumship."[29] Neo-Platonic theurgy involved the practice of communicating with the spirit world as a whole with the full knowledge that not all spirits were good or desirable. Dodds observed that the *modus operandi* in theurgic texts that describe sittings for communicating with spirits via a possessed medium resembled that of spiritism.[30] Thus, spiritism covers the spirit world as a whole and need not indicate specifically nonChristian phenomena or spirits of the dead.[31]

Paul introduces his topic in 1 Cor 12:1a with the phrase τῶν πνευματικῶν that de Boor and Lindemann interpret as *die Wirkungen des Geistes*. The *Wirkungen des Geistes* were the usual effects that emerged during communications with the spirit world in early Christian circles. Paul discusses these effects, the "spiritual things," in 12:4–11 and 14:1–40 with a variety of terms: gifts; services; activities; manifestation of the spirit; prophecy; glosso-

---

[25] Andrew Lang, "Ancient Spiritualism," in idem, *Cock Lane and Common Sense* (London: Longmans, 1894; repr. New York: AMS Press, 1970) 56–83.

[26] *The Westminster Dictionary of Church History* (ed. Jerald C. Brauer; Philadelphia: Westminister, 1971) 784.

[27] Ibid.

[28] Eric R. Dodds, *The Greeks and the Irrational*; and idem, *The Ancient Concept of Progress and other Essays on Greek Literature and Belief* (Oxford: Clarendon, 1973).

[29] Dodds, *Greeks*, 70. Similarly, Edward Langton (*Essentials of Demonology: A Study of Jewish and Christian Doctrine* [London: Epworth, 1949]) states, "The Greeks shared the commonly accepted beliefs in the possibility of men receiving communications from the spirit world. The most familiar method of spirit communication known to the Greeks was that of the oracle" (pp. 94–95).

[30] Dodds, *Greeks*, 283–311; and idem, *Ancient Concept*, 200–10. Dodds (*Ancient Concept*) states, "Similarities between ancient theurgy and modern spiritualism appear too numerous to be dismissed as pure coincidence" (p. 204). See idem, *Greeks*, 289–91, for "a séance in the Iseum."

[31] See also John E. Sutphin, *The Bible and Spirit Communication* (Starkville, MS: Metamental Missions, 1971).

lalia; and speaking, singing, blessing, and praying in a spirit. In the light of Paul's context, all of these "spiritual things" suggest a direct link with intelligent spirit beings.

Whereas commentators use the term "spiritism" to describe spirit communication as communication exclusively with the dead or spirits of divination,[32] Paul is obviously interested in only good spirits, πνεῦμα ἅγιον and πνεῦμα θεοῦ. In the light of those English versions of the Bible that employ the terms "spiritist" and "medium," the use of the term "spiritism" can be used in Paul's context for good spirits on objective grounds (i.e., "spiritism" [like πνεῦμα] indicates *any* spirit) as a translation for 1 Cor 12:1a.

Thus, an interpretation of περὶ δὲ τῶν πνευματικῶν that reflects a link with the spirit world is "now concerning spiritism" wherein Paul introduces a familiar topic to early Christians: *Verkehr mit einer unsichtbaren Welt von Geistern,*[33] or communication with the spirit world.[34] As an "-ism" the term "spiritism" maintains the plurality of Paul's text "spiritual things" by functioning grammatically in the capacity of a system that recognizes a variety of ways in which spirit beings communicate and interact with the human world.

First Corinthians 12:4–11 run the gamut of a variety of effects that the spirit world produces among the Corinthians, while 14:1–40 relate explicit experiences of the direct speech of spirit beings through human mediums. Ellis states that the "πνευματικά ['spiritual things'] are viewed as the *effectual* and *visible consequence* of the empowering πνεύματα ['spirits']."[35] The "spiritual things" then relate to matters of "spirits" who communicate from the spirit world. 1 Cor 12:4–11 and 14:1–33, 37–40 will be discussed in this context in the subsequent chapters.

---

[32] See Appendix Two.

[33] So Weinel, *Wirkungen*, 55.

[34] Note the translations of 1 Cor 12:1a in *TOB*, "phénomènes spirituels" = "spiritual phenomena," and Bayard (2001), "les expériences spirituelles" = "spiritual experiences." Ekem ("'Spiritual Gifts' or 'Spiritual Persons'") suggests that these translations "seem better to approximate the real sense in which the accusative neuter plural τα πνευματικα (1 Cor 14.1) should be understood" (p. 69 n 25). The "spiritual phenomena" and "spiritual experiences" relate to experiences with "spirits" of a spirit world.

[35] Ellis, "'Spiritual' Gifts," 134 (emphasis mine).

3. 1 Cor 12:2–3: Grammar and Confession

Paul introduces the subject of communication with the spirit world with a litotes in 12:1b, οὐ θέλω ὑμᾶς ἀγνοεῖν, "I do not want you to be ignorant," i.e., "I want you to know."[36] The object of the ignorance (ἀγνοεῖν) has already been stated in v. 1a, "now concerning spiritism."[37] Paul wants the Corinthians made aware of matters related to their dealings with the spirit world. The litotes of v. 1b is followed by two verses, vv. 2–3, that pose a variety of difficulties for scholars, both grammatically and exegetically.

Verse 2 poses the greater difficulty on grammatical grounds. The verse is an *anacolouthon*, i.e., it is not grammatically coherent, for the ὅτι . . . ἦτε clause has no main verb.[38] As Conzelmann noted, the wording and structure of the verse are unclear, suggesting that an element might have dropped out during transmission of the text.[39] As the text stands, it reads literally, "You know that when you were pagans, to mute idols just as (or whenever or however) you would be led, being carried away."

One solution among scholars is to repeat the verb ἦτε, "you were," with the participle ἀπαγόμενοι, "ones carried away," transposing the participle into a periphrastic imperfect passive.[40] Another solution reads ὡς as a resumption of ὅτι so that the verse might read, "You know that when you were pagans, how you were led to mute idols, being carried away."[41] Terence Paige notes that the use of ἄγω and ἀπάγω in the passive suggests that the Corinthians were physically "led about" in a procession to a cultic center for "images" or "idols" (πρὸς τὰ εἴδωλα), a procession known as the πομπή.[42] However one reads the sentence, it is clear that Paul makes an allusion to the Corinthians' past

---

[36] This litotes occurs in Rom 1:13 and 11:25.

[37] So Mehat, "L'enseignement," who states, "On attend l'indication de l'objet de cette ignorance que Saint Paul se propose de combler. En fait, elle a été donnée en tête de phrase: 'au sujet des choses de l'Esprit'" (p. 399).

[38] See Fee, *First Epistle*, 576.

[39] Conzelmann, *1 Corinthians*, 205, and Fee, *First Epistle*, 576.

[40] So Grudem, *Gift of Prophecy*, 156 n. 69; Fee, *First Epistle*, 576; Thiselton, *First Epistle*, 911; and Garland, *1 Corinthians*, 564. The verse would then read, "You know that when you were pagans, you were carried away, as you were led to mute idols."

[41] So Conzelmann, *1 Corinthians*, 204, n. 2, and Barrett, *First Epistle*, 278.

[42] Terence Paige, "1 Corinthians 12.2: A Pagan *Pompe*?" *JSNT* 44 (1991) 57–65. This follows Grudem (*Gift of Prophecy*, 162–64) who argued that the participle "refers to actual travel to idol temples" (p. 163). Collins (*First Corinthians*, 447) and Garland (*1 Corinthians*, 566) are sympathetic with this interpretation.

experience or frame of mind before they became Christians (ὅτε ἔθνη ἦτε, "when you were Gentiles").

Verse 3 is more of an exegetical conundrum than a grammatical one. The two confessions, "Jesus is anathema" (ἀνάθεμα Ἰησοῦς) and "Jesus is Lord" (Κύριος Ἰησοῦς) have presented scholars with *ein Rätsel*.[43] Given the titular status that Jesus received during the post-Easter period as "Lord," the confession "Jesus is Lord" is less controversial than the alternate confession.[44] Joseph A. Fitzmyer proposed that the absolute use of κύριος as a title for Jesus originated in the Jewish-Christian community of Palestine where the post-Easter Jesus would have been hailed with the Aramaic titles אדון or מרא, "Lord" (see 1 Cor 16:22).[45] Larry Hurtado observes that the use of a title reserved for Yhwh, "Lord," for an acclamation of Jesus was a Christian innovation.[46]

The confession "Jesus is anathema," however, has been the source for many scholarly reconstructions and explanations. Thiselton lists no less than twelve different proposals for the context of this confession.[47] The term "anathema" means "accursed" and comes from the LXX translation of the Hebrew חרם, "ban" or "devotion," as ἀνάθεμα. It is used in contexts for offerings to God (see Lev 27:28 [LXX]) and to that which is accursed (see Deut 7:26 [LXX]; 13:16 [LXX]).

It seems remarkable that such a confession would occur within a Christian community. Fee comments, "It is difficult for us to imagine either that anyone actually cursed Jesus in the gathered Christian assembly, or that, if he/she did, Paul would take it so casually as to speak to it only here and in this totally noncombative way."[48] Garland notes that unless the Corinthians were familiar with the confession "Jesus is anathema" in some capacity, it would have been just as strange then as it is for scholars today.[49]

The confession has been explained in several ways. Some suggest that an

---

[43] See Johan S. Vos, "Das Rätsel von 1 Kor 12:1–3," *NovT* 35 (1993) 251–69.

[44] Luke 24:34; John 20:20; 21:7; Acts 1:6; Rom 1:4,7; 1 Cor 8:6; and Phil 2:11. The title κύριος was used in the Hellenistic world for gods or human rulers and as a translation for Hebrew יהוה in the LXX.

[45] Joseph A. Fitzmyer, "The Semitic Background of the New Testament *Kyrios*-Title," in *A Wandering Aramean: Collected Aramaic Essays* (SBLMS 25; Missoula, MT: Scholars Press, 1979) 115–32. See further Werner R. Kramer, *Christ, Lord, Son of God* (trans. Brian Hardy; SBT 50; Naperville, IL: Allenson, 1966).

[46] See Larry Hurtado, *One God, One Lord: Early Christian Devotion and Ancient Jewish Monotheism* (Philadelphia: Fortress, 1988).

[47] Thiselton, *First Epistle*, 918–24.

[48] Fee, *First Epistle*, 579.

[49] Garland, *1 Corinthians*, 568.

element of Corinthian gnostics were using the confession to express disdain for the earthly Jesus as a contrast to the heavenly Christ ("Jesus is Lord"). The gnostic dualism of flesh versus spirit provided the source for the two-fold confession, on the one hand, to curse the earthly Jesus, and on the other hand, to confess the risen Jesus as Lord.[50] Others believe that the phrase "Jesus is anathema" was spoken by nonChristians, possibly the pre-Christian Paul,[51] pre-Christian Corinthians, and Jews who rejected the Lordship of Jesus.[52] Still others argue that the phrase was a rhetorical device meant as a hypothetical remark to lend emphasis by way of contrast to the main point: "Jesus is Lord."[53]

The fact that the curse is paired with an acclamation for Jesus indicates that the meaning of these confessions is not conveyed in their distinction from one another. Instead, their meanings are conveyed in the way they function together in a relationship as what someone might or might not say about Jesus. This will be discussed below in part 8.

4. 1 Cor 12:2–3: Contrast and Analogy

Not withstanding the meaning and relationship of the two confessions "Jesus is anathema" and "Jesus is Lord," one of the main issues confronting scholars for the interpretation of 1 Cor 12:1–3 is the relationship between vv. 2 and 3. In what sense does the content of v. 2 inform the content of v. 3? Or vice versa?

---

[50] See Norbert Brox, "'Ανάθεμα 'Ιησοῦς (1Kor. 12.3)," *BZ* 12 (1968) 103–11; Birger A. Pearson, "Did the Gnostics Curse Jesus?" *JBL* 86 (1967) 301–05; and Schmithals, *Gnosticism*, 124–32. Cf. 2 Cor 5:16.

[51] Jouette M. Bassler ("1 Cor 12:3 – Curse and Confession in Context," *JBL* 101 [1982] 415–18) suggests that Paul draws from his own life experience as a one-time persecutor of Christians (p. 418). See Gal 1:13–16.

[52] J. Duncan M. Derrett, "Cursing Jesus (1 Cor. XII. 3): The Jews as Religious 'Persecutors'," *NTS* 2 (1974–1975) 544–54; Talbert, *Reading Corinthians*, 81–82; Collins, *First Corinthians*, 446; and Garland, *1 Corinthians*, 570–72. Garland (*1 Corinthians*, 570) observes that *Anathema* language reflects Jewish usage, not Greek. See Deut 21:32 and Gal 3:13 for allusions to the crucified Jesus as accursed.

[53] Bruce, *1 and 2 Corinthians*, 118; Conzelmann, *1 Corinthians*, 204; Bassler, "1 Cor 12:3," 417; Mehat, "L'enseignement," 401; Fee, *First Epistle*, 581; and Hays, *First Corinthians*, 209. Bassler ("1 Cor 12:3," 417), who subscribes to the *ad hoc* argument, notes as a caveat that if Paul had created the phrase *de novo*, the Corinthians would probably have been as baffled by it as modern exegetes. Thus, W. C. van Unnik ("Jesus: Anathema or Kyrios [1 Cor. 12:3]," in *Christ and Spirit in the New Testament* [ed. B. Lindars and S. S. Smalley; Cambridge: Cambridge University Press, 1973] 113–26) expresses doubt about the *de novo* creation of the phrase.

Does v. 2 move in a direction toward or away from v. 3?[54] Johan S. Vos summarizes four different relationships posited by scholars for vv. 2 and 3, two of which are by way of contrast, and two of which are by way of analogy:[55]

(1) Contrast – Paul uses contrasting verbal ideas, v. 1, ἀγνοεῖν, "ignorance," v. 2, οἴδατε, "you know," and v. 3, γνωρίζω, "I make known," in an attempt to contrast former Corinthian ignorance with the new knowledge in v. 3,[56]

(2) Contrast – The former enslavement (ἄγεσθαι/ἀπάγεσθαι) to mute (ἄφωνα) gods (implied by εἴδωλα) in v. 2 is contrasted with the freedom of participating in the spirit (πνεύματι) with speech (λαλεῖν/λέγειν) in v. 3,[57]

(3) Analogy – The verbs ἄγεσθαι/ἀπάγεσθαι in v. 2 and the noun πνεῦμα in v. 3 both relate similar irresistible forces with which the Corinthians were driven in former times and now as Christians, i.e., pagan inspiration versus Christian inspiration,[58]

(4) Analogy – The relationship the Corinthians had in former times with the gods through the idols (εἴδωλα) is analogous to the relationship they have with Jesus through the spirit (ἐν πνεύματι).[59]

While scholars routinely see either an analogous relationship or a contrasting relationship between vv. 2 and 3, the underlying meaning of these verses might imply a "both-and" relationship (both analogy-and-contrast): an analogy between Gentile (ἔθνη) and Christian experiences with a spirit world (good and evil spirits operated identically), and a contrast between a devotion to nonChristian spiritism (v. 2) and a devotion to Christian spiritism (v. 3).

---

[54] Mehat, ("L'enseignement,") complains that many scholars focus on the problem of 12:3a and miss the main problem: "la transition entre 12,2 et 12,3" (p. 400).

[55] Vos, "Das Rätsel," 263–64.

[56] So Mehat, "L'enseignement," 401–8; Grudem, *Gift of Prophecy*, 169–70; and Collins, *First Corinthians*, 445–46, who cites other contrasts such as the Corinthians' prior experience with their present experience, dumb idols with the Holy Spirit, and cursing Jesus with an acclamation of Jesus: "The use of contrast pervades Paul's exposition of spiritual realities" (p. 446).

[57] So Morris, *1 Corinthians*, 164–65; Karl Maly, "1 Kor 12, 1–3, eine Regel zur Unterscheidung der Geister?," *BZ* 10 (1966) 82–91, esp. 86; Kistemaker, *1 Corinthians*, 414; Hays, *First Corinthians*, 208; and Garland *1 Corinthians*, 567.

[58] So Barrett, *First Epistle*, 279; Conzelmann, *1 Corinthians*, 206; Bassler, "1 Cor 12:3," 417; Harrisville, *1 Corinthians*, 206; Fee, *First Epistle*, 577–78; and Soards, *1 Corinthians*, 253–54.

[59] This is more or less a variation of #3. Vos ("Das Rätsel," 264 n. 42) cites two sources for this view, Gerhard Dautzenberg, *Urchristliche Prophetie* (BWANT 104; Stuttgart: W. Kohlhammer, 1975) 144–45; and Johan S. Osiander, *Commentar über den ersten Brief Pauli an die Korinther* (Stuttgart: C. Besler, 1847) 534.

5. 1 Cor 12:2: NonChristian Spiritism

Despite the grammatical incoherency of v. 2, the content of v. 2 contains elements that are related to Gentile (ἔθνη) religiosity.[60] The main term that suggests this is τὰ εἴδωλα, "idols." The passive verb ἀπάγω has traditionally been understood by scholars to indicate "being carried away" in ecstasy and enthusiastic frenzy (to the idols), reminiscent of some Greek cults. This argument is usually made on the proposal that Paul is comparing Hellenistic inspiration with prophecy and glossolalia that Corinthians experience as Christians.[61] But the vocabulary of v. 2 does not support evidence for ecstasy or frenzy.[62] The passive form of the verbs ἄγω and ἀπάγω is never used for psychological states of ecstasy or inspiration. The compound verb ἀπάγω appears only here in Paul's letters. Its usage elsewhere, including the LXX, gospels, and Acts, conveys the meaning of "leading someone from one place to another."[63] In v. 2 the agent doing the "leading" and "carrying" is left unexpressed. The focus then becomes the destination to which the Corinthians were once led: the idols.[64]

Scholarly interpretations for v. 2 relate that an agent of some kind is implied in the two passive forms of the verbs ἄγω and ἀπάγω. Paige suggested the Greek πομπή, wherein one is led in procession by "pagan" priests to an idol sanctuary.[65] Vos proposes that an interpretation of v. 2 revolves around the crucial term πνεῦμα. Verse 1 begins the discourse with a πνεῦμα word; v. 3 includes two πνεῦμα words. Verse 2 is left in the middle with no "expliziten

---

[60] The term ἔθνη, "nations," is used in the NT to designate all nonChristians other than the Jews. In the Vulgate the terms for the non-Jew and the nonChristian are *gentilis* and *paganus* from which English "Gentile" and "pagan" are derived. In 1 Cor 12:2 ἔθνη is translated as "Gentiles," that refers to the Corinthians' pre-Christian Greek past. See further, Jack Finegan, *Myth and Mystery: An Introduction to the Pagan Religions of the Biblical World* (Grand Rapids: Baker, 1989).

[61] So James Moffatt, *The First Epistle of Paul to the Corinthians* (New York: Harper and Brothers, 1938) 178; Barrett, *First Epistle*, 278–79; Bruce, *1 and 2 Corinthians*, 117; Conzelmann, *1 Corinthians*, 205; House, "Tongues and Mystery Religions," 134–150; Fee, *First Epistle*, 577–78; Harrisville, *1 Corinthians*, 206 Soards, *1 Corinthians*; 254; Smit, "Tongues and Prophecy," 175–90; Wolff, *Der erste Brief*, 283; and Schrage, *Der erste Brief*, 3.119–20.

[62] So Grudem, *Gift of Prophecy*, 162–64; Mehat, "L'enseignement," 397–98; Kistemaker, *1 Corinthians*, 414; and Garland, *1 Corinthians*, 565–66.

[63] BDAG, s.v.

[64] So Garland, *1 Corinthians*, 565.

[65] See n. 42 above.

Kontrastbegriff."[66] The term εἴδωλον, however, implies an agent in the same semantic range as πνεῦμα that serves as its "Kontrastbegriff," δαιμόνιον.

The term εἴδωλον is derived from the Greek verb εἴδω, "to appear," "to be like." In the LXX the term εἴδωλον occurs ninety-six times translating fifteen Hebrew terms for cultic images and the gods they represent. The term was one of contempt and ridicule for gods other than Yhwh, the basis of which can be found in the second commandment: "You shall not make for yourself an idol (εἴδωλον)" (Exod 20:4 [LXX]; Deut 5:8 [LXX]).

Polemical contempt for foreign gods and idols occurs frequently in the OT. Terry Griffith provides five elements of this polemic:[67] (1) equation of idols with gods[68]; (2) emphasis on the material and perishable nature of idols[69]; (3) idols as man-made objects[70]; (4) lifelessness of idols (i.e., dumb, blind, deaf, and dead)[71]; and (5) the unreal nature of idols.[72] Griffith observes that Hosea links idolatry with spiritual adultery wherein the terms μοιχεύω, "to commit adultery,"and πορνεύω, "to practice (sexual) immorality," occur in the same context as εἴδωλον (Hos 4:13–14,17).[73] Thus, idols were an object of disgust that brought the most severe criticism and punishment.[74]

The OT descriptions of idols with "mouths but do not speak" (Ps 115:13 [LXX]) suggest, on the one hand, a literal dynamic that stone, gold, bronze, or silver statues, in and of themselves, did not have the power for speech, and, on the other hand, a rhetorical dynamic that the gods that were believed to operate through the idols were "nothing" compared to the only one true god, Yhwh.[75]

---

[66] Vos, "Das Rätsel," 265: "Der Begriff πνεῦμα in v. 3 ist so entscheidend, daß er in dem positiven Glied des Kontrastschemas nicht gefehlt haben kann, er hat jedoch keinen expliziten Kontrastbegriff in v. 2."

[67] Terry Griffith, *Keep Yourselves from Idols: A New Look at 1 John* (Sheffield: Sheffield Academic Press, 2002) 37–38.

[68] 1 Sam 31:9, 1 Chr 16:26; Isa 48:5; Jer 14:22; Wis 15:15.

[69] Isa 44:9–20; Jer 10:3–4; Wis 15:7–9.

[70] Hos 8:4–6; 13:2; Ps 115:3–8; Isa 44:9–20; Jer 10:3–4. Griffith (*Idols*, 38 n. 37) notes that the term χειροποίητα, "idols (made by humans)," occurs in Isa 2:18; 10:11; 16:12; 19:1; 21:9; 31:7; and 46:6.

[71] Lev 14:29; 26:30; Isa 46:6; Jer 10:5; Sir 30:19; 3 Macc 4:16; Pss 115:5–7; 135:16–17.

[72] Isa 30:20–22; Jer 10:14; 13:25–27; 16:19–20; Ezek 44:10–15; Jon 2:9; Tob 14:6; Wis 11:15; 12:24.

[73] Griffith, *Idols*, 36.

[74] Jdt 8:18–19.

[75] This is the same kind of argument found in 1 Cor 8:5–6. Cf. Deut 4:35,39. The Hebrew term אֱלִילִים, "idols" or "worthless gods," indicated real gods or images through which gods were consulted. But these gods were vain, feeble, and weak in comparison to the "true God."

The literal fact that inanimate idols were incapable of anything of their own power was transposed as a metaphor onto foreign gods represented by the idols. The dumbness of idols, a typical element of Jewish polemics, is reflected in Rev 9:20, where individuals "did not repent of the works of their hands, to give up the worship of demons and idols made from gold, silver, bronze, stone, and wood, which cannot see or hear or walk." A relationship is made here between demons and idols.

A relationship between demons and idols is also made by Paul. In 1 Cor 8:4 he suggests that idols are "nothing in the world" because there is only "one God." To his Gentile converts in Galatia, Paul states that "you were enslaved to things that by nature were not gods" (Gal 4:8), i.e., these things do in fact exist but they are not what you once thought they were, "gods."[76] In 1 Cor 10:19–20 Paul asserts his belief in the sentient reality behind the idols with the term δαιμόνιον, a term Greeks used for "a godlike being":

What am I saying then? That meat sacrificed to idols (εἰδωλόθυτόν) is anything? That an idol (εἴδωλον) is anything? No, I mean that what they sacrifice [they sacrifice] to demons and not to God (δαιμονίοις καὶ οὐ θεῷ). I do not want you to become participants with demons (κοινωνοὺς τῶν δαιμονίων γίνεσθαι).

With this statement Paul appeals to his Jewish heritage in which he lent "full weight to D[eu]t. 32.17: ἔθυσαν δαιμονίοις καὶ οὐ θεῷ."[77] Thus, Paul admits that godlike beings (δαιμονίοις) exist. NonChristian Greeks used the term δαιμόνιον in a neutral sense for these gods.[78] Jews also considered δαίμονες to be the great gods that Gentiles revered.[79] For Paul, these beings were not "gods" in the Gentile sense of benevolent beings deserving of deference and worship. They did exist, but not as that which the Gentiles were duped into thinking they

---

Cf. Jer 10:10. The term אלילים is a diminutive form, related to אלוהים. The "dumb idols" (אלילים אלמים) of Hab 2:18 convey the notion of ignorance, without knowledge. Cf. Isa 56:10 for the figures of false prophecy who are "dumb dogs, unable to bark" (כלבים אלמים לא יוכלו לבנח). In reality, these figures spoke, but the content of their speech was not true knowledge.

[76] Hence, Paul's language in 1 Cor 8:5, εἰσὶν λεγόμενοι θεοί, "there are *so-called* gods."

[77] Friedrich Buschel, "εἴδωλον," *TDNT* 2. 378. Cf. Ps 95:5 [LXX]; 105:37 [LXX]; Isa 65:3,11 [LXX]. Hays (*First Corinthians*, 169) observes that Paul's source, Deut 32:17, refers to Israel, not Gentiles (ἔθνη), that is accused of sacrificing to demons.

[78] See Acts 17:18. Only here in the NT is δαιμόνιον used in the Greek sense of deity or divinity, whether good or bad, and not in the Jewish or Christian sense of demons as evil spirits.

[79] See Ps 95:5 [LXX], πάντες οἱ θεοὶ τῶν ἐθνῶν δαιμόνια, "all of the gods of the Gentiles are demons."

were.[80] Likewise, Jews and early Christians believed that δαίμονες were not the all-powerful gods who looked over Gentile nations with good intentions.[81] The δαίμονες were nefarious, deceitful πνεύματα, "spirit beings,"that communicated demonic doctrines (cf. *T. Jud.* 23:1; 1 Tim 4:1–2). Paul concurs with this,[82] but he does not provide additional information on the relationship between demons and idols.

Some evidence suggests that an empirically perceptible relationship existed between demons and idols in antiquity. One of the earliest forms of this relationship is found in the oracle of Dodona, whose prophetic medium was that of an oak tree. According to Herbert William Parke, the oak at Dodona was considered by Greeks from Homeric times onward to be an inanimate object through which the god exerted his power: "The notion of a supernatural spirit dwelling in a tree, but distinct from it, was very early established in Greece."[83] Parke states that in Homer and in all early Greek writers the oak is described as "speaking," implying that it "uttered Zeus' prophecies in human language."[84] Parke presents the testimony of a sixteenth-century author, Erasmus Stella, whose descriptions of Indo-European beliefs in "talking oaks" provide, according to Parke, a good account of like practices at Dodona:

Trees of exceptional height such as the oaks, they said, the gods dwelt in, from which, when they made inquiries, replies were heard to be given. On this account they used never to cut this kind of tree, but worshiped them piously as the homes of supernatural powers.[85]

In the first-century C.E. Palestinian Jewish text *L.A.B.* 25:9 Pseudo-Philo describes the sin of idolatry perpetrated by the tribe of Issachar. This text gives explicit evidence for communication with intelligent demons through idols:

---

[80] Garland (*1 Corinthians*) suggests this by stating, "While denying the existence of pagan gods, he [Paul] affirms the reality of virulent spiritual powers that are enemies of God" (p. 480). Paul does not necessarily deny the existence of pagan gods; he denies their benevolence and their identity given to them by Gentiles, but he does not deny their power.

[81] See Bar 4:7; *Jub.* 11:4; and Justin Martyr, *First Apology*, 5: "And not knowing that these were demons, they called them gods, and gave to each the name which each of the demons chose for himself" (ANF 1. 164).

[82] See Garland (*1 Corinthians*): "For Paul, demons are very real and exert formidable power to defile and destroy humans" (p. 480).

[83] Herbert William Parke, *The Oracles of Zeus: Dodona, Olympia, Ammon* (Cambridge, MA: Harvard University Press, 1967) 26.

[84] Ibid., 27. So Weinel (*Wirkungen*, 8): ". . . und aus dem Rauschen der Eichen in Dodona flüstern auch für ihn Geisterstimmen, nur sind es nicht gute Götter, die da reden."

[85] Parker, *Oracles*, 22–23.

"We desired to make inquiry through the demons of the idols, whether or not they would reveal things plainly."[86]

In like manner, Christian apologists described idols as media through which demons communicated in audible voices. The second-century Christian apologist Athenagoras writes of a statue in Troad that was witnessed by others to "utter oracles."[87] He speaks of other statues, statues of Alexander and Proteus, the latter of which is "likewise said to utter oracles."[88] The powers behind the statues are demons: "They who draw men to idols, then, are the aforesaid demons."[89] Minucius Felix, fl. between 160 and 300, writes of impure spirits who "hide themselves in the statues and consecrated images, and by the afflatus they give forth acquire with men the authority of a present deity . . . uttering oracles."[90] Cyprian, 200–258, writes similarly: "They are impure and wandering spirits . . . these spirits, therefore, are lurking under the statues and consecrated images: these . . . give efficiency to oracles."[91] Tertullian notes that idols are the property of "demons and unclean spirits"; these spirits are the "proprietors of idols."[92] The *Clementine Homilies* also provide evidence for idols as media through which spirits expressed themselves. A divine spirit does not inhabit an idol, but rather a demon: "For the image is neither a living creature, nor has it a divine spirit, but the demon that appeared abused the form."[93] Elsewhere, idols are described as deceptive forms of spirit communication:

For many say, We do not worship the gold or the silver, the wood or the stone, of the objects of our worship. For we also know that these are nothing but lifeless matter, and the art of mortal men. But the spirit that *dwells in them*, that we call God. Behold the immorality of those who speak thus! For when that which appears is easily proved to be nothing, they have recourse to the invisible, . . . It remains for them to show how we are to believe that these images have a divine spirit.[94]

---

[86] Cf. Frederick J. Murphy, "Retelling the Bible: Idolatry in Pseudo-Philo," *JBL* 107 (1988) 275–87.

[87] Athenagoras, *A Plea for Christians*, 26. ANF 2. 143.

[88] Ibid.

[89] Ibid.

[90] Minucius Felix, *Octavius*, 27. ANF 4. 190.

[91] Cyprian, *Treatises*, 6.6–7. ANF 5. 467.

[92] Tertullian, *On Idolatry*, 1. ANF 3. 61.

[93] *Clementine Homilies* 9.15. ANF 8. 278.

[94] *Clementine Homilies* 10.21. ANF 8. 283 (emphasis mine).

This evidence suggests that inanimate cultic objects, in and of themselves, were nothing (i.e., they were "lifeless") apart from the gods and spirits that operated through them (hence, Paul's statement οὐδὲν εἴδωλον ἐν κόσμῳ, "an idol is nothing at all" [1 Cor 8:4]).[95] An idol as an inanimate object of wood or stone was not the significance of idolatry. Rather, the utility of idols as media for communicating with the spirit world seems to have been the basis for their allure in antiquity. Paul might have had a similar notion of the relationship between demons and idols.[96]

Paul's epithet for the idols in 1 Cor 12:2, ἄφωνα, "mute" or "without voice," was not only a literal fact that an inanimate object, in and of itself, lacks the power for speech, but also was a rhetorical term of derision meant to ridicule the "doctrines" of the demons of the idols.[97] Those spirits that communicated through idols were incapable of providing true Christian knowledge, for the demons of the idols were spirits who did not recognize Jesus as *their* "Lord" (see 1 Cor 10:21).[98] Hence, the content of their communication yielded nothing according to the gospel, for the gospel was based on Jesus as Lord by virtue of his risen from the dead[99]; the demons of the idols were "silent" or "without a voice" on the matter of the gospel.[100]

The term πνεῦμα in v. 3 shares an analogous relationship with v. 2, wherein

---

[95] See BAGD, 221: "Even the pagan knows that the images of the gods are lifeless. Artem. 4, 36 ταῦτα οὐ ζῇ."

[96] Kistemaker (*1 Corinthians*) suggests that Paul's emphasis in 1 Cor 8:4 and 10:19 "is not on the wooden or stone object that the pagans revere as their idol but on the concept of *idolatry*. And that concept is much broader, because it embodies the worship of demons that are represented by an idol. Although an idol in itself is nothing, the demons that induce people to worship an idol are powerful" (p. 347, emphasis his). Weinel (*Wirkungen*, 11) notes that those who used idols as media for spirits "witnessed and experienced . . . and received proof of the existence of a mysterious world of spirit beings lying beyond these occurrences . . . mightier, wiser, and also more ruthless than human kind" (translation mine). Among Christians, the spirits of the idols were also known as νεκροὶ θεοί, "dead gods." See *Did.* 6:3 and 2 Clement 3:1. The phrase "dead gods" means severed or cut off from the "living" God of the Christians.

[97] Although BAGD, s.v., defines ἄφωνος here as "silent" and "mute," the second entry, "incapable of conveying meaning," might equally apply rhetorically to ἄφωνα in v. 2. For demons who "teach" see 1 Tim 4:1.

[98] Kistemaker (*1 Corinthians*) states for 1 Cor 10:21 that, "The Lord and demons stand diametrically opposed to each other. . . . The Corinthians must choose between Christ and Satan" (p. 348); and Collins (*First Corinthians*) who states, "To participate in idol worship is, implicitly, to deny the sovereignty of the Lord Jesus" (p. 381).

[99] See 1 Cor 15:1–19.

[100] See Isa 44:18; 1 Cor 10:14; and 2 Cor 6:16. This follows Mehat ("L'enseignement," 405, 408) who argues that εἴδωλα in v. 2 is the key term for the Corinthians' prior ignorance of the true teaching in v. 3. See 1 Cor 2:10–16 where the gospel is given by "a spirit" of God.

the "Kontrastbegriff" of πνεῦμα in v. 2 might be δαιμόνιον implied in the term εἴδωλα.[101] The terms ἔθνος, δαιμόνιον, and εἴδωλον are intertextually and contextually linked. In Ps 95:5 [LXX] a relationship between ἔθνος and δαιμόνιον is established. In 1 Cor 10:20 Paul links δαιμόνιον with εἴδωλον. In 1 Cor 12:2 Paul describes the Corinthians' former religious persuasion as ἔθνη who were led to εἴδωλα. If Paul meant by εἴδωλα in 12:2 media through which δαίμονες communicated (tacitly alluded to in 10:20), then the "both analogy-and-contrast" relationship between vv. 2 and 3 comes into sharper focus. Demons were the spirits (πνεύματα)[102] that communicated through idols with the Corinthians when they were "Gentiles." This is not only analogous to v. 3 where a spirit (πνεῦμα) is said to speak, but also contrasts with a "holy" spirit and a spirit "of God" in v. 3.

6. 1 Cor 12:3: Christian Spiritism

Whereas v. 2 is an allusion to the Corinthians' former communications with the spirit world of demons (εἴδωλα), in v. 3 Paul focuses their attention (διὸ γνωρίζω ὑμῖν, "therefore, I want you to know") on communicating with spirit beings of a higher order; a spirit world inhabited by holy spirits[103] whose allegiance is to Jesus (Κύριος Ἰησοῦς). Verses 2 and 3 form a precarious relationship. But one matter is clear. Verse 2 relates the Corinthians' knowledge of their past (οἴδατε ὅτι ὅτε ἔθνη ἦτε, "you know that when you were Gentiles"). By means of the conjunction διό, "therefore," "for this reason," v. 3 is linked with v. 2. Paul informs the Corinthians on a matter in v. 3 vis-à-vis (διό) vv. 1 and 2.

In v. 3 the risen Jesus is confessed as "Lord" by someone ἐν πνεύματι ἁγίῳ

---

[101] Vos ("Das Rätsel") states, "Im Kontrast zu v. 3 kann man . . . die Dämonen als Subjekt denken" (p. 265). This need not imply ecstatic speech or trances experienced by the participating idol worshipers. Contra Fee (*First Epistle to the Corinthians*, 578) who argues for inspired speech reminiscent of pagan cults behind v. 2. The sacrifices made to the idols served as the "fuel" that allowed the demons to become manifest and produce voices from the idols. The Greek πομπή might be behind v. 2 as Paige ("Pagan *Pompe?*") suggests. But the main point seems to be the demons who led the Corinthians into communicating with them in former times.

[102] The terms πνεῦμα and δαιμόνιον are identical in Matt 8:16; 12:45; Luke 9:39; 10:20; 11:26. Demons were spirits of an evil and pernicious order.

[103] In v. 3, "holy spirit" is singular, but see 1 Cor 14:12,32, where "spirits" is plural and, arguably, refers to "holy spirits." "Holy spirit" in v. 3 is anarthrous and can imply "a holy spirit," or one of many.

λαλῶν, "speaking in a holy spirit." This confession is often times construed as a personal profession of faith. The person who makes this confession is thought to "have the Holy Spirit," yet the person speaks "out of his own heart."[104] Stevan L. Davies observes that this sort of description for one who speaks "in a spirit" is not informed by first-century religious experience but rather by twentieth century theology:

The terminologies of present-day historical and theological usage implicitly give individual human egos control and power over the spirit. Those who possess or who are empowered by the spirit maintain supremacy over the 'spirit' they experience. Current terminology does not imply 'not I but the spirit,' but, rather, I possess or I have or I experience or I am empowered by the spirit and 'I' am ultimately in charge. . . . The idea of inspiration in New Testament scholarship is more of a romantic theory of artistic and poetic inspiration than a pre-modern idea of spirit-possession.[105]

The confession "Jesus is Lord," indeed, appears in the NT as a Christian's personal confession in recognition of the risen Jesus as "Lord." In this context, Paul clearly describes the individual who, by his/her own profession of faith, confesses the lordship of Jesus: ὁμολογήσῃς ἐν τῷ στόματί σου κύριον Ἰησοῦν, "you confess with your mouth Jesus is Lord" (Rom 10:9). The confession here is almost indistinguishable in form from the confession in 1 Cor 12:3 with one exception: whereas in Rom 10:9 "Jesus is Lord" is confessed ἐν τῷ στόματι, "with the mouth" of a Christian, in 1 Cor 12:3 "Jesus is Lord" is confessed ἐν πνεύματι ἁγίῳ, "with a holy spirit." The former indicates a personal confession of faith on the basis of individual belief and commitment.[106] The latter indicates that "a spirit" makes the confession.[107]

Some scholars do not interpret speaking ἐν πνεύματι in v. 3 as the speech of

---

[104] So Grudem, *Gift of Prophecy*, 173: "12.3b represents a confession of faith made possible only by the enabling work of the Holy Spirit. . . . The speaker is speaking out of his own heart"; Kistemaker, *1 Corinthians*, 415; and Hays, *First Corinthians*, 208.

[105] Davies, *Jesus the Healer*, 23.

[106] The personal commitment of the confessor is further reinforced in Rom 10:9 where Paul states that belief in Jesus' resurrection from the dead occurs ἐν τῇ καρδίᾳ σου, "in your heart."

[107] Dunn (*Baptism in the Holy Spirit: A Re-examination of the New Testament Teaching on the Gift of the Spirit in Relation to Pentecostalism Today* [SBT 2/5; Naperville: Allenson, 1970]) comes close to this: Paul is "obviously not thinking of a mere statement of a proposition (for anyone could say the words), but of an inspired or ecstatic utterance which did not originate in the individual's own rational consciousness" (p. 151).

a foreign spirit temporarily making use of the person's vocal chords.[108] Their focus tends to be placed on whether the prepositional phrase suggests prophetic ecstasy.[109] The premise for this focus is usually based on the argument that the confession "Jesus is Lord" is not a prophetic utterance but rather a confession of faith.[110] The crucial term in v. 3 is neither προφητεύω nor ἔκστασις but ἐν πνεύματι. Admittedly, these three expressions overlap conceptually in some contexts (see Philo, *Her.* 265). Arguments for prophetic ecstasy in v. 3 imply that comparisons can be made between it and v. 2. But, as stated earlier, the language of v. 2 does not support ecstatic speech or trance states. Arguments against ecstasy in v. 3 are implicitly made on polemical grounds of second- and third-century Christian views that Christian prophets do not speak in a trance state.[111]

An interpretation of speaking ἐν πνεύματι ἁγίῳ in v. 3 should be made from the phrase itself rather than on possible implications for prophetic ecstasy. The preposition ἐν is usually translated as instrumental "in" or "by" so that one is said to speak "in/by the Spirit." This is a common translation of the Greek text.[112] It implies that the actual speaker is the person who speaks from his own faculties by the "power of the Spirit." Such language is not fully defined by scholars beyond the qualifications that someone "has the Holy Spirit" or is "moved by the Holy Spirit." The "Holy Spirit" here is usually understood to be

---

[108] Fee (*First Epistle*) mixes language for possession and personal confession: "One who is *possessed by the Spirit* of the living God is led to the ultimate Christian confession: 'Jesus is Lord.' . . . only one who *has the Spirit* can truly make such a confession" (p. 582, emphasis mine); and Grudem, *Gift of Prophecy*, who states, "Paul did not envisage the speaker to be completely controlled by the Holy Spirit . . . The words he speaks are his own and we should not suppose that they could be taken as the Holy Spirit's words" (p. 173).

[109] So Grudem, *Gift of Prophecy*, 172–76, who concludes that in the NT "prophets do not seem to have had ecstatic experiences while prophesying" (p. 176).

[110] So Garland, *1 Corinthians*, 567: "Paul does not say anything about 'evidences of ecstasy.' He does not mention 'prophetic utterances' or how to judge them. 'Jesus is Lord' is the basic confession made by every Christian and is not a prophetic utterance."

[111] Cf. Eusebius, *Eccl. Hist.* 5.17.3, where the work of a certain Miltiades (or Alcibiades?) is mentioned: περὶ τοῦ μὴ δεῖν προφήτην ἐν ἐκστάσει λαλεῖν, "concerning the prophet who should not speak in ecstasy." Callan ("Prophecy and Ecstasy," 139) argues on the basis of this evidence that NT prophecy did not involve trance.

[112] So Moffatt, *First Epistle*, 178; Barrett, *First Epistle*, 279; Bruce, *1 and 2 Corinthians*, 118; Morris, *1 Corinthians*, 165; Harrisville, *1 Corinthians*, 206; Soards, *1 Corinthians*, 255; Kistemaker, *1 Corinthians*, 414; Wolff, *Der erste Brief*, 282; Hays, *First Corinthians*, 208–209; Collins, *First Corinthians*, 448; Thiselton, *First Epistle*, 907, who renders "through the agency of the Holy Spirit"; Garland, *1 Corinthians*, 561; Johnson, *1 Corinthians*, 218; and Keener, *1–2 Corinthians*, 99. This follows most English versions.

some impersonal force of God that empowers a person to utter "Jesus is Lord" in his or her own right.[113] By capitalizing "holy spirit" in this text, the theology of the Holy Spirit is implicitly invoked as well as all else that belongs to the orthodox view of "the Spirit" and how it was understood to function in the church, most notably through the normal faculties of a prophet and not through trance (see n. 111 above). Elsewhere in the NT, that is, in Mark 1:23 and 5:2, the prepositional phrase ἐν πνεύματι, under Semitic influence, expresses a spirit phenomenon that might depict more accurately that which is found here in v. 3 than the interpretation "has the Holy Spirit."

Mark 1:23 and 5:2 record ἄνθρωπος ἐν πνεύματι ἀκαθάρτῳ, "a man with an unclean spirit." The prepositional phrase ἐν πνεύματι rendered as "*with* a spirit" follows the Hebrew and Aramaic preposition בְּ, "with" or "having."[114] The meaning is: the man is "possessed" by the unclean spirit.[115] In the gospels, other idioms for demonic possession are ἔχειν δαιμόνιον, "to have a demon,"[116] and δαιμονίζομαι, "to be possessed by a demon."[117] In the NT, as evidenced in the gospels, there existed contempt for such possession. But this phenomenon was not restricted to demons. The term πνεῦμα is applicable to both orders of spirits, good and evil, in the NT. Both orders of spirits produced similar effects, thus the activity of a demon or a good spirit could be expressed as ἐν πνεύματι.[118]

---

[113] See Montague, *Holy Spirit*, who states, "The Holy Spirit is therefore already present in anyone who makes this confession, even if the charisms are not yet in great evidence" (p. 147).

[114] See Num 20:20; Josh 22.8; Judg 11:34; and Dan 5:2. For רוח ב (= ἐν πνεύματι) see 1QHᵃ 12, 11–13; 16.2, 11–12; 17. 6–7; 1QS 3. 6–8. See BDF §198.

[115] Throughout the narrative the spirit is shown to be inside the man. See vv. 8,15,16,18. Many English versions translate "with an unclean spirit": *KJV, ASV, NIV, NIB, NAS, NAU, RSV, NRS, NKJ, DRA, BBE, NJB*. Cf. *DBY* and *NLT*: "possessed by an unclean spirit," and *NAB*: "had an unclean spirit."

[116] Matt 11:18; Luke 4:33; 7:33; and 8:27.

[117] Matt 4:24; 8:16,28; 9:32; Mark 1:32; and Luke 8:36.

[118] Cf. the works of Gunkel, Weinel, Hopwood, Dunn, and Levison in the survey of Chapter Two. Note also that the prepositional phrase ἐν πνεύματι is used in visionary episodes wherein the human spirit leaves the body during a vision experience: Rev 1:10, 4:2 ἐγενόμην ἐν πνεύματι, "I was in the spirit," i.e., "I entered into the spirit world"; and 17:3, 21:10 ἀπήνεγκέν με ... ἐν πνεύματι, "he carried me away ... in spirit." In 1 Cor 5:3 Paul can be "absent in body" (ἀπὼν τῷ σώματι) but "present in spirit" (παρὼν δὲ τῷ πνεύματι) among the Corinthians (see also Col 2:5). This has structural parallels with 2 Cor 12:2–4, where Paul speaks of a man being "in the body" or "out of the body" during his visionary ascent to the "third heaven" (see Joseph Osei-Bonsu, "Anthropological Dualism in the New Testament," *SJT* 40 [1987] 571–90, esp. 571–72 and 585–86). Visions though are not what Paul is speaking of in 1 Cor 12:3. The context here is ἐν πνεύματι λαλῶν, "one who speaks with (by means of) a spirit," i.e., prophetic speech. It is worth noting, however, the flexibility of the prepositional phrase ἐν πνεύματι for

The prepositional phrase in Mark 1:23 and 5:2 then functions similar to the phrases in 1 Cor 12:3, ἐν πνεύματι θεοῦ λαλῶν λέγει, "one who speaks *with* a spirit of God says," i.e., "one through whom a spirit of God is speaking says," and εἰπεῖν ἐν πνεύματι ἁγίῳ, "to speak *with* a holy spirit," i.e., "to speak while possessed by a holy spirit."[119]

Grammatically, the construction ἐν πνεύματι + λαλῶν is awkward.[120] The construction depicts two acts that occur simultaneously: (1) the participle λαλῶν, "one who speaks," conveys that the organs for speech, vocal chords, tongue, and mouth, produce utterance; and (2) this occurs by the temporary possession by a spirit of God who activates the organs for speech and speaks in its own person through the medium of a physical organism, ἐν πνεύματι θεοῦ λέγει, "*with* a spirit of God says."

Maximillian Zerwick interprets the preposition ἐν in both Mark 5:2 and 1 Cor 12:3 as "with" ("sociative" ἐν).[121] This interpretation is referenced and defined by him: "One might explain the preposition as meaning that man [in Mark 5:2] was in the power of the spirit."[122] Whereas Mark 5:2 shows a "performance of the involuntary function of spirit mediumship,"[123] 1 Cor 12:3 gives evidence for a performance of the voluntary function of spirit mediumship within an established Christian community that communicates with the spirit world. Willem Berends explains the difference between the two:

---

describing two phenomena: (1) possession by spirits; and (2) visionary experiences while absent from body. In the former, πνεύματι refers to a foreign spirit. In the latter, πνεύματι refers to the human spirit, the spirit world into which the human spirit enters, or both.

[119] Even though the majority of English versions render 1 Cor 12:3 as "in" or "by the Spirit of God/ the Holy Spirit," many English versions translate the same grammatical form in 1 Cor 14:16, εὐλογῇς [ἐν] πνεύματι, as "you give a blessing *with* the spirit." Cf. *KJV, ASV, RSV, NRS, NKJ, DRA, DBY, BBE, NAB,* and *NJB*. For ברוח קודש (= ἐν πνεύματι ἁγίῳ) see 1QSb 2.24. Rabbinic literature includes many citations for persons who "speak in (with) a holy spirit" by using the prepositional phrase ברוח קודש (see Peter Schäfer, *Die Vorstellung vom heiligen Geist in der rabbinischen Literatur* [SANT 28; Munich: Kösel, 1972] 151–57, 161).

[120] See Parry, *First Epistle*, 176.

[121] Maximillian Zerwick, *A Grammatical Analysis of the Greek New Testament* (Rome: Pontifical Biblical Institute, 1996) 115, 552. See also Morton Smith, "Pauline Worship as Seen by Pagans," *HTR* 73 (1980) 241–49, who states that in 1 Cor 12:3 "if anyone speaking 'with a spirit' says 'Jesus is anathema,' that spirit is not 'of God'" (p. 245).

[122] Zerwick, *Biblical Greek* §116. Zerwick (ibid.) states further, "Thus ἐν (not without Semitic influence) is practically reduced to the expression of a general notion of association or accompaniment, which would be rendered in English by 'with': a man with an unclean spirit" (§117).

[123] So David E. Aune, "Demon; Demonology," *ISBE* 1. 922.

We have to distinguish between a demoniac and a medium. In the first case the possessed is an involuntary victim, in the second case the medium voluntarily allows another party to take over his vocal organs.[124]

The first case appears in Mark 5:2; the second case appears in 1 Cor 12:3, much like the phenomenon analyzed in Philo in Chapter Three of this book.[125] In both Mark 5:2 and 1 Cor 12:3 the prepositional phrase ἐν πνεύματι indicates that a foreign spirit is speaking from within the person: in Mark 5:2 an unclean spirit to be exorcized (cf. Mark 5:7–9); in 1 Cor 12:3 a spirit of God or a holy spirit to be heeded (λαλῶν λέγει, "one who speaks says").[126]

7. 1 Cor 12:3: The Holy Spirit or a holy spirit

The use of πνεῦμα without the definite article in v. 3 is sometimes thought to indicate "a spirit." Fee devotes ten pages to this question, noting, "Some have suggested that when Paul does not use the definite article, he means something

---

[124] Willem Berends, "The Biblical Criteria for Demon-Possession," *WTJ* 37 (1975) 342–65, esp. 357. See further Samson Eitrem, *Some Notes on the Demonology in the New Testament* (2nd ed.; Oslo: Universitesforlaget, 1966) 50. The term "medium" is not restricted to demons or evil spirits despite what G. Campbell Morgan (*The Gospel According to Mark* [New York: Fleming H. Revell, 1927] 119) once stated, "The moment the word 'medium' is employed, the word 'demonized man' or 'demonized woman' may be substituted."

[125] Cf. *Her.* 266: "For the prophet, even when he seems to speak (λέγειν δοκεῖ), is really silent, and his organs of speech, mouth and tongue, are wholly in the employ of Another," i.e., a divine spirit. Whereas to all outward appearances the person so possessed is speaking, hence, the person "seems" (δοκεῖ) to speak. But the actual speaker is a foreign spirit that temporarily makes use of the vocal chords in the same way that the human spirit functions through the physical body.

[126] The phrase ἐν πνεύματι occurs in both a negative context where the spirit is an undesired inhabitant that is ideally exorcized from its victim, and a positive context where the spirit is a welcome inhabitant that prophesies through a prophet. Eric Sorensen (*Possession and Exorcism in the New Testament and Early Christianity* [WUNT 2/157; Tübingen: J. C. B. Mohr, 2002]) notes that even though possessing spirits were ideally exorcized, the prophecies of a good daemon in the Greek world "represent a useful resource to the community, and therefore [the prophet] is not subject to exorcism," and "There is no occasion where an attempt is made to divest a prophet of his art" (p. 95). So too Padel ("Model for Possession," 14) who states that in Greek culture, "Divinity can be an unwelcome guest in a house and a female body. But it may be a welcome guest in a female body and mind when it is useful to society, i.e. in prophetic possession." This can be said of the difference between Mark 5:2 and 1 Cor 12:3. In the former, exorcism is necessary, but in the latter the possessing spirit is a good spirit who speaks on behalf of God; exorcism is not necessary.

closer to 'a spirit,' intending a sort of divine influence or 'a spirit from God,' but something less than personality, and probably not the Holy Spirit."[127] After an analysis of many Pauline spirit texts, Fee concludes that Paul never knew of "a holy spirit," but that Paul "only and always means the Spirit of the living God, the Holy Spirit himself,"[128] thus revealing a Trinitarian commitment for the interpretation of Paul.

Other scholars have noted that the anarthrous form πνεῦμα in v. 3 can mean "a holy spirit" in accord with Greek grammar.[129] Several of these scholars (Parry, Lake, and Ellis) were mentioned in Chapter One. Swartz argues that the presence of the definite article indicates the Person of the Holy Spirit and the absence of the definite article indicates Holy Spirit as God-given power.[130] "Holy Spirit" without the Greek article τό did not merely indicate an impersonal power. A holy spirit was an intelligent sentient spirit personality who was "set apart unto God" (i.e., ἅγιον, "holy") from other sentient spirits.[131]

As an argument for the definiteness of the anarthrous form πνεῦμα θεοῦ the Hebrew construct chain רוח אלוהים is sometimes invoked as the direct grammatical correspondence to the Greek πνεῦμα θεοῦ. The characteristic feature of the syntax of the Hebrew construct chain is that if the second element in the chain is definite, then the first noun has a definite reference without an affixed Hebrew article ה. If an indefinite reference is indicated by the first noun, then the construct chain is broken up with a ל affixed to the proper noun in the construct chain.[132]

This does not follow in Greek grammar where anarthrous πνεῦμα θεοῦ can

---

[127] Fee, *God's Empowering Presence*, 15.

[128] Ibid., 24.

[129] See BDF §257.

[130] Swartz, "The Holy Spirit," 136–37. Sometimes, the phrases "the Spirit of God" and "the Holy Spirit" are thought to express one nuance of difference. "The Spirit of God" is the Spirit that comes from God, and "the Holy Spirit" is sanctifying power of God. See Collins, *First Corinthians*, 448. The Greek phrases πνεύματι θεοῦ and πνεύματι ἁγίῳ, however, refer to the same reality. "A spirit of God" (πνεύματι θεοῦ) is "a spirit set apart unto God" (πνεύματι ἁγίῳ, where the adjective ἅγιον, "holy," means "consecrated to God" or "set apart unto God."). See Isaacs (*Concept of Spirit*, 97): "In 1 Cor 12:3 ἐν πνεύματι θεοῦ is synonymous with ἐν πνεύματι ἁγίῳ."

[131] Grudem (*Gift of Prophecy*, 284–85) rightly states that in their most common sense in the NT the terms πνεῦμα and πνεύματα refer to spirit beings.

[132] Paul Joüon, *A Grammar of Biblical Hebrew* (trans. T. Muraoka; 2 vols.; SB 14/II; Rome: Pontifical Biblical Institute, 1996) 2.§130b.

arguably at times mean "a spirit of God" and not "*the* spirit of God."[133]   In Hebrew, the use of רוח without the article would have likewise been understood as "a spirit" in some contexts (1 Sam 18:10 and Judg 9:23). The use of the article can also have a generic sense as הרוח in 1 Kgs 22:21 indicates. Here, "the spirit" refers to "a certain spirit" from among other spirits mentioned earlier in v. 19 (כל־צבא השמים, "the whole host of heaven") and v. 20 (ויאמר זה בכה), וזה אמר בכה, "and one [spirit] said this, another [spirit] that").[134]

In 1 Sam 16:14 the Hebrew construct chain רוח יהוה is arguably definite due to the use of a proper noun, יהוה, as the second element of the chain. This chain is broken up in the following phrase of the same verse רוח־רעה מאת יהוה, "an evil spirit from the Lord." Both phrases in the LXX lack the article in fidelity to the Hebrew text. But one wonders how informed the typical Greek-speaking Jew was of Hebrew syntax when reading the Greek πνεῦμα κυρίου.[135] From a Greek point of view this phrase is indefinite in meaning: "a spirit of the Lord." It seems possible that if the translators of the LXX wanted to convey the meaning of the Hebrew construct chain, they might have taken the liberty of adding the article to convey the meaning "*the* spirit of the Lord" just as they take the liberty to delete the article in 1 Kgs 22:21 [LXX] in order to convey the meaning of the Hebrew, "a [certain] spirit."[136]

A translation of the anarthrous dative πνεύματι as "a spirit," implying one of many, is as warranted in 1 Cor 12:3 as it is in Mark 5:2. Translators of English versions introduce theological suppositions when they translate the anarthrous phrase ἐν πνεύματι ἁγίῳ as definite and capitalized, "in *the* Holy Spirit," while the equally anarthrous phrase ἐν πνεύματι ἀκαθάρτῳ remains indefinite in

---

[133] "The spirit of God" is τὸ πνεῦμα τοῦ θεοῦ. The translation of the indefinite πνεῦμα θεοῦ as "God's Spirit" is a poor attempt to maintain the element of numerical singularity. Grammatically, if one wanted to render the phrase with an apostrophe showing possession then the indefinite would read "one of God's spirits" and not "God's Spirit." If one chooses the latter, then one might more appropriately say "God's spirit world."

[134] Unlike the Hebrew text, the LXX lacks the article with πνεῦμα, conveying, nevertheless, the meaning of the Hebrew, "a [certain] spirit."

[135] Similarly, see Jan N. Sevenster, *Do You Know Greek?: How Much Greek Could the First Jewish Christians Have Known?* (Leiden: Brill, 1968). Arguably, the Jewish translators of the LXX would have been an exception.

[136] The term אלהים is not necessarily a proper noun. The term יהוה is a proper noun. The occurrence of רוח in construct with both of these terms in the OT presents a challenge for translation. Whereas, arguably, רוח יהוה is "*the* spirit of the Lord," רוח אלהים is "*a* spirit of God." We cannot always be this pedantic about the article, though, for in some contexts, "*a* spirit of the Lord" is warranted (see 1 Sam 16:14).

translation, "with *an* unclean spirit."[137] Zerwick explains that this supposition is not necessary:

> Some may perhaps be apprehensive lest we reduce to banality certain Pauline formulae . . . , by putting ἐν πνεύματι and the like in the same class, philologically, with ἐν πνεύματι ἀκαθάρτῳ. Such apprehension is unfounded.[138]

Edward Lee Beavin observes that those who try to distinguish between "the Holy Spirit" and "a holy spirit" (e.g., Fee, nn. 127, 128 above) are unable to "clear their minds of the hypostasis prejudice," i.e., reading later Christian theology of the Holy Spirit as a Person into πνεῦμα in Paul.[139] He argues that in Wis 1:5 the English translations of the anarthrous πνεῦμα ἅγιον as "the Holy Spirit" betray this prejudice, whereas those that translate as "a holy spirit" led Beavin to conclude that "a holy spirit and the holy spirit are the same thing. Both phrases designate a spirit placed in man by God."[140]

Furthermore, both "holy spirit" and "evil spirit" are written with the definite article in the NT: τὸ πνεῦμα τὸ ἅγιον, "the holy spirit"(Acts 10:44) and τὸ πνεῦμα τὸ πονηρόν, "the evil spirit" (Acts 19:15). Admittedly, in each instance

---

[137] See Swartz, "The Holy Spirit," 125: "By long-standing tradition, such references are capitalized, and even with the anarthrous references, the translations almost invariably translate with the English definite, '*the* Holy Spirit.'" Jason David BeDuhn (*Truth in Translation: Accuracy and Bias in English Translations of the New Testament* [Lanham, MD: University Press of America, 2003] 135–60) observes that many English translations do not distinguish between the articular and anarthrous forms of "spirit." With regard to the anarthrous form some "translation teams make a habit of changing the wording 'a holy spirit' or 'holy spirit' into 'the Holy Spirit,' apparently so uncomfortable with the indefiniteness of the expression . . ." (p. 139). BeDuhn concludes, "In our survey of the use of 'spirit' in the New Testament, . . . The translators of all of the versions we are comparing allowed theological bias to interfere with their accuracy" (p. 159).

[138] Zerwick, *Biblical Greek*, §118.

[139] Edward Lee Beavin, "Ruah Hakodesh in Some Early Jewish Literature" (Ph.D. diss., Vanderbilt University, 1961) 23.

[140] Ibid. Note similarly that the *NAB* translates 2 Cor 6:6, ἐν πνεύματι ἁγίῳ as "in a holy spirit," whereas most other English versions have "in the Holy Spirit." The *NAB* provides evidence that, grammatically, ἐν πνεύματι ἁγίῳ can be translated as "in a holy spirit." Beavin (ibid.) states that "Christians [i.e., contemporary Christians] attach considerable importance to the distinction between 'The Holy Spirit' and 'a holy spirit.'" But this distinction is borne out of a perspective that sees πνεῦμα in reference to "holy spirit" in the NT through the lens of Christian theology of the Holy Spirit. To Jews and Christians of the first century "the holy spirit" and "a holy spirit" denoted the same spiritual reality because there were many holy spirits. The phrase "the holy spirit" may be a certain spirit or a generic reference to a collective plurality.

the definite article reflects context. "The evil spirit" is "a certain spirit," an anaphoric use of the article that refers to "the evil spirits" mentioned earlier in v. 13. "The holy spirit" in Acts 10:44 is a general reference to the manifestation of the holy spirit world much like that seen in Acts 2:4 where individual spirits, "a holy spirit," are mentioned.

8. 1 Cor 12:1–3: A Translation and Explanation

A translation of 1 Cor 12:1–3 becomes necessary at this point. Paul begins his discourse as follows:

> ¹Now concerning spiritism, brothers, I do not want you to be ignorant. ²You know that when you were Gentiles you were led to [communicate with spirit beings through] mute idols,[141] as often as you were impelled to do so. ³For this reason, I want you to know that nobody through whom a spirit of God is speaking can say, 'Jesus is accursed,' and only a holy spirit speaking through someone can say 'Jesus is Lord.'

One might translate v. 1a as "Now concerning communication with the spirit world." But for the sake of fidelity to Paul's pithy text the term "spiritism" conveys this meaning adequately. The liberties taken in the translation of v. 2 are substantiated in part 5 above that discussed spirits who operated through idols; spirits that Gentiles worshiped as gods but that Christians recognized and feared as demons. Verse 3 expresses two lines of thought: (1) the Corinthians' present experiences with spirits as Christians; and (2) the knowledge of a holy spirit world of God that they did not have as ἔθνη. This second point is implicitly made back in v. 2. In v. 2 the οἴδατε . . . ἦτε phrase reminds the Corinthian Christians of their former communications with spirits as unenlightened Gentiles. Verse 3 informs them of their present devotion to communication with spirits as enlightened Christians. One might rightly ask whether the information in v. 3 is a reinforcement of Paul's teaching from a previous missionary visit or if it was meant to inform new Gentile converts at Corinth who had been accepted into the fold since Paul's departure from Corinth.

Verse 3 is sometimes understood to be a "rule of thumb" for discerning spirits by the two confessions for Jesus.[142] Unless matters at Corinth had

---

[141] The term εἴδωλα in v. 2 implies δαίμονες in light of the relationship Paul makes between the two terms in 1 Cor 10:19–20.

[142] Maly, "Unterscheidung der Geister?" 82–95.

degenerated to the lowest of levels, the confession "Jesus is anathema" is seemingly too obvious a point about which Christians should be enlightened (despite Paul's insistent remark, "I want you to know"). If v. 3 was meant to inform Corinthians about how to discern evil spirits from holy spirits, then the verse does not provide a complete procedure for such discernment: that of detecting a deceitful spirit. The question arises: What if a lying spirit masquerades as a holy spirit by saying "Jesus is Lord"? Paul was undoubtedly privy to such a scenario. In 2 Cor 11:14 he claims that "Satan masquerades as an angel of light." In 1 Cor 12:10 he casually mentions "discernment of spirits." Thus, v. 3 would seem to be only a part of a more detailed account for discerning spirits (if discernment is meant here). That detail, i.e., the procedures for detecting lying spirits, is lacking.

Some see in the confession "Jesus is anathema" a tacit allusion to demonic utterance.[143] Paul never mentions πνεῦμα πονηρόν, "an evil spirit," or δαιμόνιον, "a demon," in v. 3.[144] He only refers to "a spirit of God" and "a holy spirit": "a spirit of God" cannot say "Jesus is anathema," and only "a holy spirit" can say "Jesus is Lord." The two confessions do not provide evidence for what an evil spirit might say as opposed to what a good spirit might say. Instead, the two confessions provide a contrast between what a holy spirit might and might not say about Jesus.[145] In this way Paul conveys the relationship between a spirit set apart unto God ("a holy spirit") and the risen Jesus; only these spirits can honestly confess Jesus is Lord as a sign for the congregation of the spirit's allegiance to Jesus.[146]

The idea that "a spirit of God," an otherwise Jewish expression (רוח אלהים, πνεῦμα θεοῦ), may acclaim Jesus as "Lord" seems unusually non-Jewish in the

---

[143] See Moffatt, *First Epistle*, 179; Barrett, *First Epistle*, "There were other spirits capable of inspiring speech" (p. 279); Conzelmann, *1 Corinthians*, 205; Collins, *First Corinthians*, 446; Wolff, *Der erste Brief*, 285; and Ekem, "'Spiritual Gifts' or 'Spiritual Persons,'" 65.

[144] Thiselton (*First Epistle*, 966) argues that Paul never uses the term πνεῦμα for an "evil spirit." But see the use of πνεῦμα in 1 Cor 2:12, "the spirit of the world," 2 Cor 11:4, "another spirit," i.e., a spirit that is not, at least, holy, and the disputed Paulines, 1 Tim 4:1, "deceitful spirits" who teach "demonic instructions," and Eph 6:12, "evil spiritual forces." Otherwise, Isaacs (*Concept of Spirit*, 106) states, "πνεῦμα is nowhere used of the demonic in Paul's letters."

[145] Garland (*1 Corinthians*) similarly states: Paul "does not appeal to this pronouncement to provide a criterion by which to judge spiritual utterances but to state an obvious fact with which they would readily agree: no one could say such a blasphemous thing under the inspiration of the Spirit" (p. 569).

[146] One might expect an evil spirit to curse Jesus. But the "discernment" and "testing of spirits" among early Christians shows that deceitful spirits must have been more savvy than to expose themselves in such an obvious way by cursing Jesus.

light of the reservation among Jews of the title "Lord" (מרא, אדון) for God. The roots of this may lie in Paul's personal experiences with the risen Jesus as "Lord" (Acts 9:1–19; 1 Cor 8:6; Gal 1:11–17). The spirit world of the Jews was, indeed, populated with "holy spirits" (רוחות קודש [Greek sg., πνεῦμα ἁγιωσύνης]) and "spirits of God" (רוחות אלהים [Greek sg., πνεῦμα θεοῦ]). The experiences of the earliest Christians revealed to them a spirit world wherein Jesus, as κύριος, held a position of all-powerful authority.[147] The spirits of this spirit world were "holy" insofar as they communicated their commitment to Jesus as "Lord." Thus, a clear Christian innovation in the Jewish conception of holy spirits emerges in a spirit's usage of a title for Jesus that raised Jesus to a level nearly on par with God: "Lord."[148]

The personal declaration of a spirit's devotion to Jesus as Lord was not unlike that found among human beings who expressed their commitment to Jesus with the same language (Rom 10:9). The pronouncement "Jesus is Lord" by a human medium was meant to indicate, although not always sufficiently enough, that a holy spirit had gained temporary control of the medium's vocal chords. Although this interpretation for v. 3 is unusual for NT scholarship, even emphatically denied at times,[149] spirits communicating intelligently with human beings is not unusual in the NT.

In Acts 16:18 Paul addresses a spirit that had been irritating him for several days through the mediumship of a slave girl: διαπονηθεὶς δὲ Παῦλος καὶ ἐπιστρέψας τῷ πνεύματι εἶπεν, "Paul became annoyed, turned, and *said to the spirit.*" Paul is interrogated before the Sanhedrin in Acts 23:9, some of whom speculate whether his knowledge might have been acquired from the spirit world: εἰ δὲ πνεῦμα ἐλάλησεν αὐτῷ ἢ ἄγγελος; "What if *a spirit* or an angel has *spoken to him?*" In Acts 19:13–17 Jewish priests attempt to exorcize a spirit from within a person by invoking the names of Jesus and Paul. The spirit is specifically described as being "in" the person (ὁ ἄνθρωπος [. . .] ἐν ᾧ ἦν τὸ πνεῦμα τὸ πονηρόν) through whose organism the possessing spirit responds to the Jewish exorcists: ἀποκριθὲν δὲ τὸ πνεῦμα τὸ πονηρὸν εἶπεν αὐτοῖς, "the evil spirit *answered* and *said to them.*"

---

[147] See Mehrdad Fatehi, *The Spirit's Relation to the Risen Lord in Paul: An Examination of Its Christological Implications* (WUNT 2/128; Tübingen: Mohr Siebeck, 2000) 174–76, 180–202.

[148] See Hurtado, "Religious Experience and Religious Innovation," 199. This innovation among Christians can also be seen in the designation of spirits who did not confess Jesus as "Christ." These spirits were known collectively as τὸ [πνεῦμα] τοῦ ἀντιχρίστου, "the [spirit] of antichrist" (see 1 John 4:3).

[149] So Grudem, *Gift of Prophecy*, 173.

In the NT the nouns πνεῦμα and δαιμόνιον are either the subject of the verb διδάσκω, "to teach," or qualified by its related adjectival form. One of the main tasks for the spirit world was to instruct Christians about Christ. In Luke 12:12 Jesus informs his disciples that when they are taken before synagogues, rulers, and authorities the holy spirit διδάξει ὑμᾶς ἐν αὐτῇ τῇ ὥρᾳ ἃ δεῖ εἰπεῖν, "*will teach you* at that moment what you should say." In John 14:26 Jesus informs his disciples that the holy spirit ὑμᾶς διδάξει πάντα καὶ ὑπομνήσει ὑμᾶς πάντα ἃ εἶπον ὑμῖν [ἐγώ], "*will teach you* everything and remind you of all that [I] told you." In 1 Cor 2:13 Paul claims that what he speaks comes not from the teachings of human beings but rather from teachings of the spirit world: οὐκ ἐν διδακτοῖς ἀνθρωπίνης σοφίας λόγοις ἀλλ᾽ ἐν διδακτοῖς πνεύματος, "not in words taught by human wisdom but with *words taught by a spirit*."[150] The author of 1 Tim 4:1 warns of the [holy] spirit world's prediction that many of the faithful will begin to heed deceitful spirits unawares and διδασκαλίαις δαιμονίων, "demonic instructions," i.e., "instructions *taught* by demons." The idea that a spirit "teaches" is also found outside of the NT.

In *Didache* 11 a prophet is one through whom spirits communicate. *Didache* 11:10 states that προφήτης διδάσκων τὴν ἀλήθειαν, "a prophet is *one who teaches* the truth." Presumably, this refers to the spirits that teach through a prophet since a prophet speaks ἐν πνεύματι, "with a spirit" (11:7,8,9). The church historian Eusebius records that the spirit who was speaking through Montanus had been dismissed as a holy spirit and declared a spirit of error and an arrogant spirit by the Catholic church because καθόλου καὶ πᾶσαν τὴν ὑπὸ τὸν οὐρανὸν ἐκκλησίαν βλασφημεῖν διδάσκοντος τοῦ ἀπηυθαδισμένου πνεύματος, "the arrogant spirit *taught* to blaspheme the whole Catholic church throughout the world."[151] The third- and fourth-century neo-Platonic author

---

[150] This, too, was an argument made by Justin Martry, *Hortatory to the Greeks* 8. ANF 1. 276. Paul's claim in 1 Cor 2:13 that his teachings were those "taught by a spirit" looks forward to 12:3, where a spirit confesses Jesus as "Lord" and, presumably, proceeds to communicate with those present, and 14:16 where a spirit says a blessing in a foreign language. Scholars have noted the prominence of πνεῦμα language in First Corinthians 2, 12, and 14. Some argue that 1 Cor 2:6–16 has significant parallels to the discussion of Christian prophecy in Chapters 12 and 14. See Thomas Gillespie, "Interpreting the Kerygma: Early Christian Prophecy according to 1 Corinthians 2:6-16," in *Gospel Origins and Christian Beginnings*: *Essays in Honor of James M. Robinson* (ed. J. Goehring, et al.; Sonoma, CA: Polebridge Press, 1990) 151–56; Karl O. Sandnes, *Paul – One of the Prophets*? *A Contribution to the Apostle's Self-Understanding* (WUNT 2/43; Tübingen: Mohr, 1991); and Hunt, *The Inspired Body*.

[151] Eusebius, *Eccl. Hist.* 5.16.9. Note that the spirit entered into Montanus and made use of the vocal chords in order to communicate its teaching, not unlike that seen above in the prepositional phrase ἐν πνεύματι ἁγίῳ, "with a holy spirit," in 1 Cor 12:3; 14:2,16.

Iamblichus uses the same language for different spirits that communicate with human beings: διδαχῇ μὲν γὰρ τῆς οἰκείας οὐσίας θεὸς καὶ ἄγγελος καὶ δαίμων ἀγαθὸς χρῆται πρὸς ἄνθρωπον, "a god, an angel and a good daemon *give instruction* about their proper essence to a human being."[152]

In sum, the term "spiritism" has the utility of conveying the idea of any spirit, good or evil, just as the Greek noun πνεῦμα is used for both orders of spirits (good and evil) in the NT; and, just as both orders of spirits were believed to have the capacity for didactic utterance. The use of the term "spiritism" as an introduction to Paul's exposition in 1 Cor 12:1a relates the general sense of "communication with the spirit world," either the good spirit world or the bad spirit world. Then, in vv. 2 and 3 Paul immediately distinguishes communication between the two spirit worlds: he contrasts Gentile spiritism in v. 2 with Christian spiritism in v. 3. Within Paul's stated contrast is an unspoken analogy between the activity of intelligent demons through the media of "idols" in v. 2 and the activity of holy spirits through the media of human beings in v. 3. In each instance, spirits communicated with an audible voice, either through an inanimate object or by the use of the vocal chords of a human medium.

The argument that Paul would not have been deliberately ambiguous by comparing like phenomena in vv. 2 and 3[153] misses the fact that from a dualistic perspective (deceitful spirits and truthful spirits) spirit phenomena were typically ambiguous.[154] The terse comments for "testing" or "discerning" spirits in the NT give evidence for two interrelated realities: (1) the recognized ambiguity in matters related to Christians who communicate with the spirit world; and (2) the attempts to circumvent this ambiguity through efforts of unmasking deceitful spirits.

9. 1 Cor 12:1–3: Theme and Variations

Verses 1–3 are sometimes thought of as an awkward segue into what some consider to be the main thesis of First Corinthians 12–14 beginning in v. 4,

---

[152] Iamblichus, *De myst.* 2.10. Text and translation, Emma C. Clarke et al., *Iamblichus: On the Mysteries* (Writings from the Greek World 4; SBL; Atlanta, GA: Society of Biblical Literature, 2003) 106–7.

[153] So Mehat ("L'enseignement," 402) who argues, "Avec son goût de l'antithèse, il n'aura pas souligné l'opposition entre les dons de l'Esprit et les ivresses de l'extase païenne, et se sera contenté d'allusions ambiguës?"

[154] So Hays (*First Corinthians*, 208): "The realm of the 'spiritual' is hardly unambiguous."

"gifts."[155] Mehat has observed that v. 3 contains material that is never picked up again in chaps. 12–14.[156] The confessions "Jesus is anathema" and "Jesus is Lord" as well as the term "idols" and the verbs ἄγω and ἀπάγω from v. 2 are indeed not mentioned again in the unit. The grammatical incoherency of v. 2 implies the possibility of missing material between vv. 2 and 3 that is irrecoverable.[157] The *anacolouthon* lends less textual credibility to the opening paragraph. Nonetheless, the text of vv. 1 and 3 contain elements that tie it with the rest of chaps. 12 and 14. These links suggest that πνευματικά in 12:1a was not Paul's accommodation of Corinthian language for spiritual things.[158] Rather, πνευματικά is Paul's own term for an introduction to his personal thoughts on communication with the spirit world.[159]

Several elements in 12:3 link to other elements in Paul's discourse. The term πνεῦμα in v. 3 recurs in 12:4,7,8,9,10,11,13, and 14:1,2,14,15,16,32, and 37. The phrase εἰπεῖν ἐν πνεύματι has grammatical and conceptual variants in 14:15, προσεύξομαι τῷ πνεύματι, "I will pray [with] the spirit," ψαλῶ τῷ πνεύματι, "I will sing [with] the spirit," and 14:16, εὐλογῇς [ἐν] πνεύματι, "you say a blessing [with] a spirit."

Vos suggests that οὐδείς, "no one," is an inclusive term in v. 3. In this sense, "no one who speaks with a spirit" includes all forms of inspired speech such as prophecy and glossolalia. Hence, προφητει- terms and γλωσσο- terms in chaps.

---

[155] Käsemann's argument that χαρίσματα in v. 4 is a corrective for πνευματικά in v. 1 reflects the case that Paul's real intentions were to speak of "gifts" and not so much about spiritual things in general that fascinated the Corinthians, otherwise detracting from the more important issue of God-given gifts.

[156] So Mehat, "L'enseignement," 409.

[157] Vos ("Das Rätsel," 265) suggests a reconstruction of what might have originally come after v. 2. Following the vocabulary of v. 2, πρὸς τὰ εἴδωλα ἤγεσθε, "be led to idols," he posits the missing text to have read Νυνὶ δὲ πνεύματι ἁγίῳ πρὸς τὸν Κύριον 'Ιησοῦν ἤχθητε, "Now, be led by a holy spirit to the Lord Jesus." This exegetical interpolation is not without precedent in the NT. In Gal 5:18 and Rom 8:14 a similar text appears, πνεύματι ἄγεσθαι, "to be led by a [holy] spirit." Vos's suggestion is, at best, an educated guess.

[158] The argument that πνευματικά is Corinthian terminology is usually subsumed under the theory that Paul responds to a previous Corinthian letter whenever he introduces a new subject with περὶ δέ. Thus, περὶ δέ τῶν πνευματικῶν is Corinthian terminology. This is argued by Käsemann who considered χαρίσματα a Pauline term meant to correct the Corinthians' obsession with spiritual things denoted by πνευματικά. See Chapter One.

[159] Grudem (*Gift of Prophecy*) observes: "The large number of times πνευματικὸς is used in 1 Corinthians does not necessarily imply that it was a favorite term at Corinth, or that it was used there in a specialized way which Paul was trying to correct. . . ., rather than attempting to correct the vocabulary of the Corinthians, Paul was concerned to correct their beliefs and practices with respect to the Holy Spirit" (p. 157).

12 and 14 convey experiences related to "speaking with a spirit" in v. 3.[160] Vos also notes that v. 3 is amplified and elaborated in v. 13: everyone who is of the body of Christ also shares in the same spirit.[161]

The elements "spirit," "Lord," and "God" in vv. 1 and 3 are redistributed in vv. 4–6 as "the same spirit," "the same Lord," and "the same God" with the new terms "gifts," "services," and "energies" in such a way that sets up Paul's discourse on the benefits of communicating with the spirit world in vv. 7–11. Two forms of this communication mentioned in v. 10, prophecy and glossolalia, are expounded later in chap. 14. Chapter 14 introduces the subject with the term πνευματικά, the same term that Paul began his discourse on spiritism in 12:1a. Thus, 12:1a is linked to 14:1b, binding the unit, 12–14, together.

---

[160] Vos, "Das Rätsel," 260: "'Keiner, der im Geiste Gottes redet' (v. 3b) ist der Generalnenner für 'keiner, der in Zungen redet, prophezeit, Weisheit oder Erkenntnis vorträgt, usw.'"

[161] Ibid., 261.

Chapter 5

The Manifestation of the Spirit World: 1 Cor 12:4–11

1. Introduction: πνεῦμα as "Spirit World" in Translation

The discussion thus far of communication with a "spirit world" in First
Corinthians 12 and 14 raises the issue of where in these two chapters might the
phrase "spirit world" actually appear in translation. The usual translation of τὸ
πνεῦμα in First Corinthians 12 and 14 is "the Spirit." The letter "s" is
capitalized but in the earliest Greek no distinction is made between "Spirit" and
"spirit." By the capitalization of "spirit" English translations imply that the
Greek text is referring to the way in which "spirit" came to be understood in
later church history as "the Holy Spirit." The *NAB*, however, makes the point
of translating "holy Spirit" with a lower case "h" to denote that "the Holy
Spirit," as it is written in capitals to indicate a divine Person, was not a bona
fide concept in the NT. At any rate, this begins to pave the way for the idea that
"the spirit" does not denote concepts related to the fourth-century theology of
the Holy Spirit.

By the first century C.E. the term πνεῦμα was used for different kinds of
sentient spirit beings, both good and evil.[1] A study of πνεῦμα used in the
context of sentient spirit beings in the NT reveals that antiquity had an
understanding of πνεῦμα for different spirit beings (God, humans, demons,
angels, ghosts) just as modern-day nonwestern societies.[2] Norm A. Mundhenk
notes that a proper translation of "holy spirit" in Bibles intended by missionary
efforts for distribution among nonwestern societies must include a preliminary

---

[1] The *Testaments of the Twelve Patriarchs* is a case in point. Here, the term πνεῦμα is used
for various types of spirits: "the spirit of jealousy" (*T. Jud.* 13:3); "spirits of deceit and envy"
(*T. Sim.* 3:1); "the spirit of anger" (*T. Dan* 2:4); "the spirit of hate" (*T. Gad* 1:9); "a spirit of
arrogance" and "a lying spirit" (*T. Reub.* 2:5); "the spirit of impurity" (*T. Reub.* 5:3); "a spirit
of understanding of the Lord" (*T. Levi* 2:3); "a spirit of holiness" (*T. Levi* 18:11); "a spirit of
God" (*T. Sim.* 4:4); and "the spirit of love" (*T. Gad* 4:7). To be sure, these "spirits" are not
human "inclinations" or "dispositions" described in a pre-scientific age. A term for human
inclination already existed, namely, διαβούλιος (= יצר). The *T. 12 Patr.* clearly distinguish the
human διαβούλιον from the spirits (πνεύματα) that act on it from without (see *T. Asher* 1:3,8,9;
and *T. Ben* 6:1). The Dead Sea Scrolls also make this clear distinction: בידך יצר כול רוח, "in
your [Yhwh's] hands is the inclination of every spirit" (1QHª 7.16). This includes human
spirits, referred to as רוח בשר, "spirit of flesh."

[2] See Norm A. Mundhenk, "Translating 'Holy Spirit'," *BT* 48 (1997) 201–7, esp. 203–5

assessment of that society's beliefs, understanding, and terms used for the spirit world.[3] Such an assessment is meant to avoid using "holy spirit" for many good spirits or any spirit other than "the Holy Spirit."

While this might be true for Christian theology, one rightly wonders if such a caveat does justice to the spirit world of the NT; a world better represented in present-day nonwestern societies (good and evil spirits) than by Christian theology of the Holy Spirit.[4] Mundhenk claims that while the OT refers to "a spirit of God" or "a spirit from God," these phrases should not be understood as indicating the Holy Spirit, for they do not refer to the Holy Spirit in the later Christian sense: "The Holy Spirit is not just one individual in a class of spirits."[5] It becomes clear that Mundhenk's "Christian sense" cannot be Paul's sense ("a holy spirit" and "spirits") but rather that of later Christian theology whose roots are found in the soil of Cyril of Jerusalem, Athanasius, and the Cappadocian fathers.

Paul uses the term πνεῦμα to indicate a *source* from which emanate "gifts." This is specifically denoted in 1 Cor 12:7, 8, and 11. The passive verb δίδοται in v. 7 shows that each (ἑκάστῳ) Corinthian "is given" the manifestation of the πνεῦμα; "spirit" is the active agent. This passive verb also occurs in v. 8 with the prepositions διά, "through," and κατά, "according" with the idea that each Corinthian "is given through" and "according to the spirit."[6] In v. 11 πνεῦμα is the active agent that produces (ἐνεργεῖ) the spiritual endowments listed in vv. 8–10; πνεῦμα is also said to "distribute" (διαιροῦν) them to each Corinthian as "it wills" (βούλεται). In vv. 8–10, grammatically and contextually, πνεῦμα indicates an active and personal "spirit" source from which the Corinthians receive spiritual endowments. This source may be construed as a spiritual "realm" of spirit beings.

---

[3] Ibid., 203–5.

[4] See further David Schneider, "Colossians 1:15–16 and the Philippine Spirit World," *South East Asia Journal of Theology* 15 (1974) 91–101, who argues that in the light of missionary encounters with beliefs in a spirit world in South East Asian countries, Christian theology must come to terms with the world of spirits in the NT. Similarly, Paul Hiebert ("The Flaw of the Excluded Middle," *Missiology* 10 [1982] 35–47) argued that Christians can believe in God without believing in or acknowledging a spirit world. He called this lack of belief in a spirit world the flaw of "the excluded middle," that world "between" humans and God. See also A. Khathide, "The Spirit World Awareness in the New Testament – A Missiological Challenge," *Skrif en kerk* 21 (2000) 79–92.

[5] Mundhenk, "Translating," 205.

[6] Conzelmann (*1 Corinthians*) notes, "The Spirit appears on the one hand as cause (διὰ τοῦ πνεύματος, 'through the Spirit'), and partly as norm (κατὰ τὸ αὐτὸ πνεῦμα, 'according to the same Spirit'), without it being possible to take the distinction strictly" (p. 209).

The Greek equivalent to the English phrase "spirit world" might be κόσμος πνευματικός, "a spiritual world." This phrase does not appear in Paul and would hardly make any sense in Greek.[7] But it is not unusual in the NT for other nouns to be qualified by the adjective πνευματικός, "spiritual," which, outside of the NT, might have, likewise, not made any linguistic sense in Greek.[8] The adjective πνευματικός simply means "relating to spirit." It occurs twenty-six times in the NT, twenty-four of which are found in the undisputed and disputed letters of Paul.[9] Thus John Painter suggests that πνευματικός is a Paulinism.[10]

The singular noun πνεῦμα translated as "spirit world" would function collectively much in the same way as the singular noun "world" functions to indicate a plurality of all the living beings that inhabit it. The phrase "spirit world" as a translation for πνεῦμα is already partly denoted in an adjectival form πνευματικός which indicates "that which belongs to the supernatural order of being."[11] The adjective suggests that the noun upon which it is based, πνεῦμα, can, in certain contexts, refer to the "supernatural order of being" itself, i.e., the spirit world. Likewise, Volz had argued that Hebrew רוח, "spirit," in some contexts might indicate not only a spiritual energy connecting humans with the spirit world, but also the spirit world itself.[12]

In the NT πνεῦμα denotes a "spiritual world" or a "spirit reality" that transcends the physical world. In Rev 1:10 and 4:2 John's out-of-body visionary experiences are described by the following statement: ἐγενόμην ἐν

---

[7] According to Ekem ("'Spiritual Gifts' or 'Spiritual Persons'," 55) the only non-biblical usage of the adjective πνευματικός in a spiritual sense occurs in Plutarch, *Vitae parallelae* 2.129c.

[8] See Paul's seemingly oxymoronic phrase (from a Greek perspective) σῶμα πνευματικόν, "a spiritual body," in 1 Cor 15:44. For other nouns using "spiritual" as a qualifier see Rom 1:11, χάρισμα πνευματικόν, "a spiritual gift," Rom 7:14, νόμος πνευματικός, "[the] law [is] spiritual," 1 Cor 10:3, πνευματικὸν βρῶμα, "spiritual meat," 1 Cor 10:4, πνευματικὸν πόμα, "spiritual drink," and πνευματικῆς πέτρας, "spiritual rock," Eph 1:3, εὐλογίᾳ πνευματικῇ, "spiritual blessings," Eph 5:19, ᾠδαῖς πνευματικαῖς, "spiritual songs," Eph 6:12, τὰ πνευματικὰ τῆς πονηρίας, "spiritual wickedness [i.e., evil spiritual powers]," Col 1:9, συνέσει πνευματικῇ, "spiritual understanding," Col 3:16, ᾠδαῖς πνευματικαῖς, "spiritual songs," 1 Pet 2:5, οἶκος πνευματικός, "spiritual house," and πνευματικάς θυσίας, "spiritual sacrifices."

[9] See Rom 1:11; 7:14; 15:27; 1 Cor 2:13 (2x); 2:15; 3:1; 9:11; 10:3; 10:4 (2x); 12:1; 14:1; 14:37; 15:44 (2x); 15:46 (2x); Gal 6:1; Eph 5:19; 6:12; Col 1:9; and 3:16.

[10] John Painter, "Paul and the Πνευματικοί at Corinth," in *Paul and Paulinism: Essays in Honour of C. K. Barrett* (ed. M. D. Hooker and S. G. Wilson; London: Society for Promoting Christian Knowledge, 1982) 237.

[11] BAGD, s.v. πνευματικός.

[12] Volz, *Der Geist Gottes*, 57.

πνεύματι, "I became in spirit," i.e., "I entered into the spirit world."[13] Kendell
H. Easley suggests that πνεύματι in Paul sometimes means the "realm of spirit-
reality."[14] Since the noun πνεῦμα is not used as an adjective to qualify κόσμος
in Paul's text, i.e., κόσμος πνευματικός, "a spiritual world," the noun πνεῦμα will
be translated in those contexts that denote a world of spirits as "the spirit
[world]." The term "world" will appear in brackets to indicate that even though
κόσμος does not occur in the Greek text, the meaning of πνεῦμα, nonetheless,
indicates a "world" in which spirits exist.[15]

Thus far in this book, several matters have been addressed and discussed
regarding "spirit": (1) the anarthrous πνεῦμα arguably indicates in certain
contexts "a spirit," implying one of many, and not "the Spirit" or simply
"spirit"; (2) the plural "spirits" refers to sentient spirit beings, good or evil, and
not to "gifts," "manifestations," "inspirations," or "prophetic utterances"; and
(3) the Greek noun πνεῦμα refers to a spirit world that distributes endowments
in order to facilitate communication between that world and the human world.
The existence of a spirit world in the NT is the basis from which Paul's
language of "the spirit," "the one spirit," and "spirits" will be discussed.

2. The Meaning of "the Spirit" in 1 Cor 12:4, 7

Many commentators, both Protestant and Catholic, assume that "the spirit" is
an implicit basis for the single "Holy Spirit" in contemporary Christian
theology.[16] The discussion here will be whether this is what Paul actually meant
by the expression "the spirit."

The Greek text of First Corinthians 12 and 14 shows that Paul knows of "[a]

---

[13] See *CWDNT*, s.v. ἔκστασις (VII): "I came to be in the spiritual world." Cf. 2 Cor 12:1–4.

[14] Kendell H. Easley, "The Pauline Usage of *Pneumati* as a Reference to the Spirit of God,"
JETS 27 (1984) 299–313, esp. 305.

[15] Paul's antithetical use of κόσμος, "world," and θεός, "God," may have prevented him from
qualifying the term "world" with the adjective "spiritual" in reference to "holy spirit" or "God."
In 1 Cor 2:12 Paul distinguishes τὸ πνεῦμα τοῦ κόσμου, "the spirit of the world," from τὸ πνεῦμα
τὸ ἐκ τοῦ θεοῦ, "the spirit that is from God." The "world" is the locus of a spirit that is not from
God. This, however, does not prevent him from having in mind a "spiritual realm of holy spirits
from God" by his use of τὸ πνεῦμα as shown below.

[16] So Montague, *Holy Spirit*, 148; Fee, *First Epistle*, 586; Kistemaker, *1 Corinthians*, 417;
Thomas, *Spiritual Gifts*, 24; Hays, *First Corinthians*, 210; Thiselton, *First Epistle*, 934; and
Garland, *1 Corinthians*, 576. Thiselton ("The Holy Spirit in 1 Corinthians," 224) is convinced
that fourth- and fifth-century patristic interpretations for "the Holy Spirit" are, more or less, "a
logical explication of Paul's thought."

holy spirit," "[a] spirit of God" (πνεῦμα), "the spirit" (τὸ πνεῦμα), and "spirits" (πνεύματα). Grammatically, the articular τὸ πνεῦμα indicates a category to which the anarthrous πνεῦμα and the plural πνεύματα belong.

Stanley E. Porter explains that when the article is used the substantive may represent a category of items.[17] He lists the following as examples:

Luke 10:7, "the worker (ὁ ἐργάτης) is worthy of his wage"
Matt 12:35, "the good person (ὁ ἀγαθὸς ἄνθρωπος) . . . and the evil person (καὶ ὁ πονηρὸς ἄνθρωπος)" (wherein both represent all good and evil persons)
John 10:11, "the good shepherd (ὁ ποιμὴν ὁ καλός)"
Rom 7:1, "the husband (τοῦ ἀνθρώπου) . . . for the married woman (ἡ γὰρ ὕπανδρος γυνή) is bound to the living husband"
1 Tim 3:2, "the overseer" (τὸν ἐπίσκοπον)

The article is used in a collective sense to indicate not a single entity but rather all entities that are implied by the generic referent. Another example is found in 1 John 2:22 wherein ὁ ἀντίχριστος, "*the* antichrist" is ὁ ἀρνούμενος τὸν πατέρα καὶ τὸν υἱόν, "he who denies the Father and the Son"; yet, 1 John 2:18 notes that there are ἀντίχριστοι πολλοί, "*many* antichrists." Here again the Greek article is used in a generic sense to denote a category of "many." Arguably, τὸ πνεῦμα in 1 Cor 12: 4 and 7 indicates a generic reference to the πνεύματα in 14:12 and 32 while πνεῦμα in 12:3 and 14:2c,16 indicates one of the many spirits. Hence, in context, τὸ πνεῦμα is "the spirit world" in which exist the πνεύματα as individual and distinct spirit beings.

The Dead Sea Scroll texts (DSS) show a tendency to use "spirit" (רוח) as a collective noun for a multiplicity of "spirits" (רוחות). In the spirit world of the DSS two polarizing camps exist: Belial and his spirits (רוחות בליעל, "spirits of Belial," and רוחי גורלו, "spirits of his apportioning"),[18] and God and his spirits (רוחות אלוהים היים, "spirits of the living God").[19] The implications of the

---

[17] Porter, *Idioms*, 104.

[18] See 1QS 3.10; 4.14; 1QM 13.2,4; 14.10. For other references to evil spirits see 1QHᵃ 3.18, "all the spirits of wickedness"; 1QH f 5.4, "spirits of ungodliness"; 5.6, "spirits of deceit"; 1QM 15.14, "all the wicked spirits"; and 4Q511. 1. 6, "spirits of evil." See Alexander, "The Demonology of the Dead Sea Scrolls," 331–53.

[19] See 4QS1 40. 24. 6. For other references to spirits of God see 1QHᵃ 1.11 and 4Q502. 27. 1, "spirits of eternity"; 1QHᵃ 2.4, "spirits of righteousness"; 1QHᵃ 3.22 and 11.13, "spirits of knowledge"; 1QHᵃ 13.8, "host of your [Yhwh's] spirits"; 1QM 12.9 and 19.1, "host of his [Yhwh's] spirits"; 1QHᵃ 8.12 and 4QS1 40. 24. 5, "holy spirits" or "spirits of holiness"; 1QH f 33.2, "your [Yhwh's] spirits"; 1QM 13.10, "all the spirits of truth"; and 8Q5. 2. 6, "all the

existence of a plurality of "spirits of God" on the one hand and of the existence of many "evil spirits" on the other have not always been drawn out by scholars. Both early scholarship and more recent scholarship on "spirit" in the DSS distinguish between God's Spirit, implying only one, and all other spirits, good and evil.[20]

Most of the occurrences of the singular form of רוח, "spirit," in relation to God in the DSS are qualified by the attributive adjective קודש, "holy," plus the pronominal suffix ך, כה, "your holy spirit," or ו, "his holy spirit."[21] These occurrences are grammatically related to the articular "the spirit." The phrases "holy spirits" (רוחות קודש, 1QH[a] 8.12), "your [Yhwh's] spirits" (רוחי[ך], 1QH f 33.2), and "host of your [Yhwh's] spirits" (צבא רחויך, 1QH[a] 13.8 and 1QM 12.9) are the plural forms of the singular.

In an exposition of 1 Kgs 22:19–21 Aubrey R. Johnson notes a grammatical idea that suits the singular-plural occurrences of רוח related to Yhwh: "This רוח, as a member of Yahweh's heavenly court, . . . should be thought of as an individualization within the corporate רוח or 'Spirit' of Yahweh's extended Personality."[22] Johnson's statement, despite the flaw of its explanation of רוח as Yhwh's "extended Personality," nonetheless relates the idea that "spirits," or, in this case, "a spirit," belongs to a "corporate רוח," i.e., "the spirit of God," a singular body of spirit beings. Hence, the syntactically singular suffix forms רוחך, "your spirit," and רוחו, "his spirit," in the DSS tend to incite, grammatically, the notion of a corporate "spirit" by which the *spirits* (רוחות) of God are collected under and represented. This is further substantiated by the plural suffix forms related to God, רוחיך, "your spirits" (1QH[a] 13.8; 1QH f 33.2), and רוחיו, "his spirits" (1QM 12.9; 19.1).

Related to the singular suffix forms is the singular articular form רוח הקודש, "the holy spirit."[23] The anarthrous form רוח קודש occurs five times in the non-biblical Hebrew DSS.[24] Grammatically, the anarthrous might indicate "a holy

---

spirits in your [Yhwh's] presence." Good spirits and evil spirits are not unique to the DSS but are also assumed in the LXX that makes a clear distinction between good spirits from the Lord (ἄγγελοι) and evil spirits (δαίμονες or δαιμόνια).

[20] See Millar Burrows, *More Light on the Dead Sea Scrolls* (New York: Viking Press, 1958) 280, and Arthur E. Sekki, *The Meaning of RUAH at Qumran* (SBLDS 110; Atlanta, GA: Scholar's Press, 1989).

[21] So Sekki, RUAH, 72.

[22] Aubrey R. Johnson, *The One and the Many in the Israelite Conception of God* (Cardiff: University of Wales, 1961) 16.

[23] According to Sekki only twice, 4QDe {270} 2 ii. 13–14b and 4Q506. 131–32. 11.

[24] So ibid., 72.

spirit." In 1QS 4.21 "a holy spirit" (רוח קודש) is identified with "a spirit of truth" (רוח אמת). In the light of the anarthrous, the articular form may indicate "holy spirits" in a collective sense.[25] This grammatical phenomenon related to the term "spirit" can be found in Christian literature as well.

The categorical use of the article with the term "spirit" finds a measure of support in the NT. 1 John 4:2 notes a "test" whereby one can know "the spirit of God" (τὸ πνεῦμα τοῦ θεοῦ) through the speech of "every spirit that confesses Jesus Christ . . . is of God" (πᾶν πνεῦμα ὃ ὁμολογεῖ Ἰησοῦν Χριστὸν . . . ἐκ τοῦ θεοῦ ἐστιν). The adjective πᾶν, "all" or "every," indicates a variety or, at least, a multiplicity of "spirits" from God.[26] In this context "the spirit of God" stands in a qualitatively equal relationship with "every spirit of God." Arguably, τὸ πνεῦμα τοῦ θεοῦ is πᾶν πνεῦμα ἐκ τοῦ θεοῦ ἐστιν: *"the* spirit" = *"every* spirit." One might punctuate 1 John 4:2 with a colon, "In this way you know the Spirit of God: every spirit who confesses that Jesus Christ has come in the flesh is of God." Likewise, the singular and definite phrase τὸ [πνεῦμα] τοῦ ἀντιχρίστου, "the [spirit] of antichrist," represents, collectively, "every spirit . . . who does not acknowledge Jesus is not from God" (1 John 4:3). In v. 6 these spirits are also classed as τὸ πνεῦμα τῆς πλάνης, "the spirit of error." The spirits of God are classed as τὸ πνεῦμα τῆς ἀληθείας, "the spirit of truth."[27]

Grudem notes that the singular πνεῦμα can be used in Paul for a plurality of spirits. Admittedly, Grudem does not argue this in the context of many "holy spirits" but rather in Paul's use of πνεῦμα for the human spirit. He states,

---

[25] For רוחות קודש, "holy spirits," see 1QHᵃ 8.12; 4QS1 40. 24.5.

[26] So Georg Strecker, *Johannine Letters: A Commentary on 1, 2, and 3 John* (Hermeneia; Minneapolis: Fortress, 1999) 132.

[27] The Johannine phrases "the spirit of error" and "the spirit of truth" have direct antecedents in the DSS and *T. 12 Patr.*: רוח העול, "spirit of error" (1QS); רוח אמת, "spirit of truth" (1QS); τὸ πνεῦμα τῆς πλάνης, "the spirit of error" (*T. Jud.* 20:1); and τὸ πνεῦμα τῆς ἀληθείας, "the spirit of truth" (*T. Jud.* 20:1). Earlier we saw how Athanasius and Basil rationalized the Spirit's unique and uncreated nature on the basis of 1 Cor 2:11,12 where the Spirit is said to be ἐκ τοῦ θεοῦ, "from God." Yet in 1 John 4:2 we see that πᾶν πνεῦμα . . . ἐκ τοῦ θεοῦ, "every spirit . . . from God," suggests a plurality of spirits "from God." In the light of Athanasian and Basilian exegesis, how is πᾶν πνεῦμα . . . ἐκ τοῦ θεοῦ to be understood? Nowhere in Athanasius and Basil is it stated that many spirits of God share the same nature as "the Spirit"; the many spirits are always subordinate to "the Spirit." One might point to Basil, *Hom.* 24.7 who argues, "[For], even if all things are said to be from God, the Son and the Spirit are from God in a special sense, . . . the Spirit proceeds ineffably from the Father" (trans. Haykin, *Spirit of God*, 145). This special sense is "a mystery" according to Gregory of Nazianzus, *Orations* 31.8. Basil, however, gives a bit of an expansion on this ineffable "special sense" in *On the Holy Spirit* 18.46. See Haykin, *Spirit of God*, 145–46. Nonetheless, a plurality of spirits "from God" throws into question the idea that "the Spirit" is unique and uncreated *because* it is "from God."

"When Paul speaks of human spirits, he can also show unusual variation in the use of singular and plural, using the singular for a multiplicity of spirits in Gal. 6.18: Ἡ χάρις τοῦ κυρίου ἡμῶν Ἰησοῦ Χριστοῦ μετὰ τοῦ πνεύματος ὑμῶν, ἀδελφοί (so also Phil. 4.23; cf. Phlm. 25, 2 Tim. 4.22)."[28] Arguably, this is equally applicable to Paul's use of πνεῦμα in First Corinthians 12 and 14, wherein τὸ πνεῦμα (12:4,7) occurs in contexts relating to "the spirit [world]."

The Shepherd of Hermas, a late first-century or early second-century Christian document with Jewish influence, uses similar language in a similar context for testing the utterances of spirits. Hermas *Mand.* 11.5 contains the phrase "for every spirit which is given from God" (πᾶν γὰρ πνεῦμα ἀπὸ θεοῦ δοθέν). These spirits from God are referred to collectively as "the divine spirit" (τὸ πνεῦμα τὸ θεῖον) in 11.7. This, likewise, holds true for evil spirits that the Shepherd warns of: "Do not cleave to such spirits, but refrain from them" (see 11:4). These spirits belong to "the devil" (ὁ διάβολος) and are designated collectively as "his spirit" (αὐτοῦ πνεύματι) (11.3).[29] While this conforms to grammar, Paul's phrase "the one spirit" is only partly explained by this grammatical phenomenon. The qualification "one" needs further explication.

3. The Meaning and Use of "One" in 1 Cor 12:9,11

The distinction between one Holy Spirit and many holy spirits sometimes appears in modern-day studies on spirit in early Christianity. A glaring contrast between the "one" Holy Spirit as the norm for early Christianity and a plurality of holy spirits as the norm for early Christianity occurs in the classic five-volume study *The Beginnings of Christianity*. In a discussion of the Spirit in ancient Israel and in the Synoptic gospels, the author states,

It would be natural to expect that just as the evil spirits were regarded as personal and as many, so there would be *many holy spirits*, but in point of fact there is little trace of this development. The Holy Spirit which inspires prophets is almost always *one*.[30]

---

[28] Grudem, *Gift of Prophecy*, 124 n. 13.

[29] Compare the references to both Belial's spirits and God's spirits in the DSS with the 2nd and 3rd masc. sg. pronominal suffix: "his [Belial's] spirits of destruction" (1QM 14.10); "host of his [Yhwh's] spirits" (1QM 12.9, 19:1); "his [Yhwh's] holy spirit" and "your [Yhwh's] spirit" (1QHᵃ 7.6; 9.32; 12.12; 14.13; 16.2,3,7,12; 17.26; 1QH f2.9; 1QS 8.16; CD 2.12; 1Q39. 1.6; 4Q287. 4.13; and 4Q504. 1–2).

[30] *The Beginnings of Christianity*, 1. 287 (emphasis mine).

In the final volume, *Additional Notes to the Commentary*, it is stated:

Do the Synoptics, and did the circle of Jewish thought which they represent, think that there were many bad but *only one good spirit*, or did they think that there were many of both, and that both obsessed mankind? If this question is confined to the actual fact of the existence or non-existence of many good spirits, there can be but one answer. *There were many.*[31]

Whereas one author claims that there was only "one" Holy Spirit in first-century Christianity, another author, contributing to the same work, claims that there were many holy spirits in first-century Christianity. Paul's use of ἕν, "one," as a qualifier for spirit is easily assumed to mean a numerically singular spirit reality, especially in the light of centuries of reinforcement beginning with Athanasius.[32] The issue, however, is whether "one," taken literally, describes what Paul actually meant by it.

Following on the heels of Athanasius and the Cappadocian fathers, scholars almost always assume that Paul's qualification of the spirit as "one" in 1 Cor 12:9 and 11 expresses a numerical value without any further discussion: a single (only one) Holy Spirit. Admittedly, the term "one" can have the numerical sense of "single" or "only one" in the NT.[33] The term may also carry the sense of "someone," or "a certain one."[34] In relation to God, "the Lord our God is one" (Mark 12:29), the term "one" is best understood in the sense of "supreme" or "number one," not that there is literally only one god.[35] This is the way in which Paul uses "one God" in 1 Cor 8:4–6 in order to differentiate God from all other gods.[36]

---

[31] Kirsopp Lake, "Note IX. The Holy Spirit," ibid., 5. 102 (emphasis mine).

[32] Haykin (*Spirit of God*, 86) notes, "Since both 1 Cor 12:13 and 1 Cor 12:11 qualify the Spirit with the adjective 'one', they serve as excellent proof-texts for Athanasius' attempt to distinguish the Holy Spirit from the creatures in *ep. Serap.* 3.3–4." See Athanasius, *ad Serap.* 1.27, ἕν ἐστι τὸ Πνεῦμα τὸ ἅγιον· τὰ δὲ κτίσματα πολλά (*PG* 26. 593B).

[33] See Luke 10:42; 18:22; Rom 3:12; Gal 3:20; Jas 4:12; and 2 Pet 3:8.

[34] See Matt 16:14; 18:24; 19:16; Mark 10:17; and Luke 24:18.

[35] See Stephen A. Geller, "The God of the Covenant," in *One God or Many? Concepts of Divinity in the Ancient World* (ed. Barbara Nevling Porter; Transactions of the Casco Bay Assyriological Institute 1; Chebeague Island, ME: Casco Bay Assyriological Institute, 1997) 273–319, esp. 290–97.

[36] 1 Cor 8:4–6 seems to indicate henotheism, a term meant to convey a personal devotion to a particular god without rejecting a belief in the existence of other gods or deities. The term monotheism is meant to convey a much more restricted idea that "no other god exists *except* this god." Paul is much more in line with henotheistic thinking, "there is no other god quite like this god." See Peter Hayman, "Monotheism – A Misused Word in Jewish Studies," *JJS* 42 (1991) 1–15; and H. S. Versnel, "Thrice One: Three Greek Experiments in Oneness," in *One God or Many?*, 130 n. 136.

In other contexts, "one" carries the sense of "unity" or "together." The Greek verb ἐνόω, "to unite," is derived from the Greek numeral ἕν, "one." In the NT unified "oneness" is seen in Phil 2:2, "be of one mind" (τὸ ἓν φρονοῦτες), John 10:30, "I and the Father are one" (ἐγὼ καὶ ὁ πατὴρ ἕν ἐσμεν), John 17:21,22, "so that they may by one" (ἵνα πάντες ἓν ὦσιν), and Rom 12:5, "we, though many, are one body in Christ" (οὕτως οἱ πολλοὶ ἓν σῶμά ἐσμεν ἐν Χριστῷ). This sense of "one" also illustrates that from the single parts, the whole is made up. Paul uses the "many members but one body" language in the same sense in 1 Cor 12:12 and applies this as a metaphor to the Corinthian members who, though many, are "one body" (ἓν σῶμα) in Christ (cf. 1 Cor 12:13, 27–29).

In the Corinthian church, Paul's use of the body metaphor was meant to serve as a symbol of social unity.[37] This was an attempt by Paul to explain to the Corinthians that no one member was any more important than another (hence his digression on "love" in 1 Cor 13:1–14:1a). Throughout 1 Cor 12:1–13 "the one and the many" motif occurs: "same [one] spirit, many gifts"; "same [one] Lord, many services"; "same [one] God, many workings"; and "one body, many members."[38] This motif is meant to bolster Paul's polemic here that despite diversity in gifts and abilities among the Corinthians, all are unified in "one body" by baptism in the "one spirit." Paul makes this clear in 1 Cor 12:27–30, when he comments on different functions of the Corinthian members in the church who, nevertheless, make up "Christ's body and individually parts of it" (v. 27, ὑμεῖς δέ ἐστε σῶμα Χριστοῦ καὶ μέλη ἐκ μέρους). In this capacity, the many differently gifted members function as "one." The unity or oneness is further underscored by Paul's inclusion of "Jews or Greeks, slaves or free persons" whom he declares form "one body" (see 1 Cor 12:13).

Within "the one and the many" motif it is usually suggested that "the one spirit" is to be paired with "the distributions of [many] gifts." 1 Cor 12:4 gives

---

[37] See 1 Cor 1:10 wherein Paul sets the polemical tone of the letter: "I urge you . . . that all of you agree . . . that there be no divisions (σχίσματα) among you, but that you be united in the same mind and in the same purpose." See Collins, *First Corinthians*, 460–61; and Thiselton, *First Epistle*, 997–98. Collins provides material illustrating the use of the body metaphor among the rhetoricians, philosophers, moralists, and historians contemporary with Paul. Collins (ibid., 460) notes that unlike the classical usage of the body metaphor that attributed it to nature, Paul attributes the metaphor to God.

[38] Paige, "Spirit at Corinth," 59, makes this point. On literature for "the one and many" in Greek religion and philosophy, see Michael C. Stokes, *One and Many in Presocratic Philosophy* (Center for Hellenic Studies [Washington, D.C.]; Cambridge, MA: Harvard University Press, 1971); and C. Rowe, "One and Many in Greek Religion," in *Oneness and Variety* (ed. A. Portmann and R. Ritsema; Leiden: Brill, 1976) 37–67. For the OT, see n. 22 above.

the evidence for such a pairing: "there are different distributions of gifts, but the same spirit" (διαιρέσεις δὲ χαρισμάτων εἰσίν, τὸ δὲ αὐτὸ πνεῦμα). The term αὐτό, "same," occurs with ἕν in v. 11 as a qualifier for spirit. The term not only serves the same function to describe the "oneness" of spirit but is also emphatic. The "one spirit and many gifts" motif is elaborated through the "one body and many members" motif: all of the Corinthians, as a body, share in the one spirit from which come the many gifts to each individual Corinthian. This is the common interpretation among scholars. The plural "spirits" in 1 Cor 14:12, however, provides another possible interpretation.

The identity of "spirits" as a multiplicity of good spirits is almost always seen as incompatible with Pauline pneumatology: only one good Spirit exists.[39] Paige argues that there "are not distributions of spirits as there are of gifts,"[40] a statement that does indeed reflect the Greek text in 1 Cor 12:4. Paige further argues that a multiplicity of spirits is in line with the Hellenistic concept of δαίμονες (daemons), the Hellenistic term for "spirits," and thus reflects Corinthian pneumatology instead of the Christian Holy Spirit as "one, single, unique."[41] But "one" as a qualifier for "spirit" does not always mean "single spirit."

Eph 4:3–4 uses "one" in the sense of "unity" related to spirit: "striving to preserve the unity of the spirit (ἑνότητα τοῦ πνεύματος) through the bond of peace: one (ἕν) body and one (ἕν) spirit." Here, the sense of "one spirit" indicates not a numerical value but a "oneness" as the term ἑνότητα shows. In Phil 1:27 ἑνὶ πνεύματι and μιᾷ ψυχῇ are paired. The phrase μιὰ ψυχή, "one soul," indicated *esprit de corps*, a phrase that denotes loyalty and devotion uniting the members of a group in the world of Greek political theory. Some have noted that "one spirit" in Paul might have been an intentional parallel.[42]

Other forms of "one" are used for "Lord" and "God" (εἷς) and "hope" and "faith" (μία) in Eph 4:4–5. Paul, however, always uses ἕν in relation to "body" and "spirit."[43] Such consistency may not have been arbitrary on Paul's part. As part of his polemic, Paul seems to have been conveying both the unity of the Corinthian members who form "one body" and the unity of the "spirits" in

---

[39] See 1 Cor 12:4,9,11,13.

[40] Paige, "Spirit at Corinth," 59.

[41] Ibid., 60. This sounds more Athanasian than Pauline.

[42] So Mitchell, *Paul and the Rhetoric of Reconciliation*, p. 160, esp. n. 575; and Fee, "Translation Tendenz: English Versions and Πνεῦμα in Paul," in *Holy Spirit and Christian Origins*, 355.

[43] See Rom 12:5; 15:6; 1 Cor 6:16,17; 10:17; 12:12,13,14,20; and the disputed Pauline letters: Eph 4:4; Phil 1:27; Col 3:15.

1 Cor 14:12, 32 (unified by their allegiance to God and Christ as seen in 1 Cor 12:3) who form "one spirit [world]."

Scholars have observed the "one spirit/spirits" contrast with wonderment. Harrisville believes that Paul's use of "spirits" in v. 12 "is odd. It reflects a notion of Spirit as multiple."[44] Dunn states that the use of the plurals, "spirits," in 1 Cor 14:12 and 32 "have caused some perplexity."[45] He suggests that Paul is either referring to many spirits or to many spiritual gifts. The latter suggestion is one of the usual translations of πνεύματα in 1 Cor 14:12, but it was shown in Chapter One that "gifts" and "spirits" are two different words with two different connotations. Thus, Dunn's suggestion that "spirits" refers to many good spirits needs to be reconsidered.

Other scholars have put forth views that come closer to the idea that "one spirit" expresses a unity of spirit beings, i.e., "one spirit [world]." As we saw earlier, Gunkel wondered whether in the NT age the Spirit of God was "separated" into various spirits, since 1 Cor 14:12 shows a variety of "spirits" from which various gifts are derived.[46] Weinel also considered the relationship between "the spirit" and many good spirits.[47] Similarly, Everling quoted from Georg Ludwig Hahn's *Theologie des Neuen Testaments*, "The Spirit of God referred to a multiplicity of spirits."[48] Adolf Schlatter believed that the "one spirit" was a source from which good spirits proceeded and who were subsumed under this rubric as a group.[49] According to these scholars a relationship exists between "one spirit" and many "spirits" in which the latter are a multiplicity of spirit beings who are renamed by the former: "one spirit" serves as Pauline rhetoric for united spirit realms; realms that include good spirits, i.e., spirits who are "holy" or "of God."

Paul's use of "one body" for the Corinthian church served his polemic against the schisms among the Corinthians (1 Cor 1:10–11; 3:3–4). The phrase "one spirit" does not indicate former schisms among spirits who should otherwise be "one," but rather is meant to show that all gifts, however spectacular or however small, are derived from the same source. The Corinthians probably knew this. Paul uses the phrase not to correct them on that score, but rather to enhance his polemic against the schism and disorder (1 Cor 14:33,40) among the Corinthians. Despite what some Corinthians might have

---

[44] Harrisville, *1 Corinthians*, 232.

[45] Dunn, *Jesus and Spirit*, 233.

[46] Gunkel, *Influence*, 44.

[47] Weinel, *Wirkungen*, 68.

[48] Everling, *Die paulinische Angelologie*, 40 (translation mine).

[49] Adolf Schlatter, *Paulus der Bote Jesu* (Stuttgart: Calwer, 1934; repr. 1956) 376.

thought of their spiritual abilities as a form of self-assertion (the glossalalists), all other Corinthian members received their abilities from the "same spirit [world]" as well. Every gift, however small in the eyes of some, was as important and as necessary as any other from the perspective of the spirit world of God.[50]

Rhetorically, the "one spirit" functions in the same way as the "one body." Just as there are "many members" who compose a single body, so too are there "[many] spirits" who compose a single spirit world from which the "gifts," "services," and "activities" (1 Cor 12:4–6) are rendered. Hence, the singular "one spirit" indicates a collectiveness for a plurality of spirits in 1 Cor 12: 9, 11, and 13; that plurality of spirits is mentioned in 12:10, 14:12 and 32.[51] This is a grammatical phenomenon that occurs elsewhere in Greek literature pertaining to the spirit world.

Versnel provides evidence that sometimes οἱ θεοί, "the gods," might be the same as ὁ θεός, "the god." He profits from the work of Gilbert François, who shows that the singular ὁ θεός and the plural οἱ θεοί alternate in the same contexts.[52] Versnel argues that grammatical plurality does not always imply "many," but can refer to "oneness."[53] For example, the phrase οἱ θεοί in Herodotus is plural but "from a semantic point of view refers to a unity, a oneness."[54] Arguably, from this perspective, "spirits" are "one" in a unified sense, and this fits Paul's rhetoric: "spirits" who are "one spirit."

The view that the "one spirit" is the Holy Spirit of later Christian theology does not do justice to historical exegesis: the spirit world in the mind of Paul (as we have it in First Corinthians 12 and 14) was a world of spirit beings united by their commitment to Jesus as Lord and to God as supreme Father. The charge

---

[50] See Njiru, *Charisms*, 187: "No matter how many or how large the differences, the Holy Spirit remains as the origin." Cf. *The Constitutions of the Holy Apostles*, 8.1.1, ". . . those who have received such gifts may not exalt themselves against those who have not received them; such gifts, we mean, as are for the working of miracles"; and 8.1.2, ". . . if among you also there be a man or a woman, and such a one obtains any gift, let him be humble, that God may by pleased with him" (ANF 7. 480–81).

[51] Arguably, if Paul meant "ONLY one spirit" he might have used the adjective μόνος, "only," "alone" to convey this notion more adequately. BAGD, s.v. εἷς, places the phrase "the one and the same spirit" of 1 Cor 12:11 in the category of "emphatic" rather than "single, only one."

[52] Gilbert François, *Le polythéisme et l'emploi au singulier des mots THEOS, DAIMON dans la littérature grecque d'Homère à Platon* (Paris: Société d'édition 'Les Belles Lettres,' 1957).

[53] Versnel, "Thrice One," 121.

[54] Ibid., 127.

that this interpretation reflects "polytheism" or "pantheism" is unfounded. The fact that Paul, as a Pharisee, would have believed in the existence of angels and spirits is undeniable (see Acts 23:8). He also believed in the existence of "gods" and "lords" (1 Cor 8:5) and "demons" (1 Cor 10:20–21). Furthermore, a disputed Pauline text warns of a "veneration of angels" (Col 2:18). This acknowledges a belief in angels, yet redirects any adoration away from them toward God. A similar view is found in Revelation 22:8–9: " . . . I fell down to worship at the feet of the angel who showed them [visions] to me. But he said to me, 'Don't! I am a fellow servant of yours and of your brothers the prophets and of those who keep the message of this book. Worship God.'"

As a Christian Paul confessed his devotion to one particular god, God the Father, and his commitment to one particular lord, the Lord Jesus Christ (1 Cor 8:6). This devotion was accompanied by a belief in a spirit world, as scholars past and present have observed. Paul persuaded the Corinthians to continue communicating with the spirit world (1 Cor 14:12,39,40), as he did the Thessalonians (1 Thess 5:19–20). This communication did not include a veneration of the spirits themselves (see the warning in Col 2:18). Instead, such communication (at least among Christians) was expected to be done during a service that included the worship of the one true God with a commitment to Christ as His Son and as the risen Lord.

A Christian prayer service with the intent on communicating with the spirit world is found in Herm. *Mand*. 11.9: "when the man who has the divine spirit enters among the assembly of righteous men who have faith in a divine spirit, and this assembly of men offers up a prayer to God, then the angel of the prophetic spirit comes upon him and fills the man; and this man, being filled with the holy spirit, speaks to the multitude just as the Lord wills."[55] The holy spirit world manifests itself *subsequent* to the prayers that are offered *to God by the assembly* (ἔντευξις γένηται πρὸς τὸν θεὸν τῆς συναγωγῆς τῶν ἀνδρῶν). The holy spirit world then communicates with words of intent through a medium. The medium is "the man filled with the holy spirit" who "speaks" to the assembly, i.e., a holy spirit speaks through him to the assembly of "righteous men." This congregational experience of spirit communication is akin to that seen earlier in *L.A.B.* 28.6: "And when they had sat down, a holy spirit came down upon Kenaz and dwelled in him and put him in ecstasy, and he began to prophesy, saying . . ." The manifestation of the spirit world in *L.A.B.* and the Shepherd of Hermas is not unlike that which we see in 1 Cor 12:4–11 and 1 Cor

---

[55] For a discussion of a possible meaning of "the angel of the prophetic spirit," see Jannes Reiling, *Hermas and Christian Prophecy: A Study of the Eleventh Mandate* (Leiden: Brill, 1973) 104–11.

14:1a–37, especially in the experiences denoted by the terms "prophesy" and "speaking with a spirit."

4. 1 Cor 12:4–7, 11: The Manifestation of the Spirit World

After giving the Corinthians a brief primer on Christian spiritism in 12:1–3, Paul proceeds to elaborate on the benefits of the presence of the spirit world in vv. 4–6; rhetorically, a *partitio*, or a succinct introduction of the issue that is developed further and clarified in the *confirmatio* of vv. 7–30.[56] The spirit world is a source from which are derived the different distributions (διαιρέσεις) that Paul chooses to call by three terms: χαρίσματα, "gifts" (v. 4), διακονίαι, "services" (v. 5), and ἐνεργήματα, "activities" (v. 6). Paul claims that many of each exist, but they are viewed as coming from three interrelated sources: "the same spirit" (v. 4), "the same Lord" (v. 5), and "the same God" (v. 6).

For some scholars, the so-called triadic expression in vv. 4–6, "same spirit," "same Lord," and "same God," provides evidence for a Trinitarian component already inherent in Paul. These three phrases are sometimes thought to have "Trinitarian overtones" or else are an allusion to what would become known as the three persons of the Trinity in later Christian theology.[57] A relationship among "spirit," "Lord," and "God" like that formulated during the fourth century, however, is not indicated here.[58] Instead, these three terms indicate a

---

[56] Smit, "Argument and Genre," 217–21.

[57] So Montague, *Holy Spirit*, 148; Fee, *First Epistle*, 586; Kistemaker, *1 Corinthians*, 417; Thomas, *Spiritual Gifts*, 24; Hays, *First Corinthians*, 210; Thiselton, *First Epistle*, 934; Garland, *1 Corinthians*, 576; and Maleparampil, *The 'Trinitarian' Formulae in St. Paul*, 17–49.

[58] As would be necessary for a "Trinitarian overtone" as we do find later in Athanasius, *ad. Serap.* 1.27. Hence, some scholars see no allusions to the Trinity here. Soards (*1 Corinthians*) states, "[Paul] is not in this first-century correspondence doing full-blown fourth-century Trinitarian reflection – such as was done later in great church councils and christological discussions" (p. 256); and even stronger, Collins (*First Corinthians*) states, "Paul's three parallel statements . . . should no more be construed as an expression of Trinitarian theology than the other so-called 'Trinitarian formulae' in the Pauline writings (2 Cor 1:21–22; 13:13; Gal 4:6; Rom 8:11; 15:15–16, 30). Trinitarian theology is a later theological development" (p. 449). See earlier Fernand Prat (*The Theology of Saint Paul* [2 vols.; trans. John L. Stoddard; Westminster, MD: Newman, 1958] 2. 438) who observed that in Paul, "It is not clear how τὸ Πνεῦμα could denote the Person of the Holy Spirit." Despite these historical viewpoints, others argue that the later doctrine of the Holy Spirit is inherent in the NT. So Thomas F. Torrance, *The Christian Doctrine of God: One Being Three Persons* (Edinburgh: T & T Clark, 1996) who states, "While these formulations do not give us an explicit *doctrine* of the Holy Spirit, they do more than pave the way for it, . . ." (p. 71; emphasis his). This is a true statement; a doctrine of

source from which the Corinthians receive the benefits of communicating with God's spirits. Hence, the same spirit [world], with the same Jesus as its Lord (i.e., "the spirit [world] of the Lord," [2 Cor 3:17]), and the same God as its supreme Father (i.e., "the spirit [world] of God [1 John 4:2]), is the source from which the Corinthians are "given" (δίδοται) different distributions for one sole purpose: πρὸς τὸ συμφέρον, "for the common good" (1 Cor 12:7).

In 1 Cor 4–6 Paul uses three terms that denote "spirit": πνεῦμα, κύριος, and θεός. The second and third terms, "Lord" and "God," are also referred to by the term "spirit" in the NT. In 2 Cor 3:17 "lord" and "spirit" are identical, ὁ δὲ κύριος τὸ πνεῦμα ἐστιν, "the Lord is the spirit." Similarly, in John 4:24 πνεῦμα ὁ θεός, "God is [a] Spirit." Jesus as "Lord" is πνεῦμα ζῳοποιοῦν, "a life-giving spirit" (1 Cor 15:45). Thus, all three terms indicate a supramundane spirit reality from which "gifts," "services," and "activities" are derived. The Lord Jesus Christ and God the Father are distinguished by Paul as two separate and distinct realities in 1 Cor 8:6: for Paul, there exist God and His Christ, both of whom are "[a] spirit."[59] Paul is alluding to a spirit realm or reality by the term "spirit" (v. 4) in which the "same Lord" (v. 5) and the "same God" (v. 6) inhabit as authoritative spirit personalities.

Paul's choice of terminology for manifestations of the spirit world in vv. 4–6 reflect empirical experiences. In v. 4 the noun χάρισμα, "freely given gift," employs the suffix -μα affixed to the noun χάρις, "graciousness," "favor," or "goodwill." When appended to nouns the suffix -μα designates either the result of activity or the activity itself.[60] In Paul's context, χάρισμα thus dispenses the

---

the Holy Spirit is not in the NT, yet so-called triadic formulae did "pave the way" for fourth-century Christian pneumatology. But this does not necessarily justify the legitimacy of fourth-century theology as an appropriate prism through which to view the NT.

[59]   Hence, Hurtado's term "binitarian." See Larry Hurtado, *At the Origins of Christian Worship: The Context and Character of Earliest Christian Devotion* (Grand Rapids: Eerdmans, 2000) 63–97; and ibid., *Lord Jesus Christ: Devotion to Jesus in Earliest Christianity* (Grand Rapids: Eerdmans, 2003) 151. Douglas R. de Lacey ("'One Lord' in Pauline Christology," in *Christ the Lord: Studies in Christology Presented to Donald Guthrie* [ed. Harold H. Rowdon; Leicester, England: Inter-Varsity, 1982] 191–203) claims that Paul's reinterpretation of the Godhead as a duality, God and Christ, steered towards a trinitarian understanding. De Lacey observes that the "place of the Holy Spirit in this development is another story" (202 n. 72). That story, indeed, is not Pauline, but rather is one told in the fourth century and later. Denys E. H. Whiteley (*The Theology of St. Paul* [Oxford: Basil Blackwell, 1974] 127) similarly notes, "St. Paul would probably have found it hard to understand the later problem of the 'deity' of the Holy Spirit."

[60]   See Siegfried Schatzmann, *A Pauline Theology of Charismata* (Peabody, MA: Hendrickson, 1987) 2. This can equally be said of the noun πνεῦμα, whose root πνευ- is augmented with the suffix -μα, thereby indicating the result of an active agent, i.e., the effects

activity of the spirit world among the Corinthian mediums. The noun χάρισμα in v. 4 suggests the "concrete result of bestowal"[61] of the good spirit world's gratuitous presence and activities. The noun occurs seventeen times in the NT, only one of which appears outside of the letters of Paul, in 1 Pet 4:10. Thus, χάρισμα might be considered a typically Pauline term.

Scholarly definitions tend to explain "gifts" in 1 Cor 12:4 as specially marked vocations in life or else as a freely-given "divine grace" or a "grace gift" that is expressed in some deed, act, or word for the benefit of another.[62] Too often, however, theological implications brim to the surface without clearly defining what is appropriate for Paul's context. The definitions remain ambiguous and progress no further than a general restatement of the Greek text. For instance, Käsemann defines χάρισμα as "the specific part which the individual has in the lordship and glory of Christ; and this specific part which the individual has in the Lord shows itself in a specific service and a specific vocation."[63] This has the potential for reading into the Greek later theology which reflects vocations and services of the present-day church.[64]

Rarely do scholars suggest that a spirit world lies behind the distribution of "gifts" in Paul. Almost always it is "the Spirit" or "the Holy Spirit" that is in view, with all of the later theologically-loaded implications these two phrases carry. Héring is one of the few exceptions:

In order to understand the exhortations in Chapters 12 and 14, we must bear in mind an ability latent in the human organism, of becoming a means of expression for beings (good or bad) of the invisible world. Sometimes the 'medium' loses consciousness during these 'supranormal' states, sometimes on the other hand his consciousness is seemingly intensified.[65]

These "gifts" or "graces" occur solely within Paul's context of communication with the spirit world and should not be understood in the light of later theology on "divine grace," at least in Paul. The term χάρισμα in 1 Cor 12:4 is meant to convey a gracious act of God (cf. v. 6), an act that allows the Corinthians to enter into communication with those spirits sanctioned by God to deliver

---

of moving air or wind. By metaphorical usage, πνεῦμα denoted the presence and effects of invisible spirit beings.

[61] Schatzmann, *Charismata*, 2, quoting Gotthold Hasenhüttl, *Charisma: Ordnungsprinzip der Kirche* (ed. Hans Küng and Josef Ratzinger; Freiburg: Herder KG, 1969) 104–5.

[62] For definitions of χάρισμα in Paul's context, see Garland, *1 Corinthians*, 575.

[63] Käsemann, *Essays on New Testament Themes*, 67.

[64] See Doris Donnelly, ed., *Retrieving Charisms for the Twenty-First Century* (Collegeville, MN: Liturgical Press, 1999).

[65] Héring, *First Epistle*, 122. So, too, Ellis, "Spiritual Gifts," 134.

messages of truth, consolation, and admonishment as well as to perform acts that benefit the community and foster its growth.[66] Such an act is one of "divine grace," i.e., a gift of God whereby the Corinthians reap the benefits received by communicating with the good spirit world.[67]

The presence of the spirit world is best expressed in Paul's term διακονίαι, "services," in v. 5. The noun διακονία, "service," "ministry," is used in Heb 1:14 for spirit beings sent out for service to humankind: πνεύματα εἰς διακονίαν ἀποστελλόμενα διὰ τοὺς μέλλοντας κληρονομεῖν σωτηρίαν, "spirits sent out *to serve* those who are to inherit salvation." In 2 Cor 3:8, Paul speaks of ἡ διακονία τοῦ πνεύματος, "the ministry of the spirit [world]," echoing, in a way, 1 Cor 12:5 and 7. The presence of the spirit world is specifically the spirit world of the Lord. Paul alludes to this by qualifying the "services" in v. 5 as being related to "the same Lord." The spirit world of the Lord serves those humans who come together in solidarity in their devotion and commitment to Jesus as Lord.

The activity of the spirit world is expressed in Paul's term ἐνεργήματα, "activities," "energies," in v. 6. In the most common sense, the term expresses "activity" or "experience."[68] Paul also uses the related verb ἐνέργει in v. 11. In the NT the related substantive form, ἐνέργεια, is always used of the actions or operations of spirit beings.[69] This is effectively stated by Paul when he refers to the different manifestations of the spirit world enumerated in vv. 8–10 as those that "the one and the same spirit [world] produces (ἐνεργεῖ), i.e., energizes" (v. 11). In early Christian literature the term ἐνέργεια was used to express the activity of both good and evil spirits who make their presence empirically known among humans.[70] In 1 Cor 12:3–6 Paul refers to a holy spirit (πνεύματι ἁγίῳ [v. 3]) sent out by Christ ("services . . . same Lord" [v. 5]) who carries out its work among the Corinthians ("gifts . . . same spirit [world]" [v.

---

[66] Ellis ("'Spiritual' Gifts,") observes that the "charismatic" manifestations are, in fact, due to the "powers [i.e., spirits] that lie behind and attend those manifestations" (p. 134).

[67] Recent commentators give a general explanation that is not far afield from the interpretation presented here. See Kistemaker, *1 Corinthians*, 418; Hays, *First Corinthians*, 208; Soards, *1 Corinthians*, 256; Collins, *First Corinthians*, 452; Thiselton, *First Epistle*, 930; and Garland, *1 Corinthians*, 576.

[68] BAGD, s.v. ἐνέργημα.

[69] Ibid.

[70] See Gerard Bartelink, "The 'active' demons: energein and energumenus in Early Christian Literature," *Instrumenta patristica* 28 (1996) 177–80, who chronicles the usage of the terms in relation to the devil and demons while also noting that positive contexts of ἐνέργεια occur in relation to the activity of God and angels (p. 178 n. 8).

4]) and whose operations ("activities" [ἐνεργημάτων]) are supported by the boundless reserves of God's energy ("same God who works [ἐνεργῶν] all things in all" [v. 6]).[71]

In v. 7 Paul summarizes the three successive terms "gifts," "services," and "activities" as ἡ φανέρωσις τοῦ πνεύματος, "the manifestation of the spirit [world]."[72] The term φανέρωσις, "manifestation," is derived from the verb φανερόω, "to reveal," "make known," "show," or "to become visible." The phrase "manifestation of the spirit" indicates that πνεῦμα, an invisible reality, becomes a tangible reality readily identified through the experiences denoted in the "gifts," "services," and "activities" of holy spirit beings. Hence, "manifestation of the spirit [world]" refers to a concrete presence of the spirit world among the Corinthians disclosed in such a way that is perceptible to the senses.

The spirit world is revealed through the different distributions of "gifts," "services," and "activities" enumerated in vv. 8–10.[73] Whereas many commentators speak of mainly "gifts" for this pericope (vv. 4–11), the dominant term is "spirit."[74] The "manifestation of the spirit [world]" essentially renames what Paul speaks of back in vv. 4–6: "The manifestation (gifts, services, activities) of the spirit world (the same spirit, the same Lord, the same God)."[75]

The "manifestation of the spirit [world]" is a presence among the Corinthians that is denoted in δίδοται, "is given." The passive voice of the verb further highlights the fact that the source of each "distribution" from the spirit world is not derived from a person's own talent or faculties but instead from the spirit

---

[71] Origen distinguishes the "operations" and "effects" of evil spirits from good spirits in *De princip*. 3.3.3. In using similar terminology to Paul in Latin, Origen provides an important perspective on the effects of the two spirit worlds, one good, the other bad, from a leading church father.

[72] Garland, *1 Corinthians*, 577.

[73] Grammatically, "manifestation of the spirit [world]" is ambiguous. It might either be a subjective genitive, the manifestation that the spirit world produces, or an objective genitive, that which manifests the presence of the spirit world. Paul might have been deliberately ambiguous, for within this context, he could have easily meant both. See Garland, *1 Corinthians*, 578. Njiru (*Charisms*, 119–20) makes a cogent argument that in the context of 1 Cor 12:4–11 "manifestation" should be taken as a subjective genitive.

[74] Collins (*First Corinthians*), states, "Having introduced spiritual phenomena as a point to be considered (12:1), Paul begins his reflection in a section of the letter that has the Spirit as its unifying and dominant theme. 'The same Spirit' is the phrase that holds the unit [12:4–11] together by way of ring construction (vv. 4, 11). 'Spirit' is the dominant word in the unit" (p. 449).

[75] Fee (*First Epistle*) states that the list of items in vv. 8–10 "are not only 'gifts'; they are above all *manifestations* of the Spirit's presence" (p. 591; emphasis his).

world itself.[76] That the manifestations ("gifts," "services," and "activities") are given "to each" (ἑκάστῳ) Corinthian and not to a privileged few reflects Paul's polemic directed toward those who considered themselves more pneumatically endowed than other Corinthians.[77] According to Paul, the spirit world manifests itself πρὸς τὸ συμφέρον, "for the common good," or the "advantage" of the Corinthian community.[78] The phrase does not specify who is to benefit, but the context seems to indicate that the Corinthians are in view here. Elsewhere, it is implied that manifestations of the spirit world are given in order that the community might be "built up" and "edified."[79]

Verse 11 not only reiterates the point that each Corinthian is given a portion of the manifestation of the spirit world but also the fact that the manifestation is determined by the will of the spirit world itself and not by the individual (καθὼς βούλεται, "just as it wills," in the same way that "manifestation" is "given" in v. 7). In v. 11 Paul recapitulates language from vv. 4–7 but now with "spirit" as the dominant term: "the one and the same spirit [world] (τὸ ἓν καὶ τὸ αὐτὸ πνεῦμα, cf. v. 4) produces (ἐνεργεῖ, cf. v. 6) all these things, distributing (διαιροῦν, cf. vv. 4–6) them to each (ἑκάστῳ, cf. v. 7) just as it wills."

This important verse states that the active works and effects of the spirit world, those casually mentioned in vv. 8–10 and now summed up in the phrase "all these things" (πάντα δὲ ταῦτα), are doled out to each Corinthian member according to their individual ability and inclination in the field of spirit communication. According to Paul, the spirit world does this "just as it wills" (καθὼς βούλεται), i.e., through its selection of gifts for each Corinthian who is best suited for a particular gift, in a manner that the spirit world dispenses, in a measure as it sees fit. Whereas Paul initially referred to "the same spirit," "the same Lord," and "the same God," in vv. 4–6, he now summarizes all three phrases in the one phrase, "the one and the same spirit [world]" (τὸ ἓν καὶ αὐτὸ πνεῦμα), revealing that his rhetoric had all along referred to the spirit world of God with Jesus as its Lord; God and the Lord, ultimately, have the final say as to what a holy spirit might communicate.[80]

---

[76] So Garland, *1 Corinthians*, 578. Any communication from a spirit through a human medium is not the product of the individual's mind but rather that of a foreign spirit, in this case, a holy spirit.

[77] So Collins, *First Corinthians*, 453. See 1 Cor 3:1.

[78] Ibid.

[79] Ibid. See 1 Cor 14:3–5, 12, 26.

[80] In the fourth century, however, Basil believed that the phrase "just as it wills" in 1 Cor 12:11 shows that the Spirit acts sovereignly with "independent authority befitting a lord." Thus, the Spirit is a certain, single divinity. See Haykin, *Spirit of God*, 149. But see p. 256 n. 170.

5. 1 Cor 12:8–10: The Activities of the Spirit World

Having briefly mentioned the different distributions from the spirit world (vv. 4–6) as "the manifestation of the spirit [world]" (v. 7,11), Paul gives a list in vv. 8–10 of nine of these distributions:[81] λόγος σοφίας, "a message of wisdom," λόγος γνώσεως, "a message of knowledge," (v. 8), πίστις, "faith," χαρίσματα ἰαμάτων, "gifts of healings," (v. 9), ἐνεργήματα δυνάμεων, "workings of powers [effective acts over evil spirits]," προφητεία, "prophecy," διακρίσεις πνευμάτων, "discernment of spirits," γένη γλωσσῶν, "kinds of tongues," and ἑρμηνεία γλωσσῶν, "interpretation of tongues" (v. 10).[82] Paul gives no explanatory flourish on any one of these terms and phrases. He simply presents them casually on a list to members of the Corinthian congregation who undoubtedly were privy to their full meaning.[83] Thiselton rightly notes that a translation of some of the items on the list presupposes an interpretation of no less than six terms, "each of which bristles with controversial exegetical possibilities and judgments."[84]

Scholars have wrestled with the meaning conveyed in this list of pithy references to manifestations of the spirit world.[85] The organization of the manifestations is sometimes thought to suggest the rhetorical device of *repititio* for the sake of emphasis.[86] The organization forms what appears to be a pattern in an A-B-A' arrangement, a threefold structure that highlights the endowments of the Corinthian community by the presence of the spirit world of God. The first and third groups, referring to knowledge, wisdom, and tongues, do not appear in any of the other lists of spiritual endowments in the NT.[87]

---

[81] Fee (*First Epistle*) states, "To illustrate the thesis of v. 7 Paul proceeds to offer a sizable list of ways in which the Spirit in manifested in the Christian assembly" (p. 590).

[82] Compare similar lists: Rom 12:6–8, Eph 4:11–12, 1 Pet 4:10–11.

[83] Collins (*First Corinthians*) notes, "The difficulty in understanding the precise nature of each of the gifts is compounded by the fact that the gifts appear on a list. No adequate distinguishing characteristics are cited" (p. 451).

[84] Thiselton, *First Epistle*, 952.

[85] This has led Hays (*First Corinthians*) to argue, "It is futile to speculate at length about the precise meaning of each gift, because Paul does not give us enough information to construct a clear picture" (p. 211).

[86] Collins, *First Corinthians*, 451.

[87] Garland, *1 Corinthians*, 579–80.

5.1 Verse 8: λόγος σοφίας, λόγος γνώσεως, *"Message of Wisdom" and "Message of Knowledge"*

Paul begins in v. 8, the A section, with two gifts that appear to refer to "messages" or "utterances"(λόγος)[88] received by the Corinthians from the spirit world: "for to one is given through the spirit [world] a word of wisdom, to another a word of knowledge according to the same spirit [world]."[89] The nature of this "giving" and the content of the "word" or "message" is not disclosed by Paul. Soards defines "a word of wisdom" as "God-given insight into the mysterious purposes and workings of God in and through Jesus Christ."[90] Collins suggests that 1 Cor 2:6–16 provides a Pauline commentary on the word of wisdom wherein Paul "speaks the wisdom of God hidden in mystery in the demonstrative proof of the spirit and power."[91] The "word of knowledge" is more difficult to define, but is probably parallel to the "word of wisdom."[92] Fee defines the "word of knowledge" as a "spiritual utterance of some revelatory kind."[93] This recalls the fact that for Paul utterances of both wisdom and knowledge are given "through" (διά) and "according" (κατά) to the "spirit [world]" (πνεῦμα).

Arguably, according to Paul's context here, these messages or utterances of wisdom and knowledge are those of spirits from the spirit world, possibly uttered through the Corinthian mediums who speak ἐν πνεύματι. Thus, Barrett explains these messages as a "gift of instructive discourse" bestowed by the Spirit.[94] The content of such spirit messages might be partially explained by 1 Cor 2:6–16 wherein Paul discusses "God's wisdom" (v. 7) that is revealed by God to Christians "through the spirit [world]" (v. 10) with "words taught by a spirit" (v. 13).[95] This "wisdom" is not spelled out by Paul in any detail, but it at least has something to do with the knowledge of Christ's death and the

---

[88] So Fee, *First Epistle*, 592; and Thiselton, *First Epistle*, "utterance relating to wisdom," and "discourse relating to knowledge" (p. 936).

[89] Cf. Paul's lengthy discussion on word and wisdom in 1 Cor 1:18–4:21.

[90] Soards, *1 Corinthians*, 258.

[91] Collins, *First Corinthians*, 453. So Fee, *First Epistle*, 592; and Garland, *1 Corinthians*, 581. Thus, markedly different from "the persuasive art of wisdom" (πειθοῖ[ς] σοφίας [λόγοις] 1 Cor 2:4,13).

[92] See Kistemaker, *1 Corinthians*, 421.

[93] Fee, *First Epistle*, 593.

[94] Barrett, *First Epistle*, 284.

[95] See Njiru, *Charisms*, who states, "The actual meaning of λόγος is the concrete use of a word or a discourse (cf. 1 Cor 2,3). In our text to utter the words of wisdom necessarily requires words as being taught by the Spirit, since he alone comprehends the thoughts of God" (p. 133).

meaning and implications of his resurrection from the dead as "Lord" and savior, i.e., the gospel.[96]

5.2 Verse 9a: πίστις, "Faith"

Paul continues with his list in the B section, vv. 9 and 10a, with five endowments from the spirit world: "faith," "gifts of healings," "workings of powers (effective acts over evil spirits)," "prophecy," and "discernment of spirits." "Faith" is the first of the five spiritual endowments in the B section (the third spiritual endowment in the threefold *repititio*). Many commentators agree that "faith" here does not refer to "saving faith" or "saving trust" in God required of all Christians and necessary for salvation by grace.[97] Some have appropriated "faith" within the context of the two endowments that follow in the list, "gifts of healing" and "effective acts of power," interpreting the meaning of "faith" as a gift related to performing miracles.[98] Others have posited whether inexplicable acts of faith, such as "faith to move mountains" (see Matt 17:20; 1 Cor 13:2), is meant here.[99]

Whereas specific acts of faith and the category of miracles are possible interpretations for "faith," Thiselton argues that the focus should be placed instead on the "conceptual entailments of faith in God," linking "faith" with "a message of knowledge" in v. 8.[100] This link suggests a faith that is initiated and informed by the hearing of and an understanding of the utterances of doctrinal truths by the spirits (λόγος σοφίας, λόγος γνώσεως), in the same way that Paul speaks of faith that is activated by "a hearing" (ἀκοῆς) of the gospel in Rom

---

[96] John 16:12–14 might reveal the purposes that the spirit world had in delivering messages of wisdom and knowledge in 1 Cor 12:8: "I have much more to tell you, but you cannot bear it now. But when it (ἐκεῖνος) comes, the spirit [world] of truth, it will guide you to all truth. It will speak not on its own, but it will speak what it hears, and will declare to you the things that are coming. It will glorify me, because it will take from what is mine and declare it to you." The messages of wisdom and knowledge might have contained the truths that Christ promises in the Gospel of John; truths "spoken" by the spirit [world] of truth. These messages from the good spirit world were to be identified through the speech of spirits "glorifying" Jesus, i.e., "Jesus is Lord" (cf. 1 Cor 12:3).

[97] See Robertson and Plummer, *First Epistle*, 266; Conzelmann, *1 Corinthians*, 209; Fee, *First Epistle*, 593; Kistemaker, *1 Corinthians*, 422; Hays, *First Corinthians*, 212; Collins, *First Corinthians*, 454; Thiselton, *First Epistle*, 944; and Garland, *1 Corinthians*, 581.

[98] So Robertson and Plummer, *First Epistle*, 266; Conzelmann, *1 Corinthians*, 209; Fee, *First Epistle*, 594; and Garland, *1 Corinthians*, 581–82.

[99] Hays, *First Corinthians*, 212; Collins, *First Corinthians*, 454; and Thiselton, *First Epistle*, 946. Admittedly, this too might fall under the rubric of performing miracles.

[100] Thiselton, *First Epistle*, 946.

10:17.[101] Such faith is also a gift of God (cf. Rom 3:24–25, 6:14, 12:3). As was stated earlier, the messages of knowledge and wisdom might have contained elements pertaining to the gospel.[102] If this be the case, then "faith" here is a response to these messages from the spirit world about what Christ has accomplished through his death and resurrection.[103] Through its communications with the Corinthians, the spirit world endows certain members with the comprehension of the full scope and ramifications of the truth of the gospel.[104]

5.3 Verse 9b: χαρίσματα ἰαμάτων, "Gifts of Healings"

Garland observes that the next item, "gifts of healings," is the only item in the list that is identified as a χάρισμα. He posits that this was meant to distinguish healing by the spirit from healing by the medical arts.[105] Healing with the aid of the spirit world is recorded in Matt 12:22, 28.[106] Some commentators contribute very little explanation on "healings."[107] Thiselton, however, provides six pages on "healings," more than any other major commentary on First Corinthians to date.[108] The phrase "gifts of healings" occurs only in 1 Cor 12:9, 28, and 30. The plural indicates that Paul is probably alluding to a variety of different types of gifts of healing derived from the healing power generated by the spirit world.[109] Paul writes of those who are ill and infirm in 1 Cor 11:30 as

---

[101] See Joseph A. Fitzmyer, *Romans* (AB 33; New York: Doubleday, 1993) 137–38. Cf. Acts 10:34–44.

[102] See Paul's running commentary on "God's wisdom" in 1 Cor 2:6–16.

[103] Faith seems to have been more than just a hopeful religious commitment or conviction. Faith involved a participation in the activities of the early Christian community, particularly that of communicating with the holy spirits sent from Christ. See Leander E. Keck, *The New Testament Experience of Faith* (St. Louis, MO: CBP, 1984) 100–03.

[104] Even though the knowledge of the gospel was meant to be shared by all, some persons might have been given particular insights or else been able to understand certain points that were unique to their understanding of the gospel. See 1 Cor 3:1–2: "Brothers, I could not talk to you as spiritual people (i.e., people in communication with the good spirit world), but as fleshly people, as infants in Christ. I fed you milk, not solid food, because you were unable to take it."

[105] Garland, *1 Corinthians*, 582.

[106] See Schrage, *Der erste Brief,* 3.151, who relates "gifts of healings" to the Jesus traditions of healing.

[107] Héring, Bruce, and Barrett say nothing.

[108] Thiselton, *First Epistle*, 146–51.

[109] So Collins, *First Corinthians*, 454; Thiselton, *First Epistle*, 946; and Garland, *1 Corinthians*, 582.

a judgment on their misbehavior at the sharing of the bread and of the cup of the Lord.

Collins notes that the sanctuary dedicated to Asklepios, the Greek god of healing, was located in Corinth. He suggests that Paul's "gifts of healings" among those of the church at Corinth might have been similarly experienced by Gentiles in the Asklepieion at Corinth.[110] Early Christians did not doubt the healing powers of the Gentile gods, but they ascribed such powers to the activities of evil spirits. Even here, we see that good and evil spirits were thought to produce similar effects and phenomena.[111]

5.4 Verse 10a: ἐνεργήματα δυνάμεων, "Effective Acts over Evil Spirits"

Verse 10 introduces five ministrations of the spirit world among the Corinthians. The first three occur in the B section of the *repititio* while the last two make up the A' section. The first phrase ἐνεργήματα δυνάμεων is usually translated in English versions and the commentaries as "the workings of miracles"[112] or as "miraculous powers."[113] The term "miracle" is not evident in the Greek, but the plural does not necessarily mean that what might be considered as a "miraculous" deed is to be excluded. The term ἐνεργήματα was shown earlier to mean "activities" or "energies." The -μα suffix indicates the result of activity, and in Paul's context here, the activity of spirit beings. Its formation with the genitive δυνάμεων, "powers," raises a matter of grammar for the interpretation of the phrase, whether as a subjective genitive, "activities of powers," or as an objective genitive, "powers to effect mighty activities."

The objective genitive implies the more traditional interpretation, "workings of miracles," where the "powers" are those performed by someone who has the ability to work "miracles." The subjective genitive allows for a personal interpretation of "powers" as "spirits of evil"[114] that are effectively overpowered by one with authority over evil spirits. The primary patristic and medieval texts

---

[110] Collins, *First Corinthians*, 454. The term ἰαμάτα, "healings," is used both in Paul and in the records of the cures in the Asklepieion.

[111] Cf. Lactantius, *The Divine Institutes*, 2.16,17. ANF 7. 65–66.

[112] Cf. *KJV, AV, NRSV,* and *NJB.* Barrett, *First Epistle,* 285; Bruce, *1 and 2 Corinthians,* 119; Conzelmann, *1 Corinthians,* 209; Talbert, *Reading Corinthians,* 83; Kistemaker, *1 Corinthians,* 423 ("activities that elicit miracles"); Hays, *First Corinthians,* 211; Collins, *First Corinthians,* 455 ("activities of working miracles"); and Garland, *1 Corinthians,* 582 ("powers to effect miracles").

[113] Cf. *REB* and *NIV.* Morris, *1 Corinthians,* 168; Fee, *First Epistle,* 594; and Soards, *1 Corinthians,* 259.

[114] See BAGD, s.v. δύναμις.

understood the phrase to mean the "power to cast out demons" or "unclean spirits."[115] Some modern commentators also understand the phrase to specifically refer to exorcisms.[116]

The grammar remains open to debate, but the interpretation "power over evil spirits" is defensible as either a subjective genitive or an objective genitive. Thiselton's translation, "actively effective deeds of power," a subjective genitive, allows for the inclusion for the interpretation "powers over the powers of evil."[117] Collins translates the phrase in such a way that seems to include both grammatical possibilities, "the activities of working of miracles."[118]

If the Greek refers to "powers over the powers of evil," i.e., "effective acts over evil spirits,"[119] then there seems to have been a good reason for this endowment provided as a "service" (v. 5) by the good spirit world: some Corinthian members were enabled, with power by good spirits, to drive away spirits that might have interfered with communications from the good spirit world.[120] This might have included a spirit that had infiltrated the congregation by posing as a holy spirit through its communications and speech forms, i.e., deceptively appearing as an "angel of light." In this respect, Garland notes that 2 Thess 2:9 gives evidence that the "lawless one" works powers (δύναμις) according to the working (ἐνέργεια) of Satan in the same way that God's power (δύναμις) manifests (ἐνέργεια) in 2 Cor 12:12 and Gal 3:5.[121] In other words, holy spirits and evil spirits operated similarly during spirit communication, for

---

[115] See Thiselton, *First Epistle*, 953–54. The term δύναμις does carry the meaning "forces of evil" in the disputed Pauline letters, but in Paul the singular can also mean the effective power of God and in the gospels can mean powers of heaven.

[116] So Johannes Weiss, *Der erste Korintherbrief* (KKNT; Göttingen: Vandenhoeck & Ruprecht, 1910) 301; Héring, *First Epistle*, 126; Dunn, *Jesus and the Spirit*, 210; and *EDNT* 1. 357.

[117] Thiselton, *First Epistle*, 953–54.

[118] Collins, *First Corinthians*, 455.

[119] For δύναμις as "evil spirit" see Rom 8:38; 1 Cor 15:24; Eph 1:21; 1 Pet 3:22. See BAGD, s.v. δύναμις.

[120] For the interference by an evil spirit with the communications of a good spirit, see Dan 10:13. The "prince of the kingdom of Persia" is a tutelary spirit of the Persian Kingdom that, for 21 days, blocked the spirit sent from God to communicate with Daniel until the guardian angel Michael intervened. See Louis F. Hartman and Alexander A. Di Lella, *The Book of Daniel* (AB 23; New York: Doubleday, 1977) 282. The good spirit world intervenes in the expulsion of evil or undesirable spirits in the gospels. See Matt 9:32–34 (where the Pharisaic accusation implies the spirit[world] of God), 12:28; Mark 3:29–30; Luke 9:42–43 (the unclean spirit is banished by the "majesty of God"), and 11:20. Paul also has the power over pestering spirits in Acts 16:18.

[121] Garland, *1 Corinthians*, 582.

each were bound by the same power and laws that governed such communication (δύναμις and ἐνέργεια).

The next two items in the list, "prophecy" and "discernment of spirits," items related to the speech of a spirit through a medium, might be contextually linked to the "effective acts over evil spirits."[122] These undesirable spirits, who, at times, attempted to disrupt Christians gathered for the purpose of communicating with the spirit world of God, were recognized as such through their speech forms or behavior through a medium. An evil or undesirable spirit would have been "exorcized" or "cast out" from the person through whom it spoke and banished from the congregation.[123]

5.5 Verse 10a: προφητεία, *"Prophecy"*

A substantial portion of Chapter One was devoted to prophecy in recent research on First Corinthians 12 and 14. Essentially, it was concluded that prophecy was a form of inspired speech in an intelligible human language that was meant to convey "God's plan of salvation for the world and the community and His will for the life of individual Christians."[124] The nature and phenomenon of prophecy will be more thoroughly detailed in the exegesis of texts from First Corinthians 14 below. For now, we might suggest that προφητεία be interpreted as "the gift of becoming a medium through whom spirits can speak the mother tongue of the spectators."

5.6 Verse 10a: διακρίσεις πνευμάτων, *"Discernment of Spirits"*

In Chapter One the phrase "discernment of spirits" was shown to be interpreted in several different ways by scholars. The variety of interpretations, however, was usually marked by what was believed to be a discernment of the Holy Spirit from other types of spirits, whether human, demonic, or otherwise. The "discernment of spirits" is closely related to prophecy, for both "spirits" and "prophecy" require testing.[125] Dunn interprets "discernment of spirits" as "an

---

[122] All three items occur in the B section of the *repititio* and hence are, at least rhetorically linked.

[123] Thiselton (*First Epistle*) comes close to this: "Specific human agents (not all) may receive a particular gift from the Spirit to advance the gospel against oppressive forces, for the benefit of all" (p. 956). To be sure, Thiselton's interpretation (ibid.) encompasses both spiritual and earthly forces of opposition. We recognize, however, only the spiritual forces in the Greek.

[124] Friedrich, "προφήτης," *TDNT* 6. 848.

[125] So Garland, *1 Corinthians*, 583. See 1 Thess 5:20–21 and 1 John 4:1.

evaluation, an investigating, a testing, a weighing of the prophetic utterance."[126] Similarly, Collins relates it to discerning true prophecy from false.[127] Whereas διακρίσεις carries the sense of "discern" the related verb form διακρίνειν, "to judge," occurs in 1 Cor 14:29 for judging the utterance of a prophet. But the term πνεύματα does not mean a prophetic utterance or prophecy.[128]

The plural "spirits" in Paul is similar to the plural "spirits" in 1 John 4:1, δοκιμάζετε τὰ πνεύματα, "test the spirits." The two verbs διακρίνειν and δοκιμάζειν occur within a similar semantic range. Paul uses both verbs for "testing" prophetic utterances (cf. 1 Thess 5:21, δοκιμάζειν), the "weighing" of the utterances of prophets in 1 Cor 14:29 (διακρίνειν), and here of "judging" or "discerning" spirits. For this reason, Fee suggests that "discernment of spirits" refers to the kind of "testing" and "weighing" found in both 1 John 4:1 and 1 Cor 14:29.[129]

The interpretation "evaluating prophetic utterances" implies that the prophet himself is being judged or tested for what he says. In the Pauline phrase, the discernment, however, is that of "spirits" and not of "prophets." The judging of the utterance of a prophet determined the type of spirit that gained control of the prophet's vocal chords. Prophetic utterance was inspired speech insofar as a spirit was speaking through the prophet. The "discernment" of a spirit determined whether that spirit's speech (i.e., prophecy) and behavior through a medium (a prophet) reflected Christian content and virtue.[130] Thus, Robert Thomas identifies the "discernment of spirits" as "a recognition of the spirit who prompts such an utterance."[131] The spirit was either a holy spirit or an evil spirit.

The institution of "testing" or the "discernment of spirits" seems to have been a Christian innovation in the field of spirit communication. The very idea of "testing" or "discerning spirits" implies a direct, solicited act of communi-

---

[126] Dunn, *Jesus and the Spirit*, 234.

[127] Collins, *First Corinthians*, 455.

[128] As Grudem argues (*Gift of Prophecy*, 284–85), "spirits" does not mean "prophetic utterances" (προφητείων) but rather "spirit beings" (πνεύματα). Contra Dunn and Collins.

[129] Fee, *First Epistle*, 596. He interprets "spirits," however, as human spirits of the prophets. But cf. Strecker, *The Johannine Letters*, who states, "Not only the Johannine but the Pauline school as well found itself in acute conflict with 'false spirits'" (p. 133).

[130] See Kistemaker (*1 Corinthians*) who states, "The power and influence of spirits can be discerned by their word, deed, and appearance" (p. 425).

[131] Thomas, *Understanding Spiritual Gifts*, 35. That a "prophetic utterance" is what a spirit speaks through a prophet is observed by Vincent (*Word Studies*, 3. 256), who states that "discernment of spirits" refers to "distinguishing between the different prophetic utterances, whether they proceed from true or false spirits."

cating with spirit beings. An explicit example of direct engagement with a spirit through its medium is found in Eusebius, *Eccl. Hist.* 5.16.17, where it is reported that two Catholic bishops, Zoticus of Cumana and Julian of Apamea, attempt to converse with a spirit that spoke through the Montanist prophetess Maximilla: they "tried to refute the spirit that was in Maximilla" (πεπειρᾶσθαι μὲν τὸ ἐν τῇ Μαξιμίλλῃ πνεῦμα διελέγξαι), and they were "present for the purpose of testing and conversing with the spirit as it spoke" (παρόντας εἰς τὸ δοκιμάσαι καὶ διαλεγθῆναι τῷ πνεύματι λαλοῦντι). Eusebius records elsewhere that the spirits who moved among the Montanists were believed by the Catholic church to not always have been properly tested for their veracity:

The spirit gave blessings to those who rejoiced and were proud in him, and puffed them up by the greatness of its promises. Yet sometimes it flatly condemned them completely, wisely, and faithfully, that it might seem to be critical, though but few of the Phrygians [Montanists] were deceived. But when the arrogant spirit taught to blaspheme the whole Catholic church throughout the world, because the spirit of false prophecy received from it neither honour nor entrance, for the Christians of Asia after assembling for this purpose many times and in many parts of the province, tested the recent utterances, pronounced them profane, and rejected the heresy, – then the Montanists were driven out of the church and excommunicated.[132]

The demonization of the spirits who spoke through Montanus is clearly seen in other passages of Eusebius. Montanus was accused of being "possessed by a demon and by a spirit of error" (δαιμονῶντι καὶ ἐν πλάνης πνεύματι ὑπάρχοντι) who was "disturbing the populace"(τοὺς ὄχλους ταράττοντι) (*Eccl. Hist.* 5.16.8). Others who heard the spirit speak,

as though elevated by a holy spirit and a prophetic gift, and not a little conceited, forgot the Lord's distinction, and encouraged the mind-injuring and seducing and people-misleading spirit, being cheated and deceived by it so that he could not be kept silent.[133]

These Eusebian texts come from the side of opposition that is hostile to Montanism.[134] Montanists, however, believed that the spirits were holy spirits as the above quote from Eusebius indicates, "as though elevated by a holy

---

[132] Eusebius, *Eccl. Hist.* 5.16.9. Kirsopp Lake, trans., *Eusebius: The Ecclesiastical History* (LCL; 2 vols.; Cambridge, MA: Harvard University Press, 1926) 1. 477. Montanism emerged around the mid-to-late second century.

[133] Ibid., 5.16. 8. Trans. Lake, *Eusebius*, 1. 475, 477.

[134] For the condemnation of Montanism see William Tabbernee, "The Opposition to Montanism from Church and State: A Study of the History and Theology of the Montanist Movement as Shown by the Writings and Legislation of the Orthodox Opponents of Montanism," (Ph.D. diss., University of Melbourne, 1978).

spirit" (ὡς ἁγίῳ πνεύματι . . . ἐπαιρόμενοι).[135] One of the most eminent proponents of Montanism was the church father Tertullian, who also claimed that "ecstasy is the holy spirit's operative virtue of prophecy," and "God infused into him the ecstasy, or spiritual quality, in which prophecy consists."[136]

The fact that both good and evil spirits could communicate through a medium created the potential for such a scenario; whereas one group might view the spirit as a demon or a lying spirit, another group could claim that the spirit was a good spirit.[137] The criteria for deciding which spirit was speaking

---

[135] Anti-Montanist writings show that Montanus and his circle believed that holy spirits spoke through Montanus and Montanist prophets. For instance, Cyril of Jerusalem, *Catechetical Lectures* 16.8, accuses Montanus of calling himself the Holy Spirit: "For this Montanus, . . . dared to say that he was himself the Holy Spirit." This kind of accusation misunderstands the way in which prophecy functioned among Montanists. A spirit spoke in the first person through an otherwise passive prophet as the following Montanist oracle states: "Behold, a man is like a lyre, and I [the spirit] strike him like a plectrum. The man is asleep [is in a trance] but I am awake" (Epiphanius, *Haer.* 48.4). Montanus is not speaking, i.e., he did not call himself a holy spirit, but rather the spirit speaking through him apparently identified itself as a holy spirit. The passive state of Montanus during which a spirit communicated through him is described in Eusebius as ἐν παρεκστάσει, "in an ecstasy," and πνευματοφορηθέντα, "moved [to speak] by a spirit" (*Eccl. Hist.* 5.17.2). Notice that the latter term, while used here in a derogatory way to accuse Montanus, is used of both true and false prophets in Herm. *Mand.* 11.16: ἔχεις ἀμφοτέρων τῶν προφητῶν τὴν ζωήν. δοκίμαζε . . . τὸν ἄνθρωπον . . . πνευματοφόρον εἶναι, "you have descriptions of the lives of both kinds of prophets. Test . . . the man . . . who is moved by a spirit." On Montanism, see David F. Wright, "Why Were the Montanists Condemned?" *Themelios* 2 (1976) 15–22; Walter J. Burghardt, "Primitive Montanism: Why Condemned?" in *From Faith to Faith: Essays in Honor of D. G. Miller on his 70th Birthday* (ed. D. Y. Hadidian; PTMS 31; Allison Park, PA: Pickwick, 1979) 339–56; and Ronald E. Heine, "The Role of the Gospel of John in the Montanist Controversy," *Second Century* 6 (1987) 1–19.

[136] Tertullian, *Treatise on the Soul* 11,21. ANF 3. 191,201. The acceptance of ecstasy among patristic fathers is shown by Pierre de Labriolle, *La crise montaniste* (Paris: Leroux, 1913) 555–62. Contra Knox, *Enthusiasm*, who denied that "early Christian prophecy was of the Montanist type" (p. 43).

[137] Hence, Lake (*Eusebius*) notes, "It is important that Abercius fully believed in the supernatural gift of Montanus but ascribed it to the Devil instead of to the Holy Spirit. It was the difficulty of distinguishing . . . between these two sources of inspiration which led to so much trouble" (1. 477 n. 2). Catholics accepted that Montanus was a medium through whom a spirit spoke. When they condemned his utterances, however, they did so based on the *content* of such utterances, i.e., the "bastard utterances" (νόθων ἐκφωνημάτων, *Eccl. Hist.* 5.16.8). The notion that a spirit spoke this content through a passive medium added legitimacy to the condemnation of that spirit and the ecstatic state in which such utterances were made against the church. See *Eccl. Hist.* 5.16.7 and 5.17.2–3. See further Pierre de Labriolle, "La polémique anitmontaniste contre le prophétie extatique," *RHPR* 11 (1925) 97–145. Apparently, Tertullian was either not privy to such utterances or was not convinced by the opposition. See Tertullian, *Against Marcion* 5.8. ANF 3. 447.

ultimately lay with the behavior and speech of the spirit as it spoke through the prophet.

Christians were much more discrete than Gentiles and Jews about the spirits with whom they communicated. Unlike many in antiquity, Christians judged and tested the utterances of spirits through prophets.[138] In every case, it was to be expected that the spirit exhibit a speech form that would indicate its provenance as a spirit "of God." This fine discrimination was based on statements that showed the spirit's devotion to Jesus as Lord and to Jesus who is "Christ" as having come in the flesh, suffering death, and resurrected (see 1 Cor 12:3, 1 John 4:1,2).

Hellenistic Greek texts indicate that Gentiles were also privy to distinguishing different types of spirits from one another based on their appearance among spectators during a séance and the words they uttered through mediums. This is especially so in the case of the third century Neo-Platonist Iamblichus whose writing, *On the Mysteries*, reveals a keen awareness of empirical verifications for different types of spirits based especially on various light emanations and color effects radiated by certain spirits.[139] Like early Christians before him, Iamblichus was aware of the ambiguity posed by spirit communication.[140]

Iamblichus claims that "inferior powers assume the form of the more venerable orders, and pretend to be those whose forms they assume; and hence arrogant words are uttered by them, and such as exceed the authority which they possess."[141] These inferior spirits masquerade as that which Iamblichus calls ἀληθινῶν καὶ ἀγαθῶν πνευμάτων, "genuine and good spirits," through the

---

[138] See Joseph T. Lienhard, "On 'Discernment of Spirits' in the Early Church," *TS* 41 (1980) 505–29 for patristic interpretations. Leinhard (ibid., 519–28) effectively shows how the idea of discernment of spirit beings through prophets shifted to a discernment of evil thoughts or passions within the person's own psyche wherein "spirits" were depersonalized into symbols for different sins. This was an erroneous shift that identified "spirit" with human vices, feelings, and emotions. The effects of this shift are felt in contemporary society wherein "spirit" is used to denote a feeling or a mood in such expressions as "in good spirits," "the spirit of the season," and "lift your spirit." Such a semantic range does not reflect the semantic range of "spirit" in the first century. A spirit was not a mood. A spirit was an invisible sentient personality that might, indeed, evoke a mood. See n. 1 above.

[139] See Iamblichus, *De myst.* 2.1,3,4,6,10.

[140] Iamblichus (*De myst.* 2.6) uses language similar to Paul for the benefits of communicating with the spirit world: "Moreover, the gifts (δῶρα) that arise from these manifestations (ἐπιφανειῶν) are not all equal, nor do they bear the same fruits (καρπούς)." Compare 1 Cor 12:4, "distributions of gifts (χαρίσματα)," 12:7, "manifestation (φανέρωσις) of the spirit," and Gal 5:22, "the fruit (καρπός) of the spirit."

[141] Iamblichus, *De myst.* 2.10. For Greek text see Clarke, *Iamblichus*, 108.

words they speak. Seduction through the imitation of speech forms and miraculous acts were some of the most powerful weapons wielded by deliberately deceptive spirits, especially among Christians.

In the *Constitutions of the Apostles* 8.1.2 this is given clear testimony: "Nay, the devil foretells many things, and demons about Him; and yet for all that, there is not a spark of piety in them."[142] Once a deceptive spirit successfully persuaded its non-discerning Christian audience that it was a spirit sent by God, or, at least, not an evil spirit, then the door lay open for the evil spirit world to corrupt Christians and destroy any confidence in communication with the good spirit world.[143]

At the same time, the visitation by deceptive spirits might have provided Christians, advanced in the field of spirit communication, with opportunities to refine their discernment skills. For this reason, God might have allowed deceptive spirits to manifest in a Christian circle that had already established ties with the holy spirits. By doing so, the presence of deceptive spirits would be better recognized, even in the event that the spirit claimed to be a holy spirit. This recognition might be multi-faceted, encompassing the spirit speaking and the spirit given verbal tests, or discerning the spirit through "feeling" its presence, i.e., clairsentience.[144] The deceptions of the unholy spirits would then

---

[142] ANF 7. 480–81. See further Gal 1:8; 2 Thess 2:2; Herm. *Mand.* 11.3, "But he [the false prophet] also speaks some true words (ῥήματα ἀληθῆ λαλεῖ) for the devil fills him with his spirit, to see if he can break any of the righteous"; Justin Martyr, *1 Apology* 62; *Epistle of Ignatius to Hero* 2; Clement, *The Stromata* 6.8; Origen, *Against Celsus* 6.45; Lactantius, *The Divine Institutes* 2.16,17; 7.24; and Cyprian, *Treatise* 6.7, ". . . these spirits . . . are always mixing up falsehood with truth . . ." (ANF 5. 467). The "truth" as a basis from which evil spirits mounted their deceptions and assaults is clearly stated in Tertullian (*Apol.* 47): "Everything opposed to the truth has been got up from the truth itself, the spirits of error carrying on this system of opposition, . . . by them, certain fables have been introduced, that, by their resemblance to the truth, they might impair its credibility, or vindicate their own higher claims to faith" (ANF 3. 52).

[143] Irenaeus (*Against Heresies* 1.16.3) gives the Christian view of the power of deceitful spirits to sway the undiscerning: "For when the unclean spirit of folly has gone forth, and when afterwards he finds them not waiting upon God, but occupied with mere worldly questions, then, . . . inflating the minds of those men with the notion of their being able to conceive of something beyond God, and having fitly prepared them for the reception of deceit, he implants within them the Ogdoad of the foolish spirits of wickedness" (ANF 1. 342).

[144] For an example of clairvoyant discernment, see Iamblichus, *De myst.* 3.6, "the spirit descending and entering *is seen* by the medium, both in its extent and its quality; and that he is mystically obedient to and directed by it. . . . it becomes clear to those who are in the know that it is in itself most true, most powerful, and especially well ordered concerning things about which it [the spirit] is naturally disposed to speak the truth, and what power it provides or effects" (emphasis mine). Trans. Clarke, *Iamblichus*, 133.

diminish but never fully disappear. The discernment process would proceed to a much higher level, a more subtle level, for deceptive spirits could only continue in their deceptions by inventing new methods to ensnare Christians. The Christian notion that God allows demons to test (educate?) Christians seems to be the underlying principle here.[145]

5.7 Verse 10b: γένη γλωσσῶν, "Different kinds of tongues," and ἑρμηνεία γλωσσῶν, "Interpretation (Translation) of tongues"

Speaking in tongues, or glossolalia, has been a point of considerable debate among scholars. Much of this was discussed in Chapter One. Glossolalia was inspired speech that might serve the same capacity as prophecy only if "interpreted." Otherwise, glossolalia was not meant to be regularly practiced, for it did not serve the purpose of "building up" the church; it did not convey meaning. The nature and phenomenon of glossolalia will be more thoroughly detailed in the exegesis of texts from First Corinthians 14 in Chapter Six below. For now, we might interpret one with "different kinds of tongues" as a person having the ability for becoming "a medium through whom spirits can speak in foreign languages," and "interpretation of tongues" as the gift of becoming "a medium through whom foreign languages can be translated into the mother tongue of the spectators."

6. Conclusion

In sum, Paul lists nine endowments and activities of the spirit world that occurred in the church at Corinth, many of which concerned the direct speech of spirit beings ("a message of wisdom," "a message of knowledge," "prophecy," "discernment of spirits," "different kinds of tongues," and the "interpretation of tongues"). Some explain the list as Paul's attempt to show

---

[145] See the *Clementine Homilies*: "The labor, therefore, of everyone is to be solicitous about the putting to flight of his own demons" (9.11); "Many, not knowing how they are influenced, consent to the evil thoughts suggested by the demons, as if they were the reasoning of their own souls" (9.12), (ANF 8. 277); and Clement, *Stromata* 6.8, "Scripture says that 'the devil is transformed into an angel of light.' When about to do what? Plainly, when about to prophesy" (ANF 2. 495).

that no one gift is superior than another.[146] The ordering of the list was meant to partially correct the Corinthians' concentrated focus on glossolalia and indicate that other endowments of the spirit world are equally as important as are those to whom such endowments are doled out.[147] Paul's argument in chap. 14 coupled with the fact that glossolalia is listed last might indicate Paul's intention to downplay the role of glossolalia in the Corinthian church.[148]

---

[146] See especially Mitchell (*Paul and the Rhetoric of Reconciliation*, 268), who states that in 12:4–11 Paul presents an argument "that each person has his or her own individual gifts and roles to play, each of which in its own way benefits the community."

[147] Hays (*First Corinthians*) states, "By ordering the list in this way, Paul implies that the gifts on which the Corinthians are fixated [i.e. glossolalia] are by no means the only gifts operative in the church" (p. 212).

[148] Garland (*1 Corinthians*) states, "Although Paul does not denigrate tongues as a gift, he does place greater value on those gifts that lead to service to others, and he wants the Corinthians to share this same perspective. Since he believes that grace-gifts are given to individuals with a view to the mutual benefit of the community, and since the gift of tongues used without an interpreter benefits only the speaker (and otherwise tends to foster division), he relegates tongues to the bottom of the list of gifts" (p. 575).

Chapter 6

Prophecy and Glossolalia:
The Direct Communication of Spirits through Human
Mediums in First Corinthians 14

1. Introduction

After completing his digression on "love" in 1 Cor 13:1–14:1a, Paul returns to the main topic of First Corinthians 12–14 in 14:1b, ζηλοῦτε δὲ τὰ πνευματικά, "be eager to communicate with the spirit world," with an intent to address his opinion on the occurrence of glossolalia during community worship. In 14:1b τὰ πνευματικά, "spiritual things," is the same term with which Paul began his exhortation in 12:1a, with genitive the τῶν πνευματικῶν. By returning to his exhortation on "spiritual things" in 14:1b, Paul not only connects 12:1a with 14:1b, but also isolates chap. 13 as a rhetorical unit within the larger unit of First Corinthians 12–14.[1]

From the polemical tone of chap. 14, we conclude that some Corinthians were practicing glossolalia to excess. The fact that glossolalia was not interpreted did not foster growth or promote unity among the Corinthians (1 Cor 14:2–5,13, 16–17, 23–25). One of the main dangers of glossolalia is mentioned by Paul in v. 4a: "one who speaks a tongue builds himself up." While this might be taken in a positive sense, that of indirectly serving the corporate good of at least one of the community members who is built up,[2] building up one's self can potentially serve the ego of the glossolalist, promoting hubris and self-assertion.[3] Paul's solution, therefore, was to advocate intelligible inspired speech, i.e., prophecy, that would build up the church, provide encouragement, offer solace, and give evidence that God was present in their midst (1 Cor 14:3,4b,5,25).

Paul's antithetical arguments for the practice of prophecy over that of glossolalia does not necessarily diminish the value of glossolalia in his eyes.

---

[1] See Collins, *First Corinthians*, who states, "The particle *de* ("and") connects this exhortation with the final words of the encomium on love (14:1a). Parallel with 12:13a, the exhortation completes the *inclusio* that isolates ch. 13 as a single rhetorical unit, thereby confirming the paracletic thrust of the encomium. The exhortation also serves a transitional purpose. It allows Paul to return to the specific issue at hand, namely the exercise of spiritual gifts (*pneumatika*) within the community" (p. 491).

[2] So Garland, *1 Corinthians*, 634.

[3] As Garland (ibid.) maintains. See Martin, "Tongues of Angels," 556.

Glossolalia is listed as one of the manifestations of the spirit world in 12:10. Paul wishes that all of the Corinthians may speak in tongues (14:5), and he gives thanks to God that he speaks in tongues more than any of the Corinthians (v. 18). Instead of discouraging glossolalia, he gives instructions for the proper use of glossolalia in community worship (vv. 26–28). At the conclusion of his exhortation, Paul gives a clear directive that glossolalia should not be prohibited, "Do not forbid speaking in tongues," (v. 39), provided that the tongue is interpreted so that the others may benefit from the message (vv. 16–18, 27–28). Prophecy is indeed preferable to glossolalia (v. 1, "especially that you may prophesy"). But if someone interprets glossolalia, then, like prophecy, glossolalia can build up the church (v. 5).[4]

Paul's digression on "love" in chap. 13 establishes the basis from which the proper use of glossolalia should be understood in chap. 14: love requires the gifts to be used for building up the church.[5] The first δέ in 14:1b may be an adversative, "but," with the implication that the value of "spiritual things" (including glossolalia) is not to be undermined by love. It may also be resumptive, "and," relating the idea that "spiritual things" should be practiced in accord with love. The resumptive δέ better reflects Paul's statement in 1 Cor 13:1–2: "If I speak in human and angelic tongues but do not have love, I am a resounding gong . . . If I have the gift of prophecy . . . but do not have love, I am nothing." The imperative in 14:1b, "be eager for spiritual things," then should be understood in the light of both the digression on love in chap. 13 and the imperative in 14:1a, "pursue love."[6] Thus, Paul is not setting up an antithesis between "love" and the practice of "spiritual things"; as if to say that "spiritual things" are less important and should ultimately give way to love. Love, i.e., all of its qualifications mentioned by Paul in 1 Cor 13:4–7, is the driving factor behind the practice of spiritual things, for without love spiritual things lose all their merit (12:31; 13:13).[7] The practice of "spiritual things" should continue, but only in an environment that is conducive to love among members of the congregation; an environment where there is "patience"

---

[4] See Fee, *First Epistle*, who states, "The problem is not speaking in tongues per se but speaking in tongues without interpretation–which from the context seems very likely what the Corinthians were doing" (p. 659).

[5] So Hays, *First Corinthians*, 234.

[6] So Fee, *First Epistle*, 655; Kistemaker, *1 Corinthians*, 476; Hays, *First Corinthians*, 235; and Garland, *1 Corinthians*, 631.

[7] See Garland, *1 Corinthians*, who states, "Love is to be yoked to the Corinthians' zeal for spiritual gifts. With love as their aim, it will prevent them from being zealous only for those gifts that will enable them to steal the show and outshine others [i.e., glossolalia]" (pp. 631–32).

(μακροθυμεῖ), "kindness" (χρηστεύεται), where there is "no jealousy" (οὐ ζηλοῖ), "no boasting" (οὐ περπερεύεται), "no arrogance" (οὐ φυσιοῦται), "no rudeness" (οὐκ ἀσχημονεῖ), "no seeking of self interests" (οὐ ζητεῖ τὰ ἑαυτῆς), "no quick tempers" (οὐ παροξύνεται), "no resentment" (οὐ λογίζεται τὸ κακόν), and "no rejoicing at wrong" (οὐ χαίρει ἐπὶ τῇ ἀδικίᾳ) but "rejoicing in the truth" (συγχαίρει δὲ τῇ ἀληθείᾳ).

2. Prophecy and Glossolalia: Ecstasy

Prophecy and glossolalia are usually defined on the basis of their respective speech form, the former intelligible, the latter unintelligible. The term "ecstasy" related to speech is traditionally understood to describe the manner of speech spoken by prophets in the Greek world.[8] Ecstatic speech involves the suppression of the νοῦς, "mind," of the prophet; the prophet subsequently speaks in a "mindless" (ἄγνοια) state (see Philo, *Spec.* 4.49). The speech spoken in this state is often identified by scholars with the "out of mind" state itself; many scholars presume the speech to be "crazy," "raving babble," and "nonsensical." Following this line of reasoning, ecstatic prophecy means unintelligible speech.

Scholars usually distinguish among prophets on their form of delivery, whether the speech is comprehensible and thus paraenetic speech or whether it is unintelligible speech akin to mantic prophecy in the Greek world.[9] Prophecy and glossolalia in Paul are often distinguished by scholars in this way.[10] The incomprehensible and unintelligible nature of glossolalia have convinced some that glossolalia is akin to ecstatic utterance in the surrounding Greek culture whereas prophecy, intelligible, edifying speech, was nonecstatic and in

---

[8] Ecstasy is derived from the Greek ἔκστασις, ἐξ, "out of," + ἵστημι, "to stand," and in a prophetic context refers to the "displacement" of the human spirit by a foreign spirit. The person "stands out of" him or herself while another spirit occupies the body. This is known as a state of trance (from the French *transe*, "transport," "transpire") in contemporary society. See Philo (*Q.G.* 3.9) who describes ecstasy, "For ecstasy, as its very name clearly shows, is nothing else than the departing and going out of the understanding. But the race of prophets is affected in this way."

[9] Note that according to Heraclitus (*Pyth.* 397A) the Sibyl, although speaking with μαινομένῳ στόματι, "a raving [mantic] mouth," utters plain and understandable oracles; and Lucan, *De bell. civ.* 5.186–97 where Phemonoe is "possessed" but utters "articulate speech" (*virgine voces*).

[10] See Callan, "Prophecy and Ecstasy," 137; and Robert P. Vande Kapelle, "Prophets and Mantics," in *Pagan and Christian Anxiety: A Response to E. R. Dodds* (ed. R. Smith and J. Lounibos; Lanham, MD: University Press of America, 1984) 87–111.

continuity with the biblical tradition.[11] Evidence from polemical attacks against speaking in ecstasy during the second and third centuries is also used to argue that prophecy was nonecstatic in the NT: "the false prophet speaks in ecstasy . . . . But they cannot show that any prophet, either of those in the Old Testament or of those in the New was inspired in this way" (Eusebius, *Eccl. Hist.* 5.17.2–3).

The evidence rehearsed in Plutarch, Josephus, Philo, and Pseudo-Philo in Chapter Three of this book, however, gives a different perspective. The term "ecstasy" does not describe the manner of speech spoken by a prophet as "frenzied." Instead, it describes the psychic condition in which a prophet speaks. In this state, the prophet does not speak, but rather a foreign spirit jettisons the faculties of the prophet (hence, "ecstatic") to take temporary possession of the vocal organs in order to speak to the spectators. Alistair Stewart-Sykes states:

> The different forms of delivery [comprehensible and incomprehensible speech] have been confused with different means of inspiration. In particular paraenetic prophecy has been identified with prophets who speak in possession of their normal faculties, and mantic prophecy with those who do not. The equation is a false one . . . since it is possible for a prophet not in possession of her or his faculties to deliver paraenetic guidance. . . . A possession trance may lead to either mantic or paraenetic delivery.[12]

Paul never uses the term "ecstasy" (ἔκστασις) to describe prophecy and glossolalia.[13] He simply states that each are activities of the spirit world (1 Cor 12:10; 14:2c,16): prophecy builds up the church because it is comprehensible and glossolalia is useful only if it is interpreted.

Admittedly, the term "ecstasy" is used by Philo to describe the state in which a spirit enters into a body and speaks using the vocal organs (cf. *Her.* 249). Paul seems to indicate the same phenomenon, but he does so with different terminology. He does not use the term "ecstasy" or any other terminology taken from experiences related to Hellenistic inspiration (e.g., μανία, ἐνθουσιασμός,

---

[11] See, however, Michaelsen, "Ecstasy and Possession in Ancient Israel," 28–54; and John Levison, "Prophecy in Ancient Israel: The Case of the Ecstatic Elders," *CBQ* 65 (2003) 503–21.

[12] Alistair Stewart-Sykes, "The Original Condemnation of Asian Montanism," *JEH* 50 (1999) 1–22, esp. 4–5.

[13] Forbes (*Prophecy and Inspired Speech*) observes that "it is not possible to argue any simple opposition between, say, 'ecstatic' glossolalia and 'non-ecstatic' prophecy . . . at least in Paul's theology. According to 1 Cor. 14, prophecy and glossolalia are subject to virtually identical controls" (p. 56), and, "The study of early Christian glossolalia and prophecy would be better off if these terms ['manic' and 'ecstatic'] were not used at all" (p. 106 n.6).

ἔνθεος).[14] Both prophecy and glossolalia in Paul are utterances spoken ἐν πνεύματι (12:3; 14:2c,16). This prepositional phrase is Paul's way of describing a spirit speaking through a Christian medium that probably included the psychic condition of ecstasy.[15]

3. Prophecy and Glossolalia:
Verbal Communication from the Spirit World

In Chapter One of this book, recent research on prophecy and glossolalia in First Corinthians 12 and 14 was rehearsed and analyzed. Both are forms of inspired speech. While prophecy relates to inspired intelligible utterance, i.e., the language of the spectators, glossolalia may be either a real yet unknown human language (unknown to both the speaker and the spectators) or a non-human language akin to senseless babble. The conclusion that glossolalia was bona fide human language had much to commend it. For example, 1 Cor 12:10,28 refer to different kinds (γένη) of tongues; this would imply language. The relationship between the content of glossolalia and its subsequent interpretation into intelligible language suggests that glossolalia bore cognitive content.

Furthermore, contemporary evidence for speaking real human languages unlearned by the speaker provides firsthand accounts of what Paul may mean by glossolalia. In contemporary society, the ability to speak unlearned languages is called xenoglossy. This term was coined by the French physiologist Charles Richet around the turn of the twentieth century. It is derived from the Greek ξένος, "strange," "foreign," and γλῶσσα, "tongue," "language." Paul's term glossolalia means "speaking a tongue," or "a language," possibly implying something different. If xenoglossy is related to anything in the NT, some scholars believe it is found only in Acts 2:4, λαλεῖν ἑτέραις γλώσσαις, "to speak *other* tongues." Paul's omission of ἕτερος as well as διάλεκτος from his discussion of glossolalia is thought to show that glossolalia was neither linguistic nor contained cognitive content.[16] But Paul also uses the term ἑτερογλώσσοις, "other tongues" in 1 Cor 14:21 from a citation

---

[14] Peter and Paul, however, are described by a typical Hellenistic expression for experiencing a "trance" state, ἔκστασις, in Acts 10:10, 11:15, and 22:17.

[15] Sometimes "speaking ἐν πνεύματι" is translated as "speaking in a trance" or "speaking ecstatic utterances." See n. 26 below.

[16] But like Paul, Luke uses the phrase λαλούντων γλώσσαις, "they were speaking in tongues," without the qualifiers ἑτέραις or διάλεκτοις. See Acts 10:46.

of Isa 28:11 [LXX].[17] In the context of the Isaiah passage, these "other tongues" were those of the Assyrians. Paul applies the Isaiah quotation in its modified form to members of the Corinthian community by introducing the following v. 22 with ὥστε, "therefore," "consequently." Paul seems to identify the "other tongues" (real human language) with the "tongues" that occurred among the Corinthians.

Paul never defines prophecy or glossolalia. The Corinthians, apparently, were all too familiar with the items in Paul's list of "spiritual things" in vv. 8–10; no detailed explanation was necessary.[18] He simply uses the terms "prophecy" and "glossolalia" in arguments for their proper use and function within the community. Both forms of speech are clearly related to spirit communication as 12:4–10 and 14:1b illustrate.

Unlike many scholars who go either to Paul's surrounding Greek culture or to Paul's biblical tradition in order to explain prophecy and glossolalia, certain elements within Paul's letter itself seem to explain that both prophecy and glossolalia were spoken forms of speech ἐν πνεύματι, "with a spirit," i.e., verbal communication from the spirit world.

4. Glossolalia:
A Spirit That Speaks a Foreign Language through a Prophet

In the pericope 14:13–19 Paul addresses the need for the interpretation of glossolalia in the worshiping community. Verses 16–17 give an example of a blessing that is spoken in a tongue. As a result, the spectators will not know when to respond with the "Amen" and they are not "built up."[19] In v. 16 both the speech of the one who says a blessing in an unintelligible language and the speech of the "uninstructed" who say an intelligible utterance, "Amen," are described by the same verb, λέγω, "to speak" (ἐρεῖ is future tense). This implies that the blessing, even though it is not understood, may nonetheless be human language.

The blessing is no ordinary speech of an officiating minister. The phrase εὐλογῆς [ἐν] πνεύματι, "you pronounce a blessing [with] a spirit," makes clear

---

[17] The LXX has διὰ γλώσσης ἑτέρας.

[18] Note also the pithy expressions in 1 Thess 5:19–22.

[19] Recall Paul's criticism of glossolalia in the church in 14:4.

that the blessing is spoken by a foreign spirit, "with a spirit."[20] The prepositional phrase ἐν πνεύματι is used for unintelligible inspired speech here in 14:16, for in 14:18 Paul uses the term γλώσσαις, "tongues," to refer to the linguistic content of the blessing in v. 16. Hence glossolalia is arguably the gift of becoming a medium through whom a spirit speaks a foreign language.[21]

According to Talbert, no clear evidence for spirits who spoke foreign languages through mediums exists outside of early Christian circles in the Greek world. He gives four possible exceptions:[22] (1) Herodotus, *Hist.* 8.135, where a diviner in the temple of Ptoan Apollo speaks Carian to Mys of Europa; (2) Quintilian, *Inst. Ora.* 1.35, who states "unusual voices of the more secret language which the Greeks call 'glossai'"; (3) Dio Chrysostom, *Discourse on Servants* 10, who mentions the language of the gods and refers to falsely inspired glossolalia by "persons who know two or three Persian, Median, or Assyrian words and thus fool the ignorant"; and (4) Origen, *Adv. Cel.* 7.9 who says that false prophets spoke "unintelligible vocables which sound like Hebrew or Phoenician."[23]

5. Prophecy:
A Spirit That Speaks the Language of the Christian Congregation Through a Prophet

Prophecy, likewise, can be understood as a speech form spoken ἐν πνεύματι. Ellis notes that προφητεία in 1 Cor 14:6 "represents a particular kind of prophetic, i.e., 'in the spirit' [ἐν πνεύματι] utterance."[24] Ellis's point is evident

---

[20] See *Jub.* 25:14, where "a spirit of truth descended upon the mouth" of Rebecca so that she could give a "blessing"; and *Jub.* 31:12, where Jacob "blessed" Levi and Judah when "a spirit of prophecy came down into his mouth."

[21] Kevin Quast (*Reading the Corinthian Correspondence: An Introduction* [New York: Paulist, 1994] 79) argues that glossolalia was uncontrolled spirit possession of a "frenzied fervor" variety, reminiscent of the Corinthians' pre-Christian "pagan" past. But for Paul, glossolalia was a gift of the good spirit world. Thus, holy spirits who might speak a foreign language through a prophet would do so with complete composure. Quast's analogy of glossolalia with pre-Christian Greek oracles finds little support.

[22] Talbert, *Reading Corinthians*, 90.

[23] The only clear evidence for possible glossolalia in the Jewish world might be found in the *Test. of Job* 48–52, where Job's three daughters speak in angelic dialects while praising God.

[24] Ellis, "Spiritual Gifts," 129 n. 5.

in Paul's text. According to Paul, prophecy "builds up the church" (14:3,26) and is one of the "spiritual things," i.e., "things related to communication with the spirit world" (14:1b). In 12:3 the prepositional phrase ἐν πνεύματι indicates that a spirit has gained control of the vocal organs.[25] In this instance the spirit identifies itself as a spirit of God (πνεύματι θεοῦ) or a holy spirit (πνεύματι ἁγίῳ) by its acclamation of Jesus as Lord (Κύριος ᾽Ιησοῦς). As a speech form that "builds up" the church, this kind of acclamation for Jesus would have been immediately recognizable by the Corinthians as an acclamation whose subsequent speech content included something useful for the church. Like glossolalia, prophecy can be interpreted in Paul as the gift of becoming a medium through whom a spirit speaks the language of the spectators.

The idea that prophecy is described by the prepositional phrase ἐν πνεύματι in First Corinthians 12 and 14 shows continuity with prophetic activity among rural Christians. The *Didache*, a late first-century or early second-century manual for church order, describes itinerant prophets who are to be welcomed by Christian households. Some of these prophets are recognized as false prophets if they do not exhibit "the behavior of the Lord" (*Did.* 11:8). Both the true prophet (προφήτης) and the false prophet (ψευδοπροφήτης) speak ἐν πνεύματι, "with a spirit." *Didache* 11:7 describes προφήτην λαλοῦντα ἐν πνεύματι, "a prophet who is speaking with [by means of] a spirit." Three of the qualities that distinguish a true prophet from a false prophet are said to occur while the prophet "speaks with a spirit" (ὁ λαλῶν ἐν πνεύματι, 11:8), "orders a meal with a spirit" (ὁρίζων τράπεζαν ἐν πνεύματι, 11:9), and "says with a spirit, 'Give me money'" (εἴπῃ ἐν πνεύματι· δός μοι ἀργύρια, 11:12). All of the statements are uttered by a prophet ἐν πνεύματι, indicating that a foreign spirit is speaking through the prophet.[26]

---

[25] This prepositional phrase was shown to function similarly to Mark 5:2, "a man with an unclean spirit," indicating temporary possession by a foreign spirit. In Mark the possession is an involuntary one while in 1 Cor 12:3 the possession is voluntary to facilitate communication with the spirit world. See Chapter Four above.

[26] The phrase ἐν πνεύματι in the *Didache* is sometimes translated as "in a spirit" or "in a trance." Maxwell Staniforth (*Early Christian Writings: The Apostolic Fathers* [New York: Penguin, 1968; repr. New York: Barnes & Noble, 1993] 233) translates ἐν πνεύματι in the *Didache* as "in a trance." Staniforth's translation is a paraphrase that reflects the Greek ἐν ἐκστάσις, "in ecstasy," and is based on the idea that one who speaks ἐν πνεύματι is one who is in a state of trance by virtue of a foreign spirit who has temporarily entered into the person, jettisoning the mind/spirit of the person and speaking through that person. Cyril C. Richardson (*Early Christian Fathers* [ed. idem; New York: Collier Books, 1970], 176 n. 64), notes that in the *Didache* λαλοῦντα ἐν πνεύματι means "literally, 'speaking in a spirit,' i.e., speaking while possessed by a divine or demonic spirit." Richardson's interpretation of ἐν πνεύματι in the

The actual content of prophecy is not elaborated by Paul in First Corinthians 12 and 14 but Gillespie observes that the idea of οἰκοδομεῖ, "building up," and the proclamation of the gospel "are both *functionally* and *materially* related."[27] He argues that through prophesying in the church "the gospel is heard afresh and the community is constituted anew."[28] Gillespie's argument dovetails with a spirit's acclamation of Jesus as "Lord" in 12:3. The title "Lord" for Jesus indicated his status as the savior (τοῦ κυρίου ἡμῶν Ἰησοῦ Χριστοῦ, "our Lord Jesus Christ" [1 Cor 15:57]) who died, was buried, and was raised from the dead (1 Cor 15:1–11). A spirit that identified itself as a spirit of God by its acclamation "Jesus is Lord" through a prophet demonstrated its devotion and commitment to Jesus in accord with the gospel tradition. Communication with the spirit world of a Christian nature ("building up," "encouragement," "solace," and proclamation of the gospel) could then proceed.[29]

Paul does not give any specific criteria for what a prophet might say (i.e., what a spirit might say through a prophet). Garland, however, notes that certain criteria for evaluating what a prophet says may be inferred from parts of 1 Corinthians: (1) is a prophetic utterance in accord with the tradition of Jesus

---

Didache is equally applicable to the phrases ἐν πνεύματι θεοῦ λαλῶν λέγει, "one who speaks while possessed by a spirit of God says" and ἐν πνεύματι ἁγίῳ, "while possessed by a holy spirit" in 1 Cor 12:3, πνεύματι δὲ λαλεῖ μυστήρια, "he speaks mysteries while possessed by a spirit" in 1 Cor 14:2c, and εὐλογῆς [ἐν] πνεύματι, "you give a blessing while possessed by a spirit" in 1 Cor 14:16.

[27] Gillespie, *First Theologians*, 142 (emphasis his).

[28] Ibid., 144. Cf. 1 Cor 2:6–16 where "God's wisdom," i.e., "Jesus Christ and him crucified," or "the gospel I [Paul] preached to you" (1 Cor 15:1–11), is "revealed" by the spirit world of God (2:10) and spoken in words "taught by a spirit" (2:13). In 1 Cor 2:16 the νοῦν Χριστοῦ, "mind of Christ," means "the thoughts of Christ as they are revealed by the Spirit," i.e., revealed by the spirit world (Fee, *First Epistle*, 119). Paul quotes Isa 40:13 and translates רוח, "spirit," as νοῦν, "mind" (following the LXX), suggesting Fee's interpretation. The idea that spirits communicated the gospel message is found in Tertullian who was an advocate of the Montanist prophetic movement. He states that the Montanist prophetess Prisca was a vessel through whom the spirit world of God communicated the gospel: "Through the holy prophetess Prisca the gospel is thus preached" (*De exhortatione castitatis*, 10.5).

[29] One rightly wonders if Paul was familiar with the Christological criterion in 1 John 4:2 in which a spirit is to be identified as having come from God only if it "confesses (ὁμολογεῖ) Jesus Christ has come in the flesh." Notice that a spirit is believed to "confess" an intelligible statement that directs attention to Jesus as "Christ." This confession by a spirit is also related to "prophecy" for in v. 1 "testing the spirits" is a means to determine not only the nature of the spirit but also the nature of the prophet through whom the spirit is speaking, " . . . do not believe every spirit, but test the spirits . . . for many false prophets have gone out into the world." See Aune (*Prophecy in Early Christianity*) who states, "false prophets were mediums through which evil spirits spoke" (p. 229).

(7:10; 9:14; 11:23; 12:3; 15:3); (2) is it in accord with the Scripture as interpreted through Christ (1:19,31; 4:6); (3) is it in accord with what their [the Corinthians'] apostle [Paul] has handed on to them and taught them (2:1–5; 7:25; 11:2; 15:3); (4) is it in accord with sacrificial love for others (8:1; 13:1–13); (5) does it promote the community's good (14:3–5,12,17,26); (6) does it not cause another Christian to stumble in the faith (8:7–13); and (7) does it lead outsiders to come to faith by reproving, convicting, and convincing them that God is present in their midst (14:20–25).[30] The speech of a holy spirit, presumably, must reflect these criteria in its addresses to the congregation.

The nature of prophecy in Paul may be inferred from Paul's use of ἀποκάλυψις, "revelation." Paul uses the term to refer to the gospel given to him by Christ (Gal 1:12), of God's will for his life (Gal 2:2), and of visionary experiences (2 Cor 14:1,7). "Revelation" refers to disclosures from the spirit world in verbal form, visionary form, or a combination of the two. The term is used in 1 Cor 14:6,26,30 alongside "prophets" and "prophecies." Kistemaker notes that in v. 6 the first word pair "revelation and knowledge" is enhanced by the following pair, "prophecy and teaching," so that "prophecy runs parallel to revelation, and teaching finds its counterpart in knowledge."[31] In v. 26 Paul notes that someone may "have a revelation" during the gathering of the worship community. In vv. 29–31 Paul reveals an even closer relationship between revelation and prophecy, implying that revelation is an inspired verbal communication. Eph 3:4–5 states that the μυστήριον τοῦ Χριστοῦ, "mystery of Christ," is ἀπεκαλύφθη ... ἐν πνεύματι, "revealed ... with [by means of] a spirit." Prophecy is directly related to the "revelation" of the "mystery of Christ" by means of the prepositional phrase ἐν πνεύματι. The duty of "a spirit" was to communicate, i.e., "reveal through a prophet," the gospel of Christ. This adheres to Garland's criteria for what a prophet might say.

Dunn defines prophecy in Paul as "a word of revelation."[32] Fee emphasizes the role of spirit as to the nature of revelation in v. 6 as a "kind of utterance given by the Spirit for the benefit of the gathered community."[33] Gillespie argues that "prophecy is the product of revelation (*apokalyptein*, v. 30; cf. Gal. 1:12, 16) and the medium of revelation (*apoklalypsis*, 1 Cor 14:6 and 26; cf. Rom. 1:17; 3:21; 2 Cor. 4:2–6)."[34]

While some scholars see a lack of terminological precision in Paul with

---

[30] Garland, *1 Corinthians*, 664.
[31] Kistemaker, *1 Corinthians*, 484.
[32] Dunn, *Jesus and the Spirit*, 228.
[33] Fee, *First Epistle*, 662.
[34] Gillespie, *First Theologians*, 144.

regard to prophecy, teaching, knowledge, and revelation,[35] it is clear that prophecy, at least in Paul, is a public performance by a spirit who speaks to its congregation through the agency of a human medium, some of the content of which may be described as "revelation." Forbes makes a useful distinction between "teachers" and "prophets":

Prophecy is presented in the New Testament as inspired messages. . . . Preachers (and teachers) present their material as reports of past events, past revelations, and as the considered results of their own expository labors. . . . Prophecy, on the other hand, is proclamation of revelation only just received.[36]

To be sure, this distinction between "teaching" and "prophesying" is not meant to convey the notion that prophecy does not instruct. On the contrary, in 1 Cor 14:31 prophesying contributes to "learning " (μανθάνω); in this context, "learning from another," i.e., from a spirit. The distinction here lies with the ability of the individual: whether that be the gift of becoming a medium through whom spirits communicate (the mind is temporarily disengaged), or the ability to teach from one's own resources (the mind is engaged). As Forbes notes, prophecy is divinely revealed truth rather than the result of one's own thought processes.[37]

As messages delivered by spirits from the spirit world, prophecy may have contained not only the gospel that is already found in the NT, but also revelations that were not recorded in the NT. The idea of "new prophecy" seems to emerge in the records of early Christianity during the mid- to late-second century among a prophetic group, the Montanists, named after its founder Montanus.[38] But some scholars argue that in Paul prophecy may have led to new revelations or insights about the Christian message.

---

[35] Barrett, *First Epistle*, 317; and Fee, *First Epistle*, 663.

[36] Forbes, *Prophecy and Inspired Speech*, 228.

[37] Ibid., 229. This distinction is valid only as a comparison between a person who has the gift of being a medium and one who does not but who can teach from his or her on reflections. That does not mean that "teaching" (διδαχή) in 1 Cor 12:28; 14:6,26 is not related to instruction derived from the spirit world through mediums. See n. 178 below.

[38] Eusebius, *Eccl. Hist.* 5.17.2. This "new prophecy" was attacked by opponents who believed that Montanus was inspired by evil spirits or the devil. On the issue of a closed canon and the possibility for new revelation from the spirit world, see Bruce M. Metzger, *The Canon of the New Testament: Its Origin, Development, and Significance* (Oxford: Clarendon, 1987) who states, "The insistence of [Montanism] on the continuous gift of inspiration and prophecy influenced the Church to emphasize the final authority of apostolic writings as the rule of faith. By rejecting the extravagances of Montanism, the Church took the first step toward the adoption of a closed canon of Scripture" (p. 106).

Hurtado argues that Paul's commissioning by Christ for a mission to the Gentiles without the necessity of their conversion to Torah observance was a "new revelation without true precedent in either the Jewish tradition or the emerging Christian movement."[39] He notes that among some circles of early Christianity a "culture" existed that regarded revelations as sources of direction in religious matters. From these prophetic and revelatory experiences "major religious innovations could have been stimulated."[40] Dunn also speaks of the "creative force of religious experience," implying prophetic activity may involve new revelation.[41] Forbes also argues that prophecy in Paul "has to do with new revelation, not the human development of previous revelation or other material."[42]

Nowhere in Paul is there a directive against the possibility for new revelation. Sometimes, "revelation" is used in certain contexts in the NT to denote "truths hitherto unknown."[43] The criterion for any prophecy or utterance of a spirit was based on Jesus as Lord and the gospel message. Paul warns of "a different spirit" that may impart "a different gospel" (2 Cor 11:4). Similarly in Gal 1:8 he warns of an angel from heaven "preaching a gospel other than the one that we preached to you." Likewise, in 2 Thess 2:2 the Thessalonians are cautioned, "Do not be troubled . . . by a spirit . . . allegedly from us to the effect that the day of the Lord is at hand."[44] These warnings in no way discredit new

---

[39] Hurtado, "Religious Experience and Innovation," 189. Philip (*Origins*, 226) similarly states, "His [Paul's] perception changed from one in which the Spirit functioned as bringing revelation from within the Torah, to an understanding that the Spirit brings revelation from outside the Torah. His experience of the 'glory of God' on the Damascus road provided him with the conviction that there was now a new relationship with God which now requires only the entrance into life within the sphere of the Spirit," i.e., communication with God's spirit world during the "new normal," the eschatological period before the return of Christ, initiated at Pentecost (Acts 2:1–3). The "old law" had given way to the "new law" initiated in Christ's act of redemption.

[40] Hurtado, "Religious Experience and Innovation," 199.

[41] Dunn, *Jesus and the Spirit*, 4.

[42] Forbes, *Prophecy and Inspired Speech*, 225. Cf. Gunkel, *Influence*, who wrote over a century ago: "The theology of the great apostle is the expression of his experience, not of his reading" (p. 100).

[43] Paul's "conversion" experience revealed to him personally (Gal 1:12) a truth hitherto unknown (to him) about Christ. See 2 Cor 12:1–5 that refer to "revelations" in a visionary context, revelations vouchsafed to "a certain man" alone (Paul?), implying that the content was unknown by others.

[44] This particular verse offers clear insight into the prospect that early Christians communicated with the spirit world. The statement "a spirit . . . allegedly from us" indicates that the Thessalonians were receiving communications from spirits, among whom may appear an impostor spirit.

revelation; rather they regulate any utterance by a spirit to conform to the basic gospel message that Paul received from Christ. Paul refers to advanced Christian teaching as "solid food" that the Corinthians were unable to bear (1 Cor 3:2). Whether what Paul means by "solid food" is recorded in the NT is debatable.[45]

Thus, one rightly asks, Why would early Christians communicate with spirits? Answer: To be instructed by them about Christ's life, death, and resurrection, and its significance, i.e., the gospel. That holy spirits who were "sent from heaven" were believed to address the gospel to early Christians is explicitly given in 1 Pet 1:12: ἃ νῦν ἀνηγγέλη ὑμῖν διὰ τῶν <u>εὐαγγελισαμένων</u> <u>ὑμᾶς [ἐν] πνεύματι ἁγίῳ</u> ἀποσταλέντι ἀπ᾽ οὐρανοῦ, ". . . which now have been announced to you by *those who preached the good news to you [with] a holy spirit* sent from heaven." Those who preach the good news with a holy spirit sent from heaven are those through whom a holy spirit gives instruction and didactic utterance in the gospel message, i.e., the spirit enters into the person and gives instruction by using the vocal chords, not unlike that which we have seen elsewhere thus far (or possibly through clairvoyance or clairaudience).

6. 1 Cor 14:1b–3: Translation and Explanation

Once that prophecy and glossolalia have been defined as the speech of spirits through their respective human mediums, an interpretation of 1 Cor 14:1b–3 might read as follows:

[1b]Be eager to communicate with the spirit world, especially that you might become mediums through whom spirits speak to you in your own language. [2]For if a spirit speaks through a medium in a language unknown to the spectators, that spirit cannot make itself understood to those present but only to God, for no one understands him; for the spirit uses words whose meaning is hidden from those present. [3]But if a spirit speaking through a medium utters words known to those present, this builds up, encourages, and comforts.

Paul distinguishes spirits who speak in the language of the community (prophecy) from spirits who speak in a language unknown to the community

---

[45] Barrett, *First Epistle*, 80, and Conzelmann, *1 Corinthians*, 71, seem to argue that by "solid food" Paul had more to say to the Corinthians that he had not revealed to them before. Kistemaker, *1 Corinthians*, 101, and Garland, *1 Corinthians*, 108, argue that Paul had already revealed everything to the Corinthians. Hays (*First Corinthians*, 48) believes that by the "milk vs. solid food" rhetoric, Paul is actually exposing the immaturity of certain spirit-enthusiasts who consider themselves to be more spiritually mature than other members.

(glossolalia). Once this interpretation is presented, a new and more meaningful understanding of the Greek text emerges. Several pithy Greek phrases take on more substantive meaning than what is usually found of them in most English versions.

In v. 2 those who do not understand the language that a spirit is using are those to whom the spirit does not speak: ὁ γὰρ λαλῶν γλώσσῃ οὐκ ἀνθρώποις λαλεῖ ἀλλὰ θεῷ, "for one who speaks a tongue does not speak to human beings but to God." The people are indeed spoken to, but what they hear is incomprehensible to them, hence the glossolalist, i.e., the medium through whom a spirit is speaking, "does not speak to human beings" because they derive no cognitive benefit from what the spirit says.

The next Greek phrase in v. 2, οὐδεὶς γὰρ ἀκούει, "for no one hears," refers to those who are listening to the spirit but do not know what the spirit is saying because the spirit is speaking a language that the spectators do not understand.[46] The last Greek phrase in v. 2, πνεύματι δὲ λαλεῖ μυστήρια, "one who speaks mysteries in a spirit," reveals that what the spirit utters (λαλεῖ) is that which the spectators do not understand (μυστήρια).[47] The "mysteries" are not the usual things that Paul believes have been revealed in the era of eschatological fulfillment (1 Cor 2:1; 4:1; 15:51).[48] In the context of spirits who speak languages known and unknown to the community members, it seems likely that "mysteries" refers to the words of a language whose meaning is unknown to or "hidden" from the spectators.[49]

Verse 3 relates the benefits of a spirit who speaks the language of the community members. In Paul's usual pithy manner, he states ὁ δὲ προφητεύων ἀνθρώποις λαλεῖ, "but one who prophesies does speak to human beings." The point here is that prophecy is intelligible speech that community members understand in their own language. A linguistic obstacle to understanding the message does not exist with prophecy. Furthermore, the need for an interpreter, who may or may not be available (14:28), is not necessary. Communication can

---

[46] So Fee (*First Epistle*) who states that although ἀκούω, "to hear," does not usually mean "understand" in the NT, "it is otherwise well attested. It combines the two ideas of 'hearing with the understanding'" (656 n. 16). See also Collins (*First Corinthians*) who translates, "No one understands" (p. 492); and Thiselton, *First Epistle*, 1085.

[47] Collins (*First Corinthians*, 492) notes that "mysteries" is the unexpressed but implied object of "understands" (ἀκούει).

[48] So Thiselton, *First Epistle*, 1085.

[49] See Thiselton (ibid.) who states, "Every writer uses terminology in context-dependent ways that modify a more usual meaning, and Paul's usual meaning [for "mysteries"] cannot make sense here without undermining his own argument."

proceed unencumbered by both the possibility that the message may not be linguistically understood or that an interpreter may not be present. Both glossolalia and prophecy in vv. 2,3 are described as an utterance by the same verb, λαλέω.

Paul realizes the benefits of prophecy because in v. 3 he states that prophecy is for the community's "building up" (οἰκοδομήν), "encouragement" (παράκλησιν), and "comfort" (παραμυθίαν). Collins notes that the repetition of these terms is for the sake of emphasis: they are meant as a contrast to the "mysteries" (i.e., a language unknown to the spectators) spoken by a spirit through a medium with the gift for glossolalia.[50]

The term παράκλησις has a range of meanings related to the pastoral work of individuals: "encouragement" (Rom 15:4–5); "assurance" (Luke 2:25); and "exhortation" (Phil 2:1). Garland observes that the function of prophecy in Paul is especially brought out in Acts 15:32, wherein Judas and Silas are prophets (προφῆται) whose prophesying "encouraged" (παρεκάλεσαν, from the verb παρακαλέω, "to appeal to," "to implore," "to encourage," "to cheer up," and "to urge") the believers (ἀδελφοί, literally, "the brothers").[51] The noun παράκλησις recalls these elements from its verbal form. These elements reveal the quality of the messages received from communication with the spirit world; spirits were meant to convey that which "plead, exhort, encourage, challenge, brace, console, or provide comfort."[52]

The final term παραμυθία, "comfort," "solace," is a hapax legomenon in this form in the NT.[53] BDAG (p. 769) defines it as "that which serves as encouragement to one who is depressed or in grief." Conzelmann believes the term is synonymous with παράκλησις.[54] His observation might be substantiated on the basis that Paul "always uses παραμυθεῖσθαι or its cognates in conjunction with some form of παράκλησις (1 Thess 5:14; 1 Cor 14:3; Phil 2:1)."[55]

---

[50] Collins, *First Corinthians*, 492.

[51] Garland, *1 Corinthians*, 634.

[52] Thiselton, *First Epistle*, 1088.

[53] See a variant form in Phil 2:1 and verbal forms in John 11:19,31; and 1 Thess 2:11 and 5:14.

[54] Conzelmann, *1 Corinthians*, 235.

[55] Abraham J. Malherbe, "'Pastoral Care' in the Thessalonian Church," *NTS* 36 (1990) 375–91, esp. 387.

7. 1 Cor 14:4–5: Spirits Should Speak in the Language of the Spectators Unless a Translator is Present

In vv. 4–5 Paul continues to contrast the effects and worth of prophecy with glossolalia during community worship by using the language of "building up." In v. 4 Paul places ἑαυτόν, "self," in contrast with ἐκκλησία, "the church," to show what it is that glossolalia and prophecy serve. These two nouns, "glossolalia" and "prophecy," are the object of the same verb, οἰκοδομέω, "to build"; glossolalia builds up the self, prophecy builds up the church. The "building up," or "edification," as it is sometimes translated, is a motif that may reflect Paul's earlier metaphor for the church as God's building in 1 Cor 3:9–17. Paul laid the foundation (3:10); in the church community the apostle wants the primary criterion for communicating with the spirit world, in this case prophecy, to be based on that which builds up and edifies the community.[56]

Despite Paul's polemical preference for prophecy over glossolalia, he gives one condition under which glossolalia may be practiced within the worshiping community: if a person is present who has the gift of the interpretation of tongues. In v. 5a, Paul approves speaking in tongues, θέλω δὲ πάντας ὑμᾶς λαλεῖν γλώσσαις, "I wish that all of you would speak in tongues." Indeed, glossolalia is the communication of good spirits to the community (vv. 2c, 16). Paul himself possesses the ability for glossolalia (v. 18), as well as prophecy (13:2).

But before he provides the condition for the practice of glossolalia, Paul gives two remarks on the superiority of prophecy to glossolalia. Immediately after stating his desire that all speak in tongues, Paul stresses the importance of prophecy in v. 5a, μᾶλλον δὲ ἵνα προφητεύητε, "but much more that you might prophesy" (echoing the language in v. 1).[57] Paul proceeds with a second remark which insists on the superiority of prophecy over glossolalia: μείζων δὲ ὁ προφητεύων ἢ ὁ λαλῶν γλώσσαις, "one who prophesies is greater than the one who speaks in tongues." In Paul, prophecy is always the superior gift of inspired speech. Prophecy is placed before glossolalia in the list of things related to communication with the spirit world (12:10) and other lists related to

---

[56] Thiselton, *First Epistle*, 490.

[57] See Num 11:29, where Moses says to Joshua, who is on the verge of stifling the prophesying of Eldad and Medad, that he wishes that all of the Lord's people could become prophets and act as mediums for the spirit world. Some see a relationship between this OT passage and 1 Cor 14:5 (Kistemaker, *1 Corinthians*, 481; Thiselton, *First Epistle*, 1097; and Garland, *1 Corinthians*, 634).

different functions of community members (vv. 28,29). In v. 28 prophecy occurs in second place (δεύτερον) after apostles; glossolalia appears last. In v. 29 prophets likewise occur in second place after apostles while glossolalia is found in the next to last place before "interpreters."

After stating his preference for prophecy as something "greater" than glossolalia, Paul gives the condition under which glossolalia may be exercised within the community: ἐκτὸς εἰ μὴ διερμηνεύῃ, "except if someone interprets" (v. 5c). Paul believes that interpreted glossolalia, i.e., the interpretation (translation) of an unknown language that a spirit speaks through a medium, has a value similar to that of prophecy – just as prophecy "builds up" the church so too does interpreted glossolalia: ἵνα ἡ ἐκκλησία οἰκοδομὴν λάβῃ, "so that the church may be built up." The ἵνα clause, "so that," completes Paul's pleonastic clause "except if someone interprets," thrusting interpreted glossolalia into the same category as prophecy. As Fee states, "The interpretation of the tongue brings it within the framework of intelligibility, which in turn means that it too can edify the community."[58]

The understanding of διερμηνεύω in First Corinthians 14 was rehearsed in Chapter One. Some believed it to mean "interpretation" (Thiselton, Garland), while others argued for the meaning "translation" (Hovenden, Forbes, Turner). The distinction is a fine one,[59] but if we recall that glossolalia is described by the verbs λέγω and λαλέω, this might suggest that "translate" is more appropriate than "interpret." Also, an implicit identity between the Isaiah term "other tongues [languages]" in v. 21 and "tongues" in v. 22 is made (ὥστε) in Paul's argument. The implicit identity between the passage in the book of Isaiah and Paul provides further evidence that glossolalia is an unknown human language that can be "translated" into the words of the language of members in the Corinthian community.[60]

Collins notes that διερμηνεύῃ in 1 Cor 14:5 has an unexpressed subject. He posits that the "interpreter" may be the glossalalist himself.[61] Based on the argument that glossolalia was the speech of a foreign spirit and not that of the

---

[58] Fee, *First Epistle*, 659.

[59] See BAGD, s.v., that defines διερμηνεύῃ in 1 Cor 14:5 as "explain," "interpret," but states that the meaning "translate" is also possible here.

[60] Contra Garland, *1 Corinthians*, who believes, "'Interpretation' is not translation of another language, such as Aramaic, nor is it a word-for-word translation of what was said. Rather, it interprets the significance of the utterance" (659 n. 4). But see *TAY* that translates "speaking in tongues" in 1 Cor 12:10 as "to speak in languages he never learned"; and *RHM* that translates "except if someone interprets" in 14:5c as "unless indeed he translate."

[61] Collins, *First Corinthians*, 494.

glossalalist who was merely a medium for the spirit, it may also be possible to argue that a spirit other than the one that utters the foreign language translated the language.[62] Paul distinguishes between glossolalia and the translation of glossolalia as two distinct gifts from the spirit world (12:10). This distinction might imply that some mediums existed for the sole purpose of allowing spirits to translate the foreign language of another spirit who spoke through a different medium. 1 Cor 14:27 implies that the translator of tongues is someone other than the one who speaks in tongues. But, as Collins's observation shows, the evidence in Paul suggests either possibility: that of the glossolalist as the "translator" (1 Cor 14:5), or a different person who acts as "translator" (1 Cor 14:27).

1 Cor 14:4–5 can then be rendered in the following manner:

[4]A medium through whom a spirit is speaking in a foreign language derives benefit from it for himself alone, while a spirit who speaks through a medium in the language of the spectators builds up the whole congregation. [5]I wish that all of you had acquired the gift of becoming mediums through whom spirits could speak in a foreign language; but I would rather they speak through you in your own language. For a spirit that speaks to you through a medium in your own language is of greater benefit to you than a spirit who speaks in a foreign language – unless, of course, he translates that language into your own so that the congregation may be built up.

A spirit may speak a foreign language through a medium as long as another medium for spirits who translates foreign languages is present. Otherwise, Paul preferred that spirits speak in the mother tongue of those present in the congregation (ἡ ἐκκλησία, "the church"). Prophecy was an important activity in the church. Collins states, "Prophecy seems to be a gift without which the church cannot exist."[63] Indeed, the communication of spirits in the language of the congregation provided a direct link with the spirit world of God; a link through which the church flourished and thrived because it built up the church.

---

[62] Forbes (*Prophecy and Inspired Speech*) comes close to this, "'Interpretation' (1 Corinthians 12.30, 14.5,13, etc.), is most naturally understood in its primary sense of (inspired) 'translation'" (p. 58).

[63] Collins, *First Corinthians*, 491.

8. 1 Cor 14:6–11: The Unintelligibility of Glossolalia – Paul's Musical Instrument Analogies and an Example Taken from Human Languages

In v. 6 Paul begins a new section in his exposition with both νῦν δέ, "now then," and the vocative ἀδελφοί, "brothers."[64] This shift is meant to provide an illustration of his earlier comments in vv. 2–5 on the uselessness of glossolalia in the congregation: νῦν δέ, ἀδελφοί, ἐὰν ἔλθω πρὸς ὑμᾶς γλώσσαις λαλῶν, τί ὑμᾶς ὠφελήσω ἐὰν μὴ ὑμῖν λαλήσω ἢ ἐν ἀποκαλύψει ἢ ἐν γνώσει ἢ ἐν προφητείᾳ ἢ [ἐν] διδαχῇ;, "Now brothers, if I should come to you speaking in tongues, what good will I do if I do not speak to you by way of revelation, or knowledge, or prophecy, or instruction?" The themes in this verse are picked up and elaborated later in Paul's arguments (14:14–19, 26–31, 39–40). Thus, this important verse lays the foundation for the exposition that follows, i.e., until the end of his arguments in 1 Cor 14:40. The terms "revelation" (ἀποκαλύψει), "knowledge" (γνώσει), "prophecy" (προφητείᾳ), and "instruction" (διδαχῇ) stand in contradistinction to "speaking in tongues" (γλώσσαις λαλῶν). These terms relate to intelligible communication derived from the spirit world. The meaning of each term will be discussed in this context in the exegesis below.

In vv. 7–8 Paul's illustration for the uselessness of glossolalia in the community is laid out in two analogies: τὰ ἄψυχα φωνὴν διδόντα, εἴτε αὐλὸς εἴτε κιθάρα, ἐὰν διαστολὴν τοῖς φθόγγοις μὴ δῷ, "inanimate things that produce sound, such as a flute or a harp, that do not give out tones distinctly" (v. 7); and ἄδηλον σάλπιγξ φωνὴν δῷ, "the trumpet gives an indistinct sound" (v. 8).

Some scholars argue that Paul's musical instrument analogy shows that glossolalia was inarticulate babble instead of human language. Garland believes the analogies in vv. 7 and 8 are meant to convey the idea that, like the indistinct sounds of musical instruments, glossolalia is the utterance of inarticulate noises and syllables.[65] Thiselton believes that the analogy is not about the failure to produce a pleasing melody but rather that the harp is untuned and the woodwinds are overblown, producing mere noise without any difference

---

[64] Héring (*First Epistle*, 147) argues that the νῦν δέ means something like "let us look at the facts and take a concrete example," and this carries the force of the conjunctive combination here, "well now."

[65] Garland, *1 Corinthians*, 636, who follows Schrage, *Der erste Brief*, 3. 394–96.

(distinctiveness) in sound.[66] The musical instrument analogies, however, should not necessarily be viewed as a means to determine whether glossolalia in Paul is bona fide human language or inarticulate utterances with no cognitive content. Instead, the analogies are meant to convey the idea that glossolalia is simply unintelligible.

In v. 7 Paul makes his point about the effects of indistinct tones in the "how" (πῶς) clause, πῶς γνωσθήσεται τὸ αὐλούμενον ἢ τὸ κιθαριζόμενον; "How will what is being played on the flute or harp be recognized?" The "tones" or "notes" (φθόγγοι) refer to a recognizable melody that, unless they are played with a distinction (διαστολή), will not be known to the hearers.[67]

Paul continues the analogy in v. 8 with an example from warfare (πόλεμος). He describes a trumpet (σάλπιγξ) that gives out an indistinct sound (ἄδηλον φωνήν). The result is that those who are to prepare for battle will miss their cue to rally for battle: τίς παρασκευάσεται εἰς πόλεμον; "Who will get ready for battle?"[68] The sound will not be intelligible, and the signal for battle will not be recognized. No one will benefit.

In v. 9 Paul introduces the direct application of the musical instrument analogies, οὕτως καὶ ὑμεῖς, "so also with you," to the Corinthian situation of glossolalia in the congregation. He comments, διὰ τῆς γλώσσης ἐὰν μὴ εὔσημον λόγον δῶτε, πῶς γνωσθήσεται τὸ λαλούμενον; ἔσεσθε γὰρ εἰς ἀέρα λαλοῦντες, "if because a spirit does not utter intelligible speech through a medium, how will anyone know what is being said? You might as well be speaking to the air." Paul's point in vv. 7–9 is directed to whether the speech is intelligible or unintelligible. The instruments make either a distinct (intelligible) sound or an indistinct (unintelligible) sound.[69] The indistinct sounds of a musical instrument are akin to the unintelligibility of glossolalia.

The idea of legitimate language enters Paul's exposition in vv. 10 and 11. Paul continues his polemic, but now he speaks of human language in v. 10: τύχοι γένη φωνῶν εἰσιν ἐν κόσμῳ, "there are many different languages in the

---

[66] Thiselton, *First Epistle*, 1103, who follows H. A. W. Meyer, *Critical and Exegetical Handbook to the Epistles to the Corinthians* (2 vols.; Edinburgh: T & T Clark, 1892) 2. 9.

[67] Kistemaker (*1 Corinthians*, 486) notes that flute playing was common at both funerals and weddings (Matt 9:23; 11:17) and the harp is mentioned in Pss 33:2; 137:2; 149:3; and in 150:3, an instrument that was used in temple services.

[68] The trumpet can be used as a musical instrument (Rev 18:22) or, in the OT, as an alarm for coming warfare (Jer 4:19; Joel 2:1), the beginning of a war (Judg 3:27), and the end of war (2 Sam 20:1). Paul uses it in the context of a military bugle to alert the onslaught of warfare.

[69] Fee (*First Epistle*, 664) seems to hold this view. He concludes that the perspective of vv. 7–9 is that of the hearer in the community at worship, i.e., whether the hearer will understand what is said.

world." The noun φωνή can mean "sound," "dialect," and "language."[70] In v. 8 Paul uses the noun for the "sound" of a trumpet. Here, Paul uses it for "human languages."[71] Garland observes that Paul uses the noun φωνή for "languages," because the noun γλῶσσα (that can also mean "language") is used for glossolalia.[72] Paul's play on the noun φωνή is evident in v. 10b when he states that the different languages (φωνῶν) of the world are οὐδὲν ἄφωνον, literally "none is without sound," "not heard," or here, "none is without meaning."[73]

Paul illustrates this point as an application to the Corinthian situation of glossolalia in v. 11 by the use of an inferential conjunction οὖν, "therefore": ἐὰν οὖν μὴ εἰδῶ τὴν δύναμιν τῆς φωνῆς, ἔσομαι τῷ λαλοῦντι βάρβαρος καὶ ὁ λαλῶν ἐν ἐμοὶ βάρβαρος, "Therefore, if I do not know the meaning of the language, I will be a foreigner to the one who speaks it, and one who speaks it a foreigner to me." Paul uses the phrase τὴν δύναμιν τῆς φωνῆς, "the power of the sound," or "the force of the word," to indicate the "meaning" that a certain language possessed.[74] If Paul does not know (μὴ εἰδῶ) the meaning or force of the language, he will remain a βάρβαρος, "foreigner," to the speaker and vice versa. Those who speak different languages to one another cannot be understood. Inarticulate sounding utterance, however, does not take away from that utterances' cognitive content, if it is, in fact, a known human language.[75] A Greek who heard someone speak another language would have reacted much in the same way as those in contemporary society who visit a country whose language is not their own.[76]

Paul's point in vv. 10,11 pushes glossolalia into the realm of known human language. No single individual knows all languages, but each language, nevertheless, has real cognitive meaning (οὐδὲν ἄφωνον). Some scholars view

---

[70] See Acts 14:11, where φωνή is used of the Lycaonian dialect.

[71] So Kistemaker, *1 Corinthians*, 486; Collins, *First Corinthians*, 499; and Garland, *1 Corinthians*, 637.

[72] Garland, *1 Corinthians*, 637. Thiselton (*First Epistle*, 1105) notes this as typical for modern commentators. Paul speaks of "the tongues of men" in 1 Cor 13:1, a phrase that undoubtedly refers to human languages.

[73] So Fee, *First Epistle*, 660; Kistemaker, *1 Corinthians*, 486; and Garland, *1 Corinthians*, 631.

[74] See Collins, *First Corinthians*, 499.

[75] Collins (*First Corinthians*, 497) notes that βάρβαρος was used to describe one who could not speak Greek properly, that is, Greek as a second language. Originally the term was used to distinguish Greek-speakers from those who spoke another language.

[76] Garland, *1 Corinthians*, 637, uses contemporary experiences of visiting foreign countries as an example for Paul's illustration in v. 11.

the function of these verses in the same way that vv. 7–9 function as an analogy.[77] This runs the risk, however, of placing glossolalia in the category of a noncognitive language. Fee admits as much when he states, "The point of the analogy is that 'tongues' function *like* this [human language]," i.e., glossolalia is *like* human language but is really *not* human language.[78] Paul uses analogy in vv. 7–9 with his illustration of musical instruments, but his point there focuses on the unintelligibility of glossolalia rather as to whether glossolalia bore cognitive content.

Once Paul moves the discussion forward into the realm of known human language in vv. 10–11, Paul uses the inability to understand a foreign language as an example of the effects of glossolalia on its hearers: an unknown human language cannot be understood by the congregation and, thus, provides no meaning or "building up." Just as a "foreigner" speaks to Paul in a language that he does not understand, so too, a glossolalist who speaks to the congregation will not be understood by them. Forbes states to this effect: "Paul's reference to speakers of mutually foreign languages implies that foreign languages were what he thought glossolalists spoke. The point of the comparison with unclear bugle calls then becomes their failure to communicate, rather than simply their lack of clarity."[79] Paul will give an illustration of this in 1 Cor 14:16–18.

9. 1 Cor 14:12: A Variety of Spirit Beings Required for the Church

Paul's final application here in v. 12 echoes v. 9, οὕτως καὶ ὑμεῖς, "so it is with you." Verse 9 summed up the preceding vv. 7–8 that dealt with musical analogies for glossolalia. Verse 12 does not merely summarize the preceding vv. 10–11 that dealt with human languages. Instead, v. 12 summarizes all that has preceded since 14:1b, especially vv. 6–11. In v. 12 Paul makes a recommendation to the Corinthians that prohibits the excessive practice of communicating with only those spirits who speak foreign languages. He

---

[77] Fee, *First Epistle*, 664; Kistemaker, *1 Corinthians*, 486; and Hays, *First Corinthians*, 236.

[78] Fee, *First Epistle*, 664 n. 34 (emphasis his).

[79] Forbes, *Prophecy and Inspired Speech*, 63. A musical instrument simile was used to express the relationship between a passive prophet in the hands of an active spirit in Plutarch (*Def. orac.* 414E, 418D) and Philo (*Her.* 266). Here, Paul uses a musical instrument analogy to express the uselessness of unintelligible speech.

encourages the Corinthians to communicate with as many different πνεύματα, "spirits," as possible–not only those spirits who speak foreign languages (as had been the Corinthians' practice whose effects Paul illustrates in vv. 7–11) but also those spirits that can translate the languages, as well as those that speak the mother tongue of the congregation. Fee notes that v. 12 "holds the key to much."[80]

Verse 12 has been notoriously suspect in the annals of Pauline scholarship for its use of the plural πνεύματα, "spirits." Most commentators agree that Paul actually wrote ἐπεὶ ζηλωταί ἐστε πνευμάτων, "since you are zealous for spirits,"[81] but "spirits" is almost always interpreted as something other than "spirit beings."[82] The plural πνευμάτων has been argued to mean "inspirations of the Holy Spirit," "gifts of the Holy Spirit," "human spirits moved by the Holy Spirit," "tongues of the Holy Spirit," and "manifestations of the Holy Spirit."[83] Hence many regard "spirits" to mean something more akin to πνευματικά, "spiritual things," rather than to πνεύματα, "spirits"; but "spirits" is the actual reading of the Greek text.[84]

Paige argues that the πνευμάτων of v. 12 should be understood to refer to a multiplicity of spirit beings (and not "spiritual gifts" or "manifestations") within its proper context. He follows Weiss by distinguishing between Paul's conception of the one Spirit and the Corinthians' conception for many "spirits," an allusion to their pre-Christian beliefs in a plurality of "spirits," i.e., daemons, both good and evil.[85] Paul momentarily accommodates his language to a

---

[80] Fee, *First Epistle*, 666.

[81] Barrett, *First Epistle*, 319; Bruce, *1 and 2 Corinthians*, 131; Morris, *1 Corinthians*, 189; Conzelmann, *1 Corinthians*, 237; Harrisville, *1 Corinthians*, 232; Kistemaker, *1 Corinthians*, 487; Soards, *1 Corinthians*, 286; Hays, *First Corinthians*, 236; Thiselton, *First Epistle*, 1107; Lindemann, *Der Erste Korintherbrief*, 304; and Garland, *1 Corinthians*, 638.

[82] Paul speaks of "spirits" in v. 12 in a positive sense, although not all commentators would agree (see n. 86 below). This positive sense though creates tension with the idea that there is only "one [good, holy] Spirit." Hence, "spirits" cannot mean a plurality of "good spirits" but must mean something else. Grudem (*Gift of Prophecy*) is typical: "It is true that Paul would not have used πνεύματα to refer to a multiplicity of 'Holy Spirits'" (p. 123).

[83] See Chapter One, pp. 50–52.

[84] Fee (*First Epistle*, 660 n. 4) observes that "Paul wrote πνευμάτων ('spirits'); the change to πνευματικῶν was actually made by P 1175 pc a r syᵖ co." Most modern interpretations follow the changed text (which reads "spiritual things") with the English translation "spiritual gifts." Thiselton (*First Epistle*) is typical: "It is unlikely that even the Corinthians sought inspiration from a plurality of spirits; rather they sought a plurality of manifestations (as many as possible) from God's Holy Spirit" (p. 1107).

[85] See also House, "Tongues and the Mystery Religions," 141. The sense of "daemons" here is found in Acts 17:18, that of "deities."

Corinthian slogan, "zealous for spirits," a conception of spirit that Paul does not share, i.e., a number of "spirits."[86] To support his argument that πνευμάτων in v. 12 is not thought of by Paul as a plurality of holy spirits operating among and through the Corinthian mediums, Paige suggests that the ἐπει, "since," clause be read as the conclusion of v. 11 rather than as the beginning of a since-then construction in v. 12. The οὕτως, "so," of v. 12 does not summarize what preceded it but rather has a comparative force. Paige's interpretation makes Paul compare the βάρβαρος of v. 11 with the Corinthians (ὑμεῖς, "you") in v. 12: ". . . I will be a 'barbarian' to the one speaking and the one speaking [will be] a barbarian in my view. So you are [barbarians] also because you are 'zealots for spirits.' Strive for the edification of the church that you may excel!"[87]

Paige argues that Paul believes that the Corinthians are like barbarians (those who speak foreign languages) because they are obsessed with glossolalia, i.e., "zealots for spirits." Paige implicitly identifies "spirits" with "tongues," an interpretation that places "spirits" into the category of inspired utterance.[88] Certainly, "spirits" are responsible for speaking foreign languages through the Corinthian mediums (cf. 14:2c,16), and it seems that the Corinthians were especially desirous of this gift (hence, Paul's polemic for prophecy over glossolalia throughout First Corinthians 14).

Paul though would probably not have used "spirits" to indicate glossolalia. The use of "spirits" for an inspired form of speech follows scholars who argue that "spirits" in 12:10 refers to "prophecies," "revelations," or "prophetic utterances."[89] If Paul meant glossolalia, he very well could have used the term for it, γλῶσσα, as he does many times in First Corinthians 14. Furthermore, Paul would probably have not called the glossolalists "barbarians," even though in v. 11 he uses βάρβαρος as an example for the effects of glossolalia in the

---

[86] So Paige, "Spirit at Corinth," 86–87. Paige states, "'Zealous for spirits' may be their own slogan for themselves (as Weiss), and shows the easy crossover from 'Spirit' to 'spirits' by which God's Spirit is conceived like the multiplicity of *daimones* in Greek thought" (p. 87). The idea that "zealous for spirits" is a Corinthian slogan that does not reflect Paul's belief is held by some commentators. In this sense, Paul is being sarcastic and mildly rebuking. So Robertson and Plummer, *First Epistle*, 311; Harrisville, *1 Corinthians*, 232; and Oster, *1 Corinthians*, 335.

[87] Paige, "Spirit at Corinth," 87.

[88] Ibid. This follows Fee (*First Epistle*) who believes "spirits" in v. 12 refers to the Corinthians' human spirits: "They have great zeal for their own spirits, through speaking in tongues, to be the mouthpiece of the Holy Spirit" (p. 666).

[89] See Dautzenberg, "διάκρισις πνευμάτων," 93–104; Conzelmann, *1 Corinthians*, 209; Fee, *First Epistle*, 596–97; Soards, *1 Corinthians*, 260; Collins, *First Corinthians*, 455; and Garland, *1 Corinthians*, 583.

community. The most common meaning of πνεύματα in the NT is, of course, "spirits," both good and evil.[90]

Paige's translation of v. 12 is also meant to separate περισσεύητε, "you may excel," "abound," from πνεύματα which distances Paul from the conception of a multiplicity of spirits serving the Corinthians.[91] Paige admits, however, that if the Greek text of v. 12 is read as one summarizing sentence, a since-then construction, then the "real grammatical possibility" exists for the sense of ἵνα περισσεύητε to mean, "so that you may abound (with spirits)." Paige discounts this as being a Corinthian wish more than Paul's intent.[92] He states further that "no English translation links the two (περισσεύητε and πνεύματα) anyway."[93] This, however, is not true. The *NAB* translates v. 12 in the following manner: "So with yourselves: since you strive eagerly for spirits [πνευμάτων], seek to have an abundance [περισσεύητε] of them [πνευμάτων] for building up the church."[94] This translation conforms to the "real grammatical possibility" of the Greek text:

οὕτως καὶ ὑμεῖς, ἐπεὶ ζηλωταί ἐστε πνευμάτων,[95] πρὸς τὴν οἰκοδομὴν τῆς ἐκκλησίας ζητεῖτε ἵνα περισσεύητε.

---

[90] So Grudem, *Gift of Prophecy*, 284–85, who cogently refutes the interpretation "prophecies" or "prophetic utterances" for πνεύματα. See Luke 24:37,39 (ghost); good spirits: Acts 23:8; Heb 1:14; 1 John 4:1–3; Rev 1:4; 3:1; 4:5; 5:6; evil spirits: Matt 8:16; 12:45; Luke 10:20; 11:26; Acts 19:12; 1 Tim 4:1.

[91] Paige ("Spirit at Corinth") states, "This translation also helps to separate the sense of περισσεύητε from πνεύματα" (p. 87).

[92] Ibid., 88.

[93] Ibid., 87.

[94] See also *NIV, NIB, NRS, NLT,* and *NJB,* where these versions translate "spirits" as "spiritual gifts" or "manifestations" to mean "so that you may abound with spiritual gifts," thereby linking περισσεύητε with πνεύματα. See further *WNT* that translates: "Thus also, as for yourselves, since you are those who are most eagerly desirous of spirits [spiritual powers], be desiring them in order that you may abound in them with a view to the building up of the local assembly." Here "spirits" is misinterpreted as "spiritual powers." Nonetheless, the sense of the Greek text is maintained: "desire them [spirits] in order that you may abound in them [spirits]." The UBS Handbook on First Corinthians (Paul Ellingworth and Howard A. Hatton, *A Handbook on Paul's First Letter to the Corinthians* [UBS Handbook Series; New York: United Bible Societies, 1994] 311) suggests that translators should follow *TEV* which links ζητεῖτε and περισσεύητε with πνεύματα (*TEV* interprets πνεύματα as "gifts of the Spirit" that is followed by the UBS Handbook).

[95] Note the unusual use of the genitive πνευμάτων where we might have expected the accusative πνεύματα.

Literally,

So also with yourselves, since you are eager of spirits, for the building up of the church, seek [spirits] so that you may abound [with them].

Paul not only admits of the Corinthians' zeal for spirits (ἐπεί, "since"), but also approves of this zeal by his use of the imperative ζητεῖτε, "seek,"[96] and the ἵνα clause, both of which refer to πνευμάτων, "spirits."[97] Paul does not even qualify these spirits as "holy" (πνεύματα ἅγια) but rather presumes that the Corinthians, as Christians, are seeking those spirits who belong to the Lord and God (1 Cor 12:3).[98]   While the imperative heartily approves of the Corinthians' communication with the spirit world, the ἵνα clause establishes the qualification that they seek a number of different spirits, "so that you may have an abundance (of them) for building up the church."[99]

As we saw earlier, spirits speaking the language of the worshiping community (prophecy) "built up the church." Now in v. 12 Paul speaks of abounding with spirits "for the building up of the church." Paul's reasoning for this is meant to curtail the excessive desire for only those spirits who speak foreign languages (glossolalia), which was the target of his illustrations in the preceding vv. 7–11. Paul would have the Corinthians seek not only those spirits who speak foreign languages (but only if a translator is present), but also, and with greater preference, those spirits who communicate in the language of the

---

[96] In the sense of "strive for."

[97] The ἐπεί clause functions more smoothly here in the since-then construction of this verse than reading it as the conclusion of v. 11. This follows many commentators. See Barrett, *First Epistle*, 319; Bruce, *1 and 2 Corinthians*, 131; Conzelmann, *1 Corinthians*, 233; Morris, *1 Corinthians*, 190; Soards, *1 Corinthians*, 285; Fee, *First Epistle*, 660; Kistemaker, *1 Corinthians*, 487; Collins, *First Corinthians*, 499; and Garland, *1 Corinthians*, 631.

[98] Paul uses πνεῦμα to mean "a holy spirit" in 1 Cor 14:2c, 15,16, and πνεύματα to mean "holy spirits" in 12:10 (a few of which may pass the "discernment" stage and, thus, qualify as "a holy spirit") and 14:32. Paul never qualifies his three uses of the plural πνεύματα with ἅγια, "holy." But see 2 Thess 4:8, τὸν θεὸν τὸν [καὶ] διδόντα τὸ πνεῦμα αὐτοῦ τὸ ἅγιον εἰς ὑμᾶς, "God who [also] gives his holy spirit to you," wherein "his holy spirit" connotes a generic singular for many "holy spirits" not unlike Herm. *Mand.* 11.3 wherein the devil [ὁ διάβολος] fills the false prophet with αὐτοῦ πνεύματι, "his spirit," a collective reference to the πνεύμασιν, "spirits," that the Shepherd warns against in 11.4. See also 1 QHᵃ 8.12 and 4QS1 40. 24.5, רוחות קודש, "holy spirits"; and Herm. *Sim.* 9.13 where ἅγια πνεύματα, "holy spirits," are identified with "the powers of the Son of God."

[99] The ἵνα clause functions as an infinitive of purpose: "strive for [spirits] in order to abound [with them]."

worshiping community so that all may be edified.[100] A variety of spirit beings is required for "building up the church," those that prophesy, those that speak in a foreign language, and those that are able to translate the foreign language (not to mention the other manifestations listed in 12:8–10) – hence, the plural "spirits." This is also reflected in 14:26 where "everything is done for the building up."

Paige's position may have some grammatical support.[101] His comparative reading of vv. 11–12a, however, finds little support in Paul's context.[102] The text of v. 12 does not contain any signals that Paul actually cites a Corinthian position or slogan. The phrase "zealous for spirits" occurs neither in a derogatory context nor does the plural πνεύματα, "spirits," seem to be an especially threatening term for Paul (12:10, 14:32).[103]

The idea that πνευμάτων refers to a multiplicity of good spirits in v. 12 is argued by some scholars. Héring believed that Paul means "good spirits,"[104] for

---

[100] Thiselton (*First Epistle*, 1107) believes that the imperative "seek" is meant to redirect the Corinthians' zeal away from "powers of the Spirit" (his translation of πνευμάτων) to an eagerness for the building up of the church. But this misses Paul's point throughout First Corinthians 14, and especially in vv. 6–11. Paul does redirect their zeal, not away from "spirits" but rather toward more variety of spirits, preferably those who speak the language of the congregation. Fee (*First Epistle*, 666) notes similarly, "Paul's present concern is to capitalize on their zeal, or more accurately, . . . to redirect their zeal. . . . Since they have such zeal for the manifestation of the Spirit, they should direct that zeal in corporate worship away from being 'foreigners' to one another toward the edification of one another in Christ."

[101] Paige ("Spirit at Corinth," 87 n. 51) notes that ἐπεί as "because," concluding a sentence occurs in 1 Cor 5:10; Matt 21:46; 27:6; 18:32; Luke 1:34; Heb 5:11; and 9:17.

[102] Paige's comparative reading of vv. 11–12a was suggested earlier by Joseph MacRory, *The Epistles of St. Paul to the Corinthians* (St. Louis, MO: B. Herder, 1915) 211. MacRory (ibid.), however, believed that this reading was untenable: "Some would put a full stop after: 'so also you,' taking the sense to be: so also you shall seem barbarians if you speak in tongues and there be no one to interpret. But since in that case we should naturally expect some concluding particle in the next clause: since *therefore* you are zealous, etc., and as v. 12 is a conclusion parallel to that in v. 9, where 'so also you' does not stand by itself, perhaps we may take the present verse as meaning: Wherefore do you also (as do I), since you are zealous for spirits (spiritual gifts), seek to abound unto the edifying of the Church." To be sure, whereas MacRory notes that some might place a full stop after "so also with you," Paige places a full stop after "zealous for spirits." The interpretations that result, however, are the same: "so also you are barbarians since you are zealous for spirits" (or, as Paige, "since you are obsessed with glossolalia").

[103] Garland (*1 Corinthians*) observes, "Interpreters should refrain from resorting to Corinthian slogans or quotations to solve exegetical riddles unless there is clear textual evidence that Paul is citing another's position" (p. 649).

[104] Héring, *First Epistle*, 149.

Paul does not use the term "spirits" here in a derogatory context.[105] Ellis argued that in both 1 Cor 14:12 and 14:32, "a plurality of *good spirits* must be inferred."[106] As we saw earlier, Paige argued that "zealous for spirits" in v. 12, as a Corinthian slogan, reflects the Hellenistic view of many daemons that the Corinthians might have easily confused with the Christian conception of the one Spirit (see n. 86 above). But Morton Smith noted concerning v. 12 that "Paul's pretensions prohibited the implicit comparison of [and thus confusion of] the *daimonia* [daemons] with the spirits who came to the Christians."[107] Recently, Forbes has readdressed Ellis's point that good spirits are to be inferred in v. 12. Forbes notes that "zealous for spirits" is not likely to be a Corinthian slogan since πνεύματα is attested more widely elsewhere in the NT. Forbes argues that if Ellis's position is correct, then v. 12 "emphasizes that Paul sees benevolent spiritual beings in personal terms."[108]

10. 1 Cor 14:13–19: The Need for Intelligible Communication from the Spirit World

Paul's advocacy for a diversity of spirit beings is continued in v. 13, where the inferential conjunction, διό, "for this reason," ties this verse closely to v. 12. Paul is sensitive to the Corinthians' desire for glossolalia. Thus, he states in v. 13 διὸ ὁ λαλῶν γλώσσῃ προσευχέσθω ἵνα διερμηνεύῃ, "Therefore, one who speaks a tongue should also pray that he may translate." If the Corinthians are going to continue to allow the presence of spirit beings among them who speak in foreign languages, then they must also pray for spirits who are able to translate the language. The sense of v. 13 may run as follows: "Therefore, a person through whom a spirit is speaking a foreign language should also pray for a spirit able to translate foreign languages." Only will intelligible speech

---

[105] So Garland (*1 Corinthians*) who argues, "Paul's statement is not intended to be ironic, sarcastic, or a mild rebuke" (p. 638); and Ellingworth and Hatton (*UBS Handbook*, 311): "Paul is certainly not being ironic here." This further supports the reading of v. 12 as a since-then construction.

[106] Ellis, "'Spiritual' Gifts," 134 (emphasis his). So, too, Barrett (*First Epistle*, 319): "Paul ... here thinks of various spiritual agencies producing various spiritual gifts."

[107] Smith, "Pauline Worship," 244. In this respect, Smith also notes the gift of "distinguishing between spirits" in 12:10 with the implication that "demons" were sifted out from good spirits.

[108] Forbes, "Paul's Principalities and Powers," 66 n. 18.

build up the church, and this requires an "abundance" of different spirits, thus satisfying the criterion for "spirits" in v. 12.[109]

Verses 14 and 15 continue Paul's thought that intelligible speech should be practiced in the congregation when communicating with the spirit world. These verses are often translated in the following way:

[14]ἐὰν [γὰρ] προσεύχωμαι γλώσσῃ, τὸ πνεῦμά μου προσεύχεται, ὁ δὲ νοῦς μου ἄκαρπός ἐστιν. [15]τί οὖν ἐστιν; προσεύξομαι τῷ πνεύματι, προσεύξομαι δὲ καὶ τῷ νοΐ· ψαλῶ τῷ πνεύματι, ψαλῶ δὲ καὶ τῷ νοΐ

For if I pray in a tongue, my spirit prays but my mind is fruitless. So what is to be done? I will pray with the spirit, but I will also pray with the mind. I will sing with the spirit, but I will also sing with the mind.

Some scholars believe that in v. 14 the phrase "my spirit prays but my mind is fruitless (ἄκαρπος)," indicates that the mind (νοῦς) is idle or inactive (ἄκαρπος) during glossolalia in a manner similar to the way Hellenists viewed inspiration (e.g., Plato *Ion* 534D, "the god takes away the mind of these men and uses them as his minister . . .).[110] In essence, according to this interpretation Paul contrasts "spirit" and "mind" according to Hellenistic anthropology. There, πνεῦμα denotes the part of a person that is carried away in ecstasy while νοῦς denotes that aspect of the conscience that is temporarily disengaged during inspiration producing a trance state.

Verse 15 is believed to be Paul's response that insists on the use of both the spirit and the mind while praying. Paul counters idleness of the mind while speaking (an unconscious "ecstatic" state) by demanding the use of an engaged mind (a conscious state) while speaking: "I will pray with the spirit, I will pray with the mind." Robert Jewett summarizes:

The word 'mind' (νοῦς) as used against the enthusiasts [i.e., glossolalists] in this context is the source of conscious self-control and of clear communication of ideas to other persons. When one speaks 'with the mind,' others are instructed (1 Cor 14:19b) and built up (1 Cor 14:17).[111]

---

[109] Similarly Fee (*First Epistle*) who states, "The Corinthians' practice of uninterpreted tongues is what is being challenged, not tongues as such. This is further confirmed by vv. 27–28, which again disallow uninterpreted tongues, but otherwise *regulate* the expression of the gift *when there is interpretation*" (p. 669; emphasis his).

[110] So Conzelmann, *1 Corinthians*, 237; Callan, "Prophecy and Ecstasy," 137; Hunt, *Inspired Body*, 125–26; and Collins, *First Corinthians*, 502.

[111] Robert Jewett, *Paul's Anthropological Terms: A Study of Their Use in Conflict Settings* (AGAJU 10; Leiden: Brill, 1971) 379.

This interpretation follows the common understanding that "ecstatic utterance" is always unintelligible because the mind is displaced while Paul's view insisted on the use of the mind during inspiration that produced intelligible speech.[112] In short, Paul is contrasting a trance state in v. 14 (reminiscent of the Corinthians' "pagan" past with ecstasy) with a non-trance state in v. 15.[113] It is unlikely, however, that Paul is contrasting a trance state in v. 14 with a non-trance state in v. 15. Instead, Paul seems to be distinguishing the effects of the unintelligible utterances of a spirit (v. 14) from the intelligible utterances of a spirit (v. 15) as will be shown below.[114]

Verse 14a begins an application of what Paul stated in vv. 7–13. He now makes use of himself and the worshiping congregation as an example for the effects of unintelligible speech. Paul writes, ἐὰν [γὰρ] προσεύχωμαι γλώσσῃ, "[For] if I pray in a tongue." Any utterance "in a tongue" is an utterance spoken by a spirit. Paul had revealed this idea earlier in 14:2c, πνεύματι δέ λαλεῖ μυστήρια, "he speaks mysteries (with) a spirit," and will cite it later in v. 16, where he provides an example of someone who "says a blessing with a spirit" in the context of a bewildered audience (v. 16) – bewildered because the blessing is glossolalia (v. 18). Verse 14a then can be rendered, "for if a spirit utters a prayer through me in a foreign language."

The next phrase, τὸ πνεῦμά μου προσεύχεται, "my spirit prays," is sometimes thought to mean Paul's human spirit.[115] Grammatically, if Paul meant "my spirit" it is difficult to account for his use of the article τό here.[116] In Paul, τὸ πνεῦμα usually refers to the holy spirit or the spirit of God (in my interpretation, "the spirit world of God").[117] Furthermore, Paul's spirit cannot be the source of

---

[112] A point that has, nevertheless, been cogently refuted recently by Stewart-Sykes (see n. 12 above). The texts analyzed in Plutarch, Josephus, Philo, and Pseudo-Philo showed that intelligible or rational speech was delivered in an "ecstatic" or irrational state of mind. To this effect Aune (*Prophecy in Early Christianity*) noted, "Ecstasy and rationality, however, should not be regarded as two mutually exclusive states of consciousness" (p. 33).

[113] So Thiselton, *First Epistle*, 1112–13; and Héring, *First Epistle*, who states, "According to the Apostle, it is better to speak '*tō noi*', knowing what one is saying, rather than in ecstasy" (p. 150).

[114] Forbes (*Prophecy and Inspired Speech*, 64) argues that the phrase "my mind is unfruitful" does not necessarily mean that the mind is unconscious or in a trance state. The question is not whether a trance state is indicated but rather revolves around the issue of intelligibility.

[115] Thiselton, *First Epistle*, 1110, "my innermost spiritual being;" Garland, *1 Corinthians*, 639, "innermost deepest depths."

[116] But see τὸ πνεῦμά μου in Acts 7:59; Rom 1:9; 1 Cor 16:18; and 2 Cor 2:13.

[117] See Thiselton, *First Epistle*, 1110, who notes that "Paul prefers to reserve τὸ πνεῦμα for the Spirit of God." See, however, three instances in which τὸ πνεῦμα seems to refer to the

the prayer since a foreign spirit is uttering the prayer in an unknown language (γλώσσῃ).

As Barrett states, "*My spirit* is not easy to understand."[118] Besides Paul's own human spirit, Barrett offers two other possibilities for the meaning of τὸ πνεῦμά μου: (1) the spiritual gift entrusted to Paul, or, in particular, the spiritual agency which induces Paul's inspired speech; and (2) the Holy Spirit as given to Paul. Barrett objects to (2), "To describe the Holy Spirit as in any sense *mine* is intolerable, and certainly not Pauline."[119] Thus, Barrett concludes that "my spirit" is best explained as a spiritual gift entrusted to Paul.[120]

In the light of Paul's context of "a spirit utters a prayer through me," the phrase "my spirit prays" seems to point in the direction that Barrett suggests: "spirit" as a "spiritual agency," i.e., "a spirit being," which prompts Paul's inspired praying. Héring has argued that τὸ πνεῦμά μου cannot mean "a spirit from the supernatural world."[121] But in this particular context of glossolalia as verbal communication from the spirit world, that seems to be the meaning πνεῦμα should have – a spirit uttering a prayer in a foreign language through Paul.

The issue seems to be the understanding of the personal pronoun μου, "my." The personal pronoun occurs in the genitive, literally indicating "of me." The subject of the verb προσεύχεται is τὸ πνεῦμα. A literal translation of the phrase may be "the spirit of me prays." The Greek article τό may be taken as anaphoric, i.e., not only referring back to "spirits" in v. 12 but also to the particular spirit uttering a prayer in a foreign language implied in the verb προσεύχωμαι, "I pray," i.e., "a spirit prays through me," in v. 14a.[122] Thus, "spirit" refers to a foreign spirit other than Paul's own human spirit. If this be the case, then the phrase may relate the idea, "the spirit (i.e., one of the spirits) of me (i.e., through me) prays." Paul then seems to mean, "for if a spirit utters

---

human spirit: 1 Cor 2:11; 1 Cor 5:5; and 2 Cor 7:13. In each of these cases, the article has an anaphoric function. In 1 Cor 2:11 τὸ πνεῦμα τοῦ ἀνθρώπου, "the spirit of the person," refers back to τὰ τοῦ ἀνθρώπου, "things of a person," and thus τὸ πνεῦμα. Likewise, τὸ πνεῦμα in 1 Cor 5:5 has an anaphoric function that refers back to τοιοῦτον, "this one [man]"; "the spirit" here is a reference to "this man's" spirit. In 2 Cor 7:13, τὸ πνεῦμα αὐτοῦ, "his spirit," refers back to Τίτου, "Titus."

[118] Barrett, *First Epistle*, 319 (emphasis his).

[119] Ibid., emphasis his. Barrett's point suggests that the Holy Spirit was not the sole possession of any one person but rather belongs to all Christians.

[120] Ibid., 320.

[121] Héring, *First Epistle*, 150.

[122] Barrett (*First Epistle*, 319–20) further argues that "my spirit" must also be understood in the light of the following v. 15, where πνεύματι refers to "[a] holy spirit."

a prayer through me in a foreign language, the spirit, indeed, prays [through] me."[123]

Verse 14 ends with what many believe to indicate Paul's human mind or consciousness: ὁ δὲ νοῦς μου ἄκαρπός ἐστιν, "but my mind is fruitless" or "idle." The noun νοῦς, "mind," is understood to indicate the organ of thought in which occurs the capacity for intelligible human communication and understanding. The noun νοῦς also has the meaning of "understanding" in the sense of comprehension.[124] In the context of Paul's argumentation on the effects of unintelligible speech in the worshiping community, a "fruitless mind" indicates one who lacks understanding of the utterance of the glossolalist. The person does not comprehend the language that the spirit speaks. Forbes observes, "The fact that in glossolalia 'my mind is unfruitful' (14.14), . . . it is quite clear that Paul does not think that the glossolalist normally understands his own utterance."[125]

The term νοῦς here refers to the ability to comprehend, not to an organ of the human faculties that has been displaced in a trance. Paul's point is that if a spirit prays through him in an unknown language, he will receive no benefit from the utterance. The statement "my mind is unfruitful" reveals that Paul will not understand or comprehend what the spirit is saying. Verse 14 carries the following sense: "For if a spirit utters a prayer through me in an unknown language, the spirit, indeed, is praying [through] me, but I will not be able to understand it." This follows Paul's overall argument that began in v. 6: glossolalia in and of itself is useless and serves no benefit for anyone because it remains incomprehensible.

Paul continues with his polemic for intelligible communication from the spirit world in v. 15. Before stating his intentions, he asks τί οὖν ἐστιν; "So

---

[123] See Jude 20: ἐν πνεύματι ἁγίῳ προσευχόμενοι, "pray with a holy spirit." Notice that this occurs in the context of "building up": ἐποικοδομοῦντες ἑαυτοὺς, "build yourselves up." This follows Paul's advice to the Corinthians: build up the church through communicating with the spirit world (1 Cor 14:12). See also Eph 6:18, προσευχόμενοι ἐν παντὶ καιρῷ ἐν πνεύματι, "pray at every opportunity with (by means of) a spirit"; and John 4:24, τοὺς προσκυνοῦντας αὐτὸν ἐν πνεύματι καὶ ἀληθείᾳ δεῖ προσκυνεῖν, "those who pray to him [God] must do so with (by means of) a spirit and truth." These passages relate that spirits participate and officiate in the worship and prayer service of early Christians.

[124] BAGD, s.v.

[125] Forbes, *Prophecy and Inspired Speech*, 64. Forbes (ibid., n. 42) also raises the issue as to for whom the mind is unfruitful, the glossolalist or the congregation. Clearly, it is both as Paul admits in v. 14 with himself as an example and in vv. 16–17 with the congregation as an example.

what is to be done?"[126] Paul answers this rhetorical question as an elaboration of what was stated in v. 14. Verse 15 is usually translated, "I will pray with the spirit, but I will also pray with the mind. I will sing praise with the spirit, but I will also sing praise with the mind." At face value, this translation implies that the use of both "spirit" and "mind," as the mental faculties, are to occur in tandem during the worship service.[127] Paul's point, however, is for the occurrence of intelligible utterance from the spirit world in the congregation. Hence many commentators believe that the thrust of Paul's meaning in v. 15 relates to his preference for intelligible speech as opposed to unintelligible speech mentioned in v. 14.[128]

The use of "spirit" in v. 15 is clearly related to the spirit world.[129] In other verses (12:3; 14:2c,16) the dative πνεύματι is used to denote the verbal communication of a spirit. Here it is used to express a spirit praying and singing praises: προσεύξομαι τῷ πνεύματι, "I will pray with the spirit," and ψαλῶ τῷ πνεύματι, "I will sing praises with the spirit." With these statements, Paul acknowledges that spirits should indeed utter prayers through the agency of a human medium as in glossolalia (προσεύχωμαι γλώσσῃ). But, unlike glossolalia, the spirit should be understood by those present in the congregation. This is brought out in v. 15 in the phrases προσεύξομαι δὲ καὶ τῷ νοΐ, "but I will also pray with the mind," and ψαλῶ δὲ καὶ τῷ νοΐ, "but I will also sing with the mind." Zerwick observes that τῷ νοΐ in v. 15 can have the meaning "intelligently" with the sense of intelligibility, which has been Paul's argument ever since v. 6.[130] Thus, these phrases do not so much refer to the use of the mental faculties while praying and singing as they do to uttering the prayers and songs intelligibly so that the congregation can understand what is being said.

The sense of v. 15 may run as follows: "So what is to be done? I will utter the words of a prayer spoken by the spirit, *but will also* utter the prayer intelligibly. I will sing praises by one of God's spirits, *but will also* sing praises

---

[126] Fee (*First Epistle*, 670 n. 20) states that the idiom means, "What then is the upshot of what has just been said?" For this idiomatic phrase, see Rom 4:1; 6:1; 7:7; 8:31; 9:14,30.

[127] So Garland, *1 Corinthians*, 640, who believes this implies that Paul will pray and sing with ecstasy ("spirit") but do so in full possession of his mental faculties ("mind").

[128] So Kistemaker, *1 Corinthians*, 492; Collins, *First Corinthians*, 502, who states, "Communal prayer should be such that others can understand"; Thiselton, *First Epistle*, 1113; and Garland, *1 Corinthians*, 640.

[129] Following scholars who think "spirit" in v. 15 refers to "the Holy Spirit."

[130] Zerwick, *Grammatical Analysis*, 526. Not as Garland (*1 Corinthians*, 640), "the mental faculties."

intelligibly."[131] Whereas in v. 14 the utterance of a spirit praying in an unknown language could not be understood, the combination δὲ καί, "but also," in v. 15 emphasizes Paul's recommendation that the spirit's utterance should also be linguistically understood by the gathered community. Fee observes this emphatic meaning of δὲ καί here and states that Paul means that the prayer and praises should be "in Greek for the sake of the others," i.e., the mother tongue of the congregation.[132]

Paul makes a transition in v. 16 with ἐπεί, "since," or in this case, "otherwise."[133] The 2nd person singular form of the verb εὐλογέω, "to bless," "praise," in v. 16 turns Paul's discussion onto the Corinthians themselves, εὐλογῇς, "you bless."[134] After stating that the utterances of spirits should be linguistically understood, Paul now gives a more explicit example of what happens when spirits are allowed to speak a foreign language to the congregation.

Paul begins, ἐπεὶ ἐὰν εὐλογῇς [ἐν] πνεύματι, ὁ ἀναπληρῶν τὸν τόπον τοῦ ἰδιώτου πῶς ἐρεῖ τὸ 'Αμήν ἐπὶ τῇ σῇ εὐχαριστίᾳ; ἐπειδὴ τί λέγεις οὐκ οἶδεν, "Otherwise, if you pronounce a blessing with a spirit, how shall the one who holds the place of an uninstructed say the 'Amen' to your thanksgiving since he does not know what you are saying?" Paul here uses language from traditional Jewish liturgical practice, blessing[135] and Amen.[136] The term "thanksgiving"

---

[131] Paul's use of himself, "I will utter the words of a prayer," and "I will sing praises," as an illustration for "a spirit" praying and singing praises through him recalls the basic idea of the way in which spectators perceived the performance of a spirit speaking through the physical organism of a prophet: "For the prophet, even when he *seems to speak, is really silent,* and his organs of speech, mouth and tongue, are wholly in the employ of Another (i.e., a divine spirit), ... *Unseen by us,* that Other beats on the [vocal] chords with the skill of a master-hand . . ." (Philo, *Her.* 266, emphasis mine). There is no textual evidence that Paul experienced prophetic amnesia like that discussed in Chapter 3. Nevertheless, this does not necessarily mean that Paul did not experience prophetic amnesia. The fact that he, too, was a medium for spirits who spoke both intelligible and unintelligible languages (so he claimed; see 1 Cor 13:2; 14:18) might suggest that he underwent the type of experience described of Kenaz in *L.A.B.* 28.6,10a.

[132] Fee, *First Epistle,* 670.

[133] So Fee, *First Epistle,* 671; and Collins, *First Corinthians,* 502.

[134] Fee (*First Epistle,* 673) notes: "The reason for the singular is that it corresponds to the second person singular of the person being addressed. Thus, rather than speak to all in the second plural, Paul's point is better made in the singular, with the person addressed representing those speaking in tongues in the community."

[135] From the Hebrew ברך, "to bless," "to kneel." See Exod 18:10; 2 Sam 18:28; 1 Kgs 1:48; 1 Chr 16:36; 2 Chr 2:11; and Ezra 7:27.

[136] The "Amen" is a transliteration of the Hebrew אמן, a liturgical utterance made by the whole assembly at the conclusion of prayers. Paul evidently took this from worship practices

(εὐχαριστία) was apparently interchangeable with "blessing," for Paul seems to identify the two terms in v. 16.[137]

Paul describes those unable to understand a blessing spoken by a spirit in a foreign language as ὁ ἀναπληρῶν τὸν τόπον τοῦ ἰδιώτου, "one who holds the place of the uninstructed." This phrase might refer to those whose status in the congregation is in between nonbelievers and fully committed Christians, akin to a proselyte or catechumen.[138] But Paul's context up to this point has been the edification of "the church" (ἡ ἐκκλησία). The ἰδιώτης, "uninstructed," is the person who would ordinarily say the "Amen" to the "thanksgiving" which, as Fee notes, "implies wholehearted endorsement by one who regularly affirms the praise of the living God."[139] The "uninstructed" then are not outsiders or proselytes, but rather they are the usual Christians who regularly gather as a worshiping congregation.[140] The "uninstructed" in this context do not understand the content of the blessing that the spirit is uttering. The term ἰδιώτης in this sense has the meaning of "those who do not understand," and refers to the nonexpert in contrast to a doctor or a rhetorically trained speaker.[141]

In the following v. 17 Paul elaborates the effects of this: σὺ μὲν γὰρ καλῶς εὐχαριστεῖς ἀλλ᾽ ὁ ἕτερος οὐκ οἰκοδομεῖται, "for you may very well be giving thanks, but the other is not built up." Paul does not doubt that the glossolalist is giving thanks in a human language.[142] The other (ὁ ἕτερος) who is not built up in v. 17 refers back to ἰδιώτης in v. 16. The fact that "the other" is "not built up" by the spoken "thanksgiving" is further indication that Paul is speaking of glossolalia – the spirit utters the blessing (ἐν πνεύματι) in a foreign language but glossolalia does not build up (see 1 Cor 14:2–5). The "uninstructed" are full-fledged Christian members of the community who are "'untrained' (see Acts

---

in the Jewish synagogue (1 Chr 16:36; Rom 1:25; 11:36; 15:33; and Gal 1:5). Garland (*1 Corinthians*, 642) notes that Justin Martyr (*1 Apol.* 65) recorded that the congregation says "Amen" at the conclusion of prayers and thanksgiving as a fixture in second-century Christian worship.

[137] So Collins, *First Corinthians*, 503.

[138] BAGD, s.v.

[139] Fee, *First Epistle*, 673.

[140] Fee (ibid.) notes that the "one who holds the place of the uninstructed" represents in the singular all community members who must listen to the uninterpreted language without understanding.

[141] So Garland, *1 Corinthians*, 641.

[142] The verb εὐχαριστεῖς, "you give thanks," is identified with εὐλογῇς [ἐν] πνεύματι, "you give a blessing [with] a spirit." In each case the "thanksgiving" and the "blessing" are cognitive speech forms that are, otherwise, not understood.

4:13) in the 'language' being spoken – precisely because they do not understand what is being said."[143]

Despite Paul's insistence throughout chap. 14 that glossolalia does not build up the church, in v. 18 he brings himself back into the discussion from vv. 14 and 15 and relates that his skill in glossolalia surpasses any of those of the Corinthian mediums: εὐχαριστῶ τῷ θεῷ, πάντων ὑμῶν μᾶλλον γλώσσαις λαλῶ, "I give thanks to God that I am a better medium for spirits who speak foreign languages than any of you." Kistemaker remarks that the μᾶλλον, "to a greater degree," "more," refers not so much to the frequency of speaking but rather to the quality of speaking in tongues, hence my translation, "better . . . than."[144] The fact that Paul gives thanks to God (εὐχαριστῶ τῷ θεῷ) for his ability in glossolalia reflects his general attitude toward glossolalia as a gift from the spirit world (1 Cor 12:10). Paul reaffirms the gift of glossolalia with the highest of regard. But he does so with the intent to redirect the Corinthians' attention on the use of intelligible speech in the congregation. Verse 19 serves this purpose as a response to v. 18.[145]

In v. 19 Paul returns to what has been the crux of chap. 14 so far: the practice of communicating with spirits who speak the language of the community members in order to edify of the church. Paul asserts, ἀλλὰ ἐν ἐκκλησίᾳ θέλω πέντε λόγους τῷ νοΐ μου λαλῆσαι, ἵνα καὶ ἄλλους κατηχήσω, ἢ μυρίους λόγους ἐν γλώσσῃ, "But in church I would rather speak five words that I understand so that I may instruct others, rather than ten thousand words in a tongue"[146] As in 1 Cor 14:14 Paul uses the personal pronoun μου, "my," but now in relation to "mind": τῷ νοΐ μου, "my mind." The phrase "speak five words with my mind" (πέντε λόγους τῷ νοΐ μου λαλῆσαι) is often read to indicate Paul's reliance on his mental faculties in contrast to the withdrawal of the mental faculties in uttering nonsensical glossolalia. But as we saw earlier, νοῦς in Paul's context refers to "intelligently," denoting his preference for intelligibleness of speech (14:15). Hence the translation "speak five words that I understand" relates the context behind Paul's use of νοῦς in his discussion of the comprehension and understanding of utterances in the church.

Paul's use of numbers in v. 19 is meant to further contrast unintelligible speech with the more useful intelligible speech. The number πέντε, "five,"

---

[143] Fee, *First Epistle*, 673.

[144] Kistemaker, *1 Corinthians*, 496.

[145] So Fee, *First Epistle*, 675.

[146] Collins (*First Corinthians*, 504) notes Paul's inelegant Greek: "Paul's 'prefer' is in Greek 'I wish' (*thelō*), but 'rather' (*mallon*) has been elliptically omitted (BDF 480.4)."

means something like "a few."[147] This number is contrasted to μυρίους, which is sometimes rendered as "ten thousand" but actually is an undefined and very large number that denotes myriads or countless thousands.[148] In the church Paul distinguishes speaking a few words that can be linguistically understood from a myriad of words in "a tongue," i.e., "an unknown language." Despite Paul's prowess with glossolalia (v. 18), the important point is that each member of the worshiping community be edified. Therefore, intelligible speech (τῷ νοΐ λαλῆσαι) contributes highly because others are "instructed" (ἵνα καὶ ἄλλους κατηχήσω) by it.

Paul has been contrasting glossolalia and intelligible speech ever since v. 7. Even though he has not mentioned the term "prophecy" since v. 6, his contrasts between glossolalia and praying and singing praises with τῷ νοΐ is meant to serve the same purpose as the earlier contrasts between glossolalia and prophecy in vv. 2–5. Hence the intelligible speech with which he compares glossolalia in vv. 14–19 denotes the intelligible speech of spirits through mediums; it is only in v. 15 that a spirit "prays" or "sings praises" intelligibly to all members (prophecy would be a spirit's address of some kind).

Paul's use of κατηχέω, "to give oral instruction," occurs rarely in his letters (see Rom 2:18; Gal 6:6). The verb is not the usual term for "to teach" like διδάσκω or μανθάνω. Rather, κατηχέω functions in a more specific manner to describe "informing" or "instructing" another in religious matters.[149] The use of κατηχέω in 1 Cor 14:19 in a discussion of glossolalia and prophecy is significant. It implies that instruction on "religious matters" comes from communication with the spirit world. Paul's use of κατηχέω hinges on the idea that "religious experience" is intimately related to the spirit world, in particular, to verbal communication with the spirit world. 1 Cor 14:12, as a summarizing statement for vv. 7–11 and as a segue to vv. 13–19, makes this clear.

---

[147] See Garland, *1 Corinthians*, 642.

[148] BAGD, s.v.

[149] BAGD, s.v. The terms "catechumens" and "catechism" are derived from κατηχέω; hence, in the specific sense of catechetical instruction by the spirit world.

11. 1 Cor 14:20–25: Intelligible Communication from the Spirit World Convicts Nonbelievers of the Reality of Spirit Communication

Paul transitions once more by introducing this next pericope with the inclusive term ἀδελφοί, "brothers [and sisters]." In v. 20 Paul begins by stating a negative command that reflects his attitude about the way in which the Corinthians have been excessive in their practice of communicating with spirits who speak a foreign language: ἀδελφοί, μὴ παιδία γίνεσθε ταῖς φρεσὶν ἀλλὰ τῇ κακίᾳ νηπιάζετε, ταῖς δὲ φρεσὶν τέλειοι γίνεσθε, "Brothers [and sisters], do not be children in your thinking [in matters of spirit communication]. In evil be ignorant as children, but in other matters be mature in your thinking [i.e., the purpose of spirit communication is the edification of the church]." The context of this verse is taken from what Paul has been discussing since 14:2: prophecy builds up the church, glossolalia does not; prophecy instructs, glossolalia does not. Kistemaker observes that Paul's intention in v. 20 is meant to undermine the Corinthians' practice of glossolalia: "The Corinthians were more interested in entertainment than in education. They preferred the spectacular of tongue-speaking to the specifics of doctrinal issues."[150]

Hence the Corinthians had been "children" in their thinking.[151] The contrast between "being children" (νηπιάζετε) and "being adults" (τέλειοι γίνεσθε) is meant to show the Corinthians a distinction between their desire for glossolalia and Paul's recommendation for prophecy: "do not be like children and communicate with only those spirits that speak a foreign language; but rather, be mature and communicate with the spirit world in such a way that edifies everybody."[152]

Paul follows this assertion in v. 21 with a modified text of Isa 28:11 that attempts to elaborate from Scripture his point that glossolalia is useless: ἐν τῷ νόμῳ γέγραπται ὅτι ἐν ἑτερογλώσσοις καὶ ἐν χείλεσιν ἑτέρων λαλήσω τῷ λαῷ τούτῳ καὶ οὐδ' οὕτως εἰσακούσονταί μου, λέγει κύριος, "In the law it is

---

[150] Kistemaker, *1 Corinthians*, 498.

[151] See 1 Cor 3:1 where Paul uses the term νήπιοι, "children," to describe the Corinthians.

[152] Collins (*First Corinthians*) comes close to this: "The point is that just as the bad behavior of the child is different from the maturity of the adult, so ecstatic speaking in tongues is different from the rationality of prophecy. The Christians of Corinth are to strive after prophecy (14:1); they are to be mature in their thinking" (p. 507). Despite the fact that Collins differentiates between glossolalia and prophecy on the basis of ecstasy, he gives the correct thrust of what Paul means by distinguishing "children" from the "mature": prophecy is the more mature way because it builds up the church.

written, 'With other tongues and with the lips of foreigners I will speak to this people, and even then they will not listen to me, says the Lord.'"[153] Paul is fond of quoting from Isaiah. In First Corinthians he quotes seventeen times from the OT, six of which are from Isaiah.[154] A part of Isaiah 28 is used elsewhere in Paul, namely, in an argument with the Romans where he discusses the mystery of Israel's unbelief (Rom 9:33 [Isa 28:16]). The application of the term "law" (νόμος) to Isaiah reflects Jewish practice of using "law" of the Pentateuch and Prophets.[155]

The historical setting of the Isaiah passage (that of drunken priests and prophets whose ridicule of Isaiah's message brought God's judgment upon them in the form of deportation and exile to Assyria, a people who spoke a language foreign to the Israelites) and its current application to the Corinthian situation of excessive practice of glossolalia seems to be targeted not only at the congregation in general, but also specifically at those individuals whom Paul calls "unbelievers" (ἀπίστοις) in vv. 22–24.

Paul applies the Isaiah passage to the Corinthian situation in v. 22 with ὥστε, "therefore." He mentions two types of individuals, "believers" (πιστεύουσιν) and "unbelievers." The "believers" refer to the Christians who make up the Corinthian congregation. In the NT "unbelievers" indicates those who may be either Jewish or Gentile.[156] Paul seems to use the term here in a context that does not indicate either Jew or Gentile. Paul's context revolves around the impact of prophecy and glossolalia on unbelievers; persons who seem to need proof of the reality of communicating with spirits (cf. the effects of prophecy on unbelievers in v. 25).

Verse 22 is a notoriously difficult text in the broader context of vv. 22–25: ὥστε αἱ γλῶσσαι εἰς σημεῖόν εἰσιν οὐ τοῖς πιστεύουσιν ἀλλὰ τοῖς ἀπίστοις, ἡ δὲ προφητεία οὐ τοῖς ἀπίστοις ἀλλὰ τοῖς πιστεύουσιν, "Therefore, tongues are a sign not for believers but for unbelievers, but prophecy is not for unbelievers but for believers." By itself, this verse does not seem problematic; one may reasonably ask in what way is glossolalia a sign for unbelievers?[157] Is

---

[153] See Garland, *1 Corinthians*, 646–47, for a list of differences between Paul's text and both the LXX and MT of Isa 28:11–12.

[154] See 1 Cor 1:19 (Isa 29:14); 2:9 (Isa 64:4); 2:16 (Isa 40:13); 14:21 (Isa 28:11); 15:32 (Isa 22:13); and 15:54 (Isa 25:8).

[155] See Kistemaker, *1 Corinthians*, 498. See Rom 3:19.

[156] See Matt 7:17; Mark 9:19; Luke 9:41; 1 Cor 6:6; 10:27; 14:22,23,24; 2 Cor 4:4; 1 Tim 5:8; Titus 1:15.

[157] The term σημεῖον, "sign," is not frequently used in Paul, but carries different connotations (see 2 Thess 2:9; 3:17; Rom 4:11; 15:19; 1 Cor 1:22; 2 Cor 12:12).

glossolalia meant to indicate the presence of divine activity?[158] Does it reflect the historical context of Isa 28:11, that of divine judgment?[159] The problem arises because the illustrations presented in vv. 23–25 directly contradict the statement in v. 22. In vv. 23–25 Paul shows that tongues have a negative effect on unbelievers and prophecy has a positive effect not on believers but on unbelievers. Garland rightly asks, "If tongues are a sign for unbelievers, why does he encourage them to use prophecy instead when unbelievers are present?"[160]

Paul's main point in this passage, vv. 20–25, is that the Corinthians should set an example to those who are not familiar with the practice of communicating with the spirit world. In v. 23 the "unbelievers" and "uninformed" (ἰδιῶται)[161] are described as those who "enter" (εἰσέλθωσιν) into the "whole church" that "comes together in one place."[162] Paul depicts a hypothetical scene where all members of the community are practicing glossolalia (πάντες λαλῶσιν γλώσσαις). He then describes the reaction of the unbelievers and uninformed to glossolalia: "will they not say that you are out of your mind?" The Greek term translated as "you are out of your mind," μαίνεσθε, "you are mad," occurs four other times elsewhere in the NT, all with negative connotations (John 10:20; Acts 12:15; 26:24,25). The term is typically used of cultic frenzy in the Greek world. The female devotees of Dionysius were known as "mad women" (μαίναδες). The cognate noun μανία, "madness," is sometimes used for divine inspiration.[163] Thus, some scholars believe that Paul is relating the idea that

---

[158] So Peter Roberts, "A Sign – Christian or Pagan [1 Cor 14:21–25]," *ExpTim* 90 (1979) 199–203.

[159] So Barrett, *First Epistle*, 323; Grudem, "1 Corinthians 14.20–25: Prophecy and Tongues," 381–96.

[160] Garland, *1 Corinthians*, 649.

[161] This is the same term Paul uses for those of the Christian community who are "uninstructed" in a language in v. 16. Here in v. 23 the sense may better be "uninformed," i.e., about spirit communication.

[162] Only here does Paul speak of "the whole church coming together as one." Elsewhere, "coming together," (1 Cor 11:17,20,33; 14:26), and "whole" (Rom 16:23). See Collins, *First Corinthians*, 508.

[163] A reality that prompts Forbes (*Prophecy and Inspired Speech*) to ask, "Is μαίνεσθε a rebuke, 'You are raving', or a qualified recognition of divine or daemonic activity, 'You are possessed'?" (p. 177).

outsiders might regard glossolalia as a kind of Greek religious frenzy or inspiration.[164]

This interpretation is attractive since Paul has been discussing inspiration throughout chap. 14. He certainly makes a tacit allusion to Gentile religiosity in 1 Cor 12:2. The context, however, relates the reaction of outsiders to unintelligible speech per se (λαλῶσιν γλώσσαις) and not necessarily whether they were able to discern divine activity or religious frenzy as the source for the unintelligible speech.[165] It seems likely that the only reaction that "unbelievers" and those "uninformed" would get from a group practicing glossolalia is a purely negative reaction, "you are all crazy," i.e., a rebuke, the sense μαίνεσθε has in Acts 12:15 and 26:24,25 (but in different contexts).[166] Paul is concerned with the *effect* of glossolalia on the church's missionary witness on unbelievers.[167] This is made even more evident in vv. 24 and 25:

[24]ἐὰν δὲ πάντες προφητεύωσιν, εἰσέλθῃ δέ τις ἄπιστος ἢ ἰδιώτης, ἐλέγχεται ὑπὸ πάντων, ἀνακρίνεται ὑπὸ πάντων, [25]τὰ κρυπτὰ τῆς καρδίας αὐτοῦ φανερὰ γίνεται, καὶ οὕτως πεσὼν ἐπὶ πρόσωπον προσκυνήσει τῷ θεῷ ἀπαγγέλλων ὅτι "Ὄντως ὁ θεὸς ἐν ὑμῖν ἐστιν

But if everyone is prophesying, and a certain unbeliever or uninstructed one enters, he will be convinced by everyone, judged by everyone; the secrets of his heart will be disclosed, and so he will fall down on his face and worship God, declaring, 'God is truly in your midst.'

As intelligible speech, prophecy is not only linguistically understood by the outsiders (apparently, Paul assumes their language to have been Greek, despite the cosmopolitan make-up of Corinth), but also the content of prophetic speech will be understood as that which discloses publicly the καρδία, "heart," the deepest aspect of an individual, known only to that individual (Rom 10:9).

---

[164] Conzelmann, *1 Corinthians*, 243 n. 29; Fee, *First Epistle*, 685; Smit, "Tongues and Prophecy," 183, 187, 189; Hays, *First Corinthians*, 238–39; and Collins, *First Corinthians*, 509. For other scholars who hold this view, see Forbes, *Prophecy and Inspired Speech*, 178 n. 61.

[165] See Thiselton, *First Epistle*, who states that the context of μαίνεσθε for religious frenzy in the Greek world "need not commit us to any specific theory of a conscious equivalence to Bacchic frenzy" (p. 1126). See further ibid., n. 243.

[166] So Forbes, *Prophecy and Inspired Speech*, 180 n. 68.

[167] So Garland, *1 Corinthians*, 649. It is possible that glossolalia may have been perceived by unbelievers in spirit communication as fraudulent prophetic behavior. Even in the Greek world fraudulent prophetic activity was thought possible. See Donald Lateiner, "The Perception of Deception and Gullibility in Specialists of the Supernatural (Primarily) in Athenian Literature," in *Nomodeiktes: Greek Studies in Honor of Martin Ostwald* (ed. Ralph M. Rosen and Joseph Farrell; Ann Arbor: University of Michigan Press, 1993) 179–95.

The disclosure of the heart of an individual is meant to "convince" (ἐλέγχω) the unbeliever and uninformed that the prophecy one is speaking is not derived from the person's own mind, but rather from a spirit.[168] Likewise, the unbeliever and uninformed are "judged" or "discerned" (ἀνακρίνω) by those prophesying in the church, further revealing that the prophet is acting not on his or her own, but rather as a mouthpiece for the spirit world (implied at the end of v. 25).[169] The meaning of the verb ἀνακρίνω in conjunction with prophesying is further clarified by the context of the verb in 1 Cor 2:15 where "the spiritual person (πνευματικός) judges (ἀνακρίνει) all things," i.e., "one who is in communication with spirits [possibly the prophets, possibly the spectators] judges all things." Hence in v. 24 the two terms "convince" and "judge" indicate prophetic behavior. Once those who are uninformed in the reality of spirit communication become convinced of such a reality, they will not only be convinced that spirits are speaking through the prophets, but more importantly, they will be persuaded that these spirits are those sent from God: "God is truly in your midst" (ὁ θεὸς ἐν ὑμῖν ἐστιν).[170]

A translation of vv. 23–25 based on this interpretation might run as follows:

[23]For suppose that the whole church were gathered in one place, all speaking in foreign languages, and that people entered among you who knew nothing of communicating with spirits and did not believe in it, would they not say that you are crazy? [24]But if everyone were speaking as mediums through whom spirits spoke an intelligible language, and a certain one who neither believed in nor was informed in such matters entered among you, he would be convinced by everyone that spirit communication is a reality, [and][171] judged by everyone [i.e., by the spirits speaking through the prophets]; [25]the secrets of his heart will be disclosed [by the spirit], and so he will fall down on his face and worship God and declare that God is truly in your midst.

---

[168] See BAGD, 249; and Fee *(First Epistle)* who states, "The emphasis here is on the revelatory aspect of the prophetic utterance" (p. 686). See also 1 Cor 2:11, where the hidden "things of a person" are known only to that person whereas "the spirit [world] of God" reveals all.

[169] See Collins, *First Corinthians*, who states, "The description of the Christian prophet doing something similar to what the Lord does intimates that the prophet is inspired by God. By the power and Spirit of God with which he or she is endowed the prophet performs a function properly performed by God" (p. 510).

[170] This statement does not seem to indicate that Paul believed God himself to be present, but rather that spirits sent by God, i.e., πνεῦμα θεοῦ, "a spirit of God" (see 12:3; 14:16), spoke and acted on God's behalf and by his authority. Whatever a spirit of God says is, in essence, that which God wants communicated to the church. In this way, God is present through the manifestation of his holy spirits.

[171] The Greek lacks a connective and the two phrases are joined asyndetically.

The purpose of Paul's citation of Isa 28:11 in v. 21 now becomes clearer. The historical context of Isa 28:11 seems to be a divine judgment by God upon the Israelites deported by the Assyrians who spoke a language different from that of the Israelites. The ἑτερογλώσσοις, "other languages," in Paul's approximation of this passage is identified with γλῶσσαι, "tongues," among the Corinthians in v. 22. The "other languages" in the Isaiah passage incites a negative reaction, "they will not listen (εἰσακούσονται) to me, says the Lord." Paul applies this negative reaction to the effects of glossolalia on "unbelievers" and the "uninformed" on matters relating to spirit communication.

Earlier, in v. 14:2, Paul had used similar language to describe the effects of glossolalia: "for one who speaks a tongue does not speak to humans but to God. For no one understands (ἀκούει, "listens"), but he speaks mysteries with a spirit." The verb ἀκούω, "to listen," is also used in Paul's approximation of the passage from the book of Isaiah to describe the reaction of the Israelites to the "other languages": εἰσακούσονται, "they will not listen" (Isa 28:12 [LXX] has οὐκ ἠθέλησαν ἀκούειν, "they will not come to hear," i.e., "to listen"). More significantly, Paul says that this is a saying of the "Lord" (the LXX has "God"). In Paul's context, this alludes to the fact that glossolalia is a gift from the spirit world of God; the "Lord" might indeed communicate with foreign languages via one of his spirits commissioned for this purpose. But unless the language is interpreted, "no one will listen" or, in Paul's context, "understand" (v. 2c). Just as the Israelites did not "listen" to foreign languages from "the Lord," so too will "unbelievers" and the "uninformed" not "listen" to the glossolalists in the Corinthian Christian congregation; they will say, "You are crazy."

The problem of v. 22, that it contradicts Paul's illustrations in vv. 23–25, is probably best understood from two perspectives: (1) the application of Isa 28:11 to the Corinthian situation; and (2) Paul's general belief that prophecy is preferable to glossolalia. Since prophecy should be the preferred form of communication from the spirit world, this serves those who already believe in spirit communication as a sign of "God's presence among them"; the very sign that convinces unbelievers of the reality of spirit communication. Glossolalia, however, turns unbelievers in spirit communication away from the congregation; therefore it serves as a negative sign for unbelievers similar to the reaction of the Israelites to the Assyrian language in the Isaiah passage: "they will not listen," as in 1 Cor 14:2c, "no one listens [understands]," and here in v. 23, "You are crazy." Thus, glossolalia does not build up the church; neither are believers edified nor are unbelievers convinced of the reality and function of spirit communication in the church. In v. 22 then Paul is concerned with the effects of prophecy and glossolalia on believers and unbelievers. He gives an illustration of the effects in vv. 23–25.[172]

12. 1 Cor 14:26–33: Regulations for Communication with the Spirit World

1 Cor 14:26–33 is part of a larger pericope, vv. 26–40, that brings to closure Paul's thoughts and recommendations for communicating with spirits who speak foreign languages and those who speak the language of the congregation. Paul begins with his recommendations to the Corinthians on communicating with the spirit world in v. 26: τί οὖν ἐστίν, ἀδελφοί; "So then what is to be done, brothers?" (see 14:15). The resumptive "then" (οὖν) and "brothers" indicate that Paul is tying up his polemical argument.[173] Having delivered his observations on communicating with the spirit world in chap. 12 and 14:25, Paul now gives practical advice for the regulation of such communication.

In v. 26 Paul introduces a brief list of functions in the church with a phrase that describes the church as a "gathered" community: ὅταν συνέρχησθε, "when you come together" (cf. v. 23, συνέλθῃ ἡ ἐκκλησία ὅλη, "the whole church gathers"). In this verse the term ἕκαστος, "each," indicates that the gifts that follow in the list are distributed among a variety of persons from the spirit world. Each gift in v. 26 is mentioned in other parts of chap. 14: each one ψαλμὸν ἔχει, "has a psalm" (see 14:15)[174]; διδαχὴν ἔχει, "has a teaching" (see 14:6); ἀποκάλυψιν ἔχει, "has a revelation" (see 14:6); γλῶσσαν ἔχει, "has a tongue" (see 14:2,4, 5,6,9,13,14,19,22,23); ἑρμηνείαν ἔχει, "has a translation"

---

[172] This follows Forbes (*Prophecy and Inspired Speech*), who argues that vv. 21–25 contain two different strands of argument: "One strand is his preference for prophecy due to its intelligibility, and therefore its utility for edifying the congregation, . . . The second strand is the contrast between the effects of glossolalia and prophecy on unbelievers. The two strands are intertwined in this passage, . . ." (pp. 179–80).

[173] See Collins, *First Corinthians*, 517.

[174] The term ψαλμός, "song," does not easily lend itself to a distinction of whether Paul is referring to a prayer or a sacred song of praise. Does it refer to a fresh composition or a known composition, possibly taken from the Psalms of the OT? Lindemann (*Der Erste Korintherbrief*, 313) thinks it refers to the Psalter here. Collins (*First Corinthians*, 518) suggests a Christian composition (see Col 3:16; Eph 5:19). Whatever the case may be, hymnody seems to have played an important role in the life of early Christian gatherings (see Garland, *1 Corinthians*, 657–58).

(see 14:5,13).[175] All of these gifts refer to speech acts of some kind. Two of these gifts, "a psalm" and "a tongue," are explicitly associated with uttering "with a spirit" elsewhere in chap. 14 (see 1 Cor 14:2c,15).

The other three terms in v. 26, "teaching" (διδαχήν), "revelation" (ἀποκάλυψιν), and "translation" (ἑρμηνείαν), although not explicitly qualified by ἐν πνεύματι, are also related to speech forms derived from communication with the spirit world. Revelation has to do with inspired utterances and is closely associated with prophecy in vv. 29–31.[176] Translation of glossolalia is one of the gifts from the spirit world (see 12:10) and seems intimately related to the translation of foreign languages that a spirit might speak through a prophet. This gift might also imply a gift for being a medium through whom spirits translated the foreign language of another spirit through a different prophet.[177] Teaching may either be a function of an individual whose expositions are the sum of his own thoughts and reflections or teaching may refer to a teaching delivered by a spirit through a prophet. The latter interpretation conforms, at least, to the context of Paul's recommendations and stipulations for intelligible communication from the spirit world.[178] Paul ends this statement with the main theme driving his polemic on prophecy and glossolalia: πάντα πρὸς οἰκοδομὴν γινέσθω, "everything should be done for the building up of the church" (14:3,4,5,12,17). This is Paul's final word to the Corinthians on "building up" in his exposition on communicating with the spirit world.

In vv. 27–28 Paul recapitulates language for glossolalia and the translation of it. Having come full circle from 14:2–5, Paul now lays down three strict guidelines for the use of glossolalia in the church in v. 27: (1) εἴτε γλώσσῃ τις λαλεῖ, κατὰ δύο ἢ τὸ πλεῖστον τρεῖς, "If someone speaks in a tongue, let it be

---

[175] Fee (*First Epistle*) is careful to note that this list is not intended to give order of service. The fact that "prophecy" and "discernment" are not listed here indicates that the list is not exhaustive, even though "prophecy" and "discernment" are given regulations in the following vv. 29–33 (p. 690).

[176] Fee (ibid.) observes that revelation may be "a cover word for all other forms of intelligible inspired speech, including the 'prophecies' of vv. 29–32, especially since the verb 'revealed' occurs in the context of prophecy and discernment in v. 30" (p. 691).

[177] Hence Forbes (*Prophecy and Inspired Speech*, 58) notes that "interpretation of glossolalia" is best understood as "(inspired) 'translation.'"

[178] For spirits who "teach," the verb διδάσκω, "to teach" (whose cognate noun is διδαχή, the noun Paul uses here) and its related adjectival form occur with the terms πνεῦμα or δαιμόνιον in the NT: "holy spirit" or "a spirit" (Luke 12:12; John 14:26; 1 Cor 2:13); "demonic spirits" (1 Tim 4:1). These spirits, good and evil, are thought to have the capacity for didactic utterance directed toward spectators.

two or at most three"; (2) καὶ ἀνὰ μέρος, "and each in turn"; and (3) καὶ εἷς διερμηνευέτω, "and one should translate." Paul depicts several mediums speaking foreign languages, but not all at once. They should speak "in turn." It is unclear whether εἷς, "one," specifies an individual other than the two or three glossolalists who translate or one of the glossolalists themselves who is meant to translate. As stated earlier, the evidence in Paul seems to suggest that the one who translates may either be the spirit speaking through the glossolalist (1 Cor 14:13)[179] or a spirit speaking through a different person (1 Cor 12:10,30).[180] Both may have been possible in the Corinthian church.

Verse 28 seems also to distinguish between a glossolalist and a translator: ἐὰν δὲ μὴ ᾖ διερμηνευτής, σιγάτω ἐν ἐκκλησίᾳ, ἑαυτῷ δὲ λαλείτω καὶ τῷ θεῷ, "But if there is no one to translate, let [the glossolalist] be silent in the church, but speak to himself and to God." With this statement, Paul drives home the point that untranslated glossolalia is useless in the church. Glossolalia should not even be uttered in the church unless the language can be translated so that the gathered community can understand the message, thus benefit from it and be built up.

Verses 27 and 28 are Paul's final directives on glossolalia to the Corinthians. With the idea that glossolalia is the speech of a spirit that speaks a foreign language, and that "translation" in Paul's context is an activity of the spirit world (12:10), then these verses may run as follows,

[27]If a certain spirit decides to speak a foreign language, allow two [spirits], or at most, three [to speak], one at a time, and let one [spirit] translate. [28]But if no [spirit] is present who can translate the foreign language, let the other [spirit] be silent, but speak to himself and to God.

Just as Paul provides provisos for spirits who speak foreign languages to the Corinthians, so too does he give recommendations for spirits who speak the language of the congregation in vv. 29–33. In v. 29a Paul recommends a limit to the number of prophets who should be allowed to speak: προφῆται δὲ δύο ἢ τρεῖς λαλείτωσαν, "let two or three prophets speak," presumably, one at a time (see 14:31). Paul then advises that the prophetic utterances be evaluated, as he is want to do elsewhere (Rom 12:6; 1 Thess 5:19–22): καὶ οἱ ἄλλοι διακρινέτωσαν, "and let the others judge." The "others" (ἄλλοι) indicate members of the congregation who are listening to the spirit speak through the

---

[179] So Collins, *First Corinthians*, 518; and Thiselton, *First Epistle*, 1137.
[180] Garland, *1 Corinthians*, 659.

prophet.[181] The verb διακρινέτωσαν, "let them judge," suggests ideas ranging from "discriminate," "evaluate," and possibly "discern." Paul does not suggest here that the prophets are "judged" as to their veracity, i.e., whether they are true or false prophets (much in the way that Paul advises in 12:10 to "discern [true from false] spirits").

The prophets, presumably, are those who are established in the Corinthian Christian congregation serving as mediums for the good spirit world.[182] The "others" in the congregation "evaluate carefully"[183] the prophetic utterance, i.e., that which the spirits speak through the prophets. This may have entailed discussions among the congregation as to the substantive meaning of an address by a spirit through a medium. If a particular member misunderstood the meaning, then, possibly, the spirit would resume speaking through the prophet in order to clarify points of its address.

In v. 30 Paul mentions the possibility that someone in the congregation may be given an inspiration: ἐὰν δὲ ἄλλῳ ἀποκαλυφθῇ καθημένῳ, ὁ πρῶτος σιγάτω, "but if there is a revelation given to some other person who is seated, let the first person (the medium) be silent." The verb ἀποκαλυφθῇ, "to be given a revelation," is in the passive voice and indicates that one receives some kind of insight or verbal utterance from the spirit world. Whether this is spoken by a spirit or the one to whom the revelation is given is not clear. Prophecy seems to have been a form of revelation, as stated earlier; the "disclosure" or "revelation" of matter related to the gospel. Revelations may also have been the utterances of spirits (see 14:6, 26). What is clear is that revelations occur during communication with the spirit world; the prophets are advised to cede to the one who is given a revelation, "let the first (medium) be silent" (ὁ πρῶτος σιγάτω). The one who receives a revelation is said to be "seated" (καθημένῳ), a situation that indicates a part of the gathering in which certain seated guests may have been especially sensitive to influences from the spirits visiting the Corinthian congregation.[184]

In v. 31 the γάρ, "for," seems to have a causal force that gives the reason for

---

[181] So Collins, *First Corinthians*, 519; and Garland, *1 Corinthians*, 663. Contra Fee, *First Epistle*, 694, who believes it refers to the "other prophets."

[182] See Aune (*Prophecy in Early Christianity*): "In the middle of the first century A.D. in Corinth, prophets constituted a recognizable group within the Christian community that specialized in mediating a particular form of divine revelation within the setting of congregational worship" (p. 198). So, too, Garland, *1 Corinthians*, 662.

[183] So Garland, *1 Corinthians*, 662, who follows Grudem, *Gift of Prophecy*, 64.

[184] See Collins (*First Corinthians*): "It suggests the context of the symposium during which guests would continue to be seated" (p. 519).

what was said in v. 30: δύνασθε γὰρ καθ' ἕνα πάντες προφητεύειν, ἵνα πάντες μανθάνωσιν καὶ πάντες παρακαλῶνται, "For you can all prophesy in turn, so that everyone might learn and be encouraged." Paul intends to give the congregation a sense of order. Prophets should allow others who are inspired by the spirit world to speak. Each of the prophets have an opportunity to speak if the spirit world so chooses.

The first "all" (πάντες) probably refers to only prophets. Not all of the members of the congregation had the ability for becoming a medium through whom spirits communicated. According to Paul a variety of abilities were distributed to different members of the congregation, only one of which was prophecy (see 12:28–30). The other two uses of "all" refer to the members of the congregation. Paul states the effects of spirits that speak the language of the congregation: "so that everyone might learn and be encouraged." These are the effects that build up the church. Communication with the spirit world of God delivers instruction (μανθάνω) and that which encourages (παρακαλέω; cf. παράκλησιν, 14:3). The spirits are meant to communicate matter that brings the congregation together as one, so that all have the same understanding and are of one mind (see 1:10; 12:13).

Verses 32–33 elaborate on the real presence behind prophecy and its orderliness in the congregation: καὶ πνεύματα προφητῶν προφήταις ὑποτάσσεται, οὐ γάρ ἐστιν ἀκαταστασίας ὁ θεὸς ἀλλὰ εἰρήνης, "and the spirits of the prophets are under the prophets' control, for God is not of disorder but of peace." As shown in Chapter One, scholars routinely refer to "spirits" here as "manifestations of the Holy Spirit," "spiritual utterances," or the "human spirits of the prophets" through which the Holy Spirit speaks. Grammatically, "spirits of the prophets" is ambiguous. It may refer either to the prophets' own human spirit or to spirits other than the prophets' own. The other two plural forms "spirits" in 12:10 and 14:12 indicate, at least, spirits other than human spirits.[185]

Ellis proposed that "spirits" are "angelic spirits" who speak through the

---

[185] Admittedly, Paul uses πνεῦμα for the human spirit elsewhere: 1 Cor 2:11; 5:3,4; 16:18; Gal 6:18; 1 Thess 5:23; Phil 4:23; Phlm 25; 2 Tim 4:22. See also n. 117 above. Paul, however, never uses the plural form πνεύματα to refer to "human spirits." The plural form occurs only three times in the undisputed letters of Paul, 1 Cor 12:10; 14:12,32, all of which refer to "holy spirits" (apart from those spirits "discerned" as "unholy" in 12:10). See further George F. Tittmann, "Human Spirit and Holy Spirit: Texts and Musings," *Saint Luke's Journal of Theology* 16 (1973) 20–46; and Ethelbert W. Bullinger, *Word Studies on the Holy Spirit* (London: Eyre & Spottiswoode, 1905; repr. Grand Rapids: Kregel, 1979) who states, "πνεύματα, spirits, when standing alone (without any qualifying words), is never used of men in any form, state or condition. These are spiritual beings" (p. 213).

prophets.[186]   Grudem, however, argued that nowhere does Paul describe prophetic speech as inspired by angels.[187] He does observe that "spirits" may be called "angels" in the NT (see Heb 1:7,14 based on Ps 104:4) but this identification never occurs in Paul.[188] It is true that Paul never speaks of "angels" (ἄγγελοι) in relation to prophecy. In the NT angelic mediation usually occurs in the context of visionary experiences from the spirit world as in Rev 19:9–10.[189] Ellis unnecessarily qualifies Paul's term "spirits" in 14:32 as "angelic"; as Grudem notes of Ellis's argument, "spirits" are not "angelic spirits" in Paul. This criticism, however, leads toward the unnecessary assumption that "spirits" cannot refer to a multiplicity of good spirits (so Grudem). The idea that Paul may not have in mind "*angelic* spirits" in 14:32 does not, nevertheless, nullify the possibility that by "spirits" Paul may be indicating many holy spirits as he does for "spirits" in 14:12.

Paul states that "the spirits of the prophets are under the prophets' control (προφήταις ὑποτάσσεται)." If "spirits" refer to holy spirits, then this statement seems to contradict Paul's earlier statement in 1 Cor 12:11 that the Holy Spirit manifests καθώς βούλετια, "just as it wills." The Holy Spirit is not subject to human beings. Hence an argument is sometimes made that these spirits cannot be a reference to the Holy Spirit, but rather must refer to the prophets' own human spirits.

This argument is further elaborated by scholars to show that persons inspired by the spirit remain in control of themselves in contrast to the "ecstatic" or "out of one's mind," i.e., "out of control," type of inspiration in the Greek world: prophets in Corinth prophesy in full control of their own mental faculties (their own spirits).[190] Three points, however, question the validity of this argument:

---

[186] Ellis, "Christ and Spirit," *Christ and Spirit in the New Testament*, 275.

[187] Grudem, *Gift of Prophecy*, 122 n. 10. This was a similar argument that Dibelius leveled against Everling (*Die Geisterwelt*, 74): "Die Annahme einer Engelvermittlung aber ist nicht nur in unseren Stellen nicht begründet, sondern ist auch nach der Pneumatologie des Apostels Paulus wenig glaubhaft."

[188] Paul does use the term ἄγγελος, "angel," to designate a heavenly being in Gal 1:8 and 1 Cor 13:1.

[189] See further Grudem, *Gift of Prophecy*, 121 n. 10 (6). Note the distinction between a prophet's report of revelation previously given in the form of visions and a prophet's utterances whose provenance is that of a spirit who has taken control of the vocal organs and speaks to the spectators. The latter is sometimes called "spontaneous prophetic utterance" by scholars.

[190] So Fee, *First Epistle*, who states, "With these words ['the spirits of the prophets are under the prophets' control'] Paul lifts Christian 'inspired speech' out of the category of 'ecstasy' as such and offers it as a radically different thing from the mania of the pagan cults. There is no seizure here, no loss of control; the speaker is neither frenzied nor a babbler" (p. 696); and Conzelmann, *1 Corinthians*, 244; Kistemaker, *1 Corinthians*, 510; Hays, *First Corinthians*, 243;

(1) in the context of prophecy, "ecstasy" neither indicates "out of control" behavior (in the sense of jumping and moving about senselessly) nor nonsensical speech delivered by a prophet for, as Stewart-Sykes notes, "It is possible for a prophet not in possession of her or his faculties [i.e., to be 'in ecstasy'] to deliver paraenetic guidance [i.e., 'exhortation,' 'advice,' 'counsel' in an intelligible language]"[191];

(2) scholars argue that Paul's recommendation for "order" in the congregation (1 Cor 14:33) should be identified with the prophets' state of inspiration, an identity, however, that Paul does not make[192]; and

(3) Paul's description of prophecy and glossolalia as speech delivered ἐν πνεύματι, "with a spirit" (1 Cor 12:3; 14:2c,15,16), indicates that a spirit other than the prophet's own is speaking through the agency of the prophet. Recall Philo, *Her.* 266: "The prophet, even when he seems to be speaking, really holds his peace, his organs of speech, mouth and tongue, are wholly in the employ of Another [i.e., a divine spirit]." Paul's language is different from that of Philo, but the phenomenon of a spirit communicating through the agency of a prophet holds true in both cases, whether in Paul's pithy phrase ἐν πνεύματι λαλῶν or Philo's elaborate explanations.[193]

The argument made by scholars that 1 Cor 14:32 relates the idea that prophets in Corinth were in full control of their own spirits during inspiration is based on inaccurate portrayals of "ecstasy," the attempts to distinguish Greco-Roman ideas from "unique" Christian ideas,[194] and the idea that "spirits" cannot refer to "holy spirits." Paul never writes of "ecstasy" in his text, but he does describe spirits who communicate in human languages with the terms prophecy

---

Collins, *First Corinthians*, 519–20; Thiselton, *First Epistle*, 1144; and Garland, *1 Corinthians*, 659–60.

[191] Stewart-Sykes, "Condemnation," 4. Note also the texts of Josephus, Philo, and Pseudo-Philo analyzed in Chapter Three that indicate *intelligible* speech delivered during an "ecstatic" state.

[192] Conzelmann, *1 Corinthians*, argues that, "For Paul the criterion of orderliness is apparently effective not only when it comes to the content of inspired speech (this is treated in 12:1–3), but already in the case of the phenomenon itself" (p. 244). See also Fee, *First Epistle*, 692; and Garland, *1 Corinthians*, 660, who identify human "self-control" with inspiration by the Holy Spirit that is also "controlled" in the sense that the prophets' faculties have not "wandered" from him or her during inspiration.

[193] Forbes (*Prophecy and Inspired Speech*) observes that Paul's writings cannot be expected to provide the kind of detail we find in those of a Philo. He notes that Paul never "offers an explicit definition of prophecy," and that, "We must not expect absolute terminological precision of our sources, which are occasional writings, not philosophical treatises" (p. 221).

[194] But see Levison, *Spirit*, 254 (quoted on p. 143 above).

and glossolalia, both of which, as gifts from the spirit world (12:10), are the utterances of spirits through prophets who would have spoken in a trance state.

Considering that Paul approves of the Corinthians' communicating with a variety of spirits to build up the church in 1 Cor 14:12 (especially those spirits who speak the language of the congregation), it would follow that these are the same spirits associated with prophets mentioned in 14:32. Furthermore, since the phrase "with a spirit" indicates that a certain spirit speaks through the agency of a prophet, then the "spirits of the prophets" seem to refer to these spirits in the plural who communicate with the Corinthian congregation.[195]

Paul claims that the "spirits" are "under the prophets' control" or "are subject to the prophets" (πνεύματα προφητῶν προφήταις ὑποτάσσεται). This statement seems to suggest that established mediums within the Christian community (those mediums who are specifically used by "holy spirits" sent from God) may have had the liberty of deciding whether a spirit should enter into them and speak through them. This liberty does not necessarily mean that the prophet had full control over a spirit that did the prophet's bidding like that found in magical practices described by Irenaeus, *Against Heresies* 1.13.3, or akin to diviners and their "familiar spirits" in the OT.[196] Instead, if the prophet decided that a spirit should enter him or her, the spirit world would then decide if this was appropriate for the occasion (cf. 1 Cor 12:11, hence there is no contradiction, for despite the fact that the prophet may decide for a spirit to enter him or her to speak, the decision for this ultimately lies with the "will" [βούλεται] of the spirit world).[197] If the prophet did not want a spirit to enter and speak, then the

---

[195] See the similar phrase in Rev 22:6, ὁ θεὸς τῶν πνευμάτων τῶν προφητῶν, "the God of the spirits of the prophets." These spirits are collectively known as "the spirit of prophecy" as Rev 19:10 indicates: ἡ γὰρ μαρτυρία 'Ιησοῦ ἐστιν τὸ πνεῦμα τῆς προφητείας, "for the witness of Jesus is the spirit of prophecy." Compare this with Paul's advice that a spirit of God is a witness to Jesus by its acclamation through a prophet "Jesus is Lord" in 1 Cor 12:3. See Hui, "The Spirit of Prophecy and Pauline Pneumatology," 105–08.

[196] See John Barclay Burns, "Necromancy and the Spirits of the Dead in the Old Testament," *Transactions of the Glasgow University Oriental Society* 26 (1978) 1–14; and Leda Jean Ciraolo, "Supernatural Assistants in the Greek Magical Papyri," in *Ancient Magic and Ritual Power* (ed. Marvin Meyer and Paul Mirecki; Leiden: Brill, 1995) 279–93.

[197] The idea that the spirit world of God communicates by its own authority is a Jewish idea. "A spirit of understanding," "the spirit of God," and "the divine spirit" speak as God wills them without the influence of human will, curiosity, or sensationalism. See Sir 39:6, Josephus *A.J.* 4.6.5 §119, and Herm. *Mand.* 11.6,8. See also Wiesinger (*Occult Phenomena*, 216) who rejects popular culture's fascination with spiritism: "It is not fitting that they [exalted spirits] should at a word of command be made to amuse us, simply in order to satisfy our curiosity or to serve as the object of scientific experiments." This seems to be the reasoning behind *Did.* 11:7, "While a spirit is speaking through a prophet you must not test or examine him," i.e., "you must not

spirit world would yield to the prophet's wish and not force itself upon the prophet. Hence God is not a God "of disorder but of peace" (v. 33).

Grudem provides a similar explanation,

To speak of the Holy Spirit as he works in a believer's life as being subject (ὑποτάσσεται) to the believer is not inconsistent with Pauline theology.... Paul is showing that the Holy Spirit will not force a prophet to speak, but allows the prophet himself to determine when he should speak. This is a voluntary submission in one particular function for the sake of order, and implies no theological statement about man as somehow superior to the Holy Spirit.[198]

Verses 29–33 may run as follows,

[29]Addresses made by spirits through prophets should be limited to two or three, and those present should weigh and discuss what they have heard. [30]If one attending the service is given a revelation from the spirit world, the medium should be silent. [31]For all of the mediums [have sufficient time to] prophesy one by one so that all may be instructed and all may be encouraged. [32]The spirits that manifest themselves through the mediums will obey the mediums, [33]for God is not of disorder but of harmony.

13. 1 Cor 14:37–40: Paul's Final Comments on Communication with the Spirit World of God

Paul concludes his polemic on communication with the spirit world in vv. 37–40:

[37]εἴ τις δοκεῖ προφήτης εἶναι ἢ πνευματικός, ἐπιγινωσκέτω ἃ γράφω ὑμῖν ὅτι κυρίου ἐστὶν ἐντολή· [38]εἰ δέ τις ἀγνοεῖ, ἀγνοεῖται. [39]ὥστε, ἀδελφοί [μου], ζηλοῦτε τὸ προφητεύειν καὶ τὸ λαλεῖν μὴ κωλύετε γλώσσαις· [40]πάντα δὲ εὐσχημόνως καὶ κατὰ τάξιν γινέσθω

If anyone thinks that he is a prophet or a spiritual person, he should acknowledge that what I am writing to you is a commandment of the Lord. If anyone does not acknowledge this, he is not

---

satisfy mere human curiosity or examine the spirit for the sake of worldly matters that do not contribute to building up." This does not contradict "discerning" or "testing the spirits." In *Did.* 11:7 the prophet is one who has already been verified as a truthful prophet, for in the following line, 11:8, the matter of the false prophet (ὁ ψευδοπροφήτης) is raised.

[198] Grudem, *Gift of Prophecy*, 125–26. See further Smith, "Pauline Worship," who states, "... it was the prophets' duty to keep them [the spirits] under control and make them yield the floor to their fellows (14:29–32)" (p. 247).

acknowledged. So [my] brothers and sisters, strive eagerly to prophesy, and do not forbid speaking in tongues. But let all things be done properly and in order.[199]

Paul gives the full weight of authority of his exposition on spirit communication to the Lord as being "a commandment of the Lord" (ἐντολὴ κυρίου). Paul identifies the one through whom spirits communicate in the language of the congregation (a prophet) and the "spiritual person" (πνευματικός), i.e., "one who is in communication with the world of spirits," as persons who should recognize that his recommendations on the matter of spirit communication are not his own.[200] His recommendations find their source in the Lord himself.[201]

In v. 38 Paul pronounces a strict sentence on those who are familiar with spirit communication but who do not acknowledge his polemic on prophecy and glossolalia as a command of the Lord. Paul, apparently, believes that the Corinthians will receive the same information that he is writing to them from the spirit world as well. Paul's double use of the verb ἀγνοέω, "to not to know," "to be ignorant," is the antonym of "to acknowledge" in v. 37.[202] Paul's point follows that those who communicate with spirits in a Christian context should be able to "acknowledge" that his arguments are a revelation from the Lord Jesus Christ. This not only reflects Luke's account of Paul's personal experiences with the risen Jesus in Acts 9:16,27, 13:47, 18:9, 20:24, 22:8–10,18,19, and 25:19, but also Paul's personal testimony in Gal 1:11–12. If the one who communicates with the spirit world does not "acknowledge" what Paul is writing as a commandment of the Lord, then that person "is not acknowledged." The subject of the passive verb ἀγνοεῖται, "he is not acknowledged," is God (theological passive), for those who neglect or disregard

---

[199] 1 Cor 14:33b–36 are sometimes argued as an interpolation. These verses do not bear on the subject of spiritism in Paul's exposition per se. Hence they are not treated in the exegesis here. See Collins, *First Corinthians*, 515–17.

[200] Historically, the adjective πνευματικός, "spiritual," denoted "that which pertains to spirit/spirits/spirit world." Montanist inscriptions, for example, use this adjective to describe Christians as Χρηστιανὸς πνευματικός, "a spiritual Christian." This description refers to the practice of communicating with spirit world, for in the case of Montanus, a spirit entered into him and spoke through him in the first person (Epiphanius, *Haer.* 48.4). These "spiritual Christians" were either mediums themselves or else participated in Christian services with a medium present for the purpose of communicating with the spirit world. See William Tabbernee, "Remnants of the New Prophecy: Literary and Epigraphical Sources of the Montanist Movement," *Studia Patristica* 21 (1989) 193–201, esp. 199–200.

[201] Note that Paul distinguishes his "opinion" on a matter from "a commandment of the Lord" in 1 Cor 7:25.

[202] So Fee, *First Epistle*, 712.

what the Lord has commanded will be disregarded by God.[203] This is similarly reflected in the statements of Jesus, "But whoever disowns me before men, I will disown him before my Father in heaven" (Matt 10:33); and "I do not know you" (Matt 7:22–23).

In vv. 39 and 40 Paul comes to close his lengthy exposition to the Corinthians on the appropriate way to communicate with the spirit world and its proper use and utility in the church. Paul introduces his close with ὥστε, "so," "therefore," followed by the vocative "brothers and sisters" (ἀδελφοί). Whereas in 1 Cor 14:6,20,26 Paul simply used the vocative ἀδελφοί, here the vocative is reinforced by "my" (μου) that implies a more pastoral tone than in the previous verse.[204] Paul delivers three brief imperatives on the topic of communicating with spirits who speak foreign languages and those that speak the language of the congregation.

The first imperative, "strive eagerly to prophesy," i.e., "strive eagerly to become instruments of the spirit world for speech in your own language," recalls 1 Cor 14:1b. Paul uses the infinitive form of the verb προφητεύειν to indicate continued action. By doing so, Paul impresses upon the Corinthians that not only should they be eager to seek communication with the spirit world in the present, but also this eagerness should continue and not cease (see 1 Thess 5:20).[205]

Paul then declares that glossolalia should not be prohibited in the church: "do not forbid speaking in tongues," i.e., "do not prevent spirits from speaking in foreign languages altogether." In the end, Paul's regulations and recommendations on glossolalia were not meant to stifle glossolalia in the church completely. This follows Paul's directive that glossolalia should occur in the presence of a spirit that is able to translate the language into the tongue of the congregation (1 Cor 14:5,27,28). Apparently, Paul's imperative here is meant to clarify his rhetoric on glossolalia that might be misconstrued to mean total exclusion of the practice of glossolalia in the church.

In v. 40 Paul finally reveals the full thrust of his polemic on glossolalia and prophecy: "Let all things be done properly and in order" (see v. 33). The Corinthians' excessive practice of communicating with spirits who speak foreign languages threatened the harmony of the church. Paul's final imperative emphasizes his belief in the maintenance of order in the congregation during its communication with the spirit world.

---

[203] So Fee, ibid.; Kistemaker, *1 Corinthians*, 516; Hays, *First Corinthians*, 244; Collins, *First Corinthians*, 523; and Garland, *1 Corinthians*, 674.

[204] See Kistemaker, *1 Corinthians*, 517. See 1 Cor 15:58.

[205] So ibid.

Conclusion

This book attempted to explain Paul's exposition in First Corinthians 12 and 14 in the context of religious experience. The category "religious experience" had been somewhat marginalized in biblical studies. Thiselton's statement that any discussion of First Corinthians 12 and 14 in terms of religious experience "goes against the grain of Paul" was a clear indication of this marginlization. Scholars past (Gunkel, Weinel, Hopwood) and present (Dunn, Johnson, Hurtado, Morgan-Wynne), however, have shown that the category "religious experience" offers constructive insight and understanding into early Christian experience with "spirit." The term "spirit" was shown to be NT rhetoric for religious experience. The various effects of the spirit provided experiences of a world "beyond" the human world.

Religious experiences in the NT had to do with revelations from a "spirit" source, whether in the context of visions, prophecy, or some other experience wherein spirits guided and instructed human beings. This source was argued to be "the spirit world," a phrase that finds no direct equivalent in the Greek NT, but rather is meant to reflect the meaning of τὸ πνεῦμα, "the spirit," in First Corinthians 12 and 14.

It was shown that First Corinthians 12 and 14 provided one of the most abundant sources in the NT for a study of religious experience in earliest Christianity: a congregational setting in which Christians gathered together to worship God with the intention of establishing a direct line of communication with God's spirits. Paul's polemic in these two chapters touched on two forms of inspired speech in the church: prophecy and glossolalia. Paul's use of the prepositional phrase ἐν πνεύματι described both prophecy and glossolalia as the speech of spirits through human mediums.

Communication from the spirit world was meant to build up the Corinthian church through instruction in the gospel message and possibly with new insights into the Christian life. The primary reason though for Christian prayer meetings was to worship God, to give Him thanks and praise in the name of His Son with the hope that holy spirits might manifest. The manifestation of the spirit world might or might not occur; if it did occur, then this manifestation was determined by the will of God and His spirits alone (see 1 Cor 12:11). The prayers of those gathered served as an impetus for the manifestation of God's spirits as clearly seen in the Shepherd of Hermas, *Mandate* 11.9. Such regular gatherings for prayer built up the power (ἐνέργεια) necessary for the manifestation of holy spirits. The acclamation "Jesus is Lord" indicated that a good spirit was present in the medium. An address by the spirit to the congregation would presumably follow. Among the earliest Christians the "word of God" was not read from a book; the "word of God" was verbal communication from spirits of God who *spoke* to Christians in their mother tongue.[1] Glossolalia was shown to be human language unknown to both the glossolalist and the congregation. This was primarily evident in Paul's examples in 1 Cor 14:10–11and 16–19. If the spirit spoke in a foreign language, then that language had to be translated; otherwise, such spirits were not to speak to the congregation.

The spirits accomplished this task through the agency of those gifted with the ability for becoming mediums of the spirit world, those whom Paul calls "prophets." A prophetic utterance was the utterance of a spirit through a prophet; the prophet served as the medium through which a spirit verbally expressed itself to the spectators. Such mediums were also shown to exist in the writings of four other first-century Greco-Roman authors, namely, Plutarch, Josephus, Philo, and Pseudo-Philo, three of them Jews.

Paul mentions that prophecy is for unbelievers (1 Cor 14:24), but there may have existed a rare instance in which *glossolalia* provided evidence for a certain unbeliever in spirit communication. If the unbeliever personally knew the glossolalist, and the unbeliever heard the glossolalist speak a foreign language that the unbeliever not only recognized as a bona fide language, but also knew that the glossolalist had no knowledge of, then the unbeliever might have been persuaded that another personality was at work through the glossolalist. The contemporary phenomenon of xenolalia is a good example for this, especially that seen in the case of Carlos Mirabelli (see p. 40 n. 115). But such conditions must have been rare – so rare that Paul does not even posit the idea (unless this was his original intentions in 1 Cor 14:22). Interestingly enough, in contemporary society, the knowledge of unlearned languages is a sign of demonic possession only.[2]

The popular understanding of the term "spiritism" restricts its range to include only the spirits of dead human beings. The equivalent term in Greek, πνεῦμα, however, was shown to denote not only human spirits, but also holy spirits, evil spirits (demons, unclean spirits, spirits of deceit, etc.), angels, God, and Christ. The term "spiritism" is applicable to any of these spiritual realities in the NT. Biblical scholars who identify spiritism with necromancy in the OT are influenced more by the popular, restrictive, and subjective meaning of the

---

[1] Recall Gunkel (*Influence*, 100): "The theology of the great apostle [Paul] is the expression of his *experience, not of his reading*" (emphasis mine).

[2] Rodewyk, *Possessed by Satan*, 69–74; and even earlier in the Middle Ages, Caciola, *Discernment*, 48: "Medieval texts tell of demoniacs who suddenly knew foreign languages." See also Raphel Patai, "Exorcism and Xenoglossai among the Safed Kabbalists," *Journal of American Folklore* 91 (1978) 823–35.

term "spiritism" rather than by its philological, objective basis. The prophetic contexts of רוח and πνεῦμα relate the basic meaning for the term "spiritism": "the act of communicating with spirits (of whatever kind), usually within a congregational context."

The term πνεῦμα occurs nineteen times in First Corinthians 12 and 14. The context of all these occurrences reflects the reception of "gifts" and the constant "activity" and "services" of spirit beings from a single spiritual source, the one and same spirit world of God. The particular activity of prophecy and glossolalia in First Corinthians 14 indicates even more explicitly that spirit beings communicated substantive matter from the spirit world to human spectators who met for this purpose. Thus, the potential for using "spiritism" as a translation for 1 Cor 12:1a is great.

One of the main contributions of this thesis is to that of Christian pneumatology. Since Paul is able to use the singular form πνεῦμα for a multiplicity of "human spirits" (so Grudem), this same principle was applied to his usage of the singular and the plural forms of πνεῦμα in First Corinthians 12 and 14 where spirit refers to "holy spirit." The plural form πνεύματα occurs only three times in the undisputed letters of Paul: 1 Cor 12:10, 14:12,32. In each of these instances, "spirits" referred to "holy spirits" (apart from other spirits "discerned" as "unholy" in 12:10).

Evidence was also found in the NT for the use of the spirit of God as a generic singular for many spirits. In 1 John 4 "the spirit of God" and "the spirit of truth" were used as a generic singular for "every spirit that acknowledges Jesus has come in the flesh" (1 John 4:2,6) just as "the spirit of antichrist" and "the spirit of error" were used to designate "every spirit that does not acknowledge Jesus" (1 John 4:3,6). In Paul, the phrase "the one spirit" was meant to emphasize the single spiritual source from which the different spirits derived. Although it has not been explicitly argued in this book, occurrences of "the spirit" and "the holy spirit" in other parts of the NT (especially in Acts) may also indicate the activity of "the holy spirit world."

Paul never qualifies the plural "spirits" with the adjective "holy" (πνεύματα ἅγια). But neither does Paul always qualify the singular "spirit" with the adjective "holy." At times Paul can use πνεῦμα without any qualifier, with or without the article, to denote "holy spirit" (articular – Rom 8:5,23,27; 1 Cor 14:15; 2 Cor 1:22; 3:8; Gal 3:14; 5:17,22; and anarthrous – Rom 2:29; 7:6; 8:9; 1 Cor 2:4,13; 14:2c,16; Gal 5:5,16,18,25). Such evidence suggests the possibility that the unqualified plural "spirits" in 1 Cor 14:12,32 can also fall within the range of "holy."

Later Christian theology of the Holy Spirit should not serve as a starting point for investigating the use of πνεῦμα in the NT. It has been shown that πνεῦμα in the texts of the NT reflects little, if any, of fourth-century theology on the Deity and Personhood of the Holy Spirit. The threshold between the historical criticism and the theological interpretation of πνεῦμα in the NT is seen at the point at which πνεῦμα begins to appear in formulations for a divine Person of the Godhead: the first-century πνεῦμα-world evolved into a fourth-century πνεῦμα-Person.

The earliest Christians, Jews as well as Gentiles, experienced the spirit world as it was inherited by them from Judaism. The experiences of the spirit world, however, were "Christianized" insofar as spirits were identified as "holy" or "of God" by their utterances "Jesus is Lord" (1 Cor12:3) and "Jesus Christ has come in the flesh" (1 John 4:2). This Christological component arose from experiences of a spirit world that were clearly Jewish (πνεῦμα ἅγιον [רוח קודש] and πνεῦμα θεοῦ [רוח אלהים]), but whose messages were clearly Christian, i.e., the gospel. Expressions such as τὸ πνεῦμα, "the spirit," and τὸ πνεῦμα τὸ ἅγιον, "the holy spirit," were too far removed in the NT from what they would later become known as in the pneumatological formulations of the fourth and fifth centuries: a divine Person of the Trinity. Whereas theology correctly identified personal attributes for "the spirit" and "the holy spirit" in the NT, it created a theological landscape that veiled the spirit world of holy spirits. In the NT, "the holy spirit" is a collective noun.

Recently, Christian theology has begun to posit the idea of a spirit world in the NT. Christian theology derides language for "spirits" as something related to a lower or primitive form of theology derived from animism whereas language for "the Holy Spirit" represents a higher theology of "spirit" derived from church tradition. Thus, the Nicene Creed is used as a basis and starting point to explicate the spirit world in the NT (see Noble, "The Spirit World: A Theological Approach," p. 74 n. 255 above). If Christian theology is going to examine the possibility of a spirit world in the NT, it must do so within the context, environment, and grammar of the NT itself. The LXX and Second Temple texts will also play pivotal roles. The use of ecclesiastical texts and creeds of the fourth century and later on the matter of the Holy Spirit obscures the writings of the earliest Christians.

This thesis also contributes insofar as it brings greater attention to that ambiguous aspect of "spirit" found at the crossroads of demonology and pneumatology. The survey of scholarly monographs in Chapter Two explained the fact that πνεῦμα in the NT denoted a variety of spirits by showing that the effects of good and evil spirits were similar in nature. This similarity was found in two aspects of spirit effects, that of the origin of these effects which was believed to be πνεῦμα (whether good or evil) and a spirit's performance of speech through a human agent.

Some of the effects of πνεῦμα in the NT are clearly negative and harmful. Physical descriptions of violence (Matt 8:28–33, Mark 5:2–5, Luke 4:34–36, Acts 8:7, 19:16), muteness (Matt 9:32–33), blindness (Matt 12:22), torment (Matt 12:43–45, Luke 6:18, 11:24–26), and sickness (Acts 19:12) are attributed to the effects and activities of "unclean" (ἀκάθαρτα) and "evil" (πονηρά) spirits (πνεύματα) or demons (δαίμονες) who have possessed certain individuals. These spirits also have the capacity for speech and recognition through the agency of their human hosts (see Mark 3:11, Luke 4:36, and Acts 19:13–15). Thus, evil spirits are distinct sentient personalities who may express themselves through the intermediation of a possessed human being.

The negative effects of "possession" and its primary association with evil spirits and demons in the NT gives the impression that such phenomena cannot be "of God." The question inevitably arises, "If evil spirits are personalities who may express themselves through human agents, must good spirits be restricted from doing the same?" The evidence in Philo, Pseudo-Philo, and Paul gives a resounding "No." The effects of good spirits, however, are noticeably different.

In Philo, possession by a divine spirit (πνεῦμα θεῖον) results in harmony of composure and of speech analogous to "sweet music" (*Her.* 266). In Paul, the general effects of good spirits among Christians may be reflected in his statement on the virtues that identify the "fruit of the spirit" in Gal 5:22,23: "love, joy, peace, patience, kindness, generosity, faithfulness, gentleness, and self-control." Communication with good spirits is of a higher order than that which is found in demonic possession which only serves to torment the person and others around that person.

The effects of good spirits in Paul (πνεῦμα ἅγιον, πνεῦμα θεοῦ) are particularly spelled out in First Corinthians 12 and 14. The activities and services of the spirit world of God produce only that which is beneficial to the spiritual life and welfare of the church. The positive effects of "possession" by good spirits are their performance of "praying," "singing praises," "blessing," and "thanksgiving" (1 Cor 14:15–17). Communication with good spirits involves the voluntary act of a medium who relinquishes his or her vocal chords to a foreign spirit for the purposes of Christian instruction in the church (1 Cor 12:3,29;14:26,31). This context is far removed from that of involuntary demonic possession where the possessed is a victim of an evil spirit.

Another aspect of the similar effects of the two orders of πνεῦμα in the NT is seen in the performance of spirits who communicate knowledge of Jesus' Sonship and Lordship through a possessed human agent. In Mark 3:11 and

Luke 4:34 unclean spirits recognize Jesus as "the Son of God" (ὁ υἱὸς τοῦ θεοῦ) and "the Holy One of God" (ὁ ἅγιος τοῦ θεοῦ). The spirits express this recognition directly to Jesus through the human agent they possess. This recognition provides for the belief in Jesus' time that evil spirits recognized the power of the one who could subdue and cast them out of the person whom they tormented (Acts 19:15–16).

In 1 Cor 12:3 a spirit of God or a holy spirit is expected to proclaim through a medium "Jesus is Lord" (Κύριος 'Ιησοῦς). To a certain degree, this acclamation is not unlike the unclean spirits' recognition in two respects: (1) the spirit utters through the agency of a possessed individual; and (2) the spirit acknowledges Jesus with the language of Lordship. The gospel accounts, however, depict episodes of demonic possession, whereas 1 Cor 12:3 relates the gathering of Christians who worship God during a divine service for the purpose of communicating with his spirit world.

The effects of demonic possession and possession by good spirits are alike in one respect, that of the actual state of possession. But beyond this similarity, the effects produced during the possession state are quite different. Evil spirits would not have been expected to voluntarily sing praises and give thanksgiving (presumably to God) through the human they possessed. Evil spirits also would not have been expected to prophesy the truth. False prophecy was believed to have its source with the utterances of an evil spirit (see 1 John 4:1; Herm. *Mand.* 11.3,12; Eusebius, *Eccl. Hist.* 5.1–27).

Outward manifestations of demonic possession of the kind described in the gospels seem to reveal the operation of an evil spirit more easily than the sort of artifice and guile that Paul describes of Satan in 2 Cor 11:14, "for even Satan masquerades as an angel of light." According to this passage evil spirits were able to exhibit types of behavior that mimicked good spirits. The "tests for spirits" indicates the need to unmask "deceitful spirits." Such tests would be unnecessary if the spirit was easily recognized as "evil" by its mere performance through a human agent like that depicted in the gospels. But evil spirits were also believed to be capable of speaking some truth (see 1 Tim 4:1; Herm. *Mand.* 11.3) and, apparently, were capable at times of acting with self restraint while possessing a medium. Even from the perspective of the NT, the unclean spirits' recognition of Jesus as "the Son of God" was a true statement.

The performance of an evil spirit through a human agent such as that described in the gospels may indeed have given pause to the idea of a spirit entering into an individual for the good. The violent performance of demoniacs may have contributed to the low estimation of possession and mediums in the second- and third-century church. The belief that evil spirits were capable of masquerading as good spirits may have destroyed confidence in the prospect of receiving divine guidance from the spirit world. The possibility of being deceived by an evil spirit was a reality too risky for Christians. Deception by spirits through solicited communication with the spirit world is a common theme in early Christian writings. Clement observes that "it is possible that he [a spirit] be an evil demon or a deceptive spirit *pretending in his speeches* to be what he is not" (*Homilies* 17.14). Hence the possibility of being deceived by spirits may have discouraged Christians from communicating with the spirit world, a scenario that, arguably, would have served the evil spirits who wished to suppress communication with good spirits. Spirits may also have communicated doctrines that did not correspond with the church at that time, furthering the idea that voluntary communication with the spirit world conflicted with the teachings of the church.

In the second-century church, prophetic possession rapidly declined.[3] The condemnation of Montanism by the Catholic church was not a condemnation of spirit communication per se. Initially, the content of the spirit utterances was targeted, for, in one instance, the spirit speaking through Montanus was accused of "blaspheming" against the Catholic church. This soon led to the condemnation of the spirit speaking through Montanus and his prophets. Eventually, the ecstatic state itself was condemned; only false prophets spoke in ecstasy.

By the time of Origen, possession was considered to be the primary sign that the spirit was evil (see *De. princip.* 3.3.3 for two types of demonic possession). Origen notes that "the possessed" (*energumenos*) are to be identified with the demoniacs in the gospels who were "cured by the Savior" (*De. princip.* 3.3.3). According to Origen good spirits did not "possess." Their influence on human beings was from without.[4] The notion of a spirit possessing a person was identified with demonic activity (Eusebius, *Eccl. Hist.* 5.16.3–17.4). Hence, the

---

[3] See James L. Ash, "Decline of Ecstatic Prophecy in the Early Church," *TS* 37 (1976) 227–52. To be sure, ecstatic prophecy was only one of the elements that motivated the church to affirm the apostolic writings as authoritative and final, thus ridding "new prophecy" as incompatible with the faith. Christian sects were producing sacred writings and this included Gnostics and Montanists who were branded as heretical. The church was compelled to begin to define the canon of Scripture that recognized only those writings that were apostolic. See Lee Martin McDonald, *The Formation of the Christian Biblical Canon* (Nashville: Abingdon, 1989) 104–06.

[4] The shift from possession as both divine and demonic to possession as exclusively demonic also occurred later in Western Europe during the fifteenth century: "The same behaviors that once had rendered possessed women ciphers, betokening either divine or demonic possession according to the interpretation of the audience, now were seen as clues to the indwelling of unclean spirits only"; and "Possessed behaviors and the attendant claims to have incorporated the Spirit of God were simply too ambivalent, too close to manifestations of possession by unclean spirits, to be sustained" (Caciola, *Discernment*, 313, 314).

spirit world became taboo for most Christians as a legitimate source for divine instruction. Origen stated that prophetic activity was necessary for the church in the beginning, but it ceased to be necessary later (*Contra Celsus* 7.11).

Despite the church's growing insecurities about spirit communication during the early-to-mid second century, certain groups of Christians of this time continued communicating with the holy spirit world of God. They did so though with an increasing awareness of false prophets and the impostor spirits that communicated through them. The *Didache* warns that both true and false prophets can speak ἐν πνεύματι (11:7,8,9,12). The Shepherd of Hermas likewise claims that true and false prophets are πνευματοφόρον, "moved [to speak] by a spirit" (Herm. *Mand.* 11.16). Opponents of Montanism used the same term (πνευματοφορεῖσθαι) to describe the way in which Montanus was inspired: whereas Montanus claimed that a holy spirit "moved" him to speak, others declared that an evil spirit was the source of his inspiration (cf. 2 Pet 1:21, ὑπὸ πνεύματος ἁγίου φερόμενοι ἐλάλησαν ἀπὸ θεοῦ ἄνθρωποι, "human beings *moved by a holy spirit* spoke by God"). Historically, the prophetic activity related in Montanism, the Shepherd of Hermas, and the *Didache* reflects the prophetic activity which is found in First Corinthians 12 and 14 – the activity of spirits who communicate intelligibly through Christian mediums.

Certain church fathers held spirit communication in high esteem. Irenaeus criticized those who drove prophecy out of the church, for in so doing they "sin against the spirit of God and fall into unforgivable sin" (*Against Heresies* 3.11.9). Irenaeus further claimed that prophecy and glossolalia continued, "revealing the mysteries of God" in the church of his day (ca. 180) (*Against Heresies* 5.6.1). Tertullian, the pre-eminent church father on catholic theology, remained a proponent of communicating with the spirit world as shown in his commitment to Montanism. Unfortunately, his work *De Ecstasi*, "On Ecstasy," has not survived (see Jerome, *On Illustrious Men* 24). This work may have provided a mine of information from a Christian perspective on how spirits communicated through human mediums who spoke "with a spirit," such as Montanus himself. We can only guess how Tertullian defended ecstatic prophecy in his seven-volume work *De Ecstasi*. Nevertheless, there remain sufficient evidence in his extant writings about the legitimacy of prophets who spoke "with a spirit" or in ecstasy (e.g., *Treatise on the Soul* 11, "ecstasy is the holy spirit's operative virtue of prophecy").

First-century Jewish authors were not ambivalent toward the idea of a divine or a holy spirit entering into the body of a person and using the vocal chords to communicate with an audience. Such experiences demonstrate that possession by spirits, in and of itself, was not exclusively demonic during the earliest Christian era. Possession by spirits was a means to communicate with the divine realm – a direct communication whereby spirits spoke to human beings. These spirits were "divine" (θεῖον) and "holy" (*sanctus*) spirits.

The first-century churches likewise communicated with holy spirits for the benefit of those churches. As Paul implicitly admits, such communication was not without its problems from complications that may arise from "other" spirits (see 1 Cor 12:10, "discernment of spirits"; 2 Cor 11:4, "a different spirit"; and 2 Thess 2:2, "a spirit allegedly from us"). The earliest Christians may have been much more privy to the ways in which spirits were discerned than the NT texts actually reveal. Paul's pithiness says as much. But it has been possible to show that which earliest Christian worship must have encompassed: spirits who identify themselves as loyal adherents to Jesus as Lord and to God who is above and over all. These spirits instructed the church for its building up. The spirit world of God was the source and center of the life of the church.

Appendix 1

Greek Text and Translation of
1 Cor 12:1–11 and 1 Cor 14:1–33, 37–40

1.1 1 Cor 12:1–11

Περὶ δὲ τῶν πνευματικῶν, ἀδελφοί, οὐ θέλω ὑμᾶς ἀγνοεῖν. ²Οἴδατε ὅτι ὅτε ἔθνη ἦτε πρὸς τὰ εἴδωλα τὰ ἄφωνα ὡς ἂν ἤγεσθε ἀπαγόμενοι. ³διὸ γνωρίζω ὑμῖν ὅτι οὐδεὶς ἐν πνεύματι θεοῦ λαλῶν λέγει, Ἀνάθεμα Ἰησοῦς, καὶ οὐδεὶς δύναται εἰπεῖν, Κύριος Ἰησοῦς, εἰ μὴ ἐν πνεύματι ἁγίῳ. ⁴Διαιρέσεις δὲ χαρισμάτων εἰσίν, τὸ δὲ αὐτὸ πνεῦμα· ⁵καὶ διαιρέσεις διακονιῶν εἰσιν, καὶ ὁ αὐτὸς κύριος· ⁶καὶ διαιρέσεις ἐνεργημάτων εἰσίν, ὁ δὲ αὐτὸς θεὸς ὁ ἐνεργῶν τὰ πάντα ἐν πᾶσιν. ⁷ἑκάστῳ δὲ δίδοται ἡ φανέρωσις τοῦ πνεύματος πρὸς τὸ συμφέρον. ⁸ᾧ μὲν γὰρ διὰ τοῦ πνεύματος δίδοται λόγος σοφίας, ἄλλῳ δὲ λόγος γνώσεως κατὰ τὸ αὐτὸ πνεῦμα, ⁹ἑτέρῳ πίστις ἐν τῷ αὐτῷ πνεύματι, ἄλλῳ δὲ χαρίσματα ἰαμάτων ἐν τῷ ἑνὶ πνεύματι, ¹⁰ἄλλῳ δὲ ἐνεργήματα δυνάμεων, ἄλλῳ [δὲ] προφητεία, ἄλλῳ [δὲ] διακρίσεις πνευμάτων, ἑτέρῳ γένη γλωσσῶν, ἄλλῳ δὲ ἑρμηνεία γλωσσῶν· ¹¹πάντα δὲ ταῦτα ἐνεργεῖ τὸ ἓν καὶ τὸ αὐτὸ πνεῦμα διαιροῦν ἰδίᾳ ἑκάστῳ καθὼς βούλεται.

¹Now concerning spiritism, brothers, I do not want you to be ignorant. ²You know that when you were Gentiles you were led to [communicate with spirit beings through] mute idols, as often as you were impelled to do so. ³For this reason, I want you to know that nobody through whom a spirit of God is speaking can say, 'Jesus is accursed,' and only a holy spirit speaking through someone can say 'Jesus is Lord.' ⁴There are different distributions of gifts, but the same spirit [world distributes them all]. ⁵And there are different distributions of services but the same Lord [is the source for them]. ⁶And there are different distributions of workings but the same God who works all things in all. ⁷Each [medium] is given the manifestation of the spirit [world] for the common good. ⁸Thus, the spirit [world] gives to one a message of wisdom; another is given a message of knowledge according to the same spirit [world]; ⁹another is given faith by the same spirit [world]; ¹⁰another, effective power over evil spirits; to another, the gift of becoming a medium through whom spirits can speak the language of the spectators; to another, the discernment of spirits; to another, the ability for becoming a medium through whom spirits can speak in foreign languages, and to another the gift of becoming a medium through whom foreign languages can be translated into the language of the spectators. ¹¹The one and same spirit [world] produces all of these things, distributing them to each [medium] just as it wills and sees fit.

1.2 1 Cor 14:1b–33

ζηλοῦτε δὲ τὰ πνευματικά, μᾶλλον δὲ ἵνα προφητεύητε. ²ὁ γὰρ λαλῶν γλώσσῃ οὐκ ἀνθρώποις λαλεῖ ἀλλὰ θεῷ· οὐδεὶς γὰρ ἀκούει, πνεύματι δὲ λαλεῖ μυστήρια· ³ὁ δὲ προφητεύων ἀνθρώποις λαλεῖ οἰκοδομὴν καὶ παράκλησιν καὶ παραμυθίαν. ⁴ὁ λαλῶν γλώσσῃ ἑαυτὸν οἰκοδομεῖ· ὁ δὲ προφητεύων ἐκκλησίαν οἰκοδομεῖ. ⁵θέλω δὲ πάντας ὑμᾶς λαλεῖν γλώσσαις, μᾶλλον δὲ ἵνα προφητεύητε· μείζων δὲ ὁ προφητεύων ἢ ὁ λαλῶν γλώσσαις ἐκτὸς εἰ μὴ διερμηνεύῃ, ἵνα ἡ ἐκκλησία οἰκοδομὴν λάβῃ. ⁶Νῦν δέ, ἀδελφοί, ἐὰν ἔλθω πρὸς ὑμᾶς γλώσσαις λαλῶν, τί ὑμᾶς ὠφελήσω ἐὰν μὴ ὑμῖν λαλήσω ἢ ἐν ἀποκαλύψει ἢ ἐν γνώσει ἢ ἐν προφητείᾳ ἢ [ἐν] διδαχῇ; ⁷ὅμως τὰ ἄψυχα φωνὴν διδόντα, εἴτε αὐλὸς εἴτε κιθάρα, ἐὰν διαστολὴν τοῖς φθόγγοις μὴ δῷ, πῶς γνωσθήσεται τὸ αὐλούμενον ἢ τὸ κιθαριζόμενον; ⁸καὶ γὰρ ἐὰν ἄδηλον σάλπιγξ φωνὴν δῷ, τίς παρασκευάσεται εἰς πόλεμον; ⁹οὕτως καὶ ὑμεῖς διὰ τῆς γλώσσης ἐὰν μὴ εὔσημον λόγον δῶτε, πῶς γνωσθήσεται τὸ λαλούμενον; ἔσεσθε γὰρ εἰς ἀέρα λαλοῦντες. ¹⁰τοσαῦτα εἰ τύχοι γένη φωνῶν εἰσιν ἐν κόσμῳ καὶ οὐδὲν ἄφωνον· ¹¹ἐὰν οὖν μὴ εἰδῶ τὴν δύναμιν τῆς φωνῆς, ἔσομαι τῷ λαλοῦντι βάρβαρος καὶ ὁ λαλῶν ἐν ἐμοὶ βάρβαρος. ¹²οὕτως καὶ ὑμεῖς, ἐπεὶ ζηλωταί ἐστε πνευμάτων, πρὸς τὴν οἰκοδομὴν τῆς ἐκκλησίας ζητεῖτε ἵνα περισσεύητε. ¹³διὸ ὁ λαλῶν γλώσσῃ προσευχέσθω ἵνα διερμηνεύῃ. ¹⁴ἐὰν [γὰρ] προσεύχωμαι γλώσσῃ, τὸ πνεῦμά μου προσεύχεται, ὁ δὲ νοῦς μου ἄκαρπός ἐστιν. ¹⁵τί οὖν ἐστιν; προσεύξομαι τῷ πνεύματι, προσεύξομαι δὲ καὶ τῷ νοΐ· ψαλῶ τῷ πνεύματι, ψαλῶ δὲ καὶ τῷ νοΐ. ¹⁶ἐπεὶ ἐὰν εὐλογῇς [ἐν] πνεύματι, ὁ ἀναπληρῶν τὸν τόπον τοῦ ἰδιώτου πῶς ἐρεῖ τὸ Ἀμήν ἐπὶ τῇ σῇ εὐχαριστίᾳ; ἐπειδὴ τί λέγεις οὐκ οἶδεν· ¹⁷σὺ μὲν γὰρ καλῶς εὐχαριστεῖς ἀλλ᾽ ὁ ἕτερος οὐκ οἰκοδομεῖται. ¹⁸εὐχαριστῶ τῷ θεῷ, πάντων ὑμῶν μᾶλλον γλώσσαις λαλῶ· ¹⁹ἀλλὰ ἐν ἐκκλησίᾳ θέλω πέντε λόγους τῷ νοΐ μου λαλῆσαι, ἵνα καὶ ἄλλους κατηχήσω, ἢ μυρίους λόγους ἐν γλώσσῃ. ²⁰Ἀδελφοί, μὴ παιδία γίνεσθε ταῖς φρεσίν ἀλλὰ τῇ κακίᾳ νηπιάζετε, ταῖς δὲ φρεσὶν τέλειοι γίνεσθε. ²¹ἐν τῷ νόμῳ γέγραπται ὅτι Ἐν ἑτερογλώσσοις καὶ ἐν χείλεσιν ἑτέρων λαλήσω τῷ λαῷ τούτῳ καὶ οὐδ᾽ οὕτως εἰσακούσονταί μου, λέγει κύριος. ²²ὥστε αἱ γλῶσσαι εἰς σημεῖόν εἰσιν οὐ τοῖς πιστεύουσιν ἀλλὰ τοῖς ἀπίστοις, ἡ δὲ προφητεία οὐ τοῖς ἀπίστοις ἀλλὰ τοῖς πιστεύουσιν. ²³Ἐὰν οὖν συνέλθῃ ἡ ἐκκλησία ὅλη ἐπὶ τὸ αὐτὸ καὶ πάντες λαλῶσιν γλώσσαις, εἰσέλθωσιν δὲ ἰδιῶται ἢ ἄπιστοι, οὐκ ἐροῦσιν ὅτι μαίνεσθε; ²⁴ἐὰν δὲ πάντες προφητεύωσιν, εἰσέλθῃ δέ τις ἄπιστος ἢ ἰδιώτης, ἐλέγχεται ὑπὸ πάντων, ἀνακρίνεται ὑπὸ πάντων, ²⁵τὰ κρυπτὰ τῆς καρδίας αὐτοῦ φανερὰ γίνεται, καὶ οὕτως πεσὼν ἐπὶ πρόσωπον προσκυνήσει τῷ θεῷ ἀπαγγέλλων ὅτι Ὄντως ὁ θεὸς ἐν ὑμῖν ἐστιν. ²⁶Τί οὖν ἐστιν, ἀδελφοί; ὅταν συνέρχησθε, ἕκαστος ψαλμὸν ἔχει, διδαχὴν ἔχει, ἀποκάλυψιν ἔχει, γλῶσσαν ἔχει, ἑρμηνείαν ἔχει· πάντα πρὸς οἰκοδομὴν γινέσθω. ²⁷εἴτε γλώσσῃ τις λαλεῖ, κατὰ δύο ἢ τὸ πλεῖστον τρεῖς καὶ ἀνὰ μέρος, καὶ εἷς διερμηνευέτω· ²⁸ἐὰν δὲ μὴ ᾖ διερμηνευτής, σιγάτω ἐν ἐκκλησίᾳ, ἑαυτῷ δὲ λαλείτω καὶ τῷ θεῷ. ²⁹προφῆται δὲ δύο ἢ τρεῖς

λαλείτωσαν καὶ οἱ ἄλλοι διακρινέτωσαν· ³⁰ἐὰν δὲ ἄλλῳ ἀποκαλυφθῇ
καθημένῳ, ὁ πρῶτος σιγάτω. ³¹δύνασθε γὰρ καθ' ἕνα πάντες προφητεύειν, ἵνα
πάντες μανθάνωσιν καὶ πάντες παρακαλῶνται. ³²καὶ πνεύματα προφητῶν
προφήταις ὑποτάσσεται, ³³οὐ γάρ ἐστιν ἀκαταστασίας ὁ θεὸς ἀλλὰ εἰρήνης.

¹ᵇBe eager to communicate with the spirit world, especially that you might
become mediums through whom spirits speak to you in your own language. ²For
if a spirit speaks through a medium in a language unknown to the spectators,
that spirit cannot make itself understood to those present but only to God, for
no one understands him; for the spirit uses words whose meaning is hidden from
those present. ³But if a spirit speaking through a medium utters words known
to those present, this builds up, encourages, and comforts. ⁴A medium through
whom a spirit is speaking in a foreign language derives benefit from it for
himself alone, while a spirit who speaks through a medium in the language of
the spectators builds up the whole congregation. ⁵I wish that all of you had
acquired the gift of becoming mediums through whom spirits could speak in a
foreign language; but I would rather they speak through you in your own
language. For a spirit that speaks to you through a medium in your own
language is of greater benefit to you than a spirit who speaks in a foreign
language – unless, of course, he translates that language into your own so that
the congregation may be built up. ⁶Now brothers, suppose that I were to come
to you as one through whom a spirit spoke a foreign language; what good will
I do if I do not speak to you in your own language truths hitherto unknown, or
knowledge, or as one through whom spirits spoke your own language, or
instruction? ⁷Likewise, if inanimate things that produce sound, such as a flute
or a harp, that do not give out tones distinctly, how will what is being played on
the flute or harp be recognized? ⁸And if the trumpet gives an indistinct sound,
who will get ready for battle? ⁹So it is with you, if a spirit utters something
through one of you in a foreign language, how will anyone know what is being
said? For you will be talking to the air alone. ¹⁰There are many different
languages in the world and none is without meaning. ¹¹Therefore, if I do not
know the meaning of the language, I will be a foreigner to the one who speaks
it, and the one who speaks it a foreigner to me. ¹²So also with yourselves, since
you are zealous for spirits, seek as many different kinds of spirits as possible for
building up the church. ¹³Therefore, a person through whom a spirit is speaking
a foreign language should also pray for a spirit able to translate foreign
languages. ¹⁴For if a spirit utters a prayer through me in a foreign language, the
spirit, indeed, prays [through] me, but I will not be able to understand it. ¹⁵So
what is to be done? I will utter the words of a prayer spoken by the spirit, but
will also utter the prayer intelligibly. I will sing praises by one of God's spirits,

but will also sing praises intelligibly. [16]Otherwise, if you pronounce a blessing as a medium through whom a spirit utters in a foreign language, how shall the one who holds the place of an uninstructed say the 'Amen' to your thanksgiving since he does not know what you are saying? [17]For you may very well be giving thanks, but the other is not built up. [18]I give thanks to God that I am a better medium for spirits who speak foreign languages than any of you. [19]But in church I would rather speak five words that I understand so that I may instruct others, rather than ten thousand words in a foreign language. [20]Brothers [and sisters], do not be children in your thinking [in matters of spirit communication]. In evil be ignorant as children, but in other matters be mature in your thinking. [21]In the law it is written, 'With other tongues and with the lips of foreigners I will speak to this people, and even then they will not listen to me, says the Lord.' [22]Therefore, speaking in foreign languages is a sign not for believers but [serves as a negative] sign for those who are uninstructed in spirit communication. But speaking in the language of the congregation does not edify those who are unfamiliar with spirit communication but those who are already convinced of the reality of spirit communication. [23]For suppose that the whole church were gathered in one place, all speaking in foreign languages, and that people entered among you who knew nothing of communicating with spirits and did not believe in it, would they not say that you are crazy? [24]But if everyone were speaking as mediums through whom spirits spoke an intelligible language, and a certain one who neither believed in nor was informed in such matters entered among you, he would be convinced by everyone, [and] judged by everyone; [25]the secrets of his heart will be disclosed [by the spirit], and so he will fall down on his face and worship God and declare that God is truly in your midst. [26]So what is to be done, brothers? When you come together each one has [from the spirit world] a psalm, a teaching, a revelation of truths hitherto unknown, a foreign language, and a translation. [27]If a certain spirit decides to speak a foreign language, allow two [spirits], or at most, three, one at a time, and let one spirit translate. [28]But if no spirit is present who can translate the foreign language, let the other spirit be silent, but speak to himself and to God. [29]Addresses made by spirits through prophets should be limited to two or three, and those should weigh and discuss what they have heard. [30]If one attending the service is given a revelation, the medium should be silent. [31]For all of you mediums are able to prophesy one by one so that all may be instructed and all may be encouraged. [32]The spirits that manifest themselves through the mediums will obey the mediums, [33a]for God is not of disorder but of harmony.

1.3 1 Cor 14:37–40

³⁷Εἴ τις δοκεῖ προφήτης εἶναι ἢ πνευματικός, ἐπιγινωσκέτω ἃ γράφω ὑμῖν ὅτι κυρίου ἐστὶν ἐντολή· ³⁸εἰ δέ τις ἀγνοεῖ, ἀγνοεῖται. ³⁹ὥστε, ἀδελφοί [μου], ζηλοῦτε τὸ προφητεύειν, καὶ τὸ λαλεῖν μὴ κωλύετε γλώσσαις· ⁴⁰πάντα δὲ εὐσχημόνως καὶ κατὰ τάξιν γινέσθω.

³⁷If anyone thinks that he is a medium for spirits who speak your language or a person who is otherwise in communication with the spirit world, he should acknowledge that what I am writing to you is a commandment of the Lord. ³⁸If anyone does not acknowledge this, he is not acknowledged. ³⁹So [my] brothers and sisters, strive eagerly to become mediums for spirits who speak your own language, but do not totally forbid spirits who speak foreign languages. ⁴⁰But let all things be done properly and in order.

Appendix 2

The Meaning and Usage of the Term "Spiritism"

The translation of 1 Cor 12:1a as "now concerning spiritism" requires explanation from the perspective of popular culture. The use of the term "spiritism" as a translation for matters related to a Christian context might be misunderstood because of the ways in which contemporary Christian culture and the tradition of English Bible translations use the term to denote non-Christian practices such as sorcery, divination, and necromancy. If Paul was talking about spiritism in 1 Cor 12:1a, then the term "spiritism" must be further qualified as a term whose definition is not restricted to infernal practices, but rather a definition that includes Christian forms of worship.

1. Spiritism and Popular Culture

The usage of the term "spiritism" to denote "consulting the dead" has its provenance in the spiritist movement of the mid-eighteen hundreds in the United States and Great Britain. The popular nomenclature for the movement was "spiritualism." This term designated gatherings in which persons sat around a table or in a group, sometimes holding hands in a chain-like link, in order to communicate with the deceased. These gatherings became popularly known as "séances," a French term meaning "sittings," whose use in French is usually relegated to "sittings" for the purpose of a scientific lecture or the professional gatherings of a conference.

During the time period 1850–70, "American spiritualism" played a major role in defining for the American public the practice of spiritualism as group séances held for the purpose of contacting deceased relatives, friends, and famous personages through trance mediums.[1] The rise of spiritualism in America is usually credited to the role of two sisters, Kate and Maggie Fox, who

---

[1] See Emma Hardinge, *Modern American Spiritualism* (New York: n.p., 1870; repr. New Hyde Park: University Books, 1970). See also the following studies: B. G. Brown, "Spiritualism in Nineteenth Century America" (Ph.D. diss., Boston University, 1973); E. J. Isaacs, "A History of Nineteenth Century American Spiritualism as a Religious and Social Movement" (Ph.D. diss., University of Wisconsin-Madison, 1975); L. M. Lenker, "Haunted Culture and Surrogate Space: A New Historicist Account of Nineteenth Century American Spiritualism" (Ph.D. diss., Stanford University, 1998); and R. Morantz-Sanchez, "Without Crucible or Scalpel: A Sympathetic History of American Spiritualism" (Ph.D. diss., University of Michigan, 2002).

claimed to possess mediumistic powers for communicating with spirits.[2] People who regularly attended séances were known as "spiritists," i.e., those who practiced spiritualism. Those through whom the spirits communicated were known as "mediums." A part of the scientific community investigated the activities of mediums during séances to determine whether the source of the phenomena was of human origin or otherwise.[3] Such séances sometimes had a religious overtone in the way they were conducted and in the belief that séances demonstrated survival after physical death whereby the human spirits who had "crossed over" after physical death related through mediums what the beyond was like, preparing their listeners for what was in store for them. Occasionally the messages from the alleged spirits touched on heaven, God, Christ, hell, Satan, and other realities associated with religion and faith. But more often than not, the messages were of a mundane nature.

The popular term "spiritualism" is used interchangeably with the term "spiritism." This, however, is misleading since the term "spiritualism" was originally intended to denote a nineteenth-century philosophical school of thought that defined reality in terms of spirit as opposed to materialism.[4] Spiritism, however, is the more precise term than what is usually suggested by

---

[2] See Barbara Weisberg, *Talking to the Dead: Kate and Maggie Fox and the Rise of Spiritualism* (San Francisco: Harper Collins, 2004).

[3] Trevor H. Hall, *The Medium and the Scientist: The Story of Florence Cook and William Crookes* (Buffalo: Prometheus, 1984). For a critique, see Paul Kurtz, *The Transcendental Temptation: A Critique of Religion and the Paranormal* (Amherst, NY: Prometheus, 1991) 321–57.

[4] A. J. McNichol ("Spiritualism," *NCE* [14 vols.; ed. M. R. P. McGuire et al.; New York: McGraw-Hill] 13. 587–593) states, "The term spiritualism seems to have been coined by 17th-century theologians to signify erroneous forms of mysticism, but was taken over by V. Cousin to denote his own eclectic philosophy. Its use in philosophy became common in the 19th century, both in the wider sense of systems opposed to materialism, as with T. S. Jouffry (1796–1842) and Maine de Biran, and in more restricted contexts, as referring for instance to trends of thought originating with St. Augustine. In general usage, thinkers are termed spiritualist if they maintain the existence and primacy of a reality that is distinct from, and not derived from, matter, that of itself is not subject to the determinations of time and space, and that, in its existence, is independent of a bodily frame. Such reality may be conceived as an impersonal, universal cosmic force, or as personal, either in a supreme being or in finite beings" (13. 590). As a system of thought, spiritualism is related to deism, theism, idealism, immaterialism, and forms of realism. See Robert Vaughan, *Letter and Spirit: A Discourse on Modern Philosophical Spiritualism and Its Relation to Christianity* (London, New York: Jackson & Walford, 1849).

the word spiritualism, since the interest lies in "spirits" as the objects of preference.[5]

The term "spiritism" is usually understood within its popular context of communicating with the dead. The suffix *-ism* on the English term "spirit" relates to contexts that denote spirit beings "in action" or to the belief that spirits "act upon" or "affect" human beings in some tangible manner.

Encyclopedias and lexicons of religion and theology often base definitions of spiritism on the popular understanding of it:

Belief in the possibility of communication with the spirits of the departed, and the practice of attempting such communication, usually with the help of some person (a medium) regarded as gifted to act as an intermediary with the spirit world.[6]

The spiritism movement of the late eighteen hundreds reemerged in the New Age movement of contemporary popular culture as "channeling." Jon Klimo observes this reemergence:

Except for the present, there has never been as rich a period of channeling activity and interest in it as occurred during the mid-nineteenth century under the name Spiritualism (usually termed Spiritism in Europe). What we now call channeling was called mediumship during the Spiritualist era, and channels were called mediums.[7]

---

[5] F. C. S. Schiller ("Spiritism," in *The Encyclopedia of Religion and Ethics* [13 vols.; ed. J. Hasings; New York: Charles Scribners'] 1921) stated, " Spiritualism is a popular term for what is more correctly called Spiritism" (11. 808). This finds a measure of support from the French and German terms *spiritisme* and *Spiritismus*.

[6] *NCE*, 13. 576. See further Edward A. Pace, "Spiritism," in *The Catholic Encyclopedia* (15 vols.; New York: Robert Appleton, 1912) 14. 221; Schiller, "Spiritism," in *Encyclopedia of Religion and Ethics*, 11. 805; "Spiritism," in *The Dictionary of Dogmatic Theology* (trans. Emmanuel Doronzo; ed. Pietro Pavente, et al.; Milwaukee: Bruce, 1951) 266; "Spiritualism," in *The Dictionary of Moral Theology* (ed. P. Pallazzini Westminster, MD: Newman Press, 1962) 1151; and "Spiritualism," in *The Dictionary of Christian Theology* (ed. Peter A. Angeles; San Francisco: Harper & Row, 1985) 191.

[7] Jon Klimo, *Channeling: Investigations on Receiving Information from Paranormal Sources* (Los Angeles: J. P. Tarcher, 1987; repr. Berkeley: North Atlantic Books, 1998) 95. See also Gerald A. Larue, "Channeling – Ancient and Modern," in idem, *The Supernatural, the Occult and the Bible* (Buffalo: Prometheus, 1990) 31–42, who similarly states, "Present-day channeling is a variation of mediumship. Channelers' most recent predecessors were spiritualists who conjured up spirits of dead relatives or friends for their clients" (p. 33).

2. Spiritism and English Versions of the Bible[8]

English Bibles that appeared subsequent to the American and British popular
spiritism movement of the mid to late 1800s used terms related to spiritism.
The terms "spiritist" and "medium" appear in eight mainline English versions:
RSV (1952), *NAB* (1970), *NAS* (1977), *NRS* (1979), *NKJ* (1982), *NIV* (1984),
NIB (1984), and *NAU* (1995). The necromancer in 1 Samuel 28 who conjures
the spirit of the deceased Samuel is called "a medium" in recent versions,[9]
whereas in older versions she is called "a woman with a familiar spirit."[10]

The occult Hebrew terms אוב and ידעני are translated in English versions as
either practitioners, "spiritist" and "medium,"[11] or entities, "ghosts" and
"spirits"[12] (because of an uncertain etymology [אוב] or an unclear reference
[ידעני][13]). Some versions use both "medium" (or "wizard") and "spirit" in the
same verse.[14] The usage of these English terms in modern Bibles for practices
that are an abomination to God can influence thinking about the characterization
of spiritism. Thus, "consulting the spirit world" through "mediums" can be
shown by biblical authority to go against the will of God.

Practitioners

Lev 19:31: "Do not turn to mediums (אובת) or seek out spiritists (ידענים), for
you will be defiled by them. I am the Lord your God" (cf. *NIV, NRS, NIB, NAS,
NAU, RSV* [mediums, wizards], *NAB* [mediums, fortune-tellers], *NLT*
[mediums, psychics]).

---

[8] Bible versions cited: American Standard Version (*ASV*), Bible in Basic English (*BBE*),
Darby Bible (*DBY*), Douay-Rheims (*DRA*), Kings James Version (*KJV*), the New King James
Version (*NKJ*), Revised Standard Version (*RSV*), the New Revised Standard Version (*NRS*),
Revised English Bible (*REB*), New American Bible (*NAB*), New American Standard (*NAS, NAU*
[1995]), New International Version (*NIV, NIB* [British version]), New Jerusalem Bible (*NJB*),
and the New Living Translation (*NLT*).

[9] See 1 Sam 28:7 in the following versions: *NIV, NIB, NAS, NAU, RSV, NAB, NRS* and
NKJ.

[10] See 1 Sam 28:7 in the following versions: *KJV, ASV, DRA, DBY*, and *BBE*.

[11] See Deut 18:11 in the following versions: *NIV, NIB, NAS, NAU, RSV, NRS* and *NKJ*.

[12] See Deut 18:11 in the following versions: *NRS, NAB, BBE* and *REB*.

[13] In the *BDB* citation for אוב, the reference for ידעני is "wizard" (p. 15), whereas in the
citation for ידעני, it is "familiar spirit, *always*" (p. 396 emphasis mine).

[14] See Deut 18:11 in the following versions: *NJB, DBY, KJV* and *ASV*.

Spirits
Lev 20:6: "I will set my face against the person who turns to ghosts (אובת) and spirits (ידענים)" (*KJV, ASV, REB, DRA, BBE, NAB*).

Practitioners
1 Sam 28:3: "Saul had expelled the mediums (אובת) and spiritists (ידענים) from the land" (*NIV, NRS, NIB, NAS, NAU, RSV* [mediums, wizards], *NAB* [mediums, fortune-tellers], *NLT* [mediums, psychics]).

Practitioners
2 Kgs 21:6 and 1 Chr 33:6: "He . . . consulted mediums (אובת) and spiritists (ידענים) and (thus) did much evil in the eyes of the Lord, provoking him to anger" (*NIV, NIB, NAS, NAU, NKJ*).

Spirits and Practitioners
2 Kgs 23:24: "Josiah got rid of the spirits (אובת) and wizards (ידענים) . . . . This he did to fulfill the requirements of the law written in the book that Hilkiah the priest had discovered in the temple of the Lord" (*KJV, ASV*).

English Bibles that use the terms "spiritist" and "medium" reflect the practice of a "dynamic equivalent" translation of the text in which translators render the meaning of the original language with comparable modern expressions to facilitate understanding of biblical passages. For instance, in the *KJV* of 1611, Deut 18:11 is translated by occult terminology of the time, "familiar spirit" and "wizard," whereas in the *NKJ* of 1982 the terms "spiritist" and "medium" appear. Similarly, the *NJB* translates 2 Kgs 23:24 by terminology used in contemporary New Age spiritism: "What is more, the *spirit-guides* and mediums . . . were swept away by Josiah to give effect to the words of the Law." The term "spirit-guide" recalls the older identical English term "familiar spirit," a spirit that was believed to assist or guide the medium with communications from the spirit world.

Familiar with spiritism in modern popular culture, translators seem to have used present-day conventions they believed to be comparable to ideas found in the Hebrew terminology.[15] The terms "spiritist," "medium," and "spirit-guides"

---

[15] For instance, John S. Bonnel ("The Resurgence of Spiritism," *Christianity Today* 12 [1968] 7–10) states that the woman in 1 Samuel 28 known to history as the "witch of Endor" is "nowadays . . . called a 'clairvoyant' or a 'medium'" (p. 8). See also Brooks Alexander, "Theology from the Twilight Zone: Spirit Channeling Is the Latest Fad in Upscale New Age Spiritism," *Christianity Today* 31 (1987) 22–26; and Marvin Olasky, "The Return of Spiritism:

reflect older terminology such as "wizard," "witch," and "familiar spirit." Mediums and spirit guides are condemned by contemporary Christianity on the basis of biblical authority. During the mid-nineteenth century before English Bibles were using "spiritist" and "medium" in derogatory contexts, Catholicism declared the manifestation of spirits during séances to be satanic in origin.[16] Present-day Evangelical Christianity cites biblical support for the view that any dealing with "spirit guides" is demonic in nature.[17]

Seeing How the Church Triumphed over the New Age Movement of the 1850s Can Help Us in the 1990s," *Christianity Today* 36 (1992) 20–24.

[16] The Second Plenary Council of Baltimore, MD (1866) "declares that some at least of the manifestations [during séances] are to be ascribed to Satanic intervention, and warns the faithful against lending any support to Spiritism or even, out of curiosity, seances" (Pace, "Spiritism," *CE* 14. 224). Cf. Alexius M. Lepicier, *The Unseen World: An Exposition of Catholic Theology in Its Relation to Modern Spiritism* (London: Kegan Paul, Trench, Trübner, 1909); William J. Erwood, *Spiritualism and the Catholic Church* (Philadelphia: W. J. Erwood, 1917); Herbert Thurston, *The Church and Spiritualism* (Milwaukee: Bruce, 1933; repr., 1935); and the classic Catholic stance as stated by Karl Rahner, *Visions and Prophecies* (QD 10; Freiburg: Herder, 1963)100–01: "Catholics may not take part in spiritualistic conversations and manifestations (Decree of Holy Office, April 24, 1917; *Denz.* 2182). Thus the Church forbids seances wherever, and insofar as, such parapsychological phenomena (real or supposed) are sought and are evoked in the hope of communications form the other world (from the dead, or 'spirits', etc.), ..." For recent literature of the Catholic position on spiritism see Mitch Pacwa, *Catholics and the New Age* (Ann Arbor: Servant Publications, 1992); Lynn L. Sharp, "Fighting for the Afterlife: Spiritists, Catholics, and Popular Religion in Nineteenth-Century France," *JRH* 23 (1999) 282–95; Manuel A. Vásquez, "Battling Spiritism and the Need for Catholic Orthodoxy," in *Religions of the United States in Practice 2* (ed. Colleen McDannell [Princeton, NJ: Princeton University Press, 2001]) 449–61; and Janice Glover, "Vatican and the New Age," *Catholic Insight* 11 (2003) 17–21.

[17] See John Ankerberg and John Weldon, *The Facts on Spirit Guides: How to Avoid the Seduction of the Spirit World and Demonic Powers* (Eugene, OR: Harvest Press, 1988), who state, "The Bible instructs man to reject every form of spiritism as something evil and an encounter with lying spirits" (p. 25). The motivation behind English versions that employ terms such as "medium," "spiritist," and "spirit-guides" might, arguably, not only reflect an attempt to show fidelity to the Hebrew text, but also send a message to readers that spiritism, in any age, is prohibited by God. Steven L. Jeffers ("The Cultural Power of Words: Occult Terminology in the Hebrew, Greek, Latin and English Bible" [Ph.D. diss., Florida State University, 1989]) states a similar prospect for the translators of the *KJV* of 1611: "The political function of early English translations to make the complete text of the Bible accessible led to a definite stance on priorities by the translators. . . . There was a certain intentionality by the translators to communicate particular messages and at the same time remain true to the intent of the original Biblical authors" (p. 243).

3. Spiritism and Biblical Necromancy

The terms אוב and ידעני occur in Deut 18:11 alongside the phrase דרֹשׁ אֶל־
הַמֵּתִים, "one who consults the dead," while אוב occurs in 1 Samuel 28 as a term
for the deceased. Hence, biblical precedent exists for an association, albeit
unclear, between אוב, ידעני and necromancy, "divination by the dead"
(νεκρομαντεία).[18] The terms אוב and ידעני might not always refer to spirits of
the deceased but rather to spirits that inhabited a spirit world condemned by
God that may have included at least a portion of the deceased.

Studies on spiritism often argue that modern interest in communicating with
spirits is a resurgence of the biblical practice of necromancy. Authors have
defined spiritism as a modern example of necromancy. Some of these studies
are lexical, theological, historical, or apologetic. The texts used to illustrate
spiritism are those related to divination, witchcraft, sorcery, and necromancy
(e.g., Exod 22:18; Lev 19:31; 20:6, 27; Deut 18:10–11, and 1 Samuel 28).

The Catholic Encyclopedia (1912) states, "For an account of Spiritistic
practices in antiquity, see **Necromancy**."[19] In a study originally written as a
dissertation at The Catholic University of America in 1917, and later published,
Johannes Liljencrants wrote,

While the Spiritistic movement is distinctly modern, its essential features are probably as old
as the human race. We find them in what is known as Necromancy, or the–at least presumed –
evocation of the spirits of the departed for the purpose of divination, practiced in all ages and
rather universally, but especially among pagan peoples. . . . Some of the most prominent
features of modern Spiritism are found in the ancient practices of Necromancy.[20]

Leonard Marsh chronicled the testimony of Greek, Latin, and Christian authors
bearing on the subject of communicating with spirits through mediums.[21]

---

[18] Necromancy was a form of spirit communication practiced throughout antiquity. See
Irving L. Finkel, "Necromancy in Ancient Mesopotamia," *AfO* 29 (1983) 1–17; Daniel Ogden,
Greek and Roman Necromancy (Princeton, NJ: Princeton University Press, 2001); and Robert
K. Ritner, "Necromancy in Ancient Egypt," in *Magic and Divination in the Ancient World* (ed.
L. Ciraolo and J. Seidel; Ancient Magic and Divination 2; Leiden: Brill-Styx, 2002) 89–96.
Some English versions translate Deut 18:11b as "medium, wizard, and necromancer," suggesting
a relationship between אוב, ידעני, and necromancy (*KJV, ASV, RSV* and *NJB*).

[19] Pace, "Spiritism," *Catholic Encyclopedia*, 14. 221.

[20] *Spiritism and Religion: A Moral Study* (Lynchburg, VA: J. P. Bell, 1918; repr. Cleveland:
J. T. Zubal, 1984) 9–11.

[21] *The Apocatastasis* (Burlington, VT: n.p., 1854).

Scholarly for its time, the study, however, was an apologetic defense against spiritism as the reemergence of pagan practices of antiquity:

The present spirit-phenomena and spirit-intercourse are but the reiteration of the same things which, in ancient times, were at their height about the commencement of the Christian era. . . It is plain that Christianity is, in its principles, at irreconcilable hostility with this redevelopment, and resurrection of the old spiritism, as it was at first with all the ancient forms of it.[22]

Scholarly commentaries use terminology reminiscent of spiritism to denote the similar occult practices listed in Deut 18:11: שאל אוב וידעני, "one who inquires of a ghost (or medium) or a knowing spirit (or wizard)," and דרש אל־המתים, "one who consults the dead." John A. Thompson states that in Deut 18:10–11, we learn that "all occult, superstitions, divination, sorcery, spiritualism, etc., were abominations (9,12) to Yahweh and invited his judgment."[23]   Peter C. Craigie describes vv. 10–11 as "a blanket prohibition of . . . consultation with the spirit world."[24]   Walter Brueggemann comments that vv. 10–11 refer to practices that "include consultation with 'the spirit world' and 'the dead.'"[25]   P. Kyle McCarter refers to Saul's inquiry of the necromancer in 1 Samuel 28 as a description of a "séance."[26]

In scholarly articles spiritism and necromancy are sometimes identified. In the early part of the twentieth century, the British orientalist Samuel Daiches argued in an article, "Isaiah and Spiritualism," that Isa 28:7–16 was an account of a séance in which v. 10 depicted the utterances taking place during an

---

[22] Ibid., 160, 163. See further, A. B. Morrison, *Spiritualism and Necromancy* (New York: Nelson and Phillips, 1873); Anonymous, *An Inquiry into the Teaching of Holy Scripture concerning Communication between Man and Spirits* (St. Louis: Chas. B. Cox, ca. [1890]); Rhys B. Jones, *Spiritism in Bible Light* (London: Religious Tract Society, 1921); Lewis B. Paton, *Spiritism and the Cult of the Dead in Antiquity* (New York: Macmillan, 1921); Carlyle B. Haynes, *Spiritism and the Bible* (Nashville: Southern Publishing Association, 1941); Henry J. Triezenberg, *Spiritualism: Asking the Dead* (Grand Rapids: Zondervan, 1949); Merrill F. Unger, *Biblical Demonology* (5th ed.; Wheaton, IL: Scripture Press, 1963); Elizabeth L. Hillstrom, *Testing the Spirits* (Downers Grove, IL: Inver-Varsity, 1995) 190; and Charles Salala, "Angels and Demons in Biblical Perspective," in *Issues in African Christian Theology* (eds. S. Ngewa, M. Shaw, and T. Tienou; Kampala: East African Educational Publishers, 1998) 147.

[23] *Deuteronomy: An Introduction and Commentary* (TynOTC; London: Inter-Varsity, 1974) 210.

[24] *The Book of Deuteronomy* (NICOT; Grand Rapids, MI: Eerdmans, 1976) 260.

[25] *Deuteronomy* (Abingdon Old Testament Commentary; Nashville: Abingdon, 2001) 193.

[26] *1 Samuel* (AB 8; Garden City, NY: Doubleday, 1980) 417.

evocation of the dead.[27] More recently, Thomas O. Figart called the necromancer of 1 Samuel 28 a "spiritist," recalling terminology related to spiritism.[28] Johan Lust stated that the terms אוב and ידעני "belong to the mysterious world of a belief about spirits and the dead, similar to that which can be found in modern spiritualism."[29] J. Stafford Wright devotes a section in an article that assesses the biblical ban on the אוב and ידעני entitled "The Ban on Mediumship and Spiritualism."[30] Likewise, in a discussion of necromancy in 1 and 2 Samuel, Bill T. Arnold identifies the necromancer in 1 Sam 28:3–19 as a "spiritist" and defines the terms אוב and ידעני as "medium" and "spiritist" respectively.[31]

Some scholarly Bible dictionaries and encyclopedias include an entry for "medium." The entries include references to the antidivinatory laws and the terms אוב and ידעני. The term "medium" is defined in light of the present-day understanding of spiritism: a human agent who facilitates communication with the dead for the purpose of learning the future.[32] *Vine's Expository Dictionary* explains in its entry for "Demon, Demoniac," that demons masquerade as deceased human beings by speaking through mediums:

As seducing spirits they [the demons] deceive men into the supposition that through mediums (those who have 'familiar spirits,' Lev. 20:6, 27, e.g.) they can converse with deceased human beings. Hence the destructive deception of Spiritism, forbidden in Scripture, Lev. 19:31; Deut. 18:11; Isa 8:19.[33]

Used in contexts that condemn necromancy and occultism, the term "spiritism" and its fundamental meaning, "consulting spirits," is identified with practices

---

[27] See "Isaiah and Spiritualism," *Jewish Chronicle Supplement* (July 1921) 6.

[28] Thomas O. Figart, "Saul, the Spiritist, and Samuel," *Grace Theological Journal* 11 (1970) 13–29.

[29] Johan Lust, "On Wizards and Prophets," VTSup 26 (1974) 133–42, esp. 133.

[30] J. Stafford Wright, "The Biblical Assessment of Superstition and the Occult," *Evangelical Review of Theology* 4 (1980) 102–13, esp. 108–10.

[31] Bill T. Arnold, "Necromancy and Cleromancy in 1 and 2 Samuel," *CBQ* 66 (2004) 199–213.

[32] See David E. Aune, "Medium," *ISBE* 3. 306–7; and Julia Bidmead, "Medium, Wizard," *Eerdmans Dictionary of the Bible* (ed. David Noel Freedman, et al.; Grand Rapids: Eerdmans, 2000) 878.

[33] *Vine's Expository Dictionary of Old and New Testament Words* (ed. W. E. Vine and F. F. Bruce; Grand Rapids: Fleming H. Revell, 1981) 291. See further, John P. Newport, "Spiritism and Channeling vs. Biblical Revelation and Prophecy," in idem, *The New Age Movement and the Biblical Worldview: Conflict and Dialogue* (Grand Rapids: Eerdmans, 1998) 145–211.

that are abominable to God in the OT. Thus, "spiritism," "spirits," "spiritists," and "mediums" are banned under the "law."[34]

4. Spiritism: Continuity with Prophetic Activity in the Torah, the Prophets, and the Writings

Such usage of the term "spiritism," however, elicits an exclusively negative connotation that the term itself does not necessarily convey. Despite the association of spiritism with biblical necromancy and the common definition of spiritism as communication with "the dead," a meaning dependent more on present-day popular usage and subjective attitude than upon objective definition, the term spiritism, in and of itself, does not discriminate the type of spirit that is consulted. Rather, the term designates "a spirit" of whatever kind with the potential for including good spirits.[35]

Despite the preponderance of lexical entries that define spiritism as communication with "spirits of the dead," two entries for spiritism in recent theological dictionaries define spiritism in broader terms:

The belief in the existence of spirits affecting the real world and/or humanity and that human beings can by specific means such as propitiation, ritual, initiations, etc., come into contact with spirits in order to receive their powers, alter their activity, or communicate with them. The acts, services, or works produced by a spirit,[36]

and

The belief in spirits that affect the present world and humanity, as well as the belief that humans can come in contact with these spirits and receive their powers.[37]

---

[34] The catalogue of divination and necromancy in Deut 18:10–11 is concluded in v. 12 as, "For all that do these things are an abomination to the Lord."

[35] This was even suggested by the Holy See (Pace, "Spiritism," *Catholic Encyclopedia* 14. 224) who, by a decree of March 30, 1898, "condemns Spiritistic practices, even though intercourse with the demon be excluded and *communication sought with good spirits* only" (emphasis mine).

[36] Angeles, *Dictionary of Christian Theology*, 190. Angeles's definition for the term "spiriualism" reflects the popular notion of "consulting the dead" (see ibid., 190–91). The present definition is for the term "spiritism" and reflects a more accurate understanding of consulting the spirit world.

[37] "Spiritism," in *Westminster Dictionary of Theological Terms* (ed. Donald K. McKim; Louisville: Westminster John Knox Press, 1996) 266.

According to these definitions, no specific spirit is intended by the term spiritism. Instead, the "existence of spirits" is the basis for the term and potentially covers the whole range of the spirit world, good or evil. This reflects the range of "spirit" in the OT. Hebrew רוח as it relates to spirit beings is ambiguous. It indicates either a "good spirit" (1 Sam 10:6,10; 11:6; 16:13, 14a) or a "bad spirit" (1 Sam 16:14b,15,16,23; 18:10; 19:9).[38] In an article discussing the relationship between modern spiritism and biblical necromancy, Frank B. Lewis observed, "When the biblical writers speak of spirit or of spirits they do not necessarily and always mean the spirits of dead men."[39]

Whereas the Hebrew terms אוב, "ghost," ידעני, "knowing spirit," and המתים, "the dead," are the "spirits" identified with outlawed practices in English translations of the OT, the terms רוח and πνεῦμα (LXX) also suggest, in certain contexts, the presence of spirit beings. Those English versions that translate the occult Hebrew terms אוב and ידעני as "spirits" suggest that these terms share the same semantic field with that of the term רוח as a term for "a spirit of God,"[40] indicating that all three Hebrew terms designate spirits of the spirit world. The nouns רוח and אוב, however, do not occur together in the OT.[41] But an implied association between the two terms occurs in antithetical contrasts found in texts that declare "seek not the אוב, but rather יהוה, or אל."[42]

As "spirits" that communicate with humans from the spirit world, the terms רוח and πνεῦμα share a similar context with spirits of the dead or divination in the biblical laws.[43] For instance, both Lev 20:27 and 2 Chr 24:20 depict prophetic activity. In Lev 20:27 the אוב-spirit and ידעני-spirit are "in" the man and woman from whom these spirits "speak."[44] Likewise, 2 Chr 24:20 states that

---

[38] So, too, πνεῦμα in the LXX.

[39] "The Bible and Modern Religions: VIII. Modern Spiritualism," *Int* 11 (1957) 438–54, esp. 453.

[40] See Num 24:2; 1 Sam 10:6; 11:6; 16:14–16,23; 18:10; 19:23; 1 Kgs 22:21–22; 1 Chr 12:19; and 2 Chr 24:20.

[41] Only in verb form (רוח, "to enlarge [between the thighs]," "to relieve") and different lexeme (אוב, "wine-skin") do the terms appear near one another in Job 32:19–20.

[42] See 1 Chr 10:13–14 and Isa 8:19–20.

[43] For a brief analysis of the biblical laws condemning אוב and ידעני, see Solomon A. Nigosian, "Anti-Divinatory Statements in Biblical Codes," *Near East School of Theology Theological Review* 18 (1997) 21–34. For antidivinatory laws, see Exod 22:17; Lev 19:31; 20:6,27; 2 Kgs 21:6; 23:24; 1 Chr 10:13–14; 2 Chr 33:6; Isa 8:19–20 and 19:3.

[44] On the translation of בהם as "in them" in Lev 20:27, see Samuel R. Driver, *Deuteronomy* (ICC; Edinburgh: T & T Clark, 1895; repr. 1986) 226; Alexander Heidel, *The Gilgamesh Epic and Old Testament Parallels* (Chicago: University of Chicago Press, 1946) 200; Josef Tropper, "Wizard," *DDD*, 1705; and Jacob Milgrom, *Leviticus 17–22* (AB 3A; New York: Doubleday,

"a spirit of God (רוח אלהים) put on (לבשה) Zechariah" after which Zechariah proceeds to speak. In the qal form the verb לבש has as its direct object a garment or clothing and as its subject the wearer of the garment. Here, the subject is "a spirit of God" that "puts on" Zechariah who is the direct object. The spirit is on the inside and Zechariah is the "garment" on the outside who clothes the spirit. Hence, the action of Zechariah is that of "a spirit of God" inside of him.[45]

The LXX version translates the verb לבש literally with the Greek verb ἐνδύω, "to put on." In a similar passage, 1 Chr 12:19, Johan Lust renders this verb as "and a spirit of God (πνεῦμα θεοῦ) *entered* (ἐνέδυσεν) Amasai."[46] Both Lev 20:27 and 2 Chr 24:20 then depict "spirits" that are either "in" or who have "put on [entered]" a human intermediary for the purpose of communicating. In the former the spirits (ידעני, אוב) are condemned by Yhwh in the biblical laws. In the latter the spirit is a spirit of God (רוח, πνεῦμα) that acts as a source for divine guidance and is the means whereby Yhwh communicates with his people.

The interpretation of the antidivinatory laws as a "ban on the spirit world"[47] is misleading in light of the fact that רוח and πνεῦμα designated spirits that were also denizens of a spirit world from which came Yhwh's communication and guidance through prophetic communication.[48] A blanket ban on the spirit world would include a ban on good spirits, i.e., "spirits of God," and such would nullify the activities of רוח אלהים and πνεῦμα θεοῦ. The fact that רוח אלהים played an important role in the divine instruction and communication from

---

2001) 1765. Johannes Lindblom (*Prophecy in Ancient Israel* [Philadelphia: Fortress, 1963] 87) stated that in Lev 20:27, "The diviner through whom a ghost was believed to speak must be stoned." In Isa 29:4 the אוב has "a voice," implying speech. The term ידעני always appears with אוב and never by itself. Thus, a close association exists between the אוב and the ידעני. Presumably, then, the ידעני had "a voice" as well.

[45] William M. Schniedewind ("Prophets and Prophecy in the Books of Chronicles," in *The Chronicler as Historian*, [ed. M. P. Graham, K. G. Hoglund, and S. L. McKenzie; JSOTS 238; Sheffield: Sheffield Academic Press, 1997]) states that the use of the verb לבש in 2 Chr 24:20 is an inspirational formula that depicts possession by a spirit. The verb נבא, "to prophesy," is not used for the speech of spirits through a human agent here. Schniedewind suggests that Chronicles "allows for a new kind of prophecy, a prophecy not by prophets, but by *ad hoc* inspired messengers" (p. 222). Nevertheless, the experience is the same as that expressed in certain contexts of the nifal and hithpael forms of נבא elsewhere in the OT. See esp. 1 Kgs 22:12, 21–22.

[46] Johan Lust, et al., *A Greek-English Lexicon of the Septuagint* (Part 1 A-I; Stuttgart: Deutsch Bibelgesellschaft, 1992) 151.

[47] So Craige, *Deuteronomy*, 260; and Brueggemann, *Deuteronomy*, 193.

[48] See Num 11:25; 1 Kgs 22:18–26; 1 Chr 12:19; 2 Chr 15:1; 20:14; 24:20.

Yhwh indicates that the spirit world *as a whole* did not come under the legal condemnation of the antidivinatory laws. Both prophecy and divination had a common goal: to communicate with the deity.[49]

In Deuteronomy 18 reliance on "spirits" and "mediums" (v. 11) is banned in favor of the expectation of "a prophet like Moses" (v. 15). This shows that only specific practitioners and entities of the spirit world were targeted by the Deuteronomist. Moses acts as an intermediary for Yhwh in Exod 18:15–16 where the people go to him "to consult God" and learn of "God's statutes and regulations." In Exod 33:7 Moses was responsible for establishing the "tent of meeting," where, after the preparations of burnt offerings and all of the other meticulous instructions for building and furnishing were complete, Yhwh (a spirit source) would "meet and speak" with Moses and the Israelites (see Exod 29:42–43).

Human instruments were sometimes necessary for Yhwh to communicate with Israel. Both 1 Sam 9:9 and 2 Kgs 3:11 attest that נביאים, "prophets," were required so that the Lord might be consulted "through" them (מאותו) by a third party. Consultations with Yhwh required media, whether types of divinatory equipment such as a goblet,[50] the ephod,[51] the breastpiece in which were the urim and thummim,[52] or humans.[53] Both Yhwh's and Baal's prophets were known by the same term, נביאים. Despite the fact that the term "medium" is used exclusively in contexts prohibiting occult activity for conjuring the dead or other spirits in English versions, Johan Lust observes that Yahwistic prophets, in their function as human intermediaries, can also be named by this

---

[49] See Martti Nissinen, *References to Prophecy in Neo-Assyrian Sources* (State Archives of Assyria Studies 7; Helsinki: University of Helsinki, 1998), who states, "There is a growing tendency in the study of biblical and ancient Near Eastern prophecy to consider prophecy, rather than being in contrast with divination (i.e., consulting the divine world by various means), an integral part of it" (p. 6). Cf. the literature on the relationship between prophecy and divination: Alfred Guillaume, *Prophecy and Divination Among the Hebrews and Other Semites* (London: Hodder and Stoughton, 1938); Thomas W. Overholt, *Channels of Prophecy: The Social Dynamics of Prophetic Activity* (Minneapolis: Fortress, 1989); Hans M. Barstad, "No Prophets? Recent Developments in Biblical Prophetic Research and Ancient Near Eastern Prophecy," *JSOT* 57 (1993) 39–60; H. L. Bosman, "Redefined Prophecy as Deuteronomic Alternative to Divination in Deut 18:9–22," *Acta Theologica* 1 (1996) 1–23; and Anne Marie Kitz, "Prophecy as Divination," *CBQ* 65 (2003) 22–43.

[50] Gen 44:5.

[51] Exod 28:6–13.

[52] Exod 28:15–21,30; Judg 17:5. See Cornelis Van Dam, *The Urim and Thummim: A Means of Revelation in Ancient Israel* (Winona Lake, IN: Eisenbrauns, 1997).

[53] Exod 33:9–11.

term: "The prophets were not only God's spokesmen, but also the *mediums* through whom Jahweh was to be consulted."[54]

Spiritism or "consultation with the spirit world" per se is not condemned in the OT but, rather, condemnation is laid against spirits who were not sanctioned by Yhwh (e.g., אוֹב, "spirit of divination," or "ghost," יִדְּעֹנִי, "knowing spirit," מֵתִים, "the dead," בַּעַל, "Baal," אֱלוֹהִים אֲחֵרִים, "other gods," and רְפָאִים, "rephaim" or "netherworld spirits") and this included necromancy. Spiritism refers to practices covered by terms such as "divination," "prophecy," "visions," and related practices whose objective is to obtain information and guidance from spirit sources.[55]

5. Consulting the Spirit World: בקשׁ, שׁאל, דרשׁ

The idea that spiritism relates to communication with spirits without qualification is reinforced further by the usage of divinatory terminology in which consultations occur with either Yahwistic or non-Yahwistic spirits. The verbs דרשׁ, "to consult," שׁאל, "to ask," and בקשׁ, "to seek," are used in contexts in which Yhwh or other gods and spirits are the direct object.

The verb שׁאל, "to ask," occurs in general contexts of "asking"[56] and "inquiring."[57] The verb is also used in prophetic contexts with both Yhwh and non-Yahwistic spirits.[58] Prophetic inquiry of the spirit world is implied by the use of שׁאל in these contexts. The verb בקשׁ, "to seek," is used in general contexts for "finding,"[59] "seek to take one's life,"[60] and "seek the face of

---

[54] Johan Lust, "The Mantic Function of the Prophet," *Bijdragen* 34 (1973) 234–50, esp. 234, emphasis mine.

[55] Hans Duhm (*Der Verkehr Gottes mit den Menschen im Alten Testament* [Tübingen: J. C. B. Mohr, 1926]) compares one who puts himself in the hands of spirit beings, "machte man sich die Kräfte von Geistern dienstbar," such as the necromancer in 1 Sam 28, with the way in which God might similarly communicate with humanity, "daß Gott gelegentlich auch durch Träume und psychisch veranlagte Personen Antwort erteilt (1. Sam. 28:6, 15)" (p. 37).

[56] See Judg 5:25, 8:24,26; 1 Sam 12:17,19; 1 Kgs 3:10,11; 19:4; Isa 7:11,12, and Ezra 8:22.

[57] See Gen 24:47; 32:18; 44:19; 1 Sam 14:18; and 19:22.

[58] For Yhwh, see Deut 4:32; Judg 18:5; 1 Sam 10:22; 14:37; 22:10,13,15; 23:2,4; 28:6; 30:8; 2 Sam 2:1; 5:19,23; 1 Chr 14:10; and Isa 7:11; 45:11. For other spirits, see Deut 18:12; and Ezek 21:26.

[59] See Judg 6:29; 2 Kgs 2:17; Jer 5:1; and Ezek 34:6.

[60] Exod 4:19; 1 Sam 20:1; 22:23; 23:15; 25:29; 2 Sam 4:8; 16:11; 1 Kgs 19:10,14; Pss 35:4; 38:13; 40:15; 54:5; 63:10; 70:3; 84:14; Prov 29:10; Jer 4:30; 11:21; 19:7,9; 21:7; 22:25; 34:20,21; 38:16; 44:30; 46:26 and 49:37.

rulers."[61] Although not used of foreign gods and spirits, the verb is commonly used with Yhwh as the object.[62] Lev 19:31, however, preserves an occurrence of the verb that prohibits "seeking to be defiled" by "mediums (or ghosts)" and "wizards (or spirits)." In these contexts, the verb בקש is terminology used both to prohibit guidance from wrong spirits and to seek guidance from Yhwh. Although "asking" and "inquiring" might be different in some ways from "seeking," it is difficult to discern whether the prophetic activity underlying these verbs is different.

The verb דרש with the meaning "to consult" is used primarily with Yhwh or other gods and spirits as its object. One might "consult" Yhwh, Baal, ghosts, and spirits.[63]

דרש + Yhwh, God:

Gen 25:22 – "and she went out to consult (לדרש) the Lord."
2 Kgs 3:11 – "Is there no prophet of the Lord here so that we may consult (נדרשה) the Lord through him?"
1 Sam 9:9 – "In former times in Israel, anyone who sent to consult (לדרוש) God used to say, 'Come, let us go to the seer,' for he who is now called a prophet was formerly called a seer."

דרש + gods, spirits of the dead, and Baalzebub:

Deut 12:30 – "and do not consult (תדרש) their gods."
Deut 18:11 – "one who consults (דרש) the dead."
2 Kgs 1:2 – "Go! Consult (דרשו) Baalzebub, the god of Ekron."[64]

---

[61] 1 Kgs 10:24 and Prov 29:36.

[62] For example, see 2 Sam 12:16; 21:1; 1 Chr 16:10; 2 Chr 11:16; 20:4; Pss 27:8; 105:3; Jer 50:4; Ezra 8:23; Hos 2:9; 5:6; Amos 8:12; Zech 8:21; Zeph 1:6; 2:3; and Mal 3:1.

[63] For דרש יהוה or דרש דבר יהוה, "consult (the word of) Yhwh," see Gen 25:22; Exod 18:15; 1 Sam 9:9; 1 Kgs 22:5,8; 2 Kgs 3:11; 8:8; 22:13; and 2 Chr 16:12. For other spirits and gods, see Deut 12:30; 18:11; 1 Sam 28:7; 2 Kgs 1:2,3,6,; Isa 8:19; and 19:3. The phrase "word of the Lord" indicated "words" that were spoken, not those that had been written. The "word of the Lord" is a prophetic phrase that appears almost always in prophetic and visionary contexts. See especially 1 Sam 3:1; and Lindblom, *Prophecy in Ancient Israel*, 108–22.

[64] See Burke O. Long, "The Effect of Divination upon Israelite Literature" *JBL* 92 (1973) 489–97, who observes that the דרש event is common to both Yahwistic and non-Yahwistic consultations (p. 490). See Rannfrid I. Thelle, "דרש את־יהוה: The Prophetic Act of Consulting Yhwh in Jeremiah 21,2 and 37,7," *SJOT* 12 (1998) 249–56, who states with regard to the דרש event, "It is interesting that this type of prophetic consultation is not restricted to consulting the God of Israel. Other deities are also mentioned, such as Baal Zebub, god of Ekron, and dead

According to Siegfried Wagner, in the books of Kings, Chronicles, Jeremiah, and Ezekiel the דרש event occurs in the context of a mediator or prophet responsible for mediating Yhwh's message to the inquirer.[65] Consultations with Yhwh might take place at a designated cultic center (Gen 25:22; Ps 34:4) or a non-cultic center (1 Sam 9:9; 1 Kgs 14:5 1 Kgs 1:16; 3:11; 8:8; 2 Chr 34:21). Hence, the cultic center is not an exclusive site for making inquiries to Yhwh. Wagner states, "As long as a prophet or a man of God is present, Yahweh may be consulted."[66]

In an important article rarely cited by scholars, Lust observes that by the use of the term דרש soothsaying and prophecy have similar goals. Using 1 Samuel 28 as an example, Lust explains,

Soothsaying . . . shows some striking connections with Israelite prophecy. . . . It is characterized by the use of the term *dāraš* just as in prophetic consultation. . . . Saul goes to the medium to gain information (*dāraš*) and guidance (v. 7-8). An answer is given, foretelling what is going to happen (v. 16 ss.). The same elements occur in a prophetic consultation. The main difference is that in the prophetic consultation Jahweh is the object of the *dāraš*-event, while in the consultation of the witch it is the *'ōbôt* and *jiddǝ'onîm* or the *ba'alat-'ôb* (v.7).[67]

Lust observes further that the generations after Saul considered prophets to be the opponents of non-Yahwistic prophecy. Elijah condemns Ahaziah for his consultation (דרש) of Baalzebub, and Asa is punished for inquiring (דרש) of the רפאים, "netherworld spirits."[68]

True prophecy was distinct from false prophecy not so much in method of consultation as in the source consulted. The use of identical terminology (דרש, שאל) for inquiry of Yhwh or of other gods and spirits indicates at least that similar methods were utilized for such consultations.[69] Thus, consultation with

---

spirits" (pp. 254–55). Thelle (ibid.) concludes that "an investigation of the word דרש as a designation of the act of 'consulting a deity by a prophet' provides data to demonstrate that this activity forms an important part of Biblical prophecy" (p. 255).

[65] Siegfried Wagner, "דרש," *TDOT* 3. 302.

[66] Ibid.

[67] Johan Lust, "The Mantic Function of the Prophet," 238.

[68] Ibid., 240. See 2 Kgs 1:3 and 2 Chr 16:12.

[69] Wagner, ("דרש") states, "Illegitimate 'seeking' or 'inquiring' was obviously done in the same forms and methods as the legitimate" (3. 302). So also B. Vawter and J. T. Nellis, "Necromancy," in *EDB* (trans. L. F. Hartman; New York: McGraw-Hill,1963): "The *'ōb* was consulted just as Yahweh was" (p. 1623).

Yahwistic spirits had continuity with consultations with non-Yahwistic spirits.[70] This continuity did not always mean identity, but sometimes human intermediaries may be consulted for any deity, including Yhwh. The act of consulting a deity via a prophet was a common enough occurrence both in the OT and in the broader Ancient Near East that such consultations probably shared like procedures and phenomena that accompanied them.[71]

G. V. Smith summarizes the consequence of the existence of like phenomena exhibited by the consultation of Yahwistic or non-Yahwistic spirits: "The similarities explain why the Israelites were so easily led astray by false prophets, while the differences point to the uniqueness and importance of the true prophets who faithfully delivered God's message."[72] One might consult (דרש) a spirit of divination (אוב) or the Lord (יהוה): לשאול באוב לדרוש ולא־דרש ביהוה "and he [Saul] also consulted a ghost and had not consulted the Lord" (1 Chr 10:13–14). This passage relates that two antithetical spirit sources might be similarly consulted in the דרש event; to consult באוב, literally, "with a spirit of divination," or ביהוה, literally, "with the Lord."[73] In most cases, however, the דרש event is stated to occur without any accompanying details or commentary of what actually took place.[74]

---

[70] For instance, see 1 Kgs 18:25–26 and 18:30–33, where Baal's prophets and Elijah perform similar tasks in order to receive communication from their respective gods. But Elijah does not slash himself bloody as do Baal's prophets. Compare 1 Kgs 18:38 and 2 Chr 7:1, where in both instances "fire came down from heaven and consumed the holocaust." The outward appearance of spirit communication was not always the means to determine which spirits were consulted. Both spirits of God and other spirits might be consulted through similar media and might perform similar feats (see esp. Exod 7:10–12, 20–21; and 8:1–3). After a brief analysis of texts in 1 Samuel that deal with the spirits of God, prophecy, and the evocation of Samuel by the necromancer, Carroll Stuhlmueller ("The Spirit World," *TBT* 28 [1990] 5–11) states, "In its dealing with the spirit world, prophecy needs to be tested but not suppressed" (p. 9). Stuhlmueller recognizes the careers of Moses, Ezekiel, and Daniel as those that involved direct "contact with the spirit world" (ibid., 6).

[71] See Wilson, *Prophecy and Society in Ancient Israel*; Simo Parpola, *Assyrian Prophecies*; and Nissinen, *References to Prophecy in Neo-Assyrian Sources*, 4–9, 167–68.

[72] G. V. Smith, "Prophet; Prophecy," *ISBE* 3. 989. Similarly, Lust ("Mantic Function") states, "It may be that some early traditions held that consultation of a prophet was as suspect as a visit to a wizard" (p. 235).

[73] This is reminiscent of the observation in Chapter Two that good and evil spirits functioned identically through prophetic consultations.

[74] Wagner ("דרשׁ") states with regard to Isa 8:19, "The reference to 'the spirits of the dead . . . who chirp and mutter' does not furnish any precise information as to the way in which such illegitimate inquiries were made. Once again the passage simply uses well-known expressions for 'inquiring' of a higher power" (pp. 303–4). Likewise, in Yahwistic consultation, "The way

6. The Term רוח the Basis for Spiritism

Yhwh was "spirit," and certain conditions had to be met if a tangible link was to be established between humans and that which was "spirit."[75] This is clarified by the fact that whenever Yhwh is the object of דרש, שאל, or בקש, one is understood to "consult," "ask," or "seek" that which is explicitly רוח, "spirit." Isa 31:3 states in parallel fashion, ומצרים אדם ולא־אל וסוסיהם בשׂר ולא־רוח, "The Egyptians are men, not God; their horses are flesh, not spirit." Here, אל, "God," and רוח, "spirit," are parallel. Consulting Yhwh, therefore, is equivalent to consulting "spirit," and such a consultation might arguably be characterized as רוח-*ism*.[76]

In many instances, communications from Yhwh occurred via רוח אלהים, "a spirit of God."[77] This seems to have been the more usual way in which Yhwh

---

in which one inquired of God through a prophet (cultically or non cultically) cannot be determined conclusively from Jeremiah and Ezekiel" (ibid., 302). See Gen 25:22, wherein Rebecca inquires of Yhwh: ותלך לדרש את־יהוה, "and then she went out to consult the Lord." No detail is given as to the manner in which this consultation took place. The next verse simply records that ויאמר יהוה לה, "and the Lord said to her," without recording the way in which this answer was received. Such consultations must not have been out of the ordinary in view of the casual way in which they occur in the OT.

[75] Notice the elaborate and detailed instructions for building and furnishing the dwelling and the priestly vestments that were necessary to commune with Yhwh: Exod 25–31, 35–40. The purpose for the meticulous planning and building appears in Exod 40:34–38, wherein the "cloud" or the "glory of the Lord" covered the dwelling, an indication of the manifestation of Yhwh and his spirit world. In some sense, the dwelling functioned as a sort of antenna to attract spirit natures that were sanctioned by Yhwh. Likewise, the purpose for all of the directions for the preparation of the burnt offerings in Exod 29:10–41 is indicated in vv. 42–43: "Throughout your generations this burnt offering shall be offered regularly before the Lord at the entrance of the tent of meeting, *where I will meet you and speak with you.* There, at the altar, I will meet the Israelites." Hence, the sole purpose for building the dwelling and offering sacrifices was to facilitate *spoken* communication between Yhwh and the Israelites.

[76] See Isa 45:11, "Thus says the Lord, holy one of Israel, his maker, 'Ask me (שאלוני) of things to come.'"

[77] Many of the occurrences of רוח אלהים or רוח יהוה as "a spirit of God" appear in 1 Samuel. 1 Kgs 22:21speaks of הרוח, "a certain spirit," that is sent by Yhwh to speak through the mouths of the prophets of King Ahab and in this sense can be understood as רוח יהוה, "a spirit of the Lord." Initially, the explanation for why Yhwh sanctions a spirit to become "a lying spirit" (1 Kgs 22:22–23, רוח שקר) is difficult to understand. Early Judaism depicted lying spirits as types of evil spirits under Beliar that worked against God (*T. Reub.* 2:5, πνεῦμα ψεῦδος). The question arises, how can Yhwh be the source for "a lying spirit"? On the one hand Peter J. Williams ("Lying Spirits Sent by God? The Case of Micaiah's Prophecy," in *The Trustworthiness of God: Perspectives on the Nature of Scripture* [ed. P. Helm and C. R.

communicated with humanity in the OT.[78] If the motive in divining by the spirit world was for Yhwh's guidance via רוח אלהים, then such consultations were welcome, even demanded; for only in this way might Yhwh communicate his law and directive to humanity in a form that was perceptible and understood by them.[79]

Yhwh, gods, and spirits resided in a realm that was believed to exist as a supraterrestrial invisible reality. Hence, if one inquired of Yhwh or of a ghost, it was necessary that the person have sufficient knowledge of the procedures necessary to establish a tangible link between the terrestrial and a supraterrestrial world. This prerequisite knowledge for consulting the spirit world seems to have been the property of Yhwh's prophets as well as of Baal's prophets and necromancers.[80]

Trueman; Grand Rapids: Eerdmans, 2002] 58–66) suggests that the relationship between a lying spirit and God is akin to the relationship between God and Satan found in the first chapter of Job (p. 66). As such, the lying spirit in 1 Kgs 22:22 is not God's spirit. According to Williams, the narrative does not present God as a liar, but instead is an assertion of God's sovereignty over lying spirits as was the case with God's sovereignty over Satan in Job (ibid.). On the other hand, Simon J. DeVries (*1 Kings* [WBC 12; Waco, TX: Word, 1985]) suggests that both Jeremiah and Ezekiel depict Yhwh as deceiving or enticing a prophet, and 1 Kings 22 is no different (p. 268; see Jer 20:7; Ezek 14:9). Yhwh has spoken unfavorably against the king by deceiving Ahab with a prophecy for victory. Micaiah has inside knowledge of the deceptive operations of the spirit world in Ahab's court. Micaiah recounts for Ahab this deceptive scenario in a vision after giving him Yhwh's reasons for the deception: to dupe Ahab into war in order to have him killed (1 Kgs 22:17). Micaiah's prophecy for defeat, dismissed as "evil" by Ahab (v. 18), is fulfilled "as the Lord had spoken" (v. 38). The spirit revealed to Micaiah the intentional deception it spoke through Ahab's prophets.

[78] The OT states at times that Yhwh himself is the communicating deity: Gen 17:1, 22; Exod 19:9; 33:11, 18–23.

[79] The object of the legitimate דרש event is always יהוה, "Lord," or דבר יהוה, "word of the Lord." Never is the object of the legitimate דרש event רוח אלהים or רוח יהוה. However, in many instances in the OT, communications from Yhwh occur through an agent called רוח רוח יהוה, אלהים, or simply רוח. The phrase "the spirit of God/the Lord came upon" occurs often in the context of prophecy, divine guidance, and visions. The phrase implies that Yhwh himself is not the agent that is present during the experience but rather רוח, "a spirit," that acts on his behalf. The legitimate דרש event is never elaborated any further than the fact that Yhwh was "consulted" or "sought." From the perspective of the OT, it is not impossible that Yhwh himself communicated during the consultation process. But the דרש event might have been precipitated, more often than not, by "a spirit" sent by Yhwh. Early Israelite prophecy functioned because of "a spirit of God." A classic example is 1 Kgs 22:21. Whenever Yhwh is the object of the דרש event, it is understood that the multi-dimensional spirit world of Yhwh is sought.

[80] It appears that Samuel administered a "school of prophets" in Ramah. 1 Sam 19:20 refers to הנביאים להקת, "a company of prophets," whereby Samuel served as its headmaster, שמואל עמד נצב עליהם, "Samuel standing as head over them." No detail is given for this activity other

7. Conclusion

In summary, the usage of the term "spiritism" in contexts that ban the spirit world does no justice to the evidence in the OT wherein the spirit world is not condemned. Spiritism relates to communication with the spirit world as a whole, and this seems to reflect better the usage of the verbs דרש, שאל, and בקש in contexts that both prohibit consultations with the spirit world, such as the antidivinatory laws ("bad" spiritism), and in contexts that allow consultations with the spirit world, such as those that seek after Yhwh through prophetic or divinatory means ("good" spiritism).

Suggesting contact between two seemingly different ideas such as "good" and "bad" spiritism is not without cogency. Human agents or channels were used whether in consultations with Baal, Ekron, or Yhwh. These channels were required for different spirits, be they "bad" or, at least, condemned ones (אוב, ידעני), or "good" ones (רוח יהוה, רוח אלהים). The immediate point of contact between "good" and "bad" spiritism is found in the media and procedures necessary to communicate with the spirit world, whereas the difference lie in the source consulted. The source determined the quality of the prophetic message among the people. If that source was Yhwh, then the message was unique and the prophets delivered it faithfully and consistently. The message might be one of admonishment, a warning, instruction, or salvific.

An imperfect analogy might be drawn from present-day life. A telephone can be used either to deliver messages of comfort, concern, and love or messages of deceit, hate, and anger; it can be used by a guardian or a criminal. In both instances, the medium necessary for delivering two totally different forms of communication is the same, i.e., the telephone. Also, the natural laws for such communication must be observed by both the guardian and the criminal. When this analogy is applied to communication between a visible and an invisible world the ambiguity is readily apparent: invisible spirits can stealthily disguise themselves in order to deceive or misguide. The medium is the same, that of a human intermediary, but the spirits using these human

---

than the verbs נבאים, "prophesying," and יתנבאו, "behaving as a prophet." This activity among the prophets of Samuel's prophetic guild is stated to occur as an effect of the spirit world not only on the "school of prophets" but also on the messengers sent by Saul: ותהי על־מלאכי שאול רוח אלהים ויתנבאו גם־המה, "and a spirit of God came upon the messengers of Saul and they also prophesied." See I. Mendelsohn, "Guilds in Ancient Palestine," *BASOR* 80 (1940) 17–21and idem, "Guilds in Babylonia and Assyria," *JAOS* 60 (1940) 68–72. See also the activity of the Baal prophets in 1 Kings 18. For other "schools of prophets" see 2 Kgs 2:3,5,15; 6:1,2; 22:14.

instruments to speak through might be as different as night and day. This ambiguity was the basis for the early Christian institution of "discerning" or "testing the spirits."[81]

The distinction that divination was "bad" (non-Yahwistic) and prophecy was "good" (Yahwistic) gives way to evidence *within* the OT (דרש, שאל) that such a distinction was never the case.[82] Occasionally, the distinction depends on the subjectively pejorative English usage of "divination" as relating to the "black arts" instead of an objective analysis of the contexts of the Hebrew terms in the OT.[83] The evidence shows that the spirit world was both a lawful source for divine instruction and a prohibited source, depending on that source.

---

[81] Naturally, ancient Israelites would not have used a Christological test for prophecy. The only clear criterion for distinguishing true from false prophecy in the OT is found in Deut 18:21–22 and Jer 28:9: if the pronouncement of a prophet is fulfilled, then it was given by Yhwh. The idea of true and false prophecy in the OT is a topic of some debate among scholars. For a concise article on the matter that covers the pertinent issues, see Martin McNamara, "Discernment Criteria in Israel: True and False Prophets," in *Discernment of the Spirit and of Spirits* (ed. C. Floristán and C. Duquoc [New York, NY: Seabury Press, 1979]) 3–13. Later Christian and Rabbinic exegesis of Samuel's spirit in 1 Samuel 28 made discerning comments of the nature of the manifestation, e.g., Samuel's spirit was impersonated by an evil spirit, that seem foreign to Hebrew thinking. See Klaus A. D. Smelik, "The Witch of Endor, 1 Samuel 28 in Rabbinic and Christian Exegesis till 800 AD," *VC* 33 (1979) 160–79. For a recent discussion, see Jonathan Seidel, "Necromantic Praxis in the Midrash on the Seance at En Dor," in *Magic and Divination in the Ancient World*, 97–106.

[82] Pace Harry M. Orlinsky ("The Seer in Ancient Israel," *OrAnt* 4 [1965] 153–74), who argues for an antithetical distinction between divination and prophecy: "The common Egypto-Asiatic phenomenon of divination . . . in Israel alone . . . [did not] develop into, but . . . opposed and [was] largely replaced [by] prophecy. . . . Divination nowhere developed into prophecy . . . Divination was a common Ancient Near Eastern phenomenon; prophecy is a uniquely Israelite phenomenon." (pp. 153, 170). See, however, Kitz, "Prophecy as Divination," 22–43. Note Davies (*Magic, Divination*, 73) who states, "The word 'prophecy' is mostly employed of communications from God in the Old and New Testament sense. Of necessity, therefore, it stands upon higher ground than divination in the usual heathen sense of the word. But the ordinary theological distinction is unjust and opposed to Semitic etymology. When the Israelites resorted to magic and divination, it was in the belief that Yahwe sanctioned and controlled these practices and accepted them as legitimate." Note also that the verb נחש, "practice divination," is both accepted by Yhwh (Gen 30:27; 44:5) and condemned (Deut 18:10; 2 Kgs 21:6).

[83] Just prior to the Renaissance, the term "necromancy" underwent a phonological corruption whereby the conflation of Greek *necro*, "dead" with the Latin *niger*, "black," produced the variants "nigromancy" and "negromancy," signifying divination by the "black" arts. This phonological corruption added to the already negative stigma given to the practice in the OT. So Ritner, "Necromancy," 95–95.

Appendix 3

A Statistical Analysis of πνεῦμα as "holy spirit" in the NT[1]

The Greek noun πνεῦμα, "wind," "air," "breath," "spirit," occurs three hundred and eighty four times in the NT. The intent of the present analysis is to give and describe all forms of πνεῦμα in reference to "holy spirit" (including references to "the spirit," "spirit of God," "spirit of the Lord," "spirit of Christ," and other related variations). This will include occurrences in the nominative, genitive, dative, and accusative cases, with and without the Greek article τό, the plural form πνεύματα in reference to good and evil spirits, and singular forms that are anarthrous and unqualified. The point of the analysis is to show that the utility and range of πνεῦμα as "a spirit" in the NT is much more flexible in the world and grammar of the NT than what is made of it in the fourth century theology of the Holy Spirit.

The analysis is divided by six sections: πνεῦμα in (1) the gospels; (2) Acts of the Apostles; (3) the letters of Paul (both undisputed and disputed); (4) First and Second Peter; (5) Hebrews; and (6) the Johannine epistles and Revelation. Forms with the article (articular forms) in all four cases (nominative, genitive, dative, accusative) will be treated first, then forms without the article (anarthrous forms) in all four cases, then plural forms. This will also include the use of the prepositional phrase ἐν πνεύματι.

1. Articular Forms of πνεῦμα

1.1 Articular forms of πνεῦμα as "the holy spirit" occur twenty-six times in the gospels

Nominative – Mark 1:12 τὸ πνεῦμα, Luke 3:22 τὸ πνεῦμα τὸ ἅγιον, John 14:26 τὸ πνεῦμα τὸ ἅγιον, 16:13 τὸ πνεῦμα τῆς ἀληθείας
Genitive – Matt 4:1 τοῦ πνεύματος, 12:31 τοῦ πνεύματος, 12:32 τοῦ πνεύματος

---

[1] According to W. F. Moulton and A. S. Geden, *A Concordance to the Greek New Testament* (ed. I. Howard Marshall; 6th ed.; London: T & T Clark, 2002). See also Easley, "The Pauline Use of *Pneumati* as a Reference to the Spirit of God," 299–313; D. P. Francis, "The Holy Spirit: A Statistical Inquiry," *ExpTim* 96 (1985) 136–37; Robert L. Mowery, "The articular references to the Holy Spirit in the Synoptic Gospels and Acts," *BR* 31 (1986) 26–45; Lawrence Mak, "The Use and the Omission of the Greek Definite Article with PNEUMA HAGION," M.A. thesis, Covenant Theological Seminary, 1986; and Fee, *God's Empowering Presence*, 16–24.

τοῦ ἀγίου, 28:19 τοῦ ἀγίου πνεύματος, Luke 2:26 τοῦ πνεύματος τοῦ ἀγίου, 4:14 τοῦ πνεύματος, John 7:39 τοῦ πνεύματος

Dative – Mark 12:36 τῷ πνεύματι τῷ ἁγίῳ, Luke 2:27 τῷ πνεύματι, 4:1 τῷ πνεύματι, 10:21 τῷ πνεύματι τῷ ἁγίῳ

Accusative – Matt 3:16 τὸ πνεῦμα τοῦ θεοῦ, 10:20 τὸ πνεῦμα τοῦ πατρός ὑμῶν, 12:18 τὸ πνεῦμά μου, Mark 1:10 τὸ πνεῦμα, 3:29 τὸ πνεῦμα τὸ ἅγιον, 13:11 τὸ πνεῦμα τὸ ἅγιον, Luke 2:27 τὸ πνεῦμα, 12:10 τὸ ἅγιον πνεῦμα, John 1:32 τὸ πνεῦμα, 14:17 τὸ πνεῦμα τῆς ἀληθείας, 15:26 τὸ πνεῦμα τῆς ἀληθείας

1.2 Articular forms of πνεῦμα *as "the holy spirit" occur twenty-nine times in the Acts of the Apostle*

Nominative – 8:29 τὸ πνεῦμα, 10:19 τὸ πνεῦμα, 10:44 τὸ πνεῦμα τὸ ἅγιον, 11:15 τὸ πνεῦμα τὸ ἅγιον, 13:2 τὸ πνεῦμα τὸ ἅγιον, 19:6 τὸ πνεῦμα τὸ ἅγιον, 20:23 τὸ πνεῦμα τὸ ἅγιον, 28:25 τὸ πνεῦμα τὸ ἅγιον

Genitive – 2:33 τοῦ πνεύματος τοῦ ἀγίου, 2:38 τοῦ ἀγίου πνεύματος, 4:31 τοῦ ἀγίου πνεύματος, 9:31 τοῦ ἀγίου πνεύματος, 10:45 τοῦ ἀγίου πνεύματος, 11:28 τοῦ πνεύματος, 13:4 τοῦ ἀγίου πνεύματος, 16:6 τοῦ ἀγίου πνεύματος, 21:4 τοῦ πνεύματος

Dative – 7:51 τῷ πνεύματι τῷ ἁγίῳ, 15:28 τῷ πνεύματι τῷ ἁγίῳ

Accusative – 1:16 τὸ πνεῦμα τὸ ἅγιον, 2:4 τὸ πνεῦμα, 5:3 τὸ πνεῦμα τὸ ἅγιον, 5:9 τὸ πνεῦμα κυρίου, 5:32 τὸ πνεῦμα τὸ ἅγιον, 8:18 τὸ πνεῦμα, 10:47 τὸ πνεῦμα τὸ ἅγιον, 15:8 τὸ πνεῦμα τὸ ἅγιον, 16:7 τὸ πνεῦμα Ἰησοῦ, 20:28 τὸ πνεῦμα ἅγιον

1.3 Articular forms of πνεῦμα *as "the holy spirit" and its equivalent occur thirty-seven times in the undisputed letters of Paul*

Nominative – Rom 8:16 τὸ πνεῦμα, 8:26 τὸ πνεῦμα, 1 Cor 2:10 τὸ πνεῦμα, 12:4 τὸ αὐτὸ πνεῦμα, 12:11 τὸ αὐτὸ πνεῦμα, 14:14 τὸ πνεῦμά μου, 2 Cor 3:17 τὸ πνεῦμα κυρίου, Gal 5:17 τὸ πνεῦμα

Genitive – Rom 8:2 τοῦ πνεύματος τῆς ζωῆς, 8:5 τοῦ πνεύματος, 8:23 τοῦ πνεύματος, 15:30 τοῦ πνεύματος, 1 Cor 2:10 τοῦ πνεύματος, 2:14 τοῦ πνεύματος τοῦ θεοῦ, 12:7 τοῦ πνεύματος, 12:8 τοῦ πνεύματος, 2 Cor 1:22 τοῦ πνεύματος, 3:8 τοῦ πνεύματος, 5:5 τοῦ πνεύματος, 13:13 τοῦ ἀγίου πνεύματος, Gal 3:14 τοῦ πνεύματος, 5:22 τοῦ πνεύματος, Phil 1:19 τοῦ πνεύματος, Heb 9:8 τοῦ πνεύματος τοῦ ἀγίου

Dative – Rom 12:11 τῷ πνεύματι, 1 Cor 6:11 τῷ πνεύματι τοῦ θεοῦ, 12:9 τῷ αὐτῷ πνεύματι, 12:9 τῷ ἑνὶ πνεύματι, 14:15 τῷ πνεύματι (twice)

Accusative – 1 Cor 2:10 τὸ πνεῦμα, 2:11 τὸ πνεῦμα τοῦ θεοῦ, 2:12 τὸ πνεῦμα τὸ ἐκ τοῦ θεοῦ, 3:16 τὸ πνεῦμα τοῦ θεοῦ, 12:8 τὸ αὐτὸ πνεῦμα, 2 Cor 3:17 τὸ πνεῦμα, 4:13 τὸ αὐτὸ πνεῦμα τῆς πίστεως, Gal 3:2 τὸ πνεῦμα, 3:5 τὸ πνεῦμα, 4:6 τὸ πνεῦμα τοῦ υἱοῦ αὐτοῦ, 1 Thess 4:8 τὸ πνεῦμα αὐτοῦ τὸ ἅγιον, 5:19 τὸ πνεῦμα

1.4 Articular forms of πνεῦμα as "the holy spirit" and its equivalent occur five times in the disputed letters of Paul

Nominative – 1 Tim 4:1 τὸ πνεῦμα

Genitive – Eph 4:3 τοῦ πνεύματος, 6:17 τοῦ πνεύματος

Dative – Eph 1:13 τῷ πνεύματι τῆς ἐπαγγελίας τῷ ἁγίῳ

Accusative – Eph 4:30 τὸ πνεῦμα τὸ ἅγιον τοῦ θεου

1.5 Articular forms of πνεῦμα as "the holy spirit" and its equivalent occur twice in First Peter

Nominative – 1 Pet 4:14 τὸ τῆς δόξης, τὸ τοῦ θεοῦ πνεῦμα

1.6 Articular forms of πνεῦμα as "the holy spirit" and its equivalent occur four times in Hebrews

Nominative – Heb 3:7 τὸ πνεῦμα τὸ ἅγιον, 10:15 τὸ πνεῦμα τὸ ἅγιον

Genitive – Heb 9:8 τοῦ πνεύματος τοῦ ἁγίου

Dative – no occurrences

Accusative – Heb 10:29 τὸ πνεῦμα τῆς χάριτος

1.7 Articular forms of πνεῦμα as "the holy spirit" and its equivalent occur fifteen times in the Johannine Epistles and Revelation

Nominative – 1 John 5:6 τὸ πνεῦμα (twice), Rev 2:7,11,17,29 τὸ πνεῦμα, 3:6,13,22 τὸ πνεῦμα, 14:13 τὸ πνεῦμα, 19:10 τὸ πνεῦμα τῆς προφητείας, 22:17 τὸ πνεῦμα

Genitive – 1 John 3:24 τοῦ πνεύματος

Dative – no occurrences

Accusative – 1 John 4:2 τὸ πνεῦμα τοῦ θεοῦ, 4:6 τὸ πνεῦμα τῆς ἀληθείας

2. Anarthrous Forms of πνεῦμα

2.1 Anarthrous forms of πνεῦμα *as "[a] holy spirit" and its equivalent occur sixteen times in the gospels*

Nominative – Luke 1:35 πνεῦμα ἅγιον, 2:25 πνεῦμα, 4:18 πνεῦμα κυρίου
Genitive – Matt 1:18 πνεύματος ἁγίου, 1:20 πνεύματος ἁγίου, Luke 1:15 πνεύματος ἁγίου, 1:41 πνεύματος ἁγίου, 1:67 πνεύματος ἁγίου, 4:1 πνεύματος ἁγίου
Dative – Matt 3:11 πνεύματι ἁγίῳ, 12:28 πνεύματι θεοῦ, Mark 1:8 πνεύματι ἁγίῳ, Luke 3:16 πνεύματι ἁγίῳ, John 1:33 πνεύματι ἁγίῳ
Accusative – Luke 11:13 πνεῦμα ἅγιον, John 20:22 πνεῦμα ἅγιον

2.2 Anarthrous forms of πνεῦμα *as "[a] holy spirit" and its equivalent occur sixteen times in the Acts of the Apostles*

Nominative – Acts 19:2 πνεῦμα ἅγιον
Genitive – Acts 1:2 πνεύματος ἁγίου, 2:4 πνεύματος ἁγίου, 4:8 πνεύματος ἁγίου, 4:31 πνεύματος ἁγίου, 6:3 πνεύματος, 6:5 πνεύματος ἁγίου, 7:55 πνεύματος ἁγίου, 11:24 πνεύματος ἁγίου, 13:9 πνεύματος ἁγίου, 13:52 πνεύματος ἁγίου
Dative – Acts 1:5 πνεύματι ἁγίῳ, 10:38 πνεύματι ἁγίῳ, 11:16 πνεύματι ἁγίῳ
Accusative – 8:15 πνεῦμα ἅγιον, 8:17 πνεῦμα ἅγιον, 8:19 πνεῦμα ἅγιον, 19:2 πνεῦμα ἅγιον

2.3 Anarthrous forms of πνεῦμα *as "[a] holy spirit" and its equivalent occur forty-one times in the undisputed letters of Paul*

Nominative – Rom 8:9 πνεῦμα θεοῦ
Genitive – Rom 5:5 πνεύματος ἁγίου, 7:6 πνεύματος, 8:11 αὐτοῦ πνεύματος, 15:13 πνεύματος ἁγίου, 15:19 πνεύματος θεοῦ, 1 Cor 2:4 πνεύματος, 2:13 πνεύματος, 6:19 ἁγίου πνεύματος, 2 Cor 3:6 πνεύματος, Phil 2:1 πνεύματος, 1 Thess 1:6 πνεύματος ἁγίου
Dative – Rom 2:29 πνεύματι, 8:9 πνεύματι, 8:13 πνεύματι, 8:14 πνεύματι θεοῦ, 9:1 πνεύματι ἁγίῳ, 14:17 πνεύματι ἁγίῳ, 15:16 πνεύματι ἁγίῳ, 1 Cor12:3 πνεύματι τοῦ θεοῦ, 12:3 πνεύματι ἁγίῳ, 12:13 ἐν ἑνὶ πνεύματι, 14:2 πνεύματι, 14:16 πνεύματι, 2 Cor 3:3 πνεύματι θεοῦ ζῶντος, 6:6 πνεύματι ἁγίῳ, Gal 5:5 πνεύματι, 5:16 πνεύματι, 5:18 πνεύματι, 5:25 πνεύματι, Phil 3:3 πνεύματι θεοῦ, 1 Thess 1:5 πνεύματι ἁγίῳ

Accusative – Rom 1:4 πνεύμα ἁγιωσύνης, 8:4 πνεῦμα, 8:9 πνεῦμα Χριστοῦ, 8:15 πνεῦμα υἱοθεσίας, 1 Cor 7:40 πνεῦμα θεοῦ, Gal 4:29 πνεῦμα

2.4 Anarthrous forms of πνεῦμα *as "[a] holy spirit" occur nine times in the disputed letters of Paul*

Nominative – Eph 4:4 ἓν πνεῦμα
Genitive – 2 Thess 2:13 ἁγιασμῷ πνεύματος, 2 Tim 1:14 πνεύματος ἁγίου, Tit 3:5 πνεύματος ἁγίου
Dative – Eph 2:18 ἑνὶ πνεύματι, 2:22 πνεύματι, 3:5 πνεύματι, 5:18 πνεύματι, 6:18 πνεύματι

2.5 Anarthrous forms of πνεῦμα *as "[a] holy spirit" occur four times in First and Second Peter*

Genitive – 1 Pet 1:2 ἁγιασμῷ πνεύματος, 2 Pet 1:21 πνεύματος ἁγίου
Dative – 1 Pet 1:12 πνεύματι ἁγίῳ, 4:6 πνεύματι

2.6 Anarthrous forms of πνεῦμα *as "[a] holy spirit" occur twice in Hebrews*

Genitive – Heb 2:4 πνεύματος ἁγίου, 6:4 πνεύματος ἁγίου

2.7 Anarthrous forms of πνεῦμα *as "[a] holy spirit" do not occur in the Johannine Epistles and Revelation*

2.8 Anarthrous forms of πνεῦμα *as "[a] holy spirit" occur twice in Jude*

Dative – Jude 20 πνεύματι ἁγίῳ
Accusative – Jude 19 πνεῦμα

3. Plural forms of πνεῦμα denoting evil spirits occur twenty-one times in the NT

Matt 8:16 τὰ πνεύματα, 10:1 πνευμάτων ἀκαθάρτων, 12:45 ἕτερα πνεύματα πονηρότερα
Mark 1:27 τοῖς πνεύμασι τοῖς ἀκαθάρτοις, 3:11 τὰ πνεύματα τὰ ἀκάθαρτα, 5:13 τὰ πνεύματα τὰ ἀκάθαρτα, 6:7 τῶν πνευμάτων τῶν ἀκαθάρτων
Luke 4:36 τοῖς ἀκαθάρτοις πνεύμασιν, 6:18 πνευμάτων ἀκαθάρτων, 7:21

πνευμάτων πονηρῶν, 8:2 πνευμάτων πονηρῶν, 10:20 τὰ πνεύματα, 11:26 ἕτερα πνεύματα πονηρότερα

Acts of the Apostles 5:16 πνευμάτων ἀκαθάρτων, 8:7 πνεύματα ἀκάθαρτα, 19:12 τά τε πνεύματα τὰ πονηρὰ, 19:13 τὰ πνεύματα τὰ πονηρὰ

1 Tim 4:1 πνεύμασιν πλάνοις

1 John 4:3 πᾶν πνεῦμα . . . ἐκ τοῦ θεοῦ οὐκ ἔστιν

Rev 16:13 πνεύματα τρία ἀκάθαρτα, 16:14 πνεύματα δαιμονίων

4. Plural forms of πνεῦμα denoting good spirits occur twelve times in the NT

1 Cor 14:12 πνευμάτων, 14:32 πνεύματα προφητῶν

Heb 1:7 πνεύματα, 1:14 πνεύματα, 12:9 τῶν πνευμάτων, 12:23 πνεύμασι δικαίων

1 John 4:2 πᾶν πνεῦμα . . . ἐκ τοῦ θεοῦ ἐστιν

Rev 1:4 ἑπτά πνευμάτων, 3:1 ἑπτὰ πνεύματα τοῦ θεοῦ, 4:5 τὰ ἑπτὰ πνεύματα τοῦ θεοῦ, 5:6 τὰ πνεύματα τοῦ θεοῦ, 22:6 τῶν πνευμάτων τῶν προφητῶν

5. Plural forms of πνεῦμα denoting both good and evil spirits occur twice in the NT

1 Cor 12:10 πνευμάτων, 1 John 4:1 τὰ πνεύματα

6. Singular forms of πνεῦμα, anarthrous and unqualified

The singular form of πνεῦμα anarthrous and unqualified by ἅγιος, θεός, πονηρός, and ἀκάθαρτος occurs not only in the prepositional phrase ἐν πνεύματι but also in other phrases and contexts that denote both good and evil spirits in the NT. A good spirit seems to be in view in Acts 19:2; 23:8,9; Luke 24:37 (where Christ's post-resurrection appearance to the disciples is initially believed to be that of πνεῦμα, "a spirit" [some English versions translate, "a ghost."]); Rom 8:15; 1 Cor 15:45 (in reference to Christ as "a life-giving spirit"); 2 Cor 3:6; Gal 5:18; 2 Tim 1:7; and 1 John 4:1,2. An evil spirit seems to be indicated in Acts 16:16; Luke 9:39; 13:11; 2 Cor 11:4; and Rev 18:2.

7. The dative ἐν πνεύματι in reference to "holy spirit" occurs fifty-six times in the NT

Matt 3:11 βαπτίσει ἐν πνεύματι ἁγίῳ, 12:28 ἐν πνεύματι θεοῦ ἐγὼ ἐκβάλλω, 22:43 ἐν πνεύματι καλεῖ

Mark 1:8 βαπτίσει ἐν πνεύματι, 1:23 ἄνθρωπος ἐν πνεύματι, 5:2 ἄνθρωπος ἐν πνεύματι, 12:36 εἶπεν ἐν τῷ πνεύματι τῷ ἁγίῳ

Luke 1:17 προελεύσεται ... ἐν πνεύματι, 2:27 ἦλθεν ἐν τῷ πνεύματι, 3:16 βαπτίσει ἐν πνεύματι ἁγίῳ, 4:1 ἤγετο ἐν τῷ πνεύματι, 10:21 ἠγαλλιάσατο [ἐν] τῷ πνεύματι τῷ ἁγίῳ

John 1:33 βαπτίζων ἐν πνεύματι ἁγίῳ, 4:23 προσκυνήσουσιν τῷ πατρὶ ἐν πνεύματι, 4:24 ἐν πνεύματι ... δεῖ προσκυνεῖν

Acts 1:5 ἐν πνεύματι βαπτισθήσεσθε ἁγίῳ, 11:16 βαπτισθήσεσθε ἐν πνεύματι ἁγίῳ, 15:29 φερόμενοι ἐν τῷ ἁγίῳ πνεύματι, 19:21 ἔθετο ὁ Παῦλος ἐν τῷ πνεύματι

Rom 2:29 περιτομὴ καρδίας ἐν πνεύματι, 8:9 ὑμεῖς ἐστε ... ἐν πνεύματι, 9:1 συμμαρτυρούσης μοι ... ἐν πνεύματι ἁγίῳ, 14:17 χαρὰ ἐν πνεύματι ἁγίῳ, 15:16 ἡγιασμένη ἐν πνεύματι ἁγίῳ

1 Cor 6:11 ἐδικαιώθητε ... ἐν τῷ πνεύματι τοῦ θεοῦ, 12:3 ἐν πνεύματι θεοῦ λαλῶν, 12:3 εἰπεῖν ... ἐν πνεύματι ἁγίῳ, 12:9 πίστις ἐν τῷ αὐτῷ πνεύματι, 12:9 ἐν τῷ ἑνὶ πνεύματι, 12:13 ἐν ἑνὶ πνεύματι ... ἐβαπτίσθημεν, 14:2 πνεύματι δὲ λαλεῖ, 14:15 προσεύξομαι τῷ πνεύματι, 14:15 ψαλῶ τῷ πνεύματι, 14:16 εὐλογῇς [ἐν] πνεύματι

2 Cor 3:3 ἐγγεγραμμένη ... πνεύματι θεοῦ ζῶντος, 6:6 ἐν πνεύματι ἁγίῳ, 12:18 τῷ αὐτῷ πνεύματι περιεπατήσαμεν

Gal 3:3 ἐναρξάμενοι πνεύματι, 5:5 πνεύματι ἐκ πίστεως ... ἀπεκδεχόμεθα, 5:16 πνεύματι περιπατεῖτε, 5:18 πνεύματι ἄγεσθε, 5:25 ζῶμεν πνεύματι

Eph 1:13 ἐσφραγίσθητε τῷ πνεύματι τῆς ἐπαγγελίας τῷ ἁγίῳ, 2:18 ἐν ἑνὶ πνεύματι, 2:22 συνοικοδομεῖσθε ... ἐν πνεύματι, 3:5 ἀπεκαλύφθη ... ἐν πνεύματι, 5:18 πληροῦσθε ἐν πνεύματι, 6:18 προσευχόμενοι ἐν παντὶ καιρῷ ἐν πνεύματι

Phil 1:27 στήκετε ἐν ἑνὶ πνεύματι, 3:3 πνεύματι θεοῦ λατρεύοντες

1 Thess 1:5 ἐν πνεύματι

2 Thess 2:13 ἐν ἁγιασμῷ πνεύματος (genitive!)

1 Tim 3:16 ἐδικαιώθη ἐν πνεύματι

1 Pet 1:2 πρόγνωσιν ... ἐν ἁγιασμῷ πνεύματος (genitive!), 1:12 εὐαγγελισαμένων ... [ἐν] πνεύματι ἁγίῳ

Jude 20 ἐν πνεύματι ἁγίῳ προσευχόμενοι

8. Analysis of Data

According to these data πνεῦμα with the article in reference to "the holy spirit" or its equivalent ("the spirit," "the spirit of God," "the spirit of the Lord") occurs one hundred and seventeen times in the NT. Without the article πνεῦμα occurs as "[a] holy spirit" or its equivalent ("[a] spirit of God," "[a] spirit") eighty-eight times in the NT. The distinction that is commonly made between the articular forms of πνεῦμα for "the Holy Spirit" as divine Person and the anarthrous forms of πνεῦμα for "Holy Spirit" as divine power[2] does not always suit the grammar and context of the NT text. For instance, most of the forms that occur in the nominative case are articular because πνεῦμα is simply the subject of the clause and not necessarily because of the author's intent to refer to "the Holy Spirit" as a divine Person.

Some occurrences of πνεῦμα in the nominative case, however, are anarthrous, indicating "[a] holy spirit" (Luke 1:35), "[a] spirit" (Luke 2:25), "[a] spirit of the Lord" (4:18), and "[a] spirit of God" (Rom 8:9). These nominative anarthrous occurrences reinforce the idea that the articular forms in the nominative case indicate something other than a single divinity or Person, for the anarthrous forms in the nominative case arguably indicate a sentient being, "a certain holy spirit" that implies one of many.

Furthermore, the same verb may govern either the articular or the anarthrous form of πνεῦμα (e.g., for εἶπεν/εἰπεῖν, "to say," see the articular τῷ πνεύματι τῷ ἁγίῳ in Mark 12:36, and the anarthrous πνεύματι ἁγίῳ in 1 Cor 12:3; the anarthrous πνεύματος ἁγίου in Acts 4:8, and the articular τὸ πνεῦμα τὸ ἅγιον in Acts 13:2). Thus, one may speak by "[a] holy spirit" or "the holy spirit." Something other than a distinction between "Person" (articular) and "power" (anarthrous) is meant by this phenomenon in the NT.

Another aspect of the articular forms of πνεῦμα in the NT is the anaphoric use of the Greek article τό.[3] This grammatical usage of the article refers back to a previously mentioned reality (a noun) of the same nature as that reality with which the article is used. In some cases, the anaphoric usage of the article governs instances where πνεῦμα falls in the range of "holy spirit." In Acts 2:4 τὸ πνεῦμα, "the spirit," refers back to the anarthrous πνεύματος ἁγίου, "[a] holy spirit." Acts 8:29 and 10:29 show that τὸ πνεῦμα, "the spirit," refers back to ἄγγελος τοῦ κυρίου, "an angel of the Lord" in 8:26 and 10:3. 1 John 4:6 shows that τὸ πνεῦμα τῆς ἀληθείας, "the spirit of truth," refers back to πᾶν πνεῦμα ἐκ

---

[2] See Swartz, "The Holy Spirit," 136–37; and Francis, "The Holy Spirit," 136–37.
[3] See BDF §252.

τοῦ θεοῦ, "every spirit that is from God" in 4:2. In each of these cases the articular forms of πνεῦμα are anaphoric because they refer back to "a spirit" by which "the spirit" is meant.

In other instances the anaphoric usage of the article governs instances where πνεῦμα falls in the range of "evil spirit." In Acts 16:18 τῷ πνεύματι, "the spirit," refers back to πνεῦμα πύθωνα, "an oracular spirit," or "a spirit of divination" in v. 16. In Acts 19:15,16 τὸ πνεῦμα τὸ πονηρὸν, "the evil spirit," refers back to τὰ πνεύματα τὰ πονηρὰ, "the evil spirits," in v. 13. Likewise, Luke 8:29, 9:42, and 11:24 use the articular τῷ πνεύματι τῷ ἀκαθάρτῳ, "the unclean spirit," to refer back to δαιμόνια, "demons" (8:27), πνεῦμα, "a spirit" (9:39) and δαιμόνιον, "a demon" (9:42), and δαιμόνια, "demons," (11:20).

As for Paul, the data show a surprising number of anarthrous uses of πνεῦμα for "[a] spirit," "[a] holy spirit" and "[a] spirit of God." The number of articular forms of πνεῦμα in Paul comes to thirty-seven while the number of anarthrous forms comes to forty-one. One may also argue for the anaphoric usage of articular forms in Paul. For instance, in 1 Cor 12:4 τὸ αὐτὸ πνεῦμα, "the same spirit," refers back to both πνεύματι θεοῦ, "[a] spirit of God," and πνεύματι ἁγίῳ, "[a] holy spirit," in v. 3. In 1 Cor 14:15 τῷ πνεύματι, "the spirit," refers back to the plural πνευμάτων, "spirits," in v. 12.

In the nominative case πνεῦμα almost always takes the article as the subject of a clause. In Rom 8:9, however, Paul can use πνεῦμα in the nominative case without the article to imply "[a] spirit of God." The significance of this example shows that Paul can express πνεῦμα without the article to mean, arguably, "a spirit" even in the articularly dominated nominative case. This holds true for Luke 1:35, 2:25, and 4:18.

Fee has made an analysis of πνεῦμα in Paul in order to attempt to settle the issue of whether Paul knew of "a holy spirit" or only knew of "the Holy Spirit." In the analysis Fee concludes that Paul's use of anarthrous forms of πνεῦμα are purely stylistic and have nothing to do with Paul's indication of "a spirit." Fee argues that the anarthrous usage of πνεῦμα should mean the articular "*the* Holy Spirit" or "*the* Spirit of God" in context. For instance, he believes that anarthrous forms of πνεῦμα are influenced by their articular forms that surround the anarthrous. Thus, the anarthrous can mean none other than "*the* Holy Spirit." In Rom 8:9 the anarthrous πνεῦμα θεοῦ is surrounded by six articular uses of πνεῦμα. This context "makes it certain that this [the anarthrous form] can refer only to the Holy Spirit as the Spirit of God."[4]

---

[4] Fee, *God's Empowering Presence*, 17.

Since many of the anarthrous uses of πνεῦμα are surrounded by articular uses in First Corinthians 12–14, Galatians 5, and Romans 8, Fee concludes that the anarthrous prepositional phrase ἐν πνεύματι (which he calls formulaic) is controlled by the articular uses: "Since in each case they [anarthrous uses] are surrounded by other references to the Spirit, mostly articular, it is simply not possible that Paul in these contexts means other than the Holy Spirit when using this formula as well."[5]

Fee provides two illustrations that attempt to further his argument for the improbability of the anarthrous uses to indicate "a holy spirit": (1) if Paul means "a spirit" by πνεῦμα, then the anarthrous use of θεός in the phrase πνεῦμα θεοῦ might as well mean "a spirit of *a god*" also;[6] and (2) Paul's use of the anarthrous formulaic phrases ἐν πνεύματι and ἐν σαρκί side by side, where the latter always means "in/by *the* flesh," shows that by ἐν πνεύματι Paul can only mean "in/by *the* Spirit."[7]

As to the first argument, Fee's point attempts to show that just as θεός without the article would not have been understood by Christians to mean "a certain god," so too πνεῦμα without the article (in the context of "holy spirit") would not have been understood by Christians to mean "a spirit." It is true that Jews as well as Christians would not have understood θεός in an anarthrous construction with πνεῦμα to mean "a certain god" other than the one true God. BDF notes that the article appears with θεός and κύριος "when the specific Jewish or Christian God or Lord is meant (not 'a divine being' or 'a Lord'), but it is sometimes missing especially after prepositions."[8] Hence the one and only true God can be represented in prepositional phrases, such as ἐν πνεύματι θεοῦ, without the article. But this does not mean that πνεῦμα ἅγιον and its equivalent, πνεῦμα θεοῦ, without the article cannot be understood as "a holy spirit" as BDF notes, "τὸ ἅγιον πνεῦμα ... sometimes without article as a divine spirit."[9]

As to the second argument, Fee compares two realities, σάρξ and πνεῦμα, that are contrasted in Paul. Fee notes that in the nominative and accusative these words are almost always articular whereas in the dative they are almost always anarthrous. A kind of stereotypical usage is posited by Fee for the datives πνεύματι/ἐν πνεύματι and σαρκί/ἐν σαρκί wherein the grammatically anarthrous, yet articularly translated ἐν σαρκί controls the translation of ἐν πνεύματι.

---

[5] Ibid., 23.
[6] Ibid., 19.
[7] Ibid., 24.
[8] BDF §254.
[9] Ibid., §257.

His comparison of these anarthrous prepositional phrases is meant to show that just as ἐν σαρκί cannot mean "in a flesh" but rather means "in the flesh," so too ἐν πνεύματι cannot mean "in a spirit" but rather means "in the Spirit."[10] Admittedly, in some cases the noun of a prepositional phrase does not have to be articular in order to convey an articular sense. In both the disputed and undisputed letters of Paul, Fee notes thirty-seven occurrences of πνεύματι and ἐν πνεύματι, thirty-two of which are anarthrous and five of which are articular. Fee explains that the abundant use of the anarthrous in the dative is simply a conventional or stereotypical anarthrous usage, nothing more.

A grammatical comparison of ἐν σαρκί and ἐν πνεύματι, however, yields a skewed perspective on the matter. Despite the anarthrous use of σάρξ, the only possible translation of ἐν σαρκί into English is an articular translation, "in the flesh," for "in a flesh" makes little sense. This, however, is not true for the translation of ἐν πνεύματι as "in a spirit." The translation of ἐν πνεύματι as "in a spirit" is far more possible and realistic than the translation of ἐν σαρκί as "in a flesh." For instance, in Mark 1:23 and 5:2 ἐν πνεύματι is to be translated as "with a spirit" and not "with the spirit." Admittedly, the context in Mark 5:2 is that of πνεύματι ἀκαθάρτῳ, "an unclean spirit," and not "the Holy Spirit." Some may argue that comparisons of this nature, i.e., "unclean spirit" with "holy spirit," cannot be made lest theological boundaries are ignored and broken: "the Holy Spirit" is no ordinary spirit and cannot be compared to other spirits (especially "unclean" ones), thus ἐν πνεύματι in reference to "holy spirit" can only mean "in the Holy Spirit." Such discrimination is based more on a theological critique than it is on grammar and philology as Zerwick has observed:

Some may perhaps be apprehensive lest we reduce to banality certain Pauline formulae which are dear to us and full of boundless depths of meaning, by putting ἐν Χριστῷ, ἐν πνεύματι and the like in the same class, philologically, with ἐν πνεύματι ἀκαθάρτῳ, ... Such apprehension is unfounded.[11]

Furthermore, the prepositional phrase ἐν πνεύματι occurs in the *Didache* in the contexts of both true and false prophecy. A true prophet or a false prophet may speak ἐν πνεύματι (see *Did.* 11:7,8,9,12). Nothing in the pertinent texts suggests that for the true prophet ἐν πνεύματι should translate "in the Spirit" and for the false prophet ἐν πνεύματι should translate "in a spirit," indicating

---

[10] Fee, *God's Empowering Presence*, 24.
[11] Zerwick, *Biblical Greek*, §118.

a spirit other than "the Spirit" or "the Holy Spirit." This kind of evidence shows that no clear discrimination exists for distinguishing ἐν πνεύματι as either "in a spirit" or "in the Spirit" on mere grounds of grammar and context. Furthermore, fourth-century patristic pneumatology might not be the most appropriate position from which to delineate πνεῦμα in relation to the true prophet and the false prophet during the first and second centuries.

Technically speaking, the prepositional phrase ἐν πνεύματι is anarthrous. The only translation that reflects this adequately is "in [a] spirit"; the translation "in *the* spirit" would reflect ἐν τῷ πνεύματι. Both of these translations for πνεῦμα make good sense, not only grammatically but also contextually. The use of ἐν σαρκί, as a different circumstance altogether, seems to have no effect on how one translates ἐν πνεύματι. Hence, aside from theological considerations that may or may not be historically relevant for Paul, ἐν πνεύματι in Paul may arguable by translated as "in a spirit."

Despite Fee's thorough analysis of πνεῦμα in Paul, his concluding remarks on the matter of "a holy spirit" or "the Holy Spirit" reveal the theological motivations that tend to govern his overall approach to the matter:

The evidence confirms that Paul knows no such thing as 'a spirit' or 'a holy spirit' when using πνεῦμα to refer to divine activity. He only and always means the Spirit of the living God, the Holy Spirit himself. All of this is further corroborated by a passage like 2 Cor 13:13[14], where the Holy Spirit appears in triadic formula alongside, and distinct from, Christ and the Father. If one begins with such a text as thoroughly presuppositional to Paul's understanding, as one should, and then notes how often this triadic formula is presupposed in the many soteriological texts that mention the separate activities of the triune God, it is a cause for wonder that another view of Paul's usage took root at all.[12]

9. Conclusion

The above statistical analysis encompasses πνεῦμα as "holy spirit" and its equivalence in the NT. If the range were isolated to include only the undisputed Pauline letters the variety that is found in the rest of the NT appears also in Paul: πνεῦμα, "[a] spirit"; τὸ πνεῦμα, "the spirit"; πνεῦμα ἅγιον, "[a] holy spirit"; τὸ πνεῦμα τὸ ἅγιον, "the holy spirit"; πνεῦμα θεοῦ, "[a] spirit of God"; τὸ πνεῦμα τοῦ θεοῦ, "the spirit of God"; πνεύματα, "spirits"; and in the prepositional phrases ἐν πνεύματι ἁγίῳ, "in [a] holy spirit"; ἐν πνεύματι θεοῦ, "in [a] spirit

---

[12] Fee, *God's Empowering Presence*, 24.

of God"; ἐν τῷ αὐτῷ πνεύματι, "in the same spirit"; and ἐν τῷ πνεύματι τοῦ θεοῦ, "in the spirit of God."

Fee is interested in finding patterns in the syntax of the articular and anarthrous occurrences of πνεῦμα in Paul. According to Fee, these patterns suggest theological signposts for Paul's reference to "the Holy Spirit," i.e., the articular references "influence" the anarthrous references to mean "the Holy Spirit." Such so-called patterns, however, simply reflect the usage of Greek grammar and syntax, nothing more. One cannot cogently argue that patterns in syntax and grammar signify the theological nuances that Fee posits; theology cannot be derived from grammar.

The conclusion that Paul never knew of "a holy spirit" (as Fee) is no more true than is the saying Paul never knew of "the holy spirit." Grammatically, both the anarthrous πνεῦμα ἅγιον and the articular τὸ πνεῦμα τὸ ἅγιον exist in Paul. Many English versions of the NT make no distinction between the anarthrous and articular forms; these versions are governed by Christian theological pneumatology wherein "holy spirit" in the NT is "the Holy Spirit." Such a scenario obscures the discrete distinction in the Greek texts by following a path that leads away from Paul and toward an Athanasian orthodoxy that evolved centuries later. A historical/grammatical criticism of πνεῦμα and πνεύματα in First Corinthians 12 and 14 reveals "a holy spirit," "a spirit of God," "the spirit," and "spirits." These terms designated the spirit world of God from which were derived holy spirits, among whom was "a holy spirit" or "a spirit of God."

Bibliography

1. Commentaries on First Corinthians

Barrett, C. K., *The First Epistle to the Corinthians*. HNTC. New York: Harper & Row, 1968.

Bittlinger, Arnold, *Gifts and Graces: A Commentary on 1 Corinthians 12–14*. Grand Rapids: Eerdmans, 1968.

Blomberg, Craig L., *1 Corinthians*. Grand Rapids: Zondervan, 1994.

Bruce, Frederick F., *1 and 2 Corinthians*. New Century Bible. London: Oliphants, 1971.

Collins, Raymond F., *First Corinthians*. SacPag 7. Collegeville, MN: Liturgical Press, 1999.

Conzelmann, Hans, *1 Corinthians: A Commentary on the First Epistle to the Corinthians*. Hermeneia. Philadelphia: Fortress, 1975.

De Boor, Werner, *Der erste Brief an die Korinther*. Wuppertaler Studienbibel. Leipzig: R. Brockhaus, 1968.

Ellingworth, Paul, and Howard A. Hatton, *A Handbook On Paul's First Letter to the Corinthians*. United Bible Societies Handbook Series. 2nd edition. New York: United Bible Societies, 1994.

Fee, Gordon D., *The First Epistle to the Corinthians*. NICNT. Grand Rapids: Eerdmans, 1987.

Garland, David E., *1 Corinthians*. Baker Exegetical Commentary on the New Testament. Grand Rapids: Baker Academic, 2003.

Harrisville, Roy A., *1 Corinthians*. ACNT. Minneapolis: Augsburg, 1987.

Hays, Richard B., *First Corinthians*. IBC. Louisville: John Knox, 1997.

Héring, Jean, *The First Epistle of Saint Paul to the Corinthians*. London: Epworth, 1962.

Johnson, Alan F., *1 Corinthians*. Inter-Varsity Press New Testament Commentary Series. Downers Grove, IL: Inter-Varsity Press, 2004.

Keener, Craig S., *1–2 Corinthians*. New Cambridge Bible Commentary. Cambridge: Cambridge University Press, 2005.

Kistemaker, Simon J., *Exposition of the First Epistle to the Corinthians*. Grand Rapids: Eerdmans, 1993.

Lindemann, Andreas, *Der Erste Korintherbrief*. HNT 9/1. Tübingen: J. C. B. Mohr, 2000.

MacRory, Joseph, *The Epistles of St. Paul to the Corinthians: With Introductions and Commentary*. St. Louis, MO: B. Herder, 1915.

Moffatt, James, *The First Epistle of Paul to the Corinthians*. New York: Harper and Brothers, 1938.

Morris, Leon, *The First Epistle of Paul to the Corinthians: An Introduction and Commentary*. TynNTC. Grand Rapids: Eerdmans. 1985.

Orr, William F., and James A. Walther, *1 Corinthians: A New Translation*. AB 32. Garden City, NY: Doubleday, 1976.

Oster, Richard E., *1 Corinthians*. College Press NIV Commentary. Joplin, MO: College Press, 1995.

Parry, Reginald St John, *The First Epistle of Paul the Apostle to the Corinthians*. Cambridge Greek Testament Commentaries. Cambridge: Cambridge University Press, 1926.

Robertson, Archibald, and Alfred Plummer, *A Critical and Exegetical Commentary on the First Epistle of St Paul to the Corinthians*. ICC. Edinburgh: T & T Clark, 1911.

Schrage, Wolfgang, *Der erste Brief an die Korinther*. EKKNT 7/1–4. Zurich: Benziner/Neukirchen-Vluyn: Neukirchener, 1991–2001.

Soards, Marion L., *1 Corinthians*. NIBC. Peabody, MA: Hendrickson, 1999.

Thiselton, Anthony C.,   *The First Epistle to the Corinthians*. NIGTC. Grand Rapids: Eerdmans, 2000.

Talbert, Charles H.,   *Reading Corinthians: A Literary-Theological Commentary on 1 and 2 Corinthians*. New York: Crossroad, 1992.

Weiss, Johannes, *Der Erste Korintherbrief.* KKNT. Göttingen: Vandenhoeck & Ruprecht, 1910.

Witherington, Ben, III, *Conflict and Community in Corinth: A Socio-Rhetorical Commentary on 1 and 2 Corinthians*. Grand Rapids: Eerdmans, 1995.

Wolff, Christian,   *Der erste Brief des Paulus an die Korinther*. THKNT 7.   Berlin: Evangelische Verlagsanstalt, 1996.

2. Primary Literature

Ante-Nicene Fathers: The Writings of the Fathers Down to A.D. 325. Edited by Alexander Roberts, et al. 10 vols. Peabody, MA: Hendrickson, 1994.

Charlesworth, James H., ed., *The Old Testament Pseudepigrapha*. 2 vols. Garden City, NY: Doubleday, 1983, 1985.

Clarke, Emma C., et al., *Iamblichus on the Mysteries: Translated with Introductions and Notes*. SBL Writings from the Greek World 4. Atlanta, GA: Society of Biblical Literature, 2003.

Eusebius, Text and Translation. 2 vols. LCL. Cambridge: Harvard University Press, 1926.

Holmes, Michael W., ed., *The Apostolic Fathers: Greek Texts and English Translations*. Revised edition. Grand Rapids, MI: 2005.

Jonge, Marinus de, *Testaments of the Twelve Patriarchs: A Critical Edition of the Greek Text*. Leiden: Brill, 1978.

Josephus, Text and Translation. 10 vols. LCL. Cambridge: Harvard University Press, 1926–1965.

Martínez, Florentino G. and Eibert J. C. Tigchelaar, ed., *The Dead Sea Scrolls Study Edition*. 2 vols. Leiden: Brill, 1997.

Nicene and Post-Nicene Fathers. Edited by Philip Schaff and Henry Wace. Second Series. 14 vols. Peabody, MA: Hendrickson, 1994.

Pearson, Alfred C., *Fragments of Sophocles*. 3 vols. Cambridge: Cambridge University Press, 1917.

Philo, Complete Works. 10 vols. and 2 supplementary vols. LCL. London: William Heinemann, 1929–1935.

Plutarch, Moralia. 15 vols. LCL. New York: Putnam, 1927–1928.

Pseudo-Philon, Les Antiquités bibliques. 1: Introduction et texte critique, edited by Daniel Harrington, et al. SC 229. Paris: du Cerf, 1976.

Richardson, Cyril C., ed., *Early Church Fathers*. New York: Macmillan, 1970.

Shapland, C. R. B., *The Letters of Saint Athanasius Concerning the Holy Spirit*. London: Epworth, 1951.

3. Secondary Literature

Alexander, Brooks, "Theology from the Twilight Zone: Spirit Channeling is the Latest Fad in Upscale New Age Spiritism." *Christianity Today* 31 (1987) 22–26.

Alexander, Philip S., "The Demonology of the Dead Sea Scrolls." In *The Dead Sea Scrolls After Fifty Years: A Comprehensive Assessment*, edited by James C. VanderKam and Peter W. Flint, 2. 331–53. 2 vols. Leiden: Brill, 1999.

Alfeyev, Hegumen Hilarion, "The Trinitarian Teaching of St. Gregory Nazianzen." In *The Trinity: East/West Dialogue*, edited by Melville Y. Stewart, 107–30. Studies in Philosophy and Religion 24. Boston: Kluwer Academic Publishers, 2003.

Alston, William P., *Perceiving God: The Epistemology of Religious Experience*. Ithaca, NY: Cornell University Press, 1991.

Angeles, Peter A., ed., "Spiritualism." In *The Dictionary of Christian Theology*, 190. San Francisco: Harper & Row, 1985.

__, "Spiritism." In *The Dictionary of Christian Theology*, 191. San Francisco: Harper & Row, 1985.

Ankerberg, John and John Weldon, *The Facts on Spirit Guides: How to Avoid the Seduction of the Spirit World and Demonic Powers*. Eugene, OR: Harvest Press, 1988.

Anonymous, *An Inquiry into the Teaching of Holy Scripture concerning Communication Between Man and Spirits*. St. Louis: Chas. B. Cox, ca. [1890].

Arnold, Bill T., "Necromancy and Cleromancy in 1 and 2 Samuel." *CBQ* 66 (2004) 199–213.

Arnold, Clinton E., "The 'Exorcism' of Ephesians 6.12 in Recent Research: A Critique of Wesley Carr's View of the Role of Evil Powers in First-Century AD Belief." *JSNT* 30 (1987) 71–87.

__, "Returning to the Domain of the Powers: Stoicheia as Evil Spirits in Gal 4:3, 9." *NovT* 38 (1996) 55–76.

__, *Powers of Darkness: Principalities and Powers in Paul's Letters*. Downers Grove, IL: Inter-Varsity Press, 1992.

Ashton, John, *The Religion of Paul the Apostle*. New Haven: Yale University Press, 2000.

Aune, David E., *Prophecy in Early Christianity and the Ancient Mediterranean World*. Grand Rapids: Eerdmans, 1983.

__, "Medium." *ISBE* 3. 306–7.

__, "Demon; Demonology." *ISBE* 1. 922.

Baker, David L., "The Interpretation of 1 Corinthians 12–14." *EvQ* 46 (1974) 224–34.

Balla, Peter, *Challenges to New Testament Theology: An Attempt to Justify the Enterprise*. Peabody, MA: Hendrickson, 1998.

Barstad, Hans, "No Prophets? Recent Developments in Biblical Prophetic Research and Ancient Near Eastern Prophecy." *JSOT* 57 (1993) 39–60.

Bartelink, Gerard, "The 'active' demons: energein and energumenus in Early Christian Literature." *Instrumenta patristica* 28 (1996) 177–80.

Bassler, Jouette M., "1 Cor 12:3–Curse and Confession in Context." *JBL* 101 (1982) 415–18.

Batson, C. Daniel, and W. Larry Venti, *The Religious Experience: A Social-Psychological Perspective*. Oxford: Oxford University Press, 1982.

Beare, Francis W., "Speaking with Tongues: A Critical Survey of the New Testament Evidence." *JBL* 83 (1964) 229–46.

Beavin, Edward L., "Ruah Hakodesh in Some Early Jewish Literature." Ph.D. diss., Vanderbilt University, 1961.

Behm, Johannes, "γλῶσσα." *TDNT* 1. 719–26.

Benoit, Pierre, "Pauline Angelology and Demonology: Reflexions on the Designations of the Heavenly Powers and in the Origins of Angelic Evil According to Paul." *Religious Studies Bulletin* 3 (1983) 1–18.

Berends, Willem, "The Biblical Criteria for Demon-Possession." *WTJ* 37 (1975) 347–65.

Berkhof, Hendrikus, *Christ and the Powers*. Scottdale, PA: Herald, 1977.

Best, Ernest, "The Interpretation of Tongues." *SJT* 28 (1975) 45–62.

Bevan, Edwyn, "Spirit." In *Symbolism and Belief*, idem, 150–90. Port Washington, NY: Kennikat Press, 1968. Reprint of 1938 edition.

Bidmead, Julia, "Medium, Wizard." In *Eerdmans Dictionary of the Bible*, edited by David Noel Freedman, et al., 878. Grand Rapids: Eerdmans, 2000.

Binyon, Pamela M., *The Concept of 'Spirit' and 'Demon': A Study in the Use of Different Language Describing the Same Phenomena*. Studies in the Intercultural History of Christianity 8. Frankfurt: Peter Lang, 1977.

Bonnel, John S., "The Resurgence of Spiritism." *Christianity Today* 12 (1968) 7–10.

Boring, M. Eugene, "'What are we Looking For?' Toward a Definition of the Term 'Christian Prophet.'" *SBLSP* 1973, 142–55.

___, *The Continuing Voice of Jesus: Christian Prophecy and the Gospel*. Louisville: Westminster/John Knox, 1991.

Bourguignon, Erika, *Religion, Altered States of Consciousness, and Social Change*. Columbus: Ohio State University Press, 1973.

___, *Possession*. San Francisco: Chandler & Sharp, 1976. Reprinted Prospect Heights, IL: Waveland Press, 1991.

Bretherton, Donald I., "Theology and Psychical Studies." In *Life, Death & Psychical Research: Studies on behalf of the Churches' Fellowship for Psychical and Spiritual Studies*, edited by J. D. Pearce-Higgins and G. Stanley Whitby, 241–57. London: Rider, 1973.

Brox, Norbert, "'Ἀνάθεμα Ἰησοῦς (1 Kor. 12.3)." *BZ* 12 (1968) 103–11.

Brueggemann, Walter, *Deuteronomy*. Abingdon Old Testament Commentary. Nashville: Abingdon, 2001.

Bruner, Frederick D., *A Theology of the Holy Spirit: The Pentecost Experience and the New Testament Witness*. Grand Rapids: Eerdmans, 1970.

Bullinger, Ethelbert W., *Word Studies on the Holy Spirit*. London: Eyre & Spottiswoode, 1905. Reprinted Grand Rapids: Kregel, 1979.

Burghardt, Walter J., "Primitive Montanism: Why Condemned?" In *From Faith to Faith: Essays in Honor of D. G. Miller on his 70th Birthday*, edited by D. Y. Hadidian, 339–56. PTMS 31 Allison Park, PA: Pickwick, 1979.

Burns, Barclay John, "Necromancy and the Spirits of the Dead in the Old Testament." *Transactions of the Glasgow University Oriental Society* 26 (1978) 1–15.

Burrows, Millar, *More Light on the Dead Sea Scrolls*. New York: Vicking Press, 1958.

Buschel, Friedrich, "εἴδωλον." *TDNT* 2. 378.

Butterworth, George W., *Spiritualism and Religion*. London: Society for Promoting Christian Knowledge, 1944.

Callan, Terrance, "Prophecy and Ecstasy in Greco-Roman Religion and in 1 Corinthians." *NovT* 27 (1985) 125–40.

Caciola, Nancy, *Discerning Spirits: Divine and Demonic Possession in the Middle Ages*. Ithaca, New York: Cornell University Press, 2003.

Caird, George B., *Principalities and Powers: A Study in Pauline Theology*. Oxford: Clarendon Press, 1956.

Cantwell, Laurence, *The Theology of the Trinity*. Theology Today 4. Notre Dame: Fides, 1969.

Carr, Wesley, *Angels and Principalities: The Background, Meaning, and Development of the Pauline Phrase hai archai kai hai exousiai*. Cambridge: Cambridge University Press, 1981.

Carson, Donald A., *Showing the Spirit: A Theological Exposition of 1 Corinthians 12–14*. Grand Rapids: Baker, 1987.

Cartledge, Mark J., *Charismatic Glossolalia: An Empirical-Theological Study*. Burlington, VT: Ashgate, 2002.

Charles, Robert H., *The Ascension of Isaiah*. London: Adam and Charles Black, 1900.

Ciraolo, Leda Jean, "Supernatural Assistants in the Greek Magical Papyri." In *Ancient Magic and Ritual Power*, edited by Marvin Meyer and Paul Mirecki, 279–93. Leiden: Brill, 1995.

Clark, Gordon, "Possession." In *Dictionary of the Apostolic Church*, edited by James Hastings, 340–45. New York: C. Scribner's, 1916–1918.

Cohn, Leopold, "An Apocryphal Work Ascribed to Philo of Alexandria." *JQR* 10 (1898) 277–332.

Conybeare, Frederick C., "The Demonology of the New Testament." *JQR* 8 (1896) 576–608.

Cooey, Paula M., "Fiddling While Rome Burns: The Place of Academic Theology in the Study of Religion." *HTR* 93 (2000) 35–49.

Cooke, Bernard, *Power and the Spirit of God: Toward an Experience-Based Pneumatology*. Oxford: Oxford University Press, 2004.

Cortés, Juan B. and Florence M. Gatti, *The Case Against Possessions and Exorcisms: A Historical, Biblical, and Psychological Analysis of Demons, Devils, and Demoniacs*. New York: Vantage Press, 1975.

Cox, James L., "Spirit Mediums in Zimbabwe: Religious Experience in and on Behalf of the Community." *Studies in World Christianity* 6 (2000) 190–207.

Crabtree, Adam, *Multiple Man: Explorations in Possession and Multiple Personality*. Toronto: Collins, 1985.

Craghan, John F., "Mari and Its Prophets: The Contributions of Mari to the Understanding of Biblical Prophecy." *BTB* 5 (1975) 32–55.

Craigie, Peter C., *The Book of Deuteronomy*. NICOT. Grand Rapids: Eerdmans, 1976.

Crone, Theodore M., *Early Christian Prophecy: A Study of Its Origins and Functions*. Baltimore: St. Mary's University, 1973.

Currie, Stuart D., "'Speaking in Tongues': Early Evidence outside of the New Testament Bearing on 'Glossais Lalein.'" *Int* 19 (1965) 274–94.

Daiches, Samuel, "Isaiah and Spiritualism." *Jewish Chronicle Supplement* (July 1921) 6.

Dautzenberg, Gerhard, "Zum religionsgeschichtlichen Hintergrund der διάκρισις πνευμάτων (1 Kor 12,10)." *BZ* 15 (1971) 93–104.

Davies, Stevan L., *Jesus the Healer: Possession, Trance, and the Origins of Christianity*. New York: Continuum, 1995.

Davies, T. Witton, *Magic, Divination, and Demonology Among the Hebrew and their Neighbors*. London: J. Clarke, 1898. Reprinted New York: KTAV, 1969.

Davis, Caroline Franks, *The Evidential Force of Religious Experience*. Oxford: Clarendon Press, 1989.

Davis, James A., *Wisdom and Spirit: An Investigation of 1 Corinthians 1:18–3:20 against the Background of Jewish Sapiential Traditions in the Greco-Roman Period*. New York: University Press of America, 1984.

De Lacey, Douglas R., "'One Lord' in Pauline Christology." In *Christ the Lord: Studies in Christology presented to Donald Guthrie*, edited by Harold H. Rowdon, 191–203. Leicester, England: Inter-Varsity, 1982.

De Witte Burton, Ernest, *Spirit, Soul, and Flesh: The Usage of* πνεῦμα, ψυχή, *and* σάρξ *in Greek Writings and Translated Works from the Earliest Period to 180 A.D.; and of their Equivalents* רוח, נפש, *and* בשׂר *in the Hebrew Old Testament*. Chicago: University of Chicago Press, 1918.

Derrett, J. Duncan M., "Cursing Jesus (1 Cor. XII.3): The Jews as Religious 'Persecutors.'" *NTS* 21 (1974–1975) 544–54.

Dibelius, Martin, *Die Geisterwelt im Glauben des Paulus*. Göttingen: Vandenhoeck & Ruprecht, 1909.

Di Lella, Alexander A. and Louis F. Hartman, *The Book of Daniel*. AB 23. New York: Doubleday, 1977.

Dodds, Eric R., *The Greeks and the Irrational*. Berkeley: University of California Press, 1951.

___, *Pagan and Christian in an Age of Anxiety: Some Aspects of Religious Experience from Marcus Aurelius to Constantine*. Cambridge: Cambridge University Press, 1965.

___, *The Ancient Concept of Progress and Other Essays on Greek Literature and Belief*. Oxford: Clarendon Press, 1973.

Donnelly, Doris, ed., *Retrieving the Charisms for the Twenty-First Century*. Collegeville, MN: Liturgical Press, 1999.

Driver, Samuel R., *Deuteronomy*. ICC. Edinburgh: T & T Clark, 1895. Reprinted 1986.

Duhm, Hans, *Der Verkehr Gottes mit den Menschen im Alten Testament*. Tübingen: J.C.B. Mohr, 1926.

Dunn, James D. G., *Baptism in the Holy Spirit: A Re-examination of the New Testament Teaching on the Gift of the Spirit in Relation to Pentecostalism Today*. SBT 2/5. Naperville: Allenson, 1970.

___, *Jesus and the Spirit: A Study of the Religious and Charismatic Experience of Jesus and the First Christians as Reflected in the New Testament*. London: SCM; Philadelphia: Westminster, 1975. Reprinted Grand Rapids: Eerdmans, 1997.

___, *The Christ and the Spirit, 2: Pneumatology*. Grand Rapids: Eerdmans, 1998.

Easley, Kendell H., "The Pauline Use of *Pneumati* as a Reference to the Spirit of God." *JETS* 27 (1984) 299–313.

Eitrem, Samson, *Some Notes on the Demonology in the New Testament*. 2nd ed. Oslo: Universitesforlaget, 1966.

Ekem, John D., "'Spiritual Gifts' or 'Spiritual Persons'? 1 Corinthians 12:1A Revisited." *Neot* 38 (2004) 54–74.

Ellis, E. Earle, "'Spiritual Gifts' in the Pauline Community." *NTS* 20 (1973–1974) 128–44.

___, *Prophecy and Hermeneutic in Early Christianity*. Grand Rapids: Eerdmans, 1978.

Engelsen, Nils I. J., "Glossolalia and Other Forms of Inspired Speech according to 1 Corinthians 12–14." Ph.D. diss., Yale University, 1970.

Erwood, William J., *Spiritualism and the Catholic Church*. Philadelphia: W. J. Erwood, 1917.

Esler, Philip F., "Glossolalia and the Admission of Gentiles in the Early Christian Community." *BTB* 22 (1992) 136–42.

Evans, Gillian R., *Old Arts and New Theology: The Beginnings of Theology as an Academic Discipline*. Oxford: Clarendon, 1980.

Everling, Otto, *Die paulinische Angelologie und Dämonologie: Ein biblisch-theologischer Versuch*. Göttingen: Vandenhoeck & Ruprecht, 1888.

Farley, Edward, "The Place of Theology in the Study of Religion." *Religious Studies and Theology* 5 (1985) 9–29.

Fascher, Erich, *Prophetes: Eine sprach- und religionsgeschichtliche Untersuchung*. Gießen: A. Töplemann, 1927.

Fatehi, Mehrdad, *The Spirit's Relation to the Risen Lord in Paul: An Examination of Its Christological Implications*. WUNT 2/128. Tübingen: Mohr Siebeck, 2000.

Fee, Gordon D., *God's Empowering Presence: The Holy Spirit in the Letters of Paul*. Peabody, MA: Hendrickson, 1994.

__, "Translation Tendenz: English Versions and Πνεῦμα in Paul." In *The Holy Spirit and Christian Origins: Essays in Honor of James D. G. Dunn*, edited by Graham M. Stanton, et al., 349–59. Grand Rapids: Eerdmans, 2004.

Feil, Ernst, "From the Classical Religio to the Modern Religion: Elements of a Transformation between 1550 and 1650." In *Religion in History: the Word, the Idea, the Reality*, edited by Michel Despland and Gerard Vallee, 31–43. Waterloo, Ontario: Wilfred Laurier University Press, 1992.

Feldman, Louis H., *The Biblical Antiquities of Philo*. New York: KTAV, 1971.

__, *Studies in Josephus' Rewritten Bible*. Leiden: Brill, 1998.

Figart, Thomas O., "Saul, the Spiritist, and Samuel." *Grace Theological Journal* 11 (1970) 13–29.

Finkel, Irving L., "Necromancy in Ancient Mesopotamia." *AfO* 29 (1983) 1–17.

Fitzmyer, Joseph A., "The Semitic Background of the New Testament *kyrios*-Title." In *A Wandering Aramean: Collected Aramaic Essays*, edited by Leander E. Keck, 115–32. SBLMS 25. Missoula, MT: Scholar's Press, 1979.

__, *Romans*. AB 33. New York: Doubleday, 1993.

__, "The Role of the Spirit in Luke-Acts." In *The Unity of Luke-Acts*, edited by J. Verheyden, 165–83. Leuven: Leuven University Press, 1999.

Foerster, Werner, "Der Heilige Geist im Spätjudentum." *NTS* 8 (1962) 117–34.

Foester, Friedrich W., "πύθων." *TDNT* 6. 918–19.

Fontenrose, Joseph, *The Delphic Oracle*. Berkeley: University of California, 1978.

Forbes, Christopher, "Early Christian Inspired Speech and Hellenistic Popular Religion." *NovT* 28 (1986) 257–70.

__, *Prophecy and Inspired Speech in Early Christianity and Its Hellenistic Environment*. Tübingen: Mohr, 1995. Reprinted Peabody, MA: Hendrickson, 1997.

__, "Paul's Principalities and Powers: Demythologizing Apocalyptic?" *JSNT* 82 (2001) 61–88.

Ford, J. Massyngberde, "Towards a Theology of Speaking in Tongues." *TS* 32 (1971) 3–29.

Fowler, W. Warde, *The Religious Experience of the Roman People: From the Earliest Times to the Age of Augustine*. London: Macmillan, 1922.

François, Gilbert, *Le polythéisme et l'emploi au singulier des mots THEOS, DAIMON dans la littérature grecque d'Homer à Platon*. Paris: Société d'édition 'Les Belles Lettres,' 1957.

Garrett, Clarke, *Spirit Possession and Popular Religion: From the Camisards to the Shakers*. Baltimore: Johns Hopkins University Press, 1987.

Geller, Stephen A., "The God of the Covenant." In *One God or Many? Concepts of Divinity in the Ancient World*, edited by Barbara Nevling Porter, 273–319. Transactions of Casco Bay Assyriological Institute 1. Chebeague Island, ME: Casco Bay Assyriological Institute, 1997.

Gillespie, Thomas W., *The First Theologians: A Study in Early Christian Prophecy*. Grand Rapids: Eerdmans, 1994.

Godin, André, *The Psychological Dynamics of Religious Experience*. Birmingham, AL: Religious Education Press, 1985. Translation Mary Turton of *Psychologie des expériences religieuses: La désir et la réalité*. Paris: Le Centurion, 1981.

Goodman, Felicitas, *Speaking in Tongues: A Cross-Cultural Study of Glossolalia*. Chicago: University of Chicago Press, 1972.

__, *How about Demons? Possession and Exorcism in the Modern World*. Bloomington: Indiana University Press, 1988.

Griffith, Terry, *Keep Yourselves from Idols: A New Look at 1 John*. Sheffield: Sheffield Academic Press, 2002.

Grudem, Wayne A., "1 Cor 14:20–25: Prophecy and Tongues as Signs of God's Attitude." *WTJ* 41 (1979) 381–96.

__, "A Response to Gerhard Dautzenberg on 1 Cor. 12.10." *BZ* 22 (1978) 253–70.

__, *The Gift of Prophecy in 1 Corinthians*. Lanham, MD: University Press of America, 1982. Reprinted Eugene, OR: Wipf & Stock, 1999.

Guillaume, Alfred, *Prophecy and Divination among the Hebrews and Other Semites*. London: Hodder and Stoughton, 1938.

Gundry, Robert H., "'Ecstatic Utterance' (NEB)?" *JTS* 17 (1966) 299–307.

Gunkel, Hermann, *The Influence of the Holy Spirit: The Popular View of the Apostolic Age and the Teaching of the Apostle Paul*. Philadelphia: Fortress, 1979. Translation Roy A. Harrisville and Philip A Quanbeck II of *Die Wirkungen des heiligen Geistes nach der populären Anschauung der apostolischen Zeit und nach der Lehre des Apostels Paulus*. Göttingen: Vandenhoeck & Ruprecht, 1888.

Haldar, Alfred, *Associations of Cult Prophets among the Ancient Semites*. Uppsala: Almqwist & Wiksells, 1945.

Hall, Trevor C., *The Medium and the Scientist*. Buffalo: Prometheus, 1984.

Haran, Menahem, "From Early to Classical Prophecy: Continuity and Change." *VT* 27 (1977) 385–97.

Harnack, Adolf, *History of Dogma*. 7 vols. Boston: Little, Brown, and Co., 1903. Reprinted 4 vols. New York: Dover, 1961.

Haroutunian, Joseph, "Spirit, Holy Spirit, Spiritism." *Ex Auditu* 12 (1996) 59–75.

Harrington, Daniel J., *The Hebrew Fragments of Pseudo-Philos' Liber Antiquitatum Biblicarum Preserved in the Chronicles of Jerahmeel*. SBL. Missoula, MT: University of Montana, 1974.

__, "Pseudo-Philo." In *The Old Testament Pseudapigrapha*, edited by James H. Charlesworth, 2. 299–300. 2 vols. Garden City, NY: Doubleday, 1983.

Harrisville, Roy A., "Speaking in Tongues: A Lexicographical Study." *CBQ* 38 (1976) 35–48.

Haykin, Michael A. G., *The Spirit of God: The Exegesis of 1 and 2 Corinthians in the Pneumatomachian Controversy of the Fourth Century*. Leiden: Brill, 1994.

Hayman, Peter, "Monotheism – A Misused Word in Jewish Studies." *JJS* 42 (1991) 1–15.

Haynes, Carlyle B., *Spiritism and the Bible*. Nashville: Southern Publishing Association, 1941.

Heine, Ronald E., "The Role of the Gospel of John in the Montanist Controversy." *Second Century* 6 (1987) 1–19.

Hemphill, Kenneth S., *Spiritual Gifts: Empowering the New Testament Church*. Nashville: Broadman, 1988.

Hengel, Martin, "Problems of a History of Earliest Christianity." *Bib* 78 (1997) 131–44.

Henshaw, Richard A., *Female and Male. The Cultic Personnel: The Bible and the Rest of the Ancient Near East*. PTMS 31. Allison Park, PA: Pickwick, 1994.

Hill, David T., *Greek Words and Hebrew Meanings: Studies in the Semantics of Soteriological Terms*. SNTSMS 5. Cambridge: Cambridge University Press, 1967. Reprinted Eugene, OR: Wipf & Stock, 2000.

___, *New Testament Prophecy*. London: Marshall Morgan & Scott, 1979.

Hine, Virginia J., "Pentecostal Glossolalia: Toward a Functional Interpretation." *JSSR* 8 (1969) 211–26.

Hoekema, Anthony A., *What about Tongue-Speaking?* Grand Rapids: Eerdmans, 1966.

Hollander, Harm W., and Marinus de Jonge, *The Testaments of the Twelve Patriarchs: A Commentary*. Leiden: Brill, 1985.

Holtz, Traugott, "Das Kennzeichen des Geistes [1 Kor. XII. 1–3]." *NTS* 18 (1972) 365–76.

Hopwood, Percy G. S., *The Religious Experience of the Primitive Church: The Period Prior to the Influence of Paul*. New York: Scribner's, 1937.

Horsley, Richard A., "'How can some of you say there is no resurrection of the dead?' Spiritual Elitism in Corinth." *NovT* 20 (1978) 202–31.

Horn, Friedrich W., *Das Angeld des Geistes: Studien zur paulinischen Pneumatologie*. Göttingen: Vandenhoeck & Ruprecht, 1992.

House, H. Wayne, "Tongues and Mystery Religions of Corinth." *BSac* 140 (1983) 134–50.

Hovenden, Gerald, *Speaking in Tongues: The New Testament Evidence in Context*. Sheffield: Sheffield Academic Press, 2002.

Hoyle, R. Birch, *The Holy Spirit in St. Paul*. Garden City, NY: Doubleday, 1928.

Hufford, David J., "Beings Without Bodies: An Experience-Centered Theory of the Belief in Spirits." In *Out of the Ordinary: Folklore and the Supernatural*, edited by Barbara G. Walker, 11–45. Logan, UT: Utah State University Press, 1995.

Hui, Archie, "The Spirit of Prophecy and Pauline Pneumatology." *TynBul* 50 (1999) 93–115.

Hunt, Allen R., *The Inspired Body: Paul, the Corinthians, and Divine Inspiration*. Macon, GA: Mercer University Press, 1996.

Hurd, John C., *The Origins of 1 Corinthians*. New York: Seabury Press, 1965. Reprinted Macon, GA: Mercer University Press, 1983.

Hurtado, Larry W., *One God, One Lord: Early Christian Devotion and Ancient Jewish Monotheism*. Philadelphia: Fortress, 1988.

___, "Religious Experience and Religious Innovation in the New Testament." *JR* 80 (2000) 183–205.

___, *At the Origins of Christian Worship: The Context and Character of Earliest Christian Devotion*. Grand Rapids: Eerdmans, 2000.

___, *Lord Jesus Christ: Devotion to Jesus in Earliest Christianity*. Grand Rapids: Eerdmans, 2003.

Husserl, Edmund, *Cartesian Meditations: An Introduction to Phenomenology*. Translation Dorion Cairns. Boston: Kluwer Academic Publishers, 1950.

___, *Ideas Pertaining to a Pure Phenomenology and to a Phenomenological Philosophy*. Translation W. Boyce Gibson. Boston: Nijhoff, 1983.

Isaacs, Marie E., *The Concept of Spirit: A Study of Pneuma in Hellenistic Judaism and Its Bearing on the New Testament*. HM 1. London: Heythrop College, 1976.

Isbell, Charles D., "The Origins of Prophetic Frenzy and Ecstatic Utterance in the Old Testament World." *WTJ* 11 (1976) 62–80.

Jackson, F. J. Foakes and Kirsopp Lake, eds., *The Beginnings of Christianity: The Acts of the Apostles*. 5 vols. London: Macmillan, 1920–23. Reprinted Grand Rapids: Baker 1979.

Jacobson, Howard, *A Commentary on Pseudo-Philo's Liber Antiquitatum Biblicarum*. 2 vols. AGAJU 31. Leiden: Brill, 1996.

James, Montague R., *The Biblical Antiquities of Philo*. London: Society for Promoting Christian Knowledge, 1917.

James, William, *Varieties of Religious Experience*. New York: Longmans, Green, and Co., 1902. Reprinted New York: Vintage, 1990.

Jaquith, James R., "Towards a Typology of Formal Communicative Behaviors: Glossolalia." *Anthropological Linguistics* 9 (1967) 1–8.

Jeffers, Steven L., "The Cultural Power of Words: Occult Terminology in the Hebrew, Greek, Latin, and English Bible." Ph.D. diss., Florida State University, 1989.

Jewett, Robert, *Paul's Anthropological Terms: A Study of Their Use in Conflict Settings*. AGAJU 10. Leiden: Brill, 1971.

Johnson, Aubrey, *The One and the Many in the Israelite Conception of God*. Cardiff: University of Wales, 1961.

Johnson, Bruce C., "Tongues, a Sign for Unbelievers?: A Structural and Exegetical Study of 1 Corinthians XIV. 20–25." *NTS* 25 (1979) 180–203.

Johnson, Luke Timothy, "Norms for True and False Prophecy in First Corinthians." *American Benedictine Review* 22 (1971) 29–45.

___, "Tongues, Gift of." *ABD* 6. 596–600.

___, *Religious Experience in Earliest Christianity: A Missing Dimension in New Testament Studies*. Minneapolis: Fortress, 1998.

Jones, Rhys B., *Spiritism in Bible Light*. London: Religious Tract Society, 1921.

Jones, Donald J., "Ecstaticism and the Hebrew Prophets." *Methodist Theological School* 7 (1969) 33–45.

Joüon, Paul, *A Grammar of Biblical Hebrew*. Translation T. Muraoka. 2 vols. SB 14/11. Rome: Pontifical Biblical Institute, 1996.

Käsemann, Ernst, "Ministry and Community in the New Testament." In idem, *Essays on New Testament Themes*, 63–134. Translation W. J. Montague. SBT 41. London: SCM, 1964.

Kee, Howard C., "Testaments of the Twelve Patriarchs: A New Translation and Introduction." In *The Old Testament Pseudapigrapha*, edited by James H. Charlesworth, 1. 775–828. 2 vols. Garden City, NY: Doubleday, 1983.

Keener, Craig S., *The Spirit in the Gospels and Acts: Divine Purity and Power*. Peabody, MA: Hendrickson, 1997.

Kelsey, Morton T., *Tongues Speaking: The History and Meaning of Charismatic Experience*. New York: Crossroad, 1981.

Kildahl, John P., *The Psychology of Speaking in Tongues*. San Francisco: Harper & Row, 1972.

Kisch, Guido, *Pseudo-Philo's Liber Antiquitatum Biblicarum*. Notre Dame, IN: University of Notre Dame Press, 1949.

Kitz, Anne Marie, "Prophecy as Divination." *CBQ* 65 (2003) 22–43.

Klaniczay, Gábor, and Éva Pócs, ed., *Communicating with the Spirits*. Demons, Spirits, Witches 1. Budapest: Central European University Press, 2005.

Klimo, Jon, *Channeling: Investigations on Receiving Information from Paranormal Sources*. Los Angeles: J. P. Tarcher, 1989. Reprinted Berkeley: North Atlantic Books, 1998.

Knox, Ronald, *Enthusiasm: A Chapter in the History of Religion with Special Reference to the Seventeenth and Eighteenth Centuries*. Oxford: Clarendon, 1950. Reprinted Notre Dame, IN: University of Notre Dame Press, 1995.

Kretschmar, Georg, "Der Heilige Geist in der Geschichte: Grundzüge frühchristlicher Pneumatologie." In *Gegenwart des Geistes: Aspekte der Pneumatologie*, edited by K. Rahner and H. Schlier, 92–130. QD 85. Freiburg: Herder, 1979.

Lake, Kirsopp, *The Earlier Epistles of St Paul*. London: Rivingstons, 1911.

Lampe, Geoffrey H. W., *God as Spirit*. Bampton Lectures. Oxford: Clarendon Press, 1977.

Lang, Andrew, "Ancient Spiritualism." In idem, *Cock Lane and Common Sense*, 56–83. London: Longmans, 1894. Reprinted New York: AMS, 1970.

Langton, Edward, *Essentials of Demonology: A Study of Jewish and Christian Doctrine*. London: Epworth, 1949.

Lanier, David E., "With Stammering Lips and Another Tongue: 1 Cor 14:20–22 and Isa 28:11–12." *Covenant Theological Review* 5 (1991) 255–86.

Larue, Gerald A., *The Supernatural, the Occult and the Bible*. Buffalo: Promotheus, 1990.

Lateiner, Donald, "The Perception of Deception and Gullibility in Specialists of the Supernatural (Primarily) in Athenian Literature." In *Nomodeiktes: Greek Studies in Honor of Martin Ostwald*, edited by Ralph M. Rosen and Joseph Farrell, 179–95. Ann Arbor: University of Michigan Press, 1993.

Laurentin, René, *Catholic Pentecostalism*. Garden City, NY: Doubleday, 1977.

Lepicier, Alexius M., *The Unseen World: An Exposition of Catholic Theology in Its Relation to Modern Spiritism*. London: Kegan Paul, Trench, Trübner, 1909.

Levison, John R., "The Debut of the Divine Spirit in Josephus' Antiquities." *HTR* 87 (1994) 123–38.

___, "Inspiration and the Divine Spirit in the Writings of Philo Judaeus." *JSJ* 26 (1995) 271–323.

___, "The Prophetic Spirit as an Angel According to Philo." *HTR* 88 (1995) 189–207.

___, "Prophetic Inspiration in Pseudo-Philo's *Liber Antiquitatum Biblicarum*." *JQR* 85 (1995) 299–329.

___, "Josephus' Interpretation of the Divine Spirit." *JJS* 47 (1996) 234–55.

___, *The Spirit in First Century Judaism*. Leiden: Brill, 1997.

___, "The Pluriform Foundation of Christian Pneumatology." In *Advents of the Spirit: An Introduction to the Current Study of Pneumatology*, edited by Bradford E. Hinze and D. Lyle Dabney, 65–85. Marquette Studies in Theology 30. Milwaukee: Marquette University Press, 2001.

___, "Prophecy in Ancient Israel: The Case of the Ecstatic Elders." *CBQ* 65 (2003) 503–21.

Lewis, Frank B., "The Bible and Modern Religions: VIII. Modern Spiritualism." *Int* 11 (1957) 438–54.

Lewis, Ioan M., *Ecstatic Religion: A Study of Shamanism and Spirit Possession*. Hammondsworth, England: Penguin, 1971. Reprinted New York: Routledge, 2003.

Lienhard, Joseph T., "On 'Discerning of Spirits' in the Early Church." *TS* 41 (1980) 505–29.

Liljencrants, Johannes. *Spiritism and Religion: A Moral Study*. Lynchburg, VA: J. P. Bell, 1918. Reprinted Cleveland: J. T. Zubal, 1984.

Lindblom, Johannes, *Prophecy in Ancient Israel*. Philadelphia: Fortress, 1963.

Long, Burke O., "The Effect of Divination upon Israelite Literature." *JBL* 92 (1973) 489–97.

Luck, Georg, *Arcana Mundi: Magic and the Occult in the Greek and Roman Worlds*. Baltimore: Johns Hopkins University Press, 1985.

Lust, Johan, "The Mantic Function of the Prophet." *Bijdragen* 34 (1973) 234–50.

___, "On Wizards and Prophets." VTSup 26 (1974) 133–42.

___, et al., *A Greek-English Lexicon of the Septuagint*. Part 1 A-I. Stuttgart: Deutsche Bibelgesellschaft, 1992.

Macchia, Frank D., "Sighs too Deep for Words." *Journal of Pentecostal Theology* 1 (1992) 47–73.

Mageo, Jeannette M., and Alan Howard, *Spirits in Culture, History, and Mind.* New York: Routledge, 1996.

Maleparampil, Joseph, *The "Trinitarian" Formulae in St. Paul: An Exegetical Investigation into the Meaning and Function of Those Pauline Sayings which Compositely Make Mention of God, Christ, and the Holy Spirit.* European University Studies Series 23. Theology 546. Frankfurt: Peter Lang, 1995.

Malony, H. Newton, and A. Adam Lovekin, *Glossolalia: Behavioral Science Perspectives on Speaking in Tongues.* Oxford: Oxford University Press, 1985.

Maly, Karl, "1 Kor 12, 1–3, eine Regel zur Unterscheidung der Geister?" *BZ* 10 (1966) 82–91.

March, W. Eugene, "God With Us: A Survey of Jewish Pneumatology." *Austin Seminary Bulletin* 83 (1967) 3–16.

Marsh, Leonard, *The Apocatastasis.* Burlington, VT: n.p., 1854.

Marsh, Thomas, "Holy Spirit in Early Christian Thinking." *ITQ* 45 (1978) 101–16.

Martin, Dale B., "Tongues of Angels and Other Status Indicators." *JAAR* 59 (1991) 347–89.

May, Carlyle L., "A Survey of Glossolalia and Related Phenomena in non-Christian Religions." *American Anthropologist* 58 (1956) 75–96.

McCarter, P. Kyle, *1 Samuel.* AB 8. Garden City, NY: Doubleday, 1980.

McCasland, S. Vernon, *By the Finger of God: Demon Possession and Exorcism in Early Christianity in the Light of Modern Views of Mental Illness.* New York: Macmillan, 1951.

McKim, Donald K., ed., "Spiritism." In *Westminster Dictionary of Theological Terms*, 266. Louisville: Westminster/John Knox, 1996.

McNamara, Martin, "Discernment Criteria in Israel: True and False Prophets." In *Discernment of the Spirit and of Spirits*, edited by C. Floristán and C. Anquoc, 3–13. New York: Seabury Press, 1979.

McNichol, A. J., "Spiritualism." In *The New Catholic Encyclopedia*, edited by M. R. P. McGuire, et al., 13. 587–93. 19 vols. New York: McGraw-Hill, 1965.

Mehat, André, "L'Enseignement sur 'les choses de l'esprit' (1 Corinthiens 12, 1–3)." *RHPR* 63 (1983) 395–415.

Menzies, Robert P., *The Development of Early Christian Pneumatology: with special reference to Luke-Acts.* JSNTSup 54. Sheffield: JSOT, 1991.

Meyer, Paul, "The Holy Spirit in the Pauline Letters: A Contextual Exploration." *Int* 33 (1979) 3–18.

Michaelsen, Peter, "Ecstasy and Possession in Ancient Israel: A Review of Some Recent Contributions." *SJOT* 2 (1989) 28–54.

Mikulaseh, Rodolpho H., ed., *O medium Mirabelli: o que ha de verdadeiro nos seus milagres e a sua discutida mediumnidade posta.* Santos, Brazil: Graphic Radium, 1926.

Milgrom, Jacob, *Leviticus 17–22.* AB 3A. New York: Doubleday, 2001.

Mills, Watson E., *A Theological/Exegetical Approach to Glossolalia.* Lanham, MD: University Press of America, 1985.

Mitchell, Margaret M., "Concerning ΠΕΡΙ ΔΕ in 1 Corinthians." *NovT* 31 (1989) 229–56.

___, *Paul and the Rhetoric of Reconciliation: An Exegetical Investigation of the Language and Composition of 1 Corinthians.* Louisville: Westminster/John Knox, 1992.

Moltmann, Jürgen, *The Spirit of Life: A Universal Affirmation.* Minneapolis: Fortress, 1992.

Montague, George T., *The Holy Spirit: Growth of a Biblical Tradition.* Peabody, MA: Hendrickson, 1976.

Moran, William L., "New Evidence from Mari on the History of Prophecy." *Bib* 50 (1969) 15–56.

Morgan-Wynne, John E., *Holy Spirit and Religious Experience in Christian Literature c. 90–200 A.D.* Paternoster Studies in Christian History and Thought. Eugene, OR: Wipf & Stock, 2006.

Morrison, A. B., *Spiritualism and Necromancy*. New York: Nelson and Phillips, 1873.

Mowinckel, Sigmund, "'The Spirit' and the 'Word' in the Pre-Exilic Reforming Prophets." *JBL* 53 (1934) 199–227.

__, "Ecstatic Experience and Rational Elaboration in Old Testament Prophecy." *AcOr* 13 (1935) 264–91.

Munch, P. A., "The Spirits in the Testaments of the Twelve Patriarchs." *AO* 13 (1935) 257–63.

Mundhenk, Norm A., "Translating 'Holy Spirit.'" *BT* 48 (1997) 201–07.

Murphy, Frederick J., "Retelling the Bible: Idolatry in Pseudo-Philo." *JBL* 107 (1988) 275–87.

__, *Pseudo-Philo: Rewriting the Bible*. Oxford: Oxford University Press, 1993.

Nardoni, Enrique, "The Concept of Charism in Paul." *CBQ* 55 (1993) 68–80.

Nigosian, Solomon A., "Anti-Divinatory Statements in Biblical Codes." *Near East School of Theology Theological Review* 18 (1997) 21–34.

Nissinen, Martti, *References to Prophecy in Neo-Assyrian Sources*. State Archives of Assyria Studies 7. Helsinki: University of Helsinki, 1998.

Njiru, Paul Kariuki, *Charisms and the Holy Spirit's Activity in the Body of Christ: An Exegetical-Theological Study of 1 Corinthians 12,4–11 and Romans 12,6–8*. Gregorian Theological Series 86. Rome: Gregorian University, 2002.

Noble, Thomas A., "The Spirit World: A Theological Approach." In *The Unseen World: Christian Reflections on Angels, Demons, and the Heavenly Realm*, edited by Anthony N. S. Lane, 185–223. Grand Rapids: Baker, 1996.

Noll, Stephen F., *Angels of Light, Powers of Darkness: Thinking Biblically about Angels, Satan, and Principalities*. Downers Grove, IL: Inter-Varsity, 1998.

Oesterreich, Traugott K., *Obsession and Possession by Spirits Both Good and Evil*. Trans. D. Ibberson. Chicago: de Laurence, 1935. Reprinted *Possession: Demoniacal and Other Among Primitive Races, in Antiquity, the Middle Ages and Modern Times*. Hyde Park, NY: University Books, 1966.

Ogden, Daniel, *Greek and Roman Necromancy*. Princeton: Princeton University Press, 2001.

__, *Magic, Witchcraft, and Ghosts in the Greek and Roman World: A Source Book*. Oxford: Oxford University Press, 2002.

Olasky, Marvin, "The Return of Spiritism: Seeing how the Church Triumphed Over the New Age Movement of the 1850s can help us in the 1990s." *Christianity Today* 36 (1992) 20–24.

Omara, Robert, *Spiritual Gifts in the Church: A Study of 1 Corinthians 12:1–11*. Rome: Pontificia Universitas Urbaniana, 1997.

Orlinsky, Harry M., "The Seer in Ancient Israel." *OrAnt* 4 (1965) 153–74.

Pace, Edward A., "Spiritism." In *The Catholic Encyclopedia*, edited by Charles G. Herbermann, et al., 14. 221–27. 18 vols. New York: Robert Appleton, 1912.

Padel, Ruth, "Women: Model for Possession by Greek Daemons." In *Images of Women in Antiquity*, edited by Averil Cameron and Amélie Kuhrt, 3–18. Detroit: Wayne State University Press, 1983. Reprinted 1993.

Paige, Terence P., "Spirit at Corinth: The Corinthian Concept of Spirit and Paul's Response as Seen in 1 Corinthians." Ph.D. diss., University of Sheffield, 1991.

__, "1 Corinthians 12.2: A Pagan *Pompe*?" *JSNT* 44 (1991) 57–65.

__, "Who Believes in 'Spirit?' *Pneuma* in Pagan Usage and Implications for the Gentile Christian Mission." *HTR* 95 (2002) 417–36.

Pallazzini, P., ed., "Spiritualism." In *The Dictionary of Moral Theology*, 1151. Westminster, MD: Newman Press, 1962.

Parke, Herbert W., and Donald E. W. Wormell, *The Delphic Oracle I: The History*. Oxford: Basil Blackwell, 1956.

Parke, Herbert W., *The Oracles of Zeus: Dodona, Olympian, Ammon*. Cambridge, MA: Harvard University Press, 1967.

Parpola, Simo, *Assyrian Prophecies*. State Archives of Assyria 9. Helsinki: Helsinki University Press, 1997.

Paton, Lewis B., *Spiritism and the Cult of the Dead in Antiquity*. New York: Macmillan, 1921.

Pavente, Pietro, ed., "Spiritism." In *The Dictionary of Dogmatic Theology*, 266. Translation Emmanuel Doronzo. Milwaukee: Bruce, 1951.

Pearson, Birger, "Did the Gnostics Curse Jesus?" *JBL* 86 (1967) 301–5.

__, *The Pneumatikos-Psychikos Terminology in 1 Corinthians: A Study in the Theology of the Corinthian Opponents of Paul and its Relation to Gnosticism*. SBLDS 12. Missoula, MT: Scholar's Press, 1973.

Perrot, Charles, and Pierre-Maurice Bogaert, *Pseudo-Philon, Les Antiquités Bibliques*. SC 229–30. Paris: Cerf, 1976.

Pfitzner, Victor L., "The Spirit of the Lord: The christological focus of Pauline Pneumatology." *St. Mark's Review 178* (1999) 3–11.

Philip, Finny, *The Origins of Pauline Pneumatology: The Eschatological Bestowal of the Spirit upon Gentiles in Judaism and in the Early Development of Paul's Theology*. WUNT 2/194. Tübingen: Mohr Siebeck, 2005.

Pilch, John J., "Paul's Ecstatic Trance Experiences near Damascus in Acts of the Apostles." *Hervormde Teologiese Studies* 58 (2002) 690–707.

Piñero, Antonio, "A Mediterranean View of Prophetic Inspiration: On the Concept of Inspiration in the *Liber Antiquitatum Biblicarum* by Pseudo-Philo." *Mediterranean Historical Review* 6 (1991) 5–34.

Porter, Stanley E., *Idioms of the Greek New Testament*. 2nd ed. Sheffield: JSOT, 1994.

Poythress, Vern S., "The Nature of Corinthian Glossolalia: Possible Options." *WTJ* 40 (1977–1978) 130–35.

__, "Linguistics and Sociological Analyses of Modern Tongues-Speaking: Their Contributions and Limitations." *WTJ* 42 (1979) 367–98.

Prat, Fernand, *The Theology of Saint Paul*. 2 vols. Translation John L. Stoddard. Westminster, MD: Newman Press, 1958.

Quast, Kevin, *Reading the Corinthian Correspondence: An Introduction*. New York: Paulist, 1994.

Rahner, Karl, *Visions and Prophecies*. Translation Charles Henkey and Richard Strachan. QD 10. Freiburg: Herder, 1963.

__, *Experience of the Spirit: Source of Theology*. Translation David Morland. Theological Investigations 16. New York: Crossroad, 1983.

Reiling, Jannes, *Hermas and Christian Prophecy: A Study of the Eleventh Mandate*. Leiden: Brill, 1973.

Roberts, Peter, "A Sign – Christian or Pagan [1 Cor 14:21–25]." *ExpTim* 90 (1979) 199–203.

Roberts, Jimmy J. M., "The Hand of Yahweh." *VT* 21 (1971) 244–51.

Robinson, Donald W. B., "Charismata versus Pneumatika: Paul's Method of Discussion." *Reformed Theological Review* 31 (1972) 49–55.

Robinson, Henry Wheeler, *The Christian Experience of the Holy Spirit*. New York, London: Harper, 1928.

Salala, Charles, "Angels and Demons in Biblical Perspective." In *Issues in African Christianity Theology*, edited by S. Ngewa, et al., 140–52. Kampala: East African Educational Publishing, 1998.

Samarin, William J., *Tongues of Men and Angels: The Religious Language of Pentecostalism*. New York: Macmillan, 1972.

Sandmel, Samuel, *Philo's Place in Judaism: A Study of Conceptions of Abraham in Jewish Literature*. Cincinnati: Hebrew Union College, 1956.

Sandnes, Karl O., "Prophecy – A Sign for Believers (1 Cor 14.20–25)." *Bib* 77 (1996) 1–15.

Schäfer, Peter, *Die Vorstellung vom heiligen Geist in der rabbinischen Literatur*. Munich: Kösel, 1972.

Schatzmann, Siegfried, *A Pauline Theology of Charismata*. Peabody, MA: Hendrickson, 1987.

___, "Purpose and Function of Gifts in 1 Corinthians." *Southwestern Journal of Theology* 45 (2002) 53–68.

Schiller, F. C. S., "Spiritism." In *The Encyclopedia of Religion and Ethics*, edited by James Hastings, 11. 805. 13 vols. New York: Scribner's, 1921.

Schlatter, Adolf, *Paulus der Bote Jesu*. Stuttgart: Calwer, 1934. Reprint 1956.

Schlier, Heinrich, *Principalities and Powers in the New Testament*. Freiburg: Herder, 1961.

Schmithals, Walter, *Gnosticism in Corinth: An Investigation of the Letters to the Corinthians*. Translation J. E. Steely. Nashville: Abingdon, 1971.

Schneider, David, "Colossians 1:15–16 and the Philippine Spirit World." *South East Asian Journal of Theology* 15 (1974) 91–101.

Schniedewind, William M., "Prophets and Prophecy in the Books of Chronicles." In *The Chronicler as Historian*, edited by M. P. Graham, et al., 215–30. JSOTS 238. Sheffield: Sheffield Academic Press, 1997.

Schweizer, Eduard, "Slaves of the Elements and Worshipers of Angels: Gal 4:3, 9 and Col 2:8, 18, 20." *JBL* 107 (1988) 455–68.

Sekki, Arthur E., *The Meaning of RUAH at Qumran*. SBLDS 110. Atlanta, GA: Scholars Press, 1989.

Shantz, Colleen Annette, "Paul in Ecstasy: An Examination of the Evidence for and Implications of Paul's Ecstatic Religious Experience." Ph.D. diss., The University of St. Michael's College, 2003.

Sherry, Patrick J., "Are Spirits Bodiless Persons?" *Neue Zeitschrift für systematische Theologie und Religionsphilosophie* 24 (1982) 37–52.

Shoemaker, William R., "The Use of רוח in the Old Testament, and of πνεῦμα in the New Testament." *JBL* 23 (1904) 13–67.

Smalley, Stephen S., "Spiritual Gifts and First Corinthians 12–14." *JBL* 87 (1968) 427–33.

Smit, Joop F. M., "Argument and Genre of 1 Cor 12–14." In *Rhetoric and the New Testament*, edited by Stanley E. Porter and T. H. Olbricht, 211–30. JSNTSSup 90. Sheffield: Sheffield Academic Press, 1993.

___, "Tongues and Prophecy: Deciphering 1 Cor 14, 22." *Bib* 75 (1994) 175–90.

Smith, G. V., "Prophet; Prophecy." *ISBE* 3. 986–1004.

Smith, John E., *Experience and God*. Oxford: Oxford University Press, 1968.

Smith, Morton, "Pauline Worship as Seen by Pagans." *HTR* 93 (1980) 241–494.

___, "The Occult in Josephus." In *Josephus, Judaism, and Christianity*, edited by L. H. Feldman and G. Hata, 238–48. Detroit, MI: Wayne State University Press, 1987.

Smith, Wesley D., "The So-Called Possession in Pre-Christian Greece." *Transactions and Proceedings of the American Philological Association* 96 (1965) 403–36.

Sorensen, Eric, *Possession and Exorcism in the New Testament and Early Christianity*. WUNT 2/157. Tübingen: J. C. B. Mohr, 2002.

Springsted, Eric O., "Theology and Spirituality: Or, Why Religion is Not Critical Reflection on Religious Experience." *PSB* 19 (1998) 143–59.

Stevens, George B., *The Theology of the New Testament*. Edinburgh: T & T Clark, 1899. 2nd ed. 1918. Reprint 1968.

Stevenson, Ian, *Xenoglossy: A Review and Report of a Case*. Charlottesville, VA: University of Virginia Press, 1974.

___, *Unlearned Language: New Studies in Xenoglossy*. Charlottesville, VA: University of Virginia Press, 1984.

Stewart-Sykes, Alistair, "The Original Condemnation of Asian Montanism." *JEH* 50 (1999) 1–22.

Stol, Martin, *Epilepsy in Babylonia*. Cuneiform Monographs 2. Groningen, The Netherlands: Styx, 1993.

Strecker, Georg, *The Johannine Letters: A Commentary on 1, 2, and 3 John*. Hermeneia. Minneapolis: Fortress, 1996.

Strelan, Rick, *Strange Acts: Studies in the Cultural World of the Acts of the Apostles*. BZNW 126. Berlin: Walter de Gruyter, 2004.

Stuhlmacher, Peter, *Historical Criticism and Theological Interpretation of Scripture: Toward a Hermeneutics of Consent*. Translation Roy A. Harrisville. Philadelphia: Fortress, 1977. Reprinted Eugene, OR: Wipf & Stock, 2003.

Stuhlmueller, Carroll, "The Spirit World." *TBT* 28 (1990) 5–11.

Summers, Steven, "Out of My Mind for God: A Social-Scientific Approach to Pauline Pneumatology." *Journal of Pentecostal Theology* 13 (1998) 77–106.

Sutphin, John E., *The Bible and Spirit Communication*. Starkville, MS: Metamental Missions, 1971.

Swartz, Steve, "The Holy Spirit: Person and Power. The Greek Article and *Pneuma*." *BT* 44 (1993) 24–38.

Sweet, John P. M., "A Sign for Unbelievers: Paul's Attitude to Glossolalia." *NTS* 13 (1967) 240–57.

Swete, Henry Barclay, *The Holy Spirit in the New Testament*. London: Macmillan, 1909.

___, *The Holy Spirit in the Ancient Church: A Study of Christian Teaching in the Age of the Fathers* (London: Macmillan, 1912).

Talbert, Charles H., "Paul's Understanding of the Holy Spirit: The Evidence of 1 Corinthians 12–14." In *Perspectives on the New Testament: Essays in Honor of Frank Stagg*, edited by Charles H. Talbert, 91–110. Macon, GA: Mercer University Press, 1985.

Thelle, Rannfrid I., "דרש את־יהוה: The Prophetic Act of Consulting Yhwh in Jeremiah 21,2 and 37,7." *SJOT* 12 (1998) 249–56.

Thiselton, Anthony, "The 'Interpretation' of Tongues: A New Suggestion in the Light of Greek Usage in Philo and Josephus." *JTS* 30 (1979) 15–36.

___, "The Holy Spirit in 1 Corinthians: Exegesis and Reception History in the Patristic Era." In *The Holy Spirit and Christian Origins: Essays in Honor of James D. G. Dunn*, edited by Graham Stanton, et al., 207–28. Grand Rapids: Eerdmans, 2004.

Thomas, Robert L., *Understanding Spiritual Gifts: A verse-by-verse Study of 1 Corinthians 12–14*. Grand Rapids: Kregel, 1978. Reprinted 1999.

Thurston, Herbert, *The Church and Spiritualism*. Milwaukee: Bruce, 1933. Reprinted 1935.

Tittman, George F., "Human Spirit and Holy Spirit: Texts and Musings." *Saint Luke's Journal of Theology* 16 (1973) 20–46.

Triezeberg, Henry J., *Spiritualism: Asking the Dead.* Grand Rapids: Zondervan, 1949.

Tropper, Josef, "Wizard." *DDD* 1705–7.

Turner, Max M. B., "Spiritual Gifts Then and Now." *Vox Evangelica* 15 (1985) 7–64.

__, "The Spirit of Prophecy and the Power of Authoritative Preaching in Luke-Acts: A Question of Origins." *NTS* 38 (1992) 66–88.

__, *The Holy Spirit and Spiritual Gifts in the New Testament Church and Today.* Peabody, MA: Hendrickson, 1998.

Udoette, Donatus, *Prophecy and Tongues: A Pauline Theology of Charismata for Service in the Church [1 Cor 14].* Rome: Pontificia Universitas Urbaniana, 1993.

Unger, Merrill F., *Biblical Demonology.* 5th edition. Wheaton, IL: Scripture Press, 1963.

Vande Kappelle, Robert P., "Prophets and Mantics." In *Pagan and Christian Anxiety: A Response to E. R. Dodds,* edited by Robert C. Smith and John Lounibos, 87–111. Lanham, MD: University Press of America, 1984.

Van der Hart, Rob, *The Theology of Angels and Devils.* Theology Today 36. Notre Dame, IN: Fides, 1972.

Van Unnik, W. C., "Jesus: Anathema or Kyrios [1 Cor. 12:3]." In *Christ and the Spirit in the New Testament,* edited by Barnabas Linders and S. S. Smalley, 113–26. Cambridge: Cambridge University Press, 1973.

Van Vliet, Rien, "Discerning of Spirits. What Does it Really Mean?" *Eastern Journal of Practical Theology* (1998) 17–28.

Vásquez, Manuel A., "Battling Spiritism and the Need for Catholic Orthodoxy." In *Religions of the United States in Practice 2,* edited by Colleen McDannell, 449–61. Princeton: Princeton University Press, 2001.

Vawter, Bruce, and J. T. Nellis, "Necromancy." In *EDB,* 1623. Translation Louis F. Hartman. New York: McGraw-Hill, 1963.

Vergote, Antoine, "Religious Experience." In *From Religious Experience to a Religious Attitude,* edited by A. Godin, 10–22. Chicago: Loyola University Press, 1965.

Versnal, H. S., "Thrice One: Three Greek Experiments in Oneness." In *One God or Many? Concepts of Divinity in the Ancient World,* edited by Barbara Nevling Porter, 120–45. Transactions of the Casco Bay Assyriological Institute 1. Chebeague Island, ME: Casco Bay Assyriological Institute, 1997.

Vincent, Marvin R., *Word Studies in the New Testament.* 4 vols. New York: Charles Scribner's, 1887. Reprinted in 2 vols. Grand Rapids: Eerdmans, 1985.

Volz, Paul, *Der Geist Gottes und die verwandten Erscheinungen im Alten Testament und im anschließenden Judentum.* Tübingen: Mohr, 1910.

Vos, Johan S., "Das Rätsel von 1 Kor 12:1–3." *NovT* 35 (1993) 251–69.

Wagner, Siegfried, "דרשׁ." *TDOT* 3. 302–09.

Weaver, Mary Jo, "Πνεῦμα in Philo of Alexandria." Ph.D. diss., University of Notre Dame, 1973.

Weinel, Heinrich, *Die Wirkungen des Geistes und der Geister im nachapostolischen Zeitalter bis auf Irenäus.* Freiburg, Leipzig, Tübingen: J. C. B. Mohr (Paul Siebeck), 1899.

Weisberg, Barbara, *Talking to the Dead: Kate and Maggie Fox and the Rise of Spiritualism.* San Francisco: Harper Collins, 2004.

Wiesinger, Alois, *Occult Phenomena in the Light of Theology.* Westminster, MD: Newman Press, 1957. Reprinted Fort Collins, CO: Roman Catholic Books, 1999.

Whiteley, Denys E. H., *The Theology of St. Paul.* Oxford: Basil Blackwell, 1974.

Wiebe, Phillip H., *God and Other Spirits: Intimations of Transcendence in Christian Experience.* Oxford: Oxford University Press, 2004.

Williams, Cyril C., *Tongues of the Spirit: A Study of Pentecostal Glossolalia and Related Phenomena*. Cardiff: University of Wales Press, 1981.

Williams, David M., *Receiving the Bible in Faith: Historical and Theological Exegesis*. Washington, D. C.: Catholic University of America Press, 2004.

Williams, Peter J., "Lying Spirits Sent by God? The Case of Micaiah's Prophecy." In *The Trustworthiness of God: Perspectives on the Nature of Scripture*, edited by P. Helm and C. R. Trueman, 58–66. Grand Rapids: Eerdmans, 2002.

Williamson, Ronald, *Jews in the Hellenistic World: Philo*. Cambridge Commentaries on Writings of the Jewish and Christian World 1.2. Cambridge: Cambridge University Press, 1989.

Wire, Antoinette C., *The Corinthian Women Prophets: A Reconstruction through Paul's Rhetoric*. Minneapolis: Fortress, 1990.

Wolfson, Harry A., *Philo: Foundations of Religious Philosophy in Judaism, Christianity, and Islam*. 2 vols. Cambridge, MA: Harvard University Press, 1947.

Wright, J. Stafford, "The Biblical Assessment of Superstition and the Occult." *Evangelical Review of Theology* 4 (1980) 102–13.

Wright, Walter C., "The Source of Paul's Concept of Pneuma." *Covenant Quarterly* 41 (1983) 17–26.

Zaugg, Elmer Harry, *A Genetic Study of the Spirit-Phenomena in the New Testament*. Menasha, WI: George Banta, 1917.

Zerhusen, Robert, "The Problem Tongues of 1 Cor 14: A Reexamination." *BTB* (1997) 139–52.

Zerwick, Maximilian, *Biblical Greek*. Rome: Pontifical Biblical Institute, 1994.

Zerwick, Maximilian, and Mary Grosvenor, *A Grammatical Analysis of the Greek New Testament*. Rome: Pontifical Biblical Institute, 1996.

Index of Ancient Sources

1. Old Testament and Apocrypha

Genesis
1:1	65
6:1–4	114
17:1	303
17:22	303
19:1	137
24:47	298
25:22	299, 300, 302
32:18	298
44:5	297
44:19	298

Exodus
4:19	298
7:10–12	301
7:20,21	301
8:1–3	301
18:10	248
18:15	299
18:15–16	297
19:9	303
[LXX] 20:4	160
22:17	295
22:18	291
25–31	302
28:6–13	297
28:15–21, 30	297
29:10–41	302
29:42–43	297, 302
33:7	297
33:9–11	297
33:11	303
33:18–23	303
35–40	302
40:34–38	302

Leviticus
14:29	160
19:31	288, 291, 293, 299, 295
20:6	19, 289, 291, 293, 295
20:6,27	116, 123, 142, 144
20:27	19, 291, 293, 295, 296
26:30	160
[LXX] 27:28	156

Numbers
11:25	84, 296
11:29	230
22–24	99
20:20	168
22:2–20	121
23:5,16	123
24:2,3	121, 123

Deuteronomy
4:32	298
4:35	160
4:39	160
[LXX] 5:8	160
[LXX] 7:26	156
12:30	299
[LXX] 13:16	156
18:9,12	292
18:10–11	292, 294
18:10–12	152
18:11	116, 130, 131, 288, 289, 291, 292, 293, 297, 299
18:11–12	19, 144
18:12	294, 298
18:15	297
18:21,22	305
21:32	157
32:17	161

Joshua
22:8	168

Judges
3:9,11	132
3:27	234
5:25	298
6:29	298
6:34	84
8:24,26	298
9:23	172
12:25	84
17:5	297
18:5	298

1 Samuel

9:9	297, 299, 300
10–19	142
10:6	295
10:10	295
10:22	298
11:6	295
12:17,19	298
14:18	298
14:37	298
16:13	295
16:14	88, 172, 294
16:15	295
16:16	295
16:23	295
18:10	172, 295
19:9	295
19:20	304
19:20–24	135
19:22	298
19:23	295
[LXX] 19:23	44
20:1	298
22:10	298
22:13	298
22:15	298
22:23	298
23:2	298
23:4	298
23:15	298
25:29	298
28	291, 292, 298
28:6	298
28:3	289
28:3–19	292
28:7	288, 299
28:7,8	116, 300
30:8	298
31:9	160

2 Samuel

2:1	298
4:8	298
5:19	298
5:23	298
12:16	298
16:11	298
18:28	248

20:1	234
21:1	298

1 Kings

1:16	300
1:48	248
3:10	298
3:11	298, 300
3:15	143
8:8	300
10:24	299
14:5	300
18	304
18:25,26	301
18:30–33	301
18:38	301
19:4	298
19:10	298
19:14	298
21:23	123
22:5	299
22:8	299
22:12	296
22:17	303
22:18	303
22:18–26	296
22:19–21	186
22:19–23	88
22:19	172
22:20	172
22:21	172, 303, 304
[LXX] 22:21	172
22:21–22	295, 296
22:22	303
22:22–23	128, 142, 303
22:38	303

2 Kings

1:2	300
1:2,3,6	299
1:3	300
2:3	304
2:5	304
2:15	304
2:17	298
3:11	297, 299
6:1	304
6:2	304

8:8	299
21:6	289, 295
22:13	299
22:14	304
23:24	289, 295

1 Chronicles
10:13–14	295, 301
12:19	123, 142, 295, 296
14:2–5	249
14:10	298
14:17	249
16:10	299
16:26	160
16:36	248, 249

2 Chronicles
2:11	248
7:1	301
11:16	299
15:1	296
16:12	299, 300
20:4	299
20:14	296
24:20	123, 142, 295, 296
33:6	295
34:21	300

Ezra
7:27	248
8:22	298
8:23	299

Tobit
12:11–22	137
12:12–22	59
14:6	160

Judith
| 8:18,19 | 160 |

3 Maccabees
| 4:16 | 160 |

Job
| 4:15,18 | 114 |
| 32:19–20 | 295 |

Psalms
1:43	85
27:8	299
33:2	234
34:4	300
35:4	298
38:13	298
40:15	298
54:5	298
63:10	298
70:3	298
84:14	298
[LXX] 95:5	161, 165
104:4	114, 263
[LXX] 105:37	161
115:3–8	160
115:5–7	160
[LXX] 115:13	160
135:16,17	160
137:2	234
139	85
149:3	234
150:3	234, 299

Proverbs
| 29:10 | 298 |
| 29:36 | 299 |

Wisdom
11:15	160
12:24	160
15:7–9	160
15:15	160

Sirach
| 30:19 | 160 |
| 39:6 | 122, 295 |

Isaiah
2:18	160
7:11	298
7:12	298
8:19	293, 295, 299, 302
10:11	160
16:12	160
19:1	160
19:3	295, 299
21:9	160

22:13	253		34:20,21	298
25:8	253		38:16	298
28:7–16	292		44:30	298
28:10	292		46:26	298
28:11	31, 32, 33, 35, 252,		49:37	298
	254, 257		50:4	299
[LXX] 28:11	220			
[LXX] 28:12	257		*Baruch*	
28:16	253		4:7	162
29:4	296			
29:14	253		*Ezekiel*	
30:20–22	160		8:3	84
31:3	302		9:24	84
31:7	160		11:1	84
40:13	223, 253		14:9	303
44:9–20	160		21:26	298
44:18	164		34:6	298
45:11	298, 303		44:10–15	160
46:6	160			
48:5	160		*Daniel*	
56:10	161		5:2	168
[LXX] 63:10,11	44		10:13	206
63:14	85		12:3	79
64:4	253			
[LXX] 65:3,11	161		*Hosea*	
			2:9	299
Jeremiah			4:13,14	160
1:2	145		5:6	299
2:1	145		8:4–6	160
4:19	234		13:2	160
4:30	298		14:17	160
5:1	298			
7:1	145		*Joel*	
10:3–4	160		2:1	234
10:5	160		2:28–29	25
10:10	161			
10:14	160		*Amos*	
11:1	145		8:12	299
11:21	298			
13:25–27	160		*Jonah*	
14:22	160		2:9	160
16:19–20	160			
19:7	298		*Habakkuk*	
19:9	298		2:18	161
20:7	303			
21:7	298		*Zephaniah*	
22:25	298		1:6	299
28:9	305		2:3	299

Zechariah		*Malachi*	
1:9	85	3:1	299
4:1,4	137		
8:21	299		

2. New Testament

Matthew		2:12	79
4:24	168	3:11	272, 273
7:15	89	3:22,30	92
7:15–20	56	3:29,30	206
7:17	253	5:2	59, 62, 168, 169, 170,
7:22	89		172, 222
7:22–23	268	5:2–5	272
8:16	60, 62, 165, 168, 239	5:7–10	59
8:27	79	5:8,15,16,18	168
8:28	168, 272	5:15	79
8:29–31	59	9:19	253
9:8	79	10:17	189
9:23	234	12:29	189
9:32	168		
9:32–34	206, 272	*Luke*	
10:33	268	1:17	58
11:17	234	1:34	241
11:18	168	2:25	229
12:22	204, 272	4:14	53
12:23	79	4:32	79
12:28	204, 206	4:33	168
12:35	185	4:33–35	59
12:43–45	59, 272	4:34	273
12:45	165, 239	4:34–36	272
13:43	79	4:36	272, 273
13:54	79	5:26	79
16:14	189	6:18	72, 272
17:20	203	7:33	168
18:24	189	8:27	168
18:32	241	8:36	168
19:16	189	9:39	165
21:46	241	9:41	253
27:6	241	9:42–43	206
		10:7	185
Mark		10:20	165, 239
1:12	62	10:42	189
1:23	168, 169	11:20	206
1:23–26	59	11:24–26	272
1:27	79	11:26	165, 239
1:32	168	12:12	177, 259

18:22	189
24:18	189
24:23	92
24:29	10
24:34	156
24:36–37	59, 62
24:37,39	239

John

4:2	187
4:3	187
4:6	187
4:24	196, 246
6:70	81
10:11	185
10:20	254
10:30	190
11:19	229
11:51	59
11:31	229
13:2, 27	81
14:17	73
14:26	12, 62, 70, 80, 177, 259
15:26	62
16:12,13	70
16:12–14	203
17:21,22	190

Acts of the Apostles

1:6	156
2:1–3	226
2:1–13	33, 40
2:4	62, 125, 174, 219
2:8	40
2:13	40
2:16–21	25
4:13	250
5:3–5,9	92
7:59	244
8:7	272
8:10	60
9:1–19	176
9:16, 27	267
10:3–7	54
10:10	137, 219
10:10–16	54
10:28	137
10:34–44	204

10:38	58
10:44	173, 174
10:46	219
11:15	219
12:15	254, 255
13:47	267
14:11	235, 238
15:32	229
16:16	59
16:16,18	12
16:18	176, 206
17:18	161, 237
18:9	267
19:12	239, 272
19:13–15	272
19:13–17	176
19:15	59, 62, 173, 273
19:16	272, 273
20:2	105
20:20	156
20:24	267
21:4	105
21:7	156
22:8–10	267
22:17	219
22:18	267
22:19	267
23:6	78
23:8	194, 239
23:9	12, 176
25:19	267
26:24	254, 255
26:25	254, 255

Romans

1:4	72, 156
1:7	156
1:9	244
1:11	183
1:13	155
1:17	224
1:25	249
2:18	251
2:29	271
3:12	189
3:19	253
3:21	224
3:24,25	204

4:1	247	2:9	253
4:11	253	2:10	223
4:25	86	2:10–12	64
5:1, 3–5	86	2:10–16	164
6:1	247	2:11	90, 187, 191, 245, 256, 262
6:14	204		
7:1	185	2:11,12	65, 66, 68
7:6	271	2:12	175, 184, 187
7:7	247	2:13	12, 80, 177, 183, 202, 223, 259, 271
7:13–25	103		
7:14	183	2:13–15	44
7:14–23	103	2:15	44, 183, 256
8:5,23,27	271	2:16	223, 253
8:7–13	224	3:1	44, 183, 200, 252
8:9	72, 271	3:1–2	204
8:14	179	3:2	227
8:26	35	3:3–4	192
8:26–27	86	3:9–17	230
8:31	247	3:10	230
8:38	58, 61, 206	4:1	228
9:14	247	4:6	224
9:30	247	5:3	168, 262
9:33	253	5:4	262
10:9	166, 176, 255	5:5	245
10:17	204	5:10	241
11:25	155	6:6	253
11:36	249	6:16,17	191
12:3	204	7:1	148
12:5	191	7:10	224
12:6	260	7:25	148, 224, 267
12:6–8	201	8:1	148, 224
12:15	190	8:4	161, 164
15:4,5	229	8:4–6	189
15:6	191	8:5	161, 194
15:19	253	8:5–6	160
15:27	183	8:6	156, 176, 194, 196
15:33	249	9:11	183
16:23	254	9:14	224
		10:3	183
1 Corinthians		10:4	183
1:10	190, 192, 262	10:14	164
1:19	253	10:17	191
1:19,31	224	10:19	164
1:22	253	10:19–20	161, 174
2:1	228	10:20	81, 165
2:1–5	224	10:20–21	73, 194
2:4	58, 202, 271	10:21	164
2:6–16	177, 202, 223	10:27	253

11:2	224
11:17	254
11:20	254
11:23	224
11:30	204
11:33	254
12:1	21, 44–47, 48, 49, 62, 183, 199, 215, 271, 285
12:1–3	174–180, 195
12:1–4	149
12:1–13	190
12:2	159–165, 167, 174, 254
12:2–3	154–158
12:3	15, 16, 43, 44, 48, 54, 61, 62, 72, 89, 149, 151, 153, 164, 165, 169, 170, 174, 175, 176, 177, 180,185, 203, 211, 219, 222, 223, 240, 247, 256, 264, 265, 272, 273, 274
12:3–6	198
12:4	47, 48, 49, 53, 188, 189, 190, 191, 193 , 195, 196, 197, 199, 200, 211
12:4–6	180, 193, 195, 196, 199, 200, 201
12:4–7,11	195
12:4–10	220
12:4–11	153, 154, 194, 199
12:4,7	184, 185
12:5	195, 196, 198, 206
12:6	195, 196, 197, 198, 199, 200
12:7	53, 54, 149, 188, 196, 198, 199, 200, 201, 202, 211
12:7,8,11	182
12:7,8,9,11	62
12:7–30	195
12:8	49, 200, 201, 202, 203
12:8–10	182, 198, 199, 200, 201, 220, 241
12:9	49, 53, 188, 189, 193, 201, 203, 204
12:10	38, 39, 49, 50, 53, 55, 62, 143, 175, 179, 201, 202, 205, 207–213, 216, 218, 219, 230, 231, 232, 238, 240, 241, 250, 259, 260, 261, 262, 265, 271, 276
12:11	53, 188, 189, 198, 200, 201, 263, 265
12:12	190, 191
12:13	179, 189, 190, 191, 193, 202, 262
12:14	191
12:18	16, 148, 150, 152, 154, 155, 178
12:20	191
12:27	273
12:27–29	190
12:28	204, 219, 225, 261
12:30	204, 232, 259, 261
12:31	216
13:1–14:1a	190, 215
13:1	34, 40, 235, 262
13:1–2	216
13:1–13	224
13:2	203, 230, 248
13:4–7	216
13:11	35, 36
13:13	216
14:1	47, 62, 180, 183, 216, 220, 222, 252, 268
14:1a–37	195
14:1b–3	227–229
14:1–40	153, 154
14:2	54, 62, 177, 179, 185, 218, 219, 223, 228, 230, 238, 240, 244, 247, 252, 256, 257, 264, 271
14:2,3	229
14:2–5	233, 251, 259
14:2–5,13	215
14:2,6,9	35
14:2,14,28	35
14:2,16	15, 16
14:3	222, 228, 229, 259, 263
14:3–5	200, 224
14:3,4,25	215
14:4	259
14:4–5	230–232

14:5	216, 230, 231, 232, 258, 259, 268		253, 254, 256, 258, 270
		14:22–24	253
14:5,13,27	37	14:23	101, 253, 254, 257, 258
14:6	221, 224, 225, 233, 246, 251, 258, 261, 268	14:23–25	30, 32, 33, 215, 254, 256, 258
14:6–11	35, 233–236	14:24	253, 256, 270
14:7	234, 251	14:25	54, 253, 256, 258
14:7–8	233	14:26	152, 200, 222, 224,
14:7–9	234		225, 241, 254, 258,
14:7–11	237, 240, 251		261, 268, 273
14:7–13	244	14:26–28	216
14:8	234	14:26–31	233
14:9	234, 236, 258	14:26–33	258–266, 268
14:10	234, 235	14:26–40	258
14:10–11	35, 236, 269	14:27	232, 268
14:12	16, 49, 51–52, 53, 54,	14:27,28	30, 216, 259, 260
	62, 149, 165, 185, 191,	14:28	228, 231, 260, 268
	192, 194, 200, 224,	14:29	39, 208, 231
	236–242, 243, 245,	14:29–31	224
	246, 251, 259, 262,	14:29–33	260, 266
	263, 265, 271	14:30	224, 261
14:13	232, 242, 258, 259	14:31	225, 260, 261, 273
14:13–19	29, 220, 242–251	14:32	16, 49, 52, 53, 54, 62,
14:14	29, 31, 243, 244, 246,		149, 165, 185, 192,
	247, 250, 258		240, 241, 242, 264,
14:14–15	243		265, 271
14:14–19	233, 251	14:32–33	262
14:15	29, 31, 62, 149, 240,	14:33	264, 265, 266
	243, 244, 246, 247,	14:33b–36	267
	250, 251, 265, 271	14:33,40	192
14:15–17	273	14:37	44, 62, 149, 183
14:16	39, 49, 54, 62, 149,	14:37–40	266–268
	169, 177, 185, 218,	14:38	267
	219, 220, 221, 223,	14:39	194, 216,
	230, 238, 240, 244,	14:39–40	233
	247, 248, 249, 254,	14:40	194, 233,268
	264, 271	15:1–11	223
14:16–17	215, 220, 246	15:1–19	164
14:16–18	216, 236	15:3	224
14:17	224, 259	15:24	58, 61, 206
14:18	36, 216, 221, 230, 244,	15:32	253
	248, 250, 251	15:45	196
14:19	39, 250, 251, 258	15:44	10, 183
14:20–25	32, 33, 224, 252–257	15:46	183
14:20	252, 254, 268	15:51	228
14:21	31, 33, 219, 231, 252,	15:54	253
	253, 256	15:57	223
14:22	26, 32, 33, 220, 231,	15:58	268

16:1,12	149	5:25	271
16:18	244, 262	6:1	183
16:22	156	6:6	251
		6:18	188, 262
2 Corinthians			
1:22	271	*Ephesians*	
2:13	244	1:3	183
3:8	198, 271	1:21	206
3:17	196	3:4–5	224
4:4	253	4:3,4	191
4:2–6	224	4:4,5	191
5:16	157	4:11–12	201
6:6	173	4:29–32	82
6:16	164	5:19	183, 258
7:13	245	6:12	62, 175, 183
11:4	226, 274, 276	6:18	246
11:13,14	89		
11:14	55, 79, 175	*Philippians*	
12:1–4	184	1:27	191
12:1–5	226	2:1	229
12:2–4	54, 137, 168	2:2	190
12:12	206, 253	2:7	90
14:1,7	224	2:11	156
14:14	245, 246	4:23	188, 262
Galatians		*Colossians*	
1:5	249	1:9	183
1:8	212, 226, 262	2:5	168
1:11	267	2:18	194
1:11–17	176	3:15	191
1:12	224, 226	3:16	183, 258
1:13–16	157		
1:16	224	*1 Thessalonians*	
2:2	224	1:5	58
2:20	90	2:11	229
3:5	206	4:8	73
3:13	157	5:14	229
3:14	271	5:19–20	43, 54, 194
3:20	189	5:19–22	220, 260
4:8	161	5:20	268
5:5	271	5:23	262
5:16	271		
5:17	271	*2 Thessalonians*	
5:18	179, 271	2:2	152, 212, 226, 276
5:19–21	152	2:8	89
5:22	211, 271, 273	2:9	206, 253
5:22–26	56	3:17	253
5:23	273	4:8	240

1 Timothy
3:2   185
4:1   12, 55, 72, 73, 80, 81,
                    239, 259, 274
4:1,2   162, 164, 175, 177
5:8   253

2 Timothy
4:22   188, 262

Titus
1:15   253

Philemon
25   188, 262

Hebrews
1:7   114, 263
1:14   60, 62, 66, 239, 263
1:15   198
5:11   241
6:4   82
9:17   241

James
4:5–7   82
4:12   189

1 Peter
1:12   227
2:5   183
3:4   82
3:22   206
4:10   197

2 Peter
1:21   276
3:8   189

1 John
2:18   185
2:22   185
4:1   143, 207, 208, 211, 274
4:1,2   89
4:1–3   55, 152, 239
4:2   55, 196, 223, 271, 272
4:2,3   56, 73
4:3   176, 271
4:6   73, 271

Jude
20   246

Revelation
1:4   60, 239
1:10   54, 168, 183
3:1   239
4:2   54, 168, 183
4:5   239
5:6   239
9:20   161
18:22   234
17:13   168
19:9–10   263
19:10   265
21:8   152
21:10   168
22:6   265
22:8   194

3. Jewish Pseudepigrapha

Apocalypse of Baruch
51　　　　　　79

Apocalypse of Ezra
7:55　　　　　79

1 Enoch
43:4　　　　　79
71:1　　　　　79
104:2　　　　79

Jubilees
11:4　　　　　162
24:14　　　　128
25:14　　　　221
31:12　　　　43, 128, 221

Martyrdom of Isaiah
6.10–14　　　134

Testament of Job
48:2　　　　　125
48–52　　　　221

Testaments of the 12 Patriarchs
Testament of Asher
1:3,8,9　　　181

Testament of Benjamin
5:2　　　　　72
6:1　　　　　181

Testament of Dan
2:4　　　　　181

Testament of Gad
1:9　　　　　181
4:7　　　　　181

Testament of Issachar
7:7　　　　　73

Testament of Judah
13:13　　　　181
20:1　　　　　72, 73, 187
23:1　　　　　162

Testament of Levi
2:3　　　　　181
18:11　　　　72, 181

Testament of Reuben
2:5　　　　　181, 303
5:3　　　　　181

Testament of Simeon
3:1　　　　　72, 181
4:4　　　　　72, 181

4. Dead Sea Scrolls

1QLeviticus (1Q3)
9.1.6   188

Thanksgiving Hymns (1QHᵃ)
1.11   185
2.4   185
3.18   185
3.22   185
7.6   188
7.16   181
8.12   72, 186, 187, 240
9.32   188
11.13   185
12.11–13   168
12.12   188
13.8   185, 186
14.13   188
16.2   168, 188
16.3   188
16.7   188
16.11,12   168
16.12   188
17.6,7   168
17.26   188

Hymns (1QHf)
2.9   188
5.4   185
5.6   185
33.2   185, 186

Songs of the Sabbath Sacrifice
(4QShirShabbᵃ)
40.24.5   72
40.24.6   72

War Scroll (1QM)
12.9   185, 186, 188
13.2   185
13.4   185
13.10   72, 185

14.10   185, 188
15.14   73, 185
19.1   185, 186, 188

Rule of the Blessings (1 QSb)
2.24   169

Rule of the Community (1QS)
3.6–8   168
3.10   185
3.18,19   73
4.9   73
4.14   185
4.20   73
4.21   187
4.21a   73
4.21b   73
4.23   73
8.16   73, 188
9.3   73

Damascus Document (CD)
2.12   73, 188
12.2   73

Sapiential Work (4QS1)
40.24.5   185, 240
40.24.6   185

Ritual of Marriage (4Q502)
27.1   185

Words of the Luminariesᵃ (4Q504)
1–2.5.15   188

Songs of the Sageᵇ (4Q511)
1.6   185

Hymn (8Q5)
2.6   185

5. Targums

Targum Onkelos (Tg. Onq.)
Genesis
41:38   43

Numbers
11:25–29   43
24:2   43
27:18   43

Targum Pseudo-Jonathan (Tg. Ps.-J.)
Genesis
41:38   43
45:27   43

Numbers
11:25–29   43

6. Philo of Alexandria

Heir of Divine Things (Her.)
249   125, 130, 218
259   125
265   127, 134, 135, 167
266   127, 135, 170, 236,
               248, 264, 273

The Special Laws (Spec.)
4.49   129, 141, 217

Providence (Prov.)
2.64   124

Questions and Solutions on Genesis (Q.G.)
1.6   114
1.16   114
1.92   114
3.9   217

On Flight and Finding (Fug.)
186   43

Life of Moses (Mos.)
1.274   114, 126
1.277   43, 114, 126
1.278–279   126
1.283–284   127
2.250–252   127

7. Flavius Josephus

Antiquitates Judaicae (A.J.)
4.6.2 §102–
4.6.12 §158   120

4.6.5 §118   121, 135
4.6.5 §119   122, 265
4.6.5 §121   122

8. Pseudo-Philo

Liber Antiquitatum Biblicarum (L.A.B.)
9–19, 20–24,
30–33   133
25:9   162
28.6   99, 133, 134, 194

28.6–9   133, 134
28.6,10   132, 133, 135, 248
28.10   99, 134
62.2   99, 135

9. Plutarch

Obsolescence of Oracles (De Def. orac.)
414 D   115
414 E   116, 117, 128, 236
414 F   117
418 C–D   118
418 D   128, 236

431 E–434 C 117
431 B   119
432 D   117, 134

Parallel Lives (Vitae parallelae)
2.129 C   183

10. Early Christian Writings

Athanasius of Alexandria

Epistles to Serapion
1.1   64
1.4   65, 66
1.22   65
1.27   65, 71, 189, 195
3.2   65

Athenagoras

A Plea for Christians
7, 9   129
26   163

Basil of Caesarea

On the Holy Spirit
2.4–8.21   68
9.22–23   70
13.29   66
16.37–38   70
16.38   66, 71
16.40   66
18.46   187
25.58–29.73 68

Epistles
125.3   66

Homilies (Hom.)
*Against the Sabellians, Arius, and
the Anomoeans*
24.7   187

Cassian

Conferences
1.12   136

Chrysostom

Homilies in 1 Corinthians
29.1   123

Discourse on Servants
10   221

Clement 2
3:1   164

Clement of Alexandria

Clementine Homilies
9.11   213
9.12   213
9.15   163
10.21   163
17.14   274

Instructor
2.5   129

Stromata
6.8   212, 213

Constitutions of the Holy Apostles
8.1.1   193
8.1.2   193, 212

Cyprian

Treatises
6.6–7   163
6.7   212

Cyril of Jerusalem

Catechetical Letters
16.8   210
16.12–16   64
16.23   64, 70
16.24   67

Didache
6:3   164
11   143
11:7   222, 265
11:8   56, 222, 265
11:7,8,9   177, 276
11:10   177
11:12   222, 276

Didymus the Blind

On the Holy Spirit
3   66
15   66

On the Trinity
2.457c   66

Epiphanius

Against Heresies (Haer.)
48.4   129, 210, 267

Eusebius

Ecclesiastical History (Eccl. Hist.)
5.1.14,23,25,52   81
5.1.27   274
5.16.3–17.4   275
5.16.7   210
5.16.7,16,17   111
5.16.8   209, 210
5.16.9   177, 209
5.16.17   209

5.17.1–3   111
5.17.2   210, 225
5.17.2–3   210, 218
5.17.3   167

Gregory of Nazianzus

Letter 58: To Basil
                67

Orations
31.8   187
31.10   67
31.26   67, 70
31.27   70
31.28   68
31.29   71
34.11   67

Gregory of Nyssa

Against the Macedonians
2   67
5   67

Commentary on Song of Songs
15.6,4   71

On the Soul and the Resurrection
                71

Hippolytus

Treatise on Christ and Antichrist
2   129

Ignatius

Epistle to Hero
2   212

Irenaeus

Against Heresies
1.13.3   265
1.16.3   212
3.11.9   276
5.6.1   276

Jerome

On Illustrious Men
24   276

Justin Martyr

Apology
1.5   162
1.62   212
1.65   249

Hortatory to the Greeks
8   129, 177
37.2,3   136

Lactantius

Divine Institutes
2.16.17   205, 212

Minucius Felix

Octavius
27   163

Odes of Solomon
6.1,2   129

Origen

Against Celsus
3.25   123
6.45   212
7.9   221
7.11   275

De principii (De princip.)
1.3.2   62
1.3.3   62
2.7   62

3.3.3   199, 275
3.3.4   63, 70

The Shepherd of Hermas

Similitude
9.13   60, 240

Mandate
11   143
11.3   188, 212, 240, 274
11.4   188, 240
11.5   188
11.6,8   265
11.7   188
11.9   194
11.16   56–57, 210, 276

Tertullian

Against Marcion
5.8   211

Apology
47   212

On Idolatry   163

On the Soul
11,21   210

Theodosius

Theodosian Code
16.1.2   68

Theophilus

To Autolycus
2.9   129

11. Classical and Other Ancient Writings

Aristides

In Defense of Oratory
43   136

Aristophanes

Wasps 1019–20 116

Aeschylus

Prometheus Bound
875–887   130

Cicero

On Divination (De div.)
1.9,12   113
1.114   133, 134

Heraclitus

On the Pythia (Pyth.)
397 A   217

Herodotus

Histories (Hist.)
8.135   221

Hesiod

Works and Days
125   119

Iamblichus

On the Mysteries (De myst.)
2.1,3,4,6,10   211
2.10   178, 211
3.6   212

Lucan

Civil War (Bel. Civ.)
5.169–174   130

5.186–197   217

Pharsalia
5.173–175   130

Lucian

Alexander
12   130

Plato

Apology
22 C   136
31 D   114

Ion
533 D–534 E   135, 143
534 B   144
534 C–D   135
534 D   118, 243

Meno
99 C   136

Phaedrus
244 A–245 C   143

Sophist
252 C   116

Symposium
202 E–203 A   116
203 A   115

Quintilian

Institutio Oratoria (Inst. Ora.)
1.35   221

Sophocles

Ajax
284–330   130

Strabo

Virgil

Geography (Geo.)
9.3.5   117
10.466–468   130

Aeneid
6.77–82   130

12. Mari and Babylonian Texts

Archives Royales de Mari (ARM)
X 7.5–7, 1   139
X 8.5–8, 2   139

Babylonian Diagnostic Texts
Tablet XXVI, 19–22
(20–23)   140

Index of Modern Authors

Alexander, B. 289
Alexander, P. S. 126
Alfeyev, H. H. 70
Alston, W. P. 5
Anderson, D. 66, 70
Angeles, P. 294
Ankerberg, J. 290
Arnold, B. T. 293
Arnold, C. E. 61
Ash, J. L. 275
Ashton, J. 103–105
Attridge, H. W. 120, 124
Aune, D. E. 23, 28, 42, 51, 127, 137, 142, 144, 169, 223, 244, 261, 293
Ayers, L. 63
Baker, D. L. 49
Balla, P. 7
Barrett, C. K. 45, 50, 52, 155, 158, 159, 167, 175, 202, 205, 225, 227, 237, 240, 242, 245, 254
Barstad, H. M. 297
Bartelink, G. 198
Bassler, J. M. 157–158
Beare, F. W. 24
Beavin, E. L. 173
BeDuhn, J. D. 173
Begg, C. T. 120
Behm, J. 27
Behr, J. 63–64
Benoit, P. 61
Berends, W. 170
Berkhof, H. 61
Best, E. 24
Betz, H. D. 72
Bevan, E. 59
Binyon, P. 109
Bittlinger, A. 46, 151
Blenkinsopp, J. 120
Blomberg, C. L. 45
Bogaert, P-M 132
Bonnel, J. S. 289
Borgen, P. 123
Boring, E. M. 17, 23
Bosman, H. L. 297
Bourguignon, E. 2, 42, 144
Bousset, W. 83

Bretherton, D. I. 6, 69
Brown, J. P. 103
Brown, R. E. 71
Brox, N. 157
Bruce, F. F. 27, 34, 45, 51, 157, 159, 167, 205, 237, 240
Brueggemann, W. 292, 296
Bruner, F. D. 38
Bullinger, E. W. 262
Burghardt, W. J. 210
Burnette, D. 111
Burns, J. B. 265
Burrows, M. 186
Buschel, F. 161
Butterworth, G. W. 152
Caciola, N. 111, 270, 275
Caird, G. B. 61
Callan, T. 27, 30, 31, 167, 217, 243
Campbell, T. C. 70
Cantwell, L. 62
Carr, W. 61
Carson, D. A. 39, 40, 46
Cartledge, M. J. 38
Chajes, J. H. 110
Chang, D-C 70
Charles, R. H. 134
Christou, P. 65
Ciraolo, L. J. 265
Clark, G. 117
Clarke, E. C. 178, 211, 212
Cohn, L. 131
Coleman, P. R. 68
Collins, R. F. 22, 26, 34, 44, 46, 47, 48, 51, 73, 149, 155, 158, 164, 167, 171, 175, 190, 195, 198, 199, 200, 201, 202, 203, 204, 205, 206, 208, 215, 228, 229, 231, 235, 238, 240, 243, 247, 248, 249, 250, 252, 255, 256, 258, 260, 261, 264, 268
Conybeare, F. C. 109
Conzelmann, H. 27, 34, 46, 51, 155, 157, 158, 159, 175, 182, 203, 205, 227, 229, 237, 238, 240, 243, 255, 263, 264
Cooey, P. M. 6
Cooke, B. 17

Cortés, J. B. 4
Cox, J. L. 18
Craghan, J. F. 138–139
Craigie, P. C. 292, 296
Crone, T. M. 23, 27
Cryer, F. H. 89
Currie, S. D. 24
Daiches, S. 292–293
Daley, B. E. 68
Dautzenberg, G. 50, 158, 238
Davies, S. L. 3, 42, 166
Davies, T. W. 113, 305
Davis, C. F. 8
Davis, J. A. 43
De Boor, W. 150
De Labriolle, P. 210, 211
De Lacey, D. R. 196
DeVries, S. J. 303
De Witt Burton, E. 59
Derrett, J. D. M. 157
Dibelius, M. 61, 74, 110, 145, 262
Dietzfelbinger, C. 131
Dingwall, E. J. 13
Dodds, E. R. 93, 136, 153
Donnelly, D. 197
Driver, S. R. 295
Duhm, H. 298
Dunn, J. D. G. 94–96, 109, 166, 192,
    206, 208, 224, 226
Easley, K. H. 184, 307
Eitrem, S. 170
Ekem, J. D. 45, 48, 150, 175, 183
Ellermeier, F. 138
Ellingworth, P. and Howard A. Hatton
    239, 242
Ellis, E. E. 23, 49, 52, 150, 154, 197,
    198, 221, 242, 263
Engelsen, N. I. J. 23, 27, 51, 52
Erwood, W. J. 290
Esler, P. F. 24, 34
Evans, G. R. 6
Evans-Pritchard, E. E. 42
Everling, O. 61, 192
Farley, E. 6
Fascher, E. 24
Fatehi, M. 176
Fee, G. D. 26, 30, 34, 36, 46, 47, 50, 51,
    58, 96–98, 149, 155, 156, 157, 158,

159, 165, 167, 171, 184, 191, 195,
    199, 201, 202, 203, 205, 208, 216,
    223, 224, 225, 228, 231, 234, 235,
    236, 237, 238, 240, 241, 243, 247,
    248, 249, 250, 254, 255, 256, 259,
    260, 261, 263, 264, 267, 307, 316,
    317, 318
Feil, E. 1
Feldman, L. H. 120, 121, 131, 143
Figart, T. O. 293
Finegan, J. 159
Fitzmyer, J. A. 59, 156, 204
Foerster, W. 72
Foester, F. W. 116
Fontenrose, J. 27, 101
Forbes, C. 24, 28, 29, 34, 36, 37, 73, 101,
    218, 226, 232, 236, 242, 244, 246,
    254, 255, 258, 259, 264
Ford, J. M. 38
Fortman, E. J. 15, 67
Fowler, W. W. 93
Francis, D. P. 307, 314
François, G. 193
Frazer, J. G. 111
Frend, W. H. C. 15
Friedrich, G. 144, 207
Gardner, P. 9
Garland, D. E. 29, 34, 35, 36, 45, 47, 49,
    50, 51, 155, 156, 157, 158, 159, 162,
    167, 175, 184, 195, 197, 198, 199,
    200, 201, 202, 203, 204, 205, 206,
    207, 214, 215, 216, 224, 227, 229,
    230, 231, 233, 235, 237, 238, 240,
    241, 242, 244, 247, 249, 251, 253,
    254, 255, 258, 260, 261, 264, 268
Garrett, C. 98
Gasparro, G. S. 115
Geller, S. A. 189
Gillespie, T. W. 23, 31, 49, 177, 223, 224
Goldammer, K. 103
Goodman, F. D. 2, 38, 39
Grabbe, L. L. 89
Gray, R. 120
Griffith, T. 160
Grudem, W. A. 23, 24, 25, 31, 46, 48, 50,
    51, 144, 155, 158, 159, 166, 167, 171,
    176, 179, 188, 208, 237, 239, 254,
    261, 262, 263, 266

Guillaume, A. 297
Gundry, R. 30, 34, 39
Gunkel, H. 77–80, 102, 110, 151, 192, 226, 269
Haldar, A. 139, 140
Hall, T. H. 286
Halliday, W. R. 113
Hanson, R. P. L. 67
Haran, M. 25
Hardinge, E. 285
Harnack, A. 15, 83
Haroutunian, J. 69
Harrington, D. J. 131, 132, 133
Harrisville, R. A. 24, 34, 45, 52, 158, 159, 167, 192, 237, 238
Hartman, L. F. and Alexander A. Di Lella 206
Haykin, M. A. G. 14, 62, 66, 68, 74, 187, 189, 200
Hayman, P. 189
Haynes, C. B. 292
Hays, R. B. 34, 46, 47, 49, 51, 150, 157, 158, 161, 166, 167, 178, 184, 195, 198, 201, 203, 205, 214, 216, 227, 236, 237, 255, 263, 268
Heaney, J. J. 56
Heidel, A. 295
Heine, R. E. 210
Heintz, J-G 138
Hemphill, K. S. 48
Hengel, M. 13
Henshaw, R. A. 139
Héring, J. 45, 52, 197, 206, 233, 241, 244, 245
Heron, A. 64
Hiebert, P. 182
Hill, D. 23, 35, 26, 52, 59, 98, 99, 120, 142
Hine, V. J. 39
Hoekema, A. A. 38
Holtz, T. 150
Hopwood, P. G. S. 91–93
Horn, F. W. 54, 55, 57
Horsley, R. A. 32
House, H. W. 24, 27, 49, 159, 237
Hovenden, G. 24, 31, 34, 36
Hoyle, R. B. 13
Hufford, D. J. 18

Hui, A. 43, 265
Hunt, A. R. 29, 177, 243
Hurd, J. C. 138, 148
Hurtado, L. 8, 57, 75, 156, 176, 196, 226
Husserl, E. 4
Isaacs, M. E. 58, 59, 72, 171, 175
Isbell, C. D. 25
Jacobson, H. 132
James, M. R. 131
James, W. 2
Jaquith, J. R. 38
Jeffers, A. 113
Jeffers, S. L. 290
Jewett, R. 243
Johanson, B. C. 32
Johnson, A. F. 150, 167
Johnson, A. R. 186
Johnson, L. T. 27, 40, 101–103, 110
Jones, D. J. 140
Jones, R. B. 292
Joüon, P. 171
Käsemann, E. 47, 179, 197
Keck, L. E. 204
Keener, C. S. 46, 51, 74, 167
Kelsey, M. T. 38
Khathide, A. 182
Kildahl, J. P. 38
Kisch, G. 131
Kistemaker, S. J. 26, 46, 50, 51, 158, 159, 164, 166, 167, 184, 195, 198, 202, 203, 205, 208, 216, 224, 227, 230, 234, 235, 236, 237, 240, 247, 250, 252, 253, 263, 268
Kitz, A. M. 297, 305
Klimo, J. 287
Knox, R. 96, 210
Kramer, W. R. 156
Kretschmar, G. 59, 64
Kruger, G. 83
Kurtz, P. 286
Lake, K. 49, 72, 189, 209, 210
Lampe, G. W. H. 60
Lang, A. 153
Langdon, S. 138
Langton, E. 153
Lanier, D. E. 32
Larue, G. A. 287
Lateiner, D. 255

Laurentin, R. 38
Lepicier, A. M. 290
Levison, J. R. 15, 98–101, 120, 123, 125,
    126, 132, 133, 135, 141, 143, 218,
    264
Lewis, F. B. 295
Lewis, I. M. 2, 102, 144
Lienhard, J. T. 211
Liljencrants, J. 291
Lindblom, J. 296, 299
Lindemann, A. 150, 237, 258
Littré, Ê. 141
Long, B. O. 300
Luck, G. 25, 115
Lust, J. 293, 296, 298, 300, 301
Macchia, F. D. 38
MacRory, J. 241
Macmullen, R. 64
Mageo, J. M. 18
Mak, L. 307
Malamat, A. 138
Maleparampil, J. 95, 195
Malherbe, A. J. 229
Maly, K. 158, 174
March, W. E. 72
Marsh, L. 292
Marsh, T. 71
Martin, D. B. 32, 215
May, L. C. 38
McCarter, P. K. 292
McCasland, S. V. 109
McDonald, L. M. 275
McNamara, M. 73, 305
McNichol, A. J. 286
Mehat, A. 28, 155, 157, 158, 159, 164,
    178, 179
Meinhold, P. 66
Mendelsohn, I. 304
Menzies, R. P. 15, 59, 71, 74
Meredith, A. 67, 68, 71
Metzger, B. M. 225
Meyer, P. 44
Meyer, H. A. W. 234
Michaelsen, P. 137, 218
Mikulasch, R. H. 40
Milgrom, J. 296
Mills, W. E. 24
Mitchell, M. M. 21, 148, 191, 213

Moffat, J. 159, 167, 175
Moltmann, J. 5
Montague, G. T. 150, 168, 184, 195
Moore, M. S. 121
Moore, S. D. 103
Moran, W. L. 138, 139
Morgan, G. C. 170
Morgan-Wynne, J. E. 106–107
Morris, L. 26, 45, 51, 158, 167, 205, 237,
    240
Morrison, A. B. 292
Moulton, W. F. and A. S. Geden 307
Mowery, R. L. 307
Mowinckel, S. 25
Mundhenk, N. A. 181, 182
Murphy, F. J. 132, 133, 163
Nardoni, E. 49
Nigosian, S. A. 295
Nissinen, M. 297, 301
Njiru, P. K. 51, 149, 193, 199, 202
Noble, T. A. 74
Noll, S. F. 61
Oesterley, W. O. E. 72
Oesterreich, T. K. 136
Ogden, D. 116, 291
Olasky, M. 289
Omara, R. 45
Orlinsky, H. M. 305
Orr, W. R. and J. A. Walther 50
Osei-Bonsu, J. 168
Osiander, J. S. 158
Oster, R. 52, 238
Otto, R. 91
Overholt, T. W. 297
Pace, E. A. 287, 290, 291, 294
Pacwa, M. 290
Padel, R. 2, 170
Paige, T. 44, 59, 113, 155, 165, 190, 191,
    238, 239, 241
Painter, J. 183
Parke, H. W. and D. E. W. Wormell 117
Parke, H. W. 162
Parker, S. B. 138
Parpola, S. 138, 140, 301
Parry, R. St J. 49, 169
Patai, R. 270
Paton, L. B. 292
Pearson, A. C. 116

Pearson, B. A. 44, 45, 124, 157
Perrot, C. 131
Person, R. E. 63
Pfitzner, V. L. 61
Philip, F. 74, 226
Pilch, J. J. 3, 42
Piñero, A. 132
Porter, S. E. 66, 185
Poythress, V. S. 24, 38, 39
Prat, F. 195
Proudfoot, W. 91
Quast, K. 221
Rahner, K. 5, 290
Recheis, P. A. 83
Reiling, J. 194
Richardson, C. C. 222
Ritner, R. K. 291, 306
Roberts, J. J. M. 138, 141
Roberts, P. 254
Robertson, A. and Alfred Plummer 45,
      50, 51, 52, 203, 238
Robinson, D. W. B. 49
Robinson, H. W. 90–91
Rodewyk, A. 3, 270
Ross, J. F. 138
Runia, D. T. 124
Salala, C. 292
Samarin, W. J. 38
Sandmel, S. 124
Sandnes, K. O. 32, 33, 177
Schäfer, P. 169
Schatzmann, S. S. 46, 196, 197
Schiller, F. C. S. 287
Schlatter, A. 192
Schlier, H. 61
Schmithals, W. 43, 45, 157
Schneider, D. 182
Schniedewind, W. M. 296
Schrage, W. 45, 159, 204, 233
Schweizer, E. 61
Seidel, J. 305
Sekki, A. E. 186
Sevenster, J. N. 172
Shantz, C. A. 18
Shapland, C. R. B. 64, 65
Sharp, L. L. 290
Sharpe, E. J. 87
Sherry, P. J. 9, 10, 12, 16

Shoemaker, W. R. 59
Smalley, S. S. 24
Smelik, K. A. D. 305
Smit, J. F. M. 22, 27, 159, 195, 255
Smith, G. V. 301
Smith, M. 114, 169, 242, 266
Smith, W. D. 116
Soards, M. L. 46, 51, 158, 159, 167, 195,
      198, 202, 205, 237, 238, 240
Sorensen, E. 170
Springsten, E. O. 7
Staniforth, M. 222
Stevens, G. B. 151
Stevenson, I. 40
Stewart-Sykes, A. 218, 264
Stohl, M. 140
Strecker, G. 187, 208
Strelan, R. 13
Strong, S. A. 139
Stuhlmacher, P. 13
Stuhlmueller, C. 301
Summers, S. 34
Sutphin, J. E. 153
Swartz, S. 69, 70, 171, 173, 314
Sweet, J. P. M. 24, 31, 32
Swete, H. B. 63, 86–87
Tabbernee, W. 209, 267
Talbert, C. H. 28, 46, 57, 157, 205, 221
Thelle, R. I. 300
Thiselton, A. C. 24, 35, 36, 37, 40, 47, 48,
      50, 51, 54, 69, 142, 155, 156, 167,
      175, 184, 195, 198, 201, 203, 204,
      206, 207, 228, 229, 230, 234, 235,
      237, 241, 244, 247, 255, 259, 264
Thomas, R. L. 50, 184, 195, 208
Thompson, J. A. 292
Thurston, H. 290
Tittman, G. F. 262
Torrance, T. F. 195
Triezenberg, H. J. 292
Tropper, J. 296
Turner, M. M. B. 28, 29, 34, 36, 46,
      142–143, 144
Tylor, E. B. 87
Udoette, D. 52
Unger, M. F. 292
VanDam, C. 297
Vande Kapelle, R. P. 217

Van der Hart, R. 62
VanderKam, J. C. 73
Van Unnik, W. C. 157
Van Vliet, R. 50
Vásquez, M. A. 290
Vaughan, R. 286
Vawter, B. and J. T. Nellis 301
Vergote, A. 8
Versnel, H. S. 189, 193
Vincent, M. R. 58, 208
Volz, P. 83–86, 183
Vos, J. S. 156, 158, 160, 165, 179, 180
Wach, J. 16
Wagner, S. 300, 301, 302
Weaver, M. J. 125
Weinel, H. 80–83, 85, 108, 147, 154,
    162, 164, 192
Weisberg, B. 286
Weiss, J. 206
Whiteley, D. E. H. 196
Whitley, C. F. 25

Wiebe, P. H. 11–12
Wiesinger, A. 6, 265
Wiles, M. 63
Williams, C. G. 33
Williams, D. M. 75
Williams, P. J. 303
Williamson, R. 124
Wilson, R. R. 103, 301
Wink, W. 61
Wire, A. C. 31
Witherington, B. 31
Wolff, C. 45, 48, 51, 159, 167, 175
Wolfson, H. A. 123
Wright, D. F. 210
Wright, J. S. 151, 293
Wright, W. C. 43
Yarnold, E. 68
Zaugg, E. H. 87–90
Zerhusen, R. 37, 39
Zerwick, M. 169, 173, 247, 317

Index of Subjects and Key Terms

Ambiguity
  – in dealing with spirits 55–57, 81, 82, 89, 92, 109–110, 178
Amnesia, prophetic
  – experienced by Paul 248
  – found in both Mesopotamian and Greco-Roman texts 141
  – in Babylonian diagnostic texts 140
  – in Christian texts 136, 142–143
  – in Greco-Roman texts 136
  – in Jewish texts 137
  – in the OT 137, 141–142
  – recorded among the *mahhus* in Mari texts 139–140
  – result of demonic possession 136
  – result of holy spirit possession 99, 134
Article, Greek
  – anaphoric use of 245
  – and πνεῦμα 187, 188
  – categorical use of 185, 187
  – particular use of 66
Asklepios
  – healing temple in Corinth 205

Backgrounds for πνεῦμα
  – in Paul 43–44
Balaam
  – Josephus' view on inspiration 120–123
  – Philo's view on inspiration 125–127

Christology
  – God and Christ separate spirit realities in Paul 194, 196, 198, 199
  – holy spirits utter "Lord" for Jesus 57, 176, 203, 211, 223, 226
  – holy spirits utter "Christ" for Jesus 176, 211, 223
  – Jesus is anathema 156–157
Council of Constantinople
  – dogmatic declaration of the Holy Spirit as a Deity 14, 68
Council of Nicaea
  – divinity of Holy Spirit not clear 64

Deceptive spirits
  – ability to speak some truth recognized by early Christians 82, 212
  – invisibility of provides for stealth from normal human senses 56
  – savvy 175
Deep-Trance Spirit Communication
  – Christian 166–167, 169, 170, 176
  – convicts nonbelievers of reality of 252–258
  – Greco-Roman 116–119, 153
  – invisible to spectators 128, 170
  – Jewish 119–137
  – eventually discredited of good spirits by Origen 275
Delphic oracle
  – operation of via daemons 117–119
  – possession maligned by Lamprias 115–116
  – possession supported by Cleombrotus 117–119
  – vapors theory of inspiration 117
Discernment of spirits
  – by the life of the prophet 56–57
  – by the utterances of spirits through a prophet 208
  – Iamblichus 211–212
  – refined among Christians 212–213
  – scholarly interpretations of 50–51, 207
  – the need for among Christians 56–57, 178, 208, 210
  – through clairvoyance, clairaudience, and clairsentience 56, 212

Early Judaism
  – early Christian concept of spirit as personal derived from 15, 58–59, 71–73, 84–85
  – substance of the spirit in 79
Ecstasy
  – a sign of false inspiration 167, 218
  – confused by scholars with manner of prophetic speech 27, 217–218, 244

– does not indicate exclusively
"frenzied" speech or behavior 27–28,
122, 126–127, 130, 133–135, 218,
264
– in Akkadian and Sumerian terms
138–139
– Philo's definition of 125
– psychic condition of a prophet while
a spirit expresses itself through the
prophet 28, 138–139, 218
ἐγγαστρίμυθος
– in Philo 130–131
– in Plutarch 116, 118
ἐν πνεύματι
– expressed of holy spirits 80, 165,
166, 167, 169, 170, 219, 248–249
– expressed of unclean spirits 80, 168,
169, 170
– used in both visionary and prophetic
possession contexts 168–169
– used for glossolalia in Paul
220–221, 244, 264
– used for prophecy in Paul 221–222,
224, 264

Glossolalia
– confused with Hellenistic
inspiration 221, 243–244, 254–255
– distinguished from xenolalia 33, 40,
219–220
– human language 33–37, 234–236,
249
– noncognitive language 38–39
– prohibited unless translated
230–233
– sign for unbelievers 31–33, 253
– translation of 213, 230–232, 242,
259–261
– unintelligible utterance of holy
spirits through Christian prophets
213, 220–221, 228, 242, 244

Historical criticism
– and religious experience 100
– and theological interpretation 74
History of Religions
– *Religionsgeschichtliche Schule* 7,
85, 88

Holy Spirit, the
– as a Deity unknown to Paul
195–196
– collective noun for "the spirit world
of God" 173, 183
– distinct from other spirits 63–66,
85, 108
– not called God until fourth century
67–68
– The Holy Spirit/a holy spirit 49–50,
170–174, 184
– the One Spirit 49–50, 52, 188–194
– the Same Spirit 184–188, 195, 200

Idols, media for spirit communication
– as cited in early Christian texts
163–164
– as cited among the Greeks 162
– as cited in Jewish texts 162
– cited by Paul as a contrast to
Christian spirit communication
161–162, 164–165, 174, 178
– in the OT 160–161

Josephus
– describes deep-trance spirit
communication 119–123

Liber antiquitatum biblicarum
– evidence for a holy spirit speaking
through a medium 133–135, 194

Mediums, Deep-Trance
– as Christian prophets 170, 178, 202,
220–224, 232, 262, 265
– in the OT 295–296, 297
– not restricted to evil spirits
144–145, 170
– "schools for mediums" in the OT
303–304
Montanism
– an example of Christian deep-trance
spirit communication 153, 177
– alleged problems in discernment of
spirits 209–210
– not immediately outlawed 210
– why outlawed by the Catholic
church 210

Paul
- his chosen terminology for manifestations of the spirit world 196–199
- musical instrument analogies for glossolalia 233–236
- on need for intelligibility of spirits 242–251
- regulations for spirit communication 258–266

Philo
- describes deep-trance spirit communication 126–130

πνεύματα
- behind the "spiritual things" 154
- not "gifts" of the Holy Spirit 237
- not "inspirations" or "inspired utterances" 208, 237, 238
- not "manifestations" of the Holy Spirit 237
- Paul wants Corinthians to abound with 239–242

πνευματικά
- activities or effects of spirit 150–151, 153, 154
- meaning of debated 44–47, 149–151
- not spiritual gifts 149
- things of the spirit: spiritism 151–154
- pertains to spirits 267
- versus χαρίσματα 47–49

Pneumatology
- of early Judaism that of earliest Christians 71–73
- its relation to demonology 79–80

πνευματόφορον
- "moved by a spirit" to speak 210, 276
- used of both true and false prophets 210, 276
- used later in derogatory terms by Christian anti-Montanists 276

Prophecy
- as new revelation among Christians 225–227
- function of in Christian circles 223–227

- Greco-Roman and Paul 27–28, 99
- in Judaism 97–99
- intelligible utterance of holy spirits through Christian prophets 207, 221–226, 228
- musical instrument simile for 128–129
- Old Testament and Paul 25–27

Prophetic behavior
- akin to illness 141

Religious experience
- and biblical studies 55
- and philosophy 4–5
- and psychical studies 6
- and psychology 3–4
- and social sciences 2–3, 102
- and theology 5–8, 93
- attitude by scholars toward 13
- definition of 8, 54
- distinctly Christian nature of 95
- in First Corinthians 12 and 14 54, 111
- *religio* 1, 9
- scholarly monographs on 77–107
- "spirit" as rhetoric of in the NT 8

Séance
- a gathering for spirit communication 152, 211
- meaning of compatible with activity of earliest Christian circles 152

Shepherd of Hermas, the
- *Mandate* 11.9 as spirit communication in a Christian circle 194

Social Sciences and the NT
- glossolalia 38, 39, 41, 42
- prophecy 41–42
- spirit phenomena 87–89, 103–105, 110–111
- xenolalia 40

Spirit
- analogy with "wind" 12
- and power 58
- movements in history 83, 97–98
- what is "a spirit"? 9–12

Spirit World, the
  – according to earliest Christians
  71–75, 102–103
  – as a translation for τὸ πνεῦμα
  17–18, 181–187, 195–200
  – as understood in church fathers 71
  – communication with in Christian
  circles 16, 147, 155, 194–199,
  227–268
  – consulting of in OT 298–303
  – evil blocks communication with
  holy 206
  – in biblical and theological studies
  61–62
  – in early Judaism 85, 114–115
  – instructs on religious matters 251
  – prohibited and welcomed in the OT
  298, 301, 305
  – two distinctions for communicating
  with 113
Spiritism
  – as prophecy and divination in the
  OT 296–297
  – as a term misused in popular culture
  285–287
  – Christian nature of 111, 152,
  165–170, 174, 178, 194, 266–268
  – expresses spirit communication in
  antiquity 152–153
  – in 1 Cor 12:1a 154, 174
  – in antidivinatory laws 111, 295
  – in English bible versions 111,
  288–290
  – necromancy 291–294
  – not condemned in the OT 298, 304
  – not outlawed as prophecy by early
  church fathers 210, 276
  – outlawed by contemporary
  Christianity 290
  – refers to any spirit 111, 154, 178,
  294–295
  – רוח in the OT 302–304
  – sometimes known as spiritualism
  16, 111, 286–287
Spirits
  – d(a)emons 81, 113, 117–119

  – effects of 11, 12, 78–79, 80, 82, 83,
  99, 100, 107, 108
  – have ability to teach 80, 177–178
  – holy 152, 240, 262
  – human 152, 262
  – in early Judaism 71–73, 114–115,
  185–187
  – powers yet personal 10, 60, 242
  – utter prayers and blessings through
  a medium 244–248
Spiritual gifts
  – manifestations from the spirit world
  197
  – practiced in the context of love
  216–217

Theodosian Code
  – Trinity made into Roman law 68
Theology of the Holy Spirit
  – Athanasius of Alexandria 64–66,
  187
  – Basil of Caesarea 66–67, 187
  – biblical studies 69–71
  – Cyril of Jerusalem 64
  – departure from earliest Christianity
  14, 69–75
  – fourth-century development of
  62–68
  – Gregory of Nazianzus 67–68
  – Gregory of Nyssa 67
  – incompatible with "spirits" 108–109
τὸ πνεῦμά μου
  – foreign spirit 245
  – human spirit 244–245
Trinity
  – historically not tenable for spirit in
  earliest Christianity 70, 71, 72, 108,
  152, 193, 196
  – no scholarly support for in Paul 195
  – not in the NT 70
  – scholarly support for in Paul 96,
  195

Word of the Lord
  – verbal communication from the
  spirit world 299

Wissenschaftliche Untersuchungen zum Neuen Testament
Alphabetical Index of the First and Second Series

Ådna, Jostein: Jesu Stellung zum Tempel. 2000. *Vol. II/119.*

Ådna, Jostein (Ed.): The Formation of the Early Church. 2005. *Vol. 183.*

- and *Kvalbein, Hans* (Ed.): The Mission of the Early Church to Jews and Gentiles. 2000. *Vol. 127.*

Alkier, Stefan: Wunder und Wirklichkeit in den Briefen des Apostels Paulus. 2001. *Vol. 134.*

Anderson, Paul N.: The Christology of the Fourth Gospel. 1996. *Vol. II/78.*

Appold, Mark L.: The Oneness Motif in the Fourth Gospel. 1976. *Vol. II/1.*

Arnold, Clinton E.: The Colossian Syncretism. 1995. *Vol. II/77.*

Ascough, Richard S.: Paul's Macedonian Associations. 2003. *Vol. II/161.*

Asiedu-Peprah, Martin: Johannine Sabbath Conflicts As Juridical Controversy. 2001. *Vol. II/132.*

Attridge, Harold W.: see *Zangenberg, Jürgen.*

Aune, David E.: Apocalypticism, Prophecy and Magic in Early Christianity. 2006. *Vol. 199.*

Avemarie, Friedrich: Die Tauferzählungen der Apostelgeschichte. 2002. *Vol. 139.*

Avemarie, Friedrich and *Hermann Lichtenberger* (Ed.): Auferstehung – Ressurection. 2001. *Vol. 135.*

- Bund und Tora. 1996. *Vol. 92.*

Baarlink, Heinrich: Verkündigtes Heil. 2004. *Vol. 168.*

Bachmann, Michael: Sünder oder Übertreter. 1992. *Vol. 59.*

Bachmann, Michael (Ed.): Lutherische und Neue Paulusperspektive. 2005. *Vol. 182.*

Back, Frances: Verwandlung durch Offenbarung bei Paulus. 2002. *Vol. II/153.*

Baker, William R.: Personal Speech-Ethics in the Epistle of James. 1995. *Vol. II/68.*

Bakke, Odd Magne: 'Concord and Peace'. 2001. *Vol. II/143.*

Baldwin, Matthew C.: Whose *Acts of Peter?* 2005. *Vol. II/196.*

Balla, Peter: Challenges to New Testament Theology. 1997. *Vol. II/95.*

- The Child-Parent Relationship in the New Testament and its Environment. 2003. *Vol. 155.*

Bammel, Ernst: Judaica. Vol. I 1986. *Vol. 37.*

- Vol. II 1997. *Vol. 91.*

Barton, Stephen C.: see *Stuckenbruck, Loren T.*

Bash, Anthony: Ambassadors for Christ. 1997. *Vol. II/92.*

Bauernfeind, Otto: Kommentar und Studien zur Apostelgeschichte. 1980. *Vol. 22.*

Baum, Armin Daniel: Pseudepigraphie und literarische Fälschung im frühen Christentum. 2001. *Vol. II/138.*

Bayer, Hans Friedrich: Jesus' Predictions of Vindication and Resurrection. 1986. *Vol. II/20.*

Becker, Eve-Marie: Das Markus-Evangelium im Rahmen antiker Historiographie. 2006. *Vol. 194.*

Becker, Eve-Marie and *Peter Pilhofer* (Ed.): Biographie und Persönlichkeit des Paulus. 2005. *Vol. 187.*

Becker, Michael: Wunder und Wundertäter im frührabbinischen Judentum. 2002. *Vol. II/144.*

Becker, Michael and *Markus Öhler* (Ed.): Apokalyptik als Herausforderung neutestamentlicher Theologie. 2006. *Vol. II/214.*

Bell, Richard H.: The Irrevocable Call of God. 2005. *Vol. 184.*

- No One Seeks for God. 1998. *Vol. 106.*

- Provoked to Jealousy. 1994. *Vol. II/63.*

Bennema, Cornelis: The Power of Saving Wisdom. 2002. *Vol. II/148.*

Bergman, Jan: see *Kieffer, René*

Bergmeier, Roland: Das Gesetz im Römerbrief und andere Studien zum Neuen Testament. 2000. *Vol. 121.*

Bernett, Monika: Der Kaiserkult in Judäa unter den Herodiern und Römern. 2007. *Vol. 203.*

Betz, Otto: Jesus, der Messias Israels. 1987. *Vol. 42.*

- Jesus, der Herr der Kirche. 1990. *Vol. 52.*

Beyschlag, Karlmann: Simon Magus und die christliche Gnosis. 1974. *Vol. 16.*

Bittner, Wolfgang J.: Jesu Zeichen im Johannesevangelium. 1987. *Vol. II/26.*

Bjerkelund, Carl J.: Tauta Egeneto. 1987. *Vol. 40.*

Blackburn, Barry Lee: Theios Aner and the Markan Miracle Traditions. 1991. *Vol. II/40.*

Bock, Darrell L.: Blasphemy and Exaltation in Judaism and the Final Examination of Jesus. 1998. *Vol. II/106.*

Bockmuehl, Markus N.A.: Revelation and Mystery in Ancient Judaism and Pauline Christianity. 1990. *Vol. II/36.*

Bøe, Sverre: Gog and Magog. 2001. *Vol. II/135.*

Böhlig, Alexander: Gnosis und Synkretismus. Vol. 1 1989. *Vol. 47* – Vol. 2 1989. *Vol. 48.*

Böhm, Martina: Samarien und die Samaritai bei Lukas. 1999. *Vol. II/111.*

Böttrich, Christfried: Weltweisheit – Menschheitsethik – Urkult. 1992. *Vol. II/50.*

– */ Herzer, Jens* (Ed.): Josephus und das Neue Testament. 2007. *Vol. 209.*

Bolyki, János: Jesu Tischgemeinschaften. 1997. *Vol. II/96.*

Bosman, Philip: Conscience in Philo and Paul. 2003. *Vol. II/166.*

Bovon, François: Studies in Early Christianity. 2003. *Vol. 161.*

Brändl, Martin: Der Agon bei Paulus. 2006. *Vol. II/222.*

Breytenbach, Cilliers: see *Frey, Jörg.*

Brocke, Christoph vom: Thessaloniki – Stadt des Kassander und Gemeinde des Paulus. 2001. *Vol. II/125.*

Brunson, Andrew: Psalm 118 in the Gospel of John. 2003. *Vol. II/158.*

Büchli, Jörg: Der Poimandres – ein paganisiertes Evangelium. 1987. *Vol. II/27.*

Bühner, Jan A.: Der Gesandte und sein Weg im 4. Evangelium. 1977. *Vol. II/2.*

Burchard, Christoph: Untersuchungen zu Joseph und Aseneth. 1965. *Vol. 8.*

– Studien zur Theologie, Sprache und Umwelt des Neuen Testaments. Ed. by D. Sänger. 1998. *Vol. 107.*

Burnett, Richard: Karl Barth's Theological Exegesis. 2001. *Vol. II/145.*

Byron, John: Slavery Metaphors in Early Judaism and Pauline Christianity. 2003. *Vol. II/162.*

Byrskog, Samuel: Story as History – History as Story. 2000. *Vol. 123.*

Cancik, Hubert (Ed.): Markus-Philologie. 1984. *Vol. 33.*

Capes, David B.: Old Testament Yaweh Texts in Paul's Christology. 1992. *Vol. II/47.*

Caragounis, Chrys C.: The Development of Greek and the New Testament. 2004. *Vol. 167.*

– The Son of Man. 1986. *Vol. 38.*

– see *Fridrichsen, Anton.*

Carleton Paget, James: The Epistle of Barnabas. 1994. *Vol. II/64.*

Carson, D.A., O'Brien, Peter T. and *Mark Seifrid* (Ed.): Justification and Variegated Nomism.
Vol. 1: The Complexities of Second Temple Judaism. 2001. *Vol. II/140.*

Vol. 2: The Paradoxes of Paul. 2004. *Vol. II/181.*

Chae, Young Sam: Jesus as the Eschatological Davidic Shepherd. 2006. *Vol. II/216.*

Chester, Andrew: Messiah and Exaltation. 2007. *Vol. 207.*

Ciampa, Roy E.: The Presence and Function of Scripture in Galatians 1 and 2. 1998. *Vol. II/102.*

Classen, Carl Joachim: Rhetorical Criticsm of the New Testament. 2000. *Vol. 128.*

Colpe, Carsten: Iranier – Aramäer – Hebräer – Hellenen. 2003. *Vol. 154.*

Crump, David: Jesus the Intercessor. 1992. *Vol. II/49.*

Dahl, Nils Alstrup: Studies in Ephesians. 2000. *Vol. 131.*

Daise, Michael A.: Feasts in John. 2007. *Vol. 229.*

Deines, Roland: Die Gerechtigkeit der Tora im Reich des Messias. 2004. *Vol. 177.*

– Jüdische Steingefäße und pharisäische Frömmigkeit. 1993. *Vol. II/52.*

– Die Pharisäer. 1997. *Vol. 101.*

Deines, Roland and *Karl-Wilhelm Niebuhr* (Ed.): Philo und das Neue Testament. 2004. *Vol. 172.*

Dennis, John A.: Jesus' Death and the Gathering of True Israel. 2006. *Vol. 217.*

Dettwiler, Andreas and *Jean Zumstein* (Ed.): Kreuzestheologie im Neuen Testament. 2002. *Vol. 151.*

Dickson, John P.: Mission-Commitment in Ancient Judaism and in the Pauline Communities. 2003. *Vol. II/159.*

Dietzfelbinger, Christian: Der Abschied des Kommenden. 1997. *Vol. 95.*

Dimitrov, Ivan Z., James D.G. Dunn, Ulrich Luz and *Karl-Wilhelm Niebuhr* (Ed.): Das Alte Testament als christliche Bibel in orthodoxer und westlicher Sicht. 2004. *Vol. 174.*

Dobbeler, Axel von: Glaube als Teilhabe. 1987. *Vol. II/22.*

Dryden, J. de Waal: Theology and Ethics in 1 Peter. 2006. *Vol. II/209.*

Du Toit, David S.: Theios Anthropos. 1997. *Vol. II/91.*

Dübbers, Michael: Christologie und Existenz im Kolosserbrief. 2005. *Vol. II/191.*

Dunn, James D.G.: The New Perspective on Paul. 2005. *Vol. 185.*

Dunn , James D.G. (Ed.): Jews and Christians. 1992. *Vol. 66.*

– Paul and the Mosaic Law. 1996. *Vol. 89.*

– see *Dimitrov, Ivan Z.*

–, *Hans Klein, Ulrich Luz* and *Vasile Mihoc* (Ed.): Auslegung der Bibel in orthodoxer und westlicher Perspektive. 2000. *Vol. 130.*

Ebel, Eva: Die Attraktivität früher christlicher Gemeinden. 2004. *Vol. II/178.*

Ebertz, Michael N.: Das Charisma des Gekreuzigten. 1987. *Vol. 45.*

Eckstein, Hans-Joachim: Der Begriff Syneidesis bei Paulus. 1983. *Vol. II/10.*

– Verheißung und Gesetz. 1996. *Vol. 86.*

Ego, Beate: Im Himmel wie auf Erden. 1989. *Vol. II/34.*

Ego, Beate, Armin Lange and *Peter Pilhofer* (Ed.): Gemeinde ohne Tempel – Community without Temple. 1999. *Vol. 118.*

– and *Helmut Merkel* (Ed.): Religiöses Lernen in der biblischen, frühjüdischen und frühchristlichen Überlieferung. 2005. *Vol. 180.*

Eisen, Ute E.: see *Paulsen, Henning.*

Elledge, C.D.: Life after Death in Early Judaism. 2006. *Vol. II/208.*

Ellis, E. Earle: Prophecy and Hermeneutic in Early Christianity. 1978. *Vol. 18.*

– The Old Testament in Early Christianity. 1991. *Vol. 54.*

Endo, Masanobu: Creation and Christology. 2002. *Vol. 149.*

Ennulat, Andreas: Die 'Minor Agreements'. 1994. *Vol. II/62.*

Ensor, Peter W.: Jesus and His 'Works'. 1996. *Vol. II/85.*

Eskola, Timo: Messiah and the Throne. 2001. *Vol. II/142.*

– Theodicy and Predestination in Pauline Soteriology. 1998. *Vol. II/100.*

Fatehi, Mehrdad: The Spirit's Relation to the Risen Lord in Paul. 2000. *Vol. II/128.*

Feldmeier, Reinhard: Die Krisis des Gottessohnes. 1987. *Vol. II/21.*

– Die Christen als Fremde. 1992. *Vol. 64.*

Feldmeier, Reinhard and *Ulrich Heckel* (Ed.): Die Heiden. 1994. *Vol. 70.*

Fletcher-Louis, Crispin H.T.: Luke-Acts: Angels, Christology and Soteriology. 1997. *Vol. II/94.*

Förster, Niclas: Marcus Magus. 1999. *Vol. 114.*

Forbes, Christopher Brian: Prophecy and Inspired Speech in Early Christianity and its Hellenistic Environment. 1995. *Vol. II/75.*

Fornberg, Tord: see *Fridrichsen, Anton.*

Fossum, Jarl E.: The Name of God and the Angel of the Lord. 1985. *Vol. 36.*

Foster, Paul: Community, Law and Mission in Matthew's Gospel. *Vol. II/177.*

Fotopoulos, John: Food Offered to Idols in Roman Corinth. 2003. *Vol. II/151.*

Frenschkowski, Marco: Offenbarung und Epiphanie. Vol. 1 1995. *Vol. II/79* – Vol. 2 1997. *Vol. II/80.*

Frey, Jörg: Eugen Drewermann und die biblische Exegese. 1995. *Vol. II/71.*

– Die johanneische Eschatologie. Vol. I. 1997. *Vol. 96.* – Vol. II. 1998. *Vol. 110.* – Vol. III. 2000. *Vol. 117.*

Frey, Jörg and *Cilliers Breytenbach* (Ed.): Aufgabe und Durchführung einer Theologie des Neuen Testaments. 2007. *Vol. 205.*

– and *Udo Schnelle (Ed.):* Kontexte des Johannesevangeliums. 2004. *Vol. 175.*

– and *Jens Schröter* (Ed.): Deutungen des Todes Jesu im Neuen Testament. 2005. *Vol. 181.*

–, *Jan G. van der Watt,* and *Ruben Zimmermann* (Ed.): Imagery in the Gospel of John. 2006. *Vol. 200.*

Freyne, Sean: Galilee and Gospel. 2000. *Vol. 125.*

Fridrichsen, Anton: Exegetical Writings. Edited by C.C. Caragounis and T. Fornberg. 1994. *Vol. 76.*

Gäbel, Georg: Die Kulttheologie des Hebräerbriefes. 2006. *Vol. II/212.*

Gäckle, Volker: Die Starken und die Schwachen in Korinth und in Rom. 2005. *Vol. 200.*

Garlington, Don B.: 'The Obedience of Faith'. 1991. *Vol. II/38.*

– Faith, Obedience, and Perseverance. 1994. *Vol. 79.*

Garnet, Paul: Salvation and Atonement in the Qumran Scrolls. 1977. *Vol. II/3.*

Gemünden, Petra von (Ed.): see *Weissenrieder, Annette.*

Gese, Michael: Das Vermächtnis des Apostels. 1997. *Vol. II/99.*

Gheorghita, Radu: The Role of the Septuagint in Hebrews. 2003. *Vol. II/160.*

Gordley, Matthew E.: The Colossian Hymn in Context. 2007. *Vol. II/228.*

Gräbe, Petrus J.: The Power of God in Paul's Letters. 2000. *Vol. II/123.*

Gräßer, Erich: Der Alte Bund im Neuen. 1985. *Vol. 35.*

– Forschungen zur Apostelgeschichte. 2001. *Vol. 137.*

Grappe, Christian (Ed.): Le Repas de Dieu / Das Mahl Gottes. 2004. *Vol. 169.*

Green, Joel B.: The Death of Jesus. 1988. *Vol. II/33.*

Gregg, Brian Han: The Historical Jesus and the Final Judgment Sayings in Q. 2005. *Vol. II/207.*

Gregory, Andrew: The Reception of Luke and Acts in the Period before Irenaeus. 2003. *Vol. II/169.*

Grindheim, Sigurd: The Crux of Election. 2005. *Vol. II/202.*

Gundry, Robert H.: The Old is Better. 2005. *Vol. 178.*

Gundry Volf, Judith M.: Paul and Perseverance. 1990. *Vol. II/37.*

Häußer, Detlef: Christusbekenntnis und Jesus-überlieferung bei Paulus. 2006. *Vol. 210.*

Hafemann, Scott J.: Suffering and the Spirit. 1986. *Vol. II/19.*

– Paul, Moses, and the History of Israel. 1995. *Vol. 81.*

Hahn, Ferdinand: Studien zum Neuen Testament.
Vol. I: Grundsatzfragen, Jesusforschung, Evangelien. 2006. *Vol. 191.*
Vol. II: Bekenntnisbildung und Theologie in urchristlicher Zeit. 2006. *Vol. 192.*

Hahn, Johannes (Ed.): Zerstörungen des Jerusalemer Tempels. 2002. *Vol. 147.*

Hamid-Khani, Saeed: Relevation and Concealment of Christ. 2000. *Vol. II/120.*

Hannah, Darrel D.: Michael and Christ. 1999. *Vol. II/109.*

Harrison; James R.: Paul's Language of Grace in Its Graeco-Roman Context. 2003. *Vol. II/172.*

Hartman, Lars: Text-Centered New Testament Studies. Ed. von D. Hellholm. 1997. *Vol. 102.*

Hartog, Paul: Polycarp and the New Testament. 2001. *Vol. II/134.*

Heckel, Theo K.: Der Innere Mensch. 1993. *Vol. II/53.*

– Vom Evangelium des Markus zum viergestaltigen Evangelium. 1999. *Vol. 120.*

Heckel, Ulrich: Kraft in Schwachheit. 1993. *Vol. II/56.*

– Der Segen im Neuen Testament. 2002. *Vol. 150.*

– see *Feldmeier, Reinhard.*

– see *Hengel, Martin.*

Heiligenthal, Roman: Werke als Zeichen. 1983. *Vol. II/9.*

Hellholm, D.: see *Hartman, Lars.*

Hemer, Colin J.: The Book of Acts in the Setting of Hellenistic History. 1989. *Vol. 49.*

Hengel, Martin: Judentum und Hellenismus. 1969, ³1988. *Vol. 10.*

– Die johanneische Frage. 1993. *Vol. 67.*

– Judaica et Hellenistica. Kleine Schriften I. 1996. *Vol. 90.*

– Judaica, Hellenistica et Christiana. Kleine Schriften II. 1999. *Vol. 109.*

– Paulus und Jakobus. Kleine Schriften III. 2002. *Vol. 141.*

– Studien zur Christologie. Kleine Schriften IV. 2006. *Vol. 201.*

– and *Anna Maria Schwemer:* Paulus zwischen Damaskus und Antiochien. 1998. *Vol. 108.*

– Der messianische Anspruch Jesu und die Anfänge der Christologie. 2001. *Vol. 138.*

Hengel, Martin and *Ulrich Heckel* (Ed.): Paulus und das antike Judentum. 1991. *Vol. 58.*

– and *Hermut Löhr* (Ed.): Schriftauslegung im antiken Judentum und im Urchristentum. 1994. *Vol. 73.*

– and *Anna Maria Schwemer* (Ed.): Königsherrschaft Gottes und himmlischer Kult. 1991. *Vol. 55.*

– Die Septuaginta. 1994. *Vol. 72.*

–, *Siegfried Mittmann* and *Anna Maria Schwemer* (Ed.): La Cité de Dieu / Die Stadt Gottes. 2000. *Vol. 129.*

Hentschel, Anni: Diakonia im Neuen Testament. 2007. *Vol. 226.*

Hernández Jr., Juan: Scribal Habits and Theological Influence in the Apocalypse. 2006. *Vol. II/218.*

Herrenbrück, Fritz: Jesus und die Zöllner. 1990. *Vol. II/41.*

Herzer, Jens: Paulus oder Petrus? 1998. *Vol. 103.*

– see *Böttrich, Christfried.*

Hill, Charles E.: From the Lost Teaching of Polycarp. 2005. *Vol. 186.*

Hoegen-Rohls, Christina: Der nachösterliche Johannes. 1996. *Vol. II/84.*

Hoffmann, Matthias Reinhard: The Destroyer and the Lamb. 2005. *Vol. II/203.*

Hofius, Otfried: Katapausis. 1970. *Vol. 11.*

– Der Vorhang vor dem Thron Gottes. 1972. *Vol. 14.*

– Der Christushymnus Philipper 2,6–11. 1976, ²1991. *Vol. 17.*

– Paulusstudien. 1989, ²1994. *Vol. 51.*

– Neutestamentliche Studien. 2000. *Vol. 132.*

– Paulusstudien II. 2002. *Vol. 143.*

– and *Hans-Christian Kammler:* Johannesstudien. 1996. *Vol. 88.*

Holtz, Traugott: Geschichte und Theologie des Urchristentums. 1991. *Vol. 57.*

Hommel, Hildebrecht: Sebasmata.
Vol. 1 1983. *Vol. 31.*
Vol. 2 1984. *Vol. 32.*

Horbury, William: Herodian Judaism and New Testament Study. 2006. *Vol. 193.*

Horst, Pieter W. van der: Jews and Christians in Their Graeco-Roman Context. 2006. *Vol. 196.*

Hvalvik, Reidar: The Struggle for Scripture and Covenant. 1996. *Vol. II/82.*

Jauhiainen, Marko: The Use of Zechariah in Revelation. 2005. *Vol. II/199.*

Jensen, Morten H.: Herod Antipas in Galilee. 2006. *Vol. II/215.*

Johns, Loren L.: The Lamb Christology of the Apocalypse of John. 2003. *Vol. II/167.*

Jossa, Giorgio: Jews or Christians? 2006. *Vol. 202.*

Joubert, Stephan: Paul as Benefactor. 2000. *Vol. II/124.*

Jungbauer, Harry: „Ehre Vater und Mutter". 2002. *Vol. II/146.*

Kähler, Christoph: Jesu Gleichnisse als Poesie und Therapie. 1995. *Vol. 78.*

Kamlah, Ehrhard: Die Form der katalogischen Paränese im Neuen Testament. 1964. *Vol. 7.*

Kammler, Hans-Christian: Christologie und Eschatologie. 2000. *Vol. 126.*

– Kreuz und Weisheit. 2003. *Vol. 159.*

– see *Hofius, Otfried.*

Kelhoffer, James A.: The Diet of John the Baptist. 2005. *Vol. 176.*

– Miracle and Mission. 1999. *Vol. II/112.*

Kelley, Nicole: Knowledge and Religious Authority in the Pseudo-Clementines. 2006. *Vol. II/213.*

Kieffer, René and *Jan Bergman (Ed.):* La Main de Dieu / Die Hand Gottes. 1997. *Vol. 94.*

Kierspel, Lars: The Jews and the World in the Fourth Gospel. 2006. *Vol. 220.*

Kim, Seyoon: The Origin of Paul's Gospel. 1981, [2]1984. *Vol. II/4.*

– Paul and the New Perspective. 2002. *Vol. 140.*

– "The 'Son of Man'" as the Son of God. 1983. *Vol. 30.*

Klauck, Hans-Josef: Religion und Gesellschaft im frühen Christentum. 2003. *Vol. 152.*

Klein, Hans: see *Dunn, James D.G.*

Kleinknecht, Karl Th.: Der leidende Gerechtfertigte. 1984, [2]1988. *Vol. II/13.*

Klinghardt, Matthias: Gesetz und Volk Gottes. 1988. *Vol. II/32.*

Kloppenborg, John S.: The Tenants in the Vineyard. 2006. *Vol. 195.*

Koch, Michael: Drachenkampf und Sonnenfrau. 2004. *Vol. II/184.*

Koch, Stefan: Rechtliche Regelung von Konflikten im frühen Christentum. 2004. *Vol. II/174.*

Köhler, Wolf-Dietrich: Rezeption des Matthäusevangeliums in der Zeit vor Irenäus. 1987. *Vol. II/24.*

Köhn, Andreas: Der Neutestamentler Ernst Lohmeyer. 2004. *Vol. II/180.*

Kooten, George H. van: Cosmic Christology in Paul and the Pauline School. 2003. *Vol. II/171.*

Korn, Manfred: Die Geschichte Jesu in veränderter Zeit. 1993. *Vol. II/51.*

Koskenniemi, Erkki: Apollonios von Tyana in der neutestamentlichen Exegese. 1994. *Vol. II/61.*

– The Old Testament Miracle-Workers in Early Judaism. 2005. *Vol. II/206.*

Kraus, Thomas J.: Sprache, Stil und historischer Ort des zweiten Petrusbriefes. 2001. *Vol. II/136.*

Kraus, Wolfgang: Das Volk Gottes. 1996. *Vol. 85.*

Kraus, Wolfgang and *Karl-Wilhelm Niebuhr* (Ed.): Frühjudentum und Neues Testament im Horizont Biblischer Theologie. 2003. *Vol. 162.*

– see *Walter, Nikolaus.*

Kreplin, Matthias: Das Selbstverständnis Jesu. 2001. *Vol. II/141.*

Kuhn, Karl G.: Achtzehngebet und Vaterunser und der Reim. 1950. *Vol. 1.*

Kvalbein, Hans: see *Ådna, Jostein.*

Kwon, Yon-Gyong: Eschatology in Galatians. 2004. *Vol. II/183.*

Laansma, Jon: I Will Give You Rest. 1997. *Vol. II/98.*

Labahn, Michael: Offenbarung in Zeichen und Wort. 2000. *Vol. II/117.*

Lambers-Petry, Doris: see *Tomson, Peter J.*

Lange, Armin: see *Ego, Beate.*

Lampe, Peter: Die stadtrömischen Christen in den ersten beiden Jahrhunderten. 1987, [2]1989. *Vol. II/18.*

Landmesser, Christof: Wahrheit als Grundbegriff neutestamentlicher Wissenschaft. 1999. *Vol. 113.*

– Jüngerberufung und Zuwendung zu Gott. 2000. *Vol. 133.*

Lau, Andrew: Manifest in Flesh. 1996. *Vol. II/86.*

Lawrence, Louise: An Ethnography of the Gospel of Matthew. 2003. *Vol. II/165.*

Lee, Aquila H.I.: From Messiah to Preexistent Son. 2005. *Vol. II/192.*

Lee, Pilchan: The New Jerusalem in the Book of Relevation. 2000. *Vol. II/129.*

Lichtenberger, Hermann: Das Ich Adams und das Ich der Menschheit. 2004. *Vol. 164.*

– see *Avemarie, Friedrich.*

Lierman, John: The New Testament Moses. 2004. *Vol. II/173.*

– (Ed.): Challenging Perspectives on the Gospel of John. 2006. *Vol. II/219.*

Lieu, Samuel N.C.: Manichaeism in the Later Roman Empire and Medieval China. [2]1992. *Vol. 63.*

Lindgård, Fredrik: Paul's Line of Thought in 2 Corinthians 4:16–5:10. 2004. *Vol. II/189.*

Loader, William R.G.: Jesus' Attitude Towards the Law. 1997. *Vol. II/97.*

Löhr, Gebhard: Verherrlichung Gottes durch Philosophie. 1997. *Vol. 97.*

Löhr, Hermut: Studien zum frühchristlichen und frühjüdischen Gebet. 2003. *Vol. 160.*
– see *Hengel, Martin.*

Löhr, Winrich Alfried: Basilides und seine Schule. 1995. *Vol. 83.*

Luomanen, Petri: Entering the Kingdom of Heaven. 1998. *Vol. II/101.*

Luz, Ulrich: see *Dunn, James D.G.*

Mackay, Ian D.: John's Raltionship with Mark. 2004. *Vol. II/182.*

Mackie, Scott D.: Eschatology and Exhortation in the Epistle to the Hebrews. 2006. *Vol. II/223.*

Maier, Gerhard: Mensch und freier Wille. 1971. *Vol. 12.*
– Die Johannesoffenbarung und die Kirche. 1981. *Vol. 25.*

Markschies, Christoph: Valentinus Gnosticus? 1992. *Vol. 65.*

Marshall, Peter: Enmity in Corinth: Social Conventions in Paul's Relations with the Corinthians. 1987. *Vol. II/23.*

Martin, Dale B.: see *Zangenberg, Jürgen.*

Mayer, Annemarie: Sprache der Einheit im Epheserbrief und in der Ökumene. 2002. *Vol. II/150.*

Mayordomo, Moisés: Argumentiert Paulus logisch? 2005. *Vol. 188.*

McDonough, Sean M.: YHWH at Patmos: Rev. 1:4 in its Hellenistic and Early Jewish Setting. 1999. *Vol. II/107.*

McDowell, Markus: Prayers of Jewish Women. 2006. *Vol. II/211.*

McGlynn, Moyna: Divine Judgement and Divine Benevolence in the Book of Wisdom. 2001. *Vol. II/139.*

Meade, David G.: Pseudonymity and Canon. 1986. *Vol. 39.*

Meadors, Edward P.: Jesus the Messianic Herald of Salvation. 1995. *Vol. II/72.*

Meißner, Stefan: Die Heimholung des Ketzers. 1996. *Vol. II/87.*

Mell, Ulrich: Die „anderen" Winzer. 1994. *Vol. 77.*
– see *Sänger, Dieter.*

Mengel, Berthold: Studien zum Philipperbrief. 1982. *Vol. II/8.*

Merkel, Helmut: Die Widersprüche zwischen den Evangelien. 1971. *Vol. 13.*
– see *Ego, Beate.*

Merklein, Helmut: Studien zu Jesus und Paulus. Vol. 1 1987. *Vol. 43.* – Vol. 2 1998. *Vol. 105.*

Metzdorf, Christina: Die Tempelaktion Jesu. 2003. *Vol. II/168.*

Metzler, Karin: Der griechische Begriff des Verzeihens. 1991. *Vol. II/44.*

Metzner, Rainer: Die Rezeption des Matthäusevangeliums im 1. Petrusbrief. 1995. *Vol. II/74.*
– Das Verständnis der Sünde im Johannesevangelium. 2000. *Vol. 122.*

Mihoc, Vasile: see *Dunn, James D.G..*

Mineshige, Kiyoshi: Besitzverzicht und Almosen bei Lukas. 2003. *Vol. II/163.*

Mittmann, Siegfried: see *Hengel, Martin.*

Mittmann-Richert, Ulrike: Magnifikat und Benediktus. *1996. Vol. II/90.*

Mournet, Terence C.: Oral Tradition and Literary Dependency. 2005. *Vol. II/195.*

Mußner, Franz: Jesus von Nazareth im Umfeld Israels und der Urkirche. Ed. von M. Theobald. 1998. *Vol. 111.*

Mutschler, Bernhard: Das Corpus Johanneum bei Irenäus von Lyon. 2005. *Vol. 189.*

Niebuhr, Karl-Wilhelm: Gesetz und Paränese. 1987. *Vol. II/28.*
– Heidenapostel aus Israel. 1992. *Vol. 62.*
– see *Deines, Roland*
– see *Dimitrov, Ivan Z.*
– see *Kraus, Wolfgang*

Nielsen, Anders E.: "Until it is Fullfilled". 2000. *Vol. II/126.*

Nissen, Andreas: Gott und der Nächste im antiken Judentum. 1974. *Vol. 15.*

Noack, Christian: Gottesbewußtsein. 2000. *Vol. II/116.*

Noormann, Rolf: Irenäus als Paulusinterpret. 1994. *Vol. II/66.*

Novakovic, Lidija: Messiah, the Healer of the Sick. 2003. *Vol. II/170.*

Obermann, Andreas: Die christologische Erfüllung der Schrift im Johannesevangelium. 1996. *Vol. II/83.*

Öhler, Markus: Barnabas. 2003. *Vol. 156.*
– see *Becker, Michael.*

Okure, Teresa: The Johannine Approach to Mission. 1988. *Vol. II/31.*

Onuki, Takashi: Heil und Erlösung. 2004. *Vol. 165.*

Oropeza, B. J.: Paul and Apostasy. 2000. *Vol. II/115.*

Ostmeyer, Karl-Heinrich: Kommunikation mit Gott und Christus. 2006. *Vol. 197.*
– Taufe und Typos. 2000. *Vol. II/118.*

Paulsen, Henning: Studien zur Literatur und Geschichte des frühen Christentums. Ed. von Ute E. Eisen. 1997. *Vol. 99.*

Pao, David W.: Acts and the Isaianic New Exodus. 2000. *Vol. II/130.*

Park, Eung Chun: The Mission Discourse in Matthew's Interpretation. 1995. *Vol. II/81.*

Park, Joseph S.: Conceptions of Afterlife in Jewish Insriptions. 2000. *Vol. II/121.*

Pate, C. Marvin: The Reverse of the Curse. 2000. *Vol. II/114.*

Pearce, Sarah J.K.: The Land of the Body. 2007. *Vol. 208.*

Peres, Imre: Griechische Grabinschriften und neutestamentliche Eschatologie. 2003. *Vol. 157.*

Philip, Finny: The Origins of Pauline Pneumatology. 2005. *Vol. II/194.*

Philonenko, Marc (Ed.): Le Trône de Dieu. 1993. *Vol. 69.*

Pilhofer, Peter: Presbyteron Kreitton. 1990. *Vol. II/39.*

– Philippi. Vol. 1 1995. *Vol. 87.* – Vol. 2 2000. *Vol. 119.*

– Die frühen Christen und ihre Welt. 2002. *Vol. 145.*

– see *Becker, Eve-Marie.*

– see *Ego, Beate.*

Pitre, Brant: Jesus, the Tribulation, and the End of the Exile. 2005. *Vol. II/204.*

Plümacher, Eckhard: Geschichte und Geschichten. 2004. *Vol. 170.*

Pöhlmann, Wolfgang: Der Verlorene Sohn und das Haus. 1993. *Vol. 68.*

Pokorný, Petr and *Josef B. Souček:* Bibelauslegung als Theologie. 1997. *Vol. 100.*

– and *Jan Roskovec* (Ed.): Philosophical Hermeneutics and Biblical Exegesis. 2002. *Vol. 153.*

Popkes, Enno Edzard: Die Theologie der Liebe Gottes in den johanneischen Schriften. 2005. *Vol. II/197.*

Porter, Stanley E.: The Paul of Acts. 1999. *Vol. 115.*

Prieur, Alexander: Die Verkündigung der Gottesherrschaft. 1996. *Vol. II/89.*

Probst, Hermann: Paulus und der Brief. 1991. *Vol. II/45.*

Räisänen, Heikki: Paul and the Law. 1983, ²1987. *Vol. 29.*

Rehkopf, Friedrich: Die lukanische Sonderquelle. 1959. *Vol. 5.*

Rein, Matthias: Die Heilung des Blindgeborenen (Joh 9). 1995. *Vol. II/73.*

Reinmuth, Eckart: Pseudo-Philo und Lukas. 1994. *Vol. 74.*

Reiser, Marius: Syntax und Stil des Markusevangeliums. 1984. *Vol. II/11.*

Rhodes, James N.: The Epistle of Barnabas and the Deuteronomic Tradition. 2004. *Vol. II/188.*

Richards, E. Randolph: The Secretary in the Letters of Paul. 1991. *Vol. II/42.*

Riesner, Rainer: Jesus als Lehrer. 1981, ³1988. *Vol. II/7.*

– Die Frühzeit des Apostels Paulus. 1994. *Vol. 71.*

Rissi, Mathias: Die Theologie des Hebräerbriefs. 1987. *Vol. 41.*

Roskovec, Jan: see *Pokorný, Petr.*

Röhser, Günter: Metaphorik und Personifikation der Sünde. 1987. *Vol. II/25.*

Rose, Christian: Die Wolke der Zeugen. 1994. *Vol. II/60.*

Rothschild, Clare K.: Baptist Traditions and Q. 2005. *Vol. 190.*

– Luke Acts and the Rhetoric of History. 2004. *Vol. II/175.*

Rüegger, Hans-Ulrich: Verstehen, was Markus erzählt. 2002. *Vol. II/155.*

Rüger, Hans Peter: Die Weisheitsschrift aus der Kairoer Geniza. 1991. *Vol. 53.*

Sänger, Dieter: Antikes Judentum und die Mysterien. 1980. *Vol. II/5.*

– Die Verkündigung des Gekreuzigten und Israel. 1994. *Vol. 75.*

– see *Burchard, Christoph*

– and *Ulrich Mell* (Hrsg.): Paulus und Johannes. 2006. *Vol. 198.*

Salier, Willis Hedley: The Rhetorical Impact of the Semeia in the Gospel of John. 2004. *Vol. II/186.*

Salzmann, Jorg Christian: Lehren und Ermahnen. 1994. *Vol. II/59.*

Sandnes, Karl Olav: Paul – One of the Prophets? 1991. *Vol. II/43.*

Sato, Migaku: Q und Prophetie. 1988. *Vol. II/29.*

Schäfer, Ruth: Paulus bis zum Apostelkonzil. 2004. *Vol. II/179.*

Schaper, Joachim: Eschatology in the Greek Psalter. 1995. *Vol. II/76.*

Schimanowski, Gottfried: Die himmlische Liturgie in der Apokalypse des Johannes. 2002. *Vol. II/154.*

– Weisheit und Messias. 1985. *Vol. II/17.*

Schlichting, Günter: Ein jüdisches Leben Jesu. 1982. *Vol. 24.*

Schließer, Benjamin: Abraham's Faith in Romans 4. 2007. *Vol. II/224.*

Schnabel, Eckhard J.: Law and Wisdom from Ben Sira to Paul. 1985. *Vol. II/16.*

Schnelle, Udo: see *Frey, Jörg.*

Schröter, Jens: Von Jesus zum Neuen Testament. 2007. *Vol. 204.*

– see *Frey, Jörg.*

Schutter, William L.: Hermeneutic and Composition in I Peter. 1989. *Vol. II/30.*

Schwartz, Daniel R.: Studies in the Jewish Background of Christianity. 1992. *Vol. 60.*

Schwemer, Anna Maria: see *Hengel, Martin*

Scott, Ian W.: Implicit Epistemology in the Letters of Paul. 2005. *Vol. II/205.*

Scott, James M.: Adoption as Sons of God. 1992. *Vol. II/48.*
– Paul and the Nations. 1995. *Vol. 84.*
Shum, Shiu-Lun: Paul's Use of Isaiah in Romans. 2002. *Vol. II/156.*
Siegert, Folker: Drei hellenistisch-jüdische Predigten. Teil I 1980. *Vol. 20* – Teil II 1992. *Vol. 61.*
– Nag-Hammadi-Register. 1982. *Vol. 26.*
– Argumentation bei Paulus. 1985. *Vol. 34.*
– Philon von Alexandrien. 1988. *Vol. 46.*
Simon, Marcel: Le christianisme antique et son contexte religieux I/II. 1981. *Vol. 23.*
Snodgrass, Klyne: The Parable of the Wicked Tenants. 1983. *Vol. 27.*
Söding, Thomas: Das Wort vom Kreuz. 1997. *Vol. 93.*
– see *Thüsing, Wilhelm.*
Sommer, Urs: Die Passionsgeschichte des Markusevangeliums. 1993. *Vol. II/58.*
Souček, Josef B.: see *Pokorný, Petr.*
Spangenberg, Volker: Herrlichkeit des Neuen Bundes. 1993. *Vol. II/55.*
Spanje, T.E. van: Inconsistency in Paul? 1999. *Vol. II/110.*
Speyer, Wolfgang: Frühes Christentum im antiken Strahlungsfeld. Vol. I: 1989. *Vol. 50.*
– Vol. II: 1999. *Vol. 116.*
– Vol. III: 2007. *Vol. 213.*
Stadelmann, Helge: Ben Sira als Schriftgelehrter. 1980. *Vol. II/6.*
Stenschke, Christoph W.: Luke's Portrait of Gentiles Prior to Their Coming to Faith. *Vol. II/108.*
Sterck-Degueldre, Jean-Pierre: Eine Frau namens Lydia. 2004. *Vol. II/176.*
Stettler, Christian: Der Kolosserhymnus. 2000. *Vol. II/131.*
Stettler, Hanna: Die Christologie der Pastoralbriefe. 1998. *Vol. II/105.*
Stökl Ben Ezra, Daniel: The Impact of Yom Kippur on Early Christianity. 2003. *Vol. 163.*
Strobel, August: Die Stunde der Wahrheit. 1980. *Vol. 21.*
Stroumsa, Guy G.: Barbarian Philosophy. 1999. *Vol. 112.*
Stuckenbruck, Loren T.: Angel Veneration and Christology. 1995. *Vol. II/70.*
– , *Stephen C. Barton* and *Benjamin G. Wold* (Ed.): Memory in the Bible and Antiquity. 2007. *Vol. 212.*
Stuhlmacher, Peter (Ed.): Das Evangelium und die Evangelien. 1983. *Vol. 28.*
– Biblische Theologie und Evangelium. 2002. *Vol. 146.*
Sung, Chong-Hyon: Vergebung der Sünden. 1993. *Vol. II/57.*
Tajra, Harry W.: The Trial of St. Paul. 1989. *Vol. II/35.*

– The Martyrdom of St.Paul. 1994. *Vol. II/67.*
Theißen, Gerd: Studien zur Soziologie des Urchristentums. 1979, ³1989. *Vol. 19.*
Theobald, Michael: Studien zum Römerbrief. 2001. *Vol. 136.*
Theobald, Michael: see *Mußner, Franz.*
Thornton, Claus-Jürgen: Der Zeuge des Zeugen. 1991. *Vol. 56.*
Thüsing, Wilhelm: Studien zur neutestamentlichen Theologie. Ed. von Thomas Söding. 1995. *Vol. 82.*
Thurén, Lauri: Derhethorizing Paul. 2000. *Vol. 124.*
Thyen, Hartwig: Studien zum Corpus Iohanneum. 2007. *Vol. 214.*
Tibbs, Clint: Religious Experience of the Pneuma. 2007. *Vol. II/230.*
Tolmie, D. Francois: Persuading the Galatians. 2005. *Vol. II/190.*
Tomson, Peter J. and *Doris Lambers-Petry* (Ed.): The Image of the Judaeo-Christians in Ancient Jewish and Christian Literature. 2003. *Vol. 158.*
Trebilco, Paul: The Early Christians in Ephesus from Paul to Ignatius. 2004. *Vol. 166.*
Treloar, Geoffrey R.: Lightfoot the Historian. 1998. *Vol. II/103.*
Tsuji, Manabu: Glaube zwischen Vollkommenheit und Verweltlichung. 1997. *Vol. II/93.*
Twelftree, Graham H.: Jesus the Exorcist. 1993. *Vol. II/54.*
Ulrichs, Karl Friedrich: Christusglaube. 2007. *Vol. II/227.*
Urban, Christina: Das Menschenbild nach dem Johannesevangelium. 2001. *Vol. II/137.*
Visotzky, Burton L.: Fathers of the World. 1995. *Vol. 80.*
Vollenweider, Samuel: Horizonte neutestamentlicher Christologie. 2002. *Vol. 144.*
Vos, Johan S.: Die Kunst der Argumentation bei Paulus. 2002. *Vol. 149.*
Wagener, Ulrike: Die Ordnung des „Hauses Gottes". 1994. *Vol. II/65.*
Wahlen, Clinton: Jesus and the Impurity of Spirits in the Synoptic Gospels. 2004. *Vol. II/185.*
Walker, Donald D.: Paul's Offer of Leniency (2 Cor 10:1). 2002. *Vol. II/152.*
Walter, Nikolaus: Praeparatio Evangelica. Ed. von Wolfgang Kraus und Florian Wilk. 1997. *Vol. 98.*
Wander, Bernd: Gottesfürchtige und Sympathisanten. 1998. *Vol. 104.*
Waters, Guy: The End of Deuteronomy in the Epistles of Paul. 2006. *Vol. 221.*
Watt, Jan G. van der: see *Frey, Jörg*
Watts, Rikki: Isaiah's New Exodus and Mark. 1997. *Vol. II/88.*

Wedderburn, A.J.M.: Baptism and Resurrection. 1987. *Vol. 44.*

Wegner, Uwe: Der Hauptmann von Kafarnaum. 1985. *Vol. II/14.*

Weissenrieder, Annette: Images of Illness in the Gospel of Luke. 2003. Vol. II/164.

–, *Friederike Wendt* and *Petra von Gemünden* (Ed.): Picturing the New Testament. 2005. *Vol. II/193.*

Welck, Christian: Erzählte ,Zeichen'. 1994. *Vol. II/69.*

Wendt, Friederike (Ed.): see *Weissenrieder, Annette.*

Wiarda, Timothy: Peter in the Gospels. 2000. *Vol. II/127.*

Wifstrand, Albert: Epochs and Styles. 2005. *Vol. 179.*

Wilk, Florian: see *Walter, Nikolaus.*

Williams, Catrin H.: I am He. 2000. *Vol. II/113.*

Wilson, Todd A.: The Curse of the Law and the Crisis in Galatia. 2007. *Vol. II/225.*

Wilson, Walter T.: Love without Pretense. 1991. *Vol. II/46.*

Wischmeyer, Oda: Von Ben Sira zu Paulus. 2004. *Vol. 173.*

Wisdom, Jeffrey: Blessing for the Nations and the Curse of the Law. 2001. *Vol. II/133.*

Wold, Benjamin G.: Women, Men, and Angels. 2005. *Vol. II/2001.*

– see *Stuckenbruck, Loren T.*

Wright, Archie T.: The Origin of Evil Spirits. 2005. *Vol. II/198.*

Wucherpfennig, Ansgar: Heracleon Philologus. 2002. *Vol. 142.*

Yeung, Maureen: Faith in Jesus and Paul. 2002. *Vol. II/147.*

Zangenberg, Jürgen, Harold W. Attridge and *Dale B. Martin* (Ed.): Religion, Ethnicity and Identity in Ancient Galilee. 2007. *Vol. 210.*

Zimmermann, Alfred E.: Die urchristlichen Lehrer. 1984, [2]1988. *Vol. II/12.*

Zimmermann, Johannes: Messianische Texte aus Qumran. 1998. *Vol. II/104.*

Zimmermann, Ruben: Christologie der Bilder im Johannesevangelium. 2004. *Vol. 171.*

– Geschlechtermetaphorik und Gottesverhältnis. 2001. *Vol. II/122.*

– see *Frey, Jörg*

Zumstein, Jean: see *Dettwiler, Andreas*

Zwiep, Arie W.: Judas and the Choice of Matthias. 2004. *Vol. II/187.*

For a complete catalogue please write to the publisher
Mohr Siebeck • P.O. Box 2030 • D–72010 Tübingen/Germany
Up-to-date information on the internet at www.mohr.de